ALSO BY CHAD L. WILLIAMS

Torchbearers of Democracy:
African American Soldiers in the World War I Era

Major Problems in African American History,
Second Edition (coeditor)

Charleston Syllabus:
Readings on Race, Racism, and Racial Violence (coeditor)

THE WOUNDED WORLD

THE
WOUNDED
WORLD

W. E. B. DU BOIS AND
THE FIRST WORLD WAR

CHAD L. WILLIAMS

Farrar, Straus and Giroux
New York

Farrar, Straus and Giroux
120 Broadway, New York 10271

Library of Congress Cataloging-in-Publication Data
Names: Williams, Chad Louis, 1976– author.
Title: The wounded world : W. E. B. Du Bois and the First World War /
    Chad L. Williams.
Other titles: W. E. B. Du Bois and the First World War
Description: First edition. | New York : Farrar, Straus and Giroux, 2023. |
    Includes bibliographical references and index.
Identifiers: LCCN 2022055054 | ISBN 9780374293154 (hardcover)
Subjects: LCSH: Du Bois, W. E. B. (William Edward Burghardt), 1868–1963—
    Social and political views. | World War, 1914–1918—Participation, African
    American. | World War, 1914–1918—African Americans. | United States.
    Army—African American troops. | African American soldiers—Social conditions—
    20th century. | African Americans—Social conditions—To 1964.
Classification: LCC D639.B53 W555 2023 | DDC 940.3089/
    96073—dc23/eng/20221117
LC record available at https://lccn.loc.gov/2022055054

Designed by Patrice Sheridan

Our books may be purchased in bulk for promotional, educational, or business use.
Please contact your local bookseller or the Macmillan Corporate and
Premium Sales Department at 1-800-221-7945, extension 5442,
or by email at MacmillanSpecialMarkets@macmillan.com.

www.fsgbooks.com
www.twitter.com/fsgbooks • www.facebook.com/fsgbooks

1 3 5 7 9 10 8 6 4 2

For Mom and Dad

One of the dangers of being a Black American is being schizo-phrenic, and I mean "schizophrenic" in the most literal sense. To be a Black American is in some ways to be born with the desire to be white. It's a part of the price you pay for being born here, and it affects every Black person. We can go back to Vietnam, we can go back to Korea. We can go back for that matter to the First World War. We can go back to W.E.B. Du Bois—an honorable and beautiful man—who campaigned to persuade Black people to fight in the First World War, saying that if we fight in this war to save this country, our right to citizenship can never, never again be questioned—and who can blame him? He really meant it, and if I'd been there at that moment I would have said so too perhaps . . .

—JAMES BALDWIN,
"Revolutionary Hope: A Conversation Between
James Baldwin and Audre Lorde"

A wound gives strange dignity to him who bears it.

—STEPHEN CRANE,
"An Episode of War"

CONTENTS

THE WOUNDED WORLD

PROLOGUE

THE MILD SUMMER MORNING of Wednesday, June 26, 1957, likely began as most days for the eighty-nine-year-old W. E. B. Du Bois. He woke up at his Brooklyn home, the picturesque ivy-covered brownstone at 31 Grace Court he shared with his wife, Shirley Graham. He shaved and took a leisurely bath. After dressing in his customary suit and tie, he carefully walked downstairs to the kitchen for a hearty breakfast. He always considered it the most important meal of the day.[1]

By ten o'clock, he'd settled into his study. Floor-to-ceiling bookcases lined the walls, overflowing with his massive library. Artwork and mementos provided sparse yet elegant decoration. He sat down in the leather-back chair at his desk, which was cluttered with newspapers, letters, and more books. From his window he could see the Brooklyn traffic and people passing by on the street.[2]

Even in old age, and under the pressure of the McCarthy era's full brunt, Du Bois kept himself busy. He had recently published *The Ordeal of Mansart*, the first book in what he envisioned as a trilogy of novels titled *The Black Flame*, and he eagerly anticipated completing its follow-up. There was always an article or editorial to write when he felt up to it. The government had confiscated his passport, and national speaking opportunities had dried up, but local radical groups continued to vie for his time and sage voice.

On this morning, as he began another day, Du Bois was in a reflective, even somber mood. The evening before, he had eulogized James W. Ford, one of New York's most prominent Black Communist organizers. Born in Alabama, Ford was a Fisk alum who had served in France during the First World War. In 1925, he helped organize the American Negro Labor Congress, and the following year he joined the Communist

Party, running for vice president of the United States three times on the CP ticket. Heading up the National Committee to Defend Negro Leadership, Ford continued to stand by Du Bois when most African Americans, fearful of being tarred as red, turned their backs on him. In his eulogy, Du Bois remembered Ford as a man "who walked calm and upright, insisting on his beliefs and still expressing his determination to work for a radical reform of this nation."[3]

Sitting in his office, moved by Ford's passing, Du Bois thought about his own life. He considered his work: the struggle to achieve full citizenship for African Americans, bringing freedom to all people of African descent across the globe, making democracy a reality. He had attempted every political strategy and utilized every instrument in his considerable intellectual toolbox. He always represented the race to the best of his abilities, gaining loyal supporters as well as attracting vocal opponents. His views evolved, but over nearly nine decades his belief in the humanity and beauty of Black people had never wavered.

He remembered family and friends. Many of his closest companions—Charles Young, John Hope, James Weldon Johnson, Joel Spingarn—were long departed. So too were his first wife and children. But others, over time, filled the void and made life worth living. None were more important than Shirley Graham, who, with her selflessness and comradeship, allowed Du Bois to enjoy love in his latter years.

He likely paused to think about his accomplishments. There was the unrivaled academic pedigree; the nearly twenty single-authored books; the contributions to history, sociology, anthropology, political science, philosophy, and literature that maybe, one day, his white contemporaries might fully recognize. He could take satisfaction in helping to birth a civil rights movement that, in 1957, a new generation of young leaders was fighting with inspiring success, as well as an anti-colonial struggle that, after decades, bore fruit just a few months earlier, in March, when Ghana celebrated its independence.

Indeed, he had seen and lived through much: the rise of Jim Crow, the horrors of Western colonialism, the steady erosion of democracy. Seventeen American presidents had come and gone, all disasters on the matter of protecting the rights of Black people. He had traveled the world—Europe, Africa, Asia, the Caribbean—experiencing up close the global problem of the color line as well as adding to his always evolving body of knowledge about how to confront it. He had survived the unimaginable destruction wrought by two world wars.

The first of these wars tested Du Bois's strength and convictions as had few other experiences in his life. He believed that through patriotism and military sacrifice, democracy would become a reality for African Americans. He called for his people to "close ranks" and put aside their "special grievances." He was accused of betraying the race. For more than two decades afterward, through the whirlwinds of disillusion and failure, he attempted to make sense of this history and his own place in it, a history that still haunted him.

He was far from perfect. Du Bois could not ignore the moments when he was wrong, his faith misplaced, his better judgment clouded by hope. For all his efforts, Black people continued to endure racial oppression. Greed, economic exploitation, and the subversion of democracy still ran amok. Peace remained an elusive dream, as the specter of atomic war loomed and the world teetered on the edge of catastrophe. He thought about what remained unfinished.

And he thought about the end. He did not fear dying. At many times in his long life he'd expected it to come. Death, Du Bois believed, was natural, and given the unbearable state of the world for Black folk, it was at times even welcomed.

Sitting at his desk, pondering life and his legacy, he decided to write his "final message" to the world.[4] It was short and succinct. Once completed, he sealed the note in an envelope and gave it to Shirley Graham. He included clear instructions: "To be opened after my death."[5]

PART I

HOPE

CHAPTER 1

"The present war in Europe is one of the great disasters due to race and color prejudice and it but foreshadows greater disasters in the future."[1]

DU BOIS FEARED FOR his family's safety. It was August 1914, and war engulfed Europe. His thirteen-year-old daughter, Yolande, and his wife, Nina, were scheduled to leave for England at the end of the month.[2] Yolande had received admission to the prestigious Bedales boarding school in Hampshire, where, as her father intended, she would be "trained to become a healthy woman, of broad outlook and spiritual resources, able to earn a living in some line of work which she likes and is fitted for."[3] Du Bois believed that Nina should dutifully relocate as well and settle in nearby London to provide motherly support whenever necessary.

War complicated their travel plans. The European crisis had been long in the making. The forces of nationalism, militarism, and imperialism swelled in the decades following the Franco-Prussian War of 1870–71, gripping the continent with fear, envy, and mistrust.[4] Colonial rivalries and a precarious alliance system exacerbated tensions. The fatal spark occurred in the Balkans. On June 28, 1914, a nineteen-year-old Bosnian nationalist, Gavrilo Princip, shot and killed the Archduke of Austria and heir to the throne, Franz Ferdinand, along with his wife, Sophie, in the capital city of Sarajevo. The assassination presented Germany and Kaiser Wilhelm II with an opportunity to push for the conflict they had long prepared for.

On July 28, Austria-Hungary, with Germany's backing, declared war on Serbia. The dominoes quickly began to fall. Two days later, Russia came to the defense of its Serbian ally. Germany responded in kind and, between August 1 and August 4, declared war against Russia, France, and Belgium. "Whatever our lot may be," Imperial Chancellor Theobald von Bethmann Hollweg avowed before the assembled members of the Reichstag, "the 4th of August, 1914, will remain through all eternity one of Germany's greatest days."[5] As the sun rose on August 5, Great Britain had entered the mess, creating a Triple Entente with France and Russia against the Central Powers of Germany and Austria-Hungary. All sides mobilized every young, able-bodied man for military service, with *The New York Times* estimating that seventeen million men stood at the ready to fight and possibly die in "the Colossal European War."[6] Soldiers of various nations, clad in crisp, clean uniforms of blue, red, khaki, and gray, buoyantly filled trains and prepared to travel to the front by foot and by horse. The war would be over in a matter of weeks, they believed. However, some military leaders and heads of state imagined a more ominous future. On the eve of his nation's declaration of war, the British foreign secretary, Sir Edward Grey, solemnly predicted, "The lamps are going out all over Europe; we shall not see them lit again in our lifetime."[7]

Germany, with nearly four million well-trained soldiers, advanced weapons, and seemingly boundless martial spirit, envisioned a swift and decisive victory. The Kaiser's forces, adhering to the Schlieffen Plan conceived in 1905, invaded neutral Belgium.[8] The initial wave of German cavalry and infantry experienced stiffer than expected resistance and took surprisingly heavy losses at the opening Battle of Liège. Nevertheless, Belgium's plucky defenses proved no match for Germany's deep reservoir of soldiers, superior firepower, and ruthless tactics, marked by the burning of villages and executions of civilians.[9] By August 20, Brussels had fallen, and Germany focused attention on its ultimate goal: crushing France.[10]

As Du Bois followed early news of the European disaster, he wrote to a longtime friend and London resident, Frances Hoggan. With August 28 ship passage booked for Nina and Yolande, he wanted an up-close opinion about the situation abroad and how it might affect his family. The war had quickly disrupted social and economic life in capital cities and rural countrysides alike,[11] and while Germany had not yet decided to unleash its U-boats, the safety of transatlantic travel was uncertain. Hoggan, sharing the optimistic sentiments of most middle-class Londoners in the early days of the war, informed Du Bois in her August 15 letter that though room and board had become more expensive, "life goes on almost normally." "There is not much risk in coming over," she assured him and, regarding Du Bois's loved ones, promised, "I should do my part for them in case of need." Hoggan acknowledged that "uncertainty is the great feature at present," but she believed that "as things now stand Germany will be forced by failure of supplies for the army and other armies to make peace within a not very long period."[12]

Du Bois was steadfast that his daughter, war or no war, would attend Bedales. Yet he decided to err on the side of caution and delay Yolande and Nina's Atlantic crossing until after mid-September. "I would not want them in any danger or great deprivation," he told Hoggan, although the pair, he presumed, "would not mind small inconveniences." About the war itself, Du Bois, at least for the moment, could not muster the words: "This sudden failure of civilization is simply beyond comment."[13]

~

BY AUGUST 1914, William Edward Burghardt Du Bois had scaled heights thought unimaginable for a Black person in late nineteenth- and early twentieth-century America. "I was born by a golden river and in the shadow of two great hills, five years after the Emancipation Proclamation which began the freeing of American Negro slaves," he wrote in the last of his many autobiographical remembrances.[14] The only child of Alfred Du Bois and Mary Silvina Burghardt, Du Bois came of age in the small, quintessentially New England town of Great Barrington, Massachusetts. Driven to succeed despite challenging familial circumstances, he excelled academically, devoting himself to reading Greek and Latin and browsing the shelves of the local bookstore.[15] On June 27,

1884, at the age of sixteen, the light brown–skinned prodigy graduated from high school, the star of his small class of thirteen students.[16]

Following the sudden death of his mother in March 1885, young
Du Bois set out to make a name for himself and his family by obtaining the best education possible. He enrolled and, three years later,
graduated with pride from Fisk University in Tennessee, his first experience below the Mason-Dixon line, a world, he recalled, "split into
white and black halves." He loved Fisk, crediting the school with exposing him to this new world of Black folk—full of both suffering and
striving. Fisk also set in stone his racial identity. On these formative
years, Du Bois reflected, "A new loyalty and allegiance replaced my
Americanism: henceforward I was a Negro."[17]

But he'd long desired to attend Harvard. Admitted to pursue a
second undergraduate degree, he arrived on the Cambridge campus in
September 1888. Later recollecting that he was "in Harvard, but not of
it," he nevertheless made the most of his time, learning from some
of the nation's intellectual giants—William James, George Santayana,
Albert Bushnell Hart, Nathaniel Shaler, Josiah Royce—and honing a
humanistic approach to the study of life and a commitment to democratic reasoning.[18] After graduating cum laude in 1890, he continued
at Harvard to obtain a doctorate in history, stopping along the way to
spend two transformational years—from 1893 to 1894—at the University of Berlin. The lessons he reverently absorbed in classes taught
by Gustav von Schmoller, Heinrich von Treitschke, and other German
luminaries fortified his approach to history as a science, with the power
to shape the way nations and their people understood the past, present,
and future. Du Bois's experience in Germany profoundly shaped his
intellect, cultural tastes, and character. He would sport a well-groomed
Vandyke beard and handlebar mustache for the rest of his life.[19]

Yet this product of Victorian New England and European Enlightenment thought was Black, and unashamedly so. Late into the
night of his twenty-fifth birthday, in 1893, homesick and contempla-
tive in the solitude of his candlelit Berlin boarding room, Du Bois
determined to dedicate his life's cause to the Black race. "I therefore
take the work that the Unknown lay in my hands and work for the rise

of the Negro people, taking for granted that their best development means the best development of the world," he penned in a letter to himself. "These are my plans," he added, "to make a name in science, to make a name in literature and thus to raise my race."[20] This project of racial uplift, the calling of many like-minded educated African Americans in the late nineteenth century, steeled Du Bois's sense of purpose.[21]

He could soon boast of fulfilling his personal charge from that Berlin evening. He received his Harvard Ph.D. in 1895—the first African American to do so—with his doctoral dissertation, "The Suppression of the African Slave Trade," earning distinction as the inaugural publication of the Harvard Historical Studies series. He briefly taught classics at Wilberforce University in Ohio, an unpleasant experience save for the friendships he made and the charming, dark-eyed student, Nina Gomer, he became enamored with and married on May 12, 1896. The young couple moved to Philadelphia, where Du Bois spent a year at the University of Pennsylvania researching and writing what became *The Philadelphia Negro*, a pioneering work of sociology. The segregated state of the academy ruled out the possibility of a full-time position at Penn, so in 1897 Will and Nina packed up and moved south to Atlanta University. Here Du Bois truly made his mark, producing a series of studies that cemented his status as the nation's foremost Black social scientist interrogating what had come to be known interchangeably as the "race question" and the "Negro problem."[22]

As the new century approached, the hopes of African Americans for basic equality and recognition of their humanity looked dire. The post–Civil War years had offered the promise of freedom and political inclusion in the nation's reconstructed democracy, yet the dream ended prematurely with the election of 1876, as the federal government absolved itself of responsibility to protect its Black citizens.[23] Southern white supremacists were determined to keep the Negro in his place. In 1883, the Supreme Court ruled that the Thirteenth and Fourteenth Amendments did not guarantee individual civil rights and that Congress, as it had affirmed in 1875, lacked the power to outlaw racial discrimination. One by one, Southern states, redeemed from

Republican rule, devised ways to strip African Americans of political power and access to the ballot.[24] Informal rules of segregation became sanctioned and codified with the 1896 *Plessy v. Ferguson* Supreme Court ruling, broadening a system and culture of Jim Crow that seeped into every aspect of Southern race relations.[25] The vast majority of Black Southerners toiled in near-slavery conditions as sharecroppers, trapped in a crushing cycle of debt and servitude.[26] Justice was synonymous with terror. A brutal convict leasing system, taking advantage of the Thirteenth Amendment's allowance of involuntary servitude "as punishment for a crime," epitomized the racist structure of the law and the systemic criminalization of Blackness.[27] Lynching and mob violence became endemic throughout the South and beyond. In the decade between 1890 and 1900 alone, more than twelve hundred Black people lost their lives at the hands of persons unknown.[28]

Du Bois felt the realities of race personally. Whether being a young schoolboy in Great Barrington, taking his first ride on a Jim Crow car as a Fisk undergraduate, or experiencing loneliness at Harvard and Berlin, he'd reckoned with the emotional weight of being Black.

His days in Atlanta, while remarkably productive, were also traumatic. On the evening of May 24, 1899, his two-year-old son, Burghardt, died, succumbing to a ten-day bout of diphtheria that may have been treatable had he been born on the other side of the color line. Du Bois and grief-stricken Nina, who would never be the same, buried their son in Great Barrington, not wanting his final resting place to be in the red soil of Georgia.[29] This tragedy came on the heels of the April 23 lynching of Sam Hose, a Black farmer who, after being accused of murdering his employer, was burned and mutilated before two thousand white men and women, many still adorned in their Sunday church best. An appalled Du Bois set out from his office to register a protest with editors at *The Atlanta Constitution*, but decided otherwise upon learning that Hose's charred knuckles sat on display in a downtown store window. "Something died in me that day," he reflected decades later,[30] having realized that "one could not be a calm, cool, and detached scientist while Negroes were lynched, murdered and starved."[31]

Fueled by this moral commitment, he poured all his brilliance and anguish into writing *The Souls of Black Folk*. Released in 1903, the collection of new and previously published essays—revised and organized with philosophical clairvoyance, historical audacity, literary imagination, sociological precision, autobiographical introspection, political urgency, musical lyricism, and poetic emotion—together amounted to a text that defied classification. *The Souls of Black Folk* launched Du Bois as America's foremost prophet on what he declared was "the problem of the Twentieth Century . . . the problem of the color line."[32]

In spellbinding prose, Du Bois articulated the ways in which race shaped the everyday lives of African Americans and constructed their identity. The color line, he imagined, functioned as a "vast veil," physically and spiritually dividing the Black and white worlds. The veil obscured the vision of white people, thus rendering the Negro a homogeneous "problem." As Du Bois guided his readers in the book's fourteen chapters through life on the other side of the veil, he demonstrated that Black people were not a "problem" to be resolved but a proud, gifted race, full of triumphs and sorrows, tragedies and hopes, pain and faith. Navigating the color line endowed Black people with the "peculiar sensation" of "double-consciousness," what he described as the "sense of always looking at one's self through the eyes of others, of measuring one's soul by the tape of a world that looks on in amused contempt and pity." He added, in words that encapsulated for millions the fundamental tension of being Black in America, "One ever feels his two-ness, an American, a Negro; two souls, two thoughts, two unreconciled strivings; two warring ideals in one dark body, whose dogged strength alone keeps it from being torn asunder."[33]

While Du Bois made clear from the book's outset that he was "bone of the bone and flesh of the flesh of them that live within the Veil," *The Souls of Black Folk* resonated most powerfully among college-educated African Americans who were engaged in the task of racial uplift.[34] In the chapter "Of the Training of Black Men," Du Bois articulated the responsibilities of the "Talented Tenth"—not so much an exclusive group of Black intellectuals, but an aspiration and a calling for anyone striving through work, education, artistry, and professional excellence to represent the race and contribute to its progress. This included lawyers, doctors, teachers, athletes, ministers, businessmen, and soldiers.[35] Du Bois's framing of Black leadership, like much of his thinking about the history and meaning of racial struggle, was deeply gendered and laced with patriarchy. Women, to be sure, had a place in the Talented Tenth and deserved full social and political rights. But they were the mothers of the race and, as Du Bois believed, should play their natural role while Black men stood on the front lines.[36]

Debates about the type of education African Americans should receive and its use fueled his conflict with Booker T. Washington, the powerful principal of the Tuskegee Institute in Alabama. A former slave from Virginia, Washington built Tuskegee from the ground up, advancing a gospel of industrial training that grated against Du Bois's liberal arts sensibilities. Washington coupled this with a politics of racial conciliation, reassuring Southern white supremacists—as he did in his famous September 18, 1895, speech at the Cotton States and International Exposition in Atlanta—that "in all things that are purely social we can be as separate as the fingers, yet one as the hand in all things essential to mutual progress." Washington, having offered the ideal solution to the "race problem," gained the favor of white Gilded Age philanthropists and a choke hold on money flowing into Southern colleges, including to Du Bois's Atlanta University. Using his vast connections and the muscle of what came to be known as the "Tuskegee Machine," Washington sought to crush all threats, real or perceived, to his dominance.[37]

Du Bois, believing that the time had come for open, honest criticism and asserting his manly responsibility to voice it, used the chapter "Of Mr. Booker T. Washington and Others" in *The Souls of Black Folk* to methodically lay bare his ideological differences with the Tuskegee "Wizard." The race, Du Bois insisted, needed the ballot, civic equality, and higher education beyond training for life as manual laborers, writing, "We have no right to sit silently by while the inevitable seeds are sown for a harvest of disaster to our children, black and white."[38] He also painted Washington as outside the historical tradition of Black leadership, instead anointed by white capitalists North and South to legitimize the social, political, and economic marginalization of the race.[39]

The Souls of Black Folk and his confrontation of Washington thrust Du Bois into the role of civil rights leader and spokesman for the anti-Tuskegee wing of the Talented Tenth. In 1905, along with his former Harvard classmate, the Boston firebrand William Monroe Trotter, Du Bois established the Niagara Movement, a collection of race men and women committed to the cause of full political equality and racial justice for African Americans. Against Washington's considerable resistance, the group struggled for widespread support, but nevertheless laid the groundwork for the 1909 founding of the National Association for the Advancement of Colored People (NAACP).[40]

Du Bois, relocating to New York City, assumed the position of director of research and publications for the upstart, overwhelmingly white-run organization and editor of its monthly magazine of news and opinion, *The Crisis*. His pride and joy, *The Crisis* provided him with a platform to display the full arsenal of his intellectual, political, and artistic gifts. Upon receiving their copy in the mail, readers immediately turned to his editorials for information and inspiration. To those who followed his lead and hung on to his every word, Du Bois appeared larger than life.[41]

However, beneath his unassailable veneer lay a man with faults, frailties, and vulnerabilities. He possessed an ego that far exceeded his mere five-foot-five-inch stature. Keenly aware of his significance, walking cane always in hand, Du Bois could be notoriously cold and aloof.[42] He possessed little patience for people he deemed intellectually and politically inferior. While committed to hard truth-telling, he was not above strategic dishonesty when it best suited him.[43] Unable to conceive of, much less admit to, wrongdoing, Du Bois radiated a confidence that both attracted and repulsed. He especially clashed with his white colleagues at the NAACP, who waged a constant battle to coalesce his voice as editor of *The Crisis* with the agenda of the organization in its masthead. By late 1914, many board members wanted him out.

Joel Spingarn knew and understood Du Bois better than any

other person in the NAACP. The wealthy son of Jewish immigrants, headstrong and pugnacious, Spingarn made a name for himself as a brilliant scholar of comparative literature, teaching for twelve years at Columbia University. A dispute with Columbia's president prompted his departure from the university, opening the door for a new career in civic activism that, in 1911, led him to the NAACP. His younger brother, Arthur, a founding member, headed the nascent organization's legal committee. As Du Bois's future wife, Shirley Graham, told the story years later, "Upon visiting the offices of this association," Joel "met a small, alert brown man who was enthusiastically getting together a magazine which he called *The Crisis*. Such a literary effort alone would have deeply interested the former English professor, but the man himself with his Harvard accent and continental manners intrigued him."[44]

Intrigue blossomed into admiration and ultimately a deep friendship. In Du Bois, Spingarn saw a man of letters, erudition, and the potential of a suffering race. In Spingarn, Du Bois saw an intellectual and temperamental equal who, as part of a fellow persecuted group of people, held a fierce commitment to equal rights. "He was one of those vivid, enthusiastic but clear-thinking idealists which from age to age the Jewish race has given the world," Du Bois remembered.[45] Spingarn was also proudly American, having eschewed his hyphenated identity, and he saw no reason why Black people should not be embraced as full Americans as well. He immersed himself in the work of the NAACP with fervor, spreading the gospel of the "New Abolitionism" and assuming the chairmanship in 1913. "We fought each other continuously in the councils of the Association," Du Bois recalled of these early days of, at times, painful growth, "but always our admiration and basic faith in each other kept us going hand in hand."[46] Their relationship symbolized, for both men, the promise of American democracy.[47]

Spingarn also possessed the mettle to honestly criticize his friend when the occasion arose. At the height of a bitter disagreement in October 1914 between Du Bois and the NAACP over the role of *The Crisis* and the autonomy of its editor, Spingarn wrote to Du Bois, fully aware that "I may wound your feelings deeply." "You have an extraordinary unwillingness to acknowledge that you have made a mistake, even in trifles," he brazenly diagnosed, "and if accused of one, your mind will find or even invent reasons and quibbles of any kind to prove that you were never mistaken." White coworkers and acquaintances, Spingarn believed, felt "a mingled affection and resentment" toward Du Bois. "They have come to feel that you prefer to have your own way rather than accept another way," and trembled at the possibility of "wounding your own sensitive nerves."[48]

Du Bois, respectfully, refused to back down. He thanked Spingarn for his letter and its constructive spirit. "Some of the criticism, I think, is fair. Some I am sure is not," Du Bois wrote, admitting that "my temperament is a difficult one to endure," and noting, "In my peculiar education and experience it would be miraculous if I came through normal and unwarped." But the root cause of the friction within the NAACP, he argued, was not principally due to his touchy personality but to "the inevitable American rift of the color line." "You do not realize this," he gently told his enlightened yet still-privileged comrade. "Perhaps I realize it over-much," Du Bois conceded. "But remember I've lived beside it nearly half a century."[49]

Indeed, by the fall of 1914, as the world convulsed and the fate of the twentieth century hung in the balance, arguably no other African American could articulate the significance of the color line—and what it meant for Black people in the United States and beyond—with greater insight, vision, and passion than W. E. B. Du Bois.

AT 12:00 NOON ON September 23, Nina and Yolande departed from New York aboard the steamship *St. Paul* for Liverpool.[50] In spite of the war—and unexpected passport complications Du Bois frantically sought to resolve—they arrived safely after a little more than a week at sea.[51] Du Bois was relieved. He took seriously his patriarchal responsibilities to direct the course of Yolande's education and provide for Nina's comfort. However, untethered from their presence, he could now devote more undivided attention to his work, which included thinking about the war.

Events on the battlefield unfolded quickly. By early September, after smashing through Belgium and into northern France, the German columns stood a mere thirty miles from Paris, ready to strike a final blow. The war may very well have ended at the Marne. But on September 6, the French general Joseph Joffre rallied his troops, launched a daring counterattack, and, aided by British Allied forces and critical miscalculations by German commanders, forced the Kaiser's army to retreat to the Aisne River. The weeklong nonstop storm of machine-gun fire and artillery explosion left a horrific toll: more than five hundred thousand soldiers dead, wounded, or missing.[52] The results portended things to come. Hoping to outflank each other, the "race to the sea" began, with opposing forces moving northward as rapidly as possible, mangling the countryside with miles of fortified trenches along the way.

While Nina and Yolande tried to get accustomed to their new surroundings in London and Bedales, on October 19, across the English Channel, the warring armies clashed near the Belgian town of Ypres. For more than a month they bloodied the fields of Flanders until, by mid-November, the arrival of winter weather brought the hostilities to an indecisive halt. Both sides suffered staggering casualties, with the British Expeditionary Forces severely crippled and the Belgian army virtually destroyed. The battle resulted in stalemate and entrenchment, as the Allied and German troops, also fighting determined Russian forces in the east, literally and figuratively dug in for an uncertain future.[53]

The imperial scope of the war immediately became clear as Africa was pulled into the conflict. In early August, France and Great Britain, already imagining the colonial spoils of an Allied victory, had taken control of the German-held territories of Togoland and Cameroon. An invasion of British forces from South Africa, led by Louis Botha, into German South West Africa proved unsuccessful, but fighting continued. By September, German East Africa, the Kaiser's most prized African colonial possession, also became a battleground, marked by the mobilization of native Black troops. Germany and Great Britain initially hesitated but ultimately assented to using Africans in combat against white soldiers. Yet they remained adamant against employing them on European soil, more attentive to the stability of racial hierarchy than to military necessity. France, on the other hand, decided to throw troops from its North and West African colonies into the killing fields of the Western Front. By 1915, red-capped *tirailleurs* were charging into the German lines, paying their blood tax for the privilege of being children of the empire.[54]

The African dimensions of the war sadly confirmed for Du Bois the dangers a German victory would incur to Black folk on the continent and beyond. He knew Germany well. As a young student at the University of Berlin, he had developed a profound reverence for German history, culture, and intellect. The experience also afforded him firsthand knowledge of the *Deutsches Kaiserreich*'s march toward autocracy, militarism, and empire. He'd taken classes with Heinrich von Treitschke, the acclaimed historian whom Du Bois described as "the very embodiment of united monarchical, armed, Germany."[55] He'd viewed the military parades and observed the Prussian gait of superiority with which the soldiers marched. It reminded him of the strut of the Southern white supremacist. In a curt October 9, 1914, letter to Moritz Schanz, a German diplomat who worked to propagandize his country's imperial control of East Africa, Du Bois declared, without equivocation, "I regret to say that I believe Germany is responsible for the war." He reminded Schanz of a recent statement produced by a group of "leading German scientists" who defended their nation's conduct in fueling the crisis. "Germany will fight to the end as a cultured nation, which has the might of Goethe, Beethoven, and Kant," they wrote, adding, "Those who associate with Russians and Servians and offer to the world the spectacle of letting loose mongrels and niggers on the white race have the least right to call themselves defenders of European civilization."[56] Although Du Bois held Goethe in the highest esteem, appreciated the beauty of Beethoven's music, and relished fond memories of reading Kant alongside George Santayana at Harvard, his allegiances lay with the world's Black folk, whose freedoms and aspirations were threatened by Germany. "I sincerely hope that your country will be thoroughly whipped," he told Schanz.[57]

This exchange with Schanz took place just as Du Bois finished writing "World War and the Color Line" for the November 1914 issue of *The Crisis*, his first extensive published thoughts on the European calamity. "The present war in Europe is one of the great disasters due to race and color prejudice," he warned readers, "and it but foreshadows greater disasters in the future." He made clear that the loyalties of people of color must rest with the Allied nations of England, France, and Belgium, in spite of their own terrible colonial records. A victory by the Central Powers, he rationalized, would mean "the triumph of every force calculated to subordinate darker peoples" and elevate Germany, her dream of racial dominance and world conquest realized, to "one of the most contemptible of 'Nigger' hating nations."[58] Race and the global color line stood at the heart of the war's origins. It was "not merely national jealousy" that prefigured the European bloodletting. Instead, Du Bois argued, the real causes of the war lay in "the wild quest for Imperial expansion among colored races between Germany, England and France primarily, and Belgium, Italy, Russia and Austria-Hungary in lesser degree." Driving this was "a theory of the inferiority of the darker peoples and a contempt for their rights and aspirations" espoused by the United States and embraced the world over, which by 1914 had "become all but universal in the greatest centers of modern culture."[59]

Du Bois put an even finer point on this argument for the May 1915 issue of *The Atlantic Monthly* in the essay "The African Roots of War." "Yet in a very real sense Africa is a prime cause of this terrible overturning of civilization which we have lived to see," he asserted. The 1884 Berlin Conference marked a new epoch in the history of Africa and Europe, as the partitioning of the continent—"contemptible and dishonest beyond expression"—and subsequent exploitation relied upon "lying treaties, rivers of rum, murder, assassination, mutilation, rape, and torture," all in the name of "progress." This new imperialism underwrote the maturation of late nineteenth- and early twentieth-century global capitalism. What made this development unique, Du Bois analyzed, was the complicity between the "captains of industry" and the "white workingman" in race prejudice and "exploiting 'chinks and niggers.'" With other economic spheres of influence already claimed or deemed not as profitable, the "white European mind" fixated on Africa. "The greater the concentration, the more deadly the rivalry," Du Bois wrote. The result, he argued, was the World War, a tangle of national jealousies and suspicions arising from the "spoils of trade-empire" and the desire for expansion, "not in Europe but in Asia, and particularly in Africa."[60]

Du Bois painted a bleak picture. The war served as Europe's reckoning. Africa and the darker races suffered the collateral damage. What, then, did the future hold? How could those committed to peace, like Du Bois, "remove the real causes of war"?

Democracy was the answer. "We must extend the democratic ideal to the yellow, brown, and black peoples," he faithfully declared. The eighteenth- and nineteenth-century expansion of democracy beyond the realm of the ruling elite, a remarkable development in world history, also coincided with slavery, disfranchisement, empire, and the doctrine of white supremacy. The nations of the West, therefore, faced a decision. "Suppose we have to choose between this unspeakably inhuman outrage on decency and intelligence and religion which we call the World War and the attempt to treat black men as human, sentient, responsible beings?" Du Bois believed that the answer was obvious, and that it could be done. "Democracy is a method of doing the impossible," he mused. The impossible meant providing African peoples with land, education, and political autonomy. They also needed uplift and leadership. For this, Du Bois looked to the diaspora, "the twenty-five million grandchildren of the European slave trade, spread through the Americas and now writhing desperately for freedom and a place in the world," and, first and foremost, "the ten million black folk of the United States, now a problem, then a world-salvation." A future Black world, born out of the war, shaped by democratic ideals, and led by enlightened African Americans—like himself—riveted his imagination.

⁓

DU BOIS CONTINUED TO closely monitor the war as it spilled into 1915. He had the aid of a personal war correspondent in his wife, Nina, whose letters home, mostly expressing her loneliness and need for additional money, contained periodic impressions of events in

London. Basic everyday items grew more scarce; German attacks on merchant vessels increased in regularity; shell-shocked convalescing soldiers became a regular sight.[61] "Every where one turns are troops," Nina remarked in a May 15 letter three weeks into the Second Battle of Ypres, the first use by Germany of poison gas on the Western Front. "I passed a hospital where there seemed to be such numbers of wounded soldiers some sitting out some on cots, the losses have been very heavy on both sides of late."[62]

The decision by Germany to conduct air raids on London brought the war to terrifyingly close proximity. Around 11:00 p.m. on the night of May 31, a 650-foot German zeppelin appeared over North London and released more than 120 incendiary bombs and grenades on mostly residential neighborhoods. Flames consumed forty-one buildings, and left seven people dead and another thirty-five wounded. The campaign continued into June.[63] "I've seen several bombs, two from the recent raids on London," Nina wrote that month. She professed to not being afraid, believing the Germans would opt for more important targets than where she resided; nevertheless, she acknowledged, "they don't always hit where they aim to."[64]

The May 7, 1915, sinking of the RMS *Lusitania* offered tragic evidence that the Atlantic Ocean would not buffer America from the war's destructive reach. "Isn't the sinking of the Lusitania dreadful," Nina wrote to her husband. After being torpedoed by a German U-boat, the British ocean liner sank in just eighteen minutes, killing 1,198 passengers, including 128 American citizens. President Woodrow Wilson responded to an outraged public calling for the United States to declare war on Germany, arguing, "There is such a thing as a man being too proud to fight. There is such a thing as a nation being so right that it does not need to convince others by force that it is right."[65] Meanwhile, Nina watched as demonstrations erupted in the streets of London. Signs reading DO NOTHING AMERICA in large letters plastered the windows of buses. "I wonder what the Germans will do next," she pondered.[66]

Whatever subsequent atrocities followed, Du Bois's judgment of the war, as he revealed in the June 1915 *Crisis* editorial "Lusitania," had now been set in stone. "The last horror of a horrible war is come!

It puts a period to what we have already said: European civilization has failed." He raged at the hypocrisy of those who decried the actions of Germany on the high seas while remaining silent about the rape, mutilation, and exploitation of Black and brown people across the globe: "The Great War is the lie unveiled." From the moral high ground as the European civil war raged below, Du Bois proclaimed, "It is a great privilege in the midst of this frightful catastrophe to belong to a race that can stand before Heaven with clean hands and say: we have not oppressed, we have been oppressed; we are not thieves, we are victims; we are not murderers, we are lynched!"[67]

While Du Bois stayed busy in New York, managing *The Crisis* and writing scorching editorials, Yolande, an ocean away at the Bedales school, missed her papa. "I haven't had a letter from you for years," she wrote in June, jokingly but with enough somberness to betray her emotional needs. Even with her mother nearby, being a young Black girl in a foreign country was a disorienting experience. The presence of the war undoubtedly heightened her anxieties. "Do you think America will join in the war, don't you think she ought to?" she asked her father. "I do."[68]

Du Bois did not offer his daughter an answer. He instead reminded Yolande to stay focused on the "interesting worlds" buried within her books.[69] However, her question, as well as how African Americans should respond if the United States entered the war, no doubt weighed heavily on his mind. The national Preparedness Movement, led by the former president Theodore Roosevelt and his fellow Spanish-Cuban-American War "Rough Rider" General Leonard Wood, gained momentum after the sinking of the *Lusitania*. Woodrow Wilson held firm to a policy of American neutrality but grudgingly agreed to increase the size of the military and officer corps with the June 1916 National Defense Act. Du Bois, in heart and principle, sided with such anti-militarists and peace advocates as the NAACP cofounder Jane Addams.[70] At the same time, he recognized the importance of reminding African Americans that the war, while perhaps geographically distant, held important implications for the race in both the present and the future.

Du Bois used *The Crisis* to keep readers fully abreast of the war and its significance for the Black world. He gave special attention to the African dimensions of the conflict, noting the service of colonial troops, particularly those in the French Army. The image of Black West Africans fighting for France and against German autocracy on European soil fascinated him.[71] Photos of the *tirailleurs sénégalais*, accompanied by provocative subheadings—such as "Black soldiers from Senegal fighting to protect the civilization of Europe from itself" and "Negro Senegalese, of the French colonial troops, delivering a harangue to a group of German prisoners"—appeared regularly in *The Crisis* from late 1914 to early 1917.[72]

Pictures and stories of the "Buffalo Soldiers" of the United States Regular Army rang more familiar to readers. As Jim Crow, disfranchisement, and mob violence had rendered most African Americans second-class citizens, the presence and meaning of Black troops in the Ninth and Tenth Cavalry and the Twenty-Fourth and Twenty-Fifth Infantry became especially important. Black men made up ten percent of a standing Regular Army that numbered only twenty-five thousand prior to World War I. Through heroic service in Cuba, the Philippines, and across the American West, they staked claim to the United States and their manhood, albeit in the name of empire and at the expense of the lives of indigenous peoples and other darker races.[73] Since 1868, nineteen Black soldiers had received the Medal of Honor.[74] Looking past their contradictions and choosing to focus on what they meant for the cause of African American progress, Du Bois extolled the Black Regulars in *Crisis* articles with photos, updates on their whereabouts, and profiles as "Men of the Month." As evocative symbols, they represented citizenship, Black masculinity, and leadership, the fighting arm of Du Bois's Talented Tenth.

The summer of 1916 found some of the Buffalo Soldiers in Mexico. The United States, asserting its hemispheric dominance, had meddled in the Mexican Revolution since its start in 1910. The Wilson administration formally recognized Venustiano Carranza as leader of the country, in the process betraying Carranza's adversary and former American ally, Francisco "Pancho" Villa. Aggrieved and in need of supplies, Villa and his men conducted a daring raid on Columbus, New Mexico, on March 9, 1916, resulting in the deaths of eighteen

American soldiers and civilians. Wilson promptly responded by ordering a "Punitive Expedition" to track down Villa and bring him to justice. On March 15, General John J. Pershing led roughly ten thousand
hastily assembled American troops across the border.[75]

"Black Jack" Pershing's expeditionary force included his former
unit, the Tenth Cavalry, now officered by Major Charles Young. Young
towered as the highest-ranking African American in the United States
Army. Born in Kentucky in 1864, he had military service in his blood.
Young's father, Gabriel, escaped from slavery and briefly served in the
Union Army at the tail end of the Civil War. In 1884, Young enrolled
at the venerable and thoroughly racist West Point Military Academy.
Enduring insult and isolation, he graduated in 1889, only the third
African American to do so. His varied and distinguished career began
with the Ninth Cavalry and, in 1894, with an assignment at Wilber-
force University to serve as professor of military science and tactics.[76]

Du Bois arrived at Wilberforce that same year.[77] The two men
initially bonded over their shared disdain for the school's Christmas-
time religious revival services, but soon found they had other things in
common.[78] They possessed similar tastes in music and literature. Both
were fiercely disciplined, determined to defy stereotypes, and committed to shattering barriers when it came to their careers, Du Bois
in academics and Young in the military. Indeed, Du Bois, educated at
Harvard and the University of Berlin, could appreciate as few others
Young's lonely battle to demonstrate his ability in a white supremacist
army. Most important, the two trailblazers held a deep commitment
to uplifting the race. Young, "silent, uncomplaining, brave, and efficient," as Du Bois described him, stood as a fitting model of Black
leadership—for African Americans but also for Du Bois personally.[79]
Young possessed a type of rugged Black masculinity that the highbrow doctor from Great Barrington, long an admirer of martial figures, deeply respected.[80] Du Bois, socially awkward and shy by nature,
found in Young his first true male friend.[81]

The bonds between the two men grew over the years. They confided in each other, with Young revealing the pain he experienced
during his isolating time at West Point and Du Bois sharing the hurt
of being the subject of Black New York gossip circles related to his

aloof personality and the stability of his marriage.[82] Nina Du Bois and Young's wife, Ada, also spent time together. In June and July 1915, Ada and her two children, Charles Noel and Marie Aurelia, visited Nina and Yolande in London. Charles wrote to Nina, wishing her well and expressing gratitude that she remained safely beyond the reach of "that beastly war."[83]

Along with being a dear friend and a personal hero, Young was a powerful symbol for Du Bois. The editor chronicled every achievement of Young's illustrious career, which seemed to hold no limit.[84] After the Spanish-Cuban-American War disrupted his teaching at Wilberforce, Young returned to the Ninth Cavalry, this time as a captain. The February 1912 issue of *The Crisis* featured Captain Young on the cover, dignified in his uniform, officer bars proudly displayed. He served in a number of places throughout the country and world in service of America's empire—in California as superintendent of national parks, in the Philippines to help secure the U.S. occupation, in Haiti and Liberia as a military attaché—and ascended to the rank of major. A handsome full-page photo in the January 1916 *Crisis* listed his accomplishments.[85] To the questions "Am I an American or am I a Negro? Can I be both?" that Du Bois had asked in the 1897 essay "The Conservation of Races" and echoed in *The Souls of Black Folk*, Charles Young seemingly and without contradiction answered yes.[86]

Further validation of Young's importance came on the evening of February 22, 1916, in Boston, when he accepted the NAACP Spingarn Medal. Du Bois played a pivotal role in making sure that Young became the second recipient of the prestigious award, named after Du Bois's closest white comrade, Joel Spingarn.[87] Twenty-five hundred friends, family, well-wishers, and admirers, among them the governor of Massachusetts, filled the Tremont Temple in downtown Boston, across the street from where Crispus Attucks and other heroes of the American Revolution lay buried and memorialized. Young humbly accepted the award, assuring the crowd that if and when the country needed his services, he would be "Jonny on the spot."[88] An untimely train wreck in Connecticut delayed Du Bois, preventing him from attending the ceremony. However, he reunited with his friend the next day in New

York City, where, over dinner, they celebrated Du Bois's forty-eighth birthday and toasted to the next chapter in Young's military career.[89]

Du Bois further atoned for missing the Spingarn medal fete with a tribute in the March 1916 *Crisis* simply and appropriately titled "Young." At the height of his profession, "strongly built, and physically fit" with a "certain unusually fine quality of spirit," Young was more than deserving of the NAACP's highest award. He had endured many challenges and come face-to-face with death, but, as Du Bois wrote, he survived, and, alluding to the possibility of America entering the World War, stood "ready for further sacrifices."[90]

BY THE SUMMER OF 1916, few people could question Du Bois's stature as Black America's foremost thinker and leader. On November 15 of the preceding year, Booker T. Washington had died at the age of fifty-nine, his overworked heart finally giving out. The influence of the Tuskegee principal had gradually eroded since the founding of the Niagara Movement and its progeny, the NAACP. Washington's death, Du Bois accurately deduced, marked an "epoch in the history of America" and the history of the Black freedom struggle. Du Bois opted for magnanimity in noting the passing of his adversary, writing in a *Crisis* eulogy, "He was the greatest Negro leader since Frederick Douglass, and the most distinguished man, white or black, who has come out of the South since the Civil War." While acknowledging Washington's "mistakes and shortcomings," Du Bois wrote that the times did not call for "recrimination or complaint." Instead, he encouraged Black people in America and throughout the world to "close ranks and march steadily on" toward their ultimate goal of freedom, equality, and justice.[91] With his chief rival gone from the stage, it was Du Bois's time to lead.

The first real test of his call for unity occurred in August 1916 at Amenia, New York. "There was war in Europe," he recalled of the moment, "but a war far, far away." Although he had discussed it, in his words, "from time to time with a calm detachment," his mind remained focused on the "battle in America, that war of colors which we who are black always sense as the principal thing in life." Success-fully fighting that battle required a unified front. Joel Spingarn had conceived the idea for a gathering at his Troutbeck estate in Amenia, where, Du Bois remembered, "colored and white men of all shades of opinion might sit down and rest and talk and agree on many things if not on all."[92]

When it came to conceptualizing and organizing the confer-ence, Du Bois assumed the reins. He developed the agenda and care-fully managed an ambitious interracial list of two hundred invitees that included the current and former presidents Wilson, Taft, and Roosevelt, who each declined.[93] Ultimately, fifty-five men and women representing a broad geographical and ideological cross-section of the racial uplift spectrum confirmed their attendance.[94]

The most prominent member of the Tuskegee camp to accept Du Bois's invitation was Emmett Jay Scott. In 1897, the native Texan, with a background in journalism, had landed the plum job of private secretary to Booker T. Washington. He made himself indispensable and soon became Washington's most trusted confidant, effectively serving as the brains and cunning behind-the-scenes architect of the Tuskegee Machine. He was also one of Du Bois's slyest foes, using his connections in the Black press to undermine first the Niagara Move-ment and then the NAACP. After Washington's death in 1915, Scott envisioned succeeding the Wizard, but Robert Russa Moton, from sister school Hampton Institute, was selected for the position. While disappointed by the snub, Scott remained loyal to Tuskegee, as his presence at Amenia in Moton's place reflected.[95]

Reminiscing in 1925, Du Bois ascribed mystical qualities to Joel Spingarn's rural Troutbeck manor and its sprawling property. "I had no sooner seen the place than I knew it was mine," he recollected of his arrival on the cool, misty morning of August 24. The "same slow, rocky uplift of land, the nestle of lake and the sturdy murmur of brooks and brown rivers," and the "blue and mysterious mountains" in the distance transported him back to his beloved Berkshire Hills. Du Bois and Spingarn breathed a sigh of relief as participants—Emmett Scott, the Morehouse College president John Hope, Mary Church

Terrell of the National Association of Colored Women, the *New York Age* editor Fred Moore, and others—slowly began to filter in and locate their assigned canvas tents spread out across the lawn. The rustic settings made for a congenial atmosphere and helped thaw icy relationships hardened by years of ideological conflict. Soon, Du Bois fondly remembered, they were all having a "rollicking jolly time." Between games of tennis, swims in the lake, leisurely hikes in the surrounding forest, and great meals—"miraculously steaming and perfectly cooked"—the gathered spokesmen and women of the race attended to business. They talked openly and frankly. By the last day, August 26, they came away with a balanced platform that called for "political freedom," the right to "all forms of education," and recognition of "the peculiar difficulties" facing Black people in the South. Achieving these goals would necessitate a "practical working understanding among the leaders of the colored race" and the elimination of "antiquated subjects of controversy, ancient suspicions and factional alignments." Amenia, they hoped, would only be the first of many similar gatherings in the future.[96]

Years later, Du Bois reflected, "Probably on account of our meeting the Negro race was more united and more ready to meet the problems of the world than it could possibly have been without these beautiful days of understanding."[97] Brimming with confidence as he returned to New York City, he felt that no challenge, even war, was too large to tackle.[98]

He was not, however, prepared to confront the possibility of death. A kidney stone ailed him throughout the summer. The pain had become bad enough to briefly incapacitate him during the lead-up to Amenia. By December, his condition was unbearable and required surgery. On the morning of December 15, 1916, doctors at St. Luke's Hospital prepared Du Bois for an operation on his left kidney. A nervous Joel Spingarn sent his family physician to be present, "in order to make certain," as he wrote to Du Bois in the days leading up to the procedure, "that every advantage of medical science would be placed at your disposal."[99] Surgeons successfully removed the stone. However, the blockage, undiagnosed for ten years, had left the organ irreparably damaged. After two weeks of consultation, doctors recommended the kidney's immediate removal. A second, more serious, surgery was scheduled for January 4.[100]

"They brought him down from the operating table at 1:30," Joel Spingarn wrote. The surgery, as Du Bois modestly described it, was "rather delicate."[101] Spingarn later visited, finding Du Bois asleep. The nurse offered words of reassurance. "He is unconscious, and we cannot tell yet," she said, "but he seems to have stood the operation pretty well." As Spingarn left the hospital, Du Bois's fate uncertain, he worried for his friend, but also wondered what it would mean "for twelve million people if this champion of theirs were not permitted to live."[102] NAACP colleagues and much of the Talented Tenth across the country held their collective breath, awaiting word of Du Bois's condition.[103]

For nearly three weeks, "shrouded by the curtains of pain," he convalesced. Recalling the ordeal in typically dramatic prose, Du Bois "looked death in the face and found its lineaments not unkind. But it was not my time."[104] Day by day he improved, and by January 20 he was up on his feet and moving about. On January 22 he left St. Luke's Hospital, "apparently as strong as ever, if not stronger, for the fight ahead."[105]

BY THE END OF January 1917, as Du Bois, having eluded death and fully recovered, eased back into his work at *The Crisis*, Woodrow Wilson agonized over the increasing likelihood of America going to war. Du Bois initially came to know and respect the Southern-born Wilson, who held a Ph.D. in history and government, as an academic.[106] He used Wilson's popular 1889 textbook *The State* in his civil government classes at Atlanta University,[107] and he shared with Wilson a deep fascination with the history and ultimate potential of American democracy. "Democracy is a principle with us, not a mere form of government," Wilson wrote in a 1901 *Atlantic Monthly* article. "It is for this that we love democracy: for the emphasis it puts on character; for its tendency to exalt the purposes of the average man to some high level of endeavor; for its just principle of common assent in matters in which all are concerned; for its ideals of duty and its sense of brotherhood."[108] However, the two scholars, both shaped in radically different ways by the color line, held polar opposite views on race, history, and the full inclusion of Black people in the nation's democracy.[109]

In spite of these faults, Du Bois saw reasons for optimism in Woodrow Wilson the elected officeholder, having followed his public career as president of Princeton University and as governor of New Jersey. He came to view the reform-minded Democrat as a "new type of politician." When Wilson decided to seek the presidency in 1912, promising "justice executed with liberality and cordial good feeling" for his "colored fellow-citizens," Du Bois, in a leap of faith, resigned his brief one-year membership in the Socialist Party and threw his weight behind Wilson's candidacy.[110] "On the whole, we do not believe that Woodrow Wilson admires Negroes," Du Bois wrote in his *Crisis* endorsement. But he still considered him "a cultivated scholar" with "brains" and not fanatically committed to white supremacy like other Southern Democrats.[111] After Wilson handily defeated the former president Theodore Roosevelt, who was running as a third-party Progressive, and the incumbent, William Howard Taft, Du Bois penned a firm, yet hopeful open letter to the new commander in chief. "Your inauguration to the Presidency of the United States is to the colored people, to the white South and to the nation a momentous occasion," he wrote in *The Crisis*, adding that Wilson held the potential "to become the greatest benefactor of his country since Abraham Lincoln."[112]

The folly of Du Bois's belief in Wilson soon became embarrassingly clear. Consistent with most Southern progressives, Wilson viewed Jim Crow as the most efficient means of addressing the "race question."[113] He thus put up no resistance as his cabinet, dominated by fellow Democrats from the South, diligently began segregating the federal government, starting with the Treasury and the Postal Service. Moreover, with the ghosts of Reconstruction still looming, the desire for a clean, corruption-free civil service by Wilson and his administration came at the expense of Black employees, the majority of them Republicans who had traditionally benefited from a long-standing patronage system. Good government meant a white government.

Emboldened Southern congressional Democrats advanced a host of virulently racist measures, including a federal anti-miscegenation law. Although Wilson opposed these rabid expressions of white supremacy, his more genteel version was ultimately no less devastating for African Americans in Washington and beyond, both tangibly and symbolically.[114]

Adam Patterson became one of the Wilson administration's most prominent Black victims. Patterson had come a long way from the small town of Walthall, Mississippi, where he was born on December 23, 1876. Ambition carried him to the University of Kansas, where he earned a law degree in 1900. He began practicing in Colorado, before eventually settling in Muskogee, Oklahoma, in 1904. Taking advantage of Muskogee's vibrant Black community of post-Reconstruction Exodusters, Patterson made a name for himself in both law and real estate. The move also served as an opportunity for reinvention, as he listed himself and his wife, Nellie, as white on the 1910 census. His willingness to bend the rules of race was also reflected in his politics, as he counted himself among the small national population of Black Democrats, calculating that a break from the Republican Party would translate to political and financial reward. He aggressively stumped for Wilson in 1912, winning the favor of local and state white Democratic politicians, including Senator Thomas Gore. As a result of these efforts, he received a nomination for the post of register of the Treasury, a position that, since Reconstruction, had traditionally been given to an African American.[115]

He immediately found himself in a hornet's nest. The previous Black register of the Treasury, James Napier, had nobly resigned in protest over the newly elected president's policy of racial segregation for all federal employees. The Black press looked askance at Patterson when he agreed to accept the humiliation of Jim Crow as a condition of the post, while, at the same time, white supremacists in and outside Congress furiously opposed his nomination. Rumors circulated that he would be assassinated if ever confirmed.[116] Overwhelmed, yet still hoping to remain in the good graces of white Democrats, Patterson withdrew his name, wanting, as he wrote to Wilson, not to "embarrass your administration, Mr. President."[117]

Patterson's public withdrawal and unwillingness to fight for the post earned him a savage beating in the Black press. *The Topeka Plaindealer* accused him of "laying down," while *The Washington Bee* described him as "a man with a child's mind."[118] Du Bois offered his thoughts in a blistering editorial, "Another Open Letter to Woodrow Wilson," penned for the September 1913 issue of *The Crisis*. After just six months, Du Bois fumed, "It is no exaggeration to say that every enemy of the Negro race is greatly encouraged" and scolded Wilson that "not a single act and not a single word of yours since election has given anyone reason to infer that you have the slightest interest in the colored people or desire to alleviate their intolerable position." He decried the removal of "worthy Negro officials" from the federal government while noting that the only Black man put up for office— Adam Patterson—was "a contemptible cur" whose nomination "was an insult to every Negro in the land."[119]

The Patterson embarrassment numbered only one of many points Du Bois made in his scathing critique of the president. He specifically targeted Wilson's actions in segregating the federal government, writing, "The policy adopted, whether with your consent or knowledge or not, is an indefensible attack on a people who have in the past been shamefully humiliated . . . We have appealed in the past, Mr. Wilson, to you as a man and statesman; to your sense of fairness and broad cosmopolitan outlook on the world. We renew this appeal and to it we venture to add some plain considerations of political expediency." Du Bois's plea made little difference, as the unmitigated racial disaster of the Wilson presidency continued to unfold. Despite the best efforts of the NAACP's Washington branch to fight the onslaught on the city's Black professional community, the segregation of federal employees continued apace, further aided by a 1914 directive requiring all civil service applicants to provide photo identification.

The 1915 film *The Birth of a Nation* was like salt to an open wound. Directed by D. W. Griffith and based on the book *The Clansman*, written by Wilson's former Johns Hopkins classmate Thomas Dixon, the film offered a simultaneously enthralling and grotesque rendering of the Civil War and Reconstruction era, replete with full glorification of the Ku Klux Klan. The film premiered on February 8, in Los Angeles. Ten days later, on February 18, Wilson did Dixon the favor of hosting a special screening in the East Room of the White House. Wilson professed to be "entirely unaware of the character of the play" and never offered a full public endorsement. However, the fact that he remained silent in the face of national protests—the most vociferous led by William Monroe Trotter—and offered no objections to Griffith's out-of-context quotes from his 1902 book, *A History of the American People*, conveyed a White House stamp of approval.[120] *The Birth of a Nation* became the first national blockbuster, with white audiences across the country enraptured and enraged by the visual and musical spectacle. On November 25, inspired by the film, a small group of white Georgians, led by an itinerant preacher, William Joseph Simmons, ascended Stone Mountain on the outskirts of Atlanta, burned a cross, and inaugurated the second coming of the Ku Klux Klan.[121]

Predictably, lynching and mob violence continued and became even more spectacular. On May 15, 1916, in Waco, Texas, a white mob of more than ten thousand participants reveled in the burning and mutilation of Jesse Washington, a Black farmhand accused of rape and murder. Washington was one of at least fifty Black people lynched in 1916. Wilsonian white supremacy was not confined to American soil. When U.S. Marines had disembarked at Port-au-Prince, Haiti, on July 28, 1915, Du Bois initially hoped to leverage Wilson's invasion to spread democracy and credible leadership to the hemisphere's only Black republic. However, the American occupation quickly became marred by racist brutality and economic exploitation.[122] As the 1916 presidential election neared, African Americans had no reason what-soever to support Wilson. On October 16, Du Bois received a tepid letter from the White House secretary Joseph Tumulty, who remarked that his boss could "say with a clear conscience" that he tried to live up to his "original assurances" to African Americans from four years earlier.[123] Du Bois would not be duped again. "*No intelligent Negro can vote for Woodrow Wilson*," he declared in *The Crisis*.[124]

In the months immediately following Wilson's razor-thin reelec-tion, American neutrality regarding the World War quickly became untenable. Wilson successfully campaigned on his accomplishment in keeping the United States out of the conflict and began to actively push for an American-brokered peace settlement. The February 1, 1917, resumption of unrestricted submarine warfare—a high-risk calculation by Germany that they could inflict enough damage on British vessels to end the war before the United States had time to enter and make a difference—ended those hopes. Wilson broke off diplomatic relations and began to seriously weigh the possibility of the United States joining the carnage.

A top-secret telegram from the German secretary of foreign affairs, Arthur Zimmermann, to the German ambassador to Mexico eliminated any lingering doubt in Wilson's mind. In the telegram, originally sent on January 16 and intercepted by British intelligence, Zimmermann acknowledged the likelihood of American entry into the war. In that case, Zimmermann proposed that Germany and Mexico form an alliance to "make war together, make peace together," with the ultimate prize upon victory and settlement the reacquisition of the land encompassing Texas, New Mexico, and Arizona lost in the Mexican-American War and the 1848 Treaty of Guadalupe Hidalgo. When informed by the U.S. ambassador to the United Kingdom, Walter Hines Page, of the communication, Wilson was furious. He decided to release it to the public. On March 1, the telegram appeared on newspaper front pages across the country to howls of outrage.[125]

Wilson's inauguration speech just four days later reflected the changed reality of America's involvement in the European maelstrom. "We are provincials no longer," the president somberly told his fellow Americans, who now had to view themselves as "citizens of the world." He agonized over the possibility of war, realizing the potentially horrendous consequences. The principle of staying out of European conflicts, sacrosanct since George Washington and the founding of the republic, was outdated. "There can be no turning back," Wilson said. "Our own fortunes as a nation are involved whether we would have it so or not."[126]

On the rainy evening of April 2, Wilson made the mile-long trip up Pennsylvania Avenue to address a special joint session of Congress.

He'd requested the opportunity to discuss "grave matters of national policy." As he approached the podium, anticipation and tension filled the House chamber. Reading carefully from his typewritten speech, point by point, he methodically laid out the case for war, arguing that the burden had been thrust upon the United States. America now had a solemn duty that went beyond its own narrow national interests and self-preservation.

Then he uttered the words that would frame the nation's purpose and capture the imagination of millions in the United States and beyond: "The world must be made safe for democracy." Scattered applause gradually rose to a crescendo. "We have no selfish ends to serve. We desire no conquest, no dominion. We seek no indemnities for ourselves, no material compensation for the sacrifices we shall freely make. We are but one of the champions of the rights of mankind. We shall be satisfied when those rights have been made as secure as the faith and the freedom of nations can make them." He acknowledged the danger ahead. "It is a fearful thing to lead this great peaceful people into war, into the most terrible and disastrous of all wars, civilization itself seeming to be in the balance." Nevertheless, he asserted, "the right is more precious than peace, and we shall fight for the things which we have always carried nearest to our hearts—for democracy . . . for the rights and liberties of small nations, for a universal dominion of right by such a concert of free peoples as shall bring peace and safety to all nations and make the world itself at last free." Upon concluding his speech, Wilson returned to the White House and, with the gravity of his decision bearing down on him, burst into tears.[127]

Two days later, on April 4, the United States Senate overwhelmingly approved the president's declaration of war. The House of Representatives followed suit in the early-morning hours of April 6. Later that afternoon, Wilson etched his signature on the succinct and open-ended resolution that granted him the power to "employ the entire naval and military forces of the United States and the resources of the Government to carry on war against the Imperial German Government."[128]

"I believe in the Prince of Peace. I believe that War is Murder. I

believe that armies and navies are at bottom the tinsel and braggado-
cio of oppression and wrong; and I believe that the wicked conquest
of weaker and darker nations by nations whiter and stronger but foreshadows the death of that strength."[129] These principles lay at the
heart of Du Bois's "Credo," the poetic articulation of his core values
published in 1904. He still believed what he wrote. Now the time
had arrived to test his convictions, not just in theory but in the actual
crucible of war.[130]

Du Bois's opposition to war and military service was not unconditional. He valorized Black soldiers and archetypes like Charles Young
as embodying the best manhood of the race. Moreover, Du Bois
understood war as an engine of potentially revolutionary social, political, and economic change for the colonized and racially oppressed.[131]
He needed only to look back to the Civil War, when African Americans, with Black soldiers at the liberatory tip of the Union Army's
spear, gained their freedom. As Du Bois's hero and model of racial
leadership, Frederick Douglass, famously said in an 1863 recruiting
speech, "Once let the black man get upon his person the brass letters
U.S.; let him get an eagle on his button, and a musket on his shoulder,
and bullets in his pocket, and there is no power on the earth or under
the earth which can deny that he has earned the right of citizenship
in the United States."[132] Du Bois could imagine this possibility on an
even grander scale. The war presented not only the opportunity for
African Americans to claim their full civic rights but also the chance
to remake democracy and expand it to all peoples of African descent.

Thus, with a mix of resignation, pragmatism, patriotism, and
hope, he voiced his support for America's entry into the war. In the
May edition of *The Crisis*, the first appearing after Woodrow Wilson's
declaration, Du Bois echoed the president's sorrow about stepping
into the global catastrophe. "War! It is an awful thing!" he wrote.
"It is Hell. It is the end of civilization. It is an appeal to barbarism."
And, like Wilson, he wished for the end result to be a world "where
war shall be no more." African Americans, even in the face of persecution and degradation, would do their part. Duty, to nation and to
the higher righteousness of their cause, necessitated that they "fight

shoulder to shoulder with the world." He offered a comparison, however imperfect, with the English suffragists who, in August 1914, "did not hesitate when war came" and, "although bowed beneath age-long insult and injustice," offered their patriotic service to the nation. "So will we black men fight against Germany for America," he declared. "God grant us freedom, too, in the end."[133]

War had come. And Du Bois stood ready to lead his people into battle.

CHAPTER 2

"These are the days of confusion and contradiction."[1]

A GROUP OF FOUR family members and friends found the dead body of Antoinette Rappel. The sixteen-year-old white girl from Memphis, Tennessee, had been missing since April 30, 1917. Two days later, through a thicket of trampled bushes just off Macon Road, the men of the search party spotted her bicycle propped up against a tree. Then they saw the blood and what appeared to be axe marks in the ground. They followed the bloodstained trail for about fifty feet, underneath the Wolf River bridge, when the body came into view. Rappel's clothes were torn, suggesting rape. Near the feet of the battered corpse lay her severed head, blond hair soaked in blood and blue eyes wide open in terror.[2]

The local press immediately pinned the crime on a Black perpetrator. However, the evidence gathered by the Shelby County sheriff Mike Tate pointed toward the killer being white and someone Rappel possibly knew. Nearly a week passed until Tate, under intense pressure, homed in on a Black woodcutter in his late thirties named Ell Persons. The sheriff questioned Persons twice, releasing him after each interrogation. A third arrest on May 6 and a twenty-four-hour interrogation, accompanied by "a long siege of beating," yielded a confession.[3] Still lacking firm evidence, Tate turned to a bizarre theory advanced by the French criminologist Alphonse Bertillon that the last image seen by a murder victim became permanently etched in their eyes. A judge ordered Rappel's corpse exhumed to examine her pupils. Investigators photographed the left eye and, after looking at the film, were convinced that they saw the forehead and hairline of Persons. On May 8, an all-white grand jury indicted him for murder.

As soon as word spread of Persons's "confession," mobs gathered in downtown Memphis to take the law into their own hands. Sheriff Tate quickly whisked Persons off to Nashville. For two weeks, mob leaders plotted, awaiting their opportunity. Upon learning that Persons would be transported by train back to Memphis for arraignment, they struck. The two police officers accompanying Persons in the early-morning hours of Monday, May 21, offered no resistance when a swarm of several hundred men intercepted them at Potts Camp, Mississippi. By that afternoon, crowds began to assemble at the site of Rappel's murder.

The May 22 morning editions of every local newspaper advertised the lynching. MAY RESORT TO BURNING hyped the Memphis *Commercial Appeal*. Some eager attendees, in spite of a torrential rainstorm, slept overnight to secure an up-close view. Organizers chopped down trees at the execution site to accommodate the anticipated crowd. By 9:00 a.m., as many as five thousand people had arrived. Parents sent notes to the schools of their children, asking that they be excused to take part in the festivities. The line of automobiles on Macon Road stretched for a mile and a half. The mood was carnivalesque, with vendors selling ice cream, sandwiches, and cotton candy.[4]

The ritual began with Rappel's mother, dressed in all black, making a statement. The crowd surged forward. "Let the Negro suffer as my little girl suffered, only 10 times worse," she said. "We'll burn him," the mob roared. "Yes," she responded, "burn him on the spot where he killed my little girl."[5] A group of men yanked Persons, shackled and with a heavy rope tied around his waist, out of a car. The mob went wild. After reading a perfunctory confession on Persons's behalf, the ringleaders dragged him into a prepared hollow and chained him to a log. He was doused, head to toe, in ten gallons of gasoline. A match was lit. The flames, starting at Persons's feet, slowly consumed his body. He did not make a sound. The crowd howled with delight.

After several minutes, the blazing inferno gave way to dense smoke and the smell of burning flesh. Two men rushed forward and cut off Persons's ears. Another carved out his heart. Someone then decapitated him and placed the head on a nearby post. Other anxious souvenir seekers dismembered additional parts of the body, snatched off bits of his clothing, and collected pieces of rope.

Burt Ingram, a Black automobile driver, witnessed the lynching. He could not contain his rage. He grabbed an American flag, waved it above his head, and yelled, "We're all through here, boys. Let's join the Germans." He then tore the flag to shreds. Several white men from the mob grabbed Ingram and attempted to throw him into the fire, where Persons's body still smoldered.[6]

The morning of violence climaxed with one last act of formulaic terror. Three leaders of the mob piled into a car, carrying with them what remained of Persons's body, including his decapitated head. They drove around Memphis, proudly displaying their trophy through the window. As they reached Beale Street and Rayburn, the heart of the city's Black business district, they tossed Persons's head and one of his feet at a group of African Americans. "Take this with our compliments," they shouted.[7]

In an article simply titled "The Huns," *The Independent*, a progressive weekly New York newspaper, offered a brief summation of the lynching:

> Last week a large and enthusiastic throng of the "best citizens" of Memphis, Tennessee, burned a negro at the stake after soaking him in oil and cutting off his ears.
> The world must be made safe for democracy.[8]

THE LYNCHING OF ELL PERSONS exemplified the impossible position African Americans found themselves in as the United States entered the war. The democracy that Woodrow Wilson extolled and promised to make safe around the world felt like a distant reality. Most Black people, especially in the South, paid little attention to events

overseas, as surviving the everyday challenges of white supremacy occupied enough time and attention. Those familiar with the European
carnage saw no reason to get mixed up in the quarrels of white folk.[9]

At the same time, loyalty mattered. African Americans, as in the
past, would prove their worth and fight not for what America was, but
for what it should be. Much of the Black press echoed this view, with
Du Bois leading the chorus. In the May edition of *The Crisis*, he staked
his ground in the aptly titled editorial "Loyalty." False rumors had
already begun to spread of German propaganda infiltrating Southern
Black communities. White supremacists feared that Black people could
be a potential internal enemy. Du Bois scoffed at the idea: "The Negro
is far more loyal to this country and its ideals than the white Southern
American. He has never been a disloyal rebel." African Americans, of
course, had every reason to be disloyal; white people had every reason
to worry. Nevertheless, "enslaved, raped and despised though he has
been and is," Du Bois wrote, "the Negro knows that this is his country because he helped found it, fought for its liberties and ever upheld
its ideals."[10]

More than anything, considering the gravity of the moment, the
race needed leadership. Du Bois felt singularly endowed to provide it.
After the declaration of war, the NAACP hastily scrapped its plans for
a spring national meeting in Chicago and instead committed to "a
general Negro conference" in Washington, DC, to "consider national
questions of particular importance to colored people growing out of
the present emergency."[11] Du Bois announced the proposed gathering in the May *Crisis*, stating, "The times demand that the leaders of
the American Negro counsel together as to the best course of action
present and future."[12]

The war and the meaning of African American loyalty dominated
the two-day conference on May 16 and 17, 1917. In the first session,
held at the historic First Congregational Church, William Pickens,
the dean at Morgan State College, set the tone with his address to the
gathered audience, saying, "There is no question as to the Negro's
patriotism or loyalty." However, he stressed, one should not take the
allegiance of African Americans to their country for "blind impulse

or unthinking docility." "The Negro is certainly not loyal to disfranchisement, 'jimcrowism' and lynch law," Pickens emphasized, "but he follows the star of America in spite of those evils and with the deliberate intention and fond hope of overthrowing them."[13]

The following day, with the conference venue shifting to the Colored YMCA, Du Bois took the stage. Washington, DC's, NAACP branch president and national board member Archibald Grimké introduced Du Bois, who opened the discussion on "The Policy of the American Negro in the Present Crisis."[14] He ultimately crafted the final resolution adopted by the conference, which appeared in the June issue of *The Crisis*. Speaking on behalf of twelve million Black Americans, as well as for "many other millions resident in America, in Africa, and in the islands of the seas," he reasoned that "the greatest hope for ultimate democracy" lay with the Allies. To his fellow African American citizens, he implored, "As our country it rightly demands our whole-hearted defense as well today as when with Crispus Attucks we fought for independence and with 200,000 black soldiers we helped hammer out our own freedom." He also articulated clear expectations for change, demanding an immediate end to lynching, the right to vote for both men and women, and the abolition of Jim Crow in schools, public transportation, and other areas of civic life. "These are not minor matters," he wrote. "They are not matters that can wait. They are the least that self-respecting, free, modern men can have and live." He proposed convening again two years later, in August 1919, to mark the three-hundred-year anniversary of the arrival of the first Africans, as well as to gauge progress. Until then, facing the present crisis, the race would "go forward toward Freedom without hesitation or compromise."[15]

The conference reflected Du Bois's influence and leadership. He departed Washington confident that the war could potentially be a new epoch in the historical struggle of African Americans for freedom and democracy.

Just five days after the gathering of race leaders in Washington, DC, Ell Persons was dead. The July issue of *The Crisis* included a four-page supplement devoted to the gruesome lynching and the NAACP's investigation. In the wake of Memphis, the patriotic, hopeful words of Du Bois rang hollow for many African Americans. The pugnacious Harlem-based Socialist duo of A. Philip Randolph and Chandler Owen, reflecting this mood, had no confidence in the lofty goals of the war. In the first issue of their Black radical news magazine *The Messenger*, Randolph and Owen encouraged Du Bois and other so-called spokesmen to "volunteer to go to France, if they are so eager to make the world safe for democracy . . . We would rather make Georgia safe for the Negro."[16]

~

AS ONE OF THEIR top demands, participants of the Washington conference called for the commissioning of Black officers to train and lead Black combat troops into battle. Du Bois was especially invested in this quest. For the father of the Talented Tenth, Black officers represented the pinnacle of racial leadership, manhood, and dignity.

Joel Spingarn spearheaded the effort. An active participant in the Preparedness Movement, with aspirations to serve in the army himself, Spingarn believed that a camp solely for Black officers marked an unrivaled opportunity for African Americans to demonstrate their loyalty and fitness for full citizenship.[17] He'd issued an open letter on February 15, 1917, that appeared in Black newspapers across the country, announcing plans to establish a segregated camp for Black cadets and calling for "educated colored men" of "intelligence, character and ability" to do their civic and racial duty. Knowing that his audience would bristle at the idea of a Jim Crow camp, Spingarn conceded that such an arrangement was not ideal. However, he reasoned, "the crisis is too near at hand to discuss principles and opinions" and that for the good of the country and for the progress of their race, Black men needed "to get the training that will fit you to be officers, however and wherever and whenever this training may be obtained."[18]

Much of the Black press vigorously disagreed with Spingarn. Jim Crow was wrong, they argued, and under no circumstances should responsible leaders of the race advocate for it, war or no war. "If this government cannot discuss principles and opinions so far as they related to common justice to the Negro when there is no crisis," the *Baltimore Afro-American* shot back, "perhaps a crisis is the best time to get a hearing."[19] "If we are good enough to fight," *The Chicago Defender* argued, "we are good enough to receive the same preparatory training our white brothers receive."[20]

The heated criticism put Spingarn on the defensive, but he held a trump card with Du Bois. In a confidential February 26 letter, he asked Du Bois to express support for the camp in one of his editorials.[21] In the April *Crisis* column "The Perpetual Dilemma," Du Bois publicly rallied to his friend's defense, echoing most of Spingarn's argument, but with his own distinctive voice and credibility. "We Negroes ever face it," he began, referring to the everyday pain of Jim Crow. "We must continually choose between insult and injury." With war imminent, the time for debate had passed. Du Bois saw the answer "as clear as noonday." "Give us the camp," he declared. "We did not make the damnable dilemma." He saw the segregated facility as a "temporary measure lasting four weeks and designed to FIGHT, not encourage discrimination in the army." If war came, so too would conscription. The only course of action, he believed, was to "organize the colored people for leadership and service . . . A thousand commissioned officers of colored blood is something to work for . . . Give us the camp!"

Du Bois's validation, combined with the entry of the United States into the war, had the effect Spingarn desired. On April 27, an NAACP delegation led by Spingarn met with Secretary of War Newton Baker to press their case. While acknowledging that War Department policies on the "race question" remained unsettled, Baker affirmed his support for the training of Black officers and committed to an arrangement "which was least offensive to the colored people."[22] Du Bois's backing also boosted recruitment efforts centered at Howard University and other Black colleges. By the beginning of May, some fifteen hundred young men had signed up to become officers. Most of the Black press fell in line, although some of Du Bois's most nettlesome critics continued to snipe at his decision. "Prof. 'Alphabetical' Du Bois endorses Dr. J. E. Spingarn's 'jim-crow' military training

camp proposal," mocked the *Cleveland Gazette* editor Harry Smith.
"We do not, however."[23] Du Bois returned fire with the June *Crisis*
editorial, "Officers," boldly proclaiming that the camp would be the
next chapter in the story of Black military leadership, spanning Sonni
Ali and Toussaint-Louverture and up to Charles Young.[24]

On May 19, Newton Baker gave his stamp of approval. "We have
won!" Du Bois crowed. "The camp is granted; we shall have 1,000
Negro officers in the United States Army!"[25] Although Howard University lobbied to host the camp—formally designated the Seventeenth
Provisional Training Regiment—the War Department opted for the
remote location of Fort Des Moines, Iowa, reasoning that the state's
relative absence of rigid discrimination would minimize any potential
trouble. Iowa's Black newspaper, *The Bystander*, eagerly anticipated
the cadets' arrival. "There will be brought here some of the race's
great men, as well as some of our race's great army officers."[26] Doctors, lawyers, dentists, Regular Army veterans, star athletes, ministers,
teachers, and businessmen were among the approximately 1,250 men
who streamed into Fort Des Moines from all parts of the country for
the June 18 opening of the camp.[27] Du Bois knew several of them
personally.

Matthew Virgil Boutté heeded Du Bois's call to serve. Boutté was
born on March 20, 1885, in New Iberia, Louisiana. The Bouttés were
a well-known, politically active Creole family in the area. In 1903,
Boutté left Louisiana and followed in Du Bois's footsteps by attending Fisk University. Graduating in 1908, he went on to earn a degree
in pharmacy from the University of Illinois in 1914, and he ultimately
returned to Tennessee, opening a drugstore in Nashville and joining
the Meharry Medical College faculty, teaching courses in quantitative
chemistry.[28] He also gained some military experience, spending six
months in Company "G" of the Tennessee National Guard, the only
African American reserve unit in the South.[29]

Upon arriving at Fort Des Moines, Boutté jumped headfirst into
the life of the camp. He established and served as president of the Seventeenth Provisional Training Regiment Association, using the group
to advocate on behalf of his fellow officer candidates and to build

camaraderie.[30] He quickly distinguished himself as a natural leader and one of the camp's most outstanding cadets.

As training at Fort Des Moines got under way, Boutté likely got to know Adam Patterson. After his time in Washington, DC, Patterson had licked his wounds and moved to Chicago, the Windy City beckoning as the ideal place for him to start anew. With an exploding Black population in need of services, he set up a law practice. He was also no doubt attracted to Chicago as a Democratic stronghold. He served as president of the moribund National Colored Democratic League and, despite his humiliating treatment, continued to jockey for a position in the Wilson administration.[31] Patterson sniffed another opportunity with the declaration of war and the announcement of the officers' training camp. With his legal experience, political connections, and personal savvy, he positioned himself for a promising career in the wartime army and potential future rewards.

If younger and healthier, Du Bois would have undoubtedly been alongside Boutté, Patterson, and the other remarkable Black men at Des Moines. Instead, like a proud father, he invested himself in their success, knowing that the camp and the performance of the officer candidates, on and off the battlefield, would be a referendum on his leadership and judgment.

JUST WHAT SOLDIERS THE Des Moines cadets might command remained uncertain. In the frenzied days after the United States entered the war, with enlistment policies up in the air, recruiting stations across the country summarily turned African Americans away. The Black Regular Army outfits were full and ready to fight, but the War Department had no intention of sending them to France. The Black National Guard units in Chicago, New York, Washington, DC, and Cleveland represented the only available options for African Americans to volunteer, and these units quickly met their quotas. Southern white supremacists, led by such firebrands as the Mississippi senator James Vardaman, insisted on excluding Black men from the military altogether lest they get it in their heads that they deserved to be treated as equal citizens.[32] The Selective Service Act, signed by President Wilson into law on May 18, 1917, included African Americans, with 2,290,527 Black men registering in the two draft calls of June 2 and September 12. The War Department did, however, acquiesce to the concerns of white Southerners by designating Black draftees for labor duty, with no intention of placing guns in their hands.[33] As word of this policy leaked, the Black press and the NAACP cried foul, demanding the right of African American soldiers to fight and die, if need be, on the battlefield.

The challenges facing Black soldiers and officers became deeply personal for Du Bois when controversy erupted over the future of Charles Young. Distinguished service in the Mexican Punitive Expedition had elevated Young's rank to lieutenant colonel. Given the rapid pace of promotions, he stood poised to become a brigadier general and potentially lead a yet to be determined division of Black troops. General John Pershing, soon to become commander of the American Expeditionary Forces (AEF), in fact penciled Young's name on a short list of officers to join him in France. It would be the crowning moment of Young's life and career.[34]

All seemed well as he took what should have been a routine physical examination for his promotion on May 9, 1917, in San Antonio, Texas. But the medical report came back with troubling results, and officials ordered Young to undergo subsequent tests at Letterman Army Hospital on the Presidio base in San Francisco. The following month, doctors there diagnosed him with a litany of ailments—chronic nephritis, enlargement of the heart, signs of arteriosclerosis—all serious enough to deem him unfit for active service. On June 20, confined to Letterman Hospital, a frustrated Young wrote to Du Bois. "Without an ache or pain, here I sit twirling my thumbs, when other officers are over-worked, and when I should this minute be at Des Moines helping to beat those colored officers into shape, and later to get with my whole heart and soul into the work of organization of the drafted Negro troops." He hoped that Du Bois and others could help President Wilson and Secretary of War Baker understand "the bad mental and moral effect this seemingly enforced retirement will have upon our people." The proud soldier felt embarrassed to be going on and on about his personal travails. He only desired to "work with my own in this war," above all else "for the good we can do our country."[35] Du Bois assured Young that he would "take all possible steps to bring your case to the authorities." In the meantime, he encouraged his friend to "get a good rest. It will certainly not hurt you, and be as contented as you can."[36]

Du Bois suspected treachery. He shared Young's letter with his NAACP colleague and editor of *The Nation*, Oswald Garrison Villard, as well as with Walter Lippmann of *The New Republic*, hoping that the two influential white journalists could press Secretary of War Baker on the matter. "I may, of course, be wrong," he wrote, "but I am satisfied that an attempt is being made to get him out of the army by unfair means."[37]

If only Du Bois knew the behind-the-scenes intrigue concerning Young's future that was taking place in Washington, DC, and involving none other than Woodrow Wilson. A white officer from Mississippi, Albert Dockery, who had served under Young in the Tenth Cavalry in Mexico, complained to his senator, John Sharp Williams, that he found it absolutely impossible to take orders from a Black commander. Williams forwarded the letter directly to the president. Wilson, needing to keep restless Democratic senators like Williams in his fold but, as a fellow Southerner, also sympathetic to Dockery's plight, took the extraordinary steps of personally asking Secretary of War Newton Baker to resolve the problem of Young's place in the army.[38]

Young nervously awaited his fate. His hopes received a boost on July 7, when the medical examining board looked past the damaging health report and recommended that, based on his physical appearance and record of arduous duty, "his services should be fully utilized during the present war" and that he receive a promotion to the next rank. The final decision, however, lay in the hands of War Department officials in Washington, who already viewed Young, as Baker put it to Woodrow Wilson, as "a cause of trouble." Adjutant General Henry Pinckney McCain, adhering strictly to the letter of the law, rejected the recommendation of the examining board and ordered Young placed into retirement, but with a promotion to lieutenant colonel. Newton Baker attempted to split the hairs between "active duty" and "active service" by assigning Young to Ohio to help organize a new Black militia unit that the army, in reality, never intended to mobilize. The thorny issue of Colonel Charles Young's role in the war had been mendaciously resolved.[39]

African Americans responded to news of Young's forced retirement with a mixture of heartbreak and outrage. Young, exiled in Ohio, stewed in disappointment. "It seems regrettable for both the country and our people, for I could have done good work for both," he wrote in an August letter to the *Pittsburgh Courier* editor W. P. Bayless. Nevertheless, despite the unjust circumstances, duty to nation and his oath to the flag mattered above all. "While I know the chagrin that many of our people, and not a few whites, feel in this regard, still I pray that there shall be no word of protest at this time," he advised. "We love our country too well not to desire its early success in this war." Young, patriotically, gritted his teeth and tried his best to submit "cheerfully, like a soldier."[40]

THE OUTBREAK OF WAR in 1914 set in motion forces that transformed the world, and Black America along with it. European immigration to the United States came to a screeching halt. Northern industries, with export demands from Great Britain and France booming, needed workers and began to look south to find them. African Americans paid attention. A boll weevil infestation steadily decimated cotton production, leaving many Black tenant farmers in an even worse state of destitution. Jim Crow, disfranchisement, and continued racial violence compounded the deteriorating economic conditions. So, with the attraction of jobs and the push of freedom dreams, they fled. Black Southerners, first a trickle, then a stream, and eventually a flood, bravely gathered their worldly possessions, boarded trains, and headed north. Chicago became a prime destination, as the *Defender*, with its national circulation, actively encouraged the exodus. The racial composition of New York, Philadelphia, Milwaukee, Detroit, Pittsburgh, and other urban centers also underwent dramatic transformations as a result of what would come to be known as the Great Migration.[41] Du Bois, with his sharp sociological eye, monitored the migration, predicting in *The Crisis*, "We face a social change among American Negroes of great moment, and one which needs to be watched with intelligent interest."[42]

By the following month, the eyes of the nation were fixed on the city of East St. Louis. Attracted to wartime industrial jobs, more than ten thousand African Americans from the Deep South decided to make the city their new home, unsuspectingly entering a political and economic tinderbox. Long-standing Black residents had begun to flex their muscles in city politics, emerging as a critical swing vote between Democrats and Republicans. Leaders of the Central Trades and Labor Union, fearing a loss of both political and economic influence, soon targeted Black migrants as a means to increase support among white workers and residents. In addition to branding them as strikebreakers, the union bosses blamed Black migrants for every social ill in the city, from a lack of quality housing to crime. On May 28, 1917, a mass meeting spiraled out of control and morphed into a mob intent on cleansing East St. Louis of its "Negro problem." Over the next day they attacked dozens of Black residents and destroyed property at will until the Illinois National Guard restored peace. Miraculously, no one died. But in the aftermath, Black and white people alike prepared for the inevitability of more bloodshed.[43]

Just over a month later, the storm arrived. Sporadic violence had erupted throughout June. A failed aluminum plant strike, pinned on Black workers hired by the company, further exacerbated tensions. White civic leaders became determined to rid East St. Louis of Black people for good.

Shortly after midnight on July 2, a group of Black men, fearing an ambush, mistakenly shot and killed two police officers. By sunrise, news of the shooting spread, and whites began to organize for revenge. By noon the assault was well under way. In broad daylight, mobs descended on East St. Louis's Black neighborhoods and unleashed a wave of white supremacist fury unlike anything in modern

American history. They shot, stabbed, lynched, and burned Black
men and women, young and old, healthy and infirm, with no distinction. African Americans attempted to fight back but were badly outnumbered and overpowered. Law enforcement and militia provided
them with no protection, as most either actively participated in the
massacre or watched it unfold with stony complicity. The fiery glow
of burning homes and businesses lit up the evening sky for miles. The
pogrom lasted for an explosive twenty-four hours, into July 3, until,
satisfied with their results, the mobs relented. More than seven thousand Black residents fled across the Eads and Free bridges to St. Louis
for refuge, leaving behind a community in ruins. The number of dead,
officially put at thirty-nine, likely ran into the hundreds.[44]

On Sunday, July 8, Du Bois boarded a train for East St. Louis. He
needed to see the wreckage up close and firsthand. For seven days, with
social scientific diligence, he labored to understand the magnitude of
the pogrom and its causes. He walked the desolate, smoldering streets
of the city and, with the assistance of five hired workers, twenty-five
volunteers, and the indefatigable Martha Gruening of the NAACP,
collected the personal stories of some hundred and fifty victims, along
with information concerning another fifteen hundred.[45] He may have
in fact crossed paths with Ida B. Wells-Barnett, the pioneering anti-
lynching activist who traveled to East St. Louis for her own investigation.[46] Like Wells-Barnett, Du Bois and Gruening recorded a catalog
of horrors.

In the meticulously detailed and graphically illustrated report
Du Bois published with Gruening in the September 1917 issue of *The
Crisis*, he placed blame for the pogrom squarely at the feet of union
leaders who whipped the white working-class community of East St.
Louis into a racist frenzy. However, what the massacre said about
America in the context of a war that Du Bois supported proved much
more difficult to explain. "In all the accounts given of German atrocities, no one, we believe, has accused the Germans of taking pleasure in
the sufferings of their victims," he wrote. "But these rioters combined
business and pleasure."[47] In the same issue, he penned the editorial
"Awake America," asking his countrymen to "bow our shamed heads"

and declare that "here at home we raise our hands to Heaven and pledge our sacred honor to make our own America a real land of the free." "Awake!" he shouted. "Put on they [*sic*] strength, America— put on thy beautiful robes. Become not a bye word and jest among the nations by the hypocrisy of your word and contradiction of your deeds."[48]

By the time Du Bois returned to his NAACP office on Wednesday, July 18, plans for a response from the association to the East St. Louis horror were being made. The executive committee of the NAACP's Harlem branch convened to discuss the tragedy and what to do. James Weldon Johnson steered the conversation. The multitalented diplomat, lawyer, poet, novelist, and editor had formally joined the NAACP as a field secretary the previous year, making an immediate impact by expanding the reach of the organization into the South and establishing new branches. He and Du Bois, intellectual and political soul mates, formed a tight bond. NAACP officials at the Harlem meeting first considered a mass meeting at Carnegie Hall, but recalling a comment made by Oswald Garrison Villard at the Amenia conference—that African Americans would need to begin engaging in public demonstrations of protest—Johnson suggested that a silent parade might have greater effect.[49]

At roughly 1:00 p.m. on the bright afternoon of July 28, the "Silent Protest Parade" began at Fifty-Ninth Street and Fifth Avenue. At the front of the parade, Du Bois, wearing a brimmed hat and carrying a walking stick, strode alongside James Weldon Johnson and other Black New York civic leaders. Behind them, to the melancholy sound of muffled drums, marched some ten thousand African Americans— women and children dressed in all-white gowns, men in black suits. They carried dozens of signs—"YOUR HANDS ARE FULL OF BLOOD." "WE HAVE FOUGHT FOR THE LIBERTY OF WHITE AMERICANS IN SIX WARS, OUR REWARD WAS EAST ST. LOUIS." "PATRIOTISM AND LOYALTY PRESUPPOSE PROTECTION AND LIBERTY." "MAKE AMERICA SAFE FOR DEMOCRACY." "GIVE ME A CHANCE TO LIVE." Thousands of onlookers, white and Black, lined the streets in awe at the sight, many with tears streaming down their cheeks.[50]

Black America, and Du Bois along with it, had barely caught its breath after East St. Louis when Houston erupted. On July 28, the Third Battalion of the all-Black Twenty-Fourth Infantry arrived at the outskirts of Houston, Texas, for a seven-week assignment to guard construction of a new training cantonment, Camp Logan. While the Black community welcomed the soldiers, many of whom were seasoned veterans, with open arms, white Houstonians, especially the police, viewed and treated them with disdain.[51]

Weeks of tension culminated on August 23. That afternoon, a pair of notoriously racist Houston policemen, Lee Sparks and Rufus Daniels, beat and arrested two Black soldiers who had intervened to defend the dignity of a local Black woman, Sara Travers. Rumors spread that the police killed one of the soldiers, Corporal Charles Baltimore. Some men began to talk of revenge. Baltimore returned to camp, but the sight of him, bloodied and bandaged, only increased the rage the soldiers had previously worked so hard to contain. By nightfall, the threat of mutiny hung thick in the humid Texas air.

"Get your guns boys, here comes the mob!" a soldier yelled. A shot rang out, followed by pandemonium. Other soldiers rushed to the nearest tent for weapons and, in the pitch-black darkness, began firing wildly in all directions. There was no mob, but the fuse had been lit. Sergeant Vida Henry, a thirty-five-year-old battle-hardened officer of the battalion, decided to take action, ordering his men to fall in line. Around 8:50 p.m. a column of more than one hundred Black soldiers marched down San Felipe Road and into downtown Houston. They soon began to shoot. Bullets hit several unsuspecting white residents, but the soldiers had a clear target in mind: Houston's police officers. Anyone else was collateral damage. They killed two policemen, among them Rufus Daniels, and continued to hunt for more. However, after inadvertently killing an Illinois National Guardsman, many of the men lost their will, abandoned the assault, and returned to camp. When the smoke cleared, fifteen people lay dead, with injuries taking the lives of four more in the following days.[52]

In the October issue of *The Crisis*, Du Bois attempted to make sense of the carnage and its ramifications, acknowledging from the outset that "it is difficult for one of Negro blood to write of Houston . . . Here, at last, white folk died," he grimly acknowledged. The soldiers were "disciplined men who said—'This is enough; we'll stand no more!'" He could not condone their actions. "We ask no mitigation of their punishment. They broke the law. They must suffer." But he also recognized that the men, in their desperation, were also victims.[53]

The outcome of the first of three courts-martial caused Du Bois to abandon his previous restraint. The trial of sixty-nine soldiers began on November 13. After twenty-two days, the court found fifty-eight men guilty of mutiny, assault, and murder, ordering thirteen of them to be immediately executed. Just before sunrise on the morning of December 11, army officers led the condemned soldiers to a set of gallows that had been quickly built overnight, placed ropes around their necks, and hanged them in unison. They were then buried, still wearing their uniforms, in unmarked graves.[54] "They have gone to their death. Thirteen young, strong men; soldiers who have fought for a country which never was wholly theirs; men born to suffer ridicule, injustice, and at last, death itself," Du Bois wrote in the January 1918 editorial "Thirteen." Although the race, he conceded, may have to accept their guilt and punishment, still, he cried, "We raise our clenched hands against the hundreds of thousands of white murderers, rapists, and scoundrels who have oppressed, killed, ruined, robbed, and debased their black fellow men and fellow women, and yet, today, walk scot-free, un-whipped of justice, uncondemned by millions of their white fellow citizens, and unrebuked by the President of the United States."[55]

By the end of 1917, the first combat soldiers of the American Expeditionary Forces were in France. As the pace of domestic mobilization and training quickened, thousands more prepared to board transport ships and cross the Atlantic to provide desperately needed reinforcement for the battle-weary Allied armies. Commanding General John Pershing, in France since June, envisioned the requested three million men of the AEF eventually turning the tide of the war and validating Woodrow Wilson's bold democratic vision.[56] But for Black people, including Du Bois, East St. Louis and Houston sent a clear message: the war for democracy would be fought on American soil as well.

~

A WELCOME RESPITE FROM the stress of war, racial violence, and injustice arrived on the evening of February 25, 1918. "The Editor of The Crisis will celebrate his fiftieth birthday," the lead editorial, "Jubilee," announced in advance of the milestone.[57] At the behest of *The Crisis*, hundreds of cards, poems, and letters of congratulations flowed in from every corner of the country, as well as from Haiti, Jamaica, and other points beyond. Joel Spingarn, assisted by fellow NAACP board members Mary White Ovington and James Weldon Johnson, took charge of organizing a gala celebration worthy of Du Bois's luminous stature. At New York's Civic Club, friends, family, and admirers serenaded Du Bois with testimonial after testimonial as Black America's greatest living individual. His NAACP colleagues presented him with an inscribed silver cup that read: "From the branches of the National Association for the Advancement of Colored People to W. E. Burghardt Du Bois, writer, scholar, seer, on his fiftieth birthday, February 23, 1918. Given in affectionate appreciation of his great gifts, and gratitude for the consecration of these gifts to the service of his race."[58] "The dinner was simply splendid," he wrote, genuinely touched, in a thank-you letter to Mary White Ovington the next day. "This is a case where words will fail to express all that I feel, but I am sure that you can supply some of the deficiency."[59]

The birthday fete no doubt buoyed Du Bois's spirits and provided a much-needed distraction. By the first months of 1918, the war had already tested him in ways that no other moment in his fifty years had done. As the Ell Persons lynching, the fight for Black officers, East St. Louis, Houston, Charles Young, the draft, and a constantly growing deluge of other issues demanded, Du Bois remained vocal in speaking out against racial inequality, criticizing the government, and protesting if necessary. But he also knew that the war had to be won, and African Americans had to do their part lest the race and he as its spokesman be branded as disloyal. He needed to tread carefully.

Du Bois's balancing act included maintaining a positive relationship with Secretary of War Newton Baker. The former mayor of
Cleveland, Ohio, Baker shared the belief of most of his fellow white
progressives, including Woodrow Wilson, that racial segregation, as
a matter of efficiency, remained in the best interests of both Black
and white people, and ultimately the nation. However, within the
constraints of Jim Crow, he believed in giving African Americans a
fair chance, which Du Bois recognized. Following a personal meeting with the secretary in early October, he wrote to thank Baker for
"the general way in which you have carried through your plans concerning colored soldiers. Your justice will greatly hearten the colored
people."[60] He further lauded Baker, this time publicly, in the December 1917 *Crisis*: "He has not done everything we could wish, but he
has accomplished so much more than President Wilson or any other
member of this administration that he deserves all praise."[61]

Du Bois especially noted Baker's appointment of "an official advisor who belongs to the Negro race," Emmett Scott. Recognizing the
potential of the "race question" to become explosive, the Tuskegee
Institute principal Robert Moton had presented the idea of a Black
representative in the War Department and recommended Scott for
the position. On October 5, 1917, Baker officially announced Scott
"as confidential advisor in matters affecting the interests of the
10,000,000 Negroes of the United States, and the part they are to
play in connection with the present war."[62]

The relationship between Du Bois and Emmett Scott had warmed
considerably since Joel Spingarn's Amenia gathering in 1916, to the
point that the two former adversaries could rightfully claim to be on
good terms with each other. In the same December 1917 issue in
which he praised Newton Baker, Du Bois gave Emmett Scott space
in *The Crisis* to explain his new position.[63] Booker T. Washington's
former right-hand man eagerly embraced the responsibility, along with
the prestige that came along with it. As Du Bois attempted to navigate
his relationship with the War Department, he approached Scott as an
important ally, and Scott realized the strategic value of having Du Bois
on his side. War Department business prevented Scott from attending

Du Bois's fiftieth birthday celebration, but he sent his regrets to Mary White Ovington in a warm letter, praising Du Bois's "untiring efforts in behalf of racial and human uplift" and standing as a leader of "great influence and commanding importance."[64]

Most of the correspondence between Du Bois and Scott revolved around the place and treatment of Black men in the army. Du Bois closely followed the progress of the Fort Des Moines training camp. The experiment contained plenty of challenges, but when the camp finally closed, on October 15, 1917, 639 men received commissions as captains, first lieutenants, and second lieutenants.[65] Du Bois, along with Joel Spingarn, celebrated the landmark achievement. "All is not perfect in our country today," Spingarn acknowledged, "but thank heavens, there are many, many things to be proud and grateful for."[66]

Now these officers needed Black soldiers to command. The Selective Service Act had placed the administration of the draft in the hands of local officials. In the South, this meant adhering to the customs of Jim Crow as much as the War Department would tolerate. After having the bottom-left corner of their registration cards torn off to indicate their race, African American draftees were separated from their white counterparts and overwhelmingly consigned to service battalions, commanded by white noncommissioned officers with experience in "handling" Black men, seeing them as nothing more than "laborers in uniform."[67]

Yet some Black doughboys did get the opportunity to reach France with a gun instead of a shovel. On November 29, 1917, the War Department, bowing to the demands of the Black press and admitting that it could not reasonably justify funneling all Black draftees into labor duties, created a single all-Black combat unit in the American Expeditionary Forces, the Ninety-Second Division. White men, led by General Charles Ballou, commanded the division at its highest ranks. The Des Moines graduates joined him as junior officers. The War Department, terrified at the prospect of an entire division of some twenty thousand Black soldiers in one single location, opted to spread the Ninety-Second out over seven northern and midwestern training facilities. Camp Funston in Kansas—site of the first recorded case of a virulent strain of influenza that quickly ripped through the country and like wildfire spread across the world—served as division headquarters.[68] The newly commissioned Captain Adam Patterson remained in Iowa at Camp Dodge with the 365th Infantry Regiment. Matthew Boutté, after earning his captain bars, received orders to proceed to Camp Grant, Illinois, where he organized and whipped into shape Company C of the 350th Machine Gun Battalion.[69] Fluent in French, Boutté earned another commission, this time in military intelligence, along with an appointment as the Ninety-Second Division's official interpreter.[70]

Meanwhile, the War Department had to sort out the dilemma of what to do with the Black National Guard units. The "Old Eighth" Illinois unit out of Chicago, with its full contingent of Black officers and guardsmen led by Colonel Franklin Dennison, was ready to go. The more recently created New York Fifteenth, commanded by white officers, grew quickly, with recruiting efforts aided by its band, which was led by the celebrated ragtime innovator James Reese Europe. Other smaller National Guard units from Washington, DC, Ohio, Maryland, Tennessee, and Connecticut eagerly awaited instruction. The War Department decided to establish a makeshift unit to house them all, eventually designated the Ninety-Third (Provisional) Division.

For training, the War Department sent the Eighth Illinois to Camp Logan in Houston, of all places, where tensions stemming from the mutinous actions of the Twenty-Fourth Infantry still ran high. The New York Fifteenth also had a harrowing training experience in Spartanburg, South Carolina, as local whites in the heart of the former Confederacy wanted nothing to do with the regiment of uppity Northern Black soldiers in their midst. After the regiment, fed up with continued insult and abuse, came perilously close to conducting its own version of the Houston bloodbath, the War Department quickly relocated them back north to Camp Whitman in New York State and then hastily shipped them to France. Renamed the 369th Infantry Regiment, they arrived on New Year's Day 1918 and began performing labor duties along with the thousands of other Black stevedores and Services of Supply troops, as the army did not know how else to use them. Later that month, Pershing handed the entire Ninety-Third over to the French, fulfilling a promise to give the war-weary ally an American division while also conveniently ending the confusion of what to do with this unorthodox assemblage.[71]

As the situation facing Black soldiers overseas remained uncertain, Du Bois focused on issues that African Americans faced on the home front. He pushed for more Black officers and another training camp at Fort Des Moines. He accepted a seat on the board of directors of the Circle for Negro War Relief, an interracial group founded by the white New York reformer Emilie Bigelow Hapgood that owed much of its success to the involvement of African American women, among them Matthew Boutté's impressive Fisk-educated wife, Etnah Rochon, who served as executive secretary.[72] Du Bois also forwarded the growing number of complaints he received from Black soldiers at training camps, especially in the South, to Emmett Scott.

More than any other issue, Du Bois remained personally invested in the plight of Colonel Charles Young. He heeded his friend's orders to refrain from protesting the forced retirement. But by February 1918, when it became increasingly clear that the War Department had little interest in resolving Young's fate, Du Bois went on the attack. He directed his growing anger at the adjutant general, Henry Pinckney McCain, with a series of pointed questions in *The Crisis*. He demanded that McCain clarify why Young was retired from active duty against the recommendation of the examining board, and then, strangely, reinstated but marooned in Ohio to command a National Guard regiment that did not exist.[73] Du Bois followed up the next month with a reprint of John Pershing's recommendation for Young's promotion stemming from his service in Mexico.[74] He kept up the pressure in the May issue, writing in the editorial "The Negro and the War Department" that "*Twelve million Negroes demand that Colonel Young be restored to 'active service!'*"[75]

Young decided to take matters into his own hands. On June 6, as a demonstration of his fitness to serve, he set out on horseback from his home in Wilberforce, Ohio, to travel to Washington, DC. Black newspapers chronicled every step of his valiant journey.

Sixteen days and 497 miles later, he arrived in the nation's capital and headed straight to the office of Newton Baker. The secretary of war received him politely, but Young's status in the army remained unchanged.[76]

That same month, without Charles Young commanding them, the Ninety-Second Division began preparations to depart for France. The division's domestic training experience had been chaotic and demoralizing. Spread out over seven camps, the division lacked cohesiveness and esprit de corps. Many of the Black officers, revealing the shortcomings of the Des Moines camp, did not have crucial training in artillery and other technical skills. General Ballou was determined to avoid any racial turbulence and keep the division's soldiers in their place. Following an incident involving a Black sergeant being discriminated against at a local movie theater, Ballou issued an order, Bulletin No. 35, that urged all soldiers, officers in particular, to "refrain from going where their presence will be resented" and to not provoke "race animosity" by standing up for their rights. Morale, already low, plummeted. Taken all together, Du Bois foresaw trouble on the horizon. "Is it possible that persons in the War Department wish this division to be a failure?" he asked out loud in *The Crisis*.[77]

On June 6, Matthew Boutté left for France as one of the lead officers of the Ninety-Second Division.[78] Just prior to departing from the United States, he began keeping a diary, using a small three-by-five-inch notepad he could easily travel with—and conceal. In a June 8 entry, he detailed the segregation he and other Black officers endured while crossing the Atlantic, and, channeling Du Bois and *The Souls of Black Folk*, rhetorically questioned, "How will it be when we get to France? Is it possible that the shadow will follow us there? Are we not posing as the champions of democracy?"[79]

The shadow did indeed follow him, and he soon received his answer about America's commitment to democracy. Boutté was overcome with exhilaration as his ship neared the French coast, writing in his diary, "Behold the land of France! Behold France the beautiful! Behold France the free! Behold the land where freedom is not a mockery! France the home of my forefathers!" General Ballou and his staff went into Brest—intentionally leaving Boutté behind—to confirm their sleeping arrangements at the Hotel Continental. When Boutté and the other Black officers later followed, they received orders to go to Camp Pontanezen, where they would have to sleep on boards with no mattress and a single blanket, in total disregard of their rank. Boutté returned to the hotel and, putting his French to good use, "secured the splendid rooms that had been reserved for the General and Staff."[80]

The Ninety-Second joined a steady stream of American combat divisions arriving in France by the early summer of 1918. The war had taken a dramatic turn in the spring. The March 3 Treaty of Brest-Litovsk, following the Bolshevik Revolution in October of the previous year, ended Russian involvement in the war. No longer fighting on the Eastern Front, Germany planned for a massive spring offensive, hoping to end the war before American soldiers could potentially turn the tide. The offensive, which began on March 21, got off to a successful start, with German troops advancing within seventy-five miles of Paris. However, stretched too thin over a huge swath of front and facing logistical challenges, the operation stalled and then sputtered to a halt. The American Expeditionary Forces notched its first victory in the May 28 Battle of Cantigny and later followed this up with action at Château-Thierry and Belleau Wood in the Second Battle of the Marne. Germany was pushed to the brink, and with roughly ten thousand U.S. troops arriving daily, the Allies saw victory within their grasp.[81]

Black soldiers of the Ninety-Third Division had been in the thick of the fighting. The French, with their experience utilizing colonial troops from Africa and hungry for fresh bodies, did not hesitate to throw *les soldats noirs* into battle. The division's four regiments spent March and April adjusting to life in the French Army, which entailed everything from new guns, helmets, and meal rations. By May, they were in the trenches and engaging at times in fierce combat, with the 369th in particular seeing extensive action. James Reese Europe and the regiment's band had taken France by storm with its jazzed-up sound. When two of the regiment's soldiers, Henry Johnson and Neadom Roberts, repelled a twenty-four-man raiding party on the night of May 14, killing four Germans and wounding more than a dozen more, the 369th became the perfect example of the heroism and potential of all Black troops when given a fair chance.[82]

Du Bois captured this spirit in the June 1918 *Crisis* editorial "The Black Soldier." He dedicated the issue to African American soldiers, along with "the million dark men of Africa and India, who have served in the armies of Great Britain, and to the equal, if not larger, number who are fighting for France and the other Allies." He emboldened these men to show "courage and determination," noting, "You are not fighting simply for Europe; you are fighting for the world, and you and your people are a part of the world." Exuding hope for a new epoch of democracy and self-determination for the African diaspora, he realized that his vision would not materialize overnight, but it was nevertheless "written in the stars." The first step, however, had to be "victory for the armies of the Allies."[83]

Matthew Boutté and other Black officers of the Ninety-Second, based on their first experiences overseas, would have scoffed at Du Bois's optimism. "Such a strange feeling in a place where a man is a man," Boutté wrote about the liberating sensation of being in France. White officers viewed such swelled confidence as a clear threat to their authority and the inviolability of the American color line. When Boutté arrived for duty at Bourbonne-les-Bains, his racist commanding officer, Paul Raborg from Georgia, delivered a blunt warning: "Any officer who does not make good is going to be tried for inefficiency. I am not going to have any inefficient officers in my command and if I find them they are going to be put out and I am not going to take damned long to do this thing either."[84] Boutté watched his every step and kept his company in tip-top shape.

On July 24, Raborg placed Boutté under arrest, in full view of his men, on the grounds of inefficiency. The twenty-three bogus charges levied against him, formally presented one week after his arrest, included not having a copy of the company's meal menu posted in the kitchen, failing to have the field shoes of his men satisfactorily greased, and not keeping the latrine clean enough. A stunned Boutté absorbed this cruel twist of fate in the confinement of his sleeping quarters, where he remained day and night save for one hour allowed for exercise.[85]

Raborg hoped that Boutté would defy his arrest and open himself up to further punishment. Instead, Boutté maintained his cool and on August 2 requested the counsel of a fellow Black captain, Leroy Godman.[86] A native of Columbus, Ohio, Godman had attended Howard Law School and received his juris doctor degree in 1905. In addition to his private practice, he worked for five years as assistant attorney general for the state of Ohio.[87] After earning a captaincy commission at Des Moines, he joined the Ninety-Second Division and soon found himself busy defending several African American soldiers and officers against all types of unjust accusations.[88] After a three-day proceeding during which Raborg withdrew most of his outlandish charges, Boutté was completely exonerated. The white colonel who oversaw the trial informed Boutté that his ordeal was "purely a case of prejudice" and admitted that Raborg, eventually transferred out of the division, "was unfit to command colored troops."[89]

Boutté's humiliating ordeal was not an anomaly. In General Ballou's opinion, the number of competent Black officers in his division dwarfed the majority, whose heads were "swollen with their ideas of their own importance." Ballou empowered his white officers to resort to "corrective measures," and soon more racist efficiency boards were drumming Black officers out of the Ninety-Second Division at a brisk pace.[90]

Stories of mistreatment began to trickle back to the United States. But distance and government censorship made news hard to come by. As the Ninety-Second Division and many of the Des Moines officers went through hell, Du Bois remained unaware of the severity of their plight. An ocean away, he could do little to intervene.

~

JOEL SPINGARN'S PLANS FOR a heroic career in the wartime army did not unfold as he'd initially envisioned. It started well enough when he received an officer commission of his own, becoming a major with the 311th Infantry Regiment. However, on the eve of departing for France in the fall of 1917, Spingarn came down with a debilitating

case of ulcers, which required surgery and two months of rehabilitation. Still eager to serve, he explored other possible opportunities,
including with the Ninety-Second Division.[91] Instead, in May 1918,
the War Department assigned him to the MI-4 section of the Military
Intelligence Branch (MIB). Disappointed but determined to make the
best of the situation, Spingarn began devising plans for a "constructive programme" to promote African American loyalty and address the
most urgent issues that contributed to fears of "Negro subversion." He
also had plans for Du Bois.[92]

Du Bois did not know what to expect when Joel Spingarn invited
him back to the nation's capital, on June 8. The two had just met four
days prior, on June 4, at Spingarn's downtown Washington office. At
that meeting, Spingarn updated Du Bois on his bold agenda with the
MIB after less than three weeks on the job. He wanted an advisory
committee created in the War Department to address the treatment of
Black soldiers. He wanted a crackdown on racist articles in the white
press. He wanted *The Birth of a Nation* banned throughout the country. Above all else, he wanted the government to take a stand against
mob violence. Spingarn surely boasted to Du Bois about his upcoming
June 6 appearance before the House Committee on the Judiciary at
the invitation of the Missouri congressman Leonidas Dyer, who had
introduced an anti-lynching bill in the House. Spingarn intended to
argue for the even more urgent need to pass a wartime federal anti-
lynching measure as a matter of national security.[93]

The groundwork had been laid. In a note to his wife, Amy, shortly
after the June 8 meeting with Du Bois, Spingarn wrote, "I gave him
the shock of his life." Spingarn had already begun recruiting quality
race men to join his project, and above everyone else, he craved Du
Bois as his partner in the War Department. But not just that. He asked
Du Bois to apply for an officer commission to be a captain of military
intelligence. Spingarn felt confident, as he later recounted to Amy, that
the "big vision" he proposed to Du Bois, along with the "bait of olive
drab," would secure his friend's commitment.[94]

It was a big vision indeed. Du Bois, taken aback, absorbed Spingarn's offer. As he contemplated the audacious proposal, a perfect

storm of wartime pressures, personal ambition, and competing allegiances to race, to nation, and to friend swirled in his head.

The "bait of olive drab" no doubt struck a chord. Du Bois revered
the Black military tradition and what it meant in the struggle for equal
citizenship. He likely thought of his own family history as well, one
that lacked martial distinction, despite his best attempts at exaggeration. Great-great-grandfather Tom Burghardt served a mere four days
in the Continental Army during the American Revolution. Alfred
Du Bois, the father absent from his life, had an undignified stint in the
Union Army during the Civil War, enlisting in early 1864, but getting
sick, toiling as a lowly medical attendant, and ultimately deserting.
With the honorific of "Captain" in front of his name, Du Bois could
now make his own mark.[95]

Notwithstanding the tug of his formidable ego, Du Bois also remained deeply invested in the successful outcome of the war for the
race. He believed, from the beginning of America's entry into the war,
that the great battle for world democracy would usher in a new day for
Black people. He had already sacrificed principle in supporting a Jim
Crow officers' training camp. If a position within the government—
and military intelligence, no less—would help the cause of African
American equality, he had to consider seizing the opportunity.

Then there was the fate of *The Crisis*. By the spring of 1918, following passage of the Sedition Act, the magazine had become a clear
danger in the eyes of the government and was under investigation by
at least three different agencies. Du Bois sounded the alarm at the May
board meeting, stating that "the Department of Justice has warned
us against the tone of some of the articles in The Crisis" and that
it would be necessary "to discuss the war hereafter very carefully."[96]
Faced with this new scrutiny, the magazine brought on board Charles
Studin, chairman of the NAACP legal committee, and tasked him
with approving all material, "of whatever character," before it went into
print.[97] Adding to the pressure, on June 3, the MIB director, Colonel
Marlborough Churchill, sent Studin a pointed memo, warning that
the government would not, under any circumstances, "tolerate carp-
ing and bitter utterances likely to foment disaffection and destroy the

morale of our people for the winning of the war."[98] From Du Bois's perspective, a partnership with Spingarn and the MIB, as a matter of wartime pragmatism and survival, would insulate *The Crisis*, and himself, from future persecution.[99]

While all of this mattered, perhaps the most influential factor in Du Bois's calculation was Joel Spingarn himself. Spingarn was a friend, benefactor, and confidant. Saying no to the man who quite literally helped save his life as he faced a perilous kidney surgery would be painfully difficult. But more than just peer pressure pulled at Du Bois's conscience. He believed in Spingarn. The major exuded supreme conviction, vision, and faith in America. His patriotism—and his belief that by joining the war effort, Black people could become full Americans—was contagious.[100]

Spingarn wanted an answer. Du Bois still had questions, and significant issues—most important, getting support from the NAACP board—needed to be addressed. But before walking out of Spingarn's office, Du Bois, at the very least, gave his friend every indication that he would strongly consider the offer.

This was all Spingarn needed to hear. He leapt into motion and further tilled the ground for Du Bois's possible commission, soliciting influential friends and political figures in Washington and beyond to submit letters recommending Du Bois for the post.[101] On June 10, Spingarn assured Marlborough Churchill that Du Bois had promised to "change the tone" of *The Crisis*, and that henceforth it would be "an organ of patriotic propaganda."[102]

Less than two weeks later, Du Bois took center stage at a conference of Black newspaper editors. Spingarn, with Emmett Scott's backing, pitched the idea of bringing together government officials and notable voices in the Black press to air grievances and share ideas for mutual cooperation.[103] The conference began at 10:30 on the morning of June 19 in the main auditorium of the Department of the Interior Building in Washington. Forty-one newspaper editors, publishers, and other prominent race leaders, all men, traveling at the government's expense, gathered to discuss the state of affairs facing the Negro.[104] Spingarn described the tone of discussions over the next three days as "sober and statesmanlike." They politely listened to addresses from George Creel, director of the Committee on Public Information; Secretary of War Baker; Emmett Scott; a French military officer; and the U.S. Navy assistant secretary Franklin Delano Roosevelt.[105]

Not coincidentally, Du Bois held the prime speaking position on the third day of the conference. In his speech, he stressed that he and his fellow editors were committed to promoting not just "passive loyalty" but "active, enthusiastic and self-sacrificing participation in the war." But the race had "justifiable grievances." He highlighted three specific issues—lynching, discrimination in the war effort, and segregated travel—that aroused the most outrage among Black people throughout the country. He did not expect the "Negro problem" to be solved immediately, and he explained that the race was "more than willing to wait until the war of democracy is triumphantly ended before expecting" their "full and just share of that democracy." However, the Negro did expect "that minimum of consideration which will enable him to be an efficient fighter for victory in this war."[106] This speech served as the official statement presented to War Department officials and ultimately to President Wilson.[107]

While in Washington, Du Bois tended to other business as well. Colonel Churchill felt comfortable enough with the idea of a commission for Du Bois to arrange for a physical exam, which he failed on account of his recent kidney operation. Churchill paid it no mind considering that Du Bois would be confined to a desk. Spingarn closely monitored the troubled whispers of his fellow intelligence officers as word of Du Bois's possible commission spread through the halls of the War Department and Washington government circles, apprehensions he shared with Du Bois. Nevertheless, on June 24, Du Bois submitted his formal application.

He also wrote directly to Churchill, his potential commanding officer. He felt the need to address the "questions that have arisen as to my fitness for the position which has been under discussion," questions that had nothing to do with his physical health but everything to do with his radical reputation concerning the "Negro problem." Du Bois saw "no inconsistency with or change of attitude from my

life long work and opinions" and his desire to join the Military Intelligence Branch. Echoing Spingarn's language, Du Bois explained,
"I have opportunity to push a constructive program of race relations
which is radical only in the sense of being more than most Americans
have been ready to concede to Negroes." He considered his approach
"one of far-seeing patriotism," with the ultimate goal of creating "a
union of effort among the best elements of this land on a platform
which would make it possible for self-respecting black men and patriotic white men to work together for the triumph of real democracy."
As far as what he brought to the table, Du Bois had in his corner
"large numbers of educated Negroes who believe in me and my point
of view" and the influence of *The Crisis*. He reassured Churchill that
the day-to-day functions of the magazine would fall to a managing
editor, with his role only to maintain "control over its general policy
as would prevent it at any time from doing inadvertent harm, and
make its cooperation with the military authorities more full and
intelligent." With the lure of the captaincy dangling before him,
Du Bois, who had just months earlier offered blistering criticisms of
the government, now astonishingly offered *The Crisis* as a platform
of wartime propaganda.[108]

The same week that Du Bois formally presented himself and his
services to the War Department, some eighty thousand copies of the
July issue of *The Crisis* hit newsstands and arrived in the mailboxes
of loyal subscribers. It was the "Education Number," an annual tribute to Black college graduates, the next generation of Talented Tenth
leaders.

As always, readers first cast their attention on the opening section
and Du Bois's words. The lead editorial carried a striking title: "Close
Ranks." Du Bois had, despite making his views clear since April 1917,
opted to begin the issue with a statement about the war. "This is the
crisis of the world," he declared. The year 1918 would be remembered as "the great Day of Decision, the day when the world decided
whether it would submit to military despotism and an endless armed
peace—if peace it could be called—or whether they would put down
the menace of German militarism and inaugurate the United States

of the World." For an issue devoted to education, Du Bois's musings about the war, however poetic, seemed curious, even out of place.

But what followed in the next paragraph was even more startling:

> We of the colored race have no ordinary interest in the outcome. That which the German power represents today spells death to the aspirations of Negroes and all darker races for equality, freedom and democracy. Let us not hesitate. Let us, while this war lasts, forget our special grievances and close our ranks shoulder to shoulder with our own white fellow citizens and the allied nations that are fighting for democracy. We make no ordinary sacrifice, but we make it gladly and willingly with our eyes lifted to the hills.[109]

The exact date that Du Bois wrote the editorial is unclear. He maintained in a letter to Francis E. Young, the president of the NAACP's Cleveland branch, that he penned it on June 6 and that it was "in print June 10." He also claimed, falsely, that he did not receive the "tentative offer" of the captaincy until June 15, a date later repeated in *The Crisis*.[110] Even if he did write "Close Ranks" before his June 8 meeting with Spingarn, when the possibility of the commission was presented to him, Du Bois's date falls after his June 4 meeting with Spingarn, during which they discussed the tone of *The Crisis* and the need to make it conform to government censorship expectations. "Close Ranks" was, at the very least, the product of government pressure and fear that his magazine, facing the threat of the Sedition Act, could be shut down and its editor thrown in jail.

But there is also every reason to believe that Du Bois wrote the piece with the captaincy squarely in mind. The printers' deadline for *The Crisis* always suited his purpose, meaning that he could easily have inserted "Close Ranks" at the last minute. Writing it on or shortly after his June 8 meeting with Spingarn was entirely possible. Indeed, it was on June 10, after Du Bois tentatively agreed to pursue the commission, that Spingarn reassured his superiors in the MIB that *The Crisis* would change its tone and be "an organ of patriotic propaganda." Both men knew that for the captaincy to materialize, demonstrating Du Bois's patriotic bona fides and the loyalty of *The Crisis* would be essential. Considering these factors, "Close Ranks" smelled of calculation and opportunism.[111]

Whatever the exact timing and intent of the editorial, it succeeded in soothing the nerves of skittish decision-makers in the War Department. Secretary of War Newton Baker nodded in approval and signed off on Du Bois's commission when Emmett Scott, in a June 26 meeting, showed him a copy of "Close Ranks." Baker then wrote to Churchill: "With reference to the W. E. B. Du Bois matter, it will now be satisfactory for it to go through as originally planned."[112] Before making a final decision, Churchill received a clipping of the article from Joel Spingarn in a July 6 memo titled "Changed Attitude of the Colored Press." After reading it, the colonel scribbled at the bottom, "very satisfactory."[113] With "Close Ranks," characterized by Spingarn as "evidence of the effect of M.I.B. policy," Du Bois seemed increasingly likely to add the title of captain of military intelligence to his résumé.

Then, in rapid and spectacular fashion, it all began to fall apart.

Although Du Bois had submitted a formal application, he claimed that in order to be fully comfortable in his new role in military intelligence, he needed two things: continued control of *The Crisis* and the maintenance of his salary. Both required the consent of the NAACP board. As the next scheduled meeting approached, Du Bois knew that, given the pacifist leanings of several board members, acceptance of his proposal was far from certain. Moreover, with additional time to contemplate the ramifications of what would mark a dramatic shift in his career and reputation, he began to have doubts about Spingarn's lofty plans.[114]

So perhaps, subconsciously, he hoped for a negative outcome when the board convened on July 8. That would explain why Charles Studin and Executive Secretary John Shillady characterized the presentation Du Bois delivered as lackluster. Du Bois, without much conviction, said that he was "favorably disposed toward accepting the commission offered," but wanted to maintain control of *The Crisis* and have his salary supplemented. He faced a skeptical audience. Several of the most potentially sympathetic and less pacifist members of the board were absent, including Mary White Ovington, leaving the temperamental president of the Washington, DC, branch, Archibald Grimké—consistently a thorn in Du Bois's side when it came to his role as *Crisis* editor—to chair the meeting. The board quickly and firmly rejected Du Bois's proposal, led by Grimké, who believed that a move by Du Bois into the War Department would arouse intense suspicion.[115]

Du Bois, tellingly, did not put up a fight. The next day, he wrote to Joel Spingarn and meekly informed him of the decision. "What action shall I now take?" he asked. "I am, of course, sorry for this outcome because I know you will be disappointed and that I will miss a great opportunity for service, but I am convinced that even with a full Board the proposition could be only carried by a sharp and unsatisfactory division."[116]

Spingarn fumed. Writing to Studin, Spingarn charged the board with regarding "military service as work unworthy of its members." He threatened not only to resign from the NAACP but also to publicly declare that "the organization is dangerously unpatriotic and anti-American." He would back off his threat on only one condition: the board had to endorse Du Bois's request, he demanded, "to do the highly patriotic service and constructive work which has been planned for him here."[117]

The brewing tension in the NAACP over Du Bois's captaincy merely foreshadowed the furious reaction of the African American public to "Close Ranks." As Du Bois later recalled, "The words were hardly out of my mouth when strong criticism was rained upon it."[118]

The NAACP's Washington, DC, branch, with a robust membership of seven thousand, became the center of the storm. At a standing room only meeting on July 10, emotions boiled over as speaker after speaker expressed righteous indignation toward Du Bois for his greed in wanting to draw two salaries and his hypocrisy in claiming to represent the race while behind the scenes angling for a position in the government. They also made the connection between "Close

Ranks" and Du Bois's attempt to secure the army commission, branding him a "traitor" and "Benedict Arnold." Joel Spingarn attended the meeting and bravely took up Du Bois's defense. The unruly audience shouted him down and condemned his complicity.[119] Members then took the extraordinary step of passing a resolution denouncing Du Bois's words in "Close Ranks." While reaffirming the loyalty of the race, they declared, "We see no reason for stultifying our consciences by pretending or professing to be ignorant of, or indifferent to the acts of indignity and injustice continually heaped upon us, or by admitting that they are to be excused or forgotten until they are discontinued."[120] Reporting on the "stormiest meeting ever" of the Washington branch, *The Chicago Defender* stated, "The entire N.A.A.C.P. organization is greatly stirred over what many members claim was an abandoning of the Race by Dr. DuBois."[121]

As he began to absorb blow after blow in the Black press and in private letters, Du Bois searched for encouragement from friends and colleagues.[122] "I suppose there is now bursting about you the severest storm of your useful career," wrote Archibald Pinkett, the president of the Bethel Literary and Historical Association, who had attended the raucous DC branch meeting. He reassured Du Bois that people still believed in his leadership and that he would pass this test. "If there is larger opportunity in the Army to bring to fruition your lofty ambition for the race I am persuaded that public denunciation, nor telegrams, nor letters will swerve you from your course."[123]

Du Bois especially looked to another of his closest friends, the Morehouse College president John Hope, for counsel. "A curious and critical situation has arisen," he wrote to Hope on July 12, in a letter marked "PERSONAL AND CONFIDENTIAL." He was seriously weighing Spingarn's offer, but, acknowledging talk that he had "sold out to the Government or that the Government is about to capture and muzzle me," he wondered if he could "get the consent and the cooperation of the great mass of colored people."[124] On July 22, Hope took a pause from his preparations to depart for France as a field secretary with the YMCA to respond to Du Bois and his dilemma. He was direct and reasoned: "There is just one thing that must be your guide:

'ought I to do it?'" He was also blunt, reminding Du Bois, "You look most like a fool when you try to do the expedient or politic." He asked him to seriously consider—"Do you <u>know</u> that you will be able to do constructive work or will you find yourself a secret service man pure and simple?"—and to think hard about whether this job would truly render him "efficiently patriotic."[125]

Du Bois also wrote to Joel Spingarn in an attempt to calm his apoplectic friend. "Please do not act rashly," Du Bois pleaded. The wounded editor expressed his deepest gratitude for Spingarn's "courageous defense" at the DC meeting and the battering he had received in the Black press. "Of course, we must all expect when we essay to lead a crowd that the crowd will be at times incredibly stupid." So much weighed on Du Bois's mind regarding where his duties lay. He thought of his mortality and his financial stability: "What chance a man of fifty or more would have of earning a living after this war." He thought about the NAACP and fallout from an escalation of the situation along the lines that Spingarn threatened. Finally, he thought about his responsibility as a spokesman for the race. "There is no doubt a widespread but, of course, mistaken feeling among colored people that I should not take this work." Although the masses, in his view, may have been wrong, "how far is it my duty," he asked Spingarn, "to fly in face of this opinion?" Du Bois felt, in his own tortured words, "all at sea and disposed simply to sit and wait in order to get the inspiration and see my duty clearly."[126]

Spingarn did not offer much clarity. Instead of empathizing with the obviously painful predicament Du Bois found himself in, Spingarn kept up the pressure. "I am going ahead with my plans on the assumption that you will accept and that before long all those who believe in you will approve of your decision," he wrote back, predicting that the "clamor" fomented by a "few bitter men" would "soon die down." He saw no need for Du Bois to continue as editor, so long as the board promised to return control of *The Crisis* to him after his service. Spingarn also insinuated that he would make up the financial difference of his salary.[127] "Too much depends on your coming to make any missteps now," Spingarn begged. "My whole constructive programme here is on trial, and in danger of toppling over if you do not join forces with me now."[128]

Du Bois felt conflicted as never before. A previously scheduled summer vacation to Maine and the New Jersey shore, two of his favorite getaway locations, could not have come at a more opportune time. For more than a month, spanning mid-July into late August, he attempted to distance himself from the surrounding tempest.[129]

He certainly did not look forward to the letters and news clippings that awaited him upon his return. The Black press and ordinary citizens alike vigorously debated "Close Ranks." The drumbeat of criticism continued throughout July and, building on itself, became more thunderous by the day.

Du Bois received an especially pointed letter from his longtime associate Byron Gunner, an original member of the Niagara Movement who now served as president of the National Equal Rights League. He had initially written to Du Bois on July 16, offering his congratulations on the captaincy.[130] However, as the controversy surrounding Du Bois grew, Gunner's stance toward his old friend changed. "I am finding it very difficult, in my mind, to credit to your pen the advice, 'Let us, while the war lasts, forget our special grievances,'" he wrote in his July 25 letter. They went back a long way, twenty years. "I recall the addresses I've heard you give, as I remember your wise utterances when sitting in council with you in the Niagara Movement at Buffalo and Harper's Ferry." Gunner now found himself "unable to conceive that said advice comes from you. It seems to me that the impossible has happened and I'm amazed beyond expression." He believed that the race needed to do the exact opposite of what Du Bois had advised. "Now, 'while the war lasts,' is the most opportune time for us to push and keep our 'special grievances' to the fore. This we should do for the very best interest of the democracy for which the war is being waged."[131]

Gunner likely took his cue from his fellow National Equal Rights League co-leader William Monroe Trotter. In a July 20 article for *The Boston Guardian* that also appeared in other Black newspapers, Trotter pilloried his former Niagara Movement colleague. "Wm. E.

Burghart [*sic*] DuBois, once crowned leader of the radical, uncompromising contenders for full equality, for identical rights of every kind with all other Americans, has at last finally weakened, compromised, deserted the fight, betrayed the cause of his race." Trotter credited himself for elevating Du Bois "as the best man to lead the fight for equality, human brotherhood and liberty." But his servile actions had reduced him to a "former leader." Trotter minced no words. "Any man who in the midst of a world war for world democracy dares, before this country has abolished any of its federal denials of democracy, before a single important civil political disability is removed by law or the action of the white citizenship, urge his race to forget our 'special grievances,' is not only no longer a radical, he is a compromisor, he is a deserter, he is a rank quitter of the fight for rights." Du Bois, Trotter declared, "betrays his race in the great crisis and at the time when the greatest opportunity is at hand if this race persists in demanding for itself equality and liberty while it fights in the war for democracy for all others."[132]

Trotter's words fueled the most devastating charge leveled against Du Bois: that he was a traitor to the race. Du Bois, over the years, had withstood his fair share of criticism. But never before had he been accused of being a traitor to his people. The *Cleveland Gazette* posed the question bluntly in a front-page article bearing a portrait photo of Du Bois: "Is DuBois a Traitor?" The paper's editor, Harry C. Smith, never a fan of Du Bois's, took delight in the controversy. "Dr. Booker T. Washington never took a more damaging position on race matters of vital interests than has Captain 'Web.' DuBois, editor of the Crisis," he jabbed. "Et tu Brute!"[133]

Black radicals, smelling blood, went in for the kill. Hubert Harrison, the formidable Harlem journalist and activist, entered the fray. On July 25, he published a scathingly methodical editorial in his newspaper, *The Voice*, titled "The Descent of Dr. Du Bois." Du Bois, Harrison asserted, had "palpably sinned" with his call for the race to set aside its "special grievances" for the duration of the war, an act of "cowardice" and "surrender of life, liberty, and manhood." When word broke of his quest for a captaincy, "Close Ranks," in Harrison's words, "acquired a darker and more sinister significance." He saw the two as inextricably linked, with the editorial intended to pave the way for his captaincy. Throwing Spingarn into the equation, it all added up to "deliberate, cold-blooded, purposive planning." "This ruins him as an influential person among Negroes at this time, alike whether he becomes a captain or remains an editor." In the eyes of the Black masses, whom Harrison proudly spoke on behalf of, "Du Bois is regarded much in the same way as a knight in the middle ages who had had his armor stripped from him, his arms reversed and his spurs hacked off," he mocked.[134]

Before fleeing on vacation, Du Bois made sure to offer a clarifying editorial for the August *Crisis* that he, along with Joel Spingarn, hoped would put an end to the controversy.[135] With "A Philosophy in Time of War," Du Bois drove his pen to its rhetorical extremes. "First, This is Our Country," he declared. "We have worked for it, we have suffered for it, we have fought for it; we have made its music, we have tinged its ideals, its poetry, its religion, its dreams . . ." Therefore, he believed, history and logic dictated that "if this is OUR country, then this is OUR war. We must fight it with every ounce of blood and treasure." Yes, America had sinned against its Black citizens, and yes, "a million voices with strained faces and bitter eyes" cried out against the wrongs inflicted upon them. But confronting the threat of Germany, "We shall not hesitate the fraction of a second when the God of Battles summons his dusky warriors to stand before the armposts of His Throne." A great race—"We have seen Egypt and Ethiopia, Babylon and Persia, Rome and America"—would yet again fight, "not for ourselves alone, but for the World." "I have seen the Vision and it shall not fade," he prophesized. Victory would come, but it had to be "clean and glorious, won by our manliness." So, he finally prescribed, "Patience, then, without compromise; silence without surrender; grim determination never to cease striving until we can vote, travel, learn, work and enjoy in peace—all this, and yet with it and above it all the tramp of our armies over the blood-stained lilies of France to show the world again what the loyalty and bravery of black men means."[136]

Unbeknownst to *Crisis* readers, by the time they received Du Bois's extravagant words, Spingarn's "constructive programme" had

come under attack. In a July 20 note to his wife, Spingarn continued to exude guarded confidence. "It looks like now as if I might
put through the DB matter, but there is still much work to do," he
wrote.[137] Little did he know, other officers within the MIB, leery of
his motives and protective of the turf he dared to encroach upon, took
advantage of the "Close Ranks" controversy to raise critical doubts
about Du Bois and, by extension, the major's credibility. The MIB's
lone Black intelligence officer, Walter Loving, inflicted probably the
most destructive blow to Spingarn's plans. Hubert Harrison's scathing editorial had actually been written at the request of Loving, who
subsequently shared it with Churchill as evidence of Du Bois's lack of
standing among his own people and thus his unsuitability for work
in the bureau.[138]

Woodrow Wilson, albeit indirectly, also played a key role in the
erosion of support for Spingarn's special project. Following the editor's conference, Emmett Scott and Robert Moton encouraged Wilson to speak out against lynching and its detrimental effect on Black
morale. They received backing from both Secretary of War Baker and
Churchill, who ultimately persuaded the president to act. On July
26, Wilson issued a strongly worded statement that, while making
no mention of African Americans and not singling out the South,
made clear that the "many lynchings" that had taken place throughout the country represented "a blow at the heart of ordered law and
humane justice."[139] With the president on the record, Churchill saw
no need for his branch to devote any additional time to anti-lynching
efforts and Spingarn's proposed bill.

The "big vision," as Spingarn had described it to Du Bois, never
fully launched. Churchill notified Spingarn on July 30 that his program to "solve the complex question of negro subversion" would not
be approved, on the grounds that, in reference to Emmett Scott's
operation, "there already exists an agency in the office of the Secretary of War whereby the War Department can be kept advised to
the negro question as a whole." The branch planned to restrict its
work to monitoring the morale of Black troops.[140] In a separate note,
Churchill informed Du Bois that his application for the captaincy
was rejected, his failed physical exam used as the pretext.[141] Spingarn,

demoralized, wrote to Du Bois. "I regret very much that the country is not to have the benefit of your great abilities," he lamented. "I am glad however that we planned and dreamed of these things together for our country's good."[142]

Du Bois breathed a sigh of relief. "I can only express my great sorrow at the final decision of Colonel Churchill and my sympathy with you in your efforts," he wrote to Spingarn.[143] Despite the compassionate words to his disheartened friend, the outcome, Du Bois reflected years later, "was probably by far the best result."[144]

Even with the officer commission plan dead, the matter of Du Bois's sullied reputation remained. The aggrieved editor used the September *Crisis* as a personal platform to launch a final defense of his actions and lash back at his critics. He first tried to vindicate both Spingarn and himself in the lengthy editorial "A Momentous Proposal." Misguided critics labeling him a "traitor," accusing him of "bribery," and engaging in "a corrupt bargain" with the government had exacerbated this "delicate situation." But none of it mattered now. Spingarn's special bureau would not be established. "Here the matter rests," Du Bois stated. A great opportunity had been lost. As for him, "The personal side of it is of less consequence and has left Dr. Du Bois in unruffled serenity. No one who essays to teach the multitude can long escape crucifixion," he smugly concluded.[145]

He also felt the need to further rationalize "Close Ranks." In the editorial "Our Special Grievances," he asserted that his controversial statement was "not in the slightest degree inconsistent" with the long-standing principles of the NAACP and his personal convictions. Parsing each sentence and word, he maintained that "the editorial seeks to say that the *first* duty of an American is to win the war and that to this all else is subsidiary. It declares that whatever personal and group grievances interfere with this mighty duty must wait . . . It does not say that these grievances are *not* grievances, or that the temporary setting aside of wrongs makes them right," he added, refusing to back down. "THE CRISIS says, *first* your Country, *then* your Rights!"[146]

He was not done. Continuing his stream of logic in yet another editorial, "The Reward," he acknowledged that "certain honest thinkers among us hesitate at that last sentence. They say it is all well to be idealistic, but is it not true that while we have fought for our country's battles for one hundred fifty years, we have *not* gained our rights?" He dismissed this misreading of history as "a very mischievous lie." Naming the American Revolution, the War of 1812, the Civil War, and the Spanish-Cuban-American War, he argued that "loyalty in time of trial" had resulted in the undeniable achievement of rights for the race. "God knows we have enough left to fight for, but any people who by loyalty and patriotism have gained what we have in four wars ought surely to have sense enough to give that same loyalty and patriotism a chance to win in the fifth." Pointing to the draft, the commissioning of Black officers, and President Wilson's statement against lynching, among other issues, Du Bois declared, "And we *are* winning right now." "Blessed saints! Is this *nothing?*" he asked in frustration. "Should it not discourage slackers and fools? Come, fellow black man, fight for your rights, but for God's sake have sense enough to know when you are getting what you fight for."[147]

The tumult surrounding "Close Ranks" and the captaincy did not leave Du Bois, contrary to his own words, in "unruffled serenity." Loyal friends and Talented Tenth followers continued to support him. However, among the masses of Black folk across the country, his standing as an uncompromising race leader was now in serious question. His self-aggrandizing statements and contemptuous defenses in *The Crisis* masked the inner turmoil the entire affair had wrought. He could ruminate with unparalleled poetic genius about the meaning of being Black and being American, and the heartbreaking tension between loyalty to race and loyalty to nation. But in the superheated throes of war, he had experienced firsthand this existential crisis of identity.

For the three months of June, July, and August 1918, Du Bois surely felt that he had been through a battle, one that severely tested his emotional fortitude and sense of duty. He did not emerge unscathed. His wounds cut deep. Recuperating would not be easy.

CHAPTER 3

". . . a scientific and exhaustive history of the black man in the Great War . . ."[1]

THE NINETY-SECOND DIVISION LEFT for the front on August 12, 1918. Matthew Boutté, exonerated and back with his men, was eager to get into the fray. "Thank God we have a chance to take part in this great conflict against the enemies of humanity," he penciled in his diary. He also hoped for an end to the prejudice he'd confronted in Bourbonne-les-Bains. Facing the all too real possibility of death, perhaps his white comrades would now put their focus on "fighting the Hun and not with segregating colored officers."[2]

To Boutté's dismay, he and his fellow Black officers received no respite from the racism of the United States Army. Jim Crow remained unchecked. White officers kept up their campaign of slander and disparagement. The number of Black officers continued to drop due to bogus efficiency board transfers. A few managed to hang on, among them Adam Patterson and Boutté, who forged ahead as a captain in the 365th Infantry Regiment. The Ninety-Second engaged in limited fighting through August and into September, mostly patrols and opportunistic raids in the St. Die sector. But as one Black officer, William Colson, later reflected, the men of the division "had lost all faith, military and moral" in their white commanders even before experiencing any serious combat.[3]

The nadir for the Ninety-Second Division came in the battle-scarred forests of the Argonne. The German army had been pushed back throughout the summer of 1918. Supreme Allied Commander Ferdinand Foch sensed that the time was right for a final coordinated blow. American forces had proved their mettle, but Foch remained leery of their readiness independent of French and British support. The AEF general John Pershing, determined to demonstrate his personal leadership and set Woodrow Wilson up for the head seat at the peace table, insisted that his men had to fight as an independent American army. The two generals nearly came to blows before Foch relented and allowed Pershing and the AEF to advance along a twenty-four-mile sector of the front from the Meuse River to the Argonne Forest, with the goal of capturing a critical German railway hub at Sedan. Pershing believed that the sheer size of his fighting force would turn the tide of the war in favor of the Allies for good.

However, problems hampered the Meuse-Argonne Offensive from the beginning. Pershing underestimated the challenge of moving the hulking AEF—nearly one million soldiers—into position on the front in less than two weeks. Troops and transport vehicles jammed all available roads and clogged supply lines. Making matters worse, a deadly new surge of influenza hit, taking advantage of the cold, wet, crowded conditions to cripple the army at its envisioned moment of glory.[4]

The 368th Infantry Regiment of the Ninety-Second Division was thrown into the mess. On September 20, the AEF command tasked the regiment with a complex last-minute operation of maintaining liaison between the French and American armies along the German left flank. Suddenly the 368th had a critical role in determining the success of the offensive. Like most of the AEF, they were not ready. The men were bone-tired from a rapid redeployment to the front, traveling more than three hundred miles by train, truck, and foot over a four-day period to arrive at the Argonne on September 24. They had no advance preparation for the mission and lacked the necessary maps and equipment to navigate through the treacherous barbed-wire-encrusted wooded terrain. Underestimating the challenges of the assignment and viewing the 368th as largely expendable, the white leadership of the AEF thrust the regiment into a potentially disastrous situation.

At dawn on the morning of September 26, as a heavy fog blanketed the Argonne Forest, the 368th received orders to move forward. The attack quickly devolved into chaos. German artillery shells rained from the sky. Machine-gun fire from well-hidden nests brought death from seemingly every direction. Without effective wire cutters, the men could hardly move through the thick, tangled underbrush. One white commanding officer described the terrain as "absolutely impenetrable." Communications broke down. Some men received orders to charge ahead. Others received orders to retreat. For five days, confusion, mistrust, racial discord, and blame engulfed the entire regiment. While some ordered companies performed well, as a whole the 368th struggled mightily to achieve even a small semblance of their objectives. On October 1, after advancing as far as the town of Binarville, the regiment was instructed to withdraw and was replaced with French troops. The physical losses were steep—42 men killed and 284 wounded. The damage to the reputation of the 368th, and by association the entire Ninety-Second Division, was crushing.[5]

"The 368th affair is being much discussed," Boutté wrote in an October 2 diary entry. Word of their ordeal spread like wildfire. "Colored officers come to me for information," he continued. "I tell them not to believe the reports." His was good advice. White officers, including a major who suffered a nervous breakdown during the battle, immediately placed blame on the Black officers for the regiment's alleged failure. "The cowardice shown by the men was abject," one of them wrote in his post-operation assessment.[6] In response, the commanding general Charles Ballou quickly removed thirty Black officers from duty, labeling them "worthless," "inefficient," and "untrustworthy." The army formally court-martialed five of these men on charges of cowardice and, after a series of hasty sham trials, found them guilty. Four received death sentences, the fifth life in prison. All white officers escaped accountability.[7]

The Ninety-Second Division looked to redeem itself during the final weeks of the war. In the opening days of October, the division was reassigned to occupy a sector of the Marbache, hold the line of the AEF's limited Meuse-Argonne advances in the area, and harass

German forces with frequent patrols. The Allied offensive, despite the checkered performance of the AEF, put the German army in full retreat. Three regiments of the Ninety-Second Division, including the 365th, received orders to advance on the weakened enemy positions and "push their attacks vigorously." The war was effectively over, but the operation nevertheless provided an opportunity for the division to prove its worth. The Woëvre Plain offensive commenced on November 10. For a day and a half, until the armistice went into effect on November 11 at 11:00 a.m., the division's Black soldiers gave it their all and fought extremely well. The 365th especially distinguished itself. It was a moral victory, but the 498 casualties of the tactically pointless battle undoubtedly thought otherwise.[8] Matthew Boutté was among the injured.

In addition to the continuing psychological trauma of American racism, Boutté now confronted the physical wounds of war. He eventually found himself in Base Hospital 45 at Toul, with its staff of white doctors and nurses from Virginia. He spent several excruciating weeks recovering from his injuries. The doctors pondered over what to do with the out-of-place Black officer, finally deciding to consign him to a ward with regular enlisted men. "The attention given me was practicably nil," Boutté recalled in his diary. Fortunately, he received care from two "northern Catholic white" orderlies who, upon learning that Boutté shared their faith, "promised to do all in their power to save me." "Days—dark gloomy days of sickness, of suffering, of weariness" followed, he wrote, his once exuberant spirit hardened with bitterness. "Several times I was about to give up the fight and let myself die."

A visit from John Hope, in France with the YMCA, lifted his spirits and renewed his determination "to testify to the treatment accorded colored officers and enlisted men." "No nation on earth has ever hated a group as the Americans hate Negroes," Boutté fumed in his diary. Whether it was an officer or a hospital nurse, white Americans in France remained unmoved by the pain and blood sacrifice of Black soldiers. Instead of accepting their humanity, Boutté scrawled, "It was 'that nigger' in uniform, it was 'that nigger' in suffering from wounds; it was 'that nigger' in death."

As he lay in agony, he wrote to Du Bois. "I felt that some one ought to know the things that I knew, that I had gone thru." He hoped that Du Bois, like a savior, would arrive in France. Boutté likely thought back to an earlier diary entry from August 29: "I wonder when Dr. Du Bois will reach us. For some time it has been rumored that he would be here. Who will write the history of this segregated Division?"[9]

~

AT ROUGHLY 4:00 P.M. on October 14, 1918, the NAACP board of directors convened for its monthly meeting. The eleven assembled members huddled in the editorial room of *The Crisis* at the association's 70 Fifth Avenue headquarters in New York. Occupying twelve hundred square feet, *The Crisis* office always buzzed with activity. Du Bois ensured that his eight-person staff kept busy. Preparations for the upcoming November issue would have been nearing completion, filling the fifth floor with the steady clicking of typewriters and the whirl of the multigraph machine.[10] The board members, filing in, made themselves comfortable as best they could. Joel Spingarn had finally gone to France—receiving an assignment to the front lines following the collapse of his military intelligence program—so the acting chairwoman Mary White Ovington presided.[11]

The meeting began with a discussion of standard business. The treasurer, Oswald Garrison Villard, laid out the financial health of the association, reporting that approximately ten thousand dollars sat in the General Fund, with just over six thousand in the Special Fund account. Du Bois followed with an update on the state of *The Crisis*. Although wartime paper restrictions at that time made expansion unfeasible, circulation for the month of September came in at a strong 80,500 copies sold, and revenues remained on an upward trajectory. Secretary John Shillady provided information on the current NAACP membership—39,639 and 142 active branches—along with the various issues the association was engaged in: the ongoing anti-lynching campaign, the investigation of compulsory work laws in the South, efforts to suppress *The Birth of a Nation*, the voting rights of encamped

Black soldiers. Field Secretary James Weldon Johnson reported on his activities and those of his recently appointed assistant, Walter White, a twenty-five-year-old Atlanta University alum whose light skin, blond hair, and blue eyes made him perfect for investigating Southern lynch mobs. Since the last meeting, nine cities, ranging from Davenport, Iowa, to Hawkinsville, Georgia, had filed applications to establish new NAACP branches, bringing in 538 fresh members. Charles Studin reported to the board on the work of the Legal Committee, and Du Bois talked about his preliminary plans to organize tercentenary events in commemoration of the 1619 arrival of the first twenty Africans to colonial Virginia.[12]

When it came time for new business, Oswald Garrison Villard spoke up. With the Allied offensive finally cracking Germany's entrenched forces, the end of the war loomed on the horizon. The NAACP would soon need to assess the role African Americans played in the global conflict. Villard had an idea. He suggested that the NAACP take immediate steps to compile, in a "careful and scientific" manner, all records "concerning the Negro soldier's work in the present war," with the goal of "getting out a book" by the end of the fighting.

As for who would spearhead the project, Villard believed the task fell squarely within the purview of the director of publications and research. That was Du Bois.[13]

Villard and Du Bois had a volatile personal and professional relationship. Villard, the privileged grandson of the abolitionist William Lloyd Garrison, had been, like Du Bois, a student of Albert Bushnell Hart at Harvard and earned a graduate degree in history. Their first confrontation erupted over the 1909 publication of Du Bois's book *John Brown*. Villard, also at work on a biography of Brown, wrote a scathing review in *The Nation*, which he owned, and denied a much-aggrieved Du Bois the courtesy of a published rebuttal. Distrust between the two men carried over into the founding of the NAACP and continued throughout the early years of the association. Villard questioned Du Bois's temperament and judgment, especially when it came to *The Crisis*, while Du Bois constantly pushed back against his colleague's racial paternalism. Tensions reached a head in late 1913, when Villard, irate over Du Bois's management of *The Crisis* and its strident tone, resigned as NAACP board chairman.[14]

Du Bois, considering this stormy history, absorbed Villard's proposal with mild shock.[15] But he was immediately intrigued. The personal, political, and intellectual appeals of the project began to swirl in his mind.[16] Here was a chance to embark on a major scholarly study, carried out in scientific fashion, the likes of which he had not conducted since *The Philadelphia Negro* in 1899. His political philosophies and his approach to history had evolved significantly since then. Frustrated with white scholars' abuse of the truth when it came to the history of Black people, he now exercised far less restraint in blurring the lines between scientific objectivity and propaganda to offer counternarratives of the historical record.[17] The NAACP board's proposition thus presented an opportunity to make a political statement about the causes of the World War, the central place of Black people in the Allied cause, and Du Bois's own vision of a postwar world in which African Americans and other peoples of African descent reaped the democratic gains of their sacrifices. On a personal level, he could begin to repair his credibility, damaged by "Close Ranks," and reassert his standing as the race's most formidable leader.

As the other board members in the room weighed Villard's proposal, they likely had their own motivations. The NAACP could reap significant gains in terms of membership and stature by positioning itself as the keeper of Black soldiers' historical legacy. Sympathetic members of the board such as Mary White Ovington and James Weldon Johnson no doubt also saw an opportunity to rehabilitate Du Bois's battered reputation. Villard, long weary of Du Bois devoting NAACP time to his personal scholarship and outside publications, undoubtedly hoped to use the project to control Du Bois's activities and focus them toward the exclusive benefit of the association.[18]

Villard presented a formal resolution. The NAACP would appropriate a maximum of $2,000 over a six-month period to complete the book. One board member, the Reverend Dr. Hutchens C. Bishop, the rector of Harlem's St. Philip's Episcopal Church, who'd marched alongside Du Bois in the Silent Protest Parade, seconded the motion. The resolution passed without opposition.[19]

After discussing a few more issues, such as how best to confront the ongoing scourge of lynching, Ovington adjourned the meeting.[20] It was getting late. Du Bois departed his *Crisis* office and the NAACP headquarters that evening with a new, exciting, and wholly unexpected charge: write the history of Black people in the World War and, as he surely thought, make sense of his own confusing place in that still unfolding history.

⌒

DU BOIS WASTED NO TIME in getting to work. He first pondered whether to conduct the project alone, with NAACP sponsorship, or make it a collaborative effort. Although he had never coauthored any of his previous books, he quickly saw the benefits of bringing together a team of prominent Black leaders and scholars. Telling the entire history of Black participation in the war, and its larger implications for the envisioned postwar reconstruction, posed a monumental task for a single author. Organizing an editorial and research team would address this concern and at the same time allow Du Bois to demonstrate his leadership—and relevance—in the face of continued skepticism.

He was tactical when it came to identifying potential partners. He needed individuals possessing both political clout and intellectual gravitas. Two men topped his list: Carter G. Woodson and Emmett J. Scott.

On the surface, Du Bois and Carter Woodson seemed like an ideal match. Woodson, the son of a fugitive slave from West Virginia, was a driven, fastidious student who first contacted Du Bois while he was at the University of Chicago completing his master's thesis on the Negro church. He followed in Du Bois's footsteps to Harvard, becoming at the age of thirty-seven only the second Black man to receive a Ph.D. in history, earning him the honor of being profiled as a "Man of the Month" in the July 1912 issue of *The Crisis*.[21] Woodson had established the Association for the Study of Negro Life and History (ASNLH) on September 9, 1915, and successfully published the first volume of *The Journal of Negro History* the following year. Recognizing this accomplishment and encouraging *Crisis* readers to help increase the fledgling journal's subscription numbers, Du Bois proclaimed, "Dr. Carter G. Woodson and his associates have a right to feel proud."[22]

Du Bois, however, was not one of Woodson's associates. Woodson charted a different scholarly path, one rooted in African American public-facing education and institution building.[23] While Du Bois editorialized from the tower of his Fifth Avenue NAACP office, Woodson scrapped and clawed to keep the ASNLH alive. Their approaches to the study of history also veered, with Du Bois embracing the need to combine scholarship and activism while Woodson opted for conscious detachment from racial politics. Further complicating matters, Woodson and Du Bois were both notoriously difficult to work with. Woodson possessed a prickly demeanor that made collaboration a challenge—"He is, to put it mildly, cantankerous," Du Bois wrote in 1925 regarding his fellow Harvard alum. Du Bois, meanwhile, did not take lightly any questioning of his intellectual preeminence.[24] Something would have to give.

Du Bois recounted that "when the proposition of compiling a History of the Negro in the Great War was mentioned" by the NAACP board, he "immediately thought of Mr. Woodson." Shortly after the October 14 meeting, Du Bois invited Woodson to New York at the expense of the association. Woodson could not attend, so instead Du Bois traveled to Washington, DC, home of Woodson and the ASNLH, and met with him on October 27. Du Bois emerged from their hour-long conversation optimistic about a partnership.[25]

Woodson, however, had concerns. He made them vividly clear to Du Bois in a letter he wrote that same day. In the event he agreed to the project, Woodson stated, "I would have to receive full credit for all of the work." Serving in any other capacity, he professed, "would be both dishonorable and foolish."[26] Unbeknownst to Du Bois, Woodson had already begun shopping his own idea of a historical study on African Americans in the war to various white philanthropists, foundations, and ASNLH friends. Coincidentally, the same day the NAACP board proposed the war history project to Du Bois, Woodson had sent out letters to members of his executive council requesting funds for the "successful prosecution" of an official account of the Black experience in the war, an endeavor he pressed as "a matter of the greatest importance to every servant of the truth."[27] He therefore confidently asserted to Du Bois that regardless of other books that may appear before the public, "I know that I shall still have an opportunity to make a contribution." The always cash-strapped Woodson did, however, discern a financial benefit in working with the NAACP, and he tacitly acknowledged that the two pioneering historians could make a formidable pair: "You and I are the only persons capable of doing it."[28]

Du Bois countered in a restrained October 30 letter. He proposed that they, along with Emmett Scott and George Haynes, serve as "co-equal editors of the whole work." Du Bois imagined that the "work" would be "divided into four parts and that each one of these editors write one of the parts."[29]

Du Bois made a strategic choice in selecting George Haynes as a potential fourth coeditor. Haynes held an M.A. from Yale University and a Ph.D. in economics from Columbia University, joining Du Bois and Woodson in an exclusive club of African American Ivy League doctorates. Du Bois, in fact, honored him as another "Man of the Month"—alongside Carter G. Woodson—in the July 1912 *Crisis*.[30] Haynes served as the first executive secretary of the National Urban League, founded in 1910, and went on to teach economics and sociology at Fisk University. His interest in Black migration caught the attention of the Department of Labor, which enlisted him during the war as a special assistant with the title of "Director of the Division of Negro Economics."[31] Next to Emmett Scott, Haynes remained the second most prominent African American in the federal government until he left his post in 1921. But unlike Scott, he fit Du Bois's definition of a serious scholar and could thus offer both political credibility and intellectual legitimacy.

Du Bois, who had only mentioned the idea to Haynes and not yet talked with Scott, hoped that Woodson would see the wisdom in his offer. Catering to Woodson's ego, he explained, "I am writing this proposition to you first in order to have your decision at the earliest possible moment before I approach the other gentlemen."[32]

Actually, Du Bois did not wait for Woodson's reply before turning his attention to Emmett Scott. A Du Bois–Scott union, considering their contentious Tuskegee history, seemed more far-fetched than Du Bois collaborating with Woodson. But Du Bois and Scott had remained on friendly terms during the war and through the "Close Ranks" firestorm.[33] Du Bois thus had high hopes when he and James Weldon Johnson dined with Scott on the evening of November 3 in New York to discuss forging a common postwar political agenda. After their meal, they cordially agreed on the need to overcome ideological factionalism and cooperate on various mutually shared goals. Du Bois raised the topics of the tercentenary commemoration and the promotion of consumers' cooperatives run through the National Negro Business League, both ideas Scott embraced.

But when Du Bois broached the matter of the war history, Scott demurred. He was already considering publishers for his own history. Out of courtesy, he promised to communicate with Du Bois at a later date.[34] However, this did not bode well. A book from Scott, given his high profile, would undoubtedly undermine the NAACP's work, and Du Bois along with it.

Even after absorbing this disconcerting news, Du Bois decided that a formal relationship with Scott on the war history project was still worth pursuing. He again requested Scott's cooperation in a November 8 letter, expressing his desire for the influential special assistant "to have a prominent place on this Editorial Board" and his willingness "to arrange the basis of collaboration in such a way as will best suit you." He also informed Scott that he had been in touch with Carter G. Woodson "with the same idea in mind." Du Bois attempted to show as much deference to Scott as possible. However, he could not resist a subtle swipe at his credentials, stating that he and the NAACP "intend that this shall be a complete and definitive work, done with scientific accuracy and literary skill, and based on as [*sic*] exhaustive collection of facts and documents."[35] While Du Bois, Woodson, and Haynes all held doctorates, Scott did not.

The next day, Du Bois heard back from Woodson, who emphatically rejected the idea of a four-man editorial team. "The entire work must be written by one historian assisted by well informed advisors,"

Woodson insisted. The ASNLH founder left no doubt as to whom he considered the best historian for the job. "If you think that I am qualified to write this history, employ me to do it," he fired back at Du Bois. "If you know of a more competent man in this field, you should seek him. But do not divide this task so as to bring out a hodgepodge of which the race will be ashamed. I cannot honorably attach my name to such a work." Even more troubling for Du Bois, Woodson revealed that he had been in touch with Scott about his book plans for some time prior to receiving Du Bois's proposal and he believed that Scott "will hardly cooperate with you." Woodson might have shared Du Bois's conceit about Scott's abilities—"You know that he is not an historian," he wrote—but he had no qualms about striking a deal with the well-connected Tuskegee Machine architect to further the progress of the ASNLH.[36]

The contours of Scott and Woodson's relationship became clearer when Scott, on November 10, sent an amicable reply to Du Bois, formally rejecting his invitation. He again informed Du Bois of his intentions to publish his own book, adding, "I can hardly believe, however, that my plans need interfere with your program." In a handwritten note at the bottom of the letter, Scott divulged, "I spoke with Mr. Woodson of my plans some 6 or 8 weeks ago."[37] Du Bois could now see the possibility of a partnership with Scott slipping away, while Woodson shrewdly hedged his bets by fielding collaborative offers from both men. In a matter of weeks, writing the history of Black people in the war had become its own battle, rife with double-dealing and intrigue.

THE WAR CAME TO an end on November 11, 1918. Although African American troops were in France for less than a year, they had been severely tested. The Ninety-Third Division, still attached to the French Army, had compiled an impressive record. Most notably, the 369th Infantry Regiment served valiantly on the front for 191 consecutive days, never ceding an inch of ground to the Kaiser's forces, and soon would prepare to cross the Rhine into German territory, the first American fighting unit to do so. The 370th Infantry Regiment also distinguished itself in battle, earning praise from the French and fear from the Germans, who nicknamed them the "Black Devils."[38]

Meanwhile, African American Services of Supply troops kept laboring. On the docks of Brest, Saint-Nazaire, Bordeaux, Le Havre, and Marseilles, teams of Black stevedores, at record pace, continued the backbreaking work of unloading tons of food, clothing, mail, and war matériel from sunup to sundown. Other Black labor troops, with the war over, now shouldered the unglamorous duty of cleaning up a French countryside devastated by four years of combat. The unluckiest men had the nauseating task of exhuming the rotting corpses of dead American soldiers and reburying them.[39]

As for the Ninety-Second Division, its morale hung tragically low. The targeted campaign against Black officers like Matthew Boutté was unrelenting. By the time of the armistice, their numbers in the division had precipitously dropped from eighty-two percent to fifty-eight percent.[40] The dark cloud of the 368th Infantry Regiment's alleged failure in the Meuse-Argonne also continued to hover. The five court-martialed officers sat in confinement at AEF headquarters in Chaumont, their fate uncertain.[41]

Adding to its troubles, the Ninety-Second Division faced a "whispering gallery" about its conduct with the French. White American soldiers had gone out of their way to poison the minds of French civilians by labeling Black troops as savages with tails hidden under their uniforms. It was an easy step from this to the old Southern trope of the Black beast rapist. Without a shred of evidence, white officers, including General Charles Ballou, accused their fellow Black soldiers of raping white Frenchwomen almost habitually. Ballou imposed strict orders limiting the freedom of movement of his troops and went so far as to threaten that if matters did not improve, Pershing would send the division back to the United States or break it up into labor battalions. Among white soldiers and officers in the AEF, the Ninety-Second Division became derisively labeled the "rapist division."[42]

Adam Patterson found himself at the center of the rumors surrounding the Ninety-Second and rape. On October 5, 1918, the ambitious lawyer received a promotion to major and appointment as judge advocate for the Ninety-Second Division, the first African

American in the history of the army to earn this distinction. He also became arguably the most powerful Black officer in the entire American Expeditionary Forces, one of a minuscule number of Black men who could outrank a white officer.

The situation facing his fellow Black servicemen in the Ninety-Second required all of Patterson's strength, smarts, and savvy. He personally reviewed every charge and case brought against the division's soldiers in France, including rape. Despite the rumors, only ten incidents came to his attention. Of these, seven men were found not guilty or exonerated of sexual assault. In one case, the alleged victim admitted that an American general, along with an army chaplain, forced her to testify against the accused Black sergeant.[43]

Considering what they had been through, no wonder that—perhaps more than any other group of American soldiers in France—Black troops welcomed the prospect of returning home. Homesickness quickly spread as African American servicemen yearned to be reunited with loved ones.[44] Most important, they were happy to be alive. They had survived combat, grueling labor, a devastating influenza pandemic, and, above all, American white supremacy. Black servicemen looked forward to the long journey home and, they hoped, a new beginning.

Du Bois echoed these sentiments in the dramatic "Peace" editorial headlining the December 1918 *Crisis*. "The nightmare is over. The world awakes. The long, horrible years of dreadful night are passed. Behold the sun!" he intoned. The war had been a traumatic time for Du Bois. Nina and Yolande braved the early months of the war in England, fortunately returning home in the summer of 1916 without harm. His kidney operation later that year brought him perilously close to physical death. The violence and confusion of East St. Louis, Houston, and Charles Young threatened the spiritual death of Du Bois's faith in American democracy. But the patriotic fervor of the war had engulfed him, and he found himself swept up in the tide of "100% Americanism." He would not emerge unscathed, as "Close Ranks" nearly ruined the credibility he'd spent so many years carefully cultivating. Was it all worth it? "We have dreamed. Frightfully have we dreamed unimagined, unforgettable things—all lashed with blood and tears . . . And now suddenly we awake!" he wrote. "It is done. We are sane. We are alive."[45] If the nightmare was indeed over, if the Black world, Du Bois with it, was truly sane, and if being alive now carried new meaning, documenting and revealing the history of the war assumed monumental importance.

~

THE SAME DAY AS the armistice, the NAACP board of directors met for its monthly meeting. The opening topic of business, understandably, was the status of the war history. Du Bois reported that his "first duty" was "to unite into one great effort various workers and persons of prominence whose efforts might otherwise be dissipated in other directions." He had been in touch with Woodson, Scott, and Haynes, but, he claimed, "nothing definite has yet come from this appeal." Scott had in fact made his intentions to write a book of his own quite clear. Du Bois's devious statement reflected a long pattern of obfuscating his actions from the board in order to maintain his independence.[46] He still felt that within the next three months he could lay the groundwork to begin research in the United States—"a method of procedure" that entailed examining local, state, and federal documents, press reports, and the records of philanthropic agencies all related to the organization and service of African American soldiers. In the meantime, he recommended that "at an early date" he get to France "to collect and systematize matters from French sources."[47]

Du Bois was itching to get to France for other reasons as well. From the opening guns of August 1914, he had presciently identified the connection between the war and the future of Africa. A recent statement by Lord Robert Cecil, the British parliamentary undersecretary of state for foreign affairs, that Germany should relinquish all control of her colonies in the increasingly inevitable event of an Allied victory, had sparked Du Bois's imagination. He shared his thoughts in an August 28, 1918, letter to George Foster Peabody, the influential white philanthropist and friend of Negro uplift. With peace looming, control of Germany's African colonies would be up for grabs. The

Allies, with a record of colonial exploitation Du Bois saw as "not radically" different from Germany's, could not be expected to faithfully
advocate on behalf of "the people affected." What if, Du Bois asked
Peabody, "a strong demand on the part of the Negroes of the world
against the return of the colonies to Germany could be made" as "the
moral foundation of a just peace?" Expressing unflappable confidence,
Du Bois believed that "by convention or signed petition" he could win
the support of "every Negro American of prominence to a demand
that German colonies be not restored."[48]

At the September board meeting, Du Bois encouraged the NAACP
to take immediate "steps concerning the future of Africa" and stated
his intention to pressure the Wilson administration so that "at the
Peace Conference some recognition of the rights of the Negro race
in Africa" would take place.[49] He began crafting a formal statement
of his position, sending an early version to Philip Whitwell Wilson of
the *London Daily News*. Wilson and George Peabody used their combined influence to forward Du Bois's memorandum to the American
Commission to Negotiate Peace, headed by Colonel Edward House.[50]
Toward the end of the November 11 NAACP board meeting, Du Bois
provided an update on his activities and read from his "Memorandum
on the Future of Africa," which appeared in print form in the January
1919 *Crisis* under the title "The Future of Africa."[51]

As early as January 1918, Du Bois floated the idea of "an independent Negro Central African State" administered as a protector-
ate by an international body.[52] The "Memorandum on the Future of
Africa" represented his most detailed articulation of this idea. While
the memo, divided into thirteen points, reflected Du Bois's bold application of the Wilsonian principles of self-determination to African
peoples, it also reflected his elitism and views of a hierarchically structured African diaspora. His "re-organized Africa" would, by necessity,
"be under the guidance of organized civilization." He envisioned a
"Governing International Commission" supervising Germany's former colonial holdings, along with parts of Portugal's and Belgium's
territories, until the masses of native Africans attained a sufficient
level of civilization and proved themselves capable of self-rule. The

interests of some twenty-four million African people would in the meantime be represented by the "chiefs and intelligent Negroes" of German Africa, followed by "the twelve million civilized Negroes of the United States" and other "educated persons of Negro descent" scattered across the diaspora who together, Du Bois believed, comprised "the thinking classes of the future Negro world." "We can, if we will, inaugurate on the Dark Continent a last great crusade for humanity," he mused, adding, "With Africa redeemed, Asia would be safe and Europe indeed triumphant."[53] In the hands of the diasporic Talented Tenth, Du Bois's top-down program of African uplift would humanely complete the civilizing mission of the European colonial powers and establish a crucial firewall against future imperial expansion.

Du Bois delivered an impressive presentation. The board subsequently voted to appoint a committee of three individuals "to procure a committee of twenty-five representative Negroes to present to President Wilson Dr. Du Bois' statement." Secretary John Shillady also suggested "the desirability of holding a conference or conferences on the general problem of reconstruction affecting the Negro."[54]

Du Bois effectively planted the seeds of his secondary motivation for wanting to travel to France: the organization of a Pan-African Congress during the upcoming Paris Peace Conference and the chance to formally present his memorandum concerning the future of Africa on the world stage.[55] In July 1900 he had served as chairman of the Address Committee for the Pan-African Conference, which was held at Westminster Town Hall in London and convened by the visionary Trinidadian activist Henry Sylvester Williams. At the close of the historic three-day gathering, Du Bois, in his address titled "To the Nations of the World," prophetically declared for the first time, "The problem of the twentieth century is the problem of the color line."[56] The end of the war now presented him with the tantalizing opportunity to revive the Pan-African movement and use the peace conference to shape the future of the twentieth century for Black folk.

Du Bois's plans for a Pan-African Congress meshed with his continued efforts to get the book project off the ground. This included turning to trusted allies to construct an editorial board that would offer guidance and, more important, legitimize the historical study, as negotiations with Woodson and Scott appeared destined to fail. On November 14, Du Bois sent an inquiry to Albert Bushnell Hart to gauge his interest in serving on the war history advisory board. During their Harvard days, Hart had taken a keen liking to Du Bois as an exception to the rule of inherent Negro intellectual inferiority, which he attributed to the European blood that flowed through his student's veins. Hart arranged for Du Bois's dissertation, "Suppression of the African Slave Trade," to appear as the first volume in the Harvard Historical Studies series and, in 1909, used his influence as president of the American Historical Association to allow Du Bois to deliver a landmark paper on Reconstruction at its annual meeting. More recently, like Du Bois, Hart supported America's entry into the World War.[57] And, like Du Bois, he found himself swept up into the machine of hyperpatriotism and pro-Allied propaganda. He even went so far as to join the reactionary National Security League. Du Bois did not see this as a problem, instead wisely recognizing that the endorsement of his mentor and one of the nation's leading white historians would give his war project unmatched scholarly credibility. Hart promptly replied, writing, "It would give me great pleasure to cooperate on an Advisory Board on the history of the Negro in the Great War."[58]

Du Bois also contacted several African Americans to join his team. He immediately reached out to Charles Young, asking him to participate on the editorial board, and Young unsurprisingly agreed to help his friend. Offering his "highest esteem" and "very best love," Young wrote, "I want to say that no better man than yourself could have been appointed by the National Association to write the History of the American Negro in the Great War. Nothing would please me better than to join your Editorial Board for the purposes you require."[59] Having the legendary Black officer and powerful racial symbol attached to the project would without question enhance its stature. William Taylor Burwell Williams, the Harvard-educated field director for the Slater Fund and Hampton Institute, also responded favorably to Du Bois's request.[60]

Even as the advisory board materialized, Du Bois still needed considerable help producing a book that would meet his high standards. Anticipating this challenge, he wrote to the history departments of several major universities across the country requesting information on African American students who might serve as research assistants. Some of his inquiries came up short. His Harvard classmate Evarts Greene, a professor of history at the University of Illinois, could "not at the moment think of any one whom I can recommend as qualified to serve as assistant in the compilation of the history of the American Negro in the Great War."[61] Marshall S. Brown, the dean of faculties at New York University, informed Du Bois that he had "very few colored men in my classes at the University and none of them have specialized in history."[62] Professor E. D. Adams of the Stanford University History Department responded that "no colored man or woman has ever received training in the History Department of Stanford University, and that therefore I cannot make such recommendation as you suggest."[63]

Other responses, however, were more encouraging. Max Farrand, the distinguished historian at Yale University, gave Du Bois two names, one of them Charles Harris Wesley, who'd received his master's degree in 1913 and later became—after Du Bois and Woodson—the third African American to receive a Harvard Ph.D. in history.[64] The Dartmouth professor Herbert Foster, who'd also crossed paths with Du Bois at Harvard, suggested Ernest Everett Just, the pioneering biologist and Howard University professor who, though not a historian, nevertheless earned departmental honors in history while an undergraduate.[65] The University of California history professor and former American Historical Association president H. Morse Stephens provided the names of two students. Stephens, who had begun collecting materials for a war history project of his own, kindly wrote, "Let me add in conclusion how heartily I sympathize in your project of giving the world a clear historical account of the services of the negro population of America in the great war" and offered "the best cooperation of the History Department of the University of California."[66] The renowned Harvard historian Charles Homer Haskins, a classmate of Woodrow Wilson at Johns Hopkins and close adviser to the president on his peace plans, responded to Du Bois by offering a familiar name: "The best colored student we have had in recent years is Dr. Carter G. Woodson, editor of the Journal of Negro History, who is, of course, well known to you."[67]

He most certainly was. While attempting to compile a potential editorial board and research assistance, Du Bois made a last-ditch effort to corral Woodson. In a November 12 letter, Du Bois wrote that he and the NAACP board were "sincerely desirous of having your [sic] work with us on this matter." With the scope and structure of the project changing by the day, he now proposed a history of five or six volumes, published over a period of five years, to be equally coedited by Du Bois and Woodson and funded with a hypothetical $5,000 appropriation from the NAACP. Du Bois tried his best to massage Woodson's ego and assure him that "there would be no question of your not receiving due honor." Du Bois did not, in his words, "have the power to hand it absolutely over to you," but nevertheless assured Woodson, "I realize, as too few people do, your great value as a historical student, and I want you to have full scope and untrammeled chance to do a great piece of work." Nevertheless, Du Bois's impressive magnanimity did have limitations. "If, however, you have any personal objection to working in conjunction with me, I should be very sorry to press this matter further."[68]

Woodson responded four days later, on November 16. Rightly sensing Du Bois's irritation, Woodson clarified that his desire for wanting to be sole editor did not reflect a personal objection to working with Du Bois, but instead an aversion to other individuals interfering with his scholarship. "Da Vinci could not have painted the Mona Lisa, if he had employed some one to work on the hands while he was retouching the face," Woodson scolded. He then gave Du Bois his latest offer, emphasizing that "no one has seen this agreement. It was drawn up by me." He would sign on to serve as a coequal editor for the multivolume study and work with the NAACP, but only if Du Bois met certain financial conditions. Assuming that the NAACP devoted $5,000 to the project, $2,500 would go directly into Woodson's pocket, twenty-five percent in advance and the remainder in twenty-four evenly allocated monthly payments. The remaining $2,500 would go toward expenses for the book and be "disbursed by order of said C. G. Woodson." When it came to the money, Woodson demanded full control. He continued playing hardball with Du Bois, writing that another unnamed publishing firm had tendered a similar offer and, in a paragraph marked "Confidential," stated that he continued to work with Emmett Scott on his book project. With this, he left the matter squarely in Du Bois's hands, quite possibly trembling with anger by the time he finished reading Woodson's letter.[69]

Making matters worse, any hopes of working with Scott seemingly died when Du Bois received a press release from his friend James E. Shepard, the founder and president of North Carolina Central University. A personal annotation from Shepard appeared at the bottom: "You will have to go along independent lines." Du Bois was surely stunned by what he read. The release announced that "steps have been taken to tell the full story of the Negro's participation in the Great War by Dr. Emmett J. Scott." In order to "assure a comprehensive and authoritative history," Scott had assembled a virtual who's who of scholars, activists, and other race leaders to assist him. They included the acclaimed University of Chicago sociologist Robert E. Park; Tuskegee's director of records and research, Monroe N. Work; Ralph W. Tyler, the lone accredited African American reporter in France during the war; Alice Dunbar Nelson, who had served on the Woman's Committee of the Council of National Defense; and Eva D. Bowles, the executive secretary in charge of colored work for the Young Women's Christian Association. One name undoubtedly jumped out at Du Bois more than any other: Dr. Carter G. Woodson. "Publishers of international importance will print and circulate the history," Scott crowed, with copies of the book placed "as nearly as possible in every colored home in America."[70] Although its exact date is unclear, the memo was likely issued sometime shortly after Scott learned of Du Bois's intention to write a book as well.

On the same day Woodson sent Du Bois his audacious proposal, Du Bois forwarded Scott's press release to Oswald Garrison Villard, George Foster Peabody, and L. Hollingsworth Wood, along with a memo updating them on the state of negotiations with his two antagonists.[71] Du Bois's decision to reach out to Peabody and Wood was calculated, as both men served with Emmett Scott on the ASNLH executive council. Du Bois hoped that they could use their influence, personal and financial, to broker some sort of resolution to the growing impasse concerning the book. Referring to Scott's attached announcement, Du Bois wrote, "You will note that precisely the thing is about to happen which we tried to avoid." He continued: "I have no desire at all to interfere with Mr. Scott's plans, or wishes, but he has been to say the least, lacking in frankness in going ahead with a plan almost identical with that of the N.A.A.C.P., after promising at least, cooperation." In truth, Du Bois knew full well that Scott had been thinking of a book long before the NAACP had come up with the idea. "Mr. Woodson," Du Bois noted, "has also apparently acted in the same ungenerous manner." Despite his plans rapidly falling apart, he still resisted abandoning the war history on the grounds that "Mr. Scott is not a historian or a trained writer."[72]

Du Bois unenthusiastically suggested an immediate conference with Scott and Woodson to clear the air and attempt to forge a partnership. But he knew perfectly well that the chances of success were slim to none.[73] Scott had no intention of dropping his plans for a potentially lucrative and self-promoting book that promised to solidify his leadership standing among African Americans.

Woodson also refused to play second fiddle. He brashly questioned Du Bois's commitment to the project as well as his historical credentials. "Dr. DuBois has neither the time nor the attitude to write such a work," Woodson candidly wrote to L. Hollingsworth Wood, adding that Du Bois "is now devoting himself altogether to propaganda which does not readily harmonize with history."[74] Behind the scenes, ulterior motives clashed and egos raged.

Jesse Moorland, an influential educator, minister, and social worker, hoped to make peace between the competing parties. As head of the Colored Men's Department of the YMCA, he'd labored assiduously to hold the organization accountable to serving African American soldiers during the war. Moorland had a long-standing relationship with Carter G. Woodson and knew very well of the rival book by Emmett Scott.[75] In a November 25 letter to Du Bois, Moorland wrote, "I am hearing so much of different projects of this kind, that I am inclined to think there ought to be a conference which will clear the atmosphere and make certain that we get our brains together, so that one work of the type you mention, will certainly be produced." He accurately foresaw that a flood of so-called histories of the Black experience in the war lay on the near horizon, most written for purely selfish financial gain. In the case of Du Bois's proposed book, Moorland believed that it "ought to have the backing of the best we have in both races . . . I am sure this is a time for the union of our forces and the 'scrapping' of our organizations and even of our brains, if that can be done, and bring forth a great work which shall represent the best that is in all the agencies interested." He hesitated on accepting Du Bois's request to join his advisory board until a meeting of the minds could be arranged and a coordinated effort agreed upon.[76]

Du Bois, his patience running thin, did not feel quite as noble. Four days later, he responded to Moorland, professing, "No one is more anxious than I am to have cooperation among the colored scholars and officials in this history of the Negro race." He conveyed his version of the negotiations with Emmett Scott and Carter Woodson. Scott's contract to write his own volume posed a problem, but Du Bois, cunningly shifting the blame, stated, "This as it seems to me need not necessarily interfere with the larger plan unless he wishes it." Woodson's intransigence was "more serious," with his desire to have full control of the project making, in Du Bois's eyes, "cooperation a little dubious." Du Bois, presenting himself as wholly altruistic and with no personal motive, wrote, "The only thing that I want is a scientific and complete history." He added, "If the elimination of my personal cooperation will bring this about, I shall make absolutely no difficulty on that point."[77] Du Bois, in fact, had no intention of backing down. No way would he relinquish without a fight the opportunity to reassert his leadership through authoring the definitive history of the Black experience in the war. The stakes had already become too high.

～

IN HIS CORRESPONDENCE TO Oswald Garrison Villard, George Peabody, and L. Hollingsworth Wood, Du Bois recommended, in the likelihood that a collaborative effort proved impossible, "that my contribution to the history be confined to the French side, and that I make a trip to France to collect this matter, and to do what I can at the Peace Conference for the African Colonies."[78] But he faced a serious dilemma. To get to France, he needed help, and only the most well-connected Black man in Washington could provide it: Emmett Scott.

The odds of reaching the peace conference were not in Du Bois's favor. The federal government, after tightening passport restrictions during the war, refused to allow anyone near the peace proceedings who could potentially embarrass Woodrow Wilson in his moment of triumph. Several prominent African American activists—most notably William Monroe Trotter, Ida B. Wells-Barnett, and the beauty entrepreneur Madam C. J. Walker—all attempted to get approval to travel from the State Department.[79] All were denied. Du Bois would no doubt meet the same fate, unless he used Scott's influence to obtain passage overseas. For this to happen, the increasingly volatile issue of collaboration between the two men on the book needed to be either resolved or, at the very least, temporarily pushed to the side.

With the goal of getting to France paramount in his mind, Du Bois contacted Emmett Scott's publishing agent, Frank Parker Stockbridge, to try to work out a deal. Stockbridge, the former editor of *The New York Evening Mail*, served as director of information for the American Library Association during the war and came to know Emmett Scott through their shared government work. Du Bois, aware of Stockbridge's role in publishing and marketing Scott's forthcoming book, reached out to him to forge a solution to the impasse.[80]

What the November 24 "Thanksgiving suggestion," as Du Bois phrased it in a personal memo, consisted of is not entirely clear.[81] But if the account of Walter H. Loving—the most trusted African American agent of the redesignated Military Intelligence Division—is to be believed, Stockbridge facilitated an agreement between Du Bois and Scott that benefited both parties.[82] Viewing Du Bois's book as potentially cutting into their future profits, Scott and Stockbridge aimed to eliminate the competition. Loving reported, "Dr. Du Bois and Mr. Scott have long since been enemies, but Mr. Scott was perfectly willing to cast aside all differences which might hinder the carrying out of their plan successfully. Therefore they offered to send Dr. Du Bois to France to personally collect data for the book." Scott, portrayed by Loving as concerned above all else with reaping a financial windfall from the book, would have the results of Du Bois's overseas research and, even more important, his considerable literary skills and scholarly reputation. Du Bois, in the eyes of Loving an unprincipled opportunist, would finally have Scott's political credibility, access to crucial government documents, and, most important, a passport to get to France.[83]

But time was short. The official press ship, the USS *Orizaba*, accompanying Woodrow Wilson to the peace conference, was set to depart for France on Sunday, December 1. This left less than one week for Du Bois to get his passport.

Emmett Scott, well trained in exercising power behind the scenes, adroitly began to pull the levers of influence to facilitate Du Bois's passage overseas. In a Friday, November 29, note to Stockbridge about Du Bois, Scott wrote that he had "secured all the other information necessary, in case he comes here tomorrow, so we can go over the matter together. I have secured a blank form for him and all the information necessary as to his having his application approved here in Washington and in New York. It is going to be a difficult matter to put the whole thing through in a day and a half, but I telegraphed Dr. Du Bois and shall be willing to help out in any way possible, should he come here tomorrow."[84]

He called Du Bois every hour throughout the morning and early afternoon of the twenty-ninth. He had no luck.[85] At 2:55 p.m., Scott sent Du Bois a rushed Western Union telegram: UNABLE TO GET YOU ON TELEPHONE CAN ONLY SECURE PASSPORT BY COMING TO WASHINGTON.[86] Scott, anxious in his War Department office, waited for an answer.

Du Bois received the message. He reached Scott by phone late in the afternoon, and the two discussed their potential partnership. Scott provided Du Bois with instructions for securing his passport and the departure schedule for the *Orizaba*, set to leave for France in less than forty-eight hours.[87] Realizing the urgency of the situation,

Du Bois quickly made train reservations and hopped on a late-night Pullman headed to the nation's capital.[88] As Walter Loving reported to his MID superiors, "The cunning Dr. Du Bois had been trying for weeks to get to France" and "lost no time in grasping the opportunity" presented to him.[89]

Before departing New York, Du Bois crafted a memorandum to Stockbridge based on his conversation with Scott. He began by stating that he would "be glad to cooperate with you in the compilation, writing, and editing of a history of the American Negro in the Great War." However, certain conditions applied. Du Bois listed Emmett Scott, himself, and Carter G. Woodson, in this order, as possible "co-equal editors" of the book. He preferred recognition of "the above names in the above order," but was "willing to consider any other order," such as "the inclusion of only Scott's name and my own." Woodson had become expendable. He did, however, "insist that at least my name and Mr. Scott's appear as editors-in-chief and co-equal" and that "the name of no white person should appear as editor." He could assent to Stockbridge including his name "under ours as 'Managing Editor,'" but he made it clear that this historical study of Black people must be written by Black people. He also envisioned distinguishing members of the editorial board according to race. He had no time to propose any financial arrangements and concluded by expressing his sole desire to issue "a scholarly and fairly complete book, done mainly by Negroes and put into good English."[90]

On Saturday morning, November 30, Du Bois woke up in Washington, DC. He had a full day ahead of him. Around 9:00 a.m. he ascended the steps and entered the cavernous State, War, and Navy Building at Seventeenth Street and Pennsylvania Avenue. Through the labyrinth of corridors, he made his way to Emmett Scott's office. After exchanging pleasantries, Du Bois and Scott no doubt discussed their marriage of convenience around the war history book and the necessary hurdles to overcome in getting a coveted passport.[91]

Du Bois's movements over the next several hours were dizzying. Scott escorted him to the offices of the Committee on Public Information. At 10:30 a.m., after receiving the go-ahead from CPI officials, Du Bois stepped outside and trekked roughly six blocks to 1423 New

York Avenue, which housed the State Department's Division of Passport Control.[92] They took his pictures around 11:00 a.m. Afterward, at noon, he conferred with Scott again. A half hour later, they returned to the CPI offices. Everything, for now, seemed well. At 1:00 p.m., Du Bois made another trip to the State Department, where he completed the passport application, signing an oath that he would "bear true faith and allegiance" to the Constitution of the United States.[93] With less than twenty-four hours until the *Orizaba* pushed off from Pier 5 at Hoboken, New Jersey, every second mattered.

Scott's assistance proved absolutely crucial. He had already laid the groundwork for expediting Du Bois's application, and he exerted every ounce of influence throughout the day to ensure that no unexpected complications arose. Writing directly to the CPI director, George Creel, Scott stressed that he was "exceedingly anxious" for Du Bois to gain passage on the *Orizaba* as an accredited newspaper correspondent and would consider it "a personal favor if you will assist Dr. DuBois by acquainting him with the procedure that will enable him to expedite matters so as to be a member of the party that sails tomorrow."[94] In Creel's absence, the acting CPI chairman Harvey O'Higgins cleared Du Bois to join the official press delegation as a representative of *The Crisis*. Scott also successfully coaxed the Division of Passport Control to process Du Bois's application documents on the spot and, in lieu of Du Bois's birth certificate, vouched for his citizenship and reputable character.[95]

While Scott performed magic, Du Bois made sure not to jeopardize an opportunity that would put him in elite company and now appeared almost within his grasp. In his conversations with government officials, he conveniently omitted any mention of his plans to organize a Pan-African Congress in France, a revelation that surely would have raised red flags and brought the accelerated passport approval process to a screeching halt. Du Bois had in fact written an extensive letter to Woodrow Wilson on November 27, imploring him to prioritize the rights of African Americans and other people of African descent at the peace conference and included along with it his "Memorandum on the Future of Africa." In the end, it was probably advantageous to Du Bois that the president's busy schedule would not permit a meeting the *Crisis* editor had proposed with himself and a delegation of "representative colored men."[96]

Du Bois was not alone in scrambling to finalize last-minute clearance to travel to Europe. Much to his surprise, he ran into Robert Russa Moton, also in DC at the behest of Emmett Scott to secure his passport.[97] Scott's office became an extension of the Tuskegee Machine, as he and Moton remained in constant contact throughout the war. Moton was by no means as formidable as his predecessor, Booker T. Washington, but he still took full advantage of the power his proximity to the War Department afforded. The relationship paid dividends, most notably in Moton's successful efforts to lobby Woodrow Wilson to issue a statement against mob violence.[98]

The idea of Moton going to France was initially proposed in July 1918 by Emmett Scott and the CPI.[99] The close of the war brought with it rumors of growing discontent among Black troops owing to their daily battles with American racism. With the peace conference looming, Wilson needed no additional trouble. On November 27, Scott informed Moton in a confidential telegram that Secretary of War Baker and the president himself both approved of him going to France for the purpose of, as Scott relayed to General Pershing just days later, "morale work among the colored troops."[100] As Du Bois's own passage to France hung in the balance during the frenzied morning and afternoon of November 30, he gave little consideration to the Tuskegee principal's agenda and whatever role Scott had to play in it.

Scott's exhaustive efforts and Du Bois's doggedness paid off. By 4:00 p.m., Du Bois had his passport in hand, surely jubilant over the remarkable turn of events.[101] He departed Washington, DC, that evening and arrived home at around 10:45 p.m., just in time to have dinner and get a few hours of sleep before sailing for France the next day.[102]

⁓

DESPITE DU BOIS'S ASTONISHING success in securing passage to France, the status of the war history project still contained more questions than answers. After receiving Du Bois's initial proposal, Stockbridge requested a meeting. On November 29, just before dashing off to Washington, Du Bois sent Stockbridge another memo. He could not meet with him before sailing for France. However, he did hastily compose another possible structure for the book. With more detail, he suggested that "The American Negro in the Great War" appear as a three-volume history. Volume 1, "The Black Army," would be edited by Scott and Stockbridge; Volume 2, "War Reconstruction and the Negro Race," would be overseen by Du Bois and George Haynes; and Volume 3, "Documentary History of the American Negro, 1914–1919," would be controlled by Carter G. Woodson and another still-undetermined collaborator. Du Bois said that he expected Stockbridge to write him "as soon as possible" in Paris and "enclose a proposed contract."[103] This was an ambitious endeavor, one full of potential risk but also of great reward for all parties involved. However, a definitive commitment from this quartet of luminous scholars and race men remained far from certain, as Du Bois himself very well knew.

The December 9 meeting of the NAACP board of directors offered further details on the status, however muddied, of the war history. Du Bois had left for France eight days earlier. The acting chairwoman Mary White Ovington began with her report, which included a statement on Du Bois's planned activities. "He will take part in the Pan-African Congress to be held in Paris to emphasize the internationalization of Africa and the securing of a partial self-determination for the natives of German colonies. His primary work, however, is the securing of material for the Negro history for which $2,000 was appropriated at the October Board Meeting."

Du Bois submitted his report in absentia. Offering an update on the war history, he stated, "In accordance with your vote, I have arranged to cooperate with Emmett J. Scott on a History of the Negro in the Great War. The book is to be published by Harper Brothers." This came as a surprise. After hearing of the difficulties with Emmett Scott and Carter Woodson, Oswald Garrison Villard had actually suggested dropping the endeavor altogether.[104] Now the book was back on and Du Bois was in France. He expected to return in ninety days, leaving control of *The Crisis* during his absence to his business manager, Augustus Dill, secretary Madeline Allison, and recently hired literary editor, Jessie Redmon Fauset, a gifted Ivy League–educated teacher and writer who had a keen eye for talent.[105]

The meeting became contentious. Board members were shocked by Du Bois's report. How in the world had he gotten to France, and why had he done so without permission? Why was the Pan-African Congress not being approved by the full board? And how much was this going to cost the association? Tensions flared, with Francis Grimké and William Walling especially enraged at Du Bois's actions. In retaliation, Walling pushed through a motion that whatever additional money, not to exceed $1,000, Du Bois received for his activities in France, half would come from the slim *Crisis* budget. Additionally, they attempted to rein in Du Bois and his editorial decisions by adding Secretary John Shillady and Field Secretary James Weldon Johnson as permanent members of *The Crisis* committee.[106]

Before his departure and his latest flare-up with the NAACP board, Du Bois arranged to publicize the book project for the first time in the December 1918 issue of *The Crisis*. Appearing under the caption "War History," the pronouncement read:

> The National Association for the Advancement of Colored People has appropriated funds and commissioned the Director of Publications and Research to collect the data and compile a history of the Negro in the Great War. Dr. Du Bois has invited a number of Negro scholars, soldiers and officials to form an Editorial Board, which will be able to issue an authentic, scientific and definitive history of our part in this war. The personnel of this board will be announced later. Meantime, we want the active co-operation of every person who can and will help. We want facts, letters and documents, narratives and clippings. Let us all unite to make the record complete.[107]

The open call for materials reflected Du Bois's vision of the entire race mobilizing around the construction of the war history. In his mind, despite the uncertainty surrounding the project, the groundwork had been laid. His efforts at cooperation had been sincere, or at least sincere enough for his taste. And, most important, he had a passport to France, where, as he would later write, "the destinies of mankind center."[108]

CHAPTER 4

"I have seen the wounds of France . . ."[1]

SUNDAY, DECEMBER 1, 1918, began early for Du Bois. He had arrived back at his 650 Greene Avenue home in Brooklyn late the previous night after miraculously securing his passport. Now he had to hastily prepare for an early-afternoon departure for France. Adrenaline and anticipation surely compensated for the fifty-year-old Du Bois's lack of sleep. With the future of the war history book project, the success of his Pan-African Congress, and the fate of Black people in the hands of the world's superpowers gathering at Versailles all hanging in the balance, he could rest later.

He quickly packed his clothes. An awaiting car took him to Lower Manhattan to settle travel arrangements at the French consulate and have his passport vised at the Custom House.[2] He made a brief stop at the Fifth Avenue office of *The Crisis* and finally set out by taxi for Hoboken.[3] As he neared Pier 5, he could see the USS *Orizaba* sitting in the dock, waiting to transport him and fifty-two other prominent journalists and newspaper reporters to France for the Paris Peace Conference.[4]

But he faced a potentially disastrous final obstacle. While getting ready to board, he learned that no record of his name appeared on the ship manifesto. In a panic, he "rushed in madly" to George Creel's shipboard office, where he encountered a crowd of men similarly trying to resolve their own unexpected complications. The minutes dragged on. At last, sometime around noon, Du Bois got a face-to-face meeting with the CPI director. Du Bois explained his unique circumstances while Creel checked his records. He had heard nothing from Emmett Scott or anyone else of Du Bois's approval to join the press corps. The ship had no extra room, Creel regretfully informed him. He could not sail.

Undeterred, Du Bois, as he recalled, "sat down and waited" in Creel's cabin. The scheduled departure time neared. Surely realizing the hell the *Crisis* editor would raise if denied passage, Creel, Du Bois recounted, "turned to me and handed me my credentials."[5] His act of personal civil disobedience proved successful. The letter, signed by Creel and postdated November 27, accredited Du Bois "as a member of the United States Press Delegation, visiting Europe in connection with the Peace Conference and accompanying the party of the President."[6]

At 2:15 p.m., the *Orizaba* pushed off into the Hudson River, past the Statue of Liberty and toward the Atlantic Ocean, Du Bois one of the passengers.[7]

Robert Russa Moton joined him on board. The other members of the Tuskegee leader's entourage consisted of his personal secretary, Nathan Hunt, and Lester Walton, the wide-ranging journalist and managing editor of *The New York Age*.[8] All four Black men shared a cabin, the government's Jim Crow practices remaining firmly in place.

In spite of his segregated sleeping quarters, Du Bois professed to having a "lovely time" during the cross-Atlantic journey. The ocean was rough, the weather cloudy and rainy, but he still ate well and avoided seasickness. Du Bois and Moton were far from friends, but certainly not enemies, and the trip allowed the two men to get to know each other better. Moton would write that they engaged in "many frank but pleasant talks" during their time at sea.[9] Even more than his conversations with Moton, Du Bois relished the opportunity to hold court and lecture his fellow white correspondents about the war and its connection to the global race question.[10]

On December 4, three days after Du Bois set sail for France, President Woodrow Wilson did the same. Wilson, First Lady Edith, and 150 other government officials, military personnel, diplomatic experts, foreign dignitaries, and special guests arrived in Hoboken by special train that morning. At Pier 4, the former German passenger liner USS *George Washington* awaited them. Wilson boarded first, the national anthem playing in the background. At 10:15 a.m., the ship pulled out of the dock as thousands of people on both sides of the Hudson River cheered and waved flags. A naval convoy accompanied the ship out of New York Harbor while zeppelins and army planes circled and danced overhead. Wilson and Edith waved from the bridge, soaking in the adulation and historical gravity of the moment.[11]

No American president had ever left the United States while still in office. Some of Wilson's closest advisers warned him against going. Republican foes openly questioned whether the Constitution even allowed for such an act, but the headstrong Wilson was determined to exert the full weight of his influence at the peace conference and push for his vision of a new international order highlighted by the establishment of a League of Nations.[12]

In his State of the Union address before Congress on December 2, Wilson had rationalized his decision to go to France, declaring, "The peace settlements which are now to be agreed upon are of transcendent importance, both to us and to the rest of the world." Thousands of young men had fought and died for the ideals of freedom and democracy that he espoused. He owed it to them to ensure that those ideals became enshrined in the peace. "I realize the magnitude and difficulty of the duty I am undertaking," he admitted. But as "the servant of the nation," he had a solemn duty "to give the best that is in me" to work with the European heads of government and promote the interests of the United States. He would remain easily accessible by cable and promised to make his absence "as brief as possible." When it was all said and done, he hoped to return home "with the happy assurance that it has been possible to translate into action the great ideals for which America has striven."[13]

The task before him was indeed considerable. The war—destroying empires, fracturing nations, sparking revolutions, throwing millions of lives into disarray—had devastated Europe on a scale that the American president still did not fully appreciate. From the perspective of France, Great Britain, and the other victorious Allied nations, peace meant a full recognition of Germany's guilt as well as proper recompense in the form of land and territories. Wilson planned to remain above the fray, focused not on the spoils of war but on the larger, more important vision of creating a new global future out of the ashes of the past. His talk of "democracy," "freedom," and "self-determination" aroused the aspirations of oppressed people throughout the world. What all of this meant beyond theory and rhetoric, however, remained completely uncertain. As he crossed the Atlantic, Wilson himself did not fully know. But he believed that his distinctive gifts and endowed leadership would produce historic results.

Du Bois, also en route to France with his own deep belief in democracy, hoped that his unique mission to represent Pan-Africa on the world stage and investigate the experiences of Black soldiers in the war would shape the course of the twentieth century as well.[14]

AFTER EIGHT DAYS AT SEA, the *Orizaba* steamed into the bustling port city of Brest in the early-morning hours of December 9, 1918. Du Bois had reached France. One of his first sights was hundreds of Black stevedores unloading the ship's cargo with a speed and efficiency that had become legendary by the end of the war. They worked "fast and hard" throughout the day and into the night. "These were rough workingmen but healthy," Du Bois observed, taking pride in the fact that even though they may have been, in the eyes of racist white Americans, lowly stevedores, they "bore themselves like men."[15]

Along with the rest of the ship's passengers, Du Bois disembarked under military escort the next day. After a walk through the city, he caught an early-evening train to Paris, paying the first-class price but still having to do without the comforts of a sleeping car.[16] Sixteen restless hours later, a groggy Du Bois arrived at the chaotic Gare Montparnasse. The station did not offer an endearing first impression of the French capital. "No one to collect tickets, no porters, no cabs and a surging crowd," Du Bois griped. He left Robert Moton and Lester Walton behind at the train station and proceeded with Nathan Hunt to find a hotel. The city bore the scars of war: cannons still defensively positioned; buildings and monuments protected with sandbags; women solemnly dressed in black, mourning their dead. After initially being turned away at four hotels, Du Bois found lodging at the comfortable Hôtel du Cloitre Saint-Honoré for the reasonable rate of ten francs a night. Moton checked in to the same hotel and a room directly across the hall.[17]

Their close proximity allowed Du Bois, as he wrote, to "butt in" and learn more details of Moton's special mission. President Wilson and Secretary of War Newton Baker had granted Moton, in his own words, the "authority to go anywhere and get information from any source" about the fast-spreading rumors of widespread rape and the incompetence of Black officers.[18] The need to defuse the growing anger of Black troops and encourage their peaceful return to the United States assumed an even higher priority. Du Bois also intended to investigate the "whispering gallery," but he had other objectives as well. Moreover, he was leery of associating too closely with the Tuskegee principal. "Wherever possible," he and Moton "gladly co-operated." However, with his image in mind, Du Bois emphasized to his *Crisis* followers that their "missions were distinct in every respect."[19]

John Hope awaited Moton and Du Bois in Paris. The Morehouse College president had been in France for just over three months with the YMCA, employed as a field secretary overseeing services provided to African American troops. Traveling at a breakneck pace throughout the country, Hope had encountered thousands of Black soldiers, and he knew better than most the systemic racial discrimination they had faced, which only worsened after the armistice. Having swallowed his anger and growing disillusionment, Hope welcomed the opportunity to speak freely with Du Bois and Moton. On the evening of December 14, Hope tracked down Moton, Du Bois, Walton, and Hunt at their hotel and the group all dined together. Aware that he would "have to throw myself in his way, so that he may let me talk to him," Hope made a point to fully brief Moton on the state of affairs concerning the troops before the government's handpicked Black emissary set off on his investigation under the care of military officials.[20]

Although Hope was on good terms with Moton, his friendship

and admiration for Du Bois ran deep. The two men spent the entire day of December 15 together, walking through the Parisian streets and talking, until, exhausted, they retired at the same hotel, Du Bois tucking himself into bed by the responsible time of eight o'clock.[21] They reunited again the following evening, dining, as Hope recalled, at a "characteristically French café," "quiet and decent," chatting for an hour over their meal. They undoubtedly discussed the troubling state of affairs concerning the army's treatment of Black servicemen. "I am very glad that, after all, he succeeded in getting here," Hope wrote to his wife, Lugenia, back in Atlanta. "He seems very fond of me, and I know that I am fond of him . . . I hope that he will accomplish something over here."[22]

ON DECEMBER 18, 1918, in a YMCA hut somewhere in eastern France, First Lieutenant William M. Slowe penned a heartfelt letter to Du Bois. Slowe, a dentist from Philadelphia, had spent the last six months serving as a medical officer in the 317th Supply Train of the Ninety-Second Division. It had been difficult work, and he had made do with a constant shortage of dental supplies and equipment. However, the constant humiliation he and other Black officers painfully tolerated from their fellow white officers proved even more challenging. The men of the division needed help. They needed to tell their story.

"We have learned with delight of your presence in France at this time," Slowe wrote, wishing Du Bois "all the success" and commending his efforts "for justice to all people." He had read a recent issue of *The Crisis*, which had furtively made its way overseas and into his hands. The "Close Ranks" uproar seriously damaged Du Bois's credibility in the eyes of many, but for Slowe and other Black officers, their faith in him remained steadfast. Slowe ended his note by affirming, "I believe you have gained the confidence of all of us here in France by your unselfish devotion to our cause and a display of wisdom which we admire."[23]

Du Bois eagerly wanted to see for himself what Slowe and other African American soldiers had experienced during the war.[24] John Hope, in his capacity with the YMCA, pulled the necessary strings to get an official visitor pass, and he served as Du Bois's host during a journey through the Lorraine region of northeast France.[25] They departed from Paris's Gare de l'Est on December 18, braving long lines and inspections by American military authorities. Arriving in the cold, wet darkness of night, they first stopped at Toul, a key Allied assembly point and home of the first American aero squadron units. Soldiers of various nationalities crowded the narrow streets of the old fortress city, which was ringed with imposing walls. Du Bois, dressed in a suit, stood out among the sea of khaki but eagerly adjusted to his surroundings. "It was a touch of war," he recalled, relishing the opportunity to dine and bunk in a YMCA hut and experience, however briefly, life as a soldier.[26]

Leaving Toul by car in a wintry mix of snow and rain, he traveled the roughly ten miles east to Maron. Nestled in a gently sloping valley along the banks of the Moselle River, the little red-roofed village housed no more than a few hundred residents. As he approached, Du Bois could see a tall church at the center of town, its steeple rising high above all other buildings. The surrounding farmland and the scenic Domaniale de Haye forest offered a sentimental vision of French rural innocence. Yet, as Du Bois immediately saw as he entered the town and walked its muddy streets crowded with soldiers and solemn-faced residents, Maron had been "overwhelmed and upturned" by the war.[27]

He and John Hope billeted in the tiny stone home of the Baulanger family. Madame Baulanger had lost four sons in the war. Her elderly husband, a twenty-four-year-old daughter, and an orphaned grandchild remained. A large wardrobe, a fireplace, a new iron stove, and piles of bedding filled the main room. In their cramped quarters, Du Bois and his newly adopted family dined over a meal of salad dressed in brandy and golden fried potatoes, laughing and sharing stories of the war. They were, in Du Bois's words, "so kind—so pitifully kind and thankful—so proud with us of the kindly dark soldiers."[28]

Du Bois found himself in Maron because the town was one of a dozen or so in the region accommodating the "dark soldiers" of the Ninety-Second Division. For five idle weeks after the armistice, the Ninety-Second lingered in the area, enduring the cold and mud of makeshift encampments. Du Bois for the first time took in the sight

of hundreds of Black soldiers from various parts of the United States—
Mississippi, Washington, DC, Alabama, Philadelphia—who had been
transplanted to rescue France, rushed "wholeheartedly into the business of saving the world," and now were tramping through the streets
of Maron.[29]

Major Adam Patterson greeted Du Bois upon his arrival. The
work of judge advocate for the beleaguered Ninety-Second Division
kept him busy. Fallout from the 368th Regiment's terrible experience in the Meuse-Argonne continued, as Patterson tried his best to
defend the honor of the persecuted Black officers. He also continued
to push back against false charges of rape that marred the division's
reputation. His fellow senior white officers were the main culprits. On
December 6, Colonel Allen Greer, the Ninety-Second Division's chief
of staff, wrote to the Tennessee senator Kenneth McKellar about "the
question of Negro officers and Negro troops," a matter, in his words,
of "vital importance not only from a military point of view but from
that which all Southerners have." Greer alleged that cases of rape,
both in the United States and in France, had been numerous, and that
as combatants, Black troops "have in fact been dangerous to no one
except themselves and women." He wrote that Black officers lacked
the ability to control the men under their command, mostly because
they were "engaged very largely in the pursuit of French women, it
being their first opportunity to meet white women who did not treat
them as servants."[30] Patterson knew all too well that racist officers like
Greer had the influence and power to define the legacy of the division,
and his own personal legacy along with it.

Fate seemingly brought the major and the editor together. On
November 23, from Ninety-Second Division headquarters in France,
Patterson had written Du Bois a serendipitous letter. Along with "several officers now doing service in France with the A.E.F.," he hoped
"to publish a full, complete and accurate history of the colored men
and officers in this war." A contingent of Black officers of the division,
led by himself, had already started organizing and compiling materials
and had outlined twenty-three tentative chapters. After one of their
meetings, "it was decided to ask you to help us in this work." What immediately distinguished Patterson's proposal from all the other book

ideas floating around was that, in his words, "this history will be written by men who know what took place and when." The manuscript would be presented to Du Bois for "final embellishment, criticism, revision," giving him the opportunity "to enlarge upon descriptions of battles as only an able writer with unlimited powers of imagination can."[31]

By the time Patterson's flattering letter reached the offices of *The Crisis* on December 11, Du Bois was already in France. Mary White Ovington received the letter, and she may very well have contacted Du Bois in France about its contents.[32] Regardless, when Du Bois arrived in Maron, he and Patterson discussed the subject of the war history and the support other Black officers were prepared to offer. Du Bois could not ask for a better source of information than Patterson, who as judge advocate had direct access to key personnel of the Ninety-Second Division, as well as all official records.

But Du Bois needed to hear from the men themselves. One night, in a smoke-filled YMCA hut stocked with candies and cigarettes and warmed by a rusty woodstove, Du Bois listened to their stories. His audience of battle-scarred soldiers and officers of the Ninety-Second Division—"good, brown faces with great, kind, beautiful eyes"—relished his presence and opened their hearts to him. Men near death from pneumonia. Segregated hospital beds. The thunder of exploding shells during the final days of the war. Comrades forced to endure scorn and contempt simply because of their dark skin and the officer stripes on their shoulders. Everything John Hope and Major Patterson had told him, and more. Du Bois took it all in, the "memories of bitter humiliations, determined triumphs, great victories and bugle-calls that sounded from earth to heaven." He saw their dignity and felt their pain.

He also heard their songs. On a late afternoon in Maron, he gazed out the window of the small room he had temporarily made his home. Outside, James "Tim" Brymn, the forty-four-year-old acclaimed conductor from Philadelphia, and his 350th Field Artillery Regimental band performed in front of the town pump. Little children stopped playing to gaze in astonishment. Women put down their daily wash to listen to the strange music coming from the instruments wielded with seeming magical ability by the Black men in khaki. Tears welled in Du Bois's eyes as he marveled at the sight.[33]

It was a sight that had become commonplace among African American troops and their French hosts. Brymn, James Reese Europe, Alfred Jack Thomas, and other African American bandmasters introduced France and the world to the exotic sounds of jazz during the war. With creative flair, traditional military tunes became injected with ragtime syncopation and further "jazzed" up by moments of brass, woodwind, and drum improvisation. Whether performing "La Marseillaise" in Paris before crowds in the tens of thousands, "The Memphis Blues" in Aix-les-Bains for convalescing GIs, or "On Patrol in No Man's Land" in a remote village square, the wails, whistles, blares, and blasts of the Black bands entranced audiences and transformed African American soldiers into cultural ambassadors.[34]

The significance of Du Bois's time spent with the Ninety-Second Division went beyond the practical aspects of securing support for the war history. He also forged an emotional connection with the African American soldiers and officers he encountered. Throughout the disillusioning months of war, the music of Tim Brymn and his band had provided solace, hope, and a sense of home for Black troops, and this music was now the soundtrack for the history Du Bois planned to tell. Feeling the muddy terrain of war-torn France under his feet, seeing African American troops up close for the first time and taking in their stories, he felt a more urgent and personal sense of purpose in preparing the history. The Black soldiers who previously existed largely as racial symbols in his political and historical imagination now were very real.

Du Bois undoubtedly wished for more time with the Ninety-Second Division. It had nevertheless been an incredibly fruitful and moving few days. He returned to Paris sometime during the third week in December, excited about the prospects of his book and what else he could accomplish while in France.

～

IMMEDIATELY UPON SETTLING BACK into his Paris hotel room, Du Bois wrote to friends and confidants in New York City. He envisioned them serving as the founding members of an editorial board for the history of Black people in the war. "I have spent 3 weeks of a proposed 3 months sojourn in Europe," he began. In this time, he'd become "convinced that a history of the Negro in this war done carefully and with scientific thoroughness is of vital importance to our future . . . Already forces to discredit our work are mobilizing." He could very well have been referring to white military officials engaged in the campaign of slander against African American troops and officers.

He may have also been referring to Emmett Scott. After listing the members of his potential editorial team, Du Bois wrote, "I regret to say that I have been unable to unite into one enterprise all of the proposed historians of this war." He claimed to have carried on "protracted negotiations" with Carter G. Woodson, Scott, and Scott's "white co-author," Frank Stockbridge. "These gentlemen seem to prefer to work alone or to cooperate under conditions which I deem fatal to historical accuracy or broad scholarship." Without any desire for "rivalry or competition," Du Bois declared that he would proceed with his plans, alone, but with the backing of an elite editorial team of race men and women to offer crucial credibility.[35] After three weeks in France, the deal between Du Bois, Scott, and Stockbridge had apparently fallen apart. Du Bois absolved himself of any responsibility.

The MID sleuth Walter Loving, however, uncovered a different story. Writing to his superior officer on April 28, 1919, he claimed that Du Bois, "in the very first letter" he sent to Stockbridge and Scott, "repudiated the agreement he made with the company to the effect that he would furnish them all the information he gathered concerning colored troops while in France." Loving believed that Du Bois never intended to work with Scott and had used him only to get a passport. After giving his verbal commitment, but shrewdly not signing a contract or exchanging any money, "the foxy Dr. Du Bois was off to France . . . Dr. Du Bois cleverly double crossed the Stockbridge-Scott Co.," Loving smirked.[36]

While not forgetting about the war history, Du Bois turned his attention to the other pressing matter on his Parisian agenda: the Pan-African Congress. He faced serious challenges to this project both at home and abroad. Back in New York, resistance from the NAACP board stiffened following the ugly December 9 meeting. In Paris, the situation was not much easier. The singularly focused Woodrow Wilson, who'd received a hero's welcome on the Champs-Élysées when he arrived on December 14, had no interest in the distracting issues of Black civil rights and the future of subjugated African peoples.[37]

Du Bois, undaunted, did his best to change that. He rushed around the city—the U.S. Secret Service watching his every step—visiting anyone and everyone he could to secure approval for the Pan-African Congress. He had little luck. He explained his plan to fellow journalists and members of Wilson's inner circle Walter Lippmann and Ray Stannard Baker, who expressed interest but made no effort to sway the president.[38] When Du Bois went directly to officials of the American Commission to Negotiate Peace, he received a more definitive response. "Impossible," an agitated captain told him. "The French Government would not permit it." Du Bois then responded, defiantly, "It's up to me to get French consent!"[39]

To assist him in this tall order, Du Bois turned to George H. Jackson. Jackson was the first African American to hold a position in the State Department's consular section, appointed to the French cities of Cognac and La Rochelle in 1897 by President William McKinley.[40] Jackson's diplomatic career came to an abrupt end in 1914, when he fell victim to Woodrow Wilson's segregationist purge of African Americans from the federal government.[41] He stayed in France, however, making a nice living as a businessman and becoming a prominent figure in Paris's small yet burgeoning African American expatriate community. Du Bois knew Jackson and contacted him when he reached France.[42]

On December 28, Jackson arranged for a meeting with Blaise Diagne, the Senegalese deputy to the French National Assembly.[43] Elected in 1914, Diagne was ambitious, energetic, and wholly supportive of the French colonial project. As such, he approached the war as an opportunity for West Africans to prove their loyalty to the Tricolor and achieve greater citizenship rights in the process. French military advocates of a *force noire* recruited some thirty-two thousand

West African *tirailleurs* after disastrous losses in the first five months of the war, most of them thrown into the front lines as shock troops.[44] Diagne, using the demand for more Black bodies to his advantage, sponsored a 1915 law that made the elite residents of Senegal's four communes (*originaires*) eligible for service in the regular army and, the following year, pushed through what came to be known as *la loi Diagne*, which granted these same men official French citizenship.[45] His stature rising, Diagne received the title of high commissioner of African troops from Prime Minister Georges Clemenceau and in 1918 spearheaded a recruitment drive that brought an additional sixty-three thousand desperately needed *tirailleurs sénégalais* into the French Army. When the fighting came to an end in November 1918, roughly two hundred thousand West Africans had been mobilized for military service.[46]

Diagne—without question the most powerful Black politician in France at the close of the war—immediately impressed Du Bois, who saw in the cunning deputy his continental counterpart. Here was a cultured, highly articulate African who, like Du Bois, viewed the war and military service as a pathway toward expanding the boundaries of democratic citizenship for people of African descent and the educated elite in particular.[47] Du Bois's elementary grasp of the French language made for a challenging conversation. But with Jackson's assistance, he got his point across, emphasizing to Diagne that time was of the essence.[48] With direct access to Prime Minister Clemenceau, perhaps he could make Du Bois's Pan-African dreams a reality.

Diagne proved helpful to Du Bois in other ways as well. During their meeting, in which Du Bois explained as best he could in his broken French the reasons for his visit to France, Diagne provided his new American friend with a bombshell. "Did you see what the American Mission told the French about the way Negroes should be treated?" Diagne asked excitedly. He handed Du Bois a document dated August 7, 1918, marked "Confidential."

Titled "On the Subject of Black American Troops," the memo had been written by Louis Linard of the French Mission at AEF headquarters and distributed to French officers in command of Black troops.

French officers needed to have "an exact idea of the situation of Ne-groes in the United States," Linard stated. The Black man was "an inferior being," not to be seen as the white man's equal, and racked with sexual pathologies that made him a "constant menace." This was the reason why, Linard incorrectly declared, "the black American troops in France have, by themselves, given rise to as many complaints for attempted rape as all the rest of the army." As a result, French com-manders should avoid "any pronounced degree of intimacy" between themselves and Black officers, "make a point of keeping the native can-tonment population from 'spoiling' the Negroes," and, by all means, keep Black soldiers away from white women.[49]

"I read it and sat very still," Du Bois remembered of his shocking encounter with the memo. Here was a smoking gun, never meant for public eyes, that bluntly revealed the United States Army's attempt to indoctrinate their French counterparts with the rules of American rac-ism. "Would it be possible to obtain a copy of this?" he asked Diagne as casually as possible. "Take that," Diagne responded.[50]

Du Bois's combined disgust with American white supremacy and his admiration for France's racial policies deepened considerably on the afternoon of December 29. Likely at the personal invitation of Diagne, he attended a celebration at the Palais du Trocadéro, the famed concert hall constructed for the 1878 World's Fair. The French Colonial League had organized a "Grande Fête" to honor the service, sacrifice, and loyalty of the colonial *troupes indigènes* who had fought on behalf of France during the war.[51]

A capacity audience of five thousand people filled the hall in a dramatic show of French patriotism and imperial propaganda. To thunderous applause, Diagne delivered a moving paean to France and full-throated endorsement of the *mission civilisatrice*. "From now on Frenchmen of the Mother land, Frenchmen of the colonies, let us form a union, indissoluble, indivisible, for the sake of honor and the grandeur of this country," Diagne pronounced. Following his speech, the stage filled with troops from France's various African, Asian, and Caribbean colonies, all bearing medals of commendation as testa-ments to their heroism. The crowd erupted when a tall, dignified, dark-skinned Tunisian soldier, Bakhane Diop, was honored as a Chevalier of the Legion of Honor, the medal pinned on his chest by the pioneering French colonialist Louis Archinard.[52] The Théâtre Français performed dramatic renderings of the battlefield exploits of the colonial troops, an orchestra played military marches, and singers from the opera gave a rousing rendition of the French anthem. Du Bois, misty-eyed, sat spellbound at the spectacle, which surpassed any tribute to Black men that he had ever seen.[53]

Indeed, Du Bois was intoxicated, just like many African American troops, by the performance of French color blindness.[54] His reverence for France overflowed in the March 1919 "Overseas" issue of *The Crisis*. The cover featured a painting, *The French Colonials Attack*, depicting a contingent of red-capped *tirailleurs sénégalais* charging forward with bayonets drawn.[55] In the adulatory "Vive La France!" Du Bois recounted his Trocadéro experience in moving prose. "How fine a thing to be a black Frenchman in 1919," he wrote. "Imagine such a celebration in America!"[56] Inside appeared a full-page portrait of Blaise Diagne personally signed to Du Bois "in token of admiring friendship." Diagne's prominence and the effusive praise the North and West African colonials received confirmed Du Bois's faith in the imaginative ideal of democracy and the power of Black military service to potentially transform the social and political status of African Americans. If France could value and honor her Black patriots, why not the United States?

Du Bois formally pitched the Pan-African Congress to Diagne in a New Year's Day 1919 memo. The proposal outlined Du Bois's audacious vision for a three-day gathering on February 1, 2, and 3, to place the demands of the Black world squarely before the great powers at the peace conference.[57] The fate of the congress still remained uncertain, hinging on Diagne's receptiveness to the proposal and his ability to sway the French authorities to say yes to the gathering. But, at the very least, there was cause for optimism.

～

AS THE NEW YEAR of 1919 approached, Du Bois was in an ebullient mood. Seemingly the entire world had descended on Paris, and he was there. The electric environment buzzed with chaos and promise.

Visitors filled every hotel to capacity. Trains ran late, jam-packed to the point of near suffocation. Wartime restrictions, still in place, made food scarce and such luxuries as butter and sugar nearly unattainable.[58] But the prospect of peace and a world remade anew lifted all spirits. Du Bois savored every moment.

More than anything, he relished the opportunity to be liberated from the shadow of American racism. He dined with friends, viewed the *Panthéon de la Guerre*, conversed with French and American officials, and walked the crowded Parisian streets with a freedom that eluded him in the United States. This, Du Bois imagined, was what democracy could and should look like.[59]

He enjoyed an especially pleasant Christmas with Joel Spingarn. The end of the war found Spingarn in and around Paris. He was no doubt thrilled to learn of Du Bois's successful arrival in France.[60] As they reunited over the holiday, their troubles of just a few months earlier seemed a distant memory. Spingarn, using his government connections and command of the language, also served as Du Bois's personal ambassador over the next few days, introducing him to various French officials who might be able to aid with the Pan-African Congress.[61]

Feeling more confident in his surroundings, Du Bois updated the NAACP on his activities. On Christmas Eve, he composed a memorandum outlining his "preliminary conclusions" regarding what he had observed and what he still hoped to achieve while abroad. He firmly believed that "every attempt must be made to present the case of the Darker Races of the world to the enlightened public opinion of Europe." This meant holding the Pan-African Congress, pending, of course, permission from the French government.

However, of "highest importance," Du Bois stressed, was the book. Preparing "the full history of the part which the black man has played in this war," he explained, was critical, demanding "great care and thoroughness." He planned to "spend as much time as possible" with Black soldiers and officers of the Ninety-Second and Ninety-Third Divisions in order to "collect the essential facts of their service." "THIS IS OF VITAL IMPORTANCE," he wrote. "No history can be written without it." Aside from Black officers like Adam Patterson, who pledged to work with him, Du Bois could trust no one, especially those with ties to the War Department. With Emmett Scott in mind, he wrote, "I am convinced since coming here that no cooperation with agencies which would whitewash facts or sacrifice historical thoroughness to popular appeal is for the moment thinkable." In addition to visiting various parts of France to conduct research, he also proposed short trips to England, Belgium, Germany, and "a few days in Algeria." Upon his return to the United States, he hoped to begin "the immediate preparation" of a three-volume study, fully financed with upward of $10,000 by the association, newly titled "History of the Black Man in the Revolution of 1914–1918."[62]

Another update followed on January 4. Grumblings from NAACP headquarters about Du Bois's agenda and why he was in France continued to trickle across the Atlantic. He explained and pushed back. "The difficulties of this undertaking have been and still are enormous," he wrote. He offered his version of how he got to France, beginning with the board's authorization for him to prepare the history of Black people in the Great War, his rush to get aboard the *Orizaba* press ship, and his unexpected encounter with Robert Moton, whom he suspected of being part of a "scheme" involving Emmett Scott and the War Department that had been "silently hatching for some months" to "sooth [*sic*] the bitter feeling among Negro troops." And make no mistake, he underscored, the Black soldiers were "bitter to an extent which even you cannot appreciate." Unlike Moton, he did not receive a government escort and unfettered travel privileges. He managed to secure one military permit to visit the front and, after ten days of negotiations, received authorization to inspect the Ninety-Second and Ninety-Third Divisions as a "newspaper man" along with the multitude of other reporters descending on France. He was an unwanted presence, viewed by his fellow Americans as "an object of aversion or suspicion."

Despite these challenges, Du Bois made clear that his time had not been wasted. He offered proof, enclosing the proposal for his Pan-African Congress, which, he explained, had "already been discussed and accepted in principle by black members of the French House of Deputies" and only awaited "final action." He also included a copy of the program from the Trocadéro spectacle honoring France's colonial troops and, most explosive, the "Secret Information" directive acquired from Blaise Diagne. It was, he stressed, "of the very highest importance." The world needed to see what the U.S. Army had done, even if it meant violating the law. The editor envisioned the memo appearing in *The Crisis* and stood "ready to assume personally all risks of immediate publication."

Du Bois was angry. The audacity that some of his NAACP colleagues would question his judgment and motives for going to France crossed the line from responsible oversight to personal insult. It was exceedingly unfair, he sharply wrote, for the board "not only to question my good faith but even to refuse to pay my expenses . . . Is the work which I am doing in accordance with vote of the Board in October? Do I possess the confidence of the Board in the further prosecution of this mission?"[63]

He was not about to sit on his hands and wait for answers. He had work to do and information about the Black war experience to collect. He had finally secured a visitor's pass from the army to tour the front. Black soldiers of the Ninety-Second and Ninety-Third Divisions awaited him.

~

SOMETIME DURING THE SECOND week of January, Du Bois departed from Paris and traveled to AEF headquarters at Chaumont, roughly 160 miles to the southeast in the department of Haute-Marne. He needed to watch his step. The Ninety-Second Division's new commanding general, James Erwin, had alerted army intelligence officers that "a man by name of Dubois, with visitor's pass, reported on his way to visit this Division. His presence at station of any unit will be immediately reported in <u>secret</u> enclosure to Assistant Chief of Staff, G-2 . . . Likewise, prompt report will be made to G-2 of all <u>his moves</u> and actions while at station of any unit."[64] Pershing himself also stayed informed about Du Bois's activities.[65] The standard "Visiting Correspondent's Agreement" Du Bois signed, stipulating that he "avoid all criticism of Allied Forces," possessed a heightened element of peril in his case.[66] The wrong word or move could be costly, resulting in his expulsion from France and possible imprisonment.

Captain Matthew Boutté greeted Du Bois at Chaumont. The war had left Boutté wounded in body and spirit. After convalescing in Toul from injuries sustained in the last days of combat, he was assigned to General Headquarters. There he spent the remainder of his six months in France with the AEF Visitors' Bureau.

If Boutté's frequent diary mentions of Du Bois are any indication, he must have been ecstatic upon learning that his fellow Fisk alum had reached France. While suffering in his hospital bed, enduring the racist slights of white doctors and nurses, he had written to Du Bois and John Hope, pleading for them to visit. "I felt that someone ought to know the things that I knew, that I had gone thru."[67] When Du Bois appeared at General Headquarters, Boutté's opportunity finally arrived.

With Boutté as his guide, Du Bois left Chaumont and headed west to the Le Mans embarkation zone. The area possessed a quaint timelessness. Many of the towns and villages, dotted with ancient manors and châteaus, still hearkened back to their medieval past. A principal road constructed by Julius Caesar in 50 B.C. ran through the heart of the region, and people still spoke Breton, the old Celtic language.[68]

Black soldiers had been gathering in the region since December 24, but they were already on the move. The AEF high command, in agreement with Marshal Ferdinand Foch, decided shortly after the armistice that the potential threat of rape posed by African American troops necessitated their immediate shipment out of France.[69] Even before Du Bois departed for Le Mans, parts of the Ninety-Second and Ninety-Third Divisions were traveling toward Brest.[70] If he did not hurry, most Black soldiers and officers would be headed home before he could speak with them.

As Du Bois reached Le Mans, he encountered a scene unlike any other in the history of modern warfare. The U.S. Army had hastily erected a virtual city to house and process its soldiers in preparation for their return to the United States. Located far enough from Paris yet close enough to the coast, Le Mans made for an ideal location. Railroad junctions converged, offering convenient transportation to the port cities of Brest, Bordeaux, and Saint-Nazaire. A labyrinth of tents, barracks, and drill fields stretched for miles in all directions. An entire nearby forest had been cut down to provide firewood. Throughout the French winter and well into the spring, some 250,000 American troops bathed, deloused, and had their paperwork processed and personal items inspected. During the considerable downtime, the army tried its best to keep the men busy and out of trouble, with YMCA recreation, pointless drilling, and considerable manual labor, much of it performed by Black troops.[71]

Adam Patterson was excited to see Du Bois again. Since Maron, Patterson had jumped right into his potential collaboration with Du Bois regarding the war history. Anticipating Du Bois's arrival at Chaumont, Patterson told him that he could find photos and war scenes of the Ninety-Second Division "for our work." He also conveyed the eagerness of his fellow soldiers and officers to meet the famed Black leader. "All have been expecting you daily."[72]

Word of Du Bois's appearance quickly spread among the demoralized troops of the Ninety-Second Division. They surely hoped for a more inspiring visit from Du Bois than the one they received from Robert Moton. Along with Lester Walton and Nathan Hunt, two white men, Clyde Miller of the Cleveland *Plain Dealer* and Thomas Jesse Jones of the U.S. Bureau of Education—whom Du Bois thoroughly detested—accompanied Moton on his trips outside Paris. Accorded every courtesy, Moton met with General John Pershing and other high-ranking white military and government officials to learn more about the treatment and performance of the army's African American troops. In conducting his investigation, Moton found charges of rape false and the performance of Black officers nowhere near as bad as characterized. He also used his unfettered access to Black soldiers in the Ninety-Second Division to speak to the men and offer words of wisdom for their impending return to the United

States that would have made Booker T. Washington proud. In speech after speech, he encouraged African American soldiers to go home in a "modest way" by not "striking the attitude of heroes," to "find a job as soon as possible," and to "settle down" into civilian life. Pleased with his work and validated by none other than Woodrow Wilson himself, Moton departed Europe for Tuskegee on January 8, leaving in his wake scores of angry and confused Black servicemen.[73]

With Matthew Boutté at his side, Du Bois began his tour of the Le Mans area. A thick overcoat and brimmed hat protected him from the wet winter elements. Mud from the makeshift roads caked his shoes and dirtied the bottoms of his slacks as he made the rounds from regiment to regiment of the Ninety-Second and Ninety-Third Divisions scattered around the camp and in adjacent towns. His white, stiff-collared shirt stayed clean underneath a dark sweater.[74]

Many of the soldiers Du Bois met wished that he would deliver a speech of his own to counterbalance Robert Moton's words. But, with military intelligence hovering and gagged by the "Visiting Correspondent's Agreement," he remained silent, later reflecting that he "was put under strict military surveillance and forbidden to make any public addresses to colored troops whom I visited."[75]

Instead, he discreetly talked with and listened to the men. As he did, "story after story and document after document poured into the editor's hands."[76]

At every stop during his several days in the area, the tales he heard of racial abuse multiplied, and the official records covertly supplied to him accumulated. A palpable tension filled the air as he traversed the Le Mans camp and witnessed the lengths to which the division's white officers had restricted the freedom of the Black soldiers and officers during the idle time before embarkation.[77] All spare moments were filled with what Du Bois characterized as "a drastic regime" of labor, drilling, and marches.[78] The morale-destroying General Order No. 40, issued on December 26 by General Erwin, kept Black soldiers of the Ninety-Second Division busy from 8:30 a.m. to 4:30 p.m. and threatened that any man outside his billet after 10:00 p.m. and not carrying an authorized pass would be "arrested, confined and punished."

Military police, stationed at every town, received virtually unchecked authority to "insure order and proper behavior" and, most pressing, prevent the "enlisted men from addressing or holding conversations with the women inhabitants." A number of Black officers caught innocently associating with female acquaintances had already been arrested and subjected to gross humiliation because of this edict.[79] The situation struck even General Pershing as extreme. During his January 21 visit to Le Mans, Pershing surprisingly saw no African American soldiers. In advance of the AEF commander's arrival, division officers ordered Black troops kept out of sight, either confined for inspection or remanded to work detail.[80]

The mood was even more dire at the Ninety-Second Division headquarters at nearby Mayenne. The men were, in the words of Sergeant Major Louis Pontlock, "broken down with discouragement" by the time Du Bois reached them. "We had no privileges and were same as prisoners," Pontlock later wrote in a detailed letter to Du Bois. Black troops could not even step foot outside their billets to urinate after taps and instead relieved themselves in cans. The long catalog of insults Black officers in particular endured included being slandered to the French civilian population, denied hotel accommodations, excluded from a reception hosted by the town mayor for the division's officers, and sent to labor duty for inexplicable reasons.[81]

Du Bois also learned more about the experience of the 368th Infantry Regiment in the Meuse-Argonne and its reverberations. In the crowded, dimly lit tents, he listened to accounts from Black officers themselves: the regiment failed to receive advance preparation for a complicated attack requiring careful coordination; they lacked heavy wire cutters and other crucial equipment; Major Max Elser of the Second Battalion shrank to the rear and cried in the heat of combat; other white field officers subsequently masked their incompetence by shifting blame to their African American counterparts.[82]

With so much disturbing news to receive, no wonder that throughout his time in Mayenne, military intelligence watched Du Bois, in his words, as if he were "a German spy."[83]

A conflicted picture emerged from Du Bois's conversations with

Black officers in the Ninety-Third Division. He was undoubtedly impressed with the remarkable service of the 369th "Black Rattlers" from Harlem, the success of the 370th "Old Eighth," and the exploits of the 372nd Infantry Regiment, embedded with the famous "Red Hand" 157th Infantry Division of the French Army. They had seen more combat than any other group of American soldiers, and hundreds of men left the front with medals of commendation for bravery pinned to their chests. The entire 369th received the Croix de Guerre. Indeed, their French commanders offered unqualified praise of the conduct of African American troops on and off the battlefield. With France's desperate need for soldiers buffering them from the institutionalized racism of the AEF, Black men of the Ninety-Third had done remarkably well.

But American white supremacy still proved resilient. Of the 369th's mere five Black officers, only James Reese Europe remained with the regiment by the end of the war. The 370th had arrived in France led by its pugnacious African American colonel Franklin A. Dennison, a long-serving veteran of the Chicago-based National Guard unit whose dignified uniformed presence once appeared on the cover of *The Crisis*.[84] Deeply revered by his men, Dennison had been drummed out of the regiment for "health reasons" and replaced with a white commander, an experience that all too closely mirrored that of Charles Young. In the 372nd, Colonel Herschel Tupes requested the wholesale removal of his regiment's Black officers on the grounds that "the racial distinctions which are recognized in civilian life" were immutable and prevented the development of "mutual confidence and esprit de corps."[85] A perplexed General Mariano Goybet of the French 157th Division, after receiving the request, discerned that "there is not, and there will undoubtedly never be, camaraderie between the white officers and the black officers."[86]

Black officers, Du Bois later recalled, were "bitter and disillusioned at the seemingly bottomless depths of American color hatred."[87] In spite of the circumstances, Du Bois relished their company. At La Chapelle, he lunched with Boutté, Leroy Godman, and other Black officers at the headquarters of the 366th Infantry Regiment.[88] Du

Bois deeply respected their resolve, dignity, and commitment to the race. The admiration was mutual, as the officers looked upon Du Bois as nothing less than a savior and the lone person capable of vindicating their trying experience. He spoke with Colonel Otis Duncan and other Black officers of the 370th Infantry Regiment, all of whom pledged to assist him in his efforts to tell their story.[89] The relationships he established with Black officers as they lunched, talked, and interacted would prove essential to the war history project.

Toliver T. Thompson was especially eager to partner with Du Bois. A Fort Des Moines graduate from Houston, Texas, Thompson served as acting personnel officer and assistant to the statistical officer in the Ninety-Second Division. Racism prevented him from receiving a well-deserved promotion.[90] After the armistice, biting his tongue and swallowing his pride, he remained with the Ninety-Second as the division historian. On January 8, 1919, anticipating Du Bois's visit to Le Mans, he wrote to the doctor, pitching the bold idea of "bringing together in an ASSOCIATION every NEGRO officer and soldier who was commissioned or enlisted during the period of the war." He envisioned branches in every state that, as part of its structure, would also have a "SOCIETY for HISTORICAL RESEARCH." He wanted Du Bois to serve as president. "You are the FATHER . . . Nothing is stronger or more binding than the brotherhood of arms, the federation of veterans," he wrote, adding, "These men will back you and support you in the fights which you will make for years to come."[91]

Du Bois had Matthew Boutté's loyalty as well. At some point during their time together, Boutté entrusted Du Bois with his diary to use for the book, a potentially dangerous act if discovered by military intelligence officials. General Headquarters remained on full alert concerning Du Bois's presence and assumed that they had a trustworthy set of eyes and ears in Boutté. They requested an update on Du Bois's movements. Instead of detailing his friend's activities, Boutté casually responded in a handwritten note, "Nothing new to report."[92]

Du Bois came away from his time with the Black troops, he later recalled, "utterly amazed and dumbfounded."[93] He shared his thoughts with the NAACP board in a January 12 note written from

Le Mans. "I have seen 8 regiments of Negro infantry and talked with many of their officers and men," he began. "I have also seen chaplains, YMCA men and a regiment of engineers." Then, barely able to contain his anger, he got to the point:

> I can say solemnly and without hesitation: <u>the greatest and most pressing & most important work for the NAACP is the collection writing & publication of the history of the Negro troops in France</u>. Never in my life have I heard such an astounding series of stories. You have not the faintest conception of what these men have been through. It is not only astonishing but it will arouse every ounce of sympathetic blood in your veins. I am doing all I can on this side to urge the preservation of documents & the writing of stories.

He then barked out his marching orders: "First commit the Association to the writing of this history at any cost. It must be done. It is the chance of a century." Next, he demanded, "Organize in every Branch a History Committee. Set them collect documents letters, maps, facts & the stories of personal experience from every colored soldier in their town city & county. Get sworn statements get name dates & places." He wanted these committees to get to work immediately, writing, "The Negro troops will begin to arrive in U.S. about Feb. 15 & shall stream on then until April or May."[94]

Du Bois returned to Paris after his time in Le Mans even more energized. After visiting the troops, he now wanted to see the battlefields. Matthew Boutté continued to serve as his guide.[95] In the April 1919 issue of *The Crisis*, in dramatic prose befitting the epic Du Bois imagined of his entire France expedition, he told readers about his travels.

He began his journey at Château-Thierry, the focal point of the Battle of Belleau Wood, the June 1918 counterattack against a German advance a mere fifty miles from Paris that christened the AEF as a credible fighting force. Next, he saw the "riven city" of Rheims, whose severely damaged Gothic Notre-Dame Cathedral, where French nobility had once been crowned, stood as a testament to Germany's ruthless conduct during the war.

From there he approached the surreal world of "No Man's Land." Once Edenic, the landscape had been transformed by "giant engines of death" into a "black ridge that writhes northward like a vast grave." Through the splintered remains of the Argonne's young trees, devastated "with fiery surprise," he reached the tragic city of Verdun. Between February 21 and December 18, 1916, in these surrounding forests and fields, some 306,000 French and German soldiers lost their lives in the most horrific ten months of warfare in modern history. While there, Du Bois came across African American labor troops, his "colored boys," cleaning up the remains of the "drunken ruin" of a city.

After passing through Commercy and Toul, he again returned to the Marbache sector. He stopped at Pont-à-Mousson and Nancy, taking in the familiar sight of the Moselle River. Unlike during his earlier December visit, Du Bois this time stood in the trenches, "wattled and boarded," that had been occupied by the men of the Ninety-Second Division, and he "saw where they rushed 'over the top'" in the final moments of the war. He vividly grasped the challenge they'd faced on the cool, foggy mornings of November 10 and 11 against German forces entrenched in the wooded, sloping terrain of Bois de Cheminot, Bois de la Voivrotte, and Bois Frehaut. "Innocent it looked, but the barbed wire, thick and tough, belted it like heavy bushes and huddled in hollows lay the machine-guns, nested in concrete walls, three feet thick, squatting low on the underbrush and scattering sputtering death up that silent hillside." With "grim determination" they fought, successfully advancing through the German onslaught and pushing toward the fortress city of Metz, suffering 498 strategically useless but symbolically meaningful casualties until, at 11:00 a.m. on the eleventh, the fighting ceased.[96]

Du Bois traveled farther south. He reached the "snow-covered Vosges" mountains, where "trenches circled the hills, and dug-outs nestled beneath by the battered villages." The final sites on his tour included Épinal, Domrémy, Bourbonne-les-Bains, and Chaumont before the whirlwind concluded and he returned to Paris.[97]

The significance of Du Bois's time outside Paris went beyond the treasure trove of materials he gathered and the firsthand testimonies he received. He came as close as he ever would to experiencing life as a soldier. During his time visiting the troops, he slept in the camps, endured the harsh winter weather, fraternized with the men, and received a taste of AEF racism. These moments allowed for a more intimate connection with the subjects of his war history. Most powerfully, in touring the battlefields, seeing firsthand "the entrails of Rheims and the guts of Verdun," he fully absorbed the failure of European civilization and the shocking destructiveness of war: "The trees, the land, the people were scarred and broken." He woefully passed through "villages in dust and ashes." He "saw the mud and dirt of the trenches," choked with wire, "twisted, barbed and poled, cloistered in curious, illogical places."[98] As he encountered gravesite after gravesite, the "breathless horror" of death greeted him at every turn. "I have seen the wounds of France," he wrote.[99] Du Bois, a product of Enlightenment rationality, wondered how to make sense of it all.

⁓

HE RETURNED TO PARIS sometime during the last week of January, freshly motivated, and leapt into the war history. He solicited more evidence about the record of Black soldiers during the war. First, he wrote letters to mayors of the various towns, villages, and cities that hosted Black troops, hoping to ascertain the truth about their behavior, especially concerning charges of rape.[100] He also reached out to his newfound ally Blaise Diagne. On February 1, he wrote to Diagne requesting his assistance in contacting the relevant *préfets* and *sous-préfets* for information on the conduct of Black troops in their areas, along with statements from French commanders about the performance of the Ninety-Third Division. Du Bois additionally asked for statistics and photos related to France's colonial troops who received medals and citations during the war.[101]

His work on the book, especially its connections to Africa, dovetailed with his efforts to bring the Pan-African Congress to fruition. After he had sent Diagne his proposal on New Year's Day, the two men convened on January 6 to discuss matters, just before Du Bois headed out to visit the Black troops at Le Mans. The French deputy must have expressed his pleasure at the nonconfrontational tone of Du Bois's plan and the absence of any explicit critiques of France's colonial policies.[102] Diagne assured Du Bois that he would use his influence with Prime Minister Clemenceau to allow the congress to take place.

While Du Bois visited the troops and toured the front, Diagne remained true to his word. With the opening date of the Paris Peace Conference fast approaching, Clemenceau granted him a meeting. Diagne, in the broadest of strokes, explained the rationale for the Pan-African Congress. The prime minister listened, then allegedly said, "I want to ask you one question: Does this Congress have as one of its goals sowing disaffection among African troops?" Diagne offered a definitive and reassuring no. "Go ahead with your congress," Clemenceau responded, satisfied that the gathering would in no way embarrass the French government and could perhaps generate more leverage in the peace talks by promoting his country's image of colonial benevolence.[103]

On January 30, Du Bois cabled the NAACP headquarters with good news: CLEMENCEAU PERMITS PAN-AFRICAN CONFERENCE . . . NORTH, SOUTH AMERICA, WEST INDIES, AFRICA REPRESENTED . . . CAREFULLY SELECTED DELEGATES WELCOME.[104]

He needed to work quickly. Even after pushing back Clemenceau's approved opening date a week, to February 19, Du Bois had only a small window of time, and limited resources, to pull the congress together. Mary White Ovington wired him a meager $500 in aid from the NAACP.[105] Finding a sufficient number of delegates also posed a major challenge. Once the State Department caught wind of the congress, they refused to grant passports to any African Americans who wished to attend. Du Bois looked to Parisian friends and the Black expatriate community for critical help. He leaned on Madame Calmann-Lévy, an influential white suffragist and salon hostess, and most vitally Ida Gibbs Hunt, an educated, politically conscious, multilingual Black woman who served as undersecretary for the congress. Together they aided Du Bois, who was impaired by his limited French, with logistics, publicity, and the sending out of invitations from their established offices at the Hôtel Malte, 63 rue de Richelieu.[106]

The Pan-African Congress opened on the morning of February 19 at the Grand Hotel, Boulevard des Capucines. Du Bois allowed Diagne the honor of serving as president, while he assumed the role of secretary. The composition of the fifty-seven delegates, ably recruited by Calmann-Lévy and Ida Hunt, reflected not so much a broad cross-section of the Black world but more so a showcase of the race's political and thinking elite. Only a few of the attendees had any direct connection to the African continent. Not surprisingly, the United States and African Americans were well represented. Two of Du Bois's closest confidants, John Hope and Joel Spingarn, attended in a show of support. The African American delegation also consisted of men and women already in Paris: Ida Hunt, George Jackson, Addie Hunton of the YMCA, the well-known journalist and orator Roscoe Conkling Simmons, and one Black army officer, Matthew Boutté. A picture published in the May 1919 *Crisis* showed Boutté, dressed in full uniform, standing next to Addie Hunton.

Over the course of three days the delegates met and discussed various aspects of the "race problem" as it affected people of African descent throughout the diaspora. It was a historic gathering, rich with symbolism and potential. Du Bois, however, quickly realized the challenge of forging a consensus about Africa's future, exacerbated by Blaise Diagne's adamant refusal to critique France's colonial practices. Du Bois wanted a more forceful statement condemning the European imperial powers and pushing for greater African autonomy. Instead, the final outcome, at Diagne's insistence, avoided demands for independence and radical economic reform. The resolutions, presented "in the interests of justice and humanity and for strengthening the forces of civilization," called for land adjustment, labor protections, the right to education and medical care, and the opportunity for Africans to participate in their own governmental affairs, so long as they met "the tests of surrounding culture."[107]

The congress also firmly endorsed the League of Nations. The final resolutions deemed the international body a necessary bulwark against the abuse and political marginalization of native Africans. When a colonial power behaved badly, the Pan-African delegates believed it "the duty of the League of Nations to bring the matter to the attention of the civilized world."[108]

By the time Du Bois's congress opened, Woodrow Wilson was aboard the USS *George Washington*, halfway across the Atlantic Ocean, on his way back to the United States. Since arriving triumphantly in Europe, he had spent his time laying the groundwork for the Paris Peace Conference, which formally opened on January 18. Representatives from thirty-two nations, surrounded by immaculately decorated gold walls under shimmering low-hanging chandeliers, packed into the Salle de l'Horloge at the Quai d'Orsay to begin the work of remaking the world. The first meeting of the fourteen-member League Commission took place on February 3. The British, led by two of their chief imperial architects, Lord Robert Cecil and Jan Smuts of South Africa, joined Wilson in dominating the proceedings and, in several behind-the-scenes meetings that lasted deep into the night, shaping the first iteration of the new international pact.[109]

Two weeks of frantic, high-stakes work left Wilson exhausted. But on February 14, with triumph in sight, he summoned the energy to address the peace conference. "I have the honor and as I esteem it the very great privilege of reporting in the name of the commission constituted by this conference on the formulation of a plan for the league of nations." The draft covenant was a bold document, establishing a general assembly and governing structure, processes for resolving international disputes, a court of justice, arms control, and labor protections. Germany was not allowed to join, a racial equality clause proposed by Japan had been tabled, and self-determination for people of the colonial world, especially in Africa, remained absent.[110] Wilson nevertheless touted the covenant as "a practical document and a humane document," possessing "a pulse of sympathy" and "compulsion of conscience." He ended the otherwise dry presentation with characteristic Wilsonian flourish. "Many terrible things have come out of this war, gentlemen, but some very beautiful things have come out of it. Wrong has been defeated, but the rest of the world has been more conscious than it ever was before of the majesty of right."[111] His work in Paris done, Wilson departed for Brest that night and prepared to head back to the United States, where a battle with Congress to approve the League of Nations awaited.[112]

For Du Bois, his Pan-African Congress, even more so than the talks at Versailles, marked a new epoch in the global struggle for democracy and racial progress. He spent the last weeks of February and into March promoting his success and scrambling to place the resolutions before the peace conference. Joel Spingarn again proved helpful. Spingarn shared word of the congress with George Beer, the Columbia University–trained historian and head of the Colonial Division of the American Commission to Negotiate Peace, who expressed great interest.[113] Du Bois met with Beer on March 1 in Beer's office on the Place de la Concorde.[114] From there he secured a meeting with the president's "soft spoken representative" Edward House, which likely took place on March 11.[115] House, Du Bois recalled, listened "with sympathetic interest" but promised nothing.[116] Du Bois's entrées and attempts to get to Woodrow Wilson himself ended there. The peace conference pressed ahead, without Du Bois addressing the European powers and the interests of the Black race unrepresented. Nevertheless, the Pan-African Congress, as Du Bois later reminisced, was "but a beginning."[117]

EVEN AS HE CRISSCROSSED the streets of Paris, proselytizing for the Pan-African Congress, Du Bois did not forget about the other leg of his mission, the NAACP war history. He continued to compile materials and documents. Statements from mayors throughout France vouching for the good behavior of Black troops arrived at Du Bois's hotel and temporary office at 9 rue Jasmin in the Sixteenth Arrondissement. The *soldats noirs* were not the bloodthirsty rapists the U.S. Army made them out to be.[118] They had, in fact, comported themselves with more respect and courtesy than their white American counterparts. With each story, Du Bois's anger grew, and his historical vision sharpened.

So he wrote. As a first attempt to make use of his research and comprehend his findings, he composed what he described as a "preliminary and tentative foreword to the history," titled "The Black Man in the Revolution of 1914–1918" for the March 1919 "Overseas" issue of *The Crisis*. The essay opened with a veiled message for Emmett Scott and Carter G. Woodson, along with a subtle jab: "The Association wishes to duplicate no work that others may do and it is especially anxious to co-operate to the fullest extent with all persons who know the facts and are acquainted with historical methods." After his "rapid survey of the situation" facing Black soldiers in France, he felt confident, despite some missing evidence and details, that he had the "main outlines" of the history he hoped to write. His central argument was clear: "The black soldier saved civilization in 1914–18." He began with France's colonial troops, heaping praise on the *tirailleurs sénégalais*, Blaise Diagne, and the respect they earned as personally beheld during the Trocadéro ceremony. As for America's Black troops, "the black stevedores have won a world record," Du Bois proclaimed, and the Ninety-Third Division, at "the most critical time of America's fighting," amassed a heroic record and earned the praise of their French commanders. The Ninety-Second Division, on the other hand, "went through hell." "Torn and shaken in morale" by racist commanders, the Black soldiers and officers of the division "seethed with bitterness and discontent."

In spite of it all, Du Bois asserted, "The black man never wavered." The "kindness and utter lack of prejudice among the French" provided a lifesaving counterbalance and empowering alternative to American white supremacy. Du Bois predicted that "the American army is going to return to America determined to disparage the black officer and eliminate him from the army despite his record." With history as their weapon, he declared, African Americans must not permit this to happen. More pointedly, even threateningly, he insisted that "the black officer and private" would never allow this to occur. "They return at once bitter and exalted! They will not submit to American caste and they will ever love France!"[119] He had left the United States pessimistic about the book, but as "The Black Man in the Revolu-

tion of 1914–1918" précis reflected, he was now invigorated, his research more fruitful—and unsettling—than he could have possibly
imagined.

Back in New York, his lengthy absence and the uncertainty regarding his activities continued to roil the leadership of the NAACP. Ad-
versarial members expressed concern about his extended stay overseas
and the associated costs. At the February board meeting, Archibald
Grimké of the volatile Washington, DC, branch, according to Ovington, "expressed his indignation that money had been appropriated for
a book." He felt that more immediate domestic issues deserved the
NAACP's limited resources. When the board approved $500 for the
Pan-African Congress, Grimké had refused to vote and had gone so
far as to tender his resignation.[120] The board also shot down Du Bois's
plan of returning to the United States via the Caribbean, making
stops in Haiti, Jamaica, and other islands to promote the resolutions
of the congress.[121]

Amid the tumult, Mary White Ovington remained Du Bois's
strongest supporter. She continued to back the book project. The December announcement of the war history and the March essay "The
Black Man in the Revolution of 1914–1918" successfully piqued the interests of *Crisis* readers. Ovington and Madeline Allison ably handled
a growing stream of correspondence arriving at the *Crisis* office pertaining to the historical study. Most promising was the interest from
recently discharged African American servicemen. "We are gathering
information all the time from the returning soldiers," Ovington excitedly informed Du Bois in a March 1919 letter. "They come to us, I
am glad to say, and bring us material." Ovington also informed Du
Bois that Scott and Woodson expected to publish their book in June.
She therefore suggested that Du Bois make immediate use of his overseas research and "get out a book on the Negro in France before you
attempt anything about him here in America." She encouraged him
to "think on the lines of a popular book first," based on his French
sources, and confidently believed that his recounting of "what has happened on the other side" would "sell better" than a book like Scott's.[122]

On March 22, wishing he could stay overseas longer but knowing that important matters awaited him in New York, Du Bois boarded the French transatlantic steamer *La Lorraine*.[123] The trove of "astonishing documents" he'd collected traveled separately, as he adroitly avoided the possibility of confiscation by military authorities by arranging for his friend Frederic C. Howe, a commissioner in the Department of Labor immigration service at Ellis Island, to ship them back to New York.[124]

The April "Easter" issue of *The Crisis* provided a striking view into Du Bois's mindset on the eve of his return to the United States. He riveted readers with the opening "Easter 1919" editorial. "Last April we were still at war," he reflected, and the world confronted a future that "loomed dark and beyond presage." With a grim acceptance, he and the race "doggedly, sullenly, gladly, splendidly, in varied manner, but always persistently . . . went to war." The result: "We have helped save the world. And we have saved ourselves." Black people proved themselves to be loyal citizens, shaming whites who branded the race cowardly and demonstrating the folly of African Americans who opposed the war effort. Indeed, where now were those "colored men who talked loudest against whole-hearted co-operation with the country's cause, and who protested most vehemently against those who were outspoken in their determination to place America first?" With the stinging criticisms of Hubert Harrison, William Trotter, and others flashing through his mind, he mocked, "There was talk and talk and talk." But he, not they, would have the last word. He had achieved vindication on the grandest of stages and successfully established a foundation with his Pan-African Congress, where "the whole black world is virtually represented." Black people had unquestionably won with their blood the legitimacy to "come before the world" and demand their citizenship rights "clean-handed and with pure hearts." "You must listen to us," he beseeched his white audience, his message unequivocal: "We shall never rest, we shall never cease to agitate, until we have received from the world what we have in such yeomanly fashion rendered—fair play."[125]

But lurking beneath the surface of this conviction and strident optimism lay anger and bitterness. This burst forth in the editorial "For What?" "My God! For what am I thankful this night?" he wrote. Should he be thankful for the fact that throughout his weeks in France he had been treated as a human being, free from the "curious monstrosity" of white supremacy, enjoying "the most commonplace of commonplaces"? Together, he and his French companions "could laugh and joke and think as friends." "God! It was simply human decency," he cried with incredulousness. But alas, he "had to be thankful for it because" he could not ignore the cruel fact that "I am an American Negro and white America, with saving exceptions, is cruel to everything that has black blood." During his wondrously emancipating weeks in France, he'd escaped from "the *Thing*—the hateful, murderous, dirty *Thing* which in America we call 'Nigger-hatred.'" But now he had to return to the United States, where "the *Thing*" awaited him. Nineteen nineteen would be the "year of salvation," the time for his "fellow blacks" to "join the democracy of Europe."[126]

"Easter 1919" and "For What?" formed part of Du Bois's meticulous effort to shape the narrative of his overseas expedition and, in the process, reshape his standing in the eyes of the African American public. He marshaled the full powers of his political and literary imagination to construct a series of stirring, beautifully written editorials in the March and April installments of *The Crisis* that laid the groundwork for him to reclaim the mantle of Black America's unquestioned race leader. The "Easter" issue also featured a glowing tribute to Du Bois from Charles Young. The esteemed colonel suggested that in light of all his contributions, the NAACP produce a special edition of *The Crisis*—a "Du Bois Number." It would be devoted to his inspiring words to "colored boys and girls" and include a full-page portrait that readers could cut out and frame. "We owe Dr. Du Bois so much, you know," Young gushed, "for his superior vision, his faith, probity and unswerving contending and insistence upon equity and freedom for us as American citizens."[127] While far from an impartial voice, Young, one of the most revered African Americans in the country, who maintained his dignity despite being martyred during the war, declared that among all race leaders, none stood as tall as Du Bois.

And now he returned. Like a conquering hero, victorious in his quest to truly make the world "safe for democracy" and democracy safe for the Black world, Du Bois was coming home.

PART II

DISILLUSION

CHAPTER 5

"The imperative duty of the moment is to fix in history the status of our Negro troops."[1]

ON FEBRUARY 17, 1919, in Paris, Du Bois busied himself with final preparations for the Pan-African Congress. That same day, thirty-six hundred miles across the ocean, New York City readied itself for a parade. But this would be a parade unlike any other in the city's illustrious history of grand demonstrations. The first regiment of troops from New York to fight in the World War had returned home: the 369th Infantry Regiment.

People began lining the sidewalks of Fifth Avenue early on the frigid, blue-skied winter morning of February 17. The 369th, still referred to locally as the New York Fifteenth, arrived in Lower Manhattan from Camp Upton via special trains and ferries. Few white New Yorkers had taken the ragtag Black National Guard regiment seriously before these men went to France. Today would be a different story.

"Forward, march!" Colonel William Hayward barked. In a tight formation perfected during their time embedded with the French Army, the regiment began its procession, passing under the "Victory Arch" memorial—which was still under construction—at Twenty-Fifth Street and then making the turn up Fifth Avenue. James Reese Europe and his famous band, horns blaring and kettledrums booming through the valley of skyscrapers, set the pace with the French marching song "Sambre et Meuse." In perfect lockstep, bayoneted rifles placed on their right shoulders, the regiment proceeded northward.

The crowds roared with delight and awe at the spectacle of thirteen hundred Black soldiers taking over one of New York's most prominent streets. Candies and cigarettes showered the men. From a building at Twenty-Seventh Street someone threw handfuls of silver coins that jingled off the mass of French steel helmets below. The men maintained their discipline and kept their eyes focused ahead. A host of local and state dignitaries, including the New York governor Alfred Smith, sat in the reviewing stand at Sixtieth Street. Emmett Scott represented the War Department, his book on the Black troops, without Du Bois's cooperation, well under way.

The regiment's wounded men traveled the parade route in army transports. Henry Johnson had a special ride of his own. The diminutive five-foot-four-inch, 130-pound soldier stood in the back of his open limousine like a giant. He soaked up the adoration of the crowd, waving a bouquet of red lilies in his right hand and showing off his Croix de Guerre in his left. "Oh you Henry Johnson!" "Oh you Black death!" his new admirers shouted.

The composition of the onlookers and the tone of the parade changed once the regiment crossed 110th Street. Harlem's "Black Rattlers" had now truly come home. Hayward loosened up the formation. Thousands of African Americans, small handheld flags fluttering in the wind, wildly cheered at the sight of their sons, fathers, husbands, and friends. They looked out of windows, hung from fire escapes, and stood on tenement rooftops. Little children, excused from school for the historic day, arrived dressed in army uniforms, the regiment's rattlesnake insignia emblazoned on their shoulders. The crowd spilled into the street, overwhelming the police who, at least for this day, allowed Black Harlem to revel with unrestrained freedom.

The euphoric throngs provided Jim Europe and the band, which had been playing since dawn, with a burst of energy. At the 130th Street reviewing stand, Europe decided to jazz things up with the swinging song "Here Comes My Daddy Now." Harlem roared in delight. After covering seven miles, the parade concluded at 145th Street. Subway trains awaited to take the soldiers back downtown for a celebratory meal at the Seventy-First Regiment Armory with family and guests. It punctuated what many of the men would remember for the remainder of their lives as a perfect day.

Some two million New Yorkers welcomed home the "Old Fifteenth," soon to become more widely known by the name given to it by their French comrades: the "Hellfighters." Festivities for returning Black servicemen occurred throughout the late winter and spring of 1919, North and South, in major cities and small towns alike. Serendipitously, also on February 17, Chicago celebrated the arrival of its National Guard unit, the "Old Eighth" 370th Infantry Regiment. The parade shut down the city. But nothing compared to the return of the 369th, which immediately became the stuff of lore.[2]

Du Bois surely wished he could have been there. "The reception given the old Fifteenth was the biggest you could conceive of," Mary White Ovington wrote to him during his final days in France.[3] The homecoming of the 369th and other African American soldiers to the United States stirred a variety of emotions among Black people. As they increasingly came to terms with the end of the war and what lay ahead, African Americans expressed a combination of pride, determination, anxiety, joy, and disillusionment. But perhaps most poignantly, there was hope, fragile yet sincere, that the service and sacrifice of African American soldiers would improve the citizenship status of the race.[4]

For Du Bois, this meant writing the history of the war. He had a remarkable story to tell, epic in nature, heroic, uplifting, yet profoundly unsettling. The African American public was ready to listen. Reassuring him about the prospects of his book, Mary White Ovington wrote, "The country is quite mad over the Negro soldier. You've got that to work with you."[5]

~

DU BOIS, AFTER NINE days at sea en route to New York, stepped off *La Lorraine* on March 31, 1919. He was in a fighting mood. His time in France had been both inspiring and infuriating. He felt betrayed by his government and its military, as all evidence pointed to an organized effort to slander Black soldiers and discredit the officers he had envisioned leading the race into the future. Just as egregious, in Du Bois's view, Robert Moton and Emmett Scott, the only two Black leaders with influence in the War Department and the White House, had seemingly done nothing to address the appalling discrimination African American servicemen had experienced.

The NAACP board of directors contributed to Du Bois's rage. He prepared to throw down the gauntlet at the April 14 board meeting, the first since his return. In advance of the meeting, he typed a "protest" letter, penned, as he described, "in hot indignation." He intended to make clear his anger with "the apparent attitude of the board" toward his activities in France and their audacity to impugn his "honesty and good faith."[6] However, as the meeting approached, he calmed himself, deciding not to submit the letter, likely realizing that his protest would lead to an explosion and, most important, potentially jeopardize his editorial control of *The Crisis*.

He instead prepared a lengthy but much more restrained report to the board, referring back to the votes taken at the October and November 1918 meetings that, as he interpreted, provided full authority for his France mission. He offered a detailed accounting of his accomplishments on both the Pan-African Congress and the war history. Concerning the latter, he emphasized that his work "could not have been done anywhere except in France and at the time when the Director went." He had collected enough information for "a preliminary sketch of the complete history," which he planned to publish in the May and June editions of *The Crisis*. He anticipated another three to six months of compiling additional documents from the government as well as from soldiers and officers, particularly those of the Ninety-Second Division.[7]

He remained bitter, but at such a delicate moment in his career, he knew that he needed the NAACP. He especially needed *The Crisis*, which served as his voice and the best vehicle for him to demonstrate his importance not only within the association but also throughout the country and the world.[8]

Du Bois arrived home to an America convulsing. The euphoria of the armistice and peace was fleeting and illusory. On the surface, the patriotic demands of the war had brought the disparate parts of the nation together for a victorious cause. But it had been done through force, coercion, repression, and violence.[9] President Woodrow Wilson, after a mere ten days at home, was back in Europe, working to make the world "safe for democracy" through his beloved League of Nations.[10] Oppressed people in the United States, their expectations raised during the war, demanded democracy for themselves.

Labor unrest erupted with the new calendar year of 1919. Union membership had soared during the war, along with wages and workplace protections. After the armistice, emboldened workers continued to press for their rights and higher pay, stoking fears of class warfare. In Seattle, on January 21, thirty-five thousand shipyard workers decided to test their strength by going on strike. The International Workers of the World (IWW), the American Federation of Labor (AFL), and other unions banded together in solidarity. By February, the work stoppage ballooned to encompass the entire city. This was a sign of things to come, as additional strikes broke out across the country in the following months.[11]

The federal government and nervous business leaders immediately pointed the finger at Russia. The specter of "bolshevism"—which became a catchall word for any and all things radical—caused labor tensions to increase. Fear spread that Russian Bolsheviks had infiltrated America with the goal of launching a worldwide communist revolution.[12]

Of particular concern were the returning doughboys. The War Department worried that discharged troops, emboldened by their service and quite possibly infected with radical ideas during their time in Europe, could be dangerous vectors of bolshevism. These fears were not completely far-fetched. Former soldiers, many still in uniform, participated in the Seattle strike.[13]

Daniel Mack returned home wearing his uniform. The twenty-four-year-old Black veteran hailed from the small town of Shingler, Georgia, roughly two dozen miles to the east of Albany. He fought in France with the 365th Infantry Regiment and came back to the

United States and the South proudly adorned in khaki as proof of his service.

On the afternoon of Saturday, April 5, 1919, Mack and a friend decided to head over to the neighboring town of Sylvester. While walking down a crowded street, Mack accidentally brushed against a white man, breaching one of the South's peculiar codes of racial etiquette. The man responded by hitting him. Mack hit him back. When the dust settled, Mack was the one under arrest.

Still in his army uniform, he appeared before a judge on Monday morning and pleaded not guilty to assault. But he also had something to say. "I fought for you in France to make the world safe for democracy," the aggrieved veteran declared. "I don't think you treated me right in putting me in jail and keeping me there, because I've got as much right as anybody else to walk on the sidewalk." Stunned, the judge sentenced Mack to thirty days on the chain gang, sending him out of the courtroom with a stern reminder that "this is a white man's country and you don't want to forget it."

Local whites, shocked by Mack's boldness, wanted to make the judge's message loud and clear. On April 14, a mob surrounded the jail where Mack was a prisoner. The chief of police opened the doors and let them in. Mack was seized from his cell, dragged to the edge of town, and beaten within an inch of his life with sticks, clubs, and revolver butts. Bloody and bruised, his skull fractured in multiple places, he somehow survived the attack and crawled to the home of a Black family nearby. They helped him flee the area.[14]

The NAACP investigated the incident, concluding that the roots lay in "the very great and very bitter feeling against the colored soldiers because of their supposed friendly treatment shown them by the French people while in Europe."[15] In the eyes of white supremacists, they had to be put back in their place lest other Black people become deluded with ideas of racial equality.

Daniel Mack survived the attempt on his life, but other Black veterans in early 1919 were not as fortunate. On March 14, near Pensacola, Florida, a mob set Bud Johnson aflame for allegedly attacking a white woman. In El Dorado, Arkansas, the following week, a twenty-five-year-old farmer, Frank Livingston, met a similar fate after being accused of killing his employer and his wife. In each incident, local and state officials did nothing to apprehend those responsible.[16] The NAACP investigated the cases, quickly sensing that something different and alarming was happening in the country. Black newspapers, such as *The Chicago Defender*, reported additional stories of veterans being targeted and assaulted.[17] For African Americans, the war, it seemed, had not come to an end.

MAJOR ADAM PATTERSON ARRIVED home safely. By late February, he was back in Chicago. And while Du Bois had squeezed every moment out of his final weeks in France, Patterson wasted no time in delving headfirst into their collaborative project on the history of Black soldiers in the war.

Patterson had ambitious plans. He started organizing his materials, which included the results of a questionnaire he circulated among fellow officers about their experiences, and sketching out potential chapters.[18] He envisioned a book of no more than 320 pages, with approximately fifty illustrations. He even imagined the cover—the title in gold lettering and embossed with a black buffalo, the insignia of the Ninety-Second Division. The major could not wait to press forward with the project and receive Du Bois's stamp of approval on his progress. In a March 20 letter to Du Bois, Patterson wrote, "As soon as you arrive in New York please let me know and I will forward data for your final arrangement for your criticism. Am moving along very well with my work and will write you fully when I know you are home."[19]

He did not, however, wait for Du Bois to get up to speed. In the following weeks he continued to make impressive headway on the book and even reached out to prospective publishers, making a pitch to Rand McNally and Company, which expressed interest. An initial printing of five thousand copies would amount to a cost of $3,750. "We will give you an attractive book," the firm promised, "which you could price at $2.00 without apology, and we would think you might ask $2.50 for it." Patterson, a novice to book publishing, sought both advice and validation from his much more experienced collaborator. He did not want to go with a smaller publisher but conceded to Du Bois that "it may be possible for you to drive a better bargain than this in New York."[20] Patterson hoped to take advantage of Rand McNally's interest and, if all went well, get the book out by the summer.

Throughout much of April 1919, Patterson peppered Du Bois with a steady stream of correspondence. First came a list of tentative subjects that he hoped would convey "just what is contemplated for this book." Potential chapters covering the Des Moines officers' camp and various parts of the Ninety-Second Division soon followed.[21] On April 11, a package arrived at *The Crisis* mail room that included two subjects for Du Bois's consultation and revision. Patterson intended to send Du Bois "two or three others within the next day or two," with the "intention to complete one each day." He acknowledged, "Yes it is a big job but I will try to do it."[22] True to his word, four more subjects were on their way to Du Bois's desk the next day.[23] Within the span of just a few weeks, drafts of ten of a proposed twenty-five to twenty-seven chapters had been written.[24]

Patterson's letters exuded enthusiasm and humility for the honor of working with Du Bois. "I lay no claim to being a writer," Patterson demurely wrote in an April 7 letter, "but I will do the best I can to save you as much work as possible." He eagerly sought Du Bois's opinion, conceding, "It is understood that you are the editor in chief and also that you share in the profits." But Patterson was also a shrewd politician and fast becoming an influential Chicago race man.[25] He held a genuine commitment to the historical legacy of Black soldiers along with a commitment to his own personal political and financial success. Referring to their collaboration on the book, Patterson thanked Du Bois for his "loyal support in the interest of the race and incidentally ourselves."[26]

Du Bois took a much more pragmatic approach to his relationship with Patterson. With his own political stature in mind, Du Bois looked to the man he'd described in 1912 as a "contemptible cur" to now assist in his postwar rehabilitation. He thus welcomed the prospect of working with Patterson and making use of his materials and access to other Black soldiers and officers. But he definitely did not view him as an intellectual equal.

This became clear when he finally responded to Patterson's weeks of correspondence. In a lengthy April 16 letter, Du Bois acknowledged receipt of the draft chapters, describing them as "excellent and informing."[27] However, the professor offered his ambitious understudy a dose of realism, throwing cold water on Patterson's hopes of getting the book out by the summer. "Only half of the whole book is ready," he wrote, "and it will all need very careful editing, the addition of many facts and the correction of numerous details." Du Bois did not intend to rush out a book that failed to meet his high threshold of excellence. "There is, therefore, no possible way of issuing a creditable volume before October 15." He also deflated Patterson's wildly overoptimistic prospects of the book's financial success. "First, do not deceive yourself," he lectured the major. "It is doubtful—very doubtful—if you can make any money out of this book. I think we can sell 10,000 copies—we cannot sell 100,000 copies. No book ever written has had such a sale among Negroes." Du Bois thought that he could possibly guarantee the cost of publication. But, most important, they needed to "first get the material ready." He encouraged Patterson to finish his "collection of stuff" and then he would add his own "mass of additional matter."[28]

Wasting little time pushing ahead with the project on his end, Du Bois began contacting many of the Black officers he'd met in France. His attempts at securing student research assistants prior to traveling abroad had yielded nothing, leaving the *Crisis* secretary Madeline Allison to manage the growing stream of correspondence and documents related to the war history. In lieu of formal help, Du Bois leaned on the men who pledged to support his endeavor while overseas.

Louis C. Washington sat atop Du Bois's list of officers to contact. Washington held the rank of first lieutenant in the 370th Infantry Regiment and had risen during the war to become one of the unit's top administrative officers. He'd met Du Bois in Le Mans and offered to help him with the war history. Just four days after arriving back in the States, Du Bois wrote to Washington, asking, "Will you kindly let me know how your war material is getting on, and what part of it I can see immediately?"[29]

Similar correspondence with other Black officers followed. Du Bois requested information directly from Colonel Otis Duncan, the highest-ranking Black officer in the 370th after Franklin Dennison's controversial removal. He reminded Duncan of his interest in "getting hold of the data for a history of your regiment," adding that the colonel "promised while in France to aid in this work."[30] For records on the 369th, Du Bois turned to Napoleon Bonaparte Marshall, the former Harvard track star, a well-known Harlem attorney, and a highly respected officer in the former New York Fifteenth National Guard before his transfer out of the regiment.[31]

Louis T. Wright had made a particularly strong impression on Du Bois when they met in France. Wright earned a medical degree from Harvard in 1915, graduating fourth in his class. In addition to his brilliance, he possessed a strong racial and political consciousness. During his senior year of medical school, he took a three-week leave of absence to join fellow Black Bostonians in protesting *The Birth of a Nation*. Receiving an officer's commission at Fort Des Moines in 1917, he served in the Ninety-Second Division Medical Corps in France, where he pioneered a technique for treating smallpox and achieved the rank of captain. Despite suffering from the effects of a gas attack, which earned him a Purple Heart, Wright pledged to contribute a section about the experiences of Black medical officers for Du Bois's book.[32] On April 24, Du Bois sent an inquiry to Wright about his progress, writing with a sense of urgency, "I want very much to get a complete story of your medical division in France. Have you written it up, together with documents; if you have not will you?"[33]

Du Bois prioritized reconnecting with Leroy Godman. The captain had returned to the United States and resettled in St. Louis. In his correspondence with Du Bois, the influential lawyer provided an update on the status of the Black officers court-martialed because of the Meuse-Argonne fiasco. Godman spearheaded their defense while in France, but after being mustered out of service, he could no longer represent them. Nevertheless, like Du Bois, he remained committed to their exoneration and understood the historical significance of the fight ahead. Godman offered to "gladly turn over to you whatever I have" regarding "the Argonne matter," adding that he would go over the cases in person with Du Bois. Confident that "a better and brighter record" could be made with the materials in Du Bois's hands, Godman reiterated that he was "very anxious that you should have the benefit of my knowledge of the affair."[34]

Du Bois's relationship with former soldiers like Godman shaped his plans for approaching the war history. He refused to sugarcoat what Black servicemen experienced overseas, as he conveyed directly to Frederick P. Keppel, assistant to the secretary of war. In an April 15 letter, Du Bois requested any available records on the organization and service of African American soldiers. He could have likely procured this information by different means, but he had a point to make as well, stating, "I wish these facts for use in a history of the war which I am writing and I want to say frankly that I shall criticize the war administration, particularly in France."[35]

While continuing to compile materials from various sources, he also moved ahead with coalescing support for the book project within the NAACP. The larger committee he'd envisioned while in France still existed only in his head. He did, however, establish a War History Committee composed of himself, the NAACP secretary John Shillady, Joel Spingarn, and founding NAACP board member Charles Russell, one of Du Bois's closest allies in the organization. The group met at the New York Civic Club on April 23 to discuss—for the first time since Du Bois's return from France—the status of the undertaking. They agreed that the initial sum of $2,000 would be insufficient to write the history and that a committee be appointed to raise funds. More pressing was the actual format of the book and the time frame for its completion. The group ultimately concluded that "in its opinion a one-volume history dealing specifically with the accomplishments of the Negro soldier in the war is the immediate need."[36]

But Du Bois believed that the Black public—in addition to learning of the accomplishments of their soldiers—needed to know the full truth of what transpired in France during and after the war. With this in mind, he embarked on a speaking tour to explain what he had seen and achieved while overseas. Although the Black press had covered the Pan-African Congress, the gathering remained shrouded in mystery, with questions swirling about Du Bois's motivations and what it truly accomplished. "We are represented in Paris by Dr. W. E. B. Du Bois and we are not represented in Paris by Dr. W. E. B. Du Bois," *The Richmond Planet* and its fiery editor, John Mitchell Jr., charged in the February 15 issue, wondering how Du Bois had secured a passport when William Monroe Trotter—who'd reached France and the peace conference only by posing as a cook on a transatlantic ocean liner— and others could not.[37] "That distinguished leader's lips are sealed so far as our rights and privileges in this country are concerned."[38]

Richmond therefore served as an ideal starting place for Du Bois to face these questions head-on. At Ebenezer Baptist Church at 8:00 p.m. on the evening of April 28, Du Bois spoke before an eager audience, each of whom paid twenty-five cents to attend. "Dr. Du Bois has just returned from the Congress of the Dark Races and will have a wonderful message for his hearers on this side of the water," the Richmond chapter of the NAACP promoted in advance. According to the *Planet*, Du Bois made some "startling disclosures" in his lecture.[39]

The content of his address in Richmond likely mirrored the speech he gave the following day, April 29, sponsored by the famed Bethel Literary and Historical Society in Washington, DC.[40] Considering that the DC branch of the NAACP exploded in near mutiny over Du Bois's "Close Ranks" position, the location of his address carried added importance. An overflow audience of more than a thousand men and women packed into the auditorium of the hallowed Metropolitan African Methodist Episcopal Church to hear Du Bois. The Reverend William H. Jernagin, president of the National Race Congress and a delegate at the Pan-African Congress, provided the introduction.[41] The crowd greeted Du Bois with thunderous applause and an ovation that lasted a full five minutes. *The Washington Bee* described the scene as "a demonstration of affection for one who had been, and seen, and conquered."[42]

Walter Loving stealthily sat among the throng. The omnipresent African American MID agent continued to view Du Bois as a threat and dutifully reported the contents of the *Crisis* editor's speech to his superiors. Du Bois began by attempting to yet again justify his war-time stance and his decision to accept Joel Spingarn's offer to work in military intelligence. He rationalized "Close Ranks" as both patriotic and pragmatic, explaining that because of his forceful tone, *The Crisis* had faced the threat of suppression by government officials. As far as the captaincy, he'd "consented to undertake the work" based on a sense of duty to the race and obligation to the country in its hour of need.

Du Bois then discussed his trip to France. According to Loving, he "carefully avoided the real truth" of how he got to France, refer-ring to the behind-the-scenes machinations between Du Bois, Emmett Scott, and Stockbridge. Du Bois devoted the bulk of his speech to re-counting the challenges he encountered securing a pass to travel to the front, the assistance he received—without naming them—from John Hope, Joel Spingarn, and Matthew Boutté, and his ultimate success in visiting the African American troops and collecting data for the book project. He alluded to the appalling circumstances Black soldiers faced overseas and made veiled references to Emmett Scott. However, he did not provide the audience with complete details about his find-ings. Hoping to create an air of suspense, referring to the forthcoming May issue, he ended his address by stating, "For further information regarding my trip, read the CRISIS."[43]

～

"DR. DUBOIS IS RETURNING from Europe, bringing a wealth of information, gathered first-hand, concerning the Black man's share in the Great War. The May CRISIS will be 'Negro Soldier Number'—and will tell of the Negro in the great conflict—AND SINCE!" This preview on the contents page of the April installment of *The Crisis*, while tantalizing, still failed to anticipate the thunderbolt impact of the May edition. As promised, it focused on the experiences of African American soldiers in the recently concluded war. Du Bois, however, had more ambitious—and self-serving—objectives in mind as well: first, to justify his decision to hold the Pan-African Congress; second, to firmly reestablish his standing as Black America's leading race spokesman by challenging the credibility of his top rivals; and third, to promote his book and position himself as the only individual capable of producing a historically accurate, scholarly, and uncompromised account of the Black experience in the war.

The cover art, drawn by the African American sketch artist Lorenzo Harris, set the mood. It featured an image of a sepia-toned soldier, manly and dignified, standing confidently next to a monument that was draped in a brightly colored red, white, and blue American flag. It represented "The American Negro's Record in the Great War." In one hand the soldier held a knife and in the other a chisel. With steely focus and confidence he wielded the chisel, first etching the word "Loyalty," followed by "Valor" and then "Achievement." The evocative image suggested that this proud record of African American contributions to the war, carved into stone, would withstand any challenges and survive the test of time.[44]

Du Bois began the "Opinion" page with "My Mission," a discreet rejoinder to colleagues on the NAACP board. Some unnamed people had the temerity, Du Bois wrote, to ask "WHY I went to help represent the Negro world in Africa and America and the Islands of the Sea." He offered an unequivocal response: "I went to Paris because today the destinies of mankind center there. Make no mistake as to this, my readers." Why did he not make his intentions known before departing? "Because I am not a fool," Du Bois retorted. He strategically concealed his plans, fully aware that should they become known to government officials, he would have no chance of reaching France. "When, therefore, I was suddenly informed of a chance to go to France as a newspaper correspondent, I did not talk—I went," he wrote. Once in France, "with the American Secret Service at my heels" and against all odds, he "turned to the French Government" and organized the Pan-African Congress. He accomplished the monumental feat without the support of the NAACP and a "meagre sum" of $750. "If the Negroes of the world could have maintained in Paris during the entire sitting of the Peace Conference a central headquarters with experts, clerks and helpers, they could have settled the future of Africa at a cost of less than $10,000." In spite of the board's shortsightedness and perceived insult toward him, Du Bois crowed that the Pan-African Congress now existed as a permanent body. "The world-fight for black rights is on!" he declared.[45]

Du Bois's boastful recapping of his "mission" to France served to burnish his leadership stature. The war had demonstrated that the continued problem of the color line required an international focus. And, in Du Bois's telling, no other Black person had asserted him- or herself on the global stage as he did. The Pan-African Congress architect towered not just as the voice of African Americans but now as the self-professed leader of a worldwide movement of peoples of African descent.

It was in this vein that he wrote "Returning Soldiers." The editorial revealed Du Bois in full command of the historical moment. "We are returning from war!" he announced. He, along with "tens of thousands of black men," had been "drafted into a great struggle"—a struggle in which, for France, they "fought gladly and to the last drop of blood," and "for America and her highest ideals, we fought in far-off hope." Indeed, America, "despite all its better souls have done and dreamed," remained a "shameful land," a nation of lynching, disfranchisement, ignorance, theft, and insult. "This is the country to which we Soldiers of Democracy return," Du Bois proclaimed. Directly confronting his critics and others who questioned the wisdom of supporting the war effort, he asserted, "It was right for us to fight. The faults of our country are our faults. Under similar circumstances, we would fight again." The race, however, would not submit to the prewar status quo. "But by the God of Heaven," he cried, "we are cowards and jackasses if now that that war is over, we do not marshal every ounce of our brain and brawn to fight a sterner, longer, more unbending battle against the forces of hell in our own land." And he punctuated his editorial with a rousing declaration:

> We *return*.
> We *return from fighting*.
> We *return fighting*.
> Make way for Democracy! We saved it in France, and by the Great Jehovah, we will save it in the United States of America, or know the reason why.[46]

Du Bois, with "Returning Soldiers" standing in sharp contrast to "Close Ranks," offered a militant postwar rallying cry for the race. As one enamored *Crisis* subscriber wrote, "'Returning Soldiers' alone is worth many times the magazine's weight in gold."[47]

Du Bois coupled his rhetorical rehabilitation with direct attacks on Robert Moton and Emmett Scott.[48] The editorial "Robert R. Moton" rekindled old Tuskegee rivalries. Lest readers be confused, Du Bois made a point to emphasize that pure coincidence found him on the *Orizaba* with Moton. Du Bois was more accurate in characterizing the distinct nature of their respective missions. "Dr. Moton was sent by the President of the United States and the Secretary of War to see and talk to Negro troops," he flatly stated, while "Dr. Du Bois was sent by the N.A.A.C.P. and THE CRISIS to gather the historical facts concerning Negro troops and to call a Pan-African Congress." Upon his arrival in France, Moton, Du Bois charged, "took no time to investigate or inquire" about the rampant prejudice facing Black troops. The "few speeches" he made to the troops attempted to cool their resentment. Then, apparently satisfied, Moton "rushed to catch his boat" in order to head back home to Tuskegee. "No one questions the personal integrity of Robert Russa Moton or his kindly disposition," Du Bois wrote, "but no one, friend or foe, can look these facts in the face and not feel bitter disappointment."[49]

Robert Moton failed to realize that the timeworn strategy of racial mollification would fall on the deaf ears of Black soldiers—as well as African Americans more broadly—emboldened by the war. Du Bois's *Crisis* assault forced the Tuskegee principal to engage in damage control. Not coincidentally, that same month, Moton composed an article for *The Southern Workman* to explain and defend his words and actions in France.[50] He sent Du Bois a copy of the article so that his antagonist could "know why I went to France and something of what I tried to do and some apparent concrete results." Offering Du Bois an olive branch, Moton wrote, "I am sure you will agree with me that Negro soldiers, officers no less than privates, have won lasting fame, despite the wild rumors of the 'Whispering gallery.'"[51] Du Bois's criticisms hit their mark.

Emmett Scott was next. With the confrontational open letter "To Mr. Emmett Scott," Du Bois threw all cordiality to the side and set a torch to any remaining goodwill stemming from their wartime friend-liness: "The Negro world and you will bear us witness that The Crisis and its Editor has given you loyal and unselfish co-operation, even at the cost of suspicion and criticism." Du Bois claimed that he did this out of a sense of national loyalty and a sincere belief that Scott had the best interests of Black troops at heart. However, his trip to France revealed "a state of affairs in regard to Negro troops which is simply astounding!" Du Bois demanded answers. He posed three accusatory questions to the special assistant:

> Did you know the treatment which black troops were receiving in France?
> If you did NOT know, why did you not find out?
> If you DID know, what did you do about it?[52]

The treatment of Black soldiers and officers in France genuinely shocked Du Bois, who felt blindsided by Scott's alleged deceit in re-maining silent. But this was personal. *Crisis* readers knew nothing of their secret partnership, which Du Bois purposefully kept concealed. Scott thus became the perfect foil for Du Bois to rebuild his radical credentials. As the editor of *The Richmond Planet* quipped, "Dr. Du Bois has on his 'fighting clothes.' A blind man can almost see that."[53]

The war history project contributed to Du Bois's venom toward Scott. In his earlier letter to Adam Patterson, Du Bois wrote, "Scott's book will appear in June or July. He and Stockbridge have been work-ing on it for months already." "They will get the start of us by two or three months," he conceded, "but that will not matter if our work is complete and first-class. THE CRISIS can put 1000 agents on the job."[54] He viewed Scott's book as a problem, not necessarily because of its potential quality, but because Scott, in order to enhance his own reputation, would use it to further conceal what Black servicemen truly experienced. "It is of tremendous importance for me to get hold of this material if they want the whole truth told," Du Bois wrote to Dr. Charles E. Bentley while attempting to track down Louis C. Washington and his collection of documents. "I am afraid Scott may get it, and if he does, the complaints will be suppressed."[55]

The salacious editorial "History" pulled back the curtain from Du Bois's previously behind-the-scenes conflicts with Carter G. Woodson and Emmett Scott, in particular. "Most American Negroes do not realize that the imperative duty of the moment is to fix in history the status of our Negro troops," he stressed. "Already subtle influences are preparing a fatal attack. It is repeated openly among influential persons: 'The black laborers did well—the black privates can fight—but the Negro officer is a failure.' This is not true and the facts exist to disprove it, but they must be marshalled with historical vision and scientific accuracy." After receiving his charge from the NAACP board to prepare the history, Du Bois, as he characterized events, sought to bring together "not as subordinates, but on terms of full equality—a board of three or four editors and a large consulting board of colored men." Despite these good intentions, "it immediately developed that co-operation was impossible." In Du Bois's version of their negotiations, Woodson selfishly "refused to co-operate except as Editor-in-Chief," while Scott's actions were more racially treasonous. "A white man, Mr. F. P. Stockbridge of New York, had already planned and was preparing a popular history and had secured the co-operation of Mr. Emmett Scott and others," Du Bois claimed. "Neither he or Mr. Scott wished to change their plans and neither would accept co-operation, except upon terms which we deemed impossible." With a unified effort out of the question, Du Bois magnanimously considered dropping the project. However, at the behest of the NAACP board, he went to France, masking the reality of his own motivations to make the trip.

Regarding the book, he came back from France convinced of three facts: "1. That the truth concerning Negroes in this war must be told impartially and entirely. 2. That no person in official position dare tell the whole truth. 3. That notwithstanding the unfortunate duplication of effort and multiplying of histories, it is the plain duty of the N.A.A.C.P. and THE CRISIS to compile and publish a complete history of 'The Negro in the Revolution of the Twentieth Century.'"

In coded words, he insinuated that Emmett Scott did not possess the necessary skill and honesty to write the history of African Americans in the war and that his forthcoming book lacked credibility. Du Bois's war history, to the contrary, would be sweeping, definitive, grounded in historical methodology, and uncompromised. "Such a history is, therefore, projected in three volumes, preceded by a brief forecast. The forecast will be issued as a supplement to the June CRISIS. It will be a short but complete history of the Negro in the war. It will be followed this year by Volume I of the full history; Volumes II and III will appear in 1920 and 1921." He encouraged "every reader of THE CRISIS" to "help in the compilation of this history" and to "write us immediately and let us know what co-operation we may expect."[56]

While Du Bois surely took some satisfaction in tearing down Carter G. Woodson and Emmett Scott, he eyed the larger goal of using the May 1919 issue to highlight the results of his investigative research in France and showcase his prowess as the leading historian of the Black war experience. He first addressed the explosive allegations from top white officers that the number of rapes committed by Black troops had reached epidemic proportions in France. Du Bois offered some historical context, explaining that "the charge of rape against colored Americans was invented by the white South after Reconstruction to excuse mob violence." Connecting this history to the war, he wrote, "Today the nasty and absolutely false charge returns to justify the outrageous treatment of Negroes by Americans in France." He published verbatim statements from the mayors of twenty-one French towns, all declaring that Black troops comported themselves with dignity and posed no threat, sexual or otherwise, to the civilian population. "What was the real animus back of this wholesale accusation?" he asked. "It was the fact that many Americans would rather have lost the war than to see a black soldier talking to a white woman."[57]

With the "Documents of the War" section, Du Bois completely threw caution to the wind, publishing some of the inflammatory letters and orders he'd obtained in France and covertly shipped back to the United States. He did not reveal how he acquired them but asserted he had "absolute proof of their authenticity." He provided an example of the unjust attempts to remove Black officers from command on specious grounds, a transcript of the slanderous note from the Ninety-Second Division chief of staff Allen Greer written to the Tennessee senator Kenneth McKellar, multiple instances of army-sanctioned racial discrimination and Jim Crow segregation, and a personal note from an enraged Black serviceman who, after suffering through hardship after hardship, wondered aloud "whether it will ever be possible for me to see an American (white) without wishing that he were in his Satanic Majesty's private domain."

Easily the most explosive document Du Bois revealed was the "Secret Information Concerning Black American Troops" directive that he later described as a piece of "dynamite."[58] He prefaced the document by stating that it represented "American and not French opinion," and that when the French Ministry learned of its circulation among the *préfets* and *sous-préfets*, "they ordered such copies to be collected and burned." Du Bois, as he indicated to the board while in France, was prepared to accept the consequences of publishing the memo, which had the potential to create an international uproar.[59]

As a whole, the shocking "Documents of the War" exposé offered insight into Du Bois's confrontational state of mind as well as his historical methodology in thinking about the book project. Adopting the careful scientific approach learned at Harvard under Albert Bushnell Hart and in Germany under Gustav von Schmoller, he used cold, hard evidence to shatter racist myths about Black soldiers and demonstrate the systematic nature of the army's racism. With the facts on his side, organized with impassioned clarity, Du Bois planned to present a history of African American servicemen in the war that no amount of slander and distortion could refute.

In white and Black America, the response to the May *Crisis* was stunning. The issue sent chills down the spines of white government officials who were already spooked by the twin specters of bolshevism and radicalized Black soldiers. Before the magazine hit the mails in late April, the U.S. Post Office investigator Robert Bowen brought the issue's contents to the attention of the MID chief Marlborough Churchill, who, ironically, less than a year earlier had weighed the possibility of Du Bois joining him as an officer in his branch.[60] With the wartime Espionage Act still in place, Bowen deemed the issue—and "Returning Soldiers" in particular—"seditious, insolently abusive of the country," and containing a "not too veiled threat." Postmaster General Albert Burleson supported Bowen's request to delay the release of the issue, upon further review. Some one hundred thousand copies of *The Crisis* sat in the New York City central distribution center for six days, pending a decision from the office of the postal solicitor as to its legality.[61]

Vigorous protest from *Crisis* readers and NAACP allies soon followed. Exhorted by Du Bois, incensed African Americans and NAACP supporters throughout the country inundated Burleson with more than 150 telegrams condemning his actions. The Reverend Robert W. Bagnall, one of the founders of the NAACP's Detroit branch, rallied his members to send forty messages to Burleson. G. A. Gregg, head of the Kansas City branch, did the same. The Reverend John Albert Williams, one of the most influential African American religious leaders in Omaha, editor of the *Omaha Monitor*, and president of the city's NAACP chapter, offered to personally deliver copies of the issue to his followers. Protests came from a diverse range of sympathizers, white and Black, male and female, ranging from local activists to United States congressmen, demonstrating the growing reach and political strength of the ten-year-old civil rights organization. Judge Edward O. Brown, a prominent white NAACP supporter from Chicago, wired the postmaster directly. "I cannot adequately express my disgusted resentment at such actions of postal authorities," Brown wrote in a letter to Du Bois. The former Kansas governor Arthur Capper, just beginning his first term in the United States Senate, also wired the postmaster general upon Du Bois's request and expressed his concern about the government's reactionary decision.[62] Nellie Bent from New Haven, Connecticut, had rescinded her NAACP membership in response to Du Bois's "Close Ranks" stand, but the May issue and the government's heavy-handed response prompted a change of heart. "I have just been informed that Postmaster General Burleson has ordered that no more Crisis should be sent through the mails," she wrote to Du Bois. "I am so overwrought, I can hardly write."

Not only had her faith in Du Bois been restored, but Bent pledged to personally deliver copies of the issue to all New Haven subscribers "if I have to walk for two or three days to do it."

Faced with a growing tidal wave of opposition and having no firm legal ground to bar circulation, the U.S. Post Office solicitor William Lamar deemed the issue "acceptable for mailing." Burleson ultimately relented and released it to the public.[63] By the first week of May, arguably the most remarkable *Crisis* number Du Bois had produced in his nearly ten years as editor was out and in the eager hands of subscribers.

The NAACP board did not particularly welcome the type of attention a newly radicalized Du Bois had garnered. The May issue and its ensuing controversy enflamed existing discord within the organization regarding his role as editor of *The Crisis*—and the motives behind his France trip more specifically. The longtime NAACP supporter George Foster Peabody accused Du Bois of an "amazing breach of international courtesy" in publishing the "Secret Information" directive. "I thought you were beyond limit," Peabody scolded.[64] Mary White Ovington, usually a reliable ally, thought his attacks on Robert Moton and Emmett Scott lacked dignity. "I think you must have written much of that stuff when very angry," she tsked.[65] Oswald Garrison Villard took matters a step further in *The Nation* and publicly rebuked Du Bois for his fiery tone. In the editorial "The Negro at Bay," Villard acknowledged that African Americans, after being "called upon to be heroes to fight for democracy," were understandably disillusioned after the war. "What is their spirit? A bitter one," Villard wrote. To illustrate his point, he mentioned Du Bois by name, as well as his "most dangerous and mistaken article in the *Crisis*," which declared that African Americans would "come back *fighting* for their rights and that they will continue to battle for them." "This is the counsel of madness," he retorted. "It leads nowhere but to bloodshed without result." Villard painted his fellow NAACP colleague as outside the circle of "the most enlightened members of both races," saying that his reckless advice threatened to do more harm than good.[66]

The success of the May issue and the overwhelmingly enthusiastic response by the *Crisis* readership blunted the anger of the board and the desire among certain members to rein in Du Bois. Monthly circulation topped the coveted one hundred thousand mark. Taking a victory lap of sorts, Du Bois published the following month a sampling of the positive responses he received. "I read the May, 1919, Crisis last evening," wrote P. J. Clyde-Randall of Pittsburgh. "Sad and sorrowful as were the disclosures therein, it pleased me beyond my ability to express. It shows that we had some one in France at the right time who had a heart to feel the wrongs planned and thoughtfully perpetrated upon us, as well as the ability and manhood to ferret them out and to fearlessly expose them." Oscar Price from Xenia, Ohio, voiced similar sentiments: "I have read of the great cause you have been promoting and of the terrible exposures you have made relative to our treatment in France, and I congratulate you upon the most honest and upright position of defense you have taken for the thousands of black soldiers who fought in France." Price and other loyal subscribers expressed their anger over the postmaster general's decision to delay the issue and pledged their support for Du Bois. J. Thomas Hewin, an attorney from Richmond, Virginia, seemed to take Du Bois's inspiring words in "Returning Soldiers" to heart: "Fight it out. We are with you."[67]

∽

DU BOIS ENDED THE "Documents of War" bombshell in the May *Crisis* with a request: "Will every Negro officer and soldier who reads these documents make himself a committee of one to see that the Editor of THE CRISIS receives documents, diaries and information such as will enable THE CRISIS history of the war to be complete, true and unanswerable?" He realized the importance of support from the African American public to the success of the NAACP war history. Emmett Scott already had the jump on him, and though Du Bois's overseas research had been incredibly fruitful, he still lacked Scott's easy access to official government and military records. He needed help, and in mobilizing his forces, he wanted soldiers, figuratively and literally.

Recently returned Black servicemen responded to his call with an influx of letters, documents, photographs, and personal testimonies. Elmer Carter, who served in France with the Ninety-Second Division, wrote Du Bois from Auburn, New York: "Your revelations of the conditions under which we lived and fought in the May issue of the Crisis will be a source of intense gratification to every Negro whose fortune it was to have been a member of the A.E.F.," adding, "It was the hope of every Negro officer and enlisted man that the humiliating and galling experience which he passed through in France should have the widest publicity and the Crisis should be congratulated for its exposé of some of the things that are not officially reported." He listed the names of various Black sergeants in the Ninety-Second Division who had access to official correspondence and were willing to provide them to Du Bois. "I have seen some of their copies of official documents," Carter revealed, "and they will doubtless contain some surprises even for you."[68]

"You ask me to tell you what I know concerning the treatment of the Negro Officer and enlisted man during my service in France," began a letter to Du Bois from Louis Pontlock, a former sergeant in the Ninety-Second Division's 368th Infantry Regiment. Pontlock, in eleven vivid handwritten pages, detailed instance after instance of racial discrimination stomached by himself and fellow officers of the 368th, beginning as soon as he sailed out of New York Harbor aboard the *George Washington* on June 15, 1918, until he departed the "Hell Hole" of Brest, France, in February 1919 for the return to the United States. Summing up his thoughts and underlining for effect, he ended by stating, "<u>The American Negro soldier in France was treated with the same contempt and undemocratic spirit as the American Negro citizen is treated in the United States.</u>" Pontlock ended his letter by declaring to Du Bois, "I am always at your service in the cause of my people."[69]

Charles Isum, a recently discharged sergeant in the 365th Infantry Regiment of the Ninety-Second Division, also wrote to Du Bois after reading the May issue of *The Crisis*. He expressed his pleasure that "someone has the nerve and backbone to tell the public the unvarnished facts concerning the injustice, discrimination and southern prejudice practices by the white Americans against the black Americans in France." Isum relayed his harrowing ordeal with "the southern rednecks" in charge of the Ninety-Second Division, focusing on his ensnarement in General Order No. 40, the edict issued on December 26, 1918, that severely restricted the opportunity for Black soldiers to interact with the French civilian population, especially its women. The commanding officer of his regiment ordered Isum placed under arrest after he innocently attended the wedding party of a local French family. He was sent to the guardhouse, paraded through the streets by an armed guard without any respect to his rank, and threatened with six months in Leavenworth, all "for walking on the street with white people." Aware of his rights, he challenged the legitimacy of his arrest and, much to the chagrin of the white officers intent on putting him in his place, demanded a general court-martial trial. Without valid grounds to punish Isum, the case vanished, and he received "an honorable discharge from the army, with character grade Excellent and rank of Sergeant, M.D." Isum assured Du Bois that he "could quote other instances where our boys were shamefully mistreated by the white Americans while in France."[70]

Charles Isum and other veterans did more than merely provide Du Bois with additional source material for the book. They offered further affirmation of his leadership standing, effectively legitimizing his unofficial title of spokesman for the historical legacy of African American servicemen. Their actions also reflected a strong collective historical consciousness. Black soldiers wanted their story told, but told correctly, rooted in a firm commitment to the truth, however ugly it may be.

The May *Crisis* put Du Bois once again in the national spotlight. The combination of riveting editorials, the impulsive decision of the postmaster general, and the support from African American servicemen considerably improved his reputation. He intended to capitalize on the momentum.

Du Bois barnstormed the country, delivering lectures about the Pan-African Congress and further educating the public about what he saw in France. Longtime friends and supporters in Baltimore dating back to the Niagara Movement sponsored a May 14 speech. The branch NAACP passed a resolution "on behalf of the colored people of Baltimore," thanking him "for his forethought and wisdom in planning a Pan-African Congress" as well as "for searching out invaluable documents and other facts as bases for a real history of black soldiers in the Great War."[71] Other cities on Du Bois's jam-packed itinerary included Detroit, St. Louis, and Philadelphia.[72] Throughout April and May, he delivered thirty-five lectures across fourteen states, with a combined audience of more than twenty thousand people.[73]

One of his most impressive events took place on May 18 in Chicago. The city, home to Adam Patterson and thousands of other Black veterans from the Ninety-Second and Ninety-Third Divisions, emerged as an important source of support for Du Bois's war history. In fact, he had initially asked Patterson to help arrange his Chicago speaking engagement, and the two men may have met for a consultation about their book.[74] The Chicago branch of the NAACP ultimately provided the forum for his appearance, which served the dual purpose of recruiting new members into the organization and allowing Du Bois to further promote the revelations he published in *The Crisis*.

A capacity audience of three thousand people crowded into Wendell Phillips High School to hear him speak, with more than a thousand disappointed people turned away. Many Black veterans undoubtedly sat in the audience, eagerly anticipating Du Bois's words. He entered the hall to a standing ovation and received a glowing introduction from the Chicago NAACP branch president, Judge Edward Osgood Brown. In his steady, professorial voice, Du Bois discussed the Pan-African Congress and his startling revelations about the treatment of Black soldiers overseas.[75] He conveyed some of the conversations he'd had with Frenchmen about the "Secret Information" circular and spoke of white American racial attitudes more generally, posing the rhetorical question to his audience, "Can you wonder that, so long as the memory of that circular lasts, France, and the rest of Europe, are going to smile at the professions of American democracy?" While he continued to lambaste the hypocrisy of the U.S. Army and the federal government, Du Bois also used his speech to emphasize that the war had ushered in a new era of Black leadership and militancy, declaring,

"All that the Negro saw and suffered and achieved during the war proved not only that the Negro can organize but that he can organize under his own officers, and the lesson of that is that what he can do in war he can do in peace." African American veterans would lead the way. "Those men will never be the same again," he said. "You need not ask them not to go back to what they were before . . . They cannot, for they are not the same men any more."[76]

Du Bois never professed to being a master orator. He remained fully cognizant of how his New England secular upbringing, academic training, stiff delivery, and stoic demeanor often challenged his ability to emotionally connect with his audiences. Yet what he lacked in rhetorical flair he more than made up for with the sharpness of his mind and the power of his pen. He put both to work in the June *Crisis*, announced as an issue devoted to "The History of the Negro in the War."

～

AT TIMES THROUGHOUT THE month of May, Du Bois surely paused to stop his head from spinning. Keeping up with the sheer pace and scale of domestic and global developments was no easy task. But he did just that—a testament to what made him and *The Crisis* so singularly unique. From his editorial perch he used the opening pages of the June issue to assess the state of the world and Black America in the wake of the war: the formal signing of the peace treaty, colonial unrest in Egypt and India, continued labor strife, the push to ratify the Nineteenth Amendment, the NAACP's anti-lynching campaign. The tumult of 1919 showed no signs of abating.

While keeping readers informed about events at home and abroad, he ultimately wanted them to grasp the most pressing issue of the moment: the history of Black participation in the war.

"An Essay Toward a History of the Black Man in the Great War" shone as the centerpiece of the June issue. Du Bois had already published the general framework of the essay in the March 1919 issue as "The Black Man in the Revolution of 1914–1918." With more time to think and digest his findings, he now provided a much more substantive investigation into the war experience of Black soldiers than in his previously rushed article. He also intended to demonstrate that the power to effectively tell the story of the war and its impact on Black people, in the United States and beyond, rested in his hands, and his hands alone. He acknowledged that the essay represented "only an attempt, full of the mistakes which nearness to the scene and many necessarily missing facts, such as only time can supply, combine to foil in part." Nevertheless, with enough evidence at his disposal, he felt obliged to press forward: "And yet, written now in the heat of strong memories and in the place of skulls, it contains truth which cold delay can never alter or bring back."

Du Bois made clear that Black soldiers, contrary to growing assumptions and misconceptions, played a central part in the war and the Allied victory. While mentioning Africans in the French Army and praising the Black labor troops, his primary interests lay in solidifying the record of the African American combat divisions. The Ninety-Third Division "fought magnificently," he wrote, and received "unstinted praise by the French and even commendation by the Americans." The men of the Ninety-Second Division "did all that was humanly possible under the circumstances," especially in the November 11 "Woëvre Plain Operation," where, Du Bois exaggerated, "the only thing that saved the Kaiser's army in this sector from a crushing defeat was the order to cease firing at 11 o'clock."

Despite these moments of valor, the history of African American participation in the war was one of malignant institutionalized racism. Du Bois alleged that the United States Army waged a deliberate and organized campaign against Black soldiers. "First, was the effort to get rid of Negro officers; second, the effort to discredit Negro soldiers; third, the effort to spread race prejudice in France; and fourth, the effort to keep Negroes out of the Regular Army." "These are serious charges," Du Bois acknowledged, but he offered several powerful examples, among them the unjust dismissal of Charles Young, the treatment of Black officers such as Matthew Boutté, the by-now well-known "Secret Information" memo, and a blow-by-blow account of the experience of the 368th Infantry in the Meuse-Argonne. The Ninety-Second Division, the "storm center of the Negro troops," as

Du Bois described it, "never had a fighting chance until the last day of the war."[77]

With his documentation of the racism experienced by African American soldiers, he sought to make a larger point about the war, the color line, and Black identity. If not for the "purling sea of French sympathy and kindliness," he contended, American white supremacy would have completely destroyed Black soldiers' morale, as well as their faith in democracy. This experience endowed them with a peculiar sense of disillusionment. Combined with the natural cynicism of war, the disillusionment of Black troops also stemmed from "the flat, frank realization that however high the ideals of America or however noble her tasks, her great duty as conceived by an astonishing number of able men, brave and good, as well as of other sorts of men, is to hate 'niggers.'"[78] The war placed the ugliness of the color line, "transported bodily from America," on full display for the world to see, while Black soldiers, through their both real and imagined relationships with the French, exposed its ultimate fiction.

Du Bois frequently invoked the theme of twoness in his writings, most famously in his formulation of "double-consciousness."[79] Just as double-consciousness in the American context could be empowering, the "double disillusion," as he described it, internalized by Black servicemen in France had a radicalizing effect. He had poetically conveyed this very point the previous month in "Returning Soldiers," but now he used his June essay to go further:

On the Negroes this double experience of deliberate and devilish persecution from their own countrymen, coupled with a taste of real democracy and world-old culture, was revolutionizing. They began to hate prejudice and discrimination as they had never hated it before. They began to realize its eternal meaning and complications. Far from filling them with a desire to escape from their race and country, they were filled with a bitter, dogged determination never to give up the fight for Negro equality in America. If American color prejudice counted on this war experience to break the spirit of the young Negro, it counted without its host. A new, radical Negro spirit has been born in France, which leaves us older radicals far behind. Thousands of young black men have offered their lives for the Lilies of France and they return ready to offer them again for the Sun-flowers of Afro-America.[80]

One question, perhaps the pressing question of the moment, remained for Du Bois to confront in his essay: Was it all worth it? "No adequate excuse for America's actions can be offered," he wrote. "A nation with a great disease set out to rescue civilization; it took the disease with it in virulent form and that disease of race-hatred and prejudice hampered its actions and discredited its finest professions." The profound disillusionment of Black soldiers matched Du Bois's own sense of betrayal. "On the other hand," he explained, "there is not a black soldier but who is glad he went,—glad to fight for France, the only real white Democracy; glad to have a new, clear vision of the real, inner spirit of American prejudice. The day of camouflage is past."[81] The veil had been lifted. With a clearer understanding of American racism, Black soldiers came home from the war fully prepared to fight against it.

As did Du Bois. With "An Essay Toward a History of the Black Man in the Great War," he succeeded in crafting a powerful work of history and a stirring piece of propaganda. The remarkable essay demonstrated that Du Bois, in just a matter of weeks between April and early May, had, in spite of a hectic schedule, been busy organizing his research and writing what he imagined as the framework for his book. He further whetted the appetite of *Crisis* readers for the larger historical study that would soon follow, when he would fully answer the question of whether the war—and his support for it—had truly been worth the sacrifice.

CHAPTER 6

"How great a failure and a failure in what does the World War betoken?"[1]

THE WORLD WAR TRANSFORMED African Americans in Charleston, South Carolina. The rich history of Black Charleston stretched back to the trials of slavery, through the upheavals of the Civil War and Reconstruction, and into the harsh realities of Jim Crow. As World War I approached America, the city's approximately thirty thousand Black residents, many of them educated professionals, represented one of the most dynamic communities below the Mason-Dixon line. James Weldon Johnson recognized this untapped potential when he launched a Southern recruitment drive for the NAACP in early 1917. Black civic leaders founded a new branch in February and quickly began to mobilize its members.[2]

The next month, Du Bois decided to see Charleston for himself. He spent three days in the city, delivering a lecture to twelve hundred people on "The World War and the Darker Races," taking in the sights, and learning more about the Black community's thriving businesses, churches, and other institutions.[3] He also met with Edwin Harleston, the president of Charleston's NAACP chapter, who informed him about the city's practice of not hiring Black teachers in its segregated schools. "The colored people of Charleston have stood this long enough," Du Bois wrote in *The Crisis* following his eventful visit. "They should awake and stop it."[4]

Harleston took Du Bois's charge to heart. Following a series of public meetings and petition drives throughout late 1917 and into 1918, the NAACP lobbied the South Carolina Legislature to change Charleston's teacher practices. Bowing to the pressure and wanting to save face, on February 2, 1919, the school board agreed to employ Black teachers in Black schools. The successful campaign, combined with their contributions as soldiers and civilians to the war effort, reflected a heightened assertiveness and rights consciousness on the part of the city's Black population.[5]

A little more than two years after Du Bois's visit, the city faced a reckoning. On the evening of May 10, 1919, a pair of white sailors, Robert Morton and Roscoe Coleman, left the Charleston Naval Shipyard and went downtown in search of fun. It may have started over a bootleg liquor deal gone bad. Or Morton and Coleman may have taken offense to a Black man refusing to cede the sidewalk. Whatever the spark, by 9:00 p.m., a growing number of white sailors and African Americans were engaged in a full-scale brawl. A group of sailors barged into a local Black-owned pool hall. Fists, cue sticks, bottles, and billiard balls flew. As the melee spilled outside, two sailors cornered and shot a Black man, Isaac Doctor. Rumors spread like wildfire back to the shipyard, where streams of white bluejackets, thinking one of their own had been killed, descended upon the city's Black neighborhood. They were soon joined by hordes of white civilians swelling into a vengeance-fueled crowd, armed with looted rifles and pistols, that numbered well over one thousand.

During the ensuing hours, into May 11, white mobs attacked Black people with impunity. Unsuspecting Black passengers were pulled from trolley cars and shot. Rioters broke into Black homes and businesses. A random bullet pierced the spine of a thirteen-year-old cobbler shop assistant, Peter Irving, leaving him permanently paralyzed. The city's segregated hospital could barely keep up with the inflow of bloodied patients. The arrival of naval provost guards and a detachment of marines, sent in to restore order, merely created additional problems, as they believed that African Americans had caused the riot. When young William Brown, a Black chauffeur, saw a group of sailors and marines approaching, he panicked and ran. The marines responded by opening fire and hitting him. He died a week later from his wounds.

African Americans, however, were not simply victims. Bricks, pipes, and bottles made for convenient weapons of self-defense. A number of Black people armed themselves with guns and engaged in counterattacks. A recently returned Black soldier, ready for war, put on his uniform, loaded his .38-caliber pistol, and patrolled the streets.

By 3:00 a.m. it was over. The violent energy of the mobs gradually burned out. Marines and local police cleared the streets and restored order. In the end, a total of three Black people died, with dozens more injured, some severely. The violence left Black Charleston shaken. Edwin Harleston and the NAACP pushed for a formal investigation and restitution, but little came of it. In the days and weeks following the riot, despite the efforts of Harleston and local religious leaders, both Black and white, to move forward in peace, racial tensions remained high.[6]

It was an ominous start to the summer of 1919.

∽

IF DU BOIS WANTED his book on the Black experience in the World War written, published, and released to the public by the fall of 1919, the summer months would be critical. He knew better than most African American writers of his day the challenges of book production—securing a publishing agreement, going through copyediting and making revisions, devising a marketing plan.

But beyond these practical obstacles stood a larger impediment: Du Bois himself. He demanded perfection and refused to rush his work into print. A scholar to his core, he took great pride in his research, rigorously analyzing the source material before him and infusing the facts of history with literary imagination and drama.[7] While approaching the researching of history as a science, its writing, he believed, should be treated like an art. His reading public expected nothing less.

He was not starting from scratch, for he had made some initial progress. Adam Patterson's work provided a strong potential foundation. The June "Essay Toward a History of the Black Man in the Great War" powerfully outlined the book's central themes. But finishing a book that met his high standards in the short span of just a few months required both focus and considerable help.

Du Bois first turned to Howard University's librarian Edward Christopher Williams. A native of Ohio with a passion for books, Williams graduated Phi Beta Kappa from Western Reserve University in 1892, marking the beginning of his career as a professional librarian. He spent seventeen years directing the library at his alma mater, with a pause in 1899–1900 to receive a master's degree in library science from the New York State Library School in Albany. In 1909, he left Western Reserve University to become principal of the prestigious M Street High School for African Americans in Washington, DC. His next career move was to Howard University in 1916 as the head librarian, where he immediately began to transform Howard's facilities, upgrade its holdings, and increase the competency of its staff.[8]

Du Bois needed Williams by his side. He'd envisioned the librarian being involved in the book project from the start, and on November 15, 1918, Williams had tentatively accepted an invitation to be part of Du Bois's editorial board.[9] After returning from France, Du Bois realized that Williams would be essential. A stalwart intellectual in his own right, Williams, along with overseeing Howard's library, held the position of instructor of languages and could boast of being fluent in German, Italian, Spanish, and, most important, French, a plus for the linguistically challenged Du Bois when it came to translating texts and documents. Also, because of his DC location, Williams had access to the War Department and to crucial government records pertaining to African American servicemen and their treatment.

Du Bois first considered a partnership with Williams during an April 8, 1919, visit to Washington. "I want to get a careful biography of all the available material, published and unpublished, of the Negro in the war; especially that issued by the United States Government, and I want to talk over co-operation with you for a proposed history. Please be thinking this over and I shall call you up as soon as I come. Of course, say nothing about this to others . . ."[10] Du Bois was engaged at the time in a war of words with Emmett Scott, who'd become the secretary-treasurer of Howard University when his work with the War Department concluded. Du Bois knew that Williams would have to tread carefully. Their conversations led to a formal arrangement in which Williams agreed to work during the summer on the history and take charge of procuring information from the War Department. Du Bois paid him $150 for two months of service.[11]

They made little progress. Du Bois asked him to relocate to New York for the month of July to focus solely on the book, but Williams remained in Washington.[12] "The War Department investigations have not as yet yielded much fruit," he updated Du Bois in mid-June. The vast amount of material concerning the American Expeditionary Forces remained unorganized, with records in Washington, some in France, and others in boxes awaiting shipment. Documents related specifically to Black troops were not categorized by race, even though the War Department intended to do so at some point in the future. Lastly, Williams informed Du Bois, "the department seems unwilling in the present state of things to allow an outsider to work over them." He'd offered to wade through the voluminous, messy collection of records himself, but army officials rebuffed his request.[13] Du Bois no doubt realized the impracticality, if not impossibility, of traditional archival research for the book.

African American veterans supplemented their work. Correspondence and documents from former soldiers continued to pour into the *Crisis* office after the scintillating June issue. Joseph Stevens, formerly of the Ninety-Second Division's 366th Infantry Regiment, thanked Du Bois and shared his experiences of the "segregation and prejudice that we received in France." "Your article is wonderful and if I can help you in anyway, command me."[14] Herman Davis, still laboring in France, wrote to inform Du Bois about his travails in the 804th Pioneer Infantry Regiment since the armistice.[15] Frank Drye, a first lieutenant in the 365th Infantry Regiment of the Ninety-Second Division, thanked Du Bois for his "persistent and courageous efforts [on] the behalf of the Negro Officers" and enclosed several letters and official documents that he hoped Du Bois would find useful in preparing the history.[16] Some veterans went so far as to view Du Bois as their savior. The former corporal Walker Thomas, who'd spent seventeen months overseas in France, congratulated Du Bois and lauded him as "the living MOSES."[17]

A letter from Lieutenant Robert Cheers got Du Bois's attention. "I am one of those 368th officers of the third battalion," Cheers wrote from the discharge section at Camp Upton, New York, where he along with four other officers from the regiment awaited an appeal of their sentences stemming from the Meuse-Argonne affair. Cheers had read "An Essay Toward a History of the Black Man in the Great War" and had come away inspired. He expressed his "desire to become a member of the NAACP and also a subscriber for the Crisis," adding that he and his fellow officers were "securing all the influence possible" to achieve their release and that they looked to Du Bois for additional support. "It is useless for me to tell you that the charges were false," Cheers wrote, "for you know that already."[18]

Du Bois closely followed the case of Cheers and the other accused men of the 368th. Robert Moton, despite Du Bois's harsh assessment of his actions in France, also recognized the gross unfairness of their convictions. Preferring, as was his modus operandi, to work behind the scenes, Moton successfully influenced Secretary of War Newton Baker to personally intervene in the cases. Leroy Godman continued to provide assistance as well. After reviewing testimony from the initial courts-martial and considering additional evidence, some of it provided by Godman, Baker invalidated the death sentences and dropped all charges against the officers, averting a potential tragedy.[19]

Du Bois continued to place blame for the hell that Black soldiers and officers—like those in the 368th Infantry Regiment—went through in France at the feet of Emmett Scott. The May Crisis editorial "To Mr. Emmett Scott" marked the opening salvo in what quickly escalated into a bitter public feud. With his eyes always open and his ear close to the ground, Scott got his hands on advance sheets of the magazine and also heard word of the critical speeches Du Bois delivered in Richmond and Washington, DC. He was incensed. Scott conveyed a public persona of conciliation that aimed to appease white supporters and Black critics alike. But the Tuskegee mastermind was also deeply prideful and, when necessary, could be devastatingly vindictive. Du Bois had crossed the line.[20]

Scott responded and set out to destroy Du Bois's credibility. With ghostwriting assistance from Ralph Waldo Tyler, the lone accredited Black journalist embedded with the AEF in France and a loyal supporter of the Tuskegee Machine, he submitted a rebuttal to the *New York Age* editor Fred Moore that also appeared in Black papers across the country.[21] Despite the enormity of his position, Scott declared that he "never failed during the war to take a firm stand for the rights of Negro soldiers at home and overseas." He hinted at the true motives behind Du Bois's attacks, writing, "I fear that the animating impulse back of his present inquiries has not as yet been altogether disclosed to the public," adding for good measure, "He also knows, as the record will show when necessity arises, that there were other occasions also when Dr. Du Bois probably felt I might be used for 'pulling chestnuts out of the fire' for him." Only Du Bois could recognize this as a threat to reveal the truth behind their book negotiations and how Scott was singularly responsible for getting Du Bois to France. Most damaging, Scott pulled the scab off Du Bois's "Close Ranks" wound, describing the *Crisis* editor as "discredited" and "desperate" owing to "the severe drubbing he has received in the Negro public press." Du Bois was trying to "rehabilitate himself in the eyes of the Negro world," and Scott would not be used. "I am fully prepared for any further onslaught he may make," he declared, and ended by throwing down the gauntlet: "I CALL FOR HIS 'BILL OF PARTICULARS.' I eagerly await his reply."[22]

Du Bois did not cower. Despite chidings from much of the Black press—which devoted front-page headlines and lead editorials to the Du Bois–Scott fracas—and disapproval from the NAACP, Du Bois shot back. Additionally, Scott's headlining as the keynote speaker at the NAACP's June national conference surely pricked Du Bois's ego and contributed to his anger.[23]

The July *Crisis* editorial "Our Success and Failure" was scorching. In three meticulously calculated pages, Du Bois defended himself against Emmett Scott's countercharges and returned fire. When he arrived in France, Du Bois had "heard of conditions, acts, conspiracies, wholesale oppression and cruelty of which he had had no previous inkling." White racists throughout the entire military hierarchy organized "one of the bitterest and most stinging campaigns of personal affront and insult ever attempted in a civilized land against civilized people" that left him astounded. Seizing the moral high ground, Du Bois wrote:

> THE CRISIS dislikes and avoids personal controversy. THE CRISIS knows that it is easier to criticize than to do. THE CRISIS is eager to give Mr. Scott every credit due and to make every allowance for the singular difficulty of his position. But THE CRISIS in its position as public mentor and adviser and newspaper absolutely refuses to be turned one moment from its determination to know why it was that in this the most critical period of the existence of the Negro race, 200,000 of the best blood of our young manhood—men who offered their lives for their people and their country, could be crucified, insulted, degraded and maltreated while their fathers, mothers, sisters and brothers had no adequate knowledge of the real truth.

Scott was the real traitor to the race. In Du Bois's eyes, he committed the unpardonable crime of "concealing fatal knowledge" from the Black press and the African American public more broadly. Du Bois concluded his caustic editorial with the same three questions he posed in May: "1. Did Mr. Scott know the treatment which black troops were receiving in France? 2. If Mr. Scott did *not* know, why did he not find out? 3. If he *did* know, what did he do about it?"[24]

Once more, Scott answered. In a letter that again appeared in Black newspapers nationwide, he repudiated Du Bois's "puny right to call me to account," saying that the *Crisis* editor was desperate and divisive at a time when "all elements and influences among the Negro people should be united against the common foes of genuine 'Freedom and Democracy.'" He repeated that Du Bois was "actuated by motives . . . which he dare not disclose to the public," but he still made no mention of the rancor surrounding their respective projects on the Black war experience. However, Scott exuded confidence that his book, when it reached the public, would offer full vindication. "The account of my stewardship has been laid and will be further laid before Colored Americans generally," he proclaimed, "and it is their verdict, and not Dr. Du Bois', which will be the final one reached in this matter."[25]

Du Bois gained nothing by another response. The continued vitriol, becoming more and more petty with each new editorial and letter, threatened to do greater harm than good for Du Bois's still-precarious reputation. Subsequent issues of *The Crisis* carried no mention of the feud with Scott. If Du Bois was to have anything more to say in the matter, it would come in the form of his book.

Du Bois, however, soon realized that if his book were indeed to appear in the next few months, it would find itself jockeying for space among a crowded field of other "histories" of the Black war experience. As soon as formal hostilities had come to an end with the armistice, Americans eagerly began to memorialize their role in the war. They had just been through a great adventure and, as Woodrow Wilson worked to set the terms of the peace, confidently believed that the United States would emerge from the maelstrom as the world's dominant power. For servicemen and their families, having some type of written record of their place in the war carried tremendous meaning. Publishers therefore rushed to capitalize on this market of potential consumers, churning out an eclectic array of battlefield guidebooks, pictorial volumes, and narrative histories, all promoted as offering "official" accounts of America's participation.[26]

For African American readers, a flurry of self-described "histories" of the Black experience in the war hit the public in the late spring and summer of 1919. Most of them, such as *History of the American Negro in the Great World War* by the Chicago newspaper editor William Allison Sweeny, lauded the "splendid record" of Black troops and, with ample pictures, celebrated them as symbols of loyalty, patriotism, and heroic manhood. Some books were blatant money grabs. Kelly Miller—the Howard University dean and esteemed scholar whose blistering 1917 open letter to Woodrow Wilson, "The Disgrace of Democracy," earned him the close scrutiny of federal investigators—published the hastily thrown together *Kelly Miller's Authentic History of the Negro in the World War*. Self-promoting and deceptively titled, the book actually focused on the European causes of the war and contained only one slim chapter on Black soldiers. In a scathing *Journal of Negro History* review, Carter G. Woodson lambasted Miller's work and questioned, with good reason, whether someone else had written it.[27]

As Du Bois expected, Emmett Scott's book, *Scott's Official History of the American Negro in the World War*, appeared in June 1919. Stockbridge and Scott's publishing company were bullish on its success, launching a nationwide promotional campaign and soliciting agents to sell the book with the promise of earning between $8 and $20 a day. They were also optimistic about their profits, as Scott, Stockbridge, and their marketing representative envisioned selling thousands of copies and making upward of $25,000 each. With so much money at stake, Scott and his team kept one eye on their audience and another on their competition, which included Du Bois. Scott had no idea when Du Bois's book might reach the public, but he took no chances in undercutting its potential. An advertisement boasted, "WE SAY UNHESITATINGLY that NEVER BEFORE and we doubt if there ever will be again, a book by so prominent an author as Dr. Emmett J. Scott, offered the Negro race that will be as welcome in every house as this book."[28]

In both presentation and content, Scott's book attempted to live up to its high expectations. The cover curiously mirrored the one proposed by Adam Patterson to Du Bois in their early conversations—the title in gold lettering complemented by an embossed buffalo, the insignia of the Ninety-Second Division. Inside, Scott offered thanks to the men and women who assisted him in compiling records and writing the text, with Carter G. Woodson at the top of the list. Scott heaped praise on Woodson, boasting, "His cooperation is, therefore, rightly to be prized as bringing to this work an appreciation of historical values."[29] Adding additional credibility to the book, Toliver T. Thompson provided Scott with his materials on the Ninety-Second Division. Du Bois's loss proved to be Scott's gain, with Scott emphasizing that because of Thompson's position and cachet with other Black officers, the chapters on the Ninety-Second Division "must, therefore, be regarded as official, authentic, and reliable."[30]

Explaining the motivation behind his book, Scott wrote, "In response to the natural desire and nation-wide demand for an authentic and reliable record of Negro military achievements and other of their patriotic contributions, this volume has been prepared as a lasting tribute to the American Negro's participation in the greatest war in human history."[31] True to his word, Scott devoted the majority of the book's 608 pages and thirty-one chapters to extolling the sacrifice and triumphs of African Americans, soldiers and civilians at home and abroad, as unquestionably loyal citizens. He included statements from Secretary of War Newton Baker, General John Pershing, and the recently deceased former president Theodore Roosevelt attesting to the patriotic fidelity of African Americans and the heroism of Black troops.[32] Skillfully compiled, making full use of Scott's access to official documents, the book offered detailed accountings of the various Black combat regiments and their successful records of service. Firsthand observations from Ralph Tyler during his time with the AEF provided further authenticity. Scott ultimately offered a celebratory account of the role of African Americans in the war, an important if highly sanitized declaration that Black people would not be excluded from the history of the great conflict.

Scott, however, could not simply ignore the fact that racial discrimination, as Du Bois dramatically revealed in the pages of *The Crisis*, marred the experience of most Black troops. He attempted to confront this ugly truth, and obliquely Du Bois, in chapter 30, titled "Did the Negro Soldier Get a Square Deal?" Offering the chapter as proof of his legitimacy as an "honest historian," Scott provided several examples of specific incidents of unfair treatment against African Americans, ranging from the implementation of the draft to the slandering of Black officers to the exclusion of Black workers from wartime government agencies. He acknowledged that "the Negro soldier suffered many hardships during the war, and was the victim of various forms of racial discrimination." However, these examples did not represent, as Du Bois claimed, an institutional practice of white supremacy. After all, Scott reasoned, many white soldiers suffered indignities as well, and the War Department, led by Newton Baker, possessed "a high sense of justice" toward Black troops and African Americans more broadly. Defending his own performance, Scott stressed that it was impossible for the War Department to know of every complaint, and that when a case did cross his desk, he made full effort to bring it to a positive resolution. In the end, he concluded that in spite of instances of discrimination and injustice, the "demonstrated loyalty, valor, and efficiency" of African American servicemen during the war earned them the "*right to be granted a fuller measure of justice, respect, opportunity, and fair play in time of peace!*"[33]

Du Bois offered no public reaction to the book.[34] Putting the fiscal health of his magazine ahead of his feud with Scott, he allowed advertisements to appear in *The Crisis* throughout the summer and fall, even though he must have gritted his teeth at the full-page an-nouncement that ran in the September issue, promoting Scott's "Great Book" as "The official and authentic history of the true part played by the Negro in the great World War, written by a great man whose valu-able experience, intimate connection with every phase of the direction of the great struggle, makes it possible to publish the true facts."[35] Du Bois, nevertheless, confidently believed that his book, when it appeared, would far surpass Scott's in quality and make a singular contribution.

~

PERHAPS WHAT HAPPENED IN Charleston was just an anomaly. Order had been restored relatively quickly. The rowdy sailors who sparked the riot would soon be gone. The mayor pledged to protect the lives and property of white and Black Charlestonians alike. The fragile peace of the color line seemed, at least on the surface, to remain intact.

But tensions unleashed with the end of the war, the mass demobi-lization of Black soldiers, and the heightened democratic aspirations of African American citizens rippled beyond the Palmetto State and the Deep South. Nationwide, race relations stood on a knife-edge and, with head-spinning frequency, burst into violence.

One day ahead of the Fourth of July, Black soldiers of the Tenth Cavalry engaged in a shoot-out with white residents and police in the remote western mining town of Bisbee, Arizona.[36] A week later, a mob in Longview, Texas, torched Black homes and businesses and killed one man. A Black reporter, who also served as an agent for *The Chicago Defender*, dared to tell the truth behind a lynching that occurred the previous month. After the newspaperman took up arms to defend himself, local whites struck back. In a subsequent investigation, *The Crisis* offered a twofold summary of the Longview violence: "First, simply and solely it is a fair sample of the lawlessness which at present is stalking restlessly through the nation. Secondly, it is indicative of the attitude which Negroes are determined to adopt for the future."[37]

Both assessments rang true on July 19, when Washington, DC, exploded. The demobilization of both Black and white soldiers further unsettled an already fraught racial climate in the nation's capital, transformed by wartime Black migration and a paucity of jobs to meet the postwar demand. In late June and early July, *The Washington Post* exploited the tension by running a series of inflammatory front-page articles detailing a wave of alleged attacks on the city's white women by Black men. This set the stage for the night of Saturday, July 19, when a white mob led by soldiers, sailors, and marines from neighboring Camp Meade decided to enact revenge for a reported assault on a white woman that took place the previous day. After assembling at Seventh Street and Pennsylvania Avenue around 10:30 p.m., the mob began seeking out Black victims.

Anti-Black violence engulfed the city for the entire weekend. White vigilantes attacked any unsuspecting Black person within their sights. Black passengers were pulled from streetcars and automobiles and mercilessly beaten. Residents dodged bullets as they ran and sought protection in their homes. Carter G. Woodson ducked for cover from an approaching mob near the Capitol, only to watch the mob catch another Black man and shoot him. One victim, Lawrence Johnson, was beaten with rocks and pipes in front of the White House, while Woodrow Wilson, recuperating from a case of dysentery after a day of boating on the Potomac, passively lay inside. The district police did little to stop the mayhem.[38]

Secretary of War Newton Baker and other government officials hoped that after Sunday night, the worst was over. But when *The Washington Post* announced in its Monday, July 21, edition that vigilantes planned for a 9:00 p.m. "clean-up" that promised to "cause the events of the last two evenings to pale into insignificance," both white and Black residents prepared for more. As nightfall descended, the predicted battle commenced. White mobs again gathered and went looking for Black targets. But this time African Americans countered with organized armed resistance. Recently returned Black servicemen— who, as *The Washington Bee* reported, "had served with distinction in France, some of whom had been wounded 'fighting to make the world safe for democracy'"—spearheaded the defense. Pitched battles took place in the streets. The next day, Newton Baker, anticipating yet another round of violence, finally called in federal troops, and a timely thunderstorm on Tuesday night dispelled most would-be rioters. The final tally counted four people dead, among them a young Black veteran, Randall Neale, who was later buried in Arlington National Cemetery. After touring the city shortly after the riot, James Weldon Johnson observed, "The Negroes saved themselves and saved Washington by their determination not to run, but to fight—fight in defense of their lives and their homes."[39]

For African Americans, the symbolic meaning of the riot hurt just as much as the actual violence. On July 22, the NAACP sent an urgent telegram to Woodrow Wilson, demanding action:

IN THE NAME OF 12,000,000 NEGROES OF THE UNITED STATES THE NATIONAL ASSOCIATION FOR THE ADVANCEMENT OF COLORED PEOPLE RESPECTFULLY CALLS YOUR ATTENTION TO THE SHAME PUT UPON THE COUNTRY BY THE MOBS, INCLUDING UNITED STATES SOLDIERS, SAILORS, AND MARINES, WHICH HAVE ASSAULTED INNOCENT AND UNOFFENDING NEGROES IN THE NATIONAL CAPITAL. MEN IN UNIFORM HAVE ATTACKED NEGROES ON THE STREETS AND PULLED THEM FROM STREET CARS TO BEAT THEM . . . THE EFFECT OF SUCH RIOTS IN THE NATIONAL CAPITAL UPON RACE ANTAGONISM WILL BE TO INCREASE BITTERNESS AND DANGER OF OUTBREAKS ELSEWHERE. NATIONAL ASSOCIATION FOR THE ADVANCEMENT OF COLORED PEOPLE

CALLS UPON YOU AS PRESIDENT AND COMMANDER IN CHIEF OF THE
ARMED FORCES OF THE NATION TO MAKE STATEMENT CONDEMNING
MOB VIOLENCE AND TO ENFORCE SUCH MILITARY LAW AS SITUATION
DEMANDS.[40]

Wilson did not respond.

Then came Chicago. Racial tensions in the city matched the
scorching summer heat. The return of Black and white soldiers complicated an already volatile dynamic surrounding labor, housing, and
public space. On the ninety-six-degree Sunday afternoon of July 27,
white and Black residents gathered to play and stay cool at the Lake
Michigan South Shore beach. Eugene Williams, a Black teenager, and
four of his friends, enjoying the water, inadvertently crossed the lake's
imaginary Jim Crow barrier. A white man began throwing rocks. The
boys kept swimming, casually dodging the incoming stones, even making a game of it. Then one struck Williams in the forehead. Bloodied
and barely conscious, he went under. Thirty minutes later, lifeguards
and police pulled up his dead body from the lake. African Americans
at the beach, outraged, demanded justice. Whites took this as a threat.
Fights broke out. Rumors quickly spread. By nightfall, the streets
filled with gangs of young white men terrorizing African Americans
throughout the city.

Temperatures remained sweltering on Monday, July 28. Hostilities increased as well. What began as sporadic violence the prior evening congealed into organized assaults on Black workers traveling
to and from the stockyards as well as any Black resident who found
him- or herself in the wrong place at the wrong time. Absolute chaos engulfed the city. White mobs descended on unsuspecting Black victims
while African Americans drew battle lines and defended themselves
with grim determination. By Tuesday morning, the death toll stood at
seventeen people, both white and Black.

Louis C. Washington had to fight for his life. The former 370th
Infantry Regiment first lieutenant, who'd met Du Bois in France and
pledged to assist with the war history book, was back in Chicago. On
the evening of July 28, Washington had gone out with a fellow officer

from the 370th, Michael Browning, their wives, and another couple for a group date to a South Side theater.[41] The show ended around 11:30 p.m. They looked to hail a taxi to return home, but all service had stopped owing to the riot. The couples began to walk. Crossing Grand Boulevard, Washington heard a yell. "One two three get the niggers!" A roving gang of four to six white hoodlums, eager to attack the first Black body in their sights, spotted them. They let out a cheer and shouted, "Everybody, let's get the niggers! Let's get the niggers!" Washington, Browning, and their group got as far as Forrestville Avenue before the mob caught up. Browning took a gunshot to the leg. One of the white assailants then slashed Washington with a knife. Washington, however, possessed a knife of his own. As another attacker, Clarence Metz, approached with an axe handle, Washington plunged his knife into Metz's heart. The next day, Chicago police called Washington to the Stanton Avenue station, informed him that a man had been stabbed, and locked him in a jail cell as a witness.[42]

Louis Washington was not the only Black veteran who fought back. Other ex-soldiers and officers, many also from 370th Infantry, still fondly known locally as the "Old Eighth" National Guard, put their military training to use to defend the South Side and engage in retaliatory combat with white mobs. The three-story brick armory on South Forest Avenue served as a rallying point. Former comrades convened to strategize and mobilize, making use of a stockpile of 1903 Springfield rifles and even a Browning machine gun. Thousands of armed African Americans, with veterans at the forefront, patrolled State Street, the main thoroughfare marking the Black Belt from the rest of the city. During the riot, it became known as the Hindenburg Line.[43]

Chicago was at war. On July 30, Mayor William Thompson, after four days of delay and a rising death count, finally called in the state militia. Six thousand armed troops took over the streets, setting up machine-gun units at key intersections and enforcing calm. Incidents of sporadic violence and arson took place over the next few days, but by August 3, the riot had run its course. The final numbers were staggering: 38 people—23 Black and 15 white—dead, 537 injured, more than 1,000 African Americans homeless.[44]

Coming so soon on the heels of the Washington, DC, riot, the mayhem in Chicago stunned African Americans across the country. The Black press had advertised the city as the promised land of the North to Southern migrants seeking economic opportunity and social freedom. Could Black people be safe anywhere? As the summer's death toll continued to rise, the answer seemed to be a resounding no.

For Du Bois, the violence took a shocking and personal turn on August 22 in Austin, Texas. After the war, Texas had become a hotbed of NAACP activism, with returning soldiers fueling a surge in local membership and branch expansion.[45] Austin had an especially active NAACP chapter, which raised the anxieties of white supremacists and prompted state authorities to shut it down. Alarmed by this development, Mary White Ovington had dispatched the executive secretary, John Shillady, from national headquarters to Austin to investigate. Shillady, entering dangerous territory, proceeded cautiously upon his arrival on August 20, alerting the state attorney general and the local justice of the peace of his intentions. They nevertheless saw him as a troublemaking outsider and ordered him to testify before a "court of inquiry" about his plans and the motives of the NAACP.

At 10:00 a.m. on August 22, while Shillady stood outside his hotel, a small mob of six to eight men led by a local judge, David Pickle, approached him. "I told him that his actions were inciting the negroes against the whites and would cause trouble, and warned him to leave town," Pickle recalled. Pickle and the mob, which also included the local constable, then pounced on Shillady, beating him until blood flowed freely down his face and he begged for mercy. Pickle boasted, without a hint of remorse, that his actions were in "the best interest of Austin and the State."[46] After receiving medical attention, Shillady fled the city on a train to St. Louis.[47]

While the battered and bruised secretary suffered the physical and emotional repercussions, the brazen attack represented an assault on the entire NAACP, Du Bois included. Writing in the October *Crisis*, he did not mask his disgust. That Shillady, "a gentleman of training and experience, known to social workers all over the land," could be "set upon by a judge, a constable and other officials, who have openly boasted their lawlessness and have been upheld by the Governor of the

State" offered irrefutable proof of the deep sickness of white supremacy that pervaded the South and the entire nation. "This is Texas,"
Du Bois cried. "This is the dominant white South. This is the answer
of the Coward and the Brute to Reason and Prayer. This is the thing
that America must conquer before it is civilized, and as long as Texas
is this kind of Hell, civilization in America is impossible."[48]

Rituals of violence continued to play out across the country in the
summer months of 1919 and into the fall. White mobs in Knoxville,
Tennessee, hoping to lynch a young Black man falsely accused of
murdering a white woman, rampaged throughout the night of August 30–31 in a wild melee that resulted in two deaths and required
1,110 state militiamen to put it down. The lynching of African Americans surged. In Omaha on September 28–29, a frenzied mob lynched
a suspected Black rapist, Will Brown, in one of the most horrific scenes
of the postwar period. The crowd of possibly fifteen thousand whites,
consumed with vengeance, stormed the city courthouse, attacked overwhelmed police officers, and nearly lynched Omaha's mayor, Edward
Smith, who escaped within an inch of his life. When the mob finally
got its hands on Will Brown, who declared his innocence to the end,
they hanged, shot, dragged, and burned his body in a macabre ritual
of vigilante justice. Only the arrival of federal troops, led by Leonard
Wood to protect the city's Black community, prevented an even greater
tragedy. Brown was one of seventy-six African American lynching victims in 1919, the highest yearly total since 1908. This number included at least eleven Black veterans. In Bogalusa, Louisiana, a recently
returned soldier, Lucius McCarty, after being accused of attempting
to assault a white woman, was shot, tied to the back of a car, dragged
through the town's streets, brought to the alleged victim's home, and
set on fire in front of fifteen hundred excited white people.[49]

The grisly denouement of what Du Bois's NAACP colleague
James Weldon Johnson dubbed the "Red Summer" of 1919 took place
in early October in Phillips County, Arkansas. Black sharecroppers,
led by recently returned servicemen, began organizing against the
systemic practice of local white merchants paying Black farmers sub-
stantially less money for their cotton harvests. A meeting of the Pro-

gressive Farmers and Household Union of America at a small church in Hoop Spur on the night of September 30 began quietly enough, with some one hundred men, women, and children singing songs, listening to speeches, and discussing ways to mobilize the county's Black population to stand up for their economic rights. But after weeks of threats, the union's leaders were also prepared for trouble. Many Black farmers arrived at the meeting with guns.

Accounts diverge along racial lines about what sparked the gunfight that erupted as midnight neared and a white deputy sheriff and detective drove up to the church, ostensibly to investigate reports of trouble. The aftermath, however, was clear: the detective lay dead, the deputy sheriff escaped with serious wounds, and whites in Elaine, Helena, and other surrounding towns, their fears of a Black insurrection confirmed, mobilized for race war.

In the ensuing four days, the blood of African Americans saturated the white cotton fields of Phillips County. Posses deputized by the sheriff terrorized the countryside and received complete freedom to put down the imagined uprising. They shot and killed at will. In one particularly horrifying incident, a veteran of the 369th "Hellfighters," Leroy Johnston, was pulled off a train and executed along with his three brothers, all successful professionals and businessmen. Their bodies, left on the side of a road, shredded with shotgun blasts, were virtually unrecognizable. Black people tried to defend themselves, but they were vastly outnumbered. Federal troops, called in to put a halt to the violence, aided and abetted in the massacre. Estimates of the number of dead ran from twenty-five to as high as four hundred, the latter figure most likely closer to the grim truth.[50]

Du Bois absorbed the news of the bloodshed with a mix of stunned amazement and visceral disgust. "Brothers we are in the Great Deep," he wrote in the September *Crisis* and, reluctantly, asserted the right of Black people to repulse their attackers with force if necessary. "Today we raise the terrible weapon of Self-Defense," he wrote. "When the murderer comes, he shall not longer strike us in the back. When the armed lynchers gather, we too must gather armed. When the mob moves, we propose to meet it with bricks and clubs and guns." His thoughts may have returned to the 1906 Atlanta riot, when he sat by the door of his home with a shotgun in order to protect his family.[51] But he also recognized the limits of fighting back. "We must never let justifiable self-defense against individuals become blind and lawless offense against all white folk." Desperately clinging to his postwar democratic hopes, Du Bois felt that Black people still needed to remain committed to "Civilization and Order" and the promise of America, "singing, learning and dreaming to make it and ourselves nobler and better."[52]

Woodrow Wilson inspired no confidence in Du Bois's wish for a "nobler and better" America for Black people. As the nation suffered through one of the worst periods of racial violence in its history, the president, seeing the incidents as matters out of federal jurisdiction, did nothing and said nothing. His mind and attention were elsewhere.

Wilson returned to the United States in early July from the Versailles peace conference, focused on convincing Congress to ratify the treaty and join the League of Nations. He had the support of Du Bois, who in the May *Crisis* lauded the potential of the League of Nations as "absolutely necessary to the salvation of the Negro race."[53] But the president's failure to adequately involve skeptical Republicans in the process now came back to haunt him. Opponents—led by Henry Cabot Lodge, the senior senator from Massachusetts and chairman of the Foreign Relations Committee—viewed the treaty, especially Article X, which required member nations to assist one another in the event of a military attack, as an infringement on American sovereignty. Eloquent words from the president, his mental stamina showing signs of weakness, now failed to persuade. Republicans, smelling blood, dug in. Wilson, his pride and legacy at stake, decided to take his case directly to the American people. On September 3, he boarded a train out of Washington for a barnstorming speaking tour, traveling to eleven states, making two speeches a day, exhorting the necessity of the League of Nations and railing against his Republican opponents at every stop.

Finally, on September 25 in Pueblo, Colorado, his mind and body could take no more. That night, after delivering what would be his last public speech, Edith Wilson found her husband unable to sleep, nauseous, his face twitching, and suffering an excruciating headache. White House officials canceled the tour and rushed the president back to Washington. On October 2, he awoke to numbness in his left arm and leg. As Edith attempted to help him, he lost consciousness and collapsed to the floor. The stroke left him incapacitated and mostly out of public sight for the remainder of his presidency, with Edith Wilson assuming many of the responsibilities of commander in chief. On November 19, 1919, a Senate vote failed to garner the two-thirds support necessary to ratify the Versailles treaty and American entry into the League of Nations. Wilson wanted to keep on fighting, but his deteriorated health would not allow it. The Senate took up the treaty one final time on March 19, 1920, with the same result. Defeated, politically and physically, his vision of America leading the world into a new democratic future shattered, Wilson sank into a deep depression. "I feel that I would like to go back to bed," he told his doctor, "and stay there until I either get well or die."[54]

~

IN THE MIDST OF what Du Bois later described as a period of "extraordinary and unexpected reaction" as Black people throughout the country fought for their lives, his work on the history of the war sputtered.[55] After its May 1919 meeting, the NAACP board did not discuss the project. The organization, Du Bois along with it, threw itself into understanding and addressing the violence that was convulsing the nation.[56] James Weldon Johnson took the lead in investigating the riot in Washington, DC, while Joel Spingarn, later joined by a still-shaken John Shillady and Herbert Seligmann, headed to Chicago. The NAACP also began to piece together what happened in Arkansas.

"As regrettable as are the Washington and the Chicago Riots," Johnson contemplated in the September *Crisis*, "I feel that they mark the turning point in the psychology of the whole nation regarding the Negro problem."[57] He was not entirely correct. Violent white racism continued, with few signs of slowing down. The psychology of African Americans, however, had indeed changed. Black people in the aftermath of the war determined to not accept the all-out assault on their citizenship and humanity without a fight.

Du Bois had sensed this transformation in consciousness during his time in France with the Black troops. As he wrote in "An Essay Toward a History of the Black Man in the Great War," "a new, radical Negro spirit has been born in France, which leaves us older radicals far behind."[58] This "new, radical Negro spirit" clearly exhibited itself in many of the letters he received from Black veterans. William Hewlett wrote to Du Bois as he prepared to return home to Petersburg, Virginia. Reading the August issue of *The Crisis* inspired him. Hewlett relished the "air of liberty; equality; and fraternity" he experienced in France and did not look forward to his impending return to the United States, a nation that, to the contrary, was "not democratic when dealing with her colored people." Hewlett passionately concluded his letter:

> If democracy in the United States means—disfranchisement; jimcrowism; lynch-law; biased judges; and juries; segregation; taxation without representation; and no representatives in any of the law making bodies of the United States; if that is the White American idea of true democracy—Then why did we fight Germany; why did we frown [on] her autocracy; why did black men die here in France 3300 miles from their homes—Was it to make democracy safe for white people in America—with the black race left out; if we have fought to make safe democracy for the white races, we will soon fight to make it safe for ourselves and our posterity.[59]

Hewlett and countless other Black veterans like him captured the broader spirit of militancy that swept through Black America in the immediate aftermath of the war. As announced by the Black press and a broad spectrum of radical activists, a "New Negro" had arrived, born in the war, steeled in the fires of the "Red Summer," and now determined to win the battle for democracy at home. A. Philip Randolph and Chandler Owen used *The Messenger* to position themselves at the forefront of the emerging New Negro Movement. In the pages of what they advertised as "The Only Radical Negro Magazine in America," Randolph and Owen boldly announced that the "Old Negro" represented by Du Bois and other accommodating so-called leaders had now been replaced by "New Crowd Negroes" who would not compromise and refused to turn the other cheek.[60] Two recently returned Ninety-Second Division officers, Victor Daly and William Colson, served on *The Messenger* staff. Some veterans gravitated toward a group even further to the left of the ideological spectrum, the African Blood Brotherhood (ABB). Established by Cyril Briggs, the Marxist West Indian editor of *The Crusader* newsmagazine, the ABB was a secret paramilitary organization committed to the defense of the race, the liberation of Africa, and the destruction of global capitalism. By 1922, the ABB fused with the Communist Party.[61]

Other former soldiers established organizations specifically for Black veterans. In March 1919, a group of Washington, DC–based officers, led by Captain Samuel Sewell, formerly of the Ninety-Second Division's maligned 368th Infantry Regiment, incorporated the Grand Army of Americans, with the hopes of continuing the martial bonds of fraternity created during the war.[62] They faced competition from the more radical League for Democracy (LFD), which emerged out of a series of secret meetings of disgruntled Black officers in Le Mans, France, and touted itself as "the most gigantic scheme of organization ever attempted by the race." Osceola McKaine, a charismatic, no-nonsense former officer of the Ninety-Second Division's 367th Infantry Regiment from South Carolina, served as the LFD's voice. At a June 1919 meeting in Washington, DC, McKaine addressed a raucous crowd of several hundred people, insisting that the time had come for African Americans to stand their ground and face down the lynch mobs. "The only thing with which to meet force is force," he declared. Just a few weeks later, as rioting erupted in the district, Black residents put his words into action.[63]

The federal government suspected groups such as the LFD of being part of a broader bolshevist-inspired movement to overturn American society. The nerves of government officials remained on edge following the wave of attempted bombings by anarchists in late April. On June 2, they struck again, intensifying the "Red Scare."

One of the targets was Attorney General A. Mitchell Palmer, as a bomb delivered to his home exploded and caused significant damage. Palmer tasked a young agent and Justice Department lawyer, J. Edgar Hoover, with heading a new division in the Bureau of Investigation and specifically targeting suspected radicals. With Palmer's approval, Hoover spearheaded a series of raids in November 1919 and January 1920 that placed suspected Italian and Eastern European anarchists in the crosshairs. The "Palmer Raids" led to more than ten thousand arrests, but few actual deportations, and widespread denunciation from Congress over Palmer's flagrant disregard of civil liberties. Hoover and the government also continued to vigorously investigate all perceived Black radical activity, including *The Crisis*. In a caustic August 25, 1919, speech on the House floor, Congressman James Byrnes of South Carolina warned against the postwar threat of Black radicals and held up "Returning Soldiers" as a prime example, demanding that Du Bois be charged with treason.[64]

While "Returning Soldiers" burnished his militant credentials, Du Bois occupied a precarious place in the growing New Negro Movement. Black radical New York was a small world, and Du Bois knew many of the key players, especially disillusioned former officers. He even asked some of them for help in compiling information for the war history.[65] But by and large, the new generation of African American and Caribbean militants viewed him with suspicion, if not outright disdain. "In the midst of the war when black men were giving their lives by the minute," A. Philip Randolph and Chandler Owen seethed in *The Messenger*, "Du Bois wrote his infamous 'Close Ranks' editorial in the Crisis which will rank in shame and reeking disgrace with the 'Atlanta Compromise' speech of Booker T. Washington."[66] More than anything, many Black people, and recently returned soldiers in particular, had little patience for what they perceived as the timorous agenda of the NAACP and the appeasing tactics of Du Bois himself.

This made Du Bois's support for the American Legion problematic. The national organization for veterans of the World War was spearheaded by prominent white officers and formally established during a three-day gathering in St. Louis on May 8–10, 1919. Concerning the admission of Black veterans, the delegates agreed that decision-making authority to admit new posts would be left to each individual state—a victory for Southern white segregationists.[67] Joel Spingarn attended and tried to oppose the policy, to no avail. Despite this insult, Du Bois immediately recognized the political power and symbolic importance of the American Legion. While he acknowledged the value of organizations like the Grand Army of Americans and the League for Democracy, he also emphatically believed, as he wrote in the September *Crisis*, that "every Negro soldier and sailor should fight to join the American Legion . . . Do not help the rascals to win by giving up," he urged.[68] Joel Spingarn, again, undoubtedly played a role in fueling Du Bois's patriotism.

Instead of the American Legion, many Black veterans found an organization much better suited to meeting their needs in the Universal Negro Improvement Association (UNIA), founded by Marcus Garvey. The relationship between the *Crisis* editor and the upstart UNIA leader began cordially enough in April 1915, when Garvey wrote a gracious note to a vacationing Du Bois welcoming him to his homeland of Jamaica and trusting that he had an enjoyable visit to the "sunny isle."[69] He received no reply. Garvey extended another hand of friendship a year later upon relocating to New York City, stopping by the NAACP headquarters to invite Du Bois to preside over his first public lecture on May 9, 1916, at St. Mark's Church Hall.[70] Du Bois was absent from the office that day, and his assistant later informed Garvey that though Du Bois appreciated the invitation, he would be traveling and unable to attend the speech.[71] As Garvey worked to make a name for himself and reestablish the UNIA in New York, Du Bois initially paid him little mind.[72]

That changed by the end of the war. During the time between his arrival in New York in 1916 and the close of 1918, Garvey traveled throughout Black America, sharpened his rhetorical skills, made allies in Harlem's radical circles, and emerged confident that the UNIA, with him at its helm, was destined to take the race into the future. Garvey's influence rose among the Black masses and the crop of New Negro voices who mocked Du Bois for his capitulating "Close Ranks" stance. Crowds by the hundreds, and then the thousands, filled the UNIA's meeting hall. Civil rights veterans such as William Monroe

Trotter and Ida B. Wells-Barnett found common cause with Garvey. Madam C. J. Walker became one of his most staunch supporters. The UNIA's newspaper, *The Negro World*, officially launched in the summer of 1918, spread Garvey's message of African uplift, racial pride, and economic self-determination, attracting more and more followers. As the war came to an end and the restlessness of African Americans about their postwar futures increased, Garvey became a force to be reckoned with.[73]

Not coincidentally, the UNIA's exponential growth in the spring and summer of 1919 went hand in hand with the return of Black troops to their homes and the violent backlash from whites across the country. With soaring oratory and audacious pageantry, Garvey brilliantly tapped into the race consciousness and spirit of resistance that swept through Black America and the larger African diaspora following the war. At a February 18 meeting in Baltimore co-headlined with Ida B. Wells-Barnett, Garvey drew upon the valiant service of Black soldiers to rally his supporters for the fight ahead: "Out of this war we have produced the American, or the West Indian, or the African Napoleon who will ultimately lead the 400,000,000 black people of the world to victory."[74] In New York City on the night of August 25, at a mass meeting at Carnegie Hall, Garvey did not disappoint the throngs of Black men and women who filled every seat and hung on to his every word. "They say to us in East St. Louis, 'We do not want you here.' They say to us in Chicago, 'We don't want you here.' They say to us in Washington, 'We don't want you here,' in America . . . We shall not be satisfied. Therefore we declare this: We, who have survived the war, that the same blood our brothers gave in France and Flanders to free the whites, the Belgians and the Serbians, the same blood we are prepared at any time to shed in the emancipation of the negro race."[75] For those who did not experience the magic of Garvey in person, his voice and message rang loudly through editorials in *The Negro World*. "The New Negro has fought the last battle for the white man," he wrote in the October 11 issue, "and he is now getting ready to fight for the redemption of Africa."[76] By the end of the year, Garvey claimed more than five thousand members in Harlem; UNIA chapters in twenty-five states; branches in the West

Indies, South America, and West Africa; and worldwide followers in the hundreds of thousands.[77]

Hostility between Du Bois and Garvey began with rival visions of Pan-Africanism and quickly evolved into a contest of who was best suited to speak on behalf of people of African descent in the wake of the war. Garvey's unequivocal call for an "Africa for the Africans" ran counter to Du Bois's top-down gradualist approach to uplifting the continent and the people of its diaspora. Their visions clashed in Paris, as Garvey accused Du Bois of sabotaging his handpicked emissary to represent the UNIA during the Paris Peace Conference.[78] While skeptical of Garvey the Pan-Africanist, Du Bois was especially leery of Garvey the businessman. In June 1919, Garvey announced plans to create a fleet of steamships called the Black Star Line. Soon, thousands of Garveyites were spending $5 to buy stock in the vision of Black men commanding the high seas and building a new, independent future. Even Du Bois's uncle, James Burghardt, was intrigued and wrote to ask his well-known nephew's advice on whether he and other people in his town should purchase some shares. "Don't under any circumstances invest any money on the Black Star Line," Du Bois warned. "The District Attorney of New York County has pronounced its methods fraudulent."[79]

~

ALTHOUGH DU BOIS TRIED to focus on writing what he believed would be the definitive story of the Black experience in the World War, the tumult, astonishment, and trauma of the summer overwhelmed him. He had believed that the end of the war would bring with it the dawn of a new era in the history of democracy, for Black people and the world. Instead, the world was aflame and Black people were being slaughtered. To make matters worse, Du Bois's legitimacy as a spokesman for the race was under attack, from moderates like Emmett Scott to New Negro militants like Marcus Garvey. Du Bois envisioned his book on the World War silencing his critics, reasserting his authority, and demonstrating the visionary wisdom of the call to "close ranks." But the scale and magnitude of the project, combined with practical challenges, quickly tempered his ambitions.

Joel Spingarn once again provided support. In early 1919, Du Bois's friend and NAACP colleague partnered with Alfred Harcourt and Donald Brace to form a new publishing house.[80] In a conversation with Harcourt, Spingarn mentioned Du Bois's World War book as a potential acquisition for the start-up company. Spingarn shared this with Du Bois, and Du Bois followed up with a letter to Harcourt on July 15, 1919: "Major J. E. Spingarn tells me that you might be willing to consider for publication in your new publishing house, my History of the Negro in the War . . . I shall be very glad to talk over the matter with you at your convenience. When may I call?" Harcourt responded, "I am glad to know that you are interested in Major Spingarn's suggestion that you let us see your History of the Negro in the War . . . I should like to talk to you about this."[81]

Harcourt proposed a face-to-face meeting or phone conversation with Du Bois for the following week. It is not clear whether this meeting or conversation took place. However, if it did, Harcourt would have learned that the book was nowhere near completion. Du Bois, instead, offered Harcourt another book that, though not the history of Black troops, provided the opportunity to try to make sense of his increasingly complicated and conflicted feelings about the war.

Du Bois had begun work on *Darkwater: Voices from Within the Veil* in late 1917.[82] He imagined the book as a sequel of sorts to *The Souls of Black Folk*. Adopting a similar approach to his 1903 masterpiece, Du Bois structured *Darkwater* as a collection of previously published writings, each revised and recast to fit the broader theme of the book. *Darkwater*'s central thread, however, remained in flux as the World War impeded on Du Bois's work and altered his focus. He finished an early draft around the time of his fiftieth birthday, in February 1918. He continued to prepare the manuscript throughout the fall, employing his remarkable gift of compartmentalization to modify the text at the same time as he began thinking about his next book on the World War.[83] He signed the postscript of what he most likely envisioned as a final draft on Thanksgiving Day 1918, not knowing that only days later he would be on a boat to France.[84]

For the first months of 1919, Du Bois placed *Darkwater* on the back burner, instead devoting most of his attention to the World War history. The hellish summer unsettled him, prompting a reevaluation of the meaning of the war and its perhaps darker implications for people of African descent across the globe. As fall arrived, with the war project stalled, he returned to *Darkwater*.

Du Bois took stock of events, and his place in them, during the remarkable ten months since completing what, at the time, he'd assumed to be a final draft. Much had changed, and he needed to revise *Darkwater* accordingly. He delivered a new manuscript to Harcourt, Brace & Howe in September 1919, and, to much fanfare, *Darkwater* appeared in February 1920.[85]

It was not a manifesto; readers expecting a formulaic program of action would be disappointed. Even more so than *The Souls of Black Folk*, *Darkwater* was a highly experimental text, as Du Bois balanced reworked essays with poetry, fictional short stories, and excerpts from various *Crisis* editorials. Given the context in which he finished the book, its unorthodox structure is not surprising. Despite the barbs of a younger vanguard of New Negro spokesmen and women questioning his radicalism, he possessed a singular ability to articulate through the written word the zeitgeist of Black America. *Darkwater* reflected Du Bois writing in a time of upheaval, anger, uncertainty, and confusion, for the race and himself personally. Channeling and expressing these conflicting emotions required marshaling the full range of his intellectual and artistic gifts.

He opened *Darkwater* with his "Credo," the poetic articulation of his core convictions originally published in 1904. Considering the context, the stanza on his belief in the horror of war and commitment to "the Prince of Peace" was glaring.[86] Revisiting "Credo" some sixteen years later, he strove to demonstrate his political, philosophical, and moral consistency. But readers would have been well within their right to question whether this was the same Du Bois who encouraged African Americans to rush headfirst into the most destructive conflict in modern history.

He assuaged any concerns about his credibility in the brilliant second chapter, "The Souls of White Folk." "The discovery of personal whiteness among the world's peoples is a very modern thing," he stated. The essay deconstructing the meaning of whiteness that appeared in *Darkwater* differed significantly in tone and substance from its original 1910 version published in *The Independent*. The aftermath of the war had unleashed the fury of Du Bois's prose and provided abundant evidence of the fallacy of white supremacy. The war represented nothing less than a crisis of Western civilization. "In the awful cataclysm of World War, where from beating, slandering, and murdering us the white world turned temporarily aside to kill each other, we of the Darker Peoples looked on in mild amaze," he wrote. The surprise was only "mild," as Black folk knew all too well the brutal nature of white supremacy. Though some may have been shocked by the "sudden descent of Europe into hell," most people of the African diaspora, Du Bois suspected, "looked on silently and sorrowfully, in sober thought, seeing sadly the prophecy of our own souls."[87]

He then posed a remarkable question: "How great a failure and a failure in what does the World War betoken?"[88] Not even a year had passed, and already he foresaw the war as a failure. Surely the war revealed the failure of white supremacy, the failure of European imperialism and the rivalries it fueled. But in the context of his work on the war and his personal place in it, Du Bois's question took on added poignancy. Given the virulent discrimination Black soldiers braved at home and abroad, the clear disregard of the Allies to support democracy and self-determination for peoples of African descent, and the cloudburst of racial violence that deluged the country throughout 1919, could the war, a war Du Bois supported heart and soul, presage his own failure as well? It was all too likely that his faith in democracy and the potential transformative power of war had been deeply misguided.

Du Bois's anger at this outcome tore through the pages of "The Souls of White Folk." "Conceive this nation, of all human peoples, engaged in a crusade to make the 'World Safe for Democracy'!" he roared, saying that in asserting itself as the guardian of international decency, the United States possessed no moral credibility: "In short, what is the black man but America's Belgium, and how could America condemn in Germany that which she commits, just as brutally, within her own borders?" "Instead of standing as a great example of the success of democracy and the possibility of human brotherhood," he wrote, "America has taken her place as an awful example of its pitfall and failures, so far as black and brown and yellow peoples are concerned." Restating his "African Roots of War" thesis in blunt terms, he declared, "Let me say this again and emphasize it and leave no room for mistaken meaning: The World War was primarily the jealous and avaricious struggle for the largest share in exploiting darker races." Du Bois offered little optimism. So long as Europe and America continued to hug the "delusion" of white supremacy as the basis for the continued "despising and robbing of darker peoples," he predicted, "then this is not the end of world war,—it is but the beginning!"[89]

Chapter 3 of *Darkwater*, "The Hands of Ethiopia," broadened his interpretation of the war to the whole of the African diaspora. The chapter, a revised version of "The African Roots of War," marked an addendum of sorts to his landmark 1915 *Atlantic Monthly* article and also built on his November 1918 "Memorandum on the Future of Africa."[90] Sounding more like Marcus Garvey, Du Bois warned, "If the attitude of the European and American worlds is in the future going to be based essentially upon the same policies as in the past, then there is but one thing for the trained man of darker blood to do and this is definitely and as openly as possible to organize his world for war against Europe." The best way to avoid this, he proposed, was the establishment of a "new African World State," composed of Germany's former colonies, which would "give Black Africa its physical beginnings." A governing body composed of "educated and trained men of Negro blood" would protect the rights of subjected Africans and function as an intermediary step toward independence. "Does this sound like an impossible dream?" Du Bois asked, not pausing to consider the flaws of his grandiose yet inherently paternalistic idea. Having lived through "the nightmare of 1914–1918," and having "seen the impossible happen and the unspeakable become so common as to cease to stir us," the once-fantastical idea of an "Africa for the Africans, guided by organized civilization" was indeed within the realm of possibility.[91]

Through a whipsaw of emotions, oscillating between hope and despair, *Darkwater* sustains one central theme: the meaning and future of democracy for Black folk in the postwar world. Du Bois engaged this question from multiple vantage points. In the chapter "Of Work and Wealth," focusing on East St. Louis, where "hell flamed" in July 1917, he explored the nexus between race and class in the failure to achieve industrial democracy. He addressed the right to vote in "Of the Ruling of Men," a crisis facing not only African Americans but the entire nation. "Democracy is a method of realizing the broadest measure of justice to all human beings," Du Bois believed, adding that "if America is ever to become a government built on the broadest justice to every citizen, then every citizen must be enfranchised." This included women. "The uplift of women is, next to the problem of the color line and the peace movement, our greatest modern cause," he asserted in "The Damnation of Women," a powerful articulation of his support for the Nineteenth Amendment as well as a moving ode to Black women and the unique struggles they faced. Du Bois believed that democracy, at its core, was a matter of individual opportunity and the right of every human being to achieve their full potential. "We know in America how to discourage, choke, and murder ability when it so far forgets itself as to choose a dark skin," he rued in "The Immortal Child." Without the nurturing of Black talent and a true belief in the value of education, America was lost, and democracy, Du Bois believed, would never "accomplish its greater ends."[92]

It all came back to the war. *Darkwater* represented a raw, unfiltered glimpse into Du Bois's state of mind in the wake of the global disaster and the domestic upheaval that followed it. One of the book's last chapters, "Of Beauty and Death," finds him searching for fragments of joy and life in the midst of the shattered ruins of a war-wrecked world—the tranquility of the Maine shoreline, the awe of the Grand Canyon, the wonder of Tim Brymn playing by the town pump in Maron, Lorraine. But he also reminded his readers about the trauma he and the race had just been through. "Most Americans have forgotten the extraordinary series of events which worked the feelings of black America to fever heat," he wrote just a year after the armistice. Much of this forgetting centered around the experiences of Black troops and their meaning. "The nation, also, forgot the deep resentment mixed with the pale ghost of fear which Negro soldiers call up in the breasts of the white South." He notably devoted a full paragraph to the "heroic figure" of Charles Young, his close friend, unjustly retired because of high blood pressure, a rationale that existed only "in the prejudiced heads of the Southern oligarchy who were determined that no American Negro should ever wear the stars of a General." Then there was East St. Louis, followed by Houston. So much death, and for what? Du Bois wondered. "This Death—is this Life? And is its beauty real or false?" Confronted with the senselessness of war and the arbitrary nature of death, including his own mortality, he searched for the meaning of a horrific immediate past and what the future could possibly hold for him and his people.[93]

Writing *Darkwater* proved therapeutic. It served as an opportunity to, at the very least, vent his frustrations and, at best, achieve greater clarity on the meaning of the war. With his next book in mind, Du Bois felt resolute that this defining moment in the history of the Black world needed to be written with even more analytical depth, interpretive vision, and moral urgency.

CHAPTER 7

". . . the madness was divine."[1]

IN JANUARY 1920, the inaugural issue of *The Brownies' Book* debuted to the public. Du Bois's idea for a periodical devoted to Black children reflected his long-standing belief that racial progress rested with the education of young people and their positive representation. He teamed with Augustus Dill, his *Crisis* business manager, and Jessie Fauset to support the bold venture. Promoted as a "monthly magazine for the children of the sun," *The Brownies' Book* sought to "teach Universal Love and Brotherhood for all little folk—black and brown and yellow and white."[2]

The landmark thirty-two-page first issue featured a potpourri of children-themed short stories, pictures, poems, and songs, along with letters from eager subscribers. In assembling the content, Du Bois had the World War and the symbolic potency of Black military service on his mind. Visually and textually, the magazine reminded readers of the significance of the war and at the same time promoted race pride by linking the heroism of African American troops with the youth destined to lead Black people into the future. A full-page picture displayed eight cadets from a Philadelphia Black Boy Scout troop, with one of the young men proudly carrying the American flag. Georgia Douglas Johnson, fast emerging as Black America's most well-known female poet, contributed a short verse titled "Recruit,"[3] celebrating African American soldiers as archetypes for a generation of New Negroes in the making:

Right shoulder arms, my laddie,
Step like your soldier-daddy,
The world is yours for taking,
Life, what you will, for making;
Dare boldly, be no slacker,
Black heroes are your backer,
And all your mother's dreaming
Awaits your full redeeming!
Right shoulder arms, my laddie,
Step like your soldier-daddy.[4]

A photo of a Black child, likely no more than three years old, accompanied the poem. Dressed in full military uniform—knee-high boots, belted jacket with brass buttons, overseas cap covering his head—the young recruit posed for the camera holding a swagger stick over his right shoulder, displaying a combination of youthful innocence and hopeful determination.[5]

Du Bois shared his own thoughts in a section of the magazine titled "As the Crow Flies." A minstrel representation of Black people in early-twentieth-century racist popular culture, the crow in Du Bois's artistic imagination became a symbol of beauty, power, and knowledge. "The Crow is black and O so beautiful, shining with dark blues and purples, with little hints of gold in his mighty wings," he wrote. Endowed with rare perspective, just like Black folk as a race—and Du Bois himself—and possessing the gift of second sight, the crow "flies far above the Earth, looking downward with his sharp eyes." The crow had important work to do. "What a lot of things he must see and hear and if he could only talk—and lo! The Brownies' Book has made him talk for you."

From his lofty vantage point Du Bois presented a remarkable sweep of global events from 1919. He began with the armistice and the triumphant image of "black troops nearing Metz, and the 367th colored regiment nearest the Rhine." Sensitive to his audience of young readers, he gently attempted to convey the impact of the war on both the world and the race. "Always after a great war there is much unrest, suffering, and poverty. This is because war kills human beings, leaves widows and orphans, destroys vast amounts of wealth, and disorganizes industry. The war of 1914–1918 was the greatest of human wars, and we hope the last." Du Bois wrote of the actions of the European imperial powers haggling over colonial territories coupled with political tumult from Ireland to Russia to India to Mexico.

His focus, however, remained on African Americans and the immediate history of the war. "Celebrations to welcome returning soldiers took place all over the United States," he recalled, highlighting the tremendous receptions given to the 369th and 370th Infantry Regiments in New York City and Chicago. He also emphasized that, in addition to these heroic Black soldiers, "one thousand colored officers took part in the war." Despite such moments of triumph, 1919 had been marked by great tragedy. "There have been many race riots and lynchings during the year," he noted with melancholy, listing Washington, Chicago, Omaha, Longview, Texas, and Phillips County, Arkansas, as the most horrific among a long list of horrors. Nineteen nineteen would ultimately be remembered as a year of turmoil, of unprecedented death, of the race grappling with the legacy of a war that elicited both pride and mourning. Du Bois fittingly ended "As the Crow Flies" by imploring his young readers to never forget "the thousand black boys dead for France."[6]

～

DU BOIS PLANNED, as he informed the NAACP board at the July 1919 monthly meeting, to "devote all my spare time during the next year to writing."[7] He now looked to make good on that vow. As 1920 began, he committed his energies to starting and, he hoped, finishing the highly anticipated study of African Americans in the World War.

In the October 1919 issue of *The Crisis*, he had provided a lengthy update on the project. "We are happy to announce that THE CRISIS' 'History of the Negro in the Revolution of 1914–1918' is progressing favorably," he informed readers, promising two volumes, the first a "popular narrative history, well illustrated," authored by himself and expected to arrive in the spring of 1920, followed by a second volume of "war documents," edited by Edward C. Williams, in 1921. However, in assessing his materials, he identified "some gaps which ought to be filled." He requested that readers send him information on the Black service battalions, along with any other material—personal narratives, regimental rosters, court-martial proceedings, citations and decorations for bravery, examples of relations with the French, photographs and scenes from life at the front—that would help make the history complete. "Material furnished will be returned when the lender so desires," he pledged, imagining the production of his war history as an urgent, collective endeavor. "Please act at once," he implored. "It is a patriotic service to the credit of our race."[8]

Black veterans and their families responded. Serving as Du Bois's proxy assistants, they continued to send him letters and materials between late 1919 and early 1920.[9] His archive grew almost daily. The flow of correspondence was not just one-way. He reached out directly to ex-servicemen as well, contacting them for information on specific individuals, events, and regiments.[10] For example, the lack of available records on the 369th Infantry, due to the fact that it fought with the French Army, frustrated him.[11] On December 27, 1919, he wrote to Obadiah Foster, a veteran of the 369th who had published a thirty-five-cent pamphlet account of his war service titled *The Modern Warfare and My Experience in France*, for documents on the famed "Hellfighters."[12] Foster obliged by putting Du Bois in touch with two Black sergeants from the regiment, confidently adding, "I am quite sure they can give you all the information you desire."[13]

Letters from family members of Black veterans reinforced the collective yet deeply personal significance of the war history. Hattie Lewis from Washington, DC, mailed Du Bois the official record of citation for her late husband, Kenneth Lewis, killed while serving with the 372nd Infantry Regiment in France. He'd received a posthumous Croix de Guerre with palm. "I am sending these documents hoping they may be of material benefit to the History," she wrote in her accompanying note. "After using kindly return same to me." What she entrusted to Du Bois held a truly priceless value.[14] Others sent their own documents, photographs, maps, and diaries, shouldering Du

Bois with the profound responsibility of safeguarding their materials and putting them to good use.[15]

While many Black veterans continued to support Du Bois, one very important former soldier grew increasingly restless. Months had passed since Adam Patterson last heard from his supposed coauthor about the status of their book. In late February 1920, he wrote to Du Bois, requesting an update on its publication prospects. "I have received many inquiries about it myself," Patterson gently stated, "but am in no position to give information." More personally important, he hoped for an explanation as to the nature of their deal and the credit he would receive for his already substantial contribution. "It was my intention to ask you some time ago just how my name would be connected with the authorship of this work," the major queried, careful not to press Du Bois too hard. He undoubtedly had boasted of his collaboration with the nation's preeminent Black scholar and spokesman for the race, and now, with no book in sight and his credibility on the line, he wished for Du Bois to clarify "how you had decided to indicate the fact in the publication." Patterson expressed his continued confidence in the profitability of their book, noting that despite the wave of other publications celebrating African Americans' role in the war, their contribution "will far surpass any that are on the market," especially Emmett Scott's much ballyhooed history.[16] However, Patterson also could not help but wonder if his grand plans with Du Bois would amount to anything.

Patterson received a bit of comfort in Du Bois's March 2 response to his note, with the doctor informing him that he was "now arranging the large amount of material which I have collected," including Patterson's potential chapters. Du Bois planned to "begin the actual writing of the history within a few days." He envisioned devoting two months of intense work to the book, finishing it "not later than May" and then having it "published in the summer or fall." He gave no clues as to just how he would achieve this ambitious goal. As for the matter of Patterson receiving proper credit for the disproportionate amount of work he had devoted to the project, Du Bois rather tersely wrote, "I am going to publish a list of the persons who have helped in the compiling of material and shall head this list with your name."[17] This was surely not what Patterson had in mind, as the enterprising Chicago race man assumed that his name would appear next to Du Bois's as an author, not as a mere contributor. Du Bois, however, possessed little desire to share the spotlight. The battles with Carter G. Woodson and Emmett Scott calcified his already formidable ego. This was his book, and while he had no problem giving credit to those who assisted him, the larger glory of its success would be his and his alone.

~

DU BOIS GOT TO WORK. After pushing Adam Patterson aside, he leaned more heavily on the expertise of the Howard University head librarian, Edward C. Williams. The preliminary research Williams conducted in the summer of 1919 did not bear much fruit, mostly due to Du Bois's hectic schedule, Williams's many responsibilities at Howard, and the unavailability of official records in the War Department. However, Williams did spend a few days in August examining and categorizing Du Bois's materials. After a "very hasty checking of the documents," he estimated that they had roughly 350 pages of "typewritten matter," more than enough to "have a volume of good size."[18]

Du Bois was also eager to catch up on his reading. In early January 1920, he asked Williams to supply him with a "small working bibliography" of books on the recently concluded war.[19] Some of the specific texts Du Bois mentioned focused on Germany, not surprising given his personal and intellectual attachment to the country. He had read the widely publicized *My Four Years in Germany* and *Face to Face with Kaiserism* by James Watson Gerard, the former United States ambassador to Germany, as well as the exiled German general Erich Ludendorff's memoir.[20] Du Bois appeared particularly interested in exploring the origins of the war, especially the intrigue between Germany and Russia, mentioning to Williams the names of a few authors who might offer some insight in this regard.[21] He notably listed Karl Kautsky, the pioneering Czech-Austrian theoretician whose landmark November 1914 article in the *International Socialist Review*, "Imperialism and the War," likely influenced Du Bois's thinking for his own equally prescient essay "The African Roots of War" in 1915.[22]

In requesting a working bibliography of books from Edward Williams and considering the writings of such individuals as Karl Kautsky, Du Bois attempted to construct a tentative scholarly foundation for his study of the Black experience in the war. He faced a serious obstacle in writing about a subject matter without the benefit of historical distance and analytical perspective. Historians on both sides of the Atlantic had already begun to try to make sense of the war, its causes and its ultimate lessons. However, they also formed part of the history they attempted to write, having in many cases actively promoted the war effort, blurring the lines between scholarship, activism, and propaganda in the process.[23] Du Bois now found himself squarely confronted with this very problem.

When he looked over the list of "a few general works on the Great War" provided by the Howard librarian, he surely realized that white "historians" would offer him little assistance.[24] Williams's recommendations included an assortment of serialized accounts of the fighting and popular histories of the war published between 1915 and early 1920, ranging from *Harper's Pictorial Library of the World War*, edited by Du Bois's Harvard mentor Albert Bushnell Hart, to a multivolume account of the British campaign in France written by Arthur Conan Doyle, creator of Sherlock Holmes.[25] These early works all uncritically triumphed the Allied cause and reached the same conclusion—that Germany held sole responsibility for the start of the war. They also almost completely omitted any mention of African and African American soldiers. Volume 10 of *Harper's Pictorial Library of the World War* included a lengthy profile of the 369th Infantry Regiment's white colonel, William Hayward, but only a mere anecdote on the Black soldiers he commanded.[26] In another book on the American army, authored by two French officers attached to Pershing's staff, the Ninety-Second and Ninety-Third Divisions received just a single footnote.[27] Du Bois would not have found the erasure of Black soldiers from this early historiography surprising. It simply reaffirmed the necessity of his own book.

The handful of works devoted to the history of African American troops in the war that Williams listed did nothing to shake Du Bois's confidence about his own unique contribution. He had already dismissed the hastily produced works of William Allison Sweeny, Kelly Miller, and his nemesis Emmett J. Scott as lacking academic legitimacy, representing nothing more than self-serving attempts to capitalize on Black public interest for books on the war. Some additional publications Williams brought to Du Bois's attention spoke to the paucity of credible studies of the Black experience in the conflict. A short pamphlet produced by the Hampton Institute on African Americans and Native Americans in the war and a pictorial review of Black soldiers compiled by the University of West Tennessee president Miles Vandahurst Lynk were of minimal use for Du Bois.[28] A book titled *The Complete History of the Colored Soldiers in the War*, coauthored by five Black soldiers of the Ninety-Second and Ninety-Third Divisions, had more potential. The veterans touted their collaboration as "a true history of what our boys have done right from we men who went through every part of the war."[29] This was one of a small number of books written by African American veterans who were determined to preserve their memories in print.[30] However, as far as Du Bois was concerned, the history of Black folk in the war remained incomplete and was left for him to write.

But before he could even begin to put pen to paper, he needed to organize his research. Since returning from France in the spring of 1919 with a chest of official documents and ephemera, he had amassed a remarkable personal archive. The steady stream of letters, personal testimonials, photographs, diaries, official memorandums, and regimental directives that flowed into his office provided the edifice of a potentially landmark work of social, military, and political history. Arranging and classifying his material brought out the social scientist in Du Bois.[31] While he embraced the necessity of moral advocacy in his writing, he never abandoned his Harvard and University of Berlin training when it came to the importance of collecting the necessary body of factual evidence to support his historical interpretations. The sheer volume of source material he accumulated for the war history spoke to his rigorous methodological standards as well as his high ambitions for the project itself.

Diligently laboring in his *Crisis* office, he identified a number of key subjects and themes to focus his thoughts. Whereas other books offered valorized, uncritical accounts of the Black war experience, Du Bois's work would not sugarcoat. He crafted a detailed handwritten index of his documents that included topics such as "conditions among draftees and enlisted men," "unfair restrictions placed on colored soldiers," "conduct and morale of colored troops," and the Ninety-Second Division's commanding officers Charles Ballou and Allen Greer. He also clearly intended to highlight the particularly egregious treatment of African American officers, as indicated by subject headings on "Special discrimination and indignities to colored officers" and "Charles Young."[32] Again he relied on Edward Williams for assistance, sending him around the first of the year a package of research materials to classify.[33]

As Du Bois's organization progressed, he became even more specific and increasingly meticulous, spending hours filling out dozens of small, paper-thin index cards with handwritten notes and information about his vast array of documents.[34] He sorted through piles of newspaper and journal articles, his own magazine *The Crisis* serving as an invaluable resource.[35] Then, with Madeline Allison's secretarial assistance, he organized his materials thematically and topically. Finally, he began sketching out chapter subjects. The process likely consumed several weeks of early 1920.

A significant bulk of his research focused on the Ninety-Second Division, the "storm center," in his words, of controversy regarding the battlefield contributions of Black troops to the American war effort.[36] And that is where he started writing. He envisioned three chapters on their tumultuous experience that would constitute the heart of the book. Completing these chapters would be a tall task, due in part to the overwhelming amount of research material he had collected related to the Ninety-Second. However, in his June 1919 tour de force "An Essay Toward a History of the Black Man in the Great War," he offered a broad-strokes outline of the potential structure, as well as the kernel of his argument.

He devoted a single chapter to the origins and development of the division. "The history of the Ninety-Second Division is a history of racial discrimination," he bluntly asserted in an early draft, believing that it was necessary first and foremost to understand the context surrounding the division's creation and organization before delving into its actual service and performance in France. "Try as the historian may to tell a bare and colorless outline of its activities," he wrote, "the facts are utterly inexplicable unless we bring in the continual strife inside of the organization, first to keep the Division from being a fighting unit; secondly to get rid of the Negro officers; thirdly to discredit those that could not be gotten rid of." He saw the attacks on the Ninety-Second, and its Black officers in particular, as a fait accompli, with the attempted ruin of the division effectively determined by the "white Negro-hating oligarchy" within the army and the War Department before the Fort Des Moines training camp even came to a close.[37]

After laying out the general context of controversy and racial discord surrounding the Ninety-Second Division, he began preparing a chapter that looked specifically at its various regiments and individual units. This meant assembling his copious documents and translating them into some sort of narrative form. His early drafts, lacking much literary beauty, revealed the challenge of making his collection of dry military documents come to life. But he nevertheless dedicated himself to the task, writing, arranging, and cutting and pasting at a brisk pace, even pushing past his usual bedtime of 10:00 p.m. He began a section on the history of the 365th Infantry Regiment at midnight on April 2, 1920.[38]

Du Bois continued to reach out to veterans of the Ninety-Second Division for additional facts and information, including one James William Johnson. Not to be confused with Du Bois's NAACP colleague with the similar name, this James Johnson was a Harlem attorney and former sergeant who'd fought with the 349th Field Artillery Regiment in the Ninety-Second Division during the war. In April 1919, just as Du Bois began work on the war history book, Johnson mailed him a copy of *Modern Artilleryman*, a thirty-eight-page pamphlet he and other veterans of his unit had published, chronicling their history.[39] Johnson also promised to provide Du Bois with additional "maps, orders and data."[40] On July 24, Du Bois sent Johnson a gentle reminder that he still hoped to receive these materials. Johnson obliged the following month, sending under separate cover his personal collection of documents and expressing his willingness to give Du Bois additional information related to "the manner in which the white officers executed their duties while serving at the front with our division."[41]

Du Bois decided to devote an entire chapter to the controversial 368th Infantry Regiment, its Black officers, and the travesty of their Meuse-Argonne experience. But he held off on writing it. In order to set the record straight and vindicate their legacy, his facts had to be overwhelming and his argument unimpeachable. He therefore continued to reach out to veterans of the regiment for more documents and personal details about what they witnessed. In early January, Leroy Godman sent him copies of the official findings related to the courts-martial of the regiment's Black officers. Du Bois promised to return them the next month, with Godman responding, "You may hold them as long as necessary."[42]

On March 31, Du Bois wrote to Edward Banks, who'd served under one of the Black officers accused of cowardice, to ascertain his version of events, adding, "I want this for the history and will either quote you or not as you desire."[43] In May 1919, Wellington Willard, a former sergeant in the 368th, had sent Du Bois an eye-opening letter about his commanding white officers, which Du Bois subsequently incorporated into "An Essay Toward a History of the Black Man in the World War." Du Bois and Willard corresponded again in July and August 1920, with Du Bois asking for specific information, down to the precise day and hour, regarding the actions of certain white officers in the Meuse-Argonne. Willard, while requesting anonymity, gladly obliged.[44]

As Du Bois immersed himself in research and writing, he faced two difficult yet unavoidable questions: Why did the vast majority of

African Americans support the war, and was their support justified? Du Bois knew that readers would expect and even demand answers. After all, he'd led the charge for African Americans to throw body and soul into the war effort. With "Close Ranks," he wagered both his racial and political credibility and, in the end, nearly ruined his luminous career.[45] Now, as he sat at the large wooden desk in his bookcase-lined *Crisis* office, he tried to make both historical and personal sense of what the war meant.

He confronted this formidable task in a proposed chapter appropriately titled "The Challenge." "One can only realize the attitude of colored Americans toward the war by considering just what their legal and social situation was in the United States and just what happened between 1914 and 1918," Du Bois began. He devoted the first pages to a succinct historical review of the nationwide effort to "fix the Negro first as a peon and later as a non-voting social caste" since the demise of Reconstruction, which included sharecropping, convict leasing, disfranchisement, segregation, and lynching terrorism. No wonder then, he wrote, that "the outbreak of the world war did not attract particular attention in Negro America. Their own war was too tremendous." The challenges facing the race continued as the war began in August 1914. Du Bois noted the significance of the mass migration of upward of half a million African Americans from the South to cities in the Northeast and Midwest. At the same time, Jim Crow segregation and public spectacles of mob violence remained unrelenting: "This then was the situation on the threshold of the year in which the United States entered the war."

Carrying the full weight of their second-class citizenship, African Americans now faced the agonizing predicament of their role in the American war effort and how—if at all—they should support their country. Du Bois highlighted the fight over the Des Moines officers' training camp, the mutiny of Black soldiers in Houston, the pervasive discrimination in the draft, and the tragedy of Charles Young's forced retirement. "Evidently all these things put a severe strain upon the Negro," he wrote, admitting that the "natural reaction" of most Black people to the United States entering the war "was that of indifference and even opposition." Why should the Negro fight for America, he rhetorically asked, "when he was not only not wanted in the army on terms of equality with other Americans," but as the violence of East St. Louis and countless other incidents demonstrated, "was not even treated as a human being."

He struggled to find a clear answer. Black people had every reason to be disloyal. If presented with the hypothetical opportunity of joining an invading German force, he conjectured, "thousands, perhaps hundreds of thousands of Negroes would have been ready for revolt." But "wiser counsel"—meaning himself—knew that the race had no "opportunity for moral hesitation." African Americans, he argued, "were compelled to go into the war without condition on the side of the Allies, first, because they had to insist on making their inclusion in the draft a test on their citizenship; secondly, because they had to insist on Negro officers for Negro troops and thirdly, they had to resist the attacks of the southern whites who anticipated the revolt of radical Negroes." As Du Bois framed it, the decision to support the war, by no means an easy one, ultimately came down to a combination of idealism, opportunity, and common sense. By disproving racist skeptics who doubted their loyalty and faithfully joining the war effort as both civilians and soldiers, African Americans had the rare chance to stake claim to their citizenship and assert their place in the nation's democracy.

As the chapter proceeded, Du Bois confronted his own place vis-à-vis the war. The ghost of "Close Ranks" haunted his writing, leading him to yet again explain and justify his controversial actions. He asserted that the Negro, despite professing loyalty to the nation, did indeed "stress, on entering the war, his own grievances against America . . ." And he conveniently upheld his own efforts and those of the NAACP as evidence, highlighting the June 1918 conference of African American newspaper editors, the NAACP's anti-lynching campaign, and his writings in *The Crisis*. He singled out Joel Spingarn, who in his work with the War Department and the Military Intelligence Branch had helped facilitate the editors' conference and pry a statement from an apprehensive Woodrow Wilson denouncing lynching.

Du Bois, with guarded introspection, then turned to his own personal controversy related to Spingarn, the MIB, and "Close Ranks." "The editor of The CRISIS was asked to be a member of this bureau with the rank of captain," he added almost casually, portraying himself as a passive participant in the affair and saying nothing of the notorious July 1918 editorial that, not coincidentally, accompanied his efforts to secure the commission. He intended to insert the full June 24, 1918, memo he'd written to MIB chief Marlborough Churchill explaining his fitness for the position.[46] With the pain of being labeled a traitor to the race continuing to sting, the document, Du Bois believed, would demonstrate his political consistency and reasonable logic for deciding to work for the government.

He concluded the chapter with a moving yet tortuously ambivalent defense of his support for the war:

It will thus be seen how difficult a period the Negro passed through. For a moment—and it was but a moment, it passed, but for a moment the country seemed to rise to its mightiest stature. I saw it and saw it with streaming eyes. I have been called bitter. I am bitter but here I saw all the hurts, the tears, the pain as in one country and that country was mine. The moment passed and is gone, but thank God that it came once. The war that brought slavery to most men (and indeed in the end to us) thus brought to some of us at a time new vision of freedom. We were at least free from our bonds. The inhibitions fell away. We could think with the nation and not as a mere group. We could rise to mighty selfishness. The nation, our country, the allies as champions of the little hurt folk, democracy. We were mad with the new vision. We did not examine the ideal too narrowly. Even if it was false it was good to rise from murky, long, sheathing waters and breathe air and see through lifting mist "the stars, the old and everlasting stars." How simple the problem was after all with the main trend right? With the great ideal set, what mattered the exceptions, the little evil facts? The edges of our inner dark world slipped and sought to coalesce with the surrounding half known larger

world. Great movements were our movements. Great joys and
sorrows ours. We had no longer the problem to resist thought
and scowl as they smile and laugh as they cried. We were mad—
that is the only word for it, we were mad and let it not excuse
us to say that the madness was divine. It was insanity just the
same. The primal beast was out to kill with prongs. How in the
end did all this set with our inner problem? After all it was not a
mere bargain—it was a moving wish.[47]

Du Bois's anguished prose invoked his famous exploration of
Black identity in *The Souls of Black Folk*—the challenge, as the chapter title aptly captured, of being both a Negro and an American. Du
Bois deeply believed that these two "warring ideals" could be reconciled through the hyper-nationalism and blood sacrifice of war itself.
He'd been enraptured by the possibility that Black people would no
longer be pitilessly confined as a "mere group" to their "inner dark
world" behind the veil, but allowed to join with their fellow Americans and other citizens of the world in a great crusade for democracy.
Perhaps he had been wrong. Perhaps it was insane for him to expect
that African Americans would be embraced as equal citizens after
demonstrating their loyalty and risking their lives during the war.
But he would not apologize. He would not admit guilt. In this early
draft of the manuscript, he prepared to plead temporary insanity. War
had brought out the worst in him, the nation, and the entire world.
Nevertheless, if the goal of Black people becoming full Americans was
madness, Du Bois embraced it. He could conceive of no other choice.

~

THE NAACP'S ANNUAL MEETING, taking place in Atlanta from
May 30 to June 3, 1920, offered Du Bois a pleasant interruption from
work on the war history. This was the first time the NAACP had held
the conference in a Southern city, reflecting the association's growth
beyond the urban North and Midwest and recognizing that, despite
the ongoing Great Migration, most Black people and the problems
they faced continued to reside below the Mason-Dixon line.[48] The

gathering was especially meaningful for Du Bois, as the city held a piece of his heart. He could reflect fondly on his years at Atlanta University, where he established himself as Black America's foremost scholar. But sorrowful moments, such as the lynching of Sam Hose, the 1906 Atlanta Riot, and, above all, the loss of his son, Burghardt, remained raw.

Any bittersweet emotions were swept away when, on Tuesday, June 1, his NAACP peers honored him with the prestigious Spingarn Medal "for the most distinguished service rendered to the colored race during the year 1919 by a colored American."[49]

The award ceremony on the Atlanta University campus was a perfect scene. A crowd of NAACP dignitaries, under a cloudless sky, music playing in the background, assembled in front of Stone Hall, the redbrick ivy-covered building that represented the university's commitment to academic excellence and African American progress. Du Bois basked in tributes from Mary White Ovington; Dr. Myron Winslow Adams, the acting president of Atlanta University; and, especially meaningful, John Hope, the man who vied with Charles Young as Du Bois's most significant Black friend. When, standing proudly, hands humbly clasped in front of him, he received the bronze medal from the chairman of the selection committee, Bishop John Hurst Adams, all must have seemed right for the moment—his internal battles with the NAACP put on hold, the disrespect of Emmett Scott upstaging him at the previous year's conference forgotten, the damage of "Close Ranks" a thing of the past.[50]

In awarding the Spingarn Medal to Du Bois, the NAACP certainly recognized his heroic service to the organization and the larger cause of Black civil rights. However, the committee specifically pointed to his accomplishment in convening the 1919 Pan-African Congress in France as the reason for the honor. Considering his heated battles with some board members over support for the international gathering, Du Bois had to feel a sense of vindication. His commitment to the Pan-African cause remained strong following his return from France and throughout the early months of 1920. His desire to build a self-sustaining Pan-African movement also went hand in hand with his labors to complete the history of Black people in the World War.

Du Bois always adopted a global approach to the study and writing of history.[51] His pathbreaking 1915 book, *The Negro*, a wide-ranging survey of African history and the legacies of the transatlantic slave trade, demonstrated how a consciousness of the diaspora animated his scholarly and political thought near the start of the war. "What is to be the future relation of the Negro race to the rest of the world?" he asked in the book's final chapter on "The Negro Problem."[52] Starting with his landmark 1915 *Atlantic Monthly* article, he viewed the World War as a watershed moment in the fate of Africa and, as the fighting progressed, the struggle for freedom and democracy for all peoples of African descent. This included African Americans, whose experiences in the war, embodied by the service of Black soldiers in France, expanded their vision of the world and their place in it.[53]

During his busy writing year of 1920, Du Bois drafted a proposed chapter titled "The World of Black Folk." "Is there a black world?" he rhetorically asked in the opening sentence. Black folk existed in nearly every corner of the globe and made up what he would "roughly classify as the Black race." "But do they today form a world—a conscious social organism, aware of itself and its parts?"

"Yes," he responded. "There is today a Black world." Brought together through labor and combat and facilitated by developments in transportation and global communication, people of African descent from throughout the diaspora converged in the upheaval of war to forge physical connections that had previously not been possible. But in thinking about the Black world, Du Bois went beyond just geography and interpersonal contact. "The growth of the black world has been spiritual rather than physical," he mused. His search for a Black world depended on a collective consciousness among those disparate, displaced, and dispossessed peoples who by historical experience and modern struggle made up the African diaspora.[54] In promoting the spiritual regeneration of Africa and its dispersed peoples, Du Bois saw himself as the Black world's principal evangelist.

He sketched a conceptual map of the postwar African diaspora that exposed his elitism and nationalistic bias. Although Africa represented the physical center of the Black world, its spiritual center,

Du Bois argued, "at present" lay in the United States. "That the re-birth of Africa in modern days should start in America was natural . . . America has meant emancipation of the spirit and energies of mankind in the last two centuries and this uplift could not be kept even from slaves." While the author of *Darkwater* could excoriate America for its hypocrisy, he refused to completely abandon its democratic ideals and potential.

As a product of his times, he also espoused a Pan-African vision firmly rooted in civilizationist thinking.[55] In language that would have made many of the apologists for European imperialism nod in satisfaction, Du Bois wrote, "Western slavery gave the Negro a world language and religion and modern methods of industry" so that by 1920 the eleven million displaced people of African descent in the United States were as "intelligent as the peasantry of southern Europe and with emerging classes and individuals who speak and think with the best of the modern world." African Americans, through the fires of slavery and Jim Crow, nevertheless emerged as an advanced, intel-lectually developed people.

Du Bois's rendering of the postwar Black world was at the same time profoundly hierarchical. He effectively ranked various peoples of African descent throughout the diaspora based on their rate of mod-ern evolution and their readiness for leadership in the arena of global affairs. Below African Americans on the rung of diasporic civilization stood West Indians, "who both excel and lay behind their American brothers." Observing that "the black West Indies have been in ferment since the war," leading to a breakdown in class and color divisions, Du Bois predicted that the region would take its place "among the most active of the spiritual centers of the black world." Conversely, Black folk in Central and South America, who identified along narrow national lines, belonged in his view "least consciously to the Black World."

Moving beyond the Western Hemisphere, he turned his atten-tion to Africa, a "vast and infinitely diversified continent" made up of "some 150,000,000 or more persons of Negro descent in all stages of development and degradation." The state of Africa and its future re-mained contingent on the benevolence of the European colonial powers and the ability of the most privileged Africans to take advantage of Western education and tutelage, either on the continent or in the colonial metropoles. At the top of Du Bois's list stood France's colonies, in his words, "the destined center of the first renaissance of Africa." He singled out the French Senegalese of the four communes of Gorée, Dakar, Rufisque, and Saint-Louis, where such men as his Pan-African compatriot Blaise Diagne formed "one of the most powerful group of modern Negroes" emerging from the war. In the British colonies, with the exception of the educated elite in Nigeria and Sierra Leone, "there has arisen little or no group consciousness or sense of kinship with the black world," Du Bois surmised. Even worse was the Belgian Congo, which remained in "spiritual darkness." As for those nations outside the grasp of European colonialism, Ethiopia held the most promise while Liberia could potentially become one of "the great centers of the future Negro world" if it achieved some semblance of economic independence, ideally in partnership with African Americans. Du Bois saw the "vast new economic battle" for self-determination as the principal challenge for "this disintegrated and inchoate black world," a diaspora in search of racial "spiritual unity" and material investment.[56]

His civilizationist framing of the war in relation to the African diaspora carried over into another chapter he began drafting, on the experiences of African colonial troops in the French Army, titled "Black France." He remained enamored of France and its image of racial egalitarianism. Evocative memories of his glorious time in France after the armistice, when he viewed with misty eyes the state-sponsored fetes of North and West African troops, the Senegalese deputy Blaise Diagne wielding influence, the praise showered by the French on African American soldiers, and the absence of the color line, continued to fire his imagination. They also blurred his historical vision.

Du Bois's main interest lay in the history of France's African colonial troops, particularly those from West Africa. Acknowledging that the sizable contingents of Algerian and Moroccan troops raised by France from the earliest days of colonial conquest and through the World War contained "many persons of Negro descent," he saw West

Africans as unquestionably Black, and thus central to his argument of France's racial enlightenment and successful implementation of the *mission civilisatrice*. Working from this premise, Du Bois's focus on the actions and reminiscences of French officers, such as Charles Mangin, the principal architect of the West African *force noire*, was not surprising. The most readily available documents at his disposal consisted of articles from French newspapers and journals such as *La Revue de Paris, Le Petit Journal, Revue des Deux Mondes,* and *La Dépêche Coloniale Illustrée.* All organs of colonial propaganda, they offered paeans to the blind loyalty of the Senegalese and their effective use as an expendable reservoir of manpower in defense of the motherland. Du Bois highlighted any and all mentions of the bravery of the Senegalese and their courage under fire without qualification or any deeper examination of what purpose these stories may have served.[57]

He got the most use out of a book by Alphonse Séché titled *Les Noirs.* A well-known Parisian journalist, poet, and playwright, Séché commanded a regiment of Senegalese soldiers during the war. His 1919 book, a combination of memoir, history, and propaganda, spoke to the heightened place of West African soldiers in the postwar French colonial and racial imagination. The preface, penned by none other than Séché's close friend Charles Mangin, set the tone of the book. Mangin lauded Séché for allowing readers to understand the true nature of the Senegalese *tirailleur,* "his absolute devotion to his leader, his indomitable courage, and his grateful love for the country which has delivered him from slavery and has given him the peace of France." France's "tropical domain" provided 275,000 soldiers during the war—135,000 "from Darkest Africa" who gladly paid the *impôt du sang* (blood tax) owed to France for lifting them out of savagery and into the light of French civilization.[58]

Edward Williams, applying his mastery of French, provided Du Bois with translations. Williams highlighted, with Du Bois's approval, sections that emphasized the unyielding courage of the *tirailleurs sénégalais.* Du Bois found a passage from chapter 3 of Séché's book, "L'ame des Sénégalais" ("The Soul of the Senegalese") potentially valuable:

In all the acts of the blacks, one finds this mixture of childishness and heroism, so much so that one is tempted to believe that their courage is an effect of the simplicity of their nature. Not at all. The Senegalese is brave by nature; a primitive being, he does not analyze. One gives him an order, and he obeys it, without any thought of that which may happen to him.[59]

Séché's infatuation with the sense of duty—*y a service*—that intrinsically motivated the Senegalese to abandon any concern for their own lives and bodily safety when it came to combat seemed to appeal to Du Bois. In another quote that Williams translated, Séché opined, "for it is not reflection, not conscience, it is impulse, obstinacy, instinct. It is also a total absence of fear, and absolute scorn of death, dependent no doubt as much on the Senegalese's lack of 'nerves' as upon his beliefs." The image of the loyal, grinning, happy-go-lucky Senegalese *tirailleur* became a popular minstrel-like cultural trope during the war and in postwar France that writers like Séché actively cultivated.[60] Du Bois, resentful of the disdain exhibited toward Black soldiers by white Americans both within and outside the military, chose to overlook the racism embedded in such stories and imagery and instead view France's use of African colonial troops as triumphant.[61] "From the successful experiment it remains to draw this practical conclusion," he determined: "The war has revealed a new factor of French power, the Black Army, whose general valor, as much European as Colonial, tested now, can no longer be doubted."[62]

Du Bois's work on the "Black France" chapter not coincidentally occurred at the very moment he began to contemplate the future of his burgeoning Pan-African movement and what it would potentially mean for the completion of his book. His self-imposed end-of-the-summer goal for publishing the study, like every other deadline before it, came and went. However, he could at least honestly claim tangible progress. He had organized his research materials. Key themes and arguments had been fleshed out. Several chapters had been drafted, with others beginning to materialize. Areas for additional research had been identified. He still did not know for certain what the book would look like, but an actual manuscript was taking shape, and he could envision a path forward.

Now he faced a dilemma: whether to push ahead and complete the book or instead devote his energies to convening a second Pan-African Congress in 1921. The decision really lay with him, but he nevertheless threw the question into the laps of the NAACP board of directors. In an October 27, 1920, memo to his colleagues, he wrote, "Two years ago the Board entrusted me with two tasks outside my regular duties," referring to the Pan-African Congress and the writing of the history of the war. He knew that he needed to explain why the book, which he had repeatedly promised was forthcoming, remained nowhere in sight. "I started this work with the understanding that it was to be financed by the general fund of the N.A.A.C.P.," he asserted. Instead, with no support forthcoming after his return from France, he felt "compelled either to give up the work or collect outside funds or use The CRISIS funds," which he did in retaining the summer help of Edward Williams.

Having, as Du Bois tried to spin matters, failed to support him in the war history, the board now had to decide if a second Pan-African Congress planned for the fall of 1921 would take place. "The time is propitious," he argued. "The Negroes of the world are aroused and thinking and acting as never before." A minimum commitment of $2,000 by the NAACP would be necessary for the gathering to happen. If the board chose otherwise, he saw no other alternative than for him to "resign as Secretary of the Congress, unless, of course, some other agency steps in to help."[63]

While Du Bois's mind clearly gravitated toward the Pan-African Congress as the logical endeavor to pursue, the book pulled at his heart. He had devoted tremendous time, as well as intellectual and emotional energy, to the war history, and he unquestionably felt a sense of obligation to those Black veterans who had invested their personal and collective memories in him and in the project. But he also realized—especially as he took full stock of his research materials and made significant writing progress over the spring and summer months of 1920—the overwhelming scope and breadth of the book he'd envisioned. While organizing the Pan-African Congress required time, energy, and planning, completing the book required deep thinking, historical reckoning, and intellectual courage. By framing his quandary of whether to organize the Pan-African Congress or continue with the war history as an either-or question, he created a false choice and, in doing so, offered a glimpse of his uncertainty and self-doubt when it came to the subject of the World War.

Du Bois reached out to trusted friends and colleagues for guidance and encouragement. The Reverend Garnett Waller, a Niagara Movement cofounder, writing from his home in Springfield, Massachusetts, believed that "the completion of the History and the permanent organization of The Pan-African Congress, are of paramount importance to our propaganda and ought to be completed."[64] Harry Pace, one of Du Bois's most loyal students from Atlanta University, who in 1905 had teamed with his former professor to launch the short-lived periodical *The Moon Illustrated Weekly*, offered similar counsel.[65] Pace believed that the NAACP, out of a sense of "moral obligation," should find a way to fund both endeavors.[66]

E. Burton Ceruti gave Du Bois the most advice to ponder. Ceruti, a prominent Los Angeles attorney whose friendship with Du Bois led him to help establish the city's NAACP branch in 1913, likewise believed that Du Bois need not choose between the Pan-African Congress and the book. But he also recognized that "'The History of the Negro Troops in the War' seems to be the work and the duty lying nearest at hand." Ceruti saw the benefits of the war history as "definite, certain and sure," adding, "the public, of which I am a part, has been led to expect and are now looking forward to its publication. We will all be disappointed if it should fail." Ceruti perceptively recognized that the problem regarding the book's completion went beyond mere monetary support, as Du Bois had suggested. He believed that the NAACP board, if given the opportunity to publish the book, would "readily assume the necessary obligations," and if for some reason that failed to materialize, Du Bois could "quickly and easily take a sufficient number of advance subscriptions to the work to meet necessary expense of preparation." Summarizing his thoughts, Ceruti wrote,

"Let me say that I believe both projects should be carried out. But if either must be abandoned, let it not be the History."[67]

Du Bois agreed. While remaining committed to the book, he forged ahead with plans for the second Pan-African Congress. Throughout the early months of 1921 and into the summer, he threw himself into organizing the gathering, waging a successful internal lobbying campaign among NAACP board members to secure financial support for the conference and again partnering with Blaise Diagne. An official announcement appeared in March 1921, and Du Bois promoted the congress in the pages of *The Crisis* throughout the spring and summer.[68]

Although logistical matters for the Pan-African Congress proved consuming, he did manage to find some spare moments to work on the book. He began writing a chapter on African Americans and the draft in April 1921, largely based on the official 1919 and 1920 published reports of the provost marshal general on the Selective Service System.[69] Progress, however, was incremental.

In lieu of additional written pages, Du Bois contemplated a possible new title. The name of his project remained in constant flux, but in his notes from late 1920 or early 1921 he changed the name from "The Black Man in the Revolution of 1914–1918" to "The Black Man in the War of the World."[70] This shift was revealing. The war remained a masculine affair, as Du Bois continued to narrowly focus on the experiences of Black soldiers and their manhood. The appearance of "War of the World" in the title, however, spoke to a broadened global conception of the role African Americans and other peoples of African descent played in the conflict. The choice to include this descriptive phrase at the expense of "the Revolution of 1914–1918" also held significance. With more than two years of hindsight, viewing the war as a revolutionary event that Black people benefited from became increasingly difficult for Du Bois. He started the book by imagining the World War as a transformative moment in global democracy. Chastened by the harsh truth of the immediate postwar years and increasingly burdened by the weight of history, he could now, in 1921, make no such claim.

Events in Tulsa, Oklahoma, offered yet more gut-wrenching evidence of the war's failed revolutionary potential. On Memorial Day, Monday, May 30, a nineteen-year-old shoeshiner, Dick Rowland, stepped into the elevator of the Drexel Building in downtown Tulsa to use the top-floor restroom. He inadvertently bumped into Sarah Page, a seventeen-year-old white woman who was operating the elevator. Page screamed. Rowland fled. An eyewitness claimed that Page had been assaulted and narrowly escaped being raped. The next morning, May 31, police arrested Rowland, who adamantly declared his innocence. By that afternoon, local newspapers announced preparations for a lynching.

Around 7:00 p.m. a mob of several hundred vengeance-seeking white residents descended on the county courthouse. Determined to prevent the lynching, an armed group of sixty Black Tulsans, composed mostly of war veterans, approached the courthouse as well, offering their support to the sheriff. A standoff ensured. The white mob soon swelled to nearly two thousand. By 10:00 p.m., more Black veterans arrived. Inevitably, a shot rang out. Gunfire exploded, and soon mayhem swept through the city. Beginning in the early-morning hours of June 1 and continuing throughout the day, white mobs obliterated Black Tulsa and thirty-five square blocks of the prosperous Greenwood District. Private airplanes dropped firebombs from above. Buck Franklin, a local attorney and the father of a future Harvard history doctorate recipient and Du Bois disciple, John Hope Franklin, described in vivid detail "the great holocaust" ten years later: "Lurid flames roared and belched and licked their forked tongues into the air. Smoke ascended the sky in thick, black volumes and amid it all, the planes—now a dozen or more in number—still hummed and darted here and there with the agility of natural birds of the air."[71] White mobs, aided by local police and National Guardsmen, killed heavily outnumbered Black people at will. The death toll, officially put at thirty-six, more likely ran as high as three hundred. Stories circulated of Black bodies being thrown into mass graves.[72]

Tulsa surpassed even East St. Louis in horror. The NAACP immediately set up a relief fund and dispatched Walter White from the national office to investigate. A ghastly full-page photo appeared in the July issue of *The Crisis* showing the smoldering ruins of Greenwood that one could have easily mistaken for an artillery-shelled French town in the war.[73] Du Bois, neck-deep in Pan-African Congress preparations and on his way to France, said nothing publicly about the Tulsa pogrom.

The Pan-African Congress offered a welcome respite from the tragedy of American race relations, as well as the intellectual and moral challenges of producing the war history book. "This month, streaming from the ends of Earth, Pan-Africa's children meet in London, Brussels and Paris," Du Bois romantically declared in the August 1921 issue of *The Crisis*. "It will not be a river of tumultuous waters, but rills of single hearts and thoughts forecasting mighty futures. Always Africa was. Always Africa will be. There has never been a world without its black and brown men and there never will be."[74]

An African American veteran, Rayford Logan, proved instrumental in laying the groundwork for the congress to take place. A graduate of Amherst College, Logan served in France with the 372nd Infantry Regiment of the Ninety-Third Division. The combined traumas of combat and racism had pushed him to the brink of homicidal fury. "My experience in the army left me so bitter against white Americans that I remained an expatriate in Europe," Logan later recalled. After receiving an official discharge in France, he made a precarious living as a currency speculator before settling in Paris. He kept in contact with his former high school teacher, the *Crisis* literary editor Jessie Fauset, who enlisted his services and fluency in French to assist with planning for the Pan-African Congress. Logan greeted Du Bois when the doctor arrived in Paris on August 16, 1921. He also skillfully mediated conversations between Du Bois and Blaise Diagne that resulted in a delicately crafted agreement about the congress's principal objectives.[75]

Du Bois, as usual, traveled unaccompanied by Nina. Earlier in the year, on May 12, the couple marked their twenty-fifth wedding anniversary. But by this time the marriage had become one of mutual obligations—Du Bois as responsible patriarch, Nina as dutiful wife—

and devoid of emotional fulfillment. As Du Bois's fame and stature grew, Nina gradually receded, choosing to stay out of the limelight and devote her energies to caring for Yolande, who was also bearing the scars of her father's neglect. Du Bois increasingly sought intellectual stimulation, as well as physical intimacy, in the company of other women. In the couple's correspondence, usually about mundane household matters or the latest set of challenges concerning Yolande, Nina still referred to him as her "dear Will." But they lived in separate worlds, Nina tethered to their unexciting home and Du Bois fully immersed in the exhilarating cause of Black global freedom.[76]

The opening meeting of the 1921 Pan-African Congress took place on August 27 in London. Compared with Paris two years earlier, the 110 delegates represented a much broader cross-section of the diaspora, including a significantly larger number of men from the African continent itself.[77] Jessie Fauset painted an idyllic picture of the gathering in the November issue of *The Crisis*. "We were all one family in London," she blissfully recalled. "Native African and native American stood side by side and said, 'Brother, this is my lot; tell me what is yours!'" After two days of pleasantries and general discussion, Du Bois, as chair of the proceedings, put forward a series of resolutions, "bold and glorious . . . couched in winged and unambiguous words," Fauset gushed, that received unanimous approval.

The conference then moved to Brussels. Blaise Diagne, taking his turn to hold the chair, rose in opposition to the London resolutions on the grounds that they were too radical and would anger the powers that be in the colonial metropoles. A showdown ensued between the American delegation, led by Du Bois, seeking a clear challenge to European imperial rule, and the Francophone delegation, led by the assimilationist-minded Diagne. Fauset feared that the entire conference "was destined to end in a rather disgraceful row." The final session in Paris decided the fate of the congress. Diagne and a steady parade of Francophone delegates extolled the empire and the glory of becoming Frenchmen. The Americans pushed back, with Rayford Logan again playing the indispensable role of translator. In the end, save for a paragraph critical of capitalism deemed by Diagne as unacceptably socialist, Du Bois's London resolutions achieved approval on September 5 and became the official platform of the congress moving forward. Du Bois claimed victory. He spent the remainder of his time in Europe in Geneva, advocating on behalf of the congress in meetings with League of Nations representatives and in the picturesque French Alps enjoying rest, inspired writing, and the company of Jessie Fauset.[78]

~

DU BOIS RETURNED TO the United States in late September, basking in the afterglow of his Pan-African triumph. "To the World," the five-page manifesto of the Pan-African Congress, appeared front and center in the November *Crisis*. "The absolute equality of races,—physical, political and social—is the founding stone of world peace and human advancement . . . It is the duty of the world to assist in every way the advance of the backward and suppressed groups of mankind."[79] Significant questions remained unanswered, and internal differences exposed in Brussels needed to be resolved. Nevertheless, Du Bois believed he had struck a blow for Black folk and taken an important step in fulfilling the dreams from the early buoyant months of 1919, when the world seemed rife with democratic possibility. As he wrote in "A Second Journey to Pan-Africa," published in *The New Republic*, "there is today no gainsaying the ground swell in the Negro race—the great, unresting, mighty surge." What form it would assume, Du Bois could not predict. "Who shall say until Time itself tells."[80]

Time proved short for *The Brownies' Book*, whose remarkable twenty-four-issue run came to an end in December 1921. Though well received and rich in content, the endeavor ultimately attracted too few subscribers to remain financially viable. Later in his life, Du Bois looked back at the children's magazine with great pride. He sounded a melancholy note in his final offering of "As the Crow Flies." "I am flying my last wide flight and am very, very sad," he wrote. "All the world lies dark beneath its snow and sunshine. Only the children are happy. Children are always happy. That is, most always."

As usual, Du Bois offered a bird's-eye view of domestic and global events, many of which related to the ongoing reverberations of the World War. "England and Ireland are still trying to make peace," the crow reported. "In another part of the British Empire," he added, "Egypt, the natives, among whom are a number of colored people, want also to be free from the domination of England." And "still further across the world in India, several hundred millions of brown people are much incensed at the injustices of English rule." Closer to home, "a Disarmament conference is sitting in Washington," and, the crow sardonically updated, "the peace treaty between the United States and Germany has at last been signed." Because the Senate rejected ratification of the Versailles agreement, the United States had to reach a bilateral treaty with Germany to formally end hostilities. The U.S.–German treaty, which normalized relations between the two nations, was signed in Berlin on August 25 and officially ratified on November 11, 1921, exactly two years after the armistice.

So ended Du Bois's last flight with *The Brownies' Book*. "Goodbye, dear kiddies," he wrote, looking beyond the horizon and into the uncertainty of the future. "I do not know whom I shall tell all I see hereafter. Nobody I suppose. Besides if I do not fly I shall not see. No, I am not crying. Crows cannot cry. It's a fine thing to be able to cry—sometimes."[81]

W. E. B. Du Bois, 1918 (Library of Congress Prints and Photographs Division)

Joel E. Spingarn, 1920
(W.E.B. Du Bois Papers, Robert S. Cox
Special Collections and University Archives
Research Center, UMass Amherst Libraries)

Major Charles Young in full dress
uniform, 1916 (Library of Congress
Prints and Photographs Division)

RIGHT: Major Adam E. Patterson, ca. 1918 (Emmett J. Scott, *Scott's Official History of the American Negro in the World War* [New York: Underwood & Underwood, 1919])

BELOW: Silent Protest Parade, July 28, 1917. W. E. B. Du Bois is second from right. James Weldon Johnson is walking next to Du Bois. (W.E.B. Du Bois Papers, Robert S. Cox Special Collections and University Archives Research Center, UMass Amherst Libraries)

Court martial of sixty-four members of the Twenty-Fourth Infantry on trial for mutiny and the murder of seventeen people, in Houston, Texas, August 23, 1917 (United States National Archives and Records Administration)

Emmett J. Scott, ca. 1919 (Wikimedia Commons)

Troops of the Ninety-Second Division (foreground) entering a trench in the Argonne Forest (Library of Congress Prints and Photographs Division)

Carter G. Woodson, ca. 1920 (W.E.B. Du Bois Papers, Robert S. Cox Special Collections and University Archives Research Center, UMass Amherst Libraries)

John Hope, President of Morehouse College and Du Bois's close friend, in uniform, ca. 1918. Hope served as a YMCA field secretary in France during World War I. (W.E.B. Du Bois Papers, Robert S. Cox Special Collections and University Archives Research Center, UMass Amherst Libraries)

Captain Matthew Virgil Boutté, ca. 1918 (Addie W. Hunton and Kathryn M. Johnson, *Two Colored Women with the American Expeditionary Forces* [Brooklyn: Brooklyn Eagle Press, 1920])

W. E. B. Du Bois wearing a U.S. Army helmet, likely taken in Le Mans, France, 1919 (Fisk University, John Hope and Aurelia E. Franklin Library, Special Collections)

W. E. B. Du Bois with officers of the 370th Infantry Regiment and Matthew Boutté in Le Mans, France, 1919. From left: Colonel Thomas A. Roberts, W. E. B. Du Bois, two unnamed Black officers, Captain Matthew Boutté (*The Crisis*)

Cover of the May 1919 issue of *The Crisis* (*The Crisis*)

African American man being attacked during the Chicago race riot of 1919 (Schomburg Center for Research in Black Culture, Jean Blackwell Hutson Research and Reference Division, The New York Public Library)

Universal Negro Improvement Association parade, organized in Harlem, 1920 (Schomburg Center for Research in Black Culture, Photographs and Prints Division, The New York Public Library)

W. E. B. Du Bois in his *Crisis* office, ca. 1920. During this time, Du Bois drafted several chapters of his book on the World War. (W.E.B. Du Bois Papers, Robert S. Cox Special Collections and University Archives Research Center, UMass Amherst Libraries)

-6-

15 It will thus be seen how difficult a period the Negro ~~people~~

For a moment ᴧand it was but a moment, it passed, but for a moment the country seemed to rise to its mighty statu̅e. I saw it and saw it with streaming eyes. I have been called bitter. I am bitter but here I saw all the
hurts, the tears, the pain as in one country and that country was mine.
The moment passed and is gone, but thank God that it came once. The war
that brought slavery to most men (and indeed in the end to us) thus brought
to some of us at a time new vision of freedom. We were at least free from
our bonds. The inhabi̱ṯ̇ations fell away. We could think with the nation
and ᴧnot as a mere grou̅p. We could rise to mighty un~~consciousness~~. The
nation, our country, the allies as champions of·the little hurt folk,
democracy. We were mad with the new vision. We did not examine the ~~ideal~~
too narrowly. Even if it was false it was good to rise from mu̅rky, long,
sheathing waters and breath̅e air and see through lifting mist "the stars,
the old and everlasting stars". How simple the problem was after all
with the main trend right? With the great ~~ideal~~ set, what mattered the exceptions, the little evil facts? The edges of our inn̲ker dark world
slipped and ~~thought~~ to ~~f·less~~ with the surrounding half known larger world.
~~Great~~ movements ᴧwere our movements. Great joys and sorrows ours. We had
no longer to resist. ~~The New and~~ scowl as they smile and laugh as they
cried. We were ~~made~~ that is the only word for it, we were mad and let it
not excuse us to say that the madness was divine. It was insanity just
the same. The primal beast ᴧout to kill with prongs. How in the end did
all this set with our inn̲ker problem? After all it was not a mere bargain-
it was a moving wish.

Excerpt from *The Black Man and the Wounded World* manuscript, chapter 8, "The Challenge," drafted ca. 1920 (Fisk University, John Hope and Aurelia E. Franklin Library, Special Collections, W. E. B. Du Bois Collection, *The Black Man and the Wounded World*)

Attendees of the 1921 Pan-African Congress in Belgium, 1921. W. E. B. Du Bois is standing in the center. Fourth from Du Bois's right is Blaise Diagne. Second from Du Bois's left is Jessie Fauset. (W.E.B. Du Bois Papers, Robert S. Cox Special Collections and University Archives Research Center, UMass Amherst Libraries)

Pallbearers carrying the casket of Charles Young into funeral services at Shepard Hall, New York City College, May 27, 1923 (Fisk University, John Hope and Aurelia E. Franklin Library, Special Collections, W. E. B. Du Bois Collection, *The Black Man and the Wounded World*)

General Robert Lee Bullard. Bullard's 1925 memoir and its slander of the Ninety-Second Division created a national uproar among African Americans (Library of Congress Prints and Photographs Division)

Captain Daniel Smith, ca. 1918. Smith was one of the five officers of the 368th Infantry Regiment convicted but ultimately exonerated following the 1918 Meuse-Argonne Offensive (Fisk University, John Hope and Aurelia E. Franklin Library, Special Collections, W. E. B. Du Bois Collection, *The Black Man and the Wounded World*)

African American Gold Star Mothers, July 11, 1930 (W.E.B. Du Bois Papers, Robert S. Cox Special Collections and University Archives Research Center, UMass Amherst Libraries)

W. E. B. Du Bois, seated at desk, 1935 (W.E.B. Du Bois Papers, Robert S. Cox Special Collections and University Archives Research Center, UMass Amherst Libraries)

W. E. B. Du Bois and James Weldon Johnson in Great Barrington, ca. 1928

(James Weldon Johnson and Grace Nail Johnson Papers. Yale Collection of American Literature, Beinecke Rare Book and Manuscript Library)

W. E. B. Du Bois with Japanese professors in Tokyo, 1936 (W.E.B. Du Bois Papers, Robert S. Cox Special Collections and University Archives Research Center, UMass Amherst Libraries)

W. E. B. Du Bois with fellow defendants during their trial in Washington, DC, November 1951 (W.E.B. Du Bois Papers, Robert S. Cox Special Collections and University Archives Research Center, UMass Amherst Libraries)

THE BLACK MAN AND THE WOUNDED WORLD

The Black Man and the Wounded World, table of contents, February 22, 1936. Du Bois prepared this table of contents for a funding request to the Carnegie Endowment for International Peace. (Fisk University, John Hope and Aurelia E. Franklin Library, Special Collections, W. E. B. Du Bois Collection, *The Black Man and the Wounded World*)

W. E. B. Du Bois sitting in his home library, ca. 1956 (W.E.B. Du Bois Papers, Robert S. Cox Special Collections and University Archives Research Center, UMass Amherst Libraries)

CHAPTER 8

"If now I do my duty toward America, it is possible America will do her duty toward me."[1]

"I AM DELIGHTED TO get your letter of April 4," Du Bois responded to Charles Young in a May 18, 1921, note.[2] Regular correspondence with Young had been difficult since the colonel arrived in Liberia the previous year. Young could only laugh when his first batch of mail mistakenly arrived in Siberia and not the West African nation with the similar-sounding name. Despite the distance between them and the challenges of communication, Young and Du Bois managed to remain in touch. "My best Du Bois," Young began in his April 4 letter. Seeking to combat the isolation of being away from both the country and the race he so selflessly served, Young had requested a copy of *Darkwater* and sent Du Bois a check for other books and magazine subscriptions. Their exchange revealed a personal and familial closeness that Du Bois shared with only a handful of other people in his life.[3] "Hope you, Nina and Yolande are all well and kicking high," Young wrote.[4] Du Bois assured him that they were indeed fine and that he need not worry about his own loved ones, who were at the time overseas in France: "We have heard from Ada in Paris and that she and the children are well." He also confirmed that he had taken care of Young's request to help with some outstanding bills and other financial matters in his absence.[5]

Young offered Du Bois an update on the state of affairs in Liberia and West Africa. A delegation from Marcus Garvey's Universal Negro

Improvement Association had recently arrived in Monrovia, looking to make inroads with the Liberian government.[6] "Write me from time to time what you know of the Garvey movement from that side," Du Bois requested, characterizing the UNIA's "foundation in brains and money" in the United States as "extremely shaky." Young asked Du Bois if he knew of the Conference of Africans of British West Africa, held in Accra in March 1920—"the most important thing except the World War that has happened on the West Coast"—and of the attempts to denounce it by the British colonial administrator Sir Hugh Clifford.[7] Du Bois was indeed aware of the gathering, and he reminded Young about his own efforts to advance the cause of African self-determination. "Can you not attend the Pan-African Congress in Europe this fall?" he asked. "Try and come and bring some good men with you."[8]

Despite the painful disappointment of the war and his forced retirement, Young's sense of purpose and duty remained steadfast. Following the armistice, he pondered his future. Du Bois had helped to secure a seat for him on the NAACP board and recruited him to the in-name-only editorial group of the war history book. Du Bois also asked Young to consider commanding the New York 369th/Fifteenth National Guard, Black America's most acclaimed regiment in the wake of the war. Young demurred, sensing that the racial politics surrounding the unit would prevent it from being wholly "patriotic, disciplinary and morally uplifting," he wrote.[9] Other future possibilities included a position in the War Camp Community Service or accepting a State Department offer to become military attaché to Haiti, a post Young had held from 1904 to 1907.[10]

Young ultimately chose Liberia. "Africa calls," he informed Du Bois.[11] He felt an obligation to respond and finish the work he started in Liberia as a military attaché earlier in his career. This second sojourn to Africa, however, possessed a cruel irony. Reinstated to active duty, he could not escape the hypocrisy of being too ill to command Black troops in France yet healthy enough to serve in the harsh climate of West Africa. This irony was not lost on Du Bois as well, who feared for his friend's life. In a letter to Secretary of State Robert Lansing, most likely penned without Young's knowledge, Du Bois wrote, "Colonel

Young is a man that always does his duty regardless of his personal advantage or disadvantage but as one of his dear friends I know that his former stay in Liberia was very near fatal. He had a severe case of Black Water fever. Moreover, as the War Department knows, Colonel Young was retired from the army and was not allowed to go to France on account of 'high blood pressure.' If his disability was so great as to keep him from France is it fair to send him to Africa where his life will certainly be jeopardized?"[12] Du Bois knew this mission might be Young's last.

Young had arrived in the Liberian capital of Monrovia in February 1920. He attempted to get acclimated to the inhospitable tropical environment and the ever-present threat of disease.[13] In the following months, he grappled with the frustrations of his assignment, largely stemming from the nation's political dysfunction. Liberian officials suspected him of being a spy who was laying the groundwork for an American takeover of the country along the lines of Haiti.[14] "This Liberia muddle has taken much of the brightness out of my heart," a dejected Young wrote to Du Bois in January 1921.[15]

Instead of attending the Pan-African Congress sessions in Europe as Du Bois hoped, Young prepared for an extensive trip through the West African coast. Departing from Liberia on November 21, 1921, he spent the next six weeks visiting Cameroon, Belgian Congo, and Nigeria, until the chronic nephritis he'd battled for years incapacitated him. On December 26, he was rushed to a hospital in Lagos, where nurses, knowing the severity of his condition, worked to make him as comfortable as possible. Thirteen days later, on January 8, 1922, at fifty-eight years of age, Young succumbed to kidney and heart failure, his body no longer able to support his indomitable spirit. British colonial officials and Nigerian soldiers buried him the next day with full military honors, his body interred in the European section of Ikoyi Cemetery. With Young's death, Black America lost its most respected military figure.[16]

Du Bois, seven months after he mailed off his final letter to Young, lost arguably his most treasured friend. On January 13, Du Bois received an urgent telegram from Young's mother, Arminta. I HAVE BEEN INFORMED THAT MY SON COLONEL YOUNG WAS KILLED IN LIBERIA, the message began. She asked whether Du Bois knew anything else and also requested that he contact Young's wife and ask her to return home.[17] Du Bois may very well have had the sad duty of informing Ada of her husband's possible death before she received official confirmation from the secretary of state later in the month.[18]

Charles Young's death, while perhaps anticipated, was nevertheless a crushing blow for Du Bois. No one knew better than he the pain Young felt when his country abandoned him during the war and, afterward, effectively banished him to Liberia. In the life and career of the man who devoted every ounce of energy his body could muster to the military he cherished, Du Bois saw the possibility of being a full-blooded American while maintaining a deep love of race. His struggle to write the history book and clearly articulate the war's meaning reflected this tension. Young had always served as a source of hope for Du Bois that the warring ideals of Blackness and Americanness could find peace. Now that hope was gone.

In a rare display of emotion, Du Bois shared his feelings about Young and the personal hurt of his loss in the February 1922 *Crisis* editorial "Charles Young." "The life of Charles Young," Du Bois began, "was a triumph of tragedy." Despite enduring hell at West Point and being "surrounded by insult and intrigue" throughout his years in the army, Young "set his teeth and kept his soul serene and triumphed." Du Bois was one of the few people in Young's life who, "behind the Veil," witnessed "the Hurt and Pain graven on his heart." An unshakable sense of duty, to both nation and race, defined Young's career. "It was his lodestar, his soul," Du Bois wrote, "and neither force nor reason swerved him from it." His anger briefly flashed as he recalled Young's unjust retirement during the war and the army's disregard for his life by consenting to the assignment in Liberia. "They could not stand a black American General. Therefore they sent him to the fever coast of Africa," Du Bois charged. "He is dead. But the heart of the Great Black Race, the Ancient of Days—the Undying and Eternal—rises and salutes his shining memory: Well done! Charles Young, Soldier and Man and unswerving Friend."[19]

In his *Crisis* eulogy, Du Bois, perhaps out of respect for his departed friend's love of country, suppressed his true feelings regarding the circumstances surrounding Young's career and eventual death. However, a letter Du Bois received from Samuel Burnette Pearson, a white officer who served with Young in the Ninth Cavalry, triggered Du Bois's indignation. The two men had formed a bond during their time together at Fort Duchesne, Utah, in 1899 that evolved into a genuine friendship lasting until Young's passing.[20] After reading "Charles Young" in *The Crisis*, Pearson wrote to Du Bois, taking issue with his characterization of Young's experience in the army and pointing to himself as an example of how respect for the colonel transgressed the color line. He also rejected the accusation that the army sent Young to Liberia to die, accusing Du Bois of stirring up "ill feeling."

Du Bois shot back. He acknowledged receipt of Pearson's letter and asserted that "none of the facts that you bring forward invalidate in the slightest what I have said in The Crisis." Bristling at Pearson's claim of close friendship with Young, Du Bois declared, "I have been one of Colonel Young's most intimate friends during the last twenty-five years and every statement that I have made is based on what he and his mother and his wife have told me." Yes, Young may have had friends and defenders at West Point and throughout his military career. "Nevertheless," Du Bois wrote, "it is true that he went through hell at West Point" and was constantly "surrounded by insult and intrigue in the army despite his friends and admirers there." Du Bois also refused to back down on his charge that the military knew a tour of duty in West Africa would be hazardous and put Young's life at risk. "They knew too that to keep him two years in the tropics without leave when he had repeatedly requested it was not likely to improve the health of one threatened with recurrence of black water fever." Du Bois made no apologies. "I realize that 'quarrelling' and stirring up 'ill feeling' is what the Oppressors have always called the just complaint of the oppressed," he angrily lectured Pearson. "Nevertheless, as long as I live I am going to voice my protest at the damnable race hatred in America which crucified Charles Young despite friends like you."[21]

~

BEGINNING IN MID-JANUARY 1922, Du Bois set aside his grief—and his focus on writing the war history—to embark on a whirlwind speaking tour that would stretch to late May. He typically planned for time on the lecture circuit during the opening months of each new year, when he would, as expected, promote the NAACP, but also use these opportunities to enrich himself. Unable to get by solely on his relatively paltry *Crisis* salary, the $35 to $100 he received per engagement represented a vital source of personal income.[22]

With the assistance of a speaker's bureau, he arranged an exhausting itinerary. While on the road in early 1922, he delivered forty-nine lectures in thirty-three different cities across the Midwest and the East Coast,[23] speaking at colleges, local churches, Black women's clubs, and even in the homes of longtime acquaintances. He largely focused his remarks on the recent Pan-African Congress held in August and September of the previous year. From city to city, before supportive audiences, some small, others filling every seat in the venue, Du Bois hailed the work of the Pan-African Congress as a great success that predicted a brighter future for African peoples. He also touted his leadership, aware that New Negro radicals continued to challenge his relevance.

Marcus Garvey stood at the front of that crowd. By 1922, the UNIA was at its height, with chapters in nearly every corner of the African diaspora. The attraction and power of Garvey had been on full display in August 1920, when he presided over the first International Convention of the Negro Peoples of the World, a gathering climaxed by twenty-five thousand devoted followers parading through Harlem and convening in a filled-to-capacity Madison Square Garden, where he accepted the title of "Provisional President of Africa."[24] While Du Bois attempted to write and think through the messy history of the war, Garvey used the symbolic power of Black soldiers to bring the New Negro to life. In doing so, he took direct aim at the doctor's credibility. "We are not depending on the statesmanship of fellows like Du Bois to lead this race of ours," he told a cheering audience in an August 1921 address, "but we are depending on the statesmanship of fellows like the New York Fifteenth, the West Indian regiments and the Eighth Illinois, who fought their way in France."[25]

Du Bois did not back down. By the summer of 1920, he was actively investigating the UNIA and the Black Star Line as a calamity in the making. In a December *Crisis* article devoted to Garvey, Du Bois took a measured approach, describing his rival as "an extraordinary leader of men," yet possessing "absolutely no business sense, no *flair* for real organization."[26] By early 1922, after absorbing enough of Garvey's verbal jabs, Du Bois was less polite. He devoted an April 1922 editorial, "The Demagog," to men, such as the unnamed Garvey, who "will come to lead, inflame, lie and steal. He will gather large followings and then burst and disappear." Du Bois believed that the bombast, divisiveness, false promises, and shady business tactics of his island-born nemesis represented a threat to the race and its respectability.[27]

By mid-April, Du Bois's hectic travel schedule slowed to the point where he could again devote much-needed attention to his book.[28] Back in New York and the confines of his office, he appraised the roughly typed pages of his manuscript and sifted through the carefully marked folders protecting his research materials.

With the 1921 Pan-African Congress still fresh in his mind, he returned to the role in the war played by Black folk outside the United States. A chapter titled "Black England" aimed to chronicle the experiences of West Indian and African servicemen in the British armies. He devoted considerable space to the history of the British West Indies Regiment (BWIR), which served in the Middle East and made a name for itself in the Palestine Campaign. Similar to African American troops in the United States Army, the BWIR endured racist and dehumanizing treatment, culminating in a mutiny at Taranto, Italy.[29] In drafting the chapter, Du Bois quoted liberally from an unpublished manuscript on the regiment provided by a Black Briton, Nathan Solomon Russell, along with clippings from the Barbados *Globe*, the Trinidad *West Indian*, and other newspapers.[30]

Although he highlighted the experiences of Black soldiers from other parts of the diaspora, African American troops remained Du Bois's central focus. He continued to chip away at chapters on the Ninety-Second Division, literally cutting sentence-length fragments from various sources and gluing them to the pages. He also compiled additional documents, contacting Edward Williams about obtaining any available government sources and official records in Washington now that some time had passed since the end of the war. Williams, despite his busy Howard schedule and other commitments, tried to accommodate Du Bois. "I have done what I could," he wrote, "but the result is not alluring." Few new government publications existed. Williams suggested that Du Bois come to DC to spend two or three days looking through unpublished material in the Library of Congress.[31] Du Bois possessed neither the time nor the temperament to sit in library archives and comb through unorganized boxes of documents. In lieu of engaging in traditional archival research, he was content to rely on the documents he had already amassed and the few useful published accounts of the Black experience in the war at his ready.

He gladly added *Two Colored Women With the American Expeditionary Forces*, written by Addie Waites Hunton and Kathryn Magnolia Johnson, to his bookshelf.[32] An active clubwoman, Addie Waites became involved with the YMCA and later the YWCA through her husband, Alphaeus Hunton, while also serving as a founding member of the National Association of Colored Women. Kathryn Johnson worked as one of the first field agents for the NAACP shortly after its 1909 founding, but she left the organization on bad terms in 1916 after being unceremoniously dismissed from her position.[33] When the United States entered the war, Black women activists rallied to the cause, volunteering to support their nation, gender, and race in a host of local and national organizations.[34] In the spring of 1918, Johnson and Hunton joined Helen Curtis in France as the only Black women employed with the YMCA overseas. Within the constraints and humiliation of Jim Crow segregation, they valiantly tried to meet the social and emotional needs of tens of thousands of Black troops in the AEF. During their fifteen months in France, from the coastal city of Saint-Nazaire to rest and recreation areas in and around Aix-les-Bains, the pair worked almost exclusively with Black Services of Supply troops, providing them with educational and religious services, practical resources such as books and paper to write letters home, and, most valuably, moral support and a sympathetic ear to listen to their hopes and frustrations.[35]

Johnson and Hunton dedicated their book, published in late 1920, to "the women of our race, who gave so trustingly and courageously the strongest of their young manhood to suffer and die for the cause of freedom." With what they described as "womanly comprehension," Johnson and Hunton chronicled their "heart to heart touch with thousands of men" who represented the best of the race. Most of the book focused on the Black stevedores and pioneer infantry labor troops they interacted with throughout their time in France, men largely overlooked and overshadowed in other accounts of the war by Black writers, Du Bois included. Hunton and Johnson reclaimed the dignity and humanity of these soldiers, even while exposing the terrible conditions they faced. Using the power of their memories, they viewed their book as a moral obligation and "imperative duty" to give voice to the men they served: "We have had no desire to attain to an authentic history, but have rather aimed to record our impressions and facts in a simple way."[36] It remained to be seen just how much Du Bois planned to incorporate the totality of Hunton and Johnson's remarkable book—with its centering of Black women and working-class soldiers—into his own study, which privileged the experiences of Black male Talented Tenth combatants and officers.

In the meantime, some of the veterans who had sent Du Bois materials grew restless. In October 1920, Clinton Peterson, a veteran of the 369th Infantry Regiment, lent Du Bois newspaper clippings of a serialized story he wrote and hoped to soon publish. "In mailing you the story I do so trusting that you will return," Peterson wrote Du Bois.[37] Well over a year later, Peterson's story remained in Du Bois's hands. "I have not heard anything more from you in regards to these clippings nor your own history of 'The Negro in the World War,'" Peterson inquired in a late January 1922 note to Du Bois. "Kindly advise me if you have finished with the clippings and how long before the book will be out."[38] Madeline Allison first replied on Du Bois's behalf. "I beg to say that Dr. DuBois is working on his history of 'The Negro in the World War' now," she wrote. "As soon as it is ready I will let you know."[39] Du Bois, during a six-week lull from his speaking engagements, responded the following month. "I have still your material here," he assured Peterson. "I am hoping to finish my manuscript this spring and then will return all of the material which I have. My book will be published, I trust, before fall."[40]

Peterson's note may very well have reminded Du Bois that his

chapter on the 369th Infantry remained very thin. Without the luxury of official French records, he stitched together the history of the
famed regiment using personal testimonies and published accounts.
He received some good news on April 6, when Colonel William Hayward responded positively to his request for additional information.[41]
Ever so slowly, the manuscript continued to take shape.

Then, suddenly, another opportunity to tell the history of Black
folk presented itself. The rising tide of postwar white supremacy me-
tastasized into nativist attacks on Eastern European immigrant groups
and anti-Catholic hysteria. A resurgent Ku Klux Klan spreading beyond
the South to fertile soil in the North and Midwest fueled this growing
hatred.[42] Unsettled by the national climate, the Knights of Columbus
established a historical commission with the goal of producing a series
of books documenting the experiences of various racial, ethnic, and
religious groups in the United States as a means of advancing a plural-
istic vision of the country's present and future. "The contributions of
the American Negro has a logical place in this series," the commission's
chairman Edward McSweeney wrote to Du Bois in a May 10, 1922,
letter of invitation: "I would be very much pleased if you would undertake this study immediately if your other engagements will permit."[43]

Du Bois had no time for such a project. But when McSweeney
described the book as having "an additional fervor inspired by the
patriotic impulse of this series for American 'solidarity,'" Du Bois's
interest must have been piqued.[44] Indeed, it was this very "patriotic
impulse" that had driven him to support the war. Moreover, he could
appreciate the sense of urgency motivating the book series. He quickly
accepted McSweeney's offer.[45]

Du Bois did, however, realize that the war history stood in his
way. "I think I understand about what your commission wants," Du
Bois wrote in a subsequent May 20 letter to McSweeney, who desired
to move forward with the book as soon as possible. "The time that
you mention, however, is a little short . . . I have a history of the Negro
in the Great War which I am about finishing." "I shall have this out
of the way by July 15," he claimed, saying that he would then be able
to devote his time to producing a detailed outline for the Knights of
Columbus and submit a manuscript draft by the fall.[46]

Instead of completing the history of Black troops in the war, Du Bois spent the summer of 1922 sketching out and writing the nine chapters of what became *The Gift of Black Folk: The Negroes in the Making of America*. As promised, he delivered a first draft of the manuscript in October.[47] His response to criticisms of the draft by a "historical expert" commissioned by the Knights of Columbus captured his vision of the book, along with his approach to the study and writing of Black history.[48] He admitted that *The Gift of Black Folk*, in mainly relying on secondary works, did not represent "an attempt at new research but rather an interpretation of well known facts." He acknowledged that his conclusions were "in many cases contrary to the accepted historical opinion" and, even with the reluctant inclusion of relevant footnotes, would challenge racist assumptions about Black people and their past. Unsettled white readers, including the reviewer of *The Gift of Black Folk* manuscript, frequently interpreted Du Bois's unflinching honesty about America's treatment of Black people as bitterness. He adamantly refused to change the tone of the book. "If it is bitter," he declared, "it must remain so."[49]

Du Bois devoted chapter 3 of *The Gift of Black Folk* to the history of Black soldiers in America's wars. "The day is past when historians glory in war," he declared in the opening sentence. Black soldiers, like all enlisted men, did not have the luxury of choosing whether the war in which they fought was defensive or offensive, just or unjust. But they did approach war from a unique perspective, which, in Du Bois's historical imagination, made them powerful symbols of the contested nature of African American identity. He posited that the "problem" African American soldiers faced "was always peculiar: no matter for what America fought and no matter for what her enemies fought, the American Negro always fought for his own freedom and for the self-respect of his race." He further argued that African American troops carried a "double motive—the desire to oppose the so-called enemy of his country along with his fellow white citizens, and before that, the motive of deserving well of those citizens and securing justice for his folk." Therefore, no matter the reason for or the moral righteousness of the war they served in, the cause for African American soldiers "was peculiarly just."[50]

The last pages of the chapter focused on America's most recent military conflict. "Finally we come to the World War," Du Bois casually began, "the history of which is not yet written." He still envisioned his study, only temporarily pushed aside by work on *The Gift of Black Folk*, as definitive, with all other published books not worthy of consideration. He offered a very brief survey of Black participation in the war, one that paled in comparison with his discussion of the Civil War. No use delving into extensive detail, he must have reasoned. He would finish his book and soon enough have much more to say. He did, however, offer some concluding thoughts on the historical contribution of African American soldiers to the war and the meaning of their service: "With the small chance thus afforded, Negro troops nevertheless made a splendid record and especially those under Negro officers. If they had had larger opportunity and less organized prejudice they would have done much more. Perhaps their greatest credit is from the fact that they withstood so bravely and uncomplainingly the barrage of hatred and offensive prejudice aimed against them."[51]

As Du Bois submitted the first draft of *The Gift of Black Folk* and the end of 1922 neared, he pondered the status and future of the long-anticipated history of the World War. His NAACP colleagues did as well. Nineteen twenty-two had been a busy year for the association, and urgent matters were coming to a head. The anti-lynching bill, sponsored by Leodonis Dyer and tirelessly lobbied for by James Weldon Johnson, appeared ever so close to a climactic vote in the House of Representatives.[52] The NAACP also devoted significant energy to matters in Arkansas. Following the October 1919 racial massacre in Phillips County, all-white juries, in a series of sham trials marred by armed mobs filling the courthouse, convicted seventy-nine African Americans of murder, conspiracy, and insurrection. Twelve men received sentences of death, and the NAACP led the charge to undo this miscarriage of justice and flagrant disregard of due process guaranteed by the Fourteenth Amendment. With Scipio Africanus Jones—the brilliant and bombastic African American attorney from Little Rock—spearheading efforts on the ground in Arkansas, and Moorfield Storey, the NAACP's founding president and famed lawyer, coordinating the association's national efforts, the fight to save the lives of the "Elaine Twelve" became a cause célèbre. After a number of twists and turns through the local and state courts, the United States Supreme Court agreed to take the case, with *Moore v. Dempsey* scheduled for oral arguments on January 9, 1923.[53]

At the November monthly meeting, amid a full agenda, the board raised the question of Du Bois's history of the war. The impressive June 1919 "Essay Toward a History of the Black Man in the Great War" had tantalized readers. However, nothing followed, and now, more than three years later, the association had yet to see any tangible return on its investment.

Du Bois did not attend the next board meeting, which convened at 4:00 p.m. on December 11. His whereabouts are uncertain. Nevertheless, even in absentia, he was prepared. Assistant Secretary Walter White read Du Bois's report, which included "the status of the History of the Negro Troops." Du Bois wrote that "the first rough manuscript draft of sixteen chapters of this history" sat on a table at the front of his *Crisis* office desk. He'd spent the weeks between board meetings delving into his materials and making the manuscript presentable but acknowledged that what lay before his NAACP colleagues was "in very imperfect form." "In some cases it embodies the final text," he explained, "in other cases a text which must be greatly cut down, and in other cases series of notes which must be further worked together." However, he asserted, what he had written—save for the final chapters, which remained only "partly sketched"—formed "a continuous narrative." He possessed, in his words, "endless documents of all degrees of importance, some of them official autographed documents which really belong in the government files and others of less value." By his own admission, Du Bois wrote, he faced the "main and more formidable task" of deciding what to do with this abundance of materials and weaving them into his narrative. He knew better than anyone the exceptional nature of his personal archive and the work he had put into the manuscript. He ended his report with a polite yet firm request: "May I ask that this material be handled, if at all, with great care."[54]

The manuscript was indeed rough, imperfect, and truly sprawling.

It numbered probably well over six hundred pages. A few of the six-teen chapters were finished and possessed Du Bois's distinctive voice. Others consisted of his words combined with cut-and-pasted text from primary source documents and relevant published works. Some were just a collection of newspaper clippings. As he wrote in earnest over the past two years, he had labored to develop some semblance of structure for the book. If they followed his cautionary instructions and read the manuscript, the NAACP board members might have been able to identify the central themes that Du Bois aimed to ad-dress: the origins of the war and its global context; the impact of the war on the African diaspora and the specific participation of soldiers of African descent in the French and British armies; the historical struggle of African Americans for democracy in the United States and the challenges they faced in supporting the war; and, most notably, the experiences of African American soldiers, which constituted the bulk of the manuscript and Du Bois's "infinite notes and documents."

While he claimed that his manuscript, in its admittedly rough form, possessed a "continuous narrative," that did not necessarily equate to a coherent argument. He aimed to tell a global story that spanned the entirety of the African diaspora, yet African Americans remained at the center. He acknowledged that democracy for African Americans on the eve of the war was largely nonexistent, but they—and he—chose to support the war nevertheless. He sought to dem-onstrate the heroism of the Black troops and find redeeming value in their service and sacrifice. However, in carefully sifting through the chapters Du Bois had drafted on their experience, James Weldon Johnson, Walter White, Mary White Ovington, or any other inter-ested NAACP board member would have been exposed to a devastat-ing catalog of systemic racial injustice. Du Bois had made significant progress. But more work clearly lay ahead.

~

AS THE CALENDAR TURNED TO 1923, the war project remained in the forefront of Du Bois's mind as he prepared for his annual lecture tour, which would run through the spring. He planned visits to cities in Ohio, Indiana, California, Oregon, Washington, Colorado, Ohio, and Pennsylvania. In the western states he charged $75 for each lecture, while appearances in the Midwest and East Coast demanded a $50 honorarium.[55]

A self-produced promotional card announced Du Bois's credentials and the range of potential topics he could lecture on. His list of accomplishments was necessarily brief but surprisingly modest: Harvard Ph.D., Fellow American Association Advancement of Science; Spingarn Medalist 1920; editor of *Crisis* magazine. A full biography, the card referenced, was available in *Who's Who in America*. He prepared an intriguing list of lectures: "Pan-Africa," "The Negro in American History," "Socialism and the Negro," and "Lynching."

These topics all followed the one that stood at the top of the list: "The Black Man in the Wounded World." The announcement also included a detailed subtitle: "History of Black Troops in the World War and of Black Folk Immediately Before and Since."[56]

This was not only the name of a proposed lecture, but also the new title of his long-awaited book. As with the previous titles Du Bois had toyed with over the years—"The Black Man in the Revolution of 1914–1918," "The Black Man in the War of the World"—Black troops as historical representatives of heroic masculinity and the strength of the race stood as the central focus of his story. But now they apparently no longer starred in a global revolution of democracy's triumph. Now, as Du Bois's new title suggested, Black troops were the main protagonists in a worldwide tragedy.

The main obstacle Du Bois confronted in his nearly four years of working on the war history was finding a clear conceptual thread. With the title "The Black Man in the Wounded World," he seemed to arrive at a moment of clarity. Organized around the central theme of tragedy, the project now possessed even greater potential by reflecting both the condition and the zeitgeist of the postwar world.

But this approach carried great risk. To write the book in the mode of tragedy, fully aware of his own controversial place in the history, required introspection, honesty, humility, and courage on Du Bois's part. If the world that he hoped would be transformed for the better by the war was in fact wounded, not only was the war itself a tragic failure, so too was his support for it. Confronting this harsh reality would be a tremendous intellectual and moral challenge.

In February, he set off on his lecture tour. Whether abroad or domestically, traveling was always exhilarating for Du Bois. He reflected on his time on the road in a series of editorials written for the May 1923 issue of *The Crisis*. From Denver he updated readers on his activities, having traveled some seventy-five hundred miles with "yet another 1000 before I see my office again." He had thus far delivered thirty lectures at NAACP branches, churches, colleges, and women's clubs, with ten more still scheduled.[57] He especially valued talks at schools, be it Wendell Phillips High School in Chicago or Stanford University. "To these young men and women, I spared no fact in my indictment of the attitude and crimes of white Europe and America against the black world." He estimated that he spoke to "about 7200 white folk and 4350 black folk."

Before both, with crowds as small as one hundred people and as large as twelve hundred, he lectured about the war. For his white audiences, he demonstrated that "present social divisions and antagonisms are economic rather than physical or cultural and these economic differences caused the Great War." Along with detailing what role Black folk played in the war, Du Bois insisted that "in race hate based on economic oppression lies the seed of future wars." For his Black audiences, he reminded them of "what we did in the World War and what we suffered, and what European economic imperialism has meant to us and our kind; what the future may be." Listeners received him with "careful attention and sometimes manifested approval."[58]

Du Bois, who turned fifty-four while en route to the West Coast for nearly two dozen talks, exhibited remarkable stamina. A letter to *The Crisis* from Rudolph Coffee, the rabbi of Temple Sinai in Oakland, California, recounted Du Bois's visit to the East Bay city on March 12. He began the day with a morning address for the female students at Mills College. In the afternoon he traveled the short distance to Berkeley and the University of California, where he addressed the economics class of Professor Solomon Blum. Du Bois's lecture, open to the entire university and attended by a diverse array of students, focused on "The Economic Status of the Negro in the United States." He followed that with an evening talk at the First Congregational Church in downtown Oakland, presided over by the local NAACP chairman John D. Drake.

In an auditorium and gallery filled to capacity, he lectured on "The Black Man in the Wounded World." "He appeared as a statesman recounting to his people just what the Negro had done in the World War," reported Rabbi Coffee, part of the committee hosting Du Bois in Oakland. The audience came away "thrilled by his simple, yet graphic description of the Negro soldier, without whose aid the Allies never could have won." Du Bois, Coffee continued, "clearly pointed out that Africa was the cause of the war, and because the Negroes of Africa have not yet received their due, the cause of another war has not been removed. The American Negro rendered the most valiant service, and so did those from Africa, although history accords them scant notice."[59]

Du Bois's lecture on the history of Black folk in the war delivered in Oakland and other stops along his western tour was very similar to the talk he gave in Los Angeles on February 26 at Trinity Auditorium. *The California Eagle*, the newspaper of Black Los Angeles, trumpeted his arrival, his first to the city in ten years, with a blaring headline: NEGROES' BOLDEST AND MOST FEARLESS CHAMPION OF CIVIL RIGHTS REACHES L.A. They previewed his lecture, "The Black Man and the Wounded World," by stating that the "eminent sociologist and statistician" had devoted "upward of five years to an intensive study of the Negro in America before, during and after the war." Tickets could be purchased at Smith's Drug Store at Twelfth Street and Central Avenue or from Johnson's Pharmacy at Normandie and Jefferson. The *Eagle* encouraged everyone to arrive on time in order to secure a good seat. Choirs from the city's Black churches came together with violinists and vocalists of local renown to provide "an elaborate setting to Dr. DuBois' lecture."[60]

Speaking in front of a "large and responsive audience," the *Eagle* reported, Du Bois, "scholar, writer, indefatigable fighter for interracial justice," took his rapt listeners through "The Black Man in the Wounded World."[61] "It is well to review these events," he began. Black folks, in spite of their initial skepticism, played a role in the war from the start. He pointed to France's use of their Black colonials— with their "fanatical bravery" and "unparalleled loyalty"—as well as the presence of soldiers from the British West Indies, despite England deciding early on that "this was a white man's war." But just as he'd envisioned for his book, the heart of his lecture belonged to the experience of African Americans. "The Negro had no opportunity to ask whether the war was right or wrong," he said. The race could only question, and hope, as in previous wars, "If now I do my duty toward America, it is possible America will do her duty toward me." He methodically detailed the achievements, as well as the many trials and tribulations that Black troops faced, at home and abroad, due to the army's dogged commitment to white supremacy. "I have dwelt on these facts, not because they are pleasant," Du Bois explained, "but that we may arrive at a clearer understanding of the problems coming after the war." The leaders of the Western nations had sought to maintain the prewar status quo, "to once more reduce the alleged 'inferior' Colored races to their former status of instruments of exploitation for the aggrandizement of white imperialists and the enrichment of white capitalists." In opposition, "the leaders of thought and action" of the darker world determined "to see that this is not done; to protest so loudly and effectively that it cannot be done." The key to the ongoing problem of the color line that the war had only exacerbated lay in "education and economic independence." For peace and harmony to become a reality, "men must first cease to allow their greed for tea and coffee, ivory and mahogany, to stand between them and what they know to be justice to all mankind."[62]

In broad strokes, he provided a brilliant overview of what "The Black Man in the Wounded World," in book form, could potentially look like and the argument it promised to make.[63] The positive responses he received further boosted his confidence, reassuring him that an audience for his work still existed. "I have seen tears of thanks in the eyes of strangers, joy and appreciation on the lips of friends, and with all this well-nigh infinite desire to make me comfortable and happy and to spread the truth with which I labored." He lectured calmly and quietly, "with scarcely a raising of my voice," telling no jokes, performing no theatrics. "I have simply reasoned, with fact and logic and illustration." The reactions of his growing white audiences especially pleased Du Bois. "For many years white folk shrank from my frankness and what they were pleased to term my 'bitterness,'" he reflected. Now a shifting of the winds had occurred as a result of the war and the postwar racial tumult. White people sought answers. "What is the dark world thinking? What is the race clash? What does the Negro want?" Du Bois made a point to be fair, while at the same time frank. They needed to know the truth, that "the crime of white humanity toward black is the most awful crime of the ages. Dress it and excuse it as you will—its stark and bloody filth makes every honest heart shudder."[64]

~

ON MAY 20, 1923, a commercial steamer carrying the oak-coffined body of Colonel Charles Young docked at the Quartermaster Depot in Brooklyn, New York.[65] Returning Young's body to the United States from Nigeria took more than a year from the time when Young's wife, Ada, submitted her initial request to government officials in February 1922. During that span, one diplomatic, bureaucratic, and logistical hurdle after another stood in the way of Young receiving a proper burial in the country he had dedicated his life to. Ada could only anxiously wait as the State Department worked with British colonial officials and local Nigerian authorities to make arrangements to exhume Young's corpse and have it properly preserved and transported across the Atlantic.

For Du Bois, the homecoming of Charles Young reopened an unhealed wound. In the months following Young's death, Du Bois stayed close with Ada, hoping to fill some of the void left by the loss of her husband. He felt a strong sense of obligation to his departed friend. The perpetually busy highbrow intellectual, infamous for his general aloofness toward others, devoted significant time to assisting Ada with a host of personal matters, ranging from Young's army pension to back taxes on property the couple owned in Denver. He also served as a sounding board and counselor as Ada struggled both financially and emotionally with suddenly becoming a widow.[66]

Perhaps the greatest gift Du Bois could offer her was to make sure that Charles Young not only returned to the United States but received a burial and celebration befitting his accomplishments and his significance to the race. After getting official confirmation that Young's body would arrive on American soil sometime in May 1923, Du Bois spearheaded funeral and memorial arrangements.[67] Following Young's death the previous year, Black churches, schools, and organizations across the country had held events to acknowledge his passing, but they would now pale in comparison with Young's official services. The Charles Young Post of the American Legion, recently named in his honor and led by Matthew Boutté, volunteered to take charge of Young's remains and organize a grand parade and memorial in New York City.[68] African Americans in the nation's capital also wished to pay their respects, and Du Bois worked with Shelby Davidson, the executive secretary of the NAACP's Washington, DC, branch, on plans for the city to honor Young before his final interment at Arlington National Cemetery.[69]

With Charles Young and the cruel legacy of the war weighing heavily on his mind, Du Bois was perhaps not in the mood to be reminded about his unfinished history. On May 15, Adam Patterson wrote to him. Three years earlier, he had received a promise from Du Bois that their book, incorporating the chapters he drafted, would appear in the summer of 1920. He had not heard from Du Bois since. In the meantime, the former judge advocate had established himself as a successful attorney in Chicago and a key player in the rough-and-tumble world of local Democratic politics. His City Hall connections and close ties to Mayor William Dever earned him the prestigious position of assistant corporation counsel and, along with it, status as one of the most influential African Americans in the city.[70] He also maintained a close connection with fellow Black veterans, especially former officers of the Ninety-Second Division, through a social uplift organization, the Committee of One Hundred. Patterson insisted on the "immediate return" of a collection of photographs he had sent to Du Bois. The fellow soldiers who, in good faith, loaned them to Patterson were now "clamoring for their return." "In many cases these photographs are the only ones taken by the men while in actual service," he explained.[71]

Patterson no doubt read Du Bois's response a week later with great disappointment. "I regret to say that it is physically impossible to unscramble the mass of material which I have until I have finished with it," Du Bois wrote. Only after completing the manuscript could he extract the photographs and return them. Until that time, he reassured, they remained "perfectly safe." "I realize your impatience," he said, "but I think perhaps that you do not know what a long and difficult piece of work a history like this is."[72]

The New York City memorial service for Charles Young took place on Sunday, May 27, 1923. Throughout Harlem, a feeling of melancholy and reverence permeated the late-spring air. The funeral procession began at 11:45 a.m., when members of the Harlem American Legion post named in his honor escorted the colonel's body out of the Fifteenth New York National Guard Armory on 132nd Street and Seventh Avenue. The old "Hellfighters" band struck up "The Star-Spangled Banner." At the front of the line stood Captain Boutté, serving as grand marshal, alongside the 369th veteran and Croix de Guerre recipient Sergeant A. A. Davis, who, adhering to military custom, carried the right boot of Young in his arms.[73] Joining Davis were other current and former members of the legendary Fifteenth National Guard, Brooklyn's George P. Davis Post of the American Legion, Black veterans from the Spanish-Cuban-American War, and a host of Black civic and fraternal organizations, all paying their respects.

The procession slowly snaked its way through the streets of Harlem. Upward of fifty thousand somber-faced mourners lined the streets of Lenox, St. Nicholas, and Amsterdam Avenues, heads bowed and bared as Young's flag-draped caisson passed by. Buildings along the route of the cortege were covered in black or decorated with red, white, and blue bunting.

Charles Young became only the second African American to have a public funeral in New York City. The first distinction had belonged to another celebrated Black soldier, James Reese Europe, the ragtime conductor, jazz pioneer, and 369th Infantry Regiment officer whose life came to a tragically premature end shortly after he and his world-famous band returned from France. His May 13, 1919, procession had covered much of the same Harlem ground as Young's parade some four years later and invoked similar feelings of admiration and respect.[74]

New York's tribute to Charles Young culminated at City College. As the procession came to an end along Amsterdam Avenue, YMCA volunteers ushered people into Shepard Hall, the Gothic-style campus centerpiece that housed the cavernous cathedral-like Great Hall.[75] Pallbearers placed Young's casket at the foot of the stage, upon which sat the speakers for the memorial service.[76] William Monroe Trotter laid a wreath at the coffin on behalf of the city of Boston.[77]

The Reverend Marshall Shepard, chaplain of the Charles Young Post, delivered the invocation, and Joel Spingarn spoke first, briefly reflecting on his personal friendship with Young and his admiration for Young's one hundred percent Americanism. He was followed by Theodore Roosevelt Jr., who remarked on how much his late father had admired Young and, if given the chance, would have placed Young in command of a Black regiment in the division the former president envisioned raising during the World War.

Then Du Bois rose from his seat on the stage and stepped to the rostrum. Although officially representing the NAACP, his eulogy was personal.[78] He gazed out at the two thousand mourners seated in rows before him. He looked at the coffin that encased Charles Young's body and the American flag shrouding it. Calmly and plainly, he recited the story of Young's upbringing and revisited his noble yet tragic military career, from West Point to Liberia. Young had shouldered insult and indignity, enough to make any average man quit, Du Bois recounted. But not Young. He confronted it all with a smile, recognizing his ultimate duty to both nation and race. He saw the World War as his great opportunity, the pinnacle of his life's work. The government, unable to bear the possibility of a Black general, had denied him that opportunity. Du Bois held nothing back. "I know that this audience has much sympathy with patriotism for America," he said, "but Colonel Young had that patriotism, and he died of a broken heart, a heart broken because his country, the country he loved so well and loved so well to serve, thought him unfit to head his own men in the last war." He ended with a quote from one of his favorite poets, Goethe: "Happy man whom death shall find in victory's splendor," and a final punctuation that Young would forever stand as one of the nation's bravest and most splendid citizens.[79] The *Amsterdam News* described Du Bois's address as "possibly one of the greatest he has ever made in his public career."[80]

With his raw honesty, Du Bois transformed the ceremony from one of somber praise for Charles Young to an indictment of the military and the forces of white supremacy that ultimately brought about his premature death. General Fred Winchester Sladen, commandant of West Point and a former classmate of Young's at the exclusive military academy, spoke after Du Bois. Unnerved and personally offended, Sladen set aside his prepared remarks to offer a rebuttal to Du Bois's charges. He defended the army and claimed that race played no part in Young's forced retirement.[81] Ferdinand Q. Morton, the powerful Harlem Democratic boss who controlled what came to be known as "Black Tammany," followed Sladen. Stepping into the fray, Morton concurred with Du Bois, emphasizing the "hideous injustice done this man whose dead body lies here before us." Even after the ceremony concluded to the sound of taps, the Great Hall continued to buzz from the verbal grenades Du Bois had lobbed in his speech.[82]

On the morning of June 1, Charles Young's body traveled by train to its final resting place at the nation's capital. At a stop in Philadelphia, local Black residents, among them Marian Anderson, who sang a rendition of the hymn "One Sweetly Solemn Thought," paid their respects.[83] Around 11:30 a.m. Regular Army troops from Fort Myer, Virginia, met Young's body as it pulled into Union Station. With schools closed for the day, nearly all of Black Washington, DC, came out to bid the colonel a final adieu. An estimated fifty thousand people lined Pennsylvania Avenue in silence for the funeral parade, which included the city's Black National Guardsmen, high school cadets, the Howard University ROTC, official military representatives, members of the American Legion, and scores of other unaffiliated Black World War veterans in civilian attire. Behind the police escort and caisson bearing the casket followed Dolly, the loyal horse Young rode some five hundred miles to Washington, DC, in a valiant yet futile attempt to prove his fitness to serve and lead Black troops in the war. The horse was shrouded in black, with Young's polished sword facing backward and his spurred boots, reversed, hanging in the stirrups.

The procession arrived at Arlington Cemetery and the Memorial Amphitheater around 1:00 p.m. The amphitheater had been completed in 1920, and only three other soldiers before Young had been honored there. A large crowd filled the grand structure, invited guests occupying the rows of marble benches and others standing shoulder to shoulder along the colonnade. With the Howard University choir singing in the background, army officers escorted Ada and Arminta Young to their seats. Du Bois most likely sat next to them. Pallbearers carried Young's coffin through the west portico entrance and placed it in front of the ceremonial stage, covered in a flank of flowers and wreaths. Colonel John Axton, the army chief of chaplains, who'd served with Young in the Philippines, lauded him for his leadership and dedication to the military. Major Oscar J. W. Scott, who reminisced about days in the Tenth Cavalry sharing the same tent with Young and drinking from the same canteen, considered him a friend. "The race pinned its faith in Colonel Young," Scott said, "and Colonel Young pinned his faith in the race." At the conclusion of the ceremony, a procession escorted Young to his burial site atop a small knoll overlooking the Potomac River. Taps played as he was lowered into the ground.[84]

An emotional Du Bois returned home to New York and penned one last tribute to his fallen friend. Whereas his February 1922 editorial "Charles Young" had conveyed tragedy and sorrow, the similarly titled elegy he wrote for the July 1923 *Crisis* exuded righteous anger and indignation. "The last sad ceremonies over the body of the late Colonel Young bring forward the old and familiar phases of Caucasian propaganda in the United States," Du Bois began, still seething from General Sladen's remarks at the New York memorial service. Young had persevered through "a storm of heart-breaking insult and prejudice" while at West Point, frequently referred to as "nigger," "the Load of Coal," and, mockingly, "*Mr.* Young." "And to-day," he wrote, "when it is all over and the man has lived and conquered and suffered and died, then his successful class-mates and fellow officers come forward and say: 'Young? We knew Young. He was a splendid fellow! Insulted! We never insulted him; we never saw him insulted.'" Du Bois was adamant that "unless we, who know the truth from Young's own lips, contradict these conscious and unconscious lies, this propaganda will go down in history and children will grow up to believe that merit is recognized at West Point whether clothed in black or white; and that Charles Young, Whittaker, Flipper and the rest had no unusual difficulties in that singular seat of education."[85]

Du Bois's anger was certainly about Charles Young and the gall of white so-called friends claiming to know him. But it also stemmed from the history of the war. He scoffed at the claim made by Sladen and other white army officials that illness was the sole reason behind Young's forced retirement. "We do not believe it," Du Bois wrote. "But even if it were true," he continued, "then the Government of the United States stands convicted of an even more inexcusable crime. For, if Charles Young's blood pressure was too high for him to go to France, why was it not too high for him to be sent to the even more arduous duty in the swamps of West Africa?" Du Bois then leveled the most serious of charges: "If then the United States Government retired a sick man, it murdered him by detailing him afterwards to Africa." Du Bois claimed that "the real reason" Young did not set foot on French soil had nothing to do with "his age, his blood pressure, nor his ability—it was simply that the General Staff did not want a black General in the United States Army. They knew that there was not a single white officer at the front who was Young's superior as a military man, and very few were his peers. They knew what Young could have made of the 92nd division." "God rest his sickened soul," Du Bois finished, "but give our souls no rest if we let the truth concerning him droop, overlaid with lies."[86]

~

IN THE MIDDLE OF Du Bois's efforts to properly memorialize Charles Young, chaos descended upon Tuskegee, Alabama. In late 1921, as part of a larger effort to consolidate and expand services for veterans of the World War, a Treasury Department committee issued recommendations for the creation of a national system of medical facilities for former soldiers. The location of the hospitals would allow veterans to receive care within or in close proximity to their own communities.

But, as it always did, the "Negro problem" and the peculiar nature of Jim Crow in postwar America created a different logic when it came to Black veterans. The Treasury Department committee decided to establish a single separate facility for Black veterans in the South, where an estimated three hundred thousand former Black servicemen resided. The Tuskegee Institute principal Robert Moton argued that his school would make an ideal site for the hospital, given its location and sterling reputation for not causing any trouble between the races. Northern-based civil rights and Black veteran organizations, however, vehemently opposed a hospital located below the Mason-Dixon line.[87] Washington, DC, and Howard University, they reasoned, was a much better alternative. The Treasury Department ultimately sided with Moton and approved Tuskegee for the $2.5 million, three-hundred-acre facility, composed of twenty-seven buildings and containing six hundred beds.[88]

Even with the specter of Jim Crow conditions, Black veterans desperately needed the hospital. Fearful that the presence of Black bodies would harm the morale of white veterans or, as it had during the war, inflame racial hostilities, Northern Public Health Service officials routinely segregated Black veterans at local hospitals or denied them service altogether.[89] The conditions facing Southern Black veterans seeking medical assistance were especially dire and all too often life-threatening. Isaac Webb, a disabled war veteran from Alabama and a Tuskegee graduate, shared his harrowing experience in a letter to Du Bois. At a facility in Mobile, Alabama, Webb described being "handed my food out of a window, forbidden to use the front of the hospital to enter my ward, which was on the back; given no medical attention, and forced to use the same toilet facilities fellows in advanced stages of syphilis and gonorrhea used." He watched a fellow Black veteran, just six beds from where he lay, die from tuberculosis. "Never in France," Webb wrote, "was I so humiliated and insulted, nor saw such acts of negligence and cruelty committed in a hospital as I saw in the South."[90] Other Black veterans could relate to Webb's ordeal. Some men seeking hospital care instead found themselves confined to jails or mental institutions.[91] Not surprisingly, most disabled African American ex-servicemen suffered in silence rather than submit themselves to subhuman treatment.[92]

On Abraham Lincoln's birthday, February 12, 1923, with great pomp and circumstance, government officials—among them Vice President Calvin Coolidge—Alabama state and local politicians, and Black spokesmen led by Robert Moton dedicated the grand hospital.[93] All seemed well on the surface. However, with the hospital set to open its doors on April 1, the issue of whether it would have Black physicians and nurses or would be run exclusively by whites came to an explosive head. In making the case for Tuskegee, Moton had assumed that the hospital would have an integrated staff and that Black veterans would receive care from medical professionals of their own race. However, Alabama white supremacists, ranging from the governor to the head of the state American Legion to local Tuskegee residents, insisted that all-white personnel run the hospital.[94] They imagined uppity Northern Black medical officers disrupting the peaceful equilibrium between the races. Additionally, Black control of a federal hospital with a monthly payroll of more than $65,000 represented a threat to the fundamental understanding that Black Southerners must remain in a position of political and economic inferiority to whites. The Veterans Bureau, concerned with maintaining the support of local whites, agreed and appointed an incorrigible Alabama racist, Colonel Robert H. Stanley, as director. Stanley, despite Moton's pleas, stood firm that the hospital would exclude Black doctors and nurses. A crisis seemed inevitable.

From NAACP headquarters in New York City, Du Bois closely monitored the increasingly sordid affair. He had encouraged Black soldiers to put their lives on the line for their country. Now, their minds and bodies broken, many of the same men Du Bois urged to go to war required care. The hospital crisis stood as a historical referendum on the government's treatment of Black veterans and, by extension, the legitimacy of African Americans' sacrifice during the war.

Du Bois first waded into the brewing storm with the June 1923

Crisis editorial "The Fear of Efficiency." He mused on the hypocrisy of prominent artistic, educational, and professional organizations denying outstanding African Americans the right to compete with whites in the pursuit of opportunity and greatness while simultaneously claiming that Black people lacked the necessary qualifications. Tuskegee offered a prime lesson in the speciousness of this argument and the general absurdity of white supremacy. Against the protests of many African Americans who knew better, "A great hospital for maimed Negro soldiers has been built there," Du Bois wrote. "Now come the Archpriests of Racial Separation in the United States, demanding, not merely asking, that the physicians, surgeons and officials in charge of this institution shall all be white! . . . This, we confess, has set our heads to whirling." Of course, he stated matter-of-factly, "Southern white people simply could not be asked to nurse and heal black folk," thus necessitating a separate hospital for Black veterans. But clearly Alabama's racists lacked conviction in their segregationist principles when the chance to enrich themselves flashed before their eyes. "Now comes white Alabama simply yearning for the salaries that will be paid physicians to take care of Negroes," Du Bois remarked. "Nothing more astonishing has happened in this astonishing generation."[95]

Irony became rage in the following month's issue of *The Crisis*. The July 1923 editorial "The Tuskegee Hospital" not coincidentally appeared alongside his furious paean to Charles Young. The tone of the editorial matched the mood of someone who'd just buried his best friend and Black America's most decorated soldier. Du Bois, point by point, laid out the facts of the controversy, including the error of the Harding administration making Robert Moton "a sort of referee for 12 million Negroes as to the personnel of the hospital"; the hospital opening "with a full white staff of white doctors and *white nurses* with *colored nurse-maids* for each white nurse, in order to save them from contact with colored patients!"; and the contract for burying dead soldiers being awarded to a white undertaker from Greenwood, South Carolina, before local Black undertakers could even submit a bid.

Even the levelheaded Du Bois found it all too much to comprehend. "In commenting on all this we can simply gasp," he wrote.

"Human hatred, meanness and cupidity gone stark mad! Separating races in hospitals and graveyards and fighting to put white men over a Negro hospital! Giving nurses black *maids* to do the work while the white 'ladies' eat with the internes, dance at the balls and flirt with the doctors and black men die! Lying, postponing, deceiving, threatening to keep out black doctors and nurses. What can be the result?" The hospital fiasco symbolized the madness as well as the profound tragedy of what the war now meant for most African Americans, and for Du Bois personally. "Here was a great government duty to take care of black soldiers wounded in soul and body by their awful experience in the Great War," he declared. "They ought to have been cared for without discrimination in the same hospitals and under the same circumstances as white soldiers . . . Outside of such schools as Tuskegee and the larger cities, there is no protection in central Alabama for a decent Negro pig-pen, much less for an institution to restore the life and health of those very black servants of the nation." With painful memories of the war on his mind, Charles Young dead, his faith that Black veterans could receive any semblance of justice in South shattered, and a book about the Black experience in the war in his office still incomplete, Du Bois grimly asserted that "the best way out of the mess would be to tear the hospital down and rebuild it within the confines of civilization."[96]

Subsequent events confirmed his harsh judgment. Behind-the-scenes coaxing from Robert Moton combined with public pressure from the NAACP, the National Medical Association, and the Black press compelled President Harding—eager to hang on to precious Northern Black votes—to support an all-Black staff. Rebuffed in their efforts to exclusively control the facility and the well-paying jobs that came with it, local whites turned to threat and intimidation to keep Black employees out. Moton and his family, along with several other prominent Black people associated with the school, temporarily left town for their safety.

Tensions climaxed on the night of July 3. Around 9:00 p.m., approximately seven hundred Alabama Klansmen descended on Tuskegee, announcing their arrival with a burning forty-foot cross that lit up the sky. A two-mile parade of automobiles loaded with hooded men snaked its way to the hospital grounds.[97] They did not approach the campus, likely knowing that Tuskegee Institute students, graduates, and supporters awaited them, armed with guns and more than ready to defend their school. At the hospital, guards allowed a group of twenty Klansmen to enter and search for a recently appointed Black hospital clerk, John H. Calhoun, presumably with the goal of making a lesson of him. After failing to locate Calhoun, they contented themselves with a midnight meal in the hospital commissary prepared by the chief dietitian, and they eventually departed, satisfied with their performance. In the morning, several white physicians who were part of the mob casually reappeared at their posts.[98]

While successful in creating a ghoulish spectacle, the Alabama Klan failed to account for the postwar New Negro militancy of African Americans who refused to quietly accept an attack on the hospital and, by extension, on Black veterans. The NAACP, with James Weldon Johnson at the helm, responded swiftly, pressuring the Department of Justice to open an investigation.[99] Meanwhile, letters from angry Black citizens, many of them ex-soldiers, inundated the White House and other government offices. Even the inaugural group of approximately ninety Black veterans admitted to the hospital petitioned the director of the Veterans Bureau that they not be subjected to white doctors who clearly lacked sympathy for their health and welfare.[100] Reports and editorials about events at Tuskegee filled the pages of Black newspapers, all in agreement that the federal government had to act and that African Americans must not back down in the face of Klan threats. As *The Chicago Defender* remarked, "While nobody is seeking trouble, nobody is running under fire."[101] Even the conflict-averse Robert Moton would have agreed with the *Defender*'s sentiments. Walter White recalled visiting Moton in his home during the height of the crisis. As they sat, Moton, grim-faced, pointed to a well-oiled shotgun and rifle in the corner of his room. "I've got only one time to die," he quietly told White. "If I must die now to save Tuskegee Institute, I'm ready. I've been running long enough."[102]

Du Bois was also in a fighting mood. If only Mrs. Annie Howe had known this before she placed her July 27 letter to Du Bois in the mail. Howe, a white woman from Alstead, New Hampshire, who always gave her monthly issue of *The Crisis* to the Black janitor of her apartment building, had read the "Tuskegee Hospital" editorial in the June issue. Unsettled by Du Bois's angry tone, she wondered "if something that excites you and which seems unjust and vindictive, cannot be explained in other ways." She enclosed an article from *The Outlook*, "a paper I am sure that can be trusted," about the situation at Tuskegee. The article disingenuously attributed the need for a white medical staff to a paucity of specially trained Black physicians and accused the NAACP of worsening the situation with its request for federal troops to protect the hospital.[103] "I realize there is much real injustice shown both blacks and whites in this world," Howe wrote, "but dwelling on it or over-emphasizing it seems to me harmful, not helpful." After all, she gently admonished Du Bois, "white people suffer just as much when unjustly accused as colored people do."[104]

An infuriated Du Bois took the time to respond to Howe with a three-page rebuttal, assuring her that "so far as the American Negro is concerned The Outlook cannot be trusted." He systematically debunked every erroneous claim in the *Outlook* article and ended with pointed words for his unsuspecting letter writer: "The Crisis continually has to combat the smug indifference of those people who are so afraid that mention of the evil of the world is going to induce bitterness and discontent. We are not afraid of bitterness and discontent, we are afraid of evil and we have neither patience nor respect for those people who would let the evil of the world go swaggering on because they fear lest some poor victim may raise his shackled hands to Heaven and shake with his righteous anger the foundations of hell."[105]

The situation at Tuskegee gradually improved. President Calvin Coolidge remained committed to the pledge of his recently deceased predecessor to eventually staff the hospital with Black doctors and nurses exclusively. Director Frank Hines of the Veterans Bureau stood firm in the face of continued threats from local whites and steadily proceeded to hire Black personnel. In September, Hines transferred the hospital's recalcitrant commanding officer Colonel Stanley to a facility in New Mexico and replaced him with a more sympathetic white Tennessean committed to training Black doctors. By October, the hospital's 226 patients received care from 6 Black doctors and 247 employees, 218 of whom were of the same race.[106] African Americans declared a final victory in January 1924, when Dr. Joseph H. Ward, a Black man, assumed the position of chief surgeon.

Though Du Bois surely took pleasure in this outcome, the entire experience left a sour taste in his mouth. Men who'd sacrificed their bodies on behalf of the nation in war should not have had to fight for medical treatment in peace. But, if anything, the Tuskegee hospital affair offered a vivid reminder of how much the war and its legacy still mattered.

~

IN JUNE 1923, seeking a way to connect his book on the war with a public that at one point hungrily awaited its appearance, a restless Du Bois reached out to Colonel Otis Duncan. Duncan had commanded Chicago's famed "Old Eighth" Illinois National Guard in France, where it became the 370th Infantry Regiment of the Ninety-Third Division, and he held the distinction of being the highest-ranking African American in the United States Army. "As you know, for the last four years I have been working on a history of the Negro troops," Du Bois wrote. Claiming that the book was "about done," he informed Duncan that he was "thinking of ways of bringing the facts to the public before the matter is buried in print."[107]

What Du Bois had in mind was a pageant, directed by himself and staged in Chicago's Eighth Regiment Armory. The visual, educational, and communal power of the historical pageant fascinated him. He had already produced a pageant of his own, *The Star of Ethiopia*, which delighted audiences during its three runs in New York, Washington, DC, and Philadelphia in 1913, 1915, and 1916.[108] The possibility of a similar show, now based on the relatively fresh history of Black participation in the World War, captured his imagination. With the New Negro renaissance in full swing and Chicago buzzing as one of its most important cities, the timing and location seemed right.[109]

Du Bois dreamed of quite the event. As he explained to Otis Duncan, "using soldiers, children and finally masses of little dolls, painted as soldiers," the full dramatic sweep of Black participation in the war, especially "the whole battle movement and marching of troops," would vividly come to life.[110] In a follow-up letter to Duncan after the colonel expressed his interest and willingness to cooperate, Du Bois further elaborated on his grandiose idea.[111] He envisioned the production as a mix of "lecture and pageant." The lecturer would be aided by "a map with movable figures . . . illustrating America, Europe and Africa, special parts in Europe and Africa, and special battlefields in Europe." The second part of the play would consist of ten scenes "illustrating the ten great events of the participation of the Negro in the war." He needed anywhere from fifty to five hundred "players in costume," voice amplifiers, and "special electrical lighting" in order to execute his vision and ideally surpass *The Star of Ethiopia* in extravagance. He planned to furnish the lecturer and the maps, while all other matters and expenses, he proposed, would be "attended to by the local body which undertakes it." "I think in this way," he told Duncan, while promising additional details at a later date, "a most informing and impressive spectacle could be arranged."[112]

Then, abruptly, Du Bois put his plans for the pageant on hold. The possibility of a third Pan-African Congress became a reality.[113] Organization of this next gathering had been messy. Lingering tensions from 1921—with the Francophone Africans and the congress secretary Isaac Béton—had sapped Du Bois's commitment, leaving the burden on the dutiful Rayford Logan to scrape together a meeting in Lisbon. The personal expenses of traveling to Portugal were the real source of Du Bois's disenchantment. However, when the National Association of Colored Women offered to pay his way, Du Bois, eager to save face, leapt into action and frantically took charge of the planning. He insisted on an opening session in London and fired off letters to every corner of the diaspora to secure participants. He departed for Europe on October 24.[114]

Before leaving, Du Bois worked with Jessie Fauset and Augustus Dill to set the content for the last two issues of *The Crisis* for 1923. The news items covered a range of topics: the struggles of the League of Nations, the continued disfranchisement of Black voters, the passing of the Niagara Movement cofounder and pioneering African American social activist Mary Burnett Talbert, and, naturally, the Pan-African Congress.

Of particular note, both issues revisited one of the most tragic moments of the World War. Fifty-four Black soldiers of the Twenty-Fourth Infantry Regiment remained imprisoned in Fort Leavenworth, Kansas, for their role in the August 1917 Houston rebellion. The NAACP's efforts to free the incarcerated soldiers had begun in 1921 but were revitalized when delegates to the October 1923 national meeting held in Kansas City visited the incarcerated men.[115] In the November editorial, "The Houston Martyrs," *The Crisis* asked readers to commemorate Armistice Day instead as "Houston Martyrs' Day" and to double the fifty thousand signatures the NAACP had already collected for a petition to the president demanding their release.[116] Another editorial, "Sick and in Prison," followed in the December issue, reminding readers that the thirteen soldiers executed for their participation in the violence had been "murdered on the scaffold by the American government to satisfy the bloodlust of Texas" and the soldiers remaining in prison represented a "shameful injustice."[117]

The December issue also included a tantalizing preview of the following month's publication, one that filled thousands of readers with long-overdue excitement and anticipation: "The January CRISIS will usher in the New Year with a chapter from Dr. Du Bois' History of Negro Troops in the World War—'The Black Man and the Wounded World.'"[118]

PART III

FAILURE

CHAPTER 9

". . . an Evil, a retrogression to Barbarism, a waste, a wholesale murder."[1]

"I HAVE TAKEN MANY journeys but this is the greatest," Du Bois wrote in the March 1924 issue of *The Crisis*. In his fifty-six years of life, he had traveled widely, through all the states of the "American Empire" and in multiple European nations—England, France, Germany, Belgium, Austria, Switzerland, Italy. While "intensely interesting," all these places remained "painfully white." But on this trip, he was "drifting toward darkness" and, ultimately, "the Eternal World of Black Folk."

It began, ironically, in the metropole of the world's largest empire. On October 24, 1923, Du Bois departed New York City for London and the third installment of his Pan-African congresses. The opening session took place in the council chamber of Denison House in London on November 7 and 8, with Du Bois dominating the rostrum.[2] The "Charter of Rights" he pushed forward mostly replicated the gradualist demands of the 1921 meeting. Departing London, he spent a few days in France, then traveled farther south through Spain, stopping at Barcelona and Madrid, savoring the reprieve of his brown face attracting no attention. He then arrived in Lisbon, "a lovely city, rising in great swelling of hills, deep creams and crimson above the sea and the calm Tagus," for the congress's second session.[3] Hosted by the Liga Africana, the two-day gathering on December 1 and 2 attracted no more than fifty attendees and consisted mostly of cursory presentations and pleasantries. Overall, the conference fell flat, although Du Bois, never one to admit failure, proclaimed it an unqualified success, "not as large a scene of meetings as in 1921, but more harmonious and more hopeful in spirit."[4]

While he found Europe pleasant, Du Bois declared the final leg of his overseas sojourn the "greatest" of his life thus far. "And now as a sort of ambassador of Pan-Africa I turn my face toward Africa." He departed Lisbon by boat for the Portuguese isle of Madeira, staying long enough in the little town of Funchal to enjoy a rainbow-encircled sunset and dawn, where "the fingers of God touch the hills above and they glow with green and gold." At sea again, his ship approached the Canary Islands, the snowcapped peak of the imposing Mount Teide volcano filling the horizon. From Tenerife, on Sunday, December 16, he set sail for his long-awaited final destination. After six restless, eager days, he approached the coast of Liberia, noting the exact time of 3:22 p.m. when he first caught sight of Cape Mount.[5]

A wave of emotion overcame the New England–born, Victorian-bred child of the diaspora as he set foot on African soil. "A long way—a long, long way have I come to this gate of the darkest world." He relished the darkness descending and resting "on lovely skins until brown seems so luscious and natural." He basked in the sunlight, "great gold globules and soft, heavy-scented heat that wraps you like a garment." He delighted in the laziness of everyday African life, "divine, eternal languor" that felt "right and good and true." He celebrated Christmas and welcomed in the new year of 1924 on the land of his forefathers. For the next two months, he called West Africa his home.[6]

Du Bois arrived in Liberia with the title "Envoy Extraordinary and Minister Plenipotentiary." He had pulled the necessary strings to be the American government's special representative at the second-term inauguration ceremonies of the president Charles D. B. King.[7] Much to the surprise of other foreign leaders and the consternation of the State Department, he transformed the courtesy gesture into an official ambassadorship, taking it upon himself to affirm the commitment of America and its eleven million people of African descent to Liberia's future.[8] He offered recommendations to President King about the economic development of Liberia, which included a troubling partnership with the rubber magnate Harvey Firestone. He also traveled to Sierra Leone, where during his six days in the Crown colony he spoke at a branch meeting of the National Congress of British West Africa (NCBWA) held in Freetown. Founded in the Gold Coast by J. E. Casely Hayford, a fellow editor, activist, and ardent Pan-Africanist, the NCBWA sowed important seeds for future independence movements in the region.[9]

While Du Bois took pleasure in every moment in West Africa, an ocean away, loyal subscribers of *The Crisis* received the January issue. As promised, it contained the opening of Du Bois's highly anticipated book, along with its tantalizing name and subtitle: "The Black Man and the Wounded World: A History of the Negro Race in the World War and After."

~

AMID LAST-MINUTE FRENZIED ORGANIZATION of the Pan-African Congress and preparations to travel abroad, Du Bois had found time to write and put finishing touches on the introductory chapter for his long-awaited book. He modestly named it "Interpretations." However, the chapter spoke to the grand ambitions he had for *The Black Man and the Wounded World*, as well as its groundbreaking potential.

"What is the ruling power in any given country?" Du Bois began, tracing the evolution of modern capitalism and the emergence of a world ruled by what he termed the "Dominant Wills." This narrow class of income seekers consolidated and maintained power over the masses of "wage-earners" through the wielding of wealth, propaganda, manipulation of law, and physical force. A glimmer of hope appeared in the late nineteenth century as the working class threatened the rule of the Dominant Wills through industrial unionism and the threat of the strike. The promise of "Industrial Democracy" greeted the dawning of the twentieth century.

But this would not be the case. The twentieth century, as Du Bois had predicted in 1900 and restated in *The Souls of Black Folk* three years later, would be defined by the problem of the color line. With slavery nominally abolished and the wage-earning European masses challenging for their rights, the Dominant Wills began to embrace a more profitable political and economic system. The "New Imperialism," as Du Bois described it, stemmed from "the policy of conquest, slavery, monopoly and theft in Eastern Europe, Asia, Africa, and Central and South America." To reduce the possibility of unrest, the Dominant Wills relinquished a small share of economic power to the laboring class in return for their political consent. However, even more significant was the spread of the "false scientific dogma" of race that the Dominant Wills employed to both rationalize the New Imperialism and forge solidarity with the wage-earning masses based on the seductive power of whiteness. And thus, "with scarce an articulate word of protest," Du Bois wrote, "the world in the late 19th and early 20th centuries was hurriedly divided up among European Countries and the United States into colonies owned or controlled by white civilized nations, or 'spheres of influence' dominated by them."

The reckoning came in 1914. As he had presciently argued in his 1915 article "The African Roots of War," Du Bois reiterated that "in allocating the spoils of the Earth, Europe fell into a jealous quarrel that nearly overthrew Civilization and left it mortally wounded." The war, in hindsight, had nothing to do with the expansion of democracy. Indeed, universal democracy, despite the lofty words of Woodrow Wilson and the Allies, struck fear in the hearts of the ruling elite, who used every method at their disposal to subvert and deny it. The true origins and impetus for the war was the thirst of the Dominant Wills for imperial expansion and greater wealth extracted from the land and bodies of the darker races.

This made the war—the "greatest catastrophe which the world ever knew"—much more than "simply a failure to agree" on the part of the Western imperial powers. The "God-defying dream had a thousand seeds of disaster," Du Bois asserted, certainly in the "hundred recurring points of disagreement in colonial expansion and development," but also in the unsustainability of the entire imperial system. Much sooner than later, he predicted, "the white wage-earner" would have no choice but to realize that "upholding Imperial Aggression over the darker peoples" only benefited the Dominant Wills, and that the "victims of imperial greed in Asia and Africa are human beings like himself." But Du Bois did not absolve the white working class of responsibility for the horror that befell the world. "All those modern civilized citizens who submitted voluntarily to the Dominant Wills of those who ruled the leading lands in 1914 were blood guilty of the murder of the men who fell in the war." "More guilty," however, "were those whose acts and thoughts made up the Dominant Wills and who were willing to increase their incomes at the expense of those who suffer in Europe and out, under the present industrial system." Blame for the war, therefore, lay not with nations, but with the men who led them and those who followed their lead: "Not Germany but certain Germans. Not England but certain Englishmen. Not France but certain Frenchmen." Blinded by whiteness, fueled by imperial greed, and lusting for power, "Individuals caused the Great War," Du Bois proclaimed, "did its deviltry and are guilty of its endless Crime."

The world had been left wounded, perhaps permanently so. Black folk, along with the masses of white workers in Europe and America, bore the scars. For Du Bois, the legacy of the war was now clear. And he left no room for misunderstanding how he felt: "The Great War was a Scourge, an Evil, a retrogression to Barbarism, a waste, a wholesale murder."[10]

The events of the past two years, as painful as they were, pushed him toward an understanding of the war as the ultimate tragedy. Judging from its scintillating introduction, *The Black Man and the Wounded World* promised to be unlike any other book on the war and, perhaps, Du Bois's most powerful work of history.

～

FINISHING AND PUBLISHING THIS BOOK, however, would not be easy. Much work remained to write the still-outstanding chapters and create a technically sound manuscript that, above all else, possessed Du Bois's trademark analytical voice and moving prose. He needed uninterrupted time, which meant financial assistance that the

NAACP surely would not provide. But more immediately, he wanted to know if enough interest existed among African Americans for the book.

Deciding to take the temperature of his market, he concluded "Interpretations" with a statement: "On account of its length and its frankly pro-Negro attitude, it is possible that Dr. Du Bois' history of the Negro in the World War will have to be published by subscription. In this case the possibility of publication will depend on the number of persons willing to subscribe." This was followed by a request for anyone "interested in the publication of 'The Black Man in the Wounded World' by Dr. W. E. Burghardt Du Bois and would like details as to its size, cost and date of issue when these matters have been determined on" to send their name and address to *The Crisis*.

Soon after the January issue reached the public, subscription pledges began flooding the *Crisis* mail room. They arrived from loyal readers representing every corner of the country: Mabel Burton of Philadelphia; Henry Asberry of Tacoma, Washington; Joseph August of New Orleans; Claude Green of St. Paul, Minnesota; Oscar McFarlin of Great Falls, Montana; Dudley Jackson of Springfield, Ohio; Flora Harris of Caldwell, Kansas; William Douglass of Berkeley, California. Most people took the time to carefully cut out Du Bois's request at the end of the article, write their name and address on the tiny blank space provided, and place their response in the mail. Sometimes they affixed it to a postcard. Other pledges took the form of handwritten notes, formal typed letters, and business cards. Many respondents expressed their excitement to Du Bois directly. Bradford G. Williams from Lakeland, Florida, had recently read *Darkwater* and eagerly anticipated the editor's next masterpiece. "I shall be delighted to subscribe to the new book, 'The Black Man in the Wounded World', and you may advise me at any time as to the cost," he wrote.[11]

Du Bois, on the other side of the Atlantic, still busy and basking in the euphoria of his African homecoming, was not aware of the reaction to his preview. However, when he returned to the United States around the middle of March and got up to speed on developments concerning the book, he had to be pleased.

On April 24, just before hitting the lecture circuit for speeches at several southern and midwestern cities, Du Bois arrived at his office, where he found a surprising letter forwarded by Mary White Ovington.[12] It was from Carter G. Woodson. Du Bois and Woodson had maintained a cordial if understandably guarded relationship since their dispute some five years earlier over who would write the history of the Black experience in the war. Since that time, Woodson, working tirelessly from his three-story 1538 Ninth Street office-home in Washington, DC, continued to lead the Association for the Study of Negro Life and History while holding positions at Howard University and West Virginia Collegiate Institute.[13] The two men corresponded on occasion, mostly on matters pertaining to lines of communication between *The Crisis* and *The Journal of Negro History* and Du Bois's participation at the ASNLH annual conference. They never revisited the touchy subject of the history of the war.

Du Bois most likely experienced some mild shock upon reading that Woodson might be willing to publish *The Black Man and the Wounded World*. Woodson had read Du Bois's introduction in the January issue of *The Crisis* and found it intriguing. He conveyed his interest to Mary White Ovington instead of to Du Bois directly, no doubt leery of how his overture might be received. Du Bois read Woodson's note with polite yet skeptical acknowledgment of the offer to possibly bring his manuscript to print. "If you are still of this opinion," he wrote without offering additional details, "I should be glad to hear further from you personally."[14]

Woodson responded four days later. The title "The Black Man and the Wounded World" had caught his attention. He wondered if the scope of Du Bois's manuscript would be "broader than the World War" and said that it brought to his mind "the possibility of giving the public an up-to-date message concerning the status of the Negro of today as determined by the events of the last decade or generation." Woodson, however, did not want to get Du Bois's hopes up too high. "If this is merely a history of the Negro in the World War it would be difficult to make its publication a success," he warned. "You realize that the enthusiasm of the World War is about as dead as the League of Nations. The Negroes themselves have lost interest in their own record during that upheaval, and white persons have never been anxious to publish such deeds to coming generations." He nevertheless expressed his willingness to cooperate with Du Bois "in bringing out this work" after having the opportunity to view the manuscript and to "learn exactly what your requirements are."[15]

Woodson's appraisal of the marketing prospects of a book on the war possessed some merit. Americans, by and large, looked at the war and its legacy with cynicism, if not outright bitterness. Woodson was correct in his assessment of most mainstream publishers showing little interest in the historical contributions of people of African descent. He stood on less sturdy ground, however, with his view that African Americans had "lost interest in their own record" of the war. Formal "official" history of the sort that Woodson steadfastly promoted may not have been up to the task, but Black people found various ways to express their memories of the war and its significance, especially in the realm of New Negro culture. Poems, plays, novels, even music conveyed the impact of the war as a transformative moment, for both the better and the worse.[16]

Du Bois did not follow through on Woodson's inquiry about publishing *The Black Man and the Wounded World*. With no complete manuscript to show Woodson and still hesitant to work with him, he likely deemed it best to let the matter go for the time being. But Du Bois, whether intentionally or not, tested Woodson's view on public interest in the history of the war. The following month, in the May issue of *The Crisis*, he published yet another portion of his book, the opening parts of chapter 2, titled "The Story of the War."[17]

He began in 1911, with the Universal Races Congress—what he declared at the time as "the greatest event of the twentieth century."[18] He was among the twenty-one hundred international representatives who'd convened in London between July 26 and July 29 to discuss the global problem of the color line. The lead organizer, Gustav Spiller, a prominent voice in the British Ethical Movement, saw this meeting, using "the light of modern science," as a first step in bringing the races of the East and the West together toward "a fuller understanding, the most friendly feelings, and a better co-operation."[19] Still a faithful adherent to the idea of European rationality and inevitable progress, Du Bois was enraptured by Spiller's vision and the congress's potential.[20]

Now, in hindsight, Du Bois could see the storm clouds that had threatened even this most hopeful of gatherings. A speech by the German anthropologist Felix von Luschan stood out for its menacing assertion of the permanence of "racial and national antagonism" and the rights of nations to defend their vital interests "with blood and iron" if necessary.[21]

The Agadir Crisis, occurring simultaneously with the Congress, provided the context for von Luschan's remarks. Morocco had been a flash point of tension between France and Germany since 1906. When France responded to an April 1911 revolt against Sultan Hafid by sending troops to the country, Germany, under the guise of protecting its citizens and business interests, countered by ordering the gunboat *Panther* to the port city of Agadir on July 1. "We sensed the shudder in the world and heard the hurrying of statesmen and the ominous speech of the Prime Minister," Du Bois wrote, referring to the July 21 address by David Lloyd George in London's Mansion House, where he emphatically affirmed his country's alliance with France and declared that he preferred war with Germany over Great Britain's vital interests being undermined and its national honor humiliated.[22] Talk of war had continued throughout the summer, until Germany and France stepped back from the precipice and negotiated the Treaty of Fez, which further carved up Africa and the imperial spoils that came with it.[23]

But temporary peace only affirmed alliances and hardened the possible battle lines of a war most Europeans deemed inevitable. The illusory calm quickly evaporated following the assassination of Archduke Franz Ferdinand and his wife, Sophie, on June 28, 1914. "The world caught its breath for a month," Du Bois reflected, but the chorus of war proved too great. And "so between July 28, 1914, and August 28, eight of the greatest nations of the world, representing its highest and best culture . . . declared that organized and world wide murder was the only path to salvation and peace."[24] Du Bois cast his net for blame widely. "The decision to force changes by military power was the guilt of Germany and a deep crimson guilt," he acknowledged. Nevertheless, the true "blood guilt," he argued, lay with every Western nation, America included, that thirsted for imperial wealth at the expense of people of color and the working classes, the result being "four long bloody years."

Du Bois then offered a sweeping overview of the first two years of the war as it unfolded in Europe. Germany made the fateful decision to fight Russia on the Eastern Front while moving forward with its long-standing plans to crush France. "On came the mighty German machine in never ending columns of grey." History would hinge on the First Battle of the Marne of September 1914. "This was the great decisive battle of the war, but alas! It did not end the fighting, it only began it." He specifically mentioned the presence of Black men, likely Algerian *tirailleurs*, fighting for France at the Battle of Ourcq River. With German aspirations for a quick victory thwarted, "the whole character of the war changed." Both sides entrenched and began the furious "Race to the Sea," hoping to seize control of the northern flank. "It was cold, wet, muddy and misty, and the murderous machines strewed the blood and limbs of thousands upon thousands across the black fields of Flanders." At the First Battle of Ypres, occurring in October and November, "the British army was wiped out and there it was that whole battalions of black men perished and more than 200,000 corpses rotted and stank in the mud." "Entrenched in deadlock," the end of the year found the opposing forces "sinking to confused sobbing and quivering" along two daunting battlefronts, each several hundred miles long.

The year 1915, Du Bois began in the next section, "saw the Allies confident and the Germans grim." The combined naval power of France and England inspired hopes of ending the war on the Western Front. Germany, however, countered with a massive influx of artillery that smashed Russia to the east and held the Allies in check to the west. Du Bois's excerpt ended there, with a cliff-hanging "to be continued," followed by another subscription request for readers to support publication of *The Black Man and the Wounded World*.[25]

With this second chapter, a truly singular book appeared to be in the works. No other historian, Black or white, had told the imperial origins of the war and its devastating opening months in this way. Du Bois also demonstrated a deep grasp of the battlefield history of the war and an ability to distill it into concise, lively, accessible prose. Sure enough, more subscription pledges streamed in from readers all over the country and world, from Rochester, New York, to Lander, Wyoming, to Salisbury, England, to Khartoum, Sudan.[26] "I have always been interested in your masterful literary productions," wrote the ex-serviceman Blair T. Hunt from Memphis. He looked forward to the publication of *The Black Man and the Wounded World* and promised to publicize it widely.

Hunt also reminded Du Bois of their past correspondence. "When thru the Crisis several years ago you mentioned the proposed book, I sent two pictures very valuable to me." Hunt wondered if the editor still had them.[27]

∽

DU BOIS DESCRIBED THE decade after World War I as one of "infinite effort and discouraging turmoil."[28] The remainder of 1924 and the early months of 1925 certainly reflected this. His clash with Marcus Garvey reached its ugly climax as the two iron-willed men traded increasingly personal barbs over who had the right to speak for and represent the race. Garvey, under attack from the federal government as well, was imprisoned for mail fraud in February 1925 and deported back to Jamaica two years later.[29] Turning from Garvey to his alma mater, Du Bois spearheaded an alumni and student rebellion to have the white president of Fisk University, Fayette McKenzie, removed from office.[30] He also found time to revisit *The Star of Ethiopia*, with two underwhelming stagings in Los Angeles on June 15 and 18, 1925.[31] If a battle needed to be fought, or a controversy demanded his opinion, or an opportunity to further the cause of Black freedom presented itself, Du Bois felt compelled to act.

In the summer, a national uproar directly related to the history of the World War erupted. Doubleday, Page and Company began promoting the highly anticipated release of Major General Robert Lee Bullard's memoir *Personalities and Reminiscences of the War*. By the time of the armistice, Bullard, a native of Alabama who had a long record of service in Cuba, the Philippines, and Mexico, stood just behind John Pershing as one of the most senior officers in the American Expeditionary Forces, commanding the Second Army.[32] His book would be the first published account by an officer in the AEF leadership and—in the still-unsettled historiography of American participation in the World War—would carry great weight. Advance excerpts of the book began appearing in the press by June, highlighting his criticisms of Pershing, Secretary of War Newton Baker, and the French, who he claimed lacked the discipline and fighting spirit of the British and Americans.

Of all the combat units in the AEF, only one received a full chapter treatment in Bullard's book: the Ninety-Second Division.[33] Bullard had commanded a volunteer regiment of Black Alabama troops during the Spanish-Cuban-American War. After that experience, combined with memories of his "pleasant boyhood with the Negroes," he claimed to hold "most kindly feelings toward them" and professed to have no bias toward the capabilities of Black soldiers when properly led. When it came to the "Negro problem," he believed that "politics constantly forced for them the same treatment as white men, when they were very different."

The Ninety-Second Division, which became part of the AEF Second Army in October 1918 and thus under his command, proved his point. The fallout from the Meuse-Argonne experience of the 368th Infantry Regiment brought the Ninety-Second to his attention. Bullard claimed that he did everything within his power to intervene in the trials of the five Black officers accused of cowardice and ensure fair justice, but in the end he decided there was nothing he could do. "The Negroes were a great disappointment," he wrote in his book. The physical inferiority of the Black race, in his view, made this inevitable. "The Negro, it seems cannot stand bombardment." Nature made Black soldiers a sexual threat as well. "The Negro is a more sensual man than the white man," Bullard theorized, "and at the same time he is far more offensive to white women than is a white man." Only this could explain why "this special Negro division was already charged with fifteen cases of rape." As a result, Bullard ordered that the Ninety-Second Division be sent back to the United States ahead of all other American combat divisions, telling Supreme Allied Commander Foch, "No man could be responsible for the acts of these Negroes towards Frenchwomen." "Altogether my memories of the 92nd Negro Division are a nightmare," Bullard ended. His experience left him with only one inescapable conclusion: "If you need combat soldiers, and especially if you need them in a hurry, don't put your time upon Negroes."[34]

When excerpts from Bullard's explosive chapter on the Ninety-Second Division appeared in the *Chicago Daily Tribune* and other newspapers, African Americans across the country reacted with outrage. BULLARD "A DAMNABLE LIAR," blasted the *New York Amsterdam News*.[35] BULLARD WAS NAMED FOR BOB LEE, mocked *The Chicago Defender*, referring to the general's Confederate namesake.[36] "TAKE BACK LIES," BULLARD IS TOLD, screamed *The Pittsburgh Courier*, going on to describe the memoir as "the insipid workings of the prejudiced mind of a white southern 'cracker'" from "one of the worst southern states with the worst reputation for its treatment of colored people."[37] "We learned a whole lot about the white man in the war," wrote an infuriated former officer of the Ninety-Second Division in response to Bullard's slander. "He is nothing but a beast and a devil and a hypocrite."[38]

Matthew Boutté responded as well. Speaking as a veteran of the Ninety-Second Division as well as leader of the Charles Young Post of the American Legion, Boutté called Bullard's stories "most damnable" and said that in any future wars Black people would refuse to fight under the command of racists such as he.[39]

Not surprisingly, several African Americans wrote to Du Bois directly to voice their outrage. G. H. Hammond Jr. considered Bullard's accusations a "rank injustice to the twelve million or more Negroes in the United States and blasphemy to the sacred memory of those that have made the supreme sacrifice in the service of this country." He predicted in his letter that the racist general would no doubt "be given a gold medal by the K. K. K."[40] The Reverend Walter Chenault, pastor of Bethel AME Church in New Albany, Indiana, sent Du Bois a copy of an article about the controversy from the Louisville *Courier-*

Journal. He wanted to see the book disavowed by the War Department, John Pershing, and Marshal Foch, as well as banned from all public libraries, and Bullard publicly rebuked. "This is a man's job," Chenault emphasized, "and in my judgment, can be most effectively done by the great N.A.A.C.P. and the Crisis." He hoped that Du Bois personally would "find ample time and space in which to effectively answer this vile assault upon a defenseless race."[41]

The NAACP leapt into action, demonstrating that the race was far from defenseless. After the *New York Herald-Tribune* published excerpts of Bullard's book on June 9, James Weldon Johnson immediately issued a response that appeared the following day. The national office contacted Emmett J. Scott, along with Colonel William Hayward and Hamilton Fish III from the 369th "Hellfighters" to write additional rebuttals.[42] Lastly, at its annual conference in Denver in late June, the NAACP passed a special resolution condemning Bullard's attempt to "defame and discredit the men of the Ninety-Second Division" and declaring his slanderous book "a hostile gesture, most improper in any army officer, from the element in the South that is still unenlightened and still cave-dwelling."[43]

When Du Bois arrived back in New York from Denver sometime around the first week of July, the Bullard matter and its direct connection to *The Black Man and the Wounded World* awaited him in the form of a letter from Major Adam Patterson. The former judge advocate of the Ninety-Second Division jumped headfirst into the controversy, penning a rebuttal for the June 13 issue of *The Chicago Defender*: "It is almost unbelievable that a man of General Bullard's type can be so far wrong in his observations regarding the Colored soldiers in the A. E. F., yet such is the case." With lawyerly, point-by-point precision, he drew from his own memory to present a convincing case for the ways in which the Ninety-Second Division had been the victim of a racist smear campaign, adding that white officers in the controversial Meuse-Argonne operation were the true cowards. "There are so many discrepancies and misstatements contained in General Bullard's article that they border on the ridiculous," he wrote.[44]

Three days after his *Chicago Defender* article appeared, Adam Patterson reached out to Du Bois from his City Hall office. He, along with other officers of the Ninety-Second Division, planned to write an additional series of articles for the *Chicago Tribune*. "I will need the manuscript I sent you for the history," he insisted. Patterson had contacted Du Bois the previous month, inquiring once again about the rare photographs he'd supplied for their project and requesting their return "without further annoyance." Du Bois, about to depart for California, apologized for the delay, but promised that "the book is coming one of these days."[45] The Bullard affair upped the ante. Patterson tried to remain magnanimous despite five years of Du Bois's cold shoulder. He promised his onetime collaborator that he would preserve and return the manuscript "in even better shape and with many excellent additions from some of the officers interested in making a defense." He was ready to come to New York, if necessary, and personally retrieve his materials "because of the importance of the work at hand . . . Please have it ready for me."[46]

Du Bois knew exactly the state of *The Black Man and the Wounded World*. "I find that it is quite impossible to restore or copy your manuscript," he responded matter-of-factly three weeks later. He attempted to explain to Patterson that his contribution "occupied a number of pages and has been divided according to the subjects and distributed into various parts of my manuscript. Then the manuscript was dictated and the originals filed according to chapters . . . It is simply impossible to separate the work now into its original constituent parts," Du Bois wrote. "I am sorry."

In an accompanying letter, he provided a more detailed update on the condition of the book, listing the twenty-one chapters he had in mind. The first sixteen chapters, Du Bois generously claimed, had "been written and once re-written." The remaining chapters "are planned and can be finished in a month." Offering yet another ambitious timeline for completion, he professed, "In two or three months the whole of the matter can be re-written and condensed and put in final form for the printer. If I could have the requisite help and leisure this history could be ready for publication January 1, 1926." He would need at least $2,500. "Without this sum," Du Bois rationalized, "the work will be finished but it will have to drag on as a subsidiary part of my regular work with such stenographic help as

THE CRISIS can spare." He wanted Patterson to take up the proposition with his fellow officers and members of the Committee of One Hundred. If they provided him with the money, Du Bois promised he could "concentrate upon the matter and prepare it quickly and finally." He also pledged to "give credit upon the title page to a number of persons who have helped me with manuscripts and stories including, of course, yourself."[47]

A few days later, a determined Patterson arrived at NAACP headquarters to resolve the impasse in person. The two men finally met face-to-face. They agreed to allow Patterson's personal office clerk to stay in New York and help sort through the manuscript. Du Bois, however, remained noncommittal about the results and reiterated as much in a follow-up letter after Patterson returned to Chicago. He also wanted to make clear that *The Black Man and the Wounded World* was his work, despite the former major's contribution, emphasizing that "the data which you furnished is but a very small part of the amount which I have collected." He would do what he could to supply Patterson with his materials, but offered the caveat, "I cannot be certain of my success."[48]

Sure enough, after undertaking a "cursory examination" of his research, he informed Patterson a week later in a July 22 note: "It is as I have feared . . . All of my matter is classified and packed in bundles. It is impossible for any one to go through these without disturbing my work of years. I must, therefore, do it myself." "No one can help me in this matter," he wrote, most especially Patterson's assistant, whose presence and unsolicited advice about how to run his *Crisis* office clearly rubbed Du Bois the wrong way. He could not devote any time to the project until September, but he still hoped to have the book completed by the first of the year. He again pressed Patterson for financial assistance, effectively holding the highly valued manuscript and photographs hostage.[49]

Patterson, however, did not blink. He consulted with the Committee of One Hundred—which presumably included many of the veterans who wanted their photographs and other materials returned—about raising the money Du Bois requested. They all agreed that "with reference to the difficulty in getting at the desired manuscript nothing can be done until such time as you will be able to furnish it." Patterson hoped that Du Bois would be true to his word and "give us what we want by the first of January next." Patterson also saw no reason for his assistant to waste any additional time in New York under Du Bois's hostile glare; she returned to Chicago.[50]

Perhaps spurred by Patterson, finally, in the September issue of *The Crisis*, in an editorial simply titled "Bullard," Du Bois stepped forward to have his say on the controversy. He expressed no surprise at Bullard's assault on the legacy of African American troops in the war. "This attack has been long planned and long over due," Du Bois wrote. From the start, Southern officers like Bullard, along with other "Negro haters entrenched in the Army and at Washington," feared the success of the Ninety-Second Division and began "a concerted campaign" against it. Drawing on his years of research and his own memory, Du Bois then presented the history of the Ninety-Second Division and the deliberate plan to destroy it in nine succinct, angry, no-holds-barred points, including the elimination of Charles Young as the potential leader of the division and the narrowly averted legal lynching of the Black officers unjustly persecuted for their role in the Meuse-Argonne fiasco. Du Bois's ninth and final point—part prophecy, part warning, and part promise—spoke directly to *The Black Man and the Wounded World*:

> And then after seven years, Bullard voices the re-vamped lie which was plotted in 1918 and lay awaiting forgetfulness. But we black men do not forget and there is about the writer a thousand pages of narrative and document to prove all and much more than has been written. Some day it will be published.[51]

Just as Du Bois issued his *Crisis* editorial, the Army War College was in the final stages of preparing a report on "The Use of Negro Manpower in War." The purpose of the study was to determine how best to employ Black troops in the event of a future military conflict. The War College compiled the testimony of white officers from the

Ninety-Second Division while making no effort to obtain the views of such Black officers as Adam Patterson, Matthew Boutté, and others. The final report, completed on October 25, 1925, was blistering and effectively mirrored the assessments of Bullard in his memoir. "The negro officer was a failure as a combat officer in the World War," it bluntly concluded. "Negro combat units should be officered entirely by white officers except in the grade of lieutenant," while Black officers "should be assigned in general to non-combatant units of negro troops." Under no circumstances, the report asserted, were Black officers to "be placed over white officers, noncommissioned officers or soldiers."[52] The commandant of the War College, Major General Hanson Ely, fully endorsed the report and recommended that "unless and until a more complete study be made on the subject," the conclusions "be accepted as the War Department policy in handling this problem."[53] So sealed the Jim Crow fate of Black troops in the U.S. Army.

~

MENTALLY EXHAUSTED AFTER SEVERAL months of intense travel, work, and unpleasant reminders about his unfinished book, Du Bois needed a break. He spent the end of August and the beginning of September 1925 on vacation with his wife, Nina, in his hometown of Great Barrington, having spotted a pleasant-looking inn during a recent high school reunion visit. The holiday left such an impression on him that he shared his experience with his good friend Charles Bentley: "It was a very fine and inspiring rest." He also updated Bentley on other personal and familial matters. Yolande was teaching in Baltimore, and—after accepting the wedding proposal of her beau, the Phi Beta Kappa and wunderkind poet Countee Cullen—she sported "a large and impressive diamond on one of her fingers, I forget which." As far as himself, Du Bois informed Bentley, "I have begun the work of the new year which looks interesting. I am considering first and foremost my history of the Negro soldiers."[54]

The Bullard controversy, combined with his exchange with Adam Patterson, jolted Du Bois into action. By September, he was fully re-engaged in writing *The Black Man and the Wounded World*. He not only owed it to the race; he owed it to himself to complete the book.

Du Bois directed his renewed focus on the heart of Bullard's attack: the Ninety-Second Division and the experience of the 368th. The pained conversations with dispirited Black officers in France in December and January 1918 and 1919 flashed back into his memory, and he was determined to amass as much evidence as possible to make an airtight case for vindicating the 368th. To add to his already substantial archive of letters, firsthand accounts, military orders, and court-martial records, he sought out further details about every aspect of the 368th's experience in the Meuse-Argonne battle.[55]

Throughout September and much of October 1925, he feverishly wrote and revised. "In a singular way the history of the black race in the Great War hinges about the 368th Regiment," he declared at the beginning of his pivotal chapter. "Not that it was really an unusual regiment or had an unusual history but it happened from a series of events that this regiment was thrown into the lime light and has become a matter of disputed history, intense feeling and propaganda."[56] He meticulously compiled document after document, assembling an irrefutable record of systemic discrimination, institutional failure, white incompetence, and intentional ruin of the 368th's reputation. Just as important, he humanized the maligned officers of the regiment. He included a photo of Captain Daniel Smith, one of the men convicted and ultimately cleared of charges of cowardice, along with biographical information chronicling his many years of service dating back to the Spanish-Cuban-American War. By the end of October, a draft of the chapter, well over one hundred pages in length, sat on his desk.[57]

Satisfied with his writing progress, Du Bois turned his attention again to the publication prospects of *The Black Man and the Wounded World*. In doing so, he remembered a letter from Robert Littell of the Macmillan Company that he'd received back in July. Littell had contacted Du Bois for tips on finding the next "Great American Novel" and who might be writing it. While tasked with scouting for fiction, Littell also informed Du Bois, "naturally I won't close my eyes to a good manuscript of any other kind."[58]

Almost two months later, on September 10, Du Bois responded and made a pitch for his book on the World War, explaining that he'd begun research for the project in 1919, following the armistice, and devoted the last six years to collecting and writing. "I am going to have ready on or about January first the manuscript of a work in one large volume or two moderate volumes which I have proposed to call 'The Black Man in the Wounded World.'"[59]

Du Bois must have been both pleased and slightly concerned with Littell's response. "I was very glad indeed to hear from you," Littell wrote a week later, "and I should be most interested in seeing your manuscript when it is done." Littell, however, was frank about how his Macmillan colleagues might receive Du Bois's proposal, and he did not want to "exaggerate their hospitality to a book such as you describe." He nevertheless encouraged Du Bois to submit the manuscript and looked forward to hearing from him "around the first of the year."[60]

January 1926 arrived, and Littell did not hear from Du Bois. Another deadline for completing the manuscript came and went.

International events, however, buoyed Du Bois's spirits. On December 1, European leaders had convened in London to formally sign the Locarno Treaties. Versailles may have brought peace, but continental stability proved elusive. France did not budge on punishing Germany and the fragile Weimar Republic with crippling sanctions and military neutering. The 1919 occupation of the Rhineland by French West African troops—*Die schwarze Schande* ("the Black Shame")—became an especially potent symbol of national humiliation and continued to linger into 1923, when Germany defaulted on its reparation payments, leading to the Franco-Belgian occupation of the Ruhr valley.[61] With internal dissent growing and the Weimar Republic teetering on the brink of collapse, nervous banks across Europe and in the United States encouraged a stabilization of Germany's economy in order to avert a global crisis. The August 1924 Dawes Plan—which allowed for Germany to stagger its payments, provided generous Wall Street loans, and mandated the removal of French troops from the Ruhr by January of the following year—produced a collective sigh of relief on both sides of the Atlantic. But important issues remained unresolved, especially concerning border security, military alliances, and the role of the League of Nations.[62]

Hoping to settle these thorny matters, the foreign ministers of France, Germany, and Great Britain convened on October 5, 1925, at the Swiss lakeside town of Locarno. During a five-hour boat cruise on the picturesque Lake Maggiore, they outlined the general terms of a historic pact, agreed to eleven days later and formally signed in London on December 1. The series of treaties guaranteed the western frontiers of Germany, demilitarized the Rhineland, and pledged that the signatories, which also included Belgium and Italy, would not go to war without first engaging in arbitration—and only in the case of "flagrant violation." Any disputes would be settled by the League of Nations, which Germany now entered with a permanent seat on the Council. Locarno appeared to rectify the errors of Versailles and truly end the war. Germany was optimistic, France came away pleased, and Great Britain, in the role of arbitrator of the peace, emerged content and eager to turn its attention to domestic and imperial matters. Although the Soviet Union premier Joseph Stalin, who rose to power after Lenin's death in January 1924, thumbed his nose at the entire affair, Europe and much of the world embraced "the spirit of Locarno."[63]

Du Bois voiced this mood in his March 1926 *Crisis* editorial "Peace on Earth": "At last there are signs that some of the dreams of those who fought and supported the World War may sometime be realized." Locarno offered a glimmer of hope and a pathway to healing the wounded world. The next step, Du Bois wrote, "after praising God for Locarno, is to say to Europe: Make way for the freedom of Asia and Africa. There can be no real disarmament in Europe and America if white nations must hold yellow and black folk in chains and then ever suffer the temptation to throttle each other in order to monopolize their illgotten gains." "Peace on earth is no mirage," he proclaimed. "It is a solemn, awful necessity. Its solution lies in facing cold and cruel facts."[64]

Recalling their exchange from two years earlier about the publication prospects of *The Black Man and the Wounded World*, Du Bois reached out to Carter G. Woodson. In his March 19 letter, Du Bois explained, "Since then I have been trying to finish the manuscript but, as you realize only too well, it is never possible to bring a historical treatise to a satisfactory end." He wanted to know if Woodson was still interested. "It will be a long manuscript," Du Bois warned, adding that he possessed "a still larger mass of the material upon which it has been based." He grudgingly accepted that "it is going to be impossible to get it published in its entirety but nevertheless I suppose it is my duty to try."[65]

Woodson responded positively the next day. "I can encourage you to expect serious consideration of your proposal. I shall do anything I can to have this book published." But, again, he could make no definitive promises until he examined the manuscript. Moreover, always mindful of his precarious finances, Woodson asked in a handwritten question scrawled at the bottom of his note, "Can you bear any of the expense?"[66] This was likely enough for Du Bois to consider a partnership with Woodson unfeasible.

Du Bois felt anxious. The immense size of the manuscript began to frustrate him. He conveyed as much in a follow-up note to Robert Littell at Macmillan, who remained interested in the project.[67] But Du Bois's own restlessness proved equally challenging. The postwar world remained wounded, and he needed to understand why. "I had to be a part of the revolution through which the world was going and to feel in my own soul the scars of its battle," he later reflected.[68] Whether in promoting Pan-Africa, vindicating the Black officers of the 368th Infantry, or looking hopefully to Locarno, Du Bois continued to seek some redeeming value in the war.

He finally decided to see for himself what was arguably the most revolutionary outcome of the conflict—the Soviet Union. He initially viewed the 1917 Bolshevik Revolution with a mixture of distant fascination and skepticism.[69] In the ensuing years, as he began writing what would become *The Black Man and the Wounded World*, he resisted fully engaging with the idea of revolutionary Marxism, still clinging to the best hope of liberal democracy. But by 1926, visiting the Soviet Union became both an intellectual and a political necessity.

Du Bois lagged behind many New Negroes, such as Claude McKay, who pointed to the editor's disconnect from the Soviet Union to further question his leadership and radical credentials. When a Soviet couple Du Bois had befriended offered to bankroll a visit to their home country, with the understanding that, as he later remembered, "I would be free to examine conditions and come to my own conclusions," he leapt at the opportunity.[70] He'd planned to travel to Switzerland and Germany that summer and had no problem tacking on a journey through the Soviet Union as well.

Before his July departure for Europe, he continued to devote time to the manuscript, circling back to work on chapter 10, "The Battalions of Labor." In Du Bois's historical and political imagination, the more than 150,000 African American labor troops who had toiled overseas during the war did not register as highly as the soldiers and officers of the Ninety-Second and Ninety-Third Divisions. Nevertheless, they constituted an important part of the story he hoped to tell. Along with his slew of official documents, he leaned heavily on Addie Hunton and Kathryn Johnson's book to detail the pioneer infantry regiments and made use of another contribution to the modest historiography of the Black experience in the war, *Sidelights on Negro Soldiers*, published in 1923 by the Hampton Institute instructor Charles H. Williams.[71] Du Bois may have also started thinking about an unwritten chapter 6, tentatively titled "Other Black Folk."[72]

Du Bois pushed *The Black Man and the Wounded World*—along with everything else on his perpetually full plate—to the side when he departed for Europe on July 17, 1926. He first visited Germany. Although the economy had slightly improved with the Dawes Plan, and the recently enacted Locarno Treaties had lifted the mood of the Weimar Republic, the scars of war remained visible. A heartbroken Du Bois walked the streets of Berlin and mourned his beloved Germany "struggling on the ruins of the empire and tottering under a load of poverty, oppression and disorganization."[73] Friends from the town of Eisenach, he reminisced, "had disappeared in the war, with little trace." He did not stay in Germany for long. After resolving a mishap with his visa, he departed for the main purpose of his trip.[74]

Years later, Du Bois wrote, "Never in my life have I been so stirred as by what I saw during two months in Russia."[75] He arrived in mid-August, sailing from Stettin through the Baltic and the Gulf of Finland for three days before arriving in Leningrad, what was once St. Petersburg and before that Petrograd. The sights and scenes of the city, as he wandered through Palace Square and along the shimmering Neva River, quickly enraptured Du Bois, infusing him with a reverence that in many ways mirrored his exaltation of France in the winter of 1918–19. The train ride from Leningrad to Moscow reminded him of his youthful days in southern New England, with "rolling pines and beeches, cattle and horses, grass."

His month in the Soviet capital, where he took up residence in a government-run hotel overlooking Red Square, was revelatory. With the help of friends and his ability to at least converse in French or German, he navigated the language barrier. A guide took him to schools, factories, libraries, museums, and other examples of the Soviet Union's development and the success of the revolution. He could of course not resist gathering some documents and peppering with questions the officials and teachers he met. But he mostly explored, observed, and pondered in solitude. "I wandered into all the nooks and crannies of the city unattended," he recalled. "I have trafficked on the curb and in the stores; I have watched crowds and audiences and groups." One evening he visited the mausoleum of Lenin and looked down upon the Bolshevik leader, "a little man, bold and blonde, bearded, with clipped moustache, just asleep." Poverty abounded, and the poor dress of the people betrayed their dire conditions. Nevertheless, they possessed a remarkable spirit, and Moscow buzzed with work and repair. And the color line was nowhere to be seen. For three weeks, Du Bois "sat still and gazed at this Russia, that the spirit of its life and people might enter my veins."[76]

He briefly visited other cities—Nizhny Novgorod along the Volga River, Odessa and Kiev in the Ukraine—before returning to the United States in October. The country he surveyed during his stay was "a land of enthusiasm" that, to his amazement, "had not emerged from war in 1918, on Armistice Day, but was just beginning in 1926 to breathe air free from Civil War and invasion, promoted and participated in by my own nation."⁷⁷ Du Bois believed in democracy. He and the African American soldiers at the heart of *The Black Man and the Wounded World* had fought to make the ideal a reality. But now he had seen another possibility and another future. He still needed time to assess and to study. However, as he told readers in the November *Crisis*, if what he observed with his own eyes in the Soviet Union was bolshevism, "I am a Bolshevik."⁷⁸

~

INVIGORATED BY HIS RECENT TRAVELS, Du Bois began the new year of 1927 thinking about *The Black Man and the Wounded World*. On January 3, he wrote to Robert Robinson Taylor, vice principal of Tuskegee, and informed him about the book. Du Bois hoped that given his influence and contacts, Taylor could "suggest some way in which this history can be finished and published."⁷⁹ "I have been writing on this history for the last ten years," he said. "It has been finished several times but, of course, there is always a chance for touching up and re-writing and I am doing that for now, I think, the third time." Du Bois believed that the manuscript could be done if he "put about three more months of intensive work upon it," but the question of how to publish it caused him to hesitate and delay. "I think I could get Mac-Millian [*sic*] or some other publisher of that sort to publish the work in one or two volumes, but that would mean cutting it down tremendously." This was not something he wished to do. He mentioned the possibility of working with Carter G. Woodson, but added dismissively, "I do not think that he is enthusiastic."⁸⁰

Du Bois's latest round of writing and editing again centered on the Ninety-Second Division. Going into even more detail and making use of records provided by Louis T. Wright and his scorned former coauthor Adam Patterson, he focused on the less-known elements of the division, such as its motorcycle, medical, and veterinary units and the judge advocate, finance, and accounting offices. Du Bois shared a thirty-two-page section of the book with Mary White Ovington, whose support for the project, stretching back to its genesis at the October 1918 board meeting, remained steadfast.⁸¹

Meanwhile, the patience of another veteran who'd loaned Du Bois material for *The Black Man and the Wounded World* grew thin. In August 1920, at Du Bois's request, James William Johnson, a former sergeant in the 349th Field Artillery of the Ninety-Second Division and now a Harlem attorney, had mailed a personal collection of "maps, orders, and data" for use in the war history. On May 28, 1927, Johnson wrote from his West 135th Street office to remind Du Bois of the materials he'd lent him as well as the editor's promise to return them in just a few months. Johnson's "repeated efforts" to contact Du Bois had proved unsuccessful. "Will you be good enough to let me known [*sic*] just when you will return this material," he inquired.[82]

Slightly embarrassed, Du Bois responded, "I am very sorry indeed to have kepted [*sic*] the material which you and others entrusted to me so long. I have been giving my spare time for over eight years to the preparation of my history of the Negroes in the great war." But, as with Adam Patterson, Du Bois could not return Johnson's items. "You will see how indispensable it is that this material be at my disposal until the question of publication is finally settled." He assured Johnson that his belongings remained "perfectly safe and I hope to be able to return all of the material not later than October First."[83] Johnson gave Du Bois the benefit of the doubt, writing on June 7, "I appreciate the value of Original Documents to an Author, and it is my desire to cooperate with you in the preparation of your history of the Negro in the Great War." He agreed to set plans for his materials, possibly another book or a personal memoir, aside for the time being. But, like a good attorney, he intended to hold Du Bois to his word. "In accordance with your promise I shall expect this material to be returned to me not later than October 1, 1927."[84]

The guilt of harboring the personal materials of yet another Black veteran once again ate at Du Bois's conscience and prompted him to try to find a way to finish his book. On June 15, he wrote to James Dillard, the influential white educator, benefactor of Southern Black schooling, and president of the John F. Slater Fund, to seek his assistance. "I had planned when I started to write a short history," but now, years later, "the project is much larger than I had laid out at first and I am sure that it could not be handed [*sic*] on a commercial basis."

Du Bois hoped that the well-connected Dillard would offer advice and, even better, funding to help him out of his impasse.[85]

Du Bois was intimately familiar with the world of white philanthropy and its role in shaping the production of Black knowledge. The continued existence and success of Black colleges and universities throughout the South depended on the benevolence of the Rockefellers, the Carnegies, and other Progressive Era tycoons interested in using a small slice of their vast fortunes to help with the "race problem." Just where this money went and for what purposes stood at the core of Du Bois's feud with Booker T. Washington and the Tuskegee Machine while he was at Atlanta University. Du Bois's belief that Black people must be more than laborers, and his commitment to the systematic study of Black life, had run against powerful headwinds, resulting in a constant and often losing battle for Northern money. White philanthropists functioned as gatekeepers, making the final decision about what scholarly projects received support and ultimately reached the public. A number of Du Bois's ideas had either languished or died altogether for lack of funding, and he knew that this could quite possibly be the fate of *The Black Man and the Wounded World* as well.[86]

Dillard considered Du Bois's letter. In his response, he made clear that the Slater Fund could not offer help, but he suggested the Rockefeller Foundation.[87] He also wondered whether the project "would be plain records and history, or whether there might be controversial matter."[88]

This question struck a nerve with Du Bois. He had long grown tired of supposedly enlightened white folk questioning the objectivity and potential reception of his work simply because he placed the humanity of Black people at the center of his interpretative framework. "Of course, any history must contain controversial matter," Du Bois explained. "I mean by that, history is an interpretation of facts and must, of course, be a question as to whether the interpretation is justified by facts. But scientific history tries to prevent [*sic*] all the facts and to make other facts available by careful reference. This is what I shall certainly do in the history of the Negro troops."[89]

Du Bois decided to take his case directly to the Rockefeller Foundation. On November 18, he wrote a detailed three-page letter to Raymond Fosdick, the foundation's most influential trustee and John Rockefeller Jr.'s closest adviser. Du Bois explained the genesis of the project, stating that he presently had a manuscript that "contains more than 781 type-written pages, letter size" and could very well grow to "over 1500 pages" when completed. "I realize now that I have undertaken a larger job than I can finish unaided," he admitted. But personal and intellectual pride prevented him from giving up on the project altogether, and he did not "relish the idea of surrendering my material or conclusions entirely to other hands." In order to "finish the work properly," he felt he needed "expert clerical and scientific assistance in this country, England and France," two or more graduate student assistants to track down and check his references, a research trip to explore additional sources in England, France, and Belgium, and a significant cash advance to "induce a publisher" as well as provide him with "leisure from my main work." He did not know exactly how much all this would cost, but "a maximum of $5000" seemed reasonable.

As for the book itself, *The Black Man and the Wounded World*, Du Bois summarized, was "a study of the effect of the great war on Negroes chiefly in the United States but also in the French, German, Belgian and British colonies." In focusing on the experiences of Black servicemen, his book aimed to "trace not simply their action as troops and laborers but their reaction to their treatment and environment and the effect of all this on modern culture." He added, "I hope in this history of the black troops to be absolutely honest and thorough in my examination of the truth and to spare neither white England and America nor the darker world in an endeavor to write a history which will paint war as the greatest of human catastrophies [*sic*] and race prejudice as its worthy coadjutor." Thinking back to Dillard's question about the potentially controversial nature of the book, Du Bois firmly stood his ground. "It goes without saying that anything I write is pro-Negro . . . Naturally it is going to defend the poor black and ignorant against prejudice and power. At the same time, in the past, my work in history and social science has, I think, stood up well under severe criticism."[90]

The response from 61 Broadway arrived swiftly. Raymond Fosdick delivered Du Bois's letter directly to John Rockefeller Jr., who balked at making a potentially risky investment. Rockefeller, his executive secretary wrote, held "no lack of sympathy with the objects which you have in mind." Nevertheless, he could not support Du Bois's project and clarified that it "represents one in which Mr. Rockefeller, in accordance with his principles, does not feel that he can participate."[91] For all his philanthropy and noblesse oblige toward the Negro, the young Rockefeller still represented the "Dominant Wills" whom Du Bois blamed for the cause of the war. He did not want his name attached, in any way, to such a radical reinterpretation of history.

The rejection put Du Bois in a dark mood. With his sixtieth birthday approaching, Matthew Boutté and his wife, Etnah, floated the idea of a nationwide celebration along with a sizable monetary gift. Du Bois had rather sadly spent, in his words, "all Christmas Eve and all day Christmas" pondering over their generous offer. He implored his dear friends to not attempt it. If, for some reason, "a spontaneous outburst of applause and goodwill in the shape of a gift that would give me more leisure" should appear, he would humbly accept. But they did not realize "how unlikely, how impossible any such manifestation of approval of me and my work is from either black folk or white today." He continued to bare his soul:

> It is possible that in some far off day much praise will come to my memory; although even that is not certain, for history plays curious tricks. Today, at any rate, I have a few fine and loyal friends; I have a small audience which, while it does not particularly like me personally, approves and applauds my work; but there is a company of Negroes entirely ignorant of my work and quite indifferent to it; there are very many of the envious and jealous; and there is an appalling number of those who actively dislike and hate me.

Funds for the Bouttés' envisioned "nation-wide Jubilee gift," Du Bois reminded, would have to be raised largely from white people, like the Rockefellers, and others: "Now it happens that the whites have borne the brunt of my attacks for thirty years. They are as a group sore and sensitive over my activity. They believe that I hate white folks. Even my nearest white friends shrink from me." He bore the costs of his honesty, adding, "The price that I must pay for speaking plainly is at least silence of word and deed on the part of white America." Do not worry, Du Bois assured them, lest his confessional be mistaken for depression. He remained "well and strong" and had at least another good ten years of productive living in him. "After that, if I am compelled to pass the hat, well and good. We'll pass that bridge when we come to it."[92]

∽

THE OPENING MONTHS OF 1928 afforded Du Bois little time to wallow in self-pity. If his confidence was down, a flurry of activity at the start of the year reaffirmed his personal and intellectual importance.

He turned sixty on February 23, 1928. In lieu of the national celebration envisioned by the Bouttés, a committee of friends, unbeknownst to Du Bois, worked to gather funds to purchase the deed to his family's property in Great Barrington.[93] Touched by the surprise gesture of receiving "the old Burghardt home," he hoped to acquire some old-fashioned pieces of furniture and restore them as his first steps in refurbishing the house.[94]

Even the modest purchase of used furniture needed to wait until after the costly wedding of his daughter, Yolande, to Countee Cullen. In the world of New Negro luminaries, Cullen shone as a star among stars. Their wedding spared no expense. The creator of *The Star of Ethiopia* crafted and personally directed an epic pageant, headlined by his daughter, that featured sixteen bridesmaids, ten groomsmen, and fifteen hundred impeccably dressed guests who swelled Salem Methodist Episcopal Church in Harlem on April 9. An equally large crowd of gawkers filled the streets outside. Deeming the $1,500 he splurged on the extravaganza as money well spent, the Du Bois–Cullen union would, in the eyes of the proud patriarch, lead the race into the future and cement the grand familial lineage he strove so hard to re-imagine and create. With his focus on what the marriage symbolized and much less on the actual compatibility of his daughter and son-in-law, Du Bois did not mind when Cullen traveled separately from Yolande for their Paris honeymoon, instead accompanied by his handsome best man, Harold Jackman.[95]

In the midst of elaborate wedding arrangements, Du Bois also prepared to publish *Dark Princess: A Romance.* He'd begun the novel shortly after returning from the Soviet Union, devoting most of his spare time in the subsequent months to writing his second work of fiction, as opposed to slogging through *The Black Man and the Wounded World. Dark Princess* served as Du Bois's definitive contribution to the New Negro renaissance championed by the Howard University philosopher Alain Locke and other Talented Tenth Black intellectuals.[96] In the October 1926 *Crisis* essay "The Criteria of Negro Art," Du Bois declared, without equivocation, "All Art is propaganda and ever must be, despite the wailing of the purists. I stand in shamelessness and say that whatever art I have for writing has been used always for propaganda for gaining the right of black folk to love and enjoy. I do not care a damn for any art that is not used for propaganda."[97]

Dark Princess, published by Harcourt Brace in September 1927, also represented a literary attempt to make sense of the upheavals of the postwar world. It specifically reflected Du Bois's continued fascination with India and its potential.[98] The story revolves around Matthew Towns, a Black college-educated medical student denied opportunity because of his race, and Princess Kautilya of the fictional province of Bwodpur, India. The two meet by chance in Berlin, and the princess, intrigued by Towns and the plight of his people, reveals that she is part of a secret committee of representatives of the darker world who are determined to bring an end to white supremacy. The novel unfolds from there, with Towns, on a mission, returning to the United States and serving as Du Bois's muse to offer his thoughts on everything from Marcus Garvey, to the Brotherhood of Sleeping Car Porters, to Chicago machine politics, to the Communist Party. The princess reenters Towns's life at various points in the story, as their love and unified sense of purpose and self-sacrifice grow. The novel concludes with Towns and Kautilya reunited in rural Virginia. The princess gives birth to a male heir to the throne, who is prophesized as "Messenger and Messiah to all the Darker Worlds!" The child would solve the problems that Du Bois, frustrated with the limited success of his Pan-African Congress movement, could not. As a meditation on the legacy of the World War and the future of Afro-Asian diasporic solidarity, *Dark Princess* provided him with the freedom and imagination that the writing of history—and more specifically *The Black Man and the Wounded World*—could not.[99]

Amid the whirlwind of promoting *Dark Princess*, writing post-wedding thank-you notes, and catching up on work for the NAACP and *The Crisis*, Du Bois received a hostile reminder about his unfinished book. The Black veteran James Johnson had not forgotten about his materials still in Du Bois's possession and had reached the end of his patience. As their agreed-upon October 1, 1927, deadline neared, Johnson had sent Du Bois a cordial yet pointed reminder. Du Bois was conveniently out of town at the time, and his secretary had replied on his behalf. "He has not had the time to get at the material as yet and I cannot tell you just when it will be ready; but I am sure Dr. Du Bois will do his best to get it to you in the near future."[100] Johnson had heard all this before. When he again wrote to Du Bois on May 23, 1928, the counselor-at-law dispensed with all cordialities and got right to the point. He maintained records of their correspondence, going back to 1922, and quoted verbatim the long list of Du Bois's broken promises. He demanded his materials by June 1, "thereby saving all parties concerned the embarrassment that further delay will entail?"[101]

Despite the ominous tone of Johnson's letter, Du Bois remained stubbornly defiant. "I am again sorry to be unable to comply with your request," he responded three days later. He claimed to have weaved Johnson's material throughout the manuscript, making it "simply physically impossible for me to abstract from this any particular piece of matter." The only option was a "systematic search which might take weeks and which would disarrange the work of years." He attempted to explain the book's long delay—"the fault is not mine. It lies in the magnitude of the work. Eventually the matter will be returned to you.

It cannot be returned now and I cannot set any exact date as to when it can be returned."[102]

But Johnson would have none of it. He shot back on June 4, "It is difficult for me to reconcile your present attitude with the promises to return my property contained in your letters covering a period of eight years, during which time I had reason to believe I was dealing with a gentleman of honor who would spare no effort in his endeavor to keep his word." He insisted that Du Bois return his property, adding, "Your favorable consideration of this request will indicate a small degree of appreciation of the courtesy, consideration and unselfish cooperation which I have made an honest effort to extend you." The Harlem attorney punctuated his letter with an unambiguous threat: "I trust that you will see the expediency of an amicable adjustment of this matter, thereby saving all parties concerned the needless expense, loss of time and further embarrassment that proceedings to compel compliance will entail."[103]

The possibility of a lawsuit and public humiliation spurred Du Bois to rethink his earlier stance. Over the next few weeks he took the time to sift through his archive and locate the angry ex-soldier's materials. By August 15, 1928, he had prepared five manila envelopes, each containing one of the requested documents. Johnson acknowledged receipt two days later, curtly writing, "It appears that all of the matter is intact. Thank you for your courtesy and cooperation."[104]

The ugly exchange with Johnson, on top of the bitter back-and-forth with Adam Patterson, reflected just how badly Du Bois's relationship with many of the veterans connected to *The Black Man and the Wounded World* had deteriorated. In 1919, they had viewed Du Bois as their hero and their voice. In trusting him with their personal mementos, they trusted him with their history. Nearly a decade later, with no book to show for their generosity, they felt betrayed.

The quarrel with Johnson led to a familiar pattern of Du Bois fretting over the state of his unfinished work and seeking avenues to fund its publication. In a long shot, Du Bois reached out to Henry Moe from the Guggenheim Foundation. In March, Countee Cullen became just the second African American to receive a prestigious fellowship from the foundation, due in no small part to Du Bois's endorsement of his future son-in-law's application. By that summer, Cullen was in Paris, working on his book of poetry and suffering through the rocky first months of his marriage to Yolande. Perhaps, considering Du Bois's good relations with the Guggenheim Foundation, they might be able to help.[105]

An aura of sadness accompanied his application. "I understand that you wish primarily to encourage young scholars," he acknowledged up front. At the age of sixty, attuned to his mortality, he submitted that "naturally, most of my work is done." However, while time remained for him on earth, he had "one unfinished piece of work which I feel it is my duty to conclude." He made his admittedly bold case for support, detailing the beginnings of the war history project with his trip to Paris right after the armistice. He had spent the next ten years collecting data and, in that time, "written and rewritten the manuscript." He again believed that due to its swollen size, commercial publication was impossible. But with "two or three months' work Abroad and probably six months' work in the United States, with assistants," he could "put the manuscript in final shape."[106]

Du Bois must have expected Henry Moe's response, which came just two days later. "As you understand, it is only in the event that we do not, in any year, get enough first-rate projects from first-rate young scholars that the Foundation could consider making grants to scholars of your years."[107] Du Bois did not press the matter further.

Completing the book had now become more than just a scholarly obligation. It had become a moral duty. The legacies of the war, its hopes and its disappointments, grew more and more complex with each passing year. The need to understand what it all meant and what it portended for the future gnawed at the core of Du Bois's being. This was his responsibility. The war may have failed, but he would not. Determined to press ahead, he carried the weight of the wounded world, literally and figuratively, on his shoulders.

CHAPTER 10

"I am ashamed of my own lack of foresight."[1]

IT WAS THE FALL OF 1928, election season, and Du Bois's patience neared its breaking point. Beginning with his boyhood days in Great Barrington, attending meetings of the local school board, he'd always appreciated the importance of the democratic process.[2] He saw America as a land of tremendous potential. Now another presidential election approached. The country, Du Bois feared, stood at a crossroads. Either the noble experiment of democracy would become a reality in the United States—or it would fail.

"The Possibility of Democracy in America" appeared in two parts in the September and October issues of *The Crisis*. Of all the pressing problems facing the nation, Du Bois wrote, one loomed largest in "importance and immediacy": "how far the policies of this government are going to be controlled by the vote of its citizens." For more than a generation, he observed, "the possibility of any rational consultation of the public will in this country has been fading . . . This is a serious thing."[3]

"For several years after the World War," Du Bois began the second part of his article, "I used to talk concerning the results of the War, and to say that notwithstanding the slaughter and the upheaval that always accompany war we were going to have in the world an extension of democracy as a result of the fighting." He once believed that "the democracy which formerly had ruled in restricted fields—in the election of officials, in the so-called political world—we were going to see extended into industry, so that in regard to work and wages and income, we were going to have democratic control." But now, almost a decade later, he wrote "to apologize and change my thesis." "I was wrong in what I was predicting," he admitted. The great question, as he saw it, was no longer the expansion of democracy, but whether it would be possible to merely retain the fragile democracy that currently existed. Surveying the postwar international scene, he saw that "reaction and oligarchy are beginning to hold up their heads in the world and to triumph." As for the United States, he was frank: "Here where we have essayed the greatest experiment in democracy, we have perhaps the greatest failure."[4]

Du Bois proceeded to demonstrate the extent of democracy's failure in the United States, meticulously combing through the voting statistics of each state in the national elections dating back to 1872, parsing the numbers as best he could by race. Since the war, the dearth of electoral participation by the majority of Americans, as well as overt political disfranchisement, had worsened. This was certainly the case for African Americans. He demonstrated that the South possessed all the trappings of an oligarchy, flagrantly violating the Fourteenth, Fifteenth, and Nineteenth Amendments and as a result distorting the distribution of voting power throughout the nation. The region, with its 124 electoral votes, had become, Du Bois bluntly declared, the "political dictator of the nation." The commitment to eliminating African American access to the ballot through poll taxes, literacy tests, and other nefarious tactics also resulted in the disfranchisement of millions of Southern whites. The failure of democracy was therefore not merely a problem of race or region. He insisted that "the question at issue is much larger than this and that no matter what the discussion involves, it must be discussed, or else democratic government in the United States is impossible."[5] The remarkably thorough article proved Du Bois's skill as both historian and political scientist. It also revealed just how profoundly the war and the future of democracy consumed him. "The clearing up and settling of this great question is the vastest problem that faces America today and we must begin its solution now," he wrote in an early draft of the piece. "If we do not, we face sooner or later, chaos and revolution."[6]

In the upcoming election, all signs pointed to the Republican candidate, Secretary of Commerce Herbert Hoover, becoming the thirty-first president of the United States. Calvin Coolidge's decision that summer not to seek a second term cleared the way for Hoover. With national name recognition owing to his work as director of the U.S. Food Administration during the World War and buoyed by a strong economy, Hoover faced little intraparty opposition. Struggling to find a challenger, Democrats settled on Al Smith, the governor of New York, who became the first Catholic nominee for the presidency. The campaign quickly turned ugly. To secure the Southern vote and appeal to white Democrats, Hoover fanned the flames of anti-Catholic hysteria, much to the pleasure of a resurgent Ku Klux Klan, and refuted accusations that he would be anything but firm in maintaining Jim Crow. Du Bois—done with both Republicans and Democrats and declaring in *The Crisis* that when it came to Hoover and Smith, "it does not matter a tinker's damn which of these gentlemen succeed"— voted in protest for the Socialist Party candidate Norman Thomas.[7] Hoover's Southern strategy proved effective, as he carried five states of the former Confederacy, including Texas, in coasting to a landslide electoral victory.[8]

A decade after the end of the war, a buoyant moment when African Americans had invested so much of their democratic hopes in the Allied victory, their marginalization from the political life of the nation seemed more pronounced than ever. The possibility of democracy that Du Bois wrote about in 1919 and tenuously clung to now, as 1929 approached, seemed ever more impossible.

∽

JAMES WELDON JOHNSON UNDERSTOOD Du Bois's disillusionment with the state of postwar American democracy as few other people could. Through their shared battles in the NAACP to fight for African American equality, Du Bois and Johnson had forged a close friendship. After the passing of Charles Young, Johnson ascended the ladder of Du Bois's most trusted Black male comrades. Their connection extended beyond the bustling offices of NAACP headquarters. In 1926, Johnson and his wife, Grace, purchased a summer cabin in

Du Bois's boyhood town of Great Barrington, Massachusetts. In the serenity of his "Five Acres" getaway, Johnson continued to produce poetry, including the noted collection *God's Trombones: Seven Negro Sermons in Verse*, published in 1927. Du Bois and Nina were among the select group of friends the Johnsons welcomed into their home.[9]

Johnson was well aware of another source of frustration for Du Bois, the long-gestating World War book. One of the many responsibilities Johnson shouldered as executive secretary of the NAACP was securing financial support for the work of the association. Although the grip of the Tuskegee Machine had weakened, most major philanthropies still considered the NAACP too radical. Johnson therefore relied on longtime backers of the organization, as well as his personal relationships with a cadre of wealthy New York City reformers, for monetary assistance.

These included Roger Baldwin and the American Fund for Public Service (AFPS).[10] Baldwin, a committed socialist and anti-war activist, cofounded the American Civil Liberties Union (ACLU) in 1920. In July 1922, using the million-dollar inheritance of Charles Garland, Baldwin established the AFPS to support the work of organizations and individuals committed to the goals of "social and economic freedom."[11] When Johnson became the NAACP executive secretary in 1920, Baldwin asked him to join the board of the ACLU, and after the founding of the AFPS, Johnson became a member of that decision-making body as well. This benefited the NAACP, as much-needed AFPS money, steered by Johnson, flowed into the organization's coffers.[12] Du Bois even had his own success with the fund. In early 1925, the AFPS awarded him $5,000 for a study of Black common schools in the South, yet another endeavor that diverted Du Bois's attention from *The Black Man and the Wounded World*.

With the backing of Johnson, the book came back into focus. At the November 5, 1928, meeting of the AFPS Imperialism Committee, in discussing potential projects related to "Negro work," Johnson made a case for Du Bois's study. With interest piqued, the committee asked Johnson to provide a full report on the manuscript for consideration.

Johnson shared the meeting minutes with Du Bois, who contacted the AFPS directly. "I want very much to lay before your Committee the full manuscript and material," he wrote, adding that, if possible, he wanted Roger Baldwin and others to "spend an hour or so in looking it over and deciding as to its merits and how it could best be completed and published."[13] He offered to arrange for a personal "exhibition," accompanied by "a plan for the publication of the work."[14]

On the afternoon of January 21 or 22, Roger Baldwin and his fellow AFPS board member Lewis Gannett arrived at 69 Fifth Avenue. Johnson greeted them as they reached the NAACP's fifth-floor headquarters. The men entered Du Bois's *Crisis* office.[15] *The Black Man and the Wounded World* lay before them.

What Baldwin and Gannett saw represented a decade's worth of research and writing. The display was awe-inspiring, an archive of breathtaking scope and volume: confidential and unduplicated official military orders and directives, topographic maps, letters and testimonials from Black servicemen, press reports and newspaper clippings, books and articles about the war that were produced after the armistice, dozens of photos ranging from individual studio portraits to panorama shots of entire companies.

The main focus, however, was the manuscript itself. Prepared for the moment, Du Bois guided Baldwin and Gannett through the book chapter by chapter, offering a brief description of each. The opening eight chapters covered the origins of the war, its Pan-African dimensions, and the entry of the United States and African Americans into the conflict. These were mostly done, requiring only polishing. The heart of the manuscript, however—eight chapters devoted to the experiences of Black labor and combat troops, with a heavy focus on the Ninety-Second Division—needed significant work. As his guests clearly saw and as Du Bois explained, he confronted a mountain of documents, all valuable, that continued to pose a challenge when it came to organizing and translating it all into a concise narrative. His ideas for the closing five chapters, addressing the armistice and the implications of the war, remained vague and unwritten. In total, he presented Baldwin and Gannett with a sprawling 746-page manuscript, with some chapters complete, some fully drafted, some a collage of cut-and-pasted documents and notes, that he believed would stand as the definitive study of Black folk in the World War.[16]

Du Bois catered his overview of the book to his socialist-minded audience. "The general plan and argument of the work," he explained in a follow-up letter, "is to study the effect of war upon a laboring class, who in addition to their economic handicap, are the object of bitter and deep-seated racial prejudice." The intensification of race prejudice and class exploitation offset any gains made by African Americans. "The net result of the war," he concluded, "has been to intensify color consciousness throughout the world and to bring nearer the possibility of a war across the color line deep-rooted in economic gain." He estimated that "completed and revised, the manuscript should run about 1,000 pages with perhaps 250 pages of documents."[17] Following the presentation, as Baldwin and Gannett departed NAACP headquarters, Du Bois felt optimistic about his chances for support.

Du Bois heard nothing for two months.[18] He nervously wrote the AFPS board treasurer Morris Ernst at the end of March requesting an update and, he hoped, a positive answer. He took the liberty of offering a more detailed plan of action and reassured Ernst that, with a little assistance, he could complete the manuscript and have it ready for submission to Vanguard Press, the left-wing publishing house established by the AFPS, "before Christmas."[19]

Lewis Gannett threw cold water on Du Bois's hopes in an April 5 note. He had come away impressed by Du Bois's materials and had written to James Weldon Johnson that "it looked very important." However, he felt it was "much too extensive in its present form for general public presentation." He believed that the project more appropriately fell within the undefined category of "Negro work" and not "in the field of general research." Perhaps, he suggested, Johnson might sponsor a new proposal, with more focus, that contained "a much more definite idea of presumptive cost."[20] The official rejection came on May 1, with the AFPS board informing Du Bois that "the cost involved in putting your document into shape is so great that they are not justified at the present time in making such an appropriation."[21]

A disappointed Du Bois responded cordially. "I appreciate very much what you have done for the history of Negro troops," he wrote to the board director, Scott Nearing. He admitted that his proposal lacked specifics, in part because he "was seeking advice as to just how the work should be done and what form it should take." He promised to write to Nearing if and when he could "put the matter in such shape as to make a more definite scheme."[22] While remaining humble, Du Bois had to have been frustrated. Even usually reliable racial allies did not seem to appreciate the value in supporting a history of the war that placed Black folk as its central actors.

~

ON OCTOBER 10, 1929, Du Bois received a heartwarming letter from his old Harvard professor and mentor Albert Bushnell Hart. The two men had kept in touch periodically over the years, their last correspondence in 1924 after the death of Hart's wife. "I am so pained to hear of the death of Mrs. Hart," Du Bois had written. "I remember the pleasant hours which I spent in your home and how much of my pleasure was due to her."[23] He dutifully invited Hart to his daughter's wedding. Hart, overseas at the time, not only missed the gala but, upon seeing the invitation, mistakenly believed it was the elder Du Bois who was tying the knot. "Whatever adds to your content and happiness adds to your efficiency," he wrote without judgment.

Hart used the occasion and the remainder of the letter to laud his former student. "You have done a great work for your race—and for all races in the United States." Du Bois, in Hart's view, "sometimes preached strong and unpalatable doctrine, and urged aggressive movements," which the acclaimed historian did not always see as practicable. "That makes no difference with the essential," he wrote, "which is that you have been a standing representative of the intellectual power of negroes." Hart counted Du Bois "among the chief American writers of your day" and trusted that his books, if not fully appreciated now, would be read "in years to come, as a statement of conditions in a critical time for the negro race." "You are an extremist," Hart complimented, "and so was William Lloyd Garrison," reminding his student that history served as the ultimate judge—like the moral righteousness of the abolitionist cause—of one's "courage, tenacity and conviction." He signed off, "Cordially your one time teacher and always friend."[24]

Despite the innocent mix-up of marital status, and putting aside the condescension and racial paternalism, the letter from his favorite teacher deeply touched Du Bois. With all his accomplishments, he still felt that his scholarship made little impact and his quixotic battles against the forces of evil in the world were increasingly in vain. Validation from the man he considered his historical mentor meant a great deal. Du Bois blushed in his reply: "I appreciate what you say of my work in your letter, and should like to quote it some time."[25]

He also sought Hart's advice on a major thorn in his side, *The Black Man and the Wounded World*. Nearly eleven years earlier, when he first began work on the project, Hart had agreed to serve on its advisory board. Hart, and likely even Du Bois, had forgotten about this. He provided Hart with a brief summary of the book's origins and breadth before explaining, "The thing stretched out much further than I had intended, and if published now would fill at least two good-sized volumes." He could perhaps compromise his vision by working with a commercial press to condense the work into a single volume, but he remained "very anxious to have the whole thing published." He wondered if Hart knew of any "young colored historian who is doing post-graduate work" who could assist him "for a few months or even a year." Lastly, Du Bois asked for possible funding leads that would allow him to bring the project to completion. "I think it would be an important contribution to our knowledge of the war."[26]

Hart responded sympathetically but could not offer tangible help. Having retired from active teaching at Harvard in 1926, he had limited contact with graduate students. He did suggest that "a single moderate sized volume would have much more influence than a large compendious work, and of course, it is very much easier to place."[27] Hart's counsel served as yet another sobering reminder of the challenge Du Bois faced in finishing the book.

His outreach to Hart may very well have been prompted by another letter he received at the beginning of the month. On October 1,

Kirby Page, the editor of the socialist-leaning pacifist journal *The World Tomorrow*, contacted Du Bois to solicit his views on the question of which country bore responsibility for the start of the World War. Du Bois had contributed to the magazine in the past, and its editors thought highly of him.[28] Page knew that Du Bois would offer a frank appraisal of the "war-guilt" debate, which, he noted, was "agitating Europe" and becoming an issue of "widespread interest" in the United States as well. Page sought to gather opinions from "a group of representative scholars and public spirited citizens throughout the nation" and publish his findings in a future issue of *The World Tomorrow*.[29]

On both sides of the Atlantic, the question of war guilt had indeed become a lively and at times vitriolic topic. During the war, most American historians had largely abandoned their commitment to objectivity in place of patriotic support for the Allied effort and condemnation of Germany. But by the mid-1920s, as disillusionment with the war became more widespread, historians revisited the question of who had caused the global disaster. The profession became increasingly polarized, with younger historians challenging the long-accepted "scapegoat theory" and offering a more complicated picture of responsibility, while older historians, including Albert Hart, held steadfast to the view of German guilt alone.[30]

The *World Tomorrow* issue offered Du Bois the chance to enter the fray. In his letter to Du Bois, Kirby Page posed four questions: "Do you believe that Germany and her allies were *solely* responsible for causing the World War?" "Do you believe that Germany was *more* responsible than any other Power for causing the World War?" "Do you favor all-round *cancellation* of war debts and reparations?" "In the light of all the evidence now available, do you think the United States acted wisely in *entering the war* against Germany?" Du Bois was one of the twelve hundred men and women contacted, and one of the 429 individuals who ultimately responded, including virtually every major historian in the profession, among them those at the center of the war-guilt debate.[31]

Page's questions simmered and stewed in Du Bois's mind. They struck a painful nerve. Answering them required revisiting one of the

most contentious periods of his life and the most controversial decision of his career in choosing to support the war. This was not simply
an intellectual exercise. For him, it was personal.

As he pondered his response over the next eight months, calamity struck the United States economy. The glitz of postwar prosperity
for the wealthiest Americans masked a structurally flawed financial
system that had become reliant on credit, manufacturing overproduc-
tion, banking deregulation, and reckless speculation. The warning
signs flashed throughout the spring and summer of 1929 until, on
Thursday, October 24, the stock market crashed. Billions of dollars
vanished in just a few days. The downward spiral continued throughout the panic-filled winter and into the new year as one bank after
another shuttered its doors and anxious businesses began laying off
workers. President Herbert Hoover acted quickly, but ultimately failed
to appreciate the magnitude of the crisis, assuring the American public
that a full recovery was imminent.[32]

On June 24, 1930, Du Bois finally sent Kirby Page his reply.
Without responding directly to the questionnaire, Du Bois offered
some of his most candid and introspective thoughts on the war and
his complicity in it.

He appreciated the forum Page sought to create, first and foremost because it acknowledged "that intelligent human beings change
their minds. I know this is true in my own case." He'd known all
about German militarism and its consequences, but "I did not know
as much then as I do now about the manipulations of the English and
French in international intrigue," he wrote. Du Bois, along with millions of others, had been swept off his feet "by the emotional response
of America to what seemed to be a great call to duty." Only now,
looking back with remorse, could he see "how easy and inevitable it is
for an appeal to blood and force to smash to utter negation any ideal
for which it is used." "Instead of a war to end war, or a war to save
democracy, we found ourselves during and after the war descending to
the meanest and most sordid of selfish actions, and we find ourselves
today nearer moral bankruptcy then we were in 1914."

His guilt ran deep. "I am ashamed of my own lack of foresight," he admitted, echoing his earlier confession in "The Possibility of Democracy in America." However, he continued, "war is so tremendous and terrible a thing that only those who actually experience it, can know its real meaning." The only hope for the future, he believed, as "the camouflage of military glamour" threatened to romanticize "the nasty mess" of war, was "honest and well-founded opinion."[33]

An abbreviated version of Du Bois's response appeared in the October 1930 issue of *The World Tomorrow* in a "Symposium on War Responsibility." Absent were his self-reflective musings about shame for his "lack of foresight." It is unclear whether he had any final say in how his words would appear before the public. Regardless, the honesty expressed in his original reply to Page was extraordinarily rare. He confessed to a failure in judgment in supporting the war, but by placing blame on the hyperpatriotism of the moment and the intoxicating sway of government propaganda, he also sought absolution. In the end, like all those who managed to survive the hell of the war, he was a victim. It was not his fault.

~

ALONG WITH THE QUESTION of war guilt, another controversy in the spring and summer of 1930 offered Du Bois a reminder of the war's bitter legacy. In early 1929, after years of pressure from such groups as the American War Mothers, the American Gold Star Mothers, and the American Legion, Congress passed a pilgrimage bill authorizing the War Department to sponsor trips to France for mothers and widows who had lost their sons and husbands in the war, so that they could visit their loved ones' final resting places.[34] Although the law made no mention of race, when it came time to organize the sojourns, the War Department issued a memo stating that Black mothers and widows would travel in separate groups, reasoning that the women of both races would naturally prefer to mourn in the company of their own kind. Word of the War Department's plan became public in March 1930, just before the first ships were set to sail.

The NAACP and much of the Black press cried foul. "Black mothers and widows saw their sons sent to Jim Crow military camps and into Jim Crow units during the hectic days of 1917 and 1918," *The Chicago Defender* reminded its readers. "They saw them go away willingly, secure in the belief that their sacrifices would mean something to those who remained at home. Then, these mothers saw Jim Crow units return to this country one after another, and finally awoke to the realization that their sons would return no more."[35] The NAACP promptly fired off letters of protest to President Hoover and members of Congress, demanding that the War Department reconsider.[36] Du Bois did not participate in the public pressure campaign, but made his views clear in private correspondence. William King, a member of the Illinois State Legislature, considered introducing a measure to protest the War Department's actions and sought out Du Bois's opinion. Du Bois offered a sharp response. "The segregation based mainly and specifically on race and color which the United States Government carries on is despicable, illogical and uncivilized . . . To perpetuate it in the case of the Gold Star mothers who are visiting great cemeteries where the putrid remains of their dead sons were buried very largely by Negro soldiers, is the last word in this national disgrace."[37]

After the War Department held firm to its Jim Crow plans despite pledging that "each group will receive equal accommodations, care and consideration," the NAACP and the Black press urged a complete boycott of the program.[38] "No black with self-respect will go if she has to go on that segregated ship," the *Defender* scolded. "Their boys would want them to do this. Mothers, don't shame those boys further by going to visit their graves on Jim Crow ships!"[39]

The overwhelming majority of the Black Gold Star mothers, however, did not heed this advice. The first ship, a retrofitted freight liner carrying fifty-four grieving women, departed New York on July 12, 1930. They were accompanied by Colonel Benjamin O. Davis, at the time the highest-ranking Black officer in the military, who was fluent in French. He volunteered to protect their dignity and ensure that they received every available courtesy.[40] Over the next three years, 279 Black women made the trip across the Atlantic to visit their deceased sons and husbands, voicing no complaints about their treatment and expressing gratitude to the government for giving them a once-in-a-lifetime opportunity.[41]

Du Bois's inability, along with that of other Black male leaders, to see the Gold Star Mothers as anything more than racial symbols reflected his view of the war and of the history he was writing. As the title itself revealed, African American women did not have much of a place in *The Black Man and the Wounded World*. In the hundreds of pages he'd drafted over the years, Du Bois made no mention of the home-front contributions of Emily Bigelow Hapgood, Mary Church Terrell, Susan Frazier, Mary Talbert, Ida B. Wells-Barnett, and other Black women activists.[42] In chapter 18 of his manuscript, "The War Within the War," he did decide to "lump together" an assortment of topics "all quite different and yet all shot through with this one peculiar color problem." This included a brief examination of the work of Black women during the war, based mostly on Addie Hunton and Kathryn Johnson's *Two Colored Women with the American Expeditionary Forces* and a small booklet issued by the Colored Work Committee of the YWCA.[43] Not surprisingly, he focused almost exclusively on the discrimination they faced.[44] While Du Bois could laud the labor and sacrifice of Black women, he believed that the history of the war, like that of the race more broadly, was ultimately the history of Black men.

～

IN THE WAKE OF the Gold Star Mothers tumult and Du Bois still fretting over how to complete and publish *The Black Man and the Wounded World*, James Weldon Johnson once again came to the rescue. Following the disappointment with the AFPS, Johnson encouraged Du Bois to inquire with the Rosenwald Fund. Established in 1917, this fund became the nation's most generous philanthropic organization in the arena of race relations and African American uplift. It poured millions of dollars into the construction of Black schools in the South as well as other efforts to promote racial progress, including the work of the NAACP. In 1928, Johnson had received the honor of becoming the first awardee of the newly inaugurated Rosenwald fellowships, which allowed him to take a much-needed yearlong sabbatical from the NAACP and start work on what would become his landmark sociological study of Harlem, *Black Manhattan*.[45] Du Bois maintained a good relationship with the Rosenwald Fund and its director, Edwin Embree, a descendant of Kentucky abolitionists, who had a Yale degree in philosophy and previously worked with the Rockefeller Foundation.[46] On December 19, 1930, Du Bois wrote Embree about "assistance from the Rosenwald Fund to two projects which I have in mind."[47]

Du Bois's first priority was "completion of my history of the Negro in the World War." He hoped Embree would see the merits of a project, more than a decade in the making, that, as he stressed, "I am exceedingly anxious to finish." The second endeavor Du Bois proposed was the "story of Reconstruction after the Civil War."[48]

His interest in Reconstruction stretched back to his early academic career. Although much had been written on the subject from the perspective of white Northerners and Southerners, works produced "from the point of view of the Negro," Du Bois explained to Embree, remained scarce. He was understating. The field of Reconstruction studies, stemming from Columbia University's William Archibald Dunning and his doctoral progeny, had effectively written Black people out of its history and cast the postwar experiment in multiracial democracy as an unmitigated failure. Voices like Du Bois's, dating back to the paper he'd read at the 1909 American Historical Association annual meeting, and those of Carter G. Woodson and his protégés at *The Journal of Negro History*, had been ignored and silenced.[49] White historians continued to produce book after book dismissing slavery as the cause of the war and arguing that the inherent inferiority of the Black race, as evidenced by the catastrophe of Reconstruction, justified their subordinate citizenship status in the present. The late 1929 publication of *The Tragic Era* by Claude Bowers, a racist screed masqueraded as history but nevertheless accepted as in line with the prevailing knowledge of the subject, marked a breaking point. Black scholars decried the book, and friends of Du Bois, such as James Weldon Johnson and Anna Julia Cooper, implored him to take up the task of a formal rebuttal. In her letter to Du Bois on the matter, Cooper wrote that someone needed to respond to Bowers "adequately, fully, ably, finally, and it seems to me 'Thou art the man!'"[50] Du Bois, feeling a call to duty, took this to heart.

He and Embree met in person sometime during the first week of January 1931, as hundreds of American banks continued to fail and the global economy cratered into full depression. Their conversation went well enough for Du Bois to follow up with a more formal and detailed proposal.[51] He opened with the Reconstruction project, mentioning his yearslong work on the subject starting with the 1901 *Atlantic Monthly* article on the Freedmen's Bureau that became the pivotal second chapter of *The Souls of Black Folk*, his American Historical Association paper and subsequent article in *The American Historical Review*, and chapter 5 in *The Gift of Black Folk*. "I wish now to consolidate these essays, supplement them with a more intensive study of documents, newspapers and literature and with interviews of living persons." From this he envisioned "a volume on the part that the black man has played in the development of American democracy from his Emancipation to the beginning of the 20th century."

He then transitioned to *The Black Man and the Wounded World*, this time offering some of the backstory of how he went to France after the armistice at the behest of the NAACP "to collect material for a history of the Negro in the World War, and to hold a Pan-African Congress." He'd hoped to have the book published much earlier, "but the difficulties of the World War and post-war period has made this impossible." Nevertheless, he presently had on hand "a manuscript of ten long chapters, representing a writing and re-writing of this story." Supplemented with a survey of the scholarship on the war published since 1918, his book would serve as the perfect complement to the Reconstruction project. He hoped to reach a broad audience. "I want these two pieces of work to be literature and not simply mechanical history," he explained to Embree. "That is, while based upon an unassailable foundation of fact, I want it to be an interpretation of the human soul down in language which is intelligible and beautiful."[52]

Du Bois received the official response from Embree on February 16. The Rosenwald Fund awarded Du Bois a two-year fellowship, beginning July 1, 1931, of $3,600 for the first year and $2,400 for the second. Given the lean economic times, this represented a substantial commitment.[53] Most important, Du Bois would have free rein to do his work. "We assume no responsibility and will attempt no control over your writings, nor will we supervise or censor them in any way," Embree reassured.

But Embree did feel emboldened enough to offer Du Bois some personal advice "as an individual and a friend—not as a foundation officer." "I have long felt that you have a literary gift that might well express itself occasionally in general beauty rather than advocating special aspects of the truth as you see them," he wrote. Du Bois, in his view, was naturally "sensitive to the racial problems" of the world and "stated one side forcibly and brilliantly." Embree, however, wished that he would divert some of his ability toward "more general writing" and take advantage of the opportunity offered by the fellowship to "undertake at least one important composition in a non-controversial field." "I know you would enjoy purely creative writing and I am sure you would do it well," he ended, and looked forward to discussing the matter further when the opportunity to meet in person arose.[54]

Du Bois was long familiar with this attitude among his white so-called friends. That Embree viewed Du Bois, the author of two novels and dozens of short stories and poems, as not having taken advantage of his "literary gift" revealed his limited knowledge of Du Bois's corpus and his approach to writing. Du Bois, with deliberate intention and care, infused beauty into everything he penned. Embree's conception of "general beauty" meant not focusing on race and the truth of white supremacy. His advice also exposed the conundrum facing Black historians, like Du Bois, who challenged the prevailing racist scholarship of their fields. Du Bois held an unwavering commitment to telling history from the perspective of Black people, and he knew that for this reason, most white readers would view anything he wrote as controversial.

Embree's shortsightedness and racial paternalism did not dampen Du Bois's gratitude at receiving the Rosenwald fellowship. "I thank you very much indeed for the grant that has been made. I deeply appreciate it," he wrote to Embree. He also expressed his willingness to discuss Embree's "suggestion in general literature," adding, "I realize the force of what you say."[55] Du Bois certainly disagreed with

Embree's suggestion and characterization of his work. Nevertheless, even with his worldwide acclaim and pedigree, Du Bois remained well aware that the fate of his scholarship and such projects as the history of the World War rested in the hands of white philanthropists.

Du Bois updated the NAACP board on his good fortune. He reminded his colleagues of their decision in 1918 to approve his trip to France to begin work on the history of Black troops in the war. "I collected data and have since then collected more here but have never been able to secure enough time and clerical assistance to bring the manuscript to a point of publication." He also mentioned James Weldon Johnson's suggestion that he write the history of Black folk during Reconstruction, an undertaking that with newfound time and funding seemed more appealing. Du Bois saw *The Black Man and the Wounded World* and the embryonic book on Reconstruction as linked, believing that the "two studies would make a history of the American Negro from the political and social point of view, from emancipation to the present time." He proposed allocating the initial $3,600 to costs for a literary assistant, to *The Crisis* for "editorial assistance," and for "books, travel and research."[56]

He could not have asked for a more welcome development and undoubtedly breathed a huge sigh of relief. After multiple failed appeals for funding, he'd finally succeeded. With the Rosenwald award, he now had the time and resources to complete *The Black Man and the Wounded World*.

WITH MUCH-NEEDED MONEY IN his pocket and free time to think, Du Bois began to envision his book as a larger meditation on the meaning of war and on the future possibilities of peace. He shared his ideas in a speech, "The Economics of War," delivered on October 26, 1931, at the Mecca Temple in New York. The day before that, sitting behind the wheel of his well-maintained 1928 Willys-Knight sedan, he'd been one of the 56,312 drivers who crossed the newly built George Washington Bridge during the first twenty-four hours of its opening to automobile traffic.[57] As he "looked down from its high and magnificent triumph," Du Bois told his audience, he could not escape the irony that the bridge's height would allow for American battleships to sail easily beneath it. With the nation gripped by depression, the United States continued to spend ungodly sums of taxpayer dollars on its military and on preparation for war, a perverse "contradiction in logic" that exposed just how much America and the world had failed to learn the lessons of 1914–18.

As he did in the opening of the second chapter of *The Black Man and the Wounded World*, Du Bois took his audience back to 1911 and the Agadir Crisis. This spark in the "rivalry for Income and Profits" made the unthinkable—"a war amongst the civilized nations of the earth"—a reality. And, as Agadir had demonstrated, "the main area of that fight was not Europe but Africa and Asia, South America and the islands of the sea" and the colonial riches extracted from them. "Such profit was worth fighting for," Du Bois argued, "and that is the reason that the world went to war in 1914." But instead of a war to end all wars, as Woodrow Wilson and others had claimed, the exact opposite occurred. He minced no words. "There has not been a single year, if even a single day, since the World War Armistice, that the world has not been engaged in organized murder somewhere upon its surface, and in practically every case the leading civilized countries of Europe and America have been chief among the fighters, or instigating the fight or at least sitting armed on the sidelines ready for eventualities." Recollecting the World War further steeled his pacifist convictions and his critique of American democracy, domestically and globally. "Thus," he ended, "the real economics of war prove to us that pacifism, like all thorough-going reform, can only be had at great cost, and that the main problem of the United States is whether we will pay this cost or whether we prefer to continue to be one of the great armed powers of the world with our feet on the necks of mankind and our hands in their pockets."[58]

While the legacy of the World War—and the book about it—circled in his mind, Du Bois also began to think more and more about the historical period that preceded it, Reconstruction. He likely chuckled when he opened and read the September 11 letter from

Alfred Harcourt that arrived at his desk. "My spies tell me the very interesting news that you are at work on a history of the Reconstruction period," the esteemed publisher wrote. With his interest piqued, Harcourt hoped that Du Bois, assuming he had not already committed to another firm, would discuss the project with him.[59]

Du Bois confirmed Harcourt's sleuthing in his September 23 reply. He did indeed have a book in mind, with the working title "The Black Man in the Reconstruction of Freedom in America, from 1860–1876." Du Bois had a bold thesis, contending that "the real hero and center of human interest in this period is the slave who is being emancipated." Historians, he said, putting it mildly, almost universally focused on "the white business men of the South and the Southern slave holders." As a result, "what the Negro did and what the Negro thought has been glossed over and forgotten." "I am going, therefore, to write a history from this point of view," he asserted. In this straightforward declaration lay the kernel for a radical reinterpretation of Reconstruction.

But there was more. He also pitched another book. "I am going to add next year as a second volume 'The Black Man and the Wounded World,'" describing it as "the part which Negro troops took in the World War and its significance for the world today."[60]

Du Bois's idea of *The Black Man and the Wounded World* as a second volume to *Black Reconstruction* made perfect sense. Reconstruction and the World War constituted the two defining moments in the history of modern American democracy and the struggle of African Americans for citizenship. Scholars did not yet fully comprehend their significance, due in large part to denying the central role played by Black folk. Du Bois, rightfully so, saw himself as uniquely qualified to tell both stories, which together revealed how the failure to achieve full democracy for African Americans in the nineteenth century due to white supremacy and economic exploitation created the conditions, domestically and globally, for another even more catastrophic failure to achieve democracy on a worldwide scale in the twentieth century.

After recovering from a brief illness, Harcourt responded to Du Bois: "What you say about your history 'The Black Man in the

Reconstruction' promises a really interesting book. I should like to hear more about it at your convenience." He encouraged Du Bois to drop by his office at any time, or he would be just as happy to come visit him at his NAACP office.[61] Harcourt made no mention of the proposed sequel on the Black experience in the World War.

Du Bois did not press the matter. He, as well as Harcourt, had perhaps forgotten that they'd briefly discussed the first incarnation of the book in late 1919 before partnering to publish *Darkwater*. Even though the nearly eight-hundred-page manuscript of *Black Man and the Wounded World*, however rough and sprawling, demanded his attention, Du Bois, in his mind, had already begun to give the history of Reconstruction—of which he had not written a single word—greater priority. On October 21, 1931, he provided Harcourt with a detailed four-page, seven-point outline of his main arguments for the book.[62] Harcourt quickly read it and wrote back the following day to convey his enthusiasm for the "splendid" proposal. "It's a book that you probably can do better than anyone else."[63] They met a few days later at Harcourt's office to discuss the project further. By the end of the month, Du Bois had put his signature on a contract.[64]

∾

DU BOIS BEGAN WORK on *Black Reconstruction* in the early months of 1932, with America in crisis and the tragic legacies of the World War surrounding him at every turn. The Great Depression showed no signs of abating. President Herbert Hoover's prediction that the economic calamity sparked in the fall of 1929 would be short-lived proved disastrously wrong. Unemployment steadily rose, reaching 8.7 percent in 1930, climbing to 15.9 percent in 1931 and then to a staggering 23.6 percent in 1932. Industrial production in all sectors plummeted. Banks continued to collapse, and on July 8 the stock market, closing at 41.22, hit rock bottom, a ninety percent drop from its 1929 high. Severe drought and dust storms in the Midwest and Southern Plains left farms dry and barren. Destitute and displaced families wandered the countryside and traveled west along dusty highways to try to start anew. In major cities, homeless encampments and blocks-long soup lines became common sights.[65]

African Americans felt the brunt of the devastation. Conditions in the South became more dire. Black farmers, with the price of cotton steadily plummeting, were fortunate to earn twenty-five cents a day. As white landowners decreased the size of their farms, Black share-croppers and their families found themselves homeless. Black skilled workers also faced considerable hardship, as white bosses prioritized hiring white workers. In search of any semblance of hope, tens of thousands of African Americans abandoned the South for cities north and west, further fueling the Great Migration that began during the World War. They found little respite. Already the last hired and the first fired, Black people swelled the ranks of the unemployed in cities like Chicago, Philadelphia, and Detroit, where the jobless rates soared as high as 60 percent.[66]

Du Bois experienced the despair in Harlem up close. In January 1928, he and Nina had moved into the newly developed Paul Law-rence Dunbar Apartments at 226 West 150th Street. Built by John D. Rockefeller Jr. specifically for working-class African Americans, the complex soon became a hub for the Talented Tenth and New Negro renaissance literati. Du Bois initially delighted in the spacious seven-room fifth-floor apartment that had been meticulously renovated to meet his tastes and spatial needs. By 1932, however, he felt the sting of every monthly rent payment.[67] Most other Harlemites suffered even worse. The unemployment rate hovered around 50 percent. Income for skilled workers and Black professionals alike fell significantly. The dismal economic situation exacerbated such social problems as health care, juvenile delinquency, and crime. With no help coming from the federal government, charitable groups and organizations like the Ur-ban League tried to provide as much relief as they could.[68] The local Charles Young Post of the American Legion, headed by Du Bois's longtime friend Matthew Boutté, stepped up to support out-of-work veterans. Boutté served as chairman of the local employment commis-sion for the Legion's national drive, covering Harlem.[69]

Harlem's Black veterans, like other ex-soldiers of the Great War, sought immediate relief in the form of overdue pay for their army ser-vice. Veteran groups such as the American Legion and the more radical Veterans of Foreign Wars had lobbied for early payment of their adjusted compensation bonus, which had been approved by Congress in 1924 over President Calvin Coolidge's veto. The onset of the Depression added greater urgency to their demand. The new president, Hoover, rebuffed the idea of early payment, reasoning that it would necessitate an increase in taxes and further stall any hope for a quick economic recovery. Veterans decided to ramp up the pressure. In January 1932, some ten thousand former servicemen and their families, dubbing themselves the Bonus Expeditionary Force, marched into Washington, DC, and encamped along the flats of the Anacostia River. Their shantytown, mockingly called Hooverville, symbolized the failure of the nation to meet its obligations to its most indebted citizens.

Race played a significant role in the government's opposition to the issuance of early bonuses. The United States Chamber of Commerce argued that granting bonuses to Black veterans would incentivize them to cease working and thereby hurt the economy. African American former soldiers remained politicized by their war experience and expected full compensation for their sacrifices. As many as thirty-five hundred Black veterans formed part of the Bonus Army and swelled the campgrounds by June. Unlike during the war, the color line did not define this army. Reporting on the camp, the *New York Amsterdam News* observed, "Mister James Crow, pestilence of the South, is conspicuous by his absence here in this orderly setting where black and white alike share the hardships of hunger and impoverished circumstances in brotherly socialization, eating and drinking from the same mess hall and fountain."[70] Roy Wilkins, the former editor of the *Kansas City Call* who arrived in New York in September 1931 as assistant secretary to Walter White, investigated conditions at the camp for the NAACP. He came away impressed, remarking, "There is more real democracy in that camp than there is for the Negro outside it."[71]

The image of the camp, with Black and white veterans in solidarity, became too much for Hoover to stomach. On July 28, the president issued orders to evict the protesters. Led by General Douglas MacArthur, federal troops, supported by a tank battalion commanded by Major George Patton, charged into the camp, bayonets drawn. With shocking force, they cleared out anyone standing in their way.

Clouds of tear gas brought back memories of the Western Front. Encampments were burned to the ground. The Bonus marchers and their families, beaten and bloodied, eventually dispersed and returned to their homes throughout the country. The unprecedented attack, however, did not break their political will. Samuel McDonald, a veteran of the 369th Infantry who'd been expelled from the camp, encouraged African Americans to abandon their past party allegiances and vote Democrat in the upcoming presidential election. "A vote for the Republican party is a vote for our fore-parents, not for ourselves," he declared. "This bonus bill is dead and the Republicans killed it. That leaves us with only the Democrats to look to for relief."[72]

The 1932 election would be pivotal. A vocal segment of the Black press, with *The Pittsburgh Courier* and its pugnacious editor Robert Vann leading the charge, voiced its opposition to the Republicans and the man occupying the White House. Du Bois and *The Crisis* joined the chorus. "The indictment which Americans of Negro descent have against Herbert Hoover is long, and to my mind, unanswerable," Du Bois wrote in a November editorial, rattling off a catalog of outrages including Hoover's acquiescence to disfranchisement, his nomination of white supremacists to federal positions, and his "outrageous discrimination based on color," specifically mentioning the Gold Star Mothers. "No one in our day has helped disfranchisement and race hatred more than Herbert Hoover."[73] To little surprise, Hoover suffered a landslide defeat at the hands of Franklin Roosevelt. The New York governor—whom Du Bois first met in 1918 when Roosevelt, then assistant secretary of the navy, addressed the conference of Black newspaper editors in Washington, DC—tallied 57.4 percent of the popular vote and carried all but six states. Most Black voters, in the end, decided that throwing their lot in with the Democrats was still a bridge too far. Du Bois also could not bring himself to vote for Roosevelt and again opted for the Socialist Party candidate, Norman Thomas. Nevertheless, the election planted the seeds for a potentially seismic shift in African American voting behavior.[74]

In 1932, Germany also held elections for a new president. A charismatic former soldier in the Bavarian Reserve Infantry, Adolf Hitler, challenged the legendary former general Paul von Hindenburg for control of the country. Railing against the Weimar Republic, communists, Jews, and the Treaty of Versailles, which he portrayed as a vindictive assault on Germany's honor, Hitler amassed a loyal following and transformed the National Socialist German Workers' Party (NSDAP), also known as the Nazis, into a political force. But even with his fiery oratory and the Nazis' tactics of intimidation, Hitler failed to defeat Hindenburg in the April 1932 runoff election. Most observers, relieved, thought that the Nazi Party was done and Hitler's blazing star had flickered out. Their assumption would prove premature.[75]

WHILE DU BOIS, as was his nature, paid close attention to domestic and global affairs, he also contended with personal and professional crises. The Depression had worsened his always precarious financial situation. The apartment he owned on St. Nicholas Avenue and rented out was badly underwater, with the mortgage at risk of default. The two policies he held with the National Benefit Life Insurance Company became worthless when the Black-owned business collapsed in 1931 and went into court-ordered receivership. His daughter, Yolande, added to the family fiscal woes. Du Bois subsidized her Baltimore apartment and the college tuition of her new husband, Arnette Williams, all the while putting off payment of the divorce settlement owed to her former husband, Countee Cullen.[76]

Du Bois's tense relationship with Emmett J. Scott once again flared up, this time threatening to land the two longtime rivals in court. In the April 1932 issue of *The Crisis*, Du Bois penned a critical editorial about Howard University and the abilities of its secretary-treasurer.[77] Scott considered it an attack on his character and threatened to sue Du Bois for libel. Despite Du Bois claiming that his personal relations with Scott had "always been pleasant," bitter memories that stretched back to the Niagara-Tuskegee days, as well as their fight over writing the history of Black troops in the World War, died hard. Du Bois adamantly rejected demands that he print a full retraction and apology, informing Arthur Spingarn, "If I have to go to jail, I'll go."[78] The ugly spat between the two Sigma Pi Phi (Boulé) brothers was embarrassing enough for leaders of the exclusive African American Greek-letter fraternity to intervene and facilitate a behind-the-scenes resolution before matters devolved any further. Du Bois ultimately published a restrained corrective in the January 1933 *Crisis*, apologizing for the unintended injury to Scott and his "integrity, ability, or zeal in behalf of Howard University."[79]

As Du Bois avoided a messy lawsuit, the situation within the NAACP became especially toxic. At the core of the problem was Walter White, who took over as executive secretary following James Weldon Johnson's retirement at the end of 1930. Du Bois believed that White lacked the temperament and intellectual ability to handle the job. His top-down micromanaging leadership style aggravated Du Bois—who valued creative independence and organizational fluidity—to no end. As *Crisis* revenues significantly declined owing to the Depression, White attempted to reel in the magazine by tightening its budget and pushing for more lighthearted content. Du Bois refused to play along. By the end of 1932, as subscriptions continued to plummet, circulation dropped, and the budget was trimmed to the bone, *The Crisis* faced the very real prospect of suspending operations. Du Bois was eager to escape New York. To help alleviate the financial burden of his beloved journal, as well as get much-needed distance from Walter White, he accepted a five-month visiting professorship at Atlanta University.[80]

Some twenty-two years had passed since Du Bois, along with his wife and daughter, had left Atlanta and its bittersweet memories, moving to New York to build the NAACP. Now he returned to the city and the university that made him famous, leaving Nina behind at their Harlem apartment, a reflection of the state of their marriage. He took up residence in a spacious room on the Spelman campus and quickly settled back into academic life. The atmosphere proved stimulating and intellectually rejuvenating, as he relished the opportunity to interact and engage with energetic graduate and undergraduate students, the next generation of Talented Tenth race leaders.[81] He immediately delved into work on *Black Reconstruction* and boned up for his return to the classroom.[82]

Teaching afforded him the opportunity to engage more deeply with Marxist theory and the development of communism. He had no love for the CPUSA, which he accused of taking advantage of poor, ignorant African Americans, most notably with Scottsboro, the cause célèbre case involving nine Black youths in Alabama who'd been accused of rape and were on trial for their lives.[83] Yet he still posed the question to *Crisis* readers in the June 1932 issue, "Is communism, as illustrated in Russia and America, a theory good for the world and for the American Negro?" "The world is ill," he diagnosed, invoking the title and theme of his unfinished book on the Great War. "It has desperate economic problems intertwined with its problems of racial prejudice." This required serious study and thought. "After all," he wrote, "our problems are not to be solved by emotions, but by deep concerted intelligence."[84]

Du Bois followed his own advice. The two classes he taught during the spring semester of 1933 at Atlanta University—"Karl Marx and the Negro" and "Economic History of the Negro"—allowed him to read, think, and learn alongside the students who reverentially sat in his seminars and absorbed his lectures. Consuming every book he could get his hands on, he compressed what for any normal person would be years of study into just a few months, and he soon amassed what he considered an unrivaled personal library on Marxism and scientific socialism. He worked through his thoughts and what he described as a "new racial philosophy" in the 1933 issues of *The Crisis*, praising Marx but still asserting that the German philosopher's theories required modification "so far as Negroes are concerned."[85] While essential to recognizing the need for "fundamental change in our economic methods," Du Bois wrote, Marxism ultimately failed to address the realities of race and the color line as both a domestic American and global imperialist phenomenon.[86] He needed more time to think, research, and test his ideas. But he had taken the first important steps on an intellectual and political journey that would change his life.[87]

∼

DU BOIS KNEW THAT his days with the NAACP and as editor of *The Crisis* were quite likely coming to an end. Although John Hope had yet to tender an offer for a permanent position on the Atlanta University faculty, needing ultimate approval from the trustees, Du

Bois expected this to happen. As he shuttled back and forth between New York and Atlanta, the financial health of *The Crisis* continued to deteriorate, and frustrations with Walter White and the NAACP's ideological direction worsened. Only a drastic overhaul of the association's leadership structure and program would convince Du Bois that his relationship with the NAACP was worth salvaging.[88]

He hoped that a second Amenia conference might spark a long-overdue reset. In December 1932, he and Joel Spingarn agreed upon the need for another gathering similar to the one in 1916, considering the rudderless state of the NAACP and the emergence of a new generation of Black leaders and thinkers pushing for more radical, economically rooted approaches to the race problem. Informal planning took place throughout the early months of 1933 until the board gave the conference formal approval in March.

The thirty-three men and women carefully selected by Du Bois to participate in the weekend-long conference began arriving at Spingarn's manicured eight-hundred-acre Troutbeck estate in the early evening of Friday, August 18. NAACP fixtures James Weldon Johnson, Mary White Ovington, William Pickens, Ernest and Lillian Alexander, Walter White, and, of course, Du Bois represented the old guard. But most of the attendees, with an average age of thirty and spanning a variety of backgrounds, exemplified the youthful energy seeking to find different solutions to the questions of race, gender, structural inequality, leadership, and collective organization. The "Young Turks" of Howard University, as Du Bois nicknamed them, led the charge, with Ralph Bunche, Abram Harris, Sterling Brown, and Emmett Dorsey pushing the importance of African American labor solidarity and economic self-determination. Also present was Charles Hamilton Houston, the former World War I officer and dean of Howard University Law School who had begun to play an increasingly important role in the legal campaigns of the NAACP.[89]

Over four days, interspersed, as Du Bois recollected, with "swimming and glorious food" along with hikes, tennis, and canoeing, the Amenia conferees talked, debating the best course of action for the race moving forward. Formal sessions on various topics took place under a large tent on the lawn, while informal conversations held over meals, during moments of socialization, and late into the night in the smaller sleeping tents were even more memorable. The final resolutions emphasized the importance of unity of purpose, a rejection of both communism and fascism as realistic solutions, the imperative of economic independence, and the need for the NAACP to prioritize issues of labor and capital alongside its traditional civil liberties agenda. Du Bois, as elder statesman, came away pleased but with guarded optimism. As he mused in the October 1933 issue of *The Crisis*, "Perhaps the second Amenia conference will not be as epoch-making as the first, but on the other hand, it is just as possible that it will be more significant for the future than any conference which colored people have yet held."[90]

He quickly tested the unity of Amenia and, more critically, the relevance of his voice and leadership in the NAACP. As part of his "new racial philosophy," he began making the case for African Americans to pool their scarce resources and form economic cooperatives. From Atlanta, where he'd secured another semester of teaching, he lobbed the bombshell editorial "Segregation" in the first *Crisis* issue of 1934, blasting open the door to a debate that he knew would go beyond any specific remedy to address the plight of African Americans but would force a reckoning with the core philosophy and agenda of the NAACP itself. "The thinking colored people of the United States must stop being stampeded by the word segregation," he declared, making a clear distinction between forced de jure discrimination as a condition of inferiority and the need for the race to take advantage of, and even embrace, "voluntary segregation and cooperation" as a matter of both pride and survival. Yes, continue to fight against discrimination. But "never in the world should our fight be against association with ourselves because by that very token we give up the whole argument that we are worth associating with."[91] The editorial caught the NAACP board by surprise and left Walter White, who insisted that Du Bois publish his rebuttal in the next issue of *The Crisis*, flummoxed. Du Bois dismissed him.[92]

Instead, the agitated editor pressed even harder the following month and challenged the NAACP directly. Providing evidence in the form of early statements and annual reports, Du Bois asserted, "As a matter of fact, the Association, while it has from time to time discussed the larger aspects of this matter, has taken no general stand and adopted no general philosophy." Although the NAACP clearly opposed discrimination based on race, it needed to accept the cold reality of segregation as a matter of fact and the futility of "tilting against windmills."

Du Bois offered two illustrative examples of the NAACP effectively supporting Jim Crow, both related to the World War. One was the decision to fight for a separate training camp for Black officers. In this case, African Americans "scored a tremendous triumph against the Color Line by their admitted and open policy of segregation," he argued. The NAACP at the time believed that "a separate Negro camp and Negro officers was infinitely better than no camp and no Negro officers and that was the only practical choice that lay before them." Du Bois next pointed to the dilemma of establishing separate hospitals for Black people and, specifically, the uproar surrounding the veterans hospital at Tuskegee as a prime example of the "contradiction and paradox of the problem of race segregation" facing the NAACP and the race. While the NAACP initially opposed locating the facility in the South, "once established," he wrote, "we fought to defend the Tuskegee hospital and give it the widest opportunity." Black veterans remained segregated there, but attended to by "an efficient Negro staff" who cared for their needs better than white doctors or nurses ever would. The NAACP, Du Bois asserted, "never denied the recurrent necessity of united separate action on the part of Negroes for self-defense and self-development." He viewed this as a matter of "race pride and race loyalty, Negro ideals and Negro unity."[93]

He kept up his drumbeat in the following issues of *The Crisis*. Black newspapers across the country covered the NAACP infighting and attempted to make sense of Du Bois's new stance. Some went so far as to liken him to Booker T. Washington.[94]

William Monroe Trotter would undoubtedly have had much to say about Du Bois and the segregation debate, but by early 1934 the once-indomitable civil rights leader was in a dark place. Trotter's influence had steadily declined since 1919. The growth of the NAACP, along with the din of New Negro radicals during the immediate postwar period, increasingly drowned out his voice on the national stage. *The Boston Guardian* struggled to stay afloat, and Trotter's health deteriorated. Perhaps above all else, he was frustrated and heartbroken at the resiliency of white supremacy and the slow pace of progress in the struggle for African American racial equality. It all became too much to bear. In the early-morning hours of April 7, just as the sun began to rise on his sixty-second birthday, Trotter, depressed and despondent, threw himself off the roof of his three-story building at 42 Cunard Street in the Roxbury section of Boston. He did not survive the fall.[95]

Trotter's tragic death hit Du Bois hard. A portrait of the legendary activist graced the May 1934 cover of *The Crisis*, and Du Bois penned a heartfelt tribute to his old comrade, writing, "Monroe Trotter was a man of heroic proportions, and probably one of the most selfless of Negro leaders during all our American history." They shared much of that history, having attended Harvard together, bonding in their criticism of Booker T. Washington, and partnering in the founding of the Niagara Movement. But Du Bois, with the NAACP, and Trotter, with the uncompromising Equal Rights League, gradually grew apart, Trotter punctuating their divide with his scathing critique of Du Bois and "Close Ranks," labeling him a traitor to the race and "rank quitter in the fight for rights." They never reconciled. Trotter proceeded with his militant program, standing, as Du Bois wrote, "unflinchingly for fighting separation and discrimination." "On this battle line he fought a long, exhausting fight for over a quarter of a century," tragically with little to show for it. Trotter's life and career served as an example of the need to oppose segregation when warranted, but to embrace "voluntary racial organization" when necessary. The race needed "not one but a thousand lives, like that of Monroe Trotter" to achieve victory. Du Bois reflected on his death:

> I can see a man of sixty, tired and disappointed, facing poverty and defeat. Standing amid indifferent friends and triumphant enemies. So he went to the window of his Dark Tower, and beckoned

to Death; up from where She lay among the lilies. And Death, like a whirlwind, swept up to him. I shall think of him as lying silent, cold and still; at last at peace, dreamless and serene. Let no trump of doom disturb him from his perfect and eternal rest.[96]

In the same issue, Du Bois's battle over the direction of the NAACP came to a head. Du Bois pushed the board to make a definitive statement on segregation, putting forth a resolution that acknowledged the association's opposition to "the underlying principle of racial segregation" but also admitting that it "always recognized and encouraged" Black institutions and would continue to do so. The board, instead, voted and approved a revised resolution, affirming that the NAACP "is opposed both to the principle and the practice of enforced segregation of human beings on the basis of race and color" that "by its very existence carries with it the implication of a superior and inferior group and invariably results in the imposition of a lower status on the group deemed inferior." Du Bois boldly published and, in the same column, mocked the decision and the board's apparent lack of race pride. "Does it believe in Negro business enterprise of any sort? Does it believe in Negro history, Negro literature and Negro art? Does it believe in Negro spirituals?" He promised to say more the following month.[97]

Du Bois had gone too far. The board responded by effectively muzzling him, voting that *The Crisis* remained the organ of the NAACP and that no salaried officer could criticize the association in the pages of the magazine without advance approval.[98] Du Bois was incredulous. In a telegram to Joel Spingarn on May 21, upon learning of the board's actions, he said, "Of course my resignation is now inevitable."[99]

He made good on that inevitability with a letter to the board on June 1. In his thirty-five years of public service, he noted, "my contribution to the settlement of the Negro problems has been mainly candid criticism based on a careful effort to know the facts. I have not always been right, but I have been sincere, and I am unwilling at this late day to be limited in the expression of my honest opinions in the way in which the Board proposes." *The Crisis*, never the simple mouthpiece of the association, was, under his stewardship, an organ of "free and uncensored expression." Seeing no other choice, he resigned.[100] The board voted to take no action on it, hoping to find a resolution to the impasse.[101] But Du Bois was done. In a June 26 letter that he shared with the public, he confirmed his resignation and announced his full separation from the NAACP effective July 1. "My program for economic readjustment has been totally ignored. My demand for a change in personnel has been considered as mere petty jealousy, and my protest against our mistakes and blunders has been looked upon as disloyalty to the organization." The only recourse, he determined, was "complete and final withdrawal," not out of hopelessness or profound respect for the NAACP but because, as he wrote, "I personally can do nothing more."[102]

With typical flourish, so came to an end Du Bois's remarkable twenty-four-year career with the NAACP and as editor of *The Crisis*. In that time, more than anyone else, he shaped public opinion about the race question in America and the possibility of democracy for Black people throughout the world. For his part, he seemed at peace. He had already lined up another semester of teaching at Atlanta University, a full-time position on the faculty as professor of sociology appeared imminent, and, free from the burdens of *The Crisis* and his battles with Walter White, he could now devote much-needed time and focus to his writing projects, *Black Reconstruction* and *The Black Man and the Wounded World*.

IN THE MIDST OF his fight with the NAACP and ultimate departure from the association, Du Bois still managed to carve out the time and focus to bring *Black Reconstruction* to completion. On June 3, 1933, he provided Edwin Embree at the Rosenwald Foundation with an update on his activities as the generous two-year fellowship came to a close. "I have given as a result of this grant two years of intensive study to the part which Negroes played in Reconstruction," he wrote. During this time, he had amassed "a considerable library on the subject," enlisted the help of teachers and students, and "kept up a clerical force of one to three persons." Harcourt Brace and Company eagerly awaited publishing the book, and Du Bois anticipated, with predictable exaggeration when it came to self-imposed deadlines, providing them with a manuscript by July 1.

He could not tout similar progress for *The Black Man and the Wounded World*. With the benefit of historical distance, and free from grappling with his own conflicted personal memories and guilt, the Reconstruction era proved much easier to write about than the World War. It was history, whereas the World War and its aftermath was the present. "I had, naturally, hoped to do a great deal more than this; one book on Reconstruction and one on the history of the Negro, before, during and since the World War," he informed Embree, "but historical and social research is endless." For Du Bois, the war, along with its disastrous outcomes, did indeed seem increasingly endless. And, like the war itself, he seemed increasingly resigned to failure when it came to progress on *The Black Man and the Wounded World*. "Although I am in a way disappointed," he admitted, "perhaps this is as much as I ought to expect."[103]

In the summer of 1933, the condition of the *Black Reconstruction* manuscript in many ways mirrored that of *The Black Man and the Wounded World*. It was nearly twice as long as it needed to be for publication, stuffed with documents and figures and lacking Du Bois's signature prose. And yet he forged ahead, devoting nearly every day through the summer and into the fall, including Saturdays and Sundays, to paring down, polishing, and ultimately finishing the first draft.[104] On December 1, he mailed the manuscript, all eleven hundred pages, to Alfred Harcourt. After spending an hour at his desk skimming through the manuscript, the publisher was thoroughly impressed and congratulated Du Bois on his "really brilliant performance."[105]

The book, however, remained far from done. Both Du Bois and Harcourt agreed that additional work was necessary to make it error proof and immune from criticism. With the backing of Harcourt, along with an endorsement from Edwin Embree, Du Bois received a $1,000 subsidy from the Carnegie Corporation in late March 1934 to complete revisions.[106] In addition to his team of Atlanta University students, he enlisted the help of fellow scholars, including E. Franklin Frazier, Rayford Logan, and Sterling Brown, to track down sources and references.[107] Du Bois worked feverishly, determined to complete what he described to his longtime London friend Ruth Anna Fisher as "my magnum opus."[108]

On May 12, 1934, he sent off a revised and what he hoped would be a nearly finished version,[109] but the massive size of the manuscript became alarmingly clear as it entered the production phase. Alfred Harcourt wrote to Du Bois on June 14 that even with their best efforts to squeeze as many words as possible onto each page, the book would run to 716 pages and have to be sold at the potentially prohibitive Depression-era cost of $5.00.[110] Du Bois continued to revise, tinker with, and sand down the manuscript over the next several months in order to transform it into what he described as "a piece of literature."[111] "My method of writing is a method of 'after-thoughts,'" he wrote to Alfred Harcourt in November as production costs skyrocketed. "I mean that after all the details of commas, periods, spelling and commas, there comes the final and to me the most important work of polishing and re-setting and even re-stating."[112]

Black Reconstruction finally rolled off the press and into the public on June 13, 1935. It was indeed a monumental achievement. Du Bois delivered on his promise of centering Black people, as slaves and then as freedpeople, as the main historical actors in the drama of the Civil War and its social, political, and economic aftermath. While still grounded in his long-held views of Reconstruction, the book and its theoretical framing reflected Du Bois's recent immersion in Marxist theory. By withdrawing their labor and fleeing to the Union lines—what Du Bois likened to a "general strike"—slaves forced the inevitability of emancipation upon Lincoln and ultimately destroyed the Confederacy from within. The fate of Reconstruction hinged on the question of work and the place of freedpeople as a new proletariat in the Southern economy. The many achievements of the era, from schooling to political office holding, ultimately crumbled under the desire of Northern capitalists, the Southern oligarchy, and complicit working-class whites to violently keep Black people as a caste of exploited serfs. The "revolution" of 1876 signaled not only the end of Reconstruction but also the beginning of the modern race problem and the effective removal of Black people as citizens from the body politic. The true "unending tragedy of Reconstruction," Du Bois powerfully demonstrated by the final pages of the book, "is the utter inability of the American mind to grasp its real significance, its national and worldwide implications."[113] Smart readers would have understood this statement as a shot at Claude Bowers and his scurrilous book *The Tragic Era*, one of the many authors and texts Du Bois excoriated in the concluding chapter, "Propaganda of History." Offering a searing indictment of the historical profession and the historiography of Reconstruction, Du Bois declared, "I stand at the end of this writing, literally aghast at what American historians have done to this field."[114] But he also believed that with *Black Reconstruction* the field would never be the same.

The immediate reception of the book further boosted his confidence. Glowing reviews and notes of congratulations flowed in from friends, colleagues, and even antagonists. Shirley Graham, quickly ascending to the top of the list of Du Bois's extramarital affections, could hardly contain her enthusiasm. "Words cannot express how thrilled I am," she gushed. "Every line, every word filled me and inspired me with the determination to be, to give, to dream only the best."[115] James Weldon Johnson applauded his longtime friend. "You have done a grand piece of work in Black Reconstruction—and no one else could have done it," he penned from Great Barrington.[116] His fellow historian Benjamin Brawley sounded a similar note in his brief review of the book. "If honesty and truth mean anything in scholarship, this book should go far in revising the traditional view of one of the most critical periods in our history."[117] Emmett Scott, moving past his legal battles with Du Bois from three years earlier, wrote, "The Negro people of the United States—in fact, the colored peoples of the world, owe you a sincere debt of gratitude for your monumental work," adding that because of his "virile pen" and setting forth of facts, "it will not be easy in the future for so-called historians to smear the Negroes' part in that lamentable period."[118] "I appreciate your kind words of June 27th," Du Bois replied.[119]

Du Bois, without question, made a remarkable historiographical intervention. He also contributed a profound statement about democracy and its tortured development since Reconstruction, through the World War, and up to the present. Reconstruction represented a moment when democracy, not only in the United States but throughout the world, could have been transformed. The roots of the horror of 1914–18 came from the seeds planted with the premature demise of Reconstruction. Du Bois made this clear in the penultimate chapter, "Back Toward Slavery," writing, "One can only say to all this that whatever the South gained through its victory in the revolution of 1876 has been paid for at a price which literally staggers humanity. Imperialism, the exploitation of colored labor throughout the world, thrives upon the approval of the United States, and the United States gives that approval because of the South. World war waits on and supports imperial aggression and international jealousy."[120] The curtailment of democracy as a result of America's abandonment of Reconstruction not only led to the World War but portended another global catastrophe in the future. As Du Bois reflected, "If the Reconstruction of Southern states, from slavery to free labor, and from aristocracy to industrial democracy, had been conceived as a major national program of America, whose accomplishment at any price was well worth the effort, we should be living today in a different world."[121]

"War and especially civil strife leave terrible wounds," Du Bois wrote toward the end of *Black Reconstruction*. "It is the duty of humanity to heal them."[122] Du Bois had succeeded in writing the history of one defining moment for Black people and its importance for the fate of democracy, in the United States and beyond. Now, once again, he turned his attention to another defining moment, the Great War, and looked to complete the story of the wounded world.

CHAPTER 11

"I think I can do something which will have
influence on future knowledge with regard to war
and colored people."[1]

DU BOIS LOVED HIS NEWSPAPERS. As part of his always meticulously
scripted daily routine, he made a point of staying abreast of current
events and, especially, international affairs.[2] During his editorship of
The Crisis, along with most of the major Black weeklies—*The Chicago Defender, New York Amsterdam News, The Pittsburgh Courier,
Baltimore Afro-American*—a copy of *The New York Times* remained
a constant presence in the office. While a resident at the Dunbar
Apartments, he had the Sunday issue of the *Times* delivered to his
door, along with firm instructions for the paperboy not to disturb
him by ringing the bell.[3] When he relocated to Atlanta for his visiting
professorship in January 1933, he gladly paid the $2.50 for a three-
month subscription to *The Atlanta Constitution*.[4] While not quite up
to the standards of *The New York Times*, at least for the time being,
it would do.

Less than a week into the new semester at Atlanta University, as
he sat down to read the Tuesday, January 31, 1933, edition of the
Constitution, Du Bois was greeted with a jarring headline: HITLER
HEADS GERMAN FUSION GOVERNMENT AS NATIONALISTS JOIN HANDS TO
SAVE NATION.

Despite Adolf Hitler's defeat in the 1932 presidential election,
the fractious German parliament failed to cobble together a governing

coalition. The Nazis still held enough power for Hitler to make a play for the chancellorship. The weeks of January 1933 had been rife with behind-the-scenes intrigue, backstabbing, and secret negotiations. Finally, on January 30 at a little past 11:00 a.m., as anxious crowds filled the streets, President Hindenburg, in a leap of faith, appointed Hitler chancellor. Jubilant Nazi supporters by the thousands marched throughout the night in triumph, their torches illuminating the sky.[5]

Despite the excitement in Berlin, to most Germans and almost all outside observers, the ascension of Hitler as chancellor elicited no real cause for alarm. Reading further into his newspaper, Du Bois would have scoured an article conveying reactions from various world capitals to Hitler's feat. In Washington, DC, "little apprehension was voiced concerning the effect the appointment might have on international relations," the *Constitution* reported, reflecting the widespread view that the responsibilities of governing would curb Hitler's worst instincts.[6] The new chancellor had other plans. In his first public statement upon assuming power, he declared, "After a thirteen-year struggle the National Socialist movement has succeeded in breaking through to the government; the struggle to win the German nation, however, is only beginning."[7]

Du Bois detested Hitler. With his intimate knowledge of German history, Du Bois knew all too well the martial and ultranationalist soil from which Hitler emerged. He saw Hitler's anti-Semitism and belief in Aryan supremacy as especially contemptible and said so in the pages of *The Crisis*. In the May 1933 editorial "The Jews," he wrote, "It seems impossible that in the middle of the 20th Century a country like Germany could turn to race hatred as a political expedient."[8] But while Du Bois certainly viewed Hitler as repugnant, the Nazi leader, in the end, differed little, he believed, from the white supremacist demagogues in America. "Wouldn't it be fine to invite Hitler to lecture at a few white Southern colleges?" he jeered in the October 1933 *Crisis*. "They might not understand his German but his race nonsense would fit beautifully."[9]

By the fall of 1933, however, Hitler's consolidation of power was deadly serious. Using an unprecedented propaganda campaign spearheaded by Joseph Goebbels, combined with the brute force of the paramilitary *Sturmabteilung* (SA) and the Gestapo secret police, the Nazis eliminated any and all political opposition. On July 14, the Reichstag decreed the NSDAP the only legitimate political party in Germany.[10] With the Nazi domestic takeover proceeding at lightning speed, Hitler turned his attention to foreign affairs. On October 14, at the League of Nations–sponsored Geneva Disarmament Conference, refusing once and for all to be bound by what he saw as the disgraceful and unfairly punitive Versailles Treaty, he withdrew Germany from both the conference and the league. France, in response, announced that it could not disarm so long as Germany remained a threat. Sure enough, Hitler promptly began formulating plans for a massive expansion of the German military.[11]

Du Bois recognized the significance of Geneva. In the December 1933 *Crisis* editorial titled "Peace," with the traumatic memories of 1914–18 on his mind, he pleaded for readers to awake from their complacency and understand the gravity of what the world faced. "We laugh gently at the disarmament conference in Geneva," he warned. "We do not even treat the matter seriously. We see no threat in the failure of this conference to our own flesh and blood, to our comfort, to our dreams, to literature and art."[12] He saw not only peace but the very future of democracy in grave danger. "Will it all end in fascism?" Du Bois mused two months later in the February 1934 *Crisis.* "We don't know but one thing is certain, it will all end."[13]

~

IN THE SUMMER OF 1934, as he finished work on *Black Reconstruction*, Du Bois renewed his ongoing quest for financial support for *The Black Man and the Wounded World.* The Social Science Research Council (SSRC), with its interdisciplinary mission of confronting the pressing social and public policy issues of the day, was an ideal match for him.[14] The organization made their grants, as stated in the brochure Du Bois received for the 1935–36 cycle, "available to mature scholars . . . without reference to age, whose capacity for productive research has been effectively demonstrated by published work." The sixty-six-year-old Du Bois, his mind sharper than ever, clearly met the criteria. Also in his favor, the awards were "designed to aid in completing rather than initiating projects."[15]

On July 19, Du Bois sent a letter to Donald Young, the SSRC secretary, expressing interest in applying for a grant. With his Reconstruction book covering the years between 1850 and 1876, he now aimed to follow it "with a study of the Negro race from 1876 until after the World War." He hoped to spend the next year consolidating and rewriting, with the goal of getting the book out in 1936 or 1937.[16]

After two months of back-and-forth correspondence, Du Bois submitted his formal application sometime during the second week of October.[17] As in his many prior appeals to foundations and philanthropies, he offered background on *The Black Man and the Wounded World* and explained why it remained unfinished. Du Bois desired "clerical help, money for buying books, and time for writing." He especially wanted to get his hands on and delve into recently published "post-war revelations and reports in English, French, German and other languages." Estimating, based on the soaring costs of preparing *Black Reconstruction*, that revising, completing, and seeing *The Black Man and the Wounded World* all the way through to publication would cost $5,000, he asked for a grant-in-aid of at least $1,000, ideally $2,000 if the SSRC could be so generous. Touting the depth of his research, he noted, "I think I may say that there is nothing in print that covers the ground which I am endeavoring to cover in this project."[18]

Du Bois was again on the road, this time in Prairie View, Texas, attending a conference on the economic conditions of African Americans in the state, when Donald Young's note arrived at his Atlanta University office on March 20, 1935. His secretary forwarded Du Bois the good news. "I am glad to inform you that the Committee on Grants-in-Aid has voted you the sum of $600, or as much thereof as may be needed in 1935–36, for the completion of your history of the Negro troops in the World War," Young wrote. While less than Du Bois requested, the amount fell within the range of most SSRC grants.[19] Du Bois expressed his gratitude for the award as well as for the validation from his social science peers. "May I thank you and the Committee very much for the grant that you have made," he replied to Young.[20] John Hope, always in his corner, also congratulated Du Bois on his success.[21] The grant, however modest, gave Du Bois a helpful shot in the arm and boosted his hopes for completing the manuscript. On April 1, he received the first $300 check, with the second installment arriving on July 1.[22]

But he also had bigger plans in mind. At the same time as he wooed the SSRC for support, he'd reached out to the Oberlaender Trust, which had been established in early 1931 with a $1 million gift from the textile businessman Gustav Oberlaender with the goal of promoting "a better understanding of the German-speaking peoples by American people and vice versa." Their grants provided for a period of study in a German-speaking country and were open to "editors and writers, public health workers, professors and students" interested in a range of subjects of public interest, including race relations.[23]

Du Bois had excitedly contacted the trust in 1931 with a plan to visit Germany and conduct research on its former African colonies.[24] Although this did not materialize, in the following years he kept up his correspondence with the trust and its secretary, Wilbur Thomas, hoping to find a topic that would stick. In an October 1934 inquiry, as he began to refocus on *The Black Man and the Wounded World*, Du Bois broached the possibility of investigating the contentious issue of France's postwar stationing of African troops in the Rhineland, which had become a staple of Nazi propaganda. In late January 1935, Du Bois sat down with Thomas at the Oberlaender Trust's 225 South Fifteenth Street headquarters in Philadelphia.[25] After sharing ideas, Du Bois decided to submit a much safer proposal on February 7, concentrating on German industrial education and comparing it with the system for African Americans in the United States.

This would do. On April 17, Du Bois received word from Thomas that the trust was willing to offer a "small grant for a trip to Germany and Austria" based on the project.[26] Eager to try to elevate Germany's image in America as concerns about the Third Reich and Hitler's ambitions continued to mount, the Oberlaender needed Du Bois just as much as he needed it. A few weeks later, he followed up with a more detailed six-month plan of study.[27] The possibility of a funded overseas trip seemed within a hairsbreadth of becoming a reality. Sure enough, on June 12 he received word of a $1,600 stipend to travel to Germany.[28]

Du Bois undoubtedly held some interest in comparative industrial educational systems in the United States and Germany, but he would have proposed any plan if it met the approval of the Oberlaender trustees and allowed him to spend time abroad.[29] He not only wanted to observe the Third Reich himself; he wanted to use the opportunity to travel more widely and further understand the developments of fascism and communism and their relation to democracy. Upon learning of the Oberlaender's willingness to fund him, he began exploring the possibility of again visiting the Soviet Union as well as seeing China and Japan. While not explicitly connected to his book, this international trip was all about making sense of the wounded world.

⌒

AS HE PREPARED TO travel to Europe and Asia, a crisis on the African continent commanded his attention. Stretching back to the 1880s, Italy had eyed Ethiopia as the prize possession of its East African imperial foothold. When Benito Mussolini rose to power, he trained his sights on Ethiopia, and in March 1934 he publicly announced his desire to grab control of the proudly independent country. On December 5, a deadly shoot-out in Walwal, a town in a disputed region of the Somali-Ethiopian border, gave the Italian dictator the excuse he needed to move forward with war plans.[30]

Du Bois had seen it coming. In the June 1926 issue of *The Crisis*, he'd penned the prescient editorial "Italy and Abyssinia." "What Italy wants is Abyssinia," Du Bois forecasted. "She has wanted Abyssinia a long time." He also predicted, correctly, that England and France, in spite of the Treaty of Versailles, the League of Nations, and Locarno, would not stand in the way of Italy's "high-handed program of theft, lying and slavery."[31]

By the start of 1935, as war appeared imminent, Du Bois began to fully immerse himself in the fate of Ethiopia. He played a prominent

role in the "Hands Off Ethiopia" campaign, a broad leftist international movement to fight against Italian aggression.[32] Throughout the
spring and summer of 1935, he delivered speeches and corresponded
with groups such as the American Committee on the Ethiopia Crisis.[33] On September 25, he took the stage at Madison Square Garden
as one of the speakers for a protest meeting organized by the American League Against War and Fascism. "Why now has the world public opinion been so extraordinarily aroused today over a procedure
which was commonplace yesterday?" Du Bois asked, looking out at
the crowd of ten thousand people, a quarter of whom were Black.
"Because the World War has taught most of Europe and America
that the continuing conquest, exploitation and oppression of colored
peoples by white is unreasonable and impossible and if persisted in will
overthrow civilization."[34]

On October 3, the first of some seven hundred thousand Italian
troops crossed the Eritrean border into Ethiopia. The start of the war
coincided almost prophetically with an article Du Bois published that
same month in the journal *Foreign Affairs* titled "Inter-Racial Implications of the Ethiopian Crisis: A Negro View." He could have named it
"The African Roots of Future War." "There seems to be little doubt
that the demand of certain states to participate in an increased colonial exploitation of Africa was a principal cause of the World War,"
he wrote, restating his still valid thesis from 1915 and adding that
Europe's continued imperialist greed "heightens the danger of another similar conflagration." He pointed to Germany and its renewed
colonial aspirations, asking, "But if Italy takes her pound of flesh by
force, does anyone suppose that Germany will not make a similar attempt?" He also predicted that Japan would mirror Europe's actions
in Asia. What proved true in 1914–18, he concluded, remained undeniable in 1935: "Economic exploitation based on the excuse of race
prejudice is the program of the white world. Italy states it openly and
plainly."[35] But he also believed that Black people across the diaspora,
African Americans included, would rally around Ethiopia and demand
freedom and self-determination, by force if necessary.

Contemplating the seeds of a possible second world war pulled
Du Bois back to his unfinished history of the first. He had exhausted

his funding options with most major philanthropies and foundations. However, the Carnegie Corporation, which had provided last-minute support for *Black Reconstruction*, remained untapped. Du Bois specifically eyed the potential of the Carnegie Endowment for International Peace, originally established by the steel tycoon in 1910 and charged with the goal of eliminating the causes of global warfare.

James T. Shotwell held the position of director of the endowment's Division of Economics and History. A distinguished historian of European politics and international relations at Columbia University, Shotwell, like Du Bois, had close connections to the World War. He'd volunteered as chairman of the Committee on Public Information's National Board for Historical Service, was handpicked as a special adviser to Woodrow Wilson in preparation for the Versailles conference, and sailed with the president to Paris in December 1918 as part of the American Commission to Negotiate Peace.[36] Following the peace conference, the Carnegie Foundation appointed him lead editor of an ambitious project, *Economic and Social History of the World War*, what he later described as "a collection of national series dealing with the economic and social effects of the war upon some sixteen European countries."[37] Shotwell brought the project to a close in 1937 with 152 volumes, believing, as he told *The New York Times*, that "the wealth of data covered in these volumes would, if read and understood by the people of the world, be a real preventative of war."[38] With their similar backgrounds and their commitment to using history as a means to promote peace, who better than Shotwell to see the value of Du Bois's book?

On January 16, 1936, Du Bois wrote to Shotwell at his Columbia University office to inquire about support. He briefed his fellow World War scholar on the background of his project, stating that he initially conceived the book "simply as an historical record," but as it recently swirled in his mind, and after reviewing some of the recent literature on the war, he'd begun to "conceive of this history as a potent tract for peace. The unnecessary suffering and intrigue, the effect of the war upon the Negro peoples today, the Italian-Ethiopian aftermath, all makes me certain that I could write a volume which would be an effective attack upon the war from the point of view of the so-called lesser peoples." He estimated that finishing the book involved "the entire re-writing, verification of authorities and copying of documents," with "clerical and skilled help" amounting to $3,000.[39]

Shotwell responded eleven days later, writing that he was "very much interested indeed in the plan of your history of the Negro in the World War." But he offered a caveat for his enthusiasm. Financing for the nearly complete *Economic and Social History of the World War* came out of a special Carnegie Corporation fund that was exhausted. He nevertheless asked Du Bois to send him a table of contents.[40] On February 4, Du Bois wrote back and promised Shotwell "a detailed list of chapters and subjects."[41]

The next day, Du Bois hit the road. He packed February with speaking engagements, still his favorite means of connecting with the Black public as well as earning extra money. He left Jim Crow Atlanta on February 5 on the 6:05 p.m. train to New York City.[42] He gave a February 8 speech in Rochester, New York, and then quickly turned back south for a pair of February 9 speeches in Baltimore and Washington, DC, on "Italy and Ethiopia." He briefly returned to Atlanta before again packing his bags for more lectures. After a swing through Birmingham, Alabama, on February 14, where he spoke on "The Economic Crisis Among American Negroes" to an audience of approximately one thousand people—with, by his estimate, maybe twenty-five white people sprinkled in—he went on to Peoria, arriving on February 16, a Sunday. From there he spent the next two days in Chicago, where the brutal winter weather fell below fifteen degrees. In between lectures on "Italy and Ethiopia" and "Literature and Art Among American Negroes," he found time to brave the elements and catch a movie.[43] His time on the circuit ended in Muncie, Indiana, on February 19, with a speech on "The Future of the Darker Races."[44] At Muncie he took a sleeper car to Cincinnati and from there headed directly back to Atlanta, arriving home, exhausted, on the evening of February 20 at around 7:00 p.m.[45]

Terrible news greeted him. At 3:00 that afternoon, John Hope had died. After fighting a bout of pneumonia for a week, Hope had taken a sudden turn for the worse, and, already weakened with a bad heart, his body failed him. "It is a very terrible loss which I cannot yet realize," he confided, stunned, in a note to his friend Virginia Alexander the next day.[46] Funeral services took place on February 24, with seven hundred friends, colleagues, dignitaries, and students crowding into Sale Hall Chapel on the Morehouse campus before Hope was buried in the shadow of the Atlanta University administration building.[47] Du Bois later wrote of the man who, next to Charles Young, stood as his most intimate Black confidant: "In his premature dying, John Hope, above everything, left friends; not a great number, but a few persons who feel that with him, honest and unselfish devotion to duty has lost a beautiful exemplar; and that they have lost something inexpressibly near and absolutely irreplaceable."[48]

In the days immediately following Hope's death, Du Bois swallowed his grief by responding to James Shotwell's request to see an outline of *The Black Man and the Wounded World*. Sitting in the quietude of his Atlanta University office, he carefully sifted through and reviewed the enormous manuscript and stacks of documents. The narrative table of contents he ultimately prepared for Shotwell presented a book like none other and, with further revisions, promised to be truly pathbreaking.

The dazzling opening chapter, "Interpretations," first published in *The Crisis* in January 1924, remained. He thought that the second chapter, "The Story of the War," his "succinct attempt to epitomize the main movements of the war," could potentially be omitted, and he envisioned completely rethinking the third chapter, "The World of Black Folk," which would now "show how the exploitation of the darker races by white Europe and America made their connection with the world organization so close that despite everything they were drawn into the war." The "Black France" chapter was done, while "Black England," incomplete, needed to account for new books to reflect how "participation of black troops intensified the Negro problems in the various English colonies." He had twenty random pages for the chapter "Other Black Folk," which required more research and factual grounding. He presumably hoped to expand this significantly.

The book, as he outlined and described, then pivoted to the "Negroes in America." Chapters 7 and 8, on the state of Black America, covered the "hesitations and internal conditions" facing Black people when "called upon to help in the war." The subsequent five chapters dealt with the draft, labor battalions, and the Ninety-Third Division, with specific treatments on the Eighth Illinois and the Fifteenth New York. He recognized that "the kernel of the story," his chapter 14 on the Ninety-Second Division, would need to be "divided up and condensed" from its current 144 pages. He possessed ample material for the following chapter on the histories of the 365th, 366th, and 367th infantry regiments of the Ninety-Second Division, although it remained very rough and inelegantly written. Chapter 16, on the 368th Infantry Regiment and the plight of its Black officers, evidenced by its 114-page length, was key. "The whole story shows the extraordinary interaction of war and race prejudice," he explained.

What could be interpreted as the third section of the book addressed the aftermath of the war and its historical and political legacy. Chapter 17 examined the armistice and how the riots and clashes following the return of Black troops "had economic and industrial causes." Chapter 18, "The War Within the War," sixty-seven written pages, proposed to explore "what went on in the United States during and after the War in the treatment of Negroes within and without the army." Chapters 19, 20, and 21, titled respectively "Behind the Lines," "The End," and "The Beginning," were, as Du Bois clarified, "planned at first as a summary of the factual material brought together in this study." But as he read and reevaluated his manuscript, Du Bois now imagined a different ending for the book. He intended to write at least two new chapters "to show the utter failure of war as a solution of a major social problem or of any other pressing problem." He saw in the World War "the germ of the depression and social anarchy which followed it." His study would therefore speak to the present and respond to "the urgent demand for the solution of economic problems which shall include the solution of race problems." He made a note of the date—February 22, 1936—that he finished his reappraisal of *The Black Man and the Wounded World*.[49]

On February 26, two days after John Hope's funeral, Du Bois shared the framework for his book with James Shotwell. He really wished that Shotwell could examine the manuscript in person, to see and feel its uniqueness, and also so Du Bois could, as he wrote, "emphasize a little better my feeling that this could be a most effective, practical peace document." "Usually we talk about peace in the abstract," he argued, "but here is a chance to see what war means in the concrete as applied to people who are already under social difficulties, and what interest American Negroes and the Negroes in the world have in world peace."[50]

A personal meeting between Du Bois and Shotwell would have likely resulted in the same outcome. On March 12, Shotwell passively informed Du Bois that the Carnegie Endowment for International Peace was not in a position to help. He reiterated that all available funds for a project like this had been invested in the *Economic and Social History of the World War*. His hands were tied. "I think you know my sympathy for the kind of work you are doing," Shotwell noted, further remarking that Du Bois's project contained "another appeal and a very strong one" that lay outside the purview of the Carnegie Endowment. He suggested that Du Bois inquire with the Russell Sage Foundation and the Milbank Fund, "or some such organization devoted to American problems"—meaning the race problem—adding that his division was "distinctly international." Shotwell, soon to travel to Europe himself, fully sponsored by the Carnegie Endowment, offered his best wishes and sincere regrets.[51]

As Du Bois absorbed this latest reminder of his place at the margins of the mainstream historical profession, Ethiopia continued to suffer. Mussolini, with the war boosting his popularity, scoffed at belated sanctions imposed by the League of Nations and pressed forward even more aggressively. Italy's military might and sheer ruthlessness, as seen in its use of poison gas, methodically decimated the ragtag Ethiopian forces, with casualties soaring into the tens of thousands. On May 2, 1936, Emperor Haile Selassie, accepting the inevitability of defeat, left the capital of Addis Ababa and fled to England. The following month, on June 30, he addressed the League of Nations

Assembly. Stepping to the podium amid the jeers and taunts of Italian journalists, Selassie delivered a speech for the ages, lambasting the league for failing to support his country and for legitimizing Italy's actions. "Apart from the Kingdom of the Lord there is not on this earth any nation that is superior to any other," he declared. "Should it happen that a strong Government finds it may with impunity destroy a weak people, then the hour strikes for that weak people to appeal to the League of Nations to give its judgment in all freedom. God and history will remember your judgment."[52]

THE SAME DAY AS Haile Selassie gave his historic speech, Du Bois was on a train to Berlin. He departed New York on Friday, June 5, on the SS *St. Louis* for his Oberlaender-sponsored trip to Germany. During the nine pleasant days at sea, his mind raced with anticipation.[53] Eight years had passed since he'd last traveled abroad. The world had changed. He followed global events as closely as possible, but *The New York Times*, *The Atlanta Constitution*, and other newspapers he regularly consumed were poor substitutes for in-person study and up-close observation. Du Bois imagined himself as the eyes, ears, and voice of the race. As such, he promised to keep readers of his new weekly column in *The Pittsburgh Courier* abreast of his adventures and findings, excusing the three-month lag from when his evocative accounts would appear in print.[54]

Du Bois's ship docked at Southampton in England on June 15.[55] He spent ten days in London, visiting friends and acquaintances and enjoying some of the nightlife before crossing the English Channel for Belgium. Departing from Brussels on a second-class train ticket, he arrived at the German capital just after midnight on July 1.[56]

He entered a radically different country from the one he'd last observed in 1926. Since jettisoning the League of Nations in October 1933, Hitler had made good on his vow to rebuild the German military. He tested the mettle of France and her international allies on March 7, 1936, ordering troops to occupy the demilitarized Rhineland. Despite the flagrant violation of the Treaty of Versailles, France lodged only a toothless protest with the League, Great Britain took a hands-off approach, and the American president Franklin Roosevelt kept his plans for a Florida fishing trip.[57] Hitler's bold act further swelled German confidence as the country prepared to host the 1936 Olympic Games. The Reich was on its best behavior and, determined to exhibit its resurgence to the world, had removed all overtly anti-Jewish signs and propaganda. Observers and tourists alike openly wondered whether the worst forms of hostility facing the Jews had passed and if Hitler's Germany, its economy booming and prosperity flowing, was really that bad.[58] Friends and colleagues warned Du Bois ahead of time not to be deceived, with the anthropologist Franz Boas predicting that the Germans would be "particularly courteous to you and show you Potemkin villages."[59]

Potemkin villages or not, Du Bois wasted no time in making Germany his temporary home. An Oberlaender representative met him at the train and escorted the doctor to his flat, "neat, clean and quiet," in the Grunewald area of southwestern Berlin, complete with the basic amenities of a couch-bed, a desk and chair, a small table with a reading lamp and a telephone.[60] But he was eager to get out of the city. As much as he adored Berlin, visitors would soon start pouring in for the Olympic Games, including thousands of pompous, overly patriotic Americans whom Du Bois no doubt hoped to avoid.[61]

He devoted late July through the bulk of August to travel and sightseeing. A week spent walking through the streets of Paris and reconnecting with acquaintances likely recalled memories of his fateful visit after the armistice.[62] But most of his time was devoted to soaking up as much of Germany as he could. Even with its descent into fascism, the nation, with its rich history and culture, continued to pull at his heartstrings. He enjoyed Dresden in late July. He took in the impressive sights of Nuremberg, "one of those ancient tales in stone, which loses the air of reality." Munich, "a city of the theater, of music, of marvelous old buildings, and of beer," in the first week of August proved unforgettable.[63] He spent four days alone in the German Museum of Science and Technology, exploring the roughly seventy thousand exhibits, a statue of his beloved Goethe greeting him at the entrance.[64] He further indulged himself at Bayreuth in northern Bavaria, his visit coinciding with the annual summer music festival devoted to Wagner. He joined the throng of international opera lovers who flocked to the city of forty thousand, splurging on the $7.50 ticket that most townspeople could not afford, the theater two miles from the home where he stayed beginning on August 18.[65] "The musical dramas of Wagner," Du Bois rhapsodized, "tell of human life as he lived it, and no human being, white or black, can afford not to know them if he would know life."[66]

While he still squeezed in some additional travel throughout the country, he spent most of September and October in Berlin,[67] at least trying to justify the stated purpose of his Oberlaender fellowship by visiting some industrial schools and speaking with various German officials. "Germany in general is not seeking to use industry and industrial processes as a means of education, but on the contrary is using education as a means of carrying on and perfecting industry," he observed. The state, Du Bois clearly saw, controlled industry. "Who now controls the State?" he asked.[68] The answer was, without any doubt, the Führer. "Hitler set up a tyranny," Du Bois wrote once safely out of Germany. Hitler had created "a state with a mighty police force, a growing army, a host of spies and informers, a secret espionage, backed by swift and cruel punishment, which might vary from loss of job to imprisonment, incommunicado, and without trial, to cold murder."[69] And the overwhelming majority of the German people consented to it all. As he prepared to depart in late October, Du Bois clearly saw that the new German state with Hitler at the dictatorial helm posed a grave threat to peace and democracy.[70]

Disappointingly, his plans to visit the Soviet Union fell through due to visa complications. Instead, he contented himself with a ten-day excursion on the Trans-Siberian Express for the eastern leg of his world trip that would take him to Manchukuo, China, and Japan. "The scenic interest of the journey is heightened by the mighty panorama of social construction being carried on across the breadth of this vast country," the promotional pamphlet touted, further adding, "Throughout the route the traveler has the opportunity to observe the lives and customs and the new culture of the innumerable peoples freed by the October Revolution from centuries of oppression."[71]

The train ride did not disappoint. Du Bois relished the beauty of the Soviet landscape, "wide, wild and wonderful," monotonous for hundreds of miles, "yet varying infinitely in succession of village and town, swamp and forest, noble rivers."[72] A brief stopover in Moscow offered just enough time to take in the sights of new construction since his visit in 1926 and to send his granddaughter a postcard.[73] From his sleeper car window, a rolling panorama of the "new Russia" and its progress unfolded before his eyes.[74] Toward the tail end of the journey, the train skirted along the southern lip of Lake Baikal, "a jewel hung in space at that fateful spot where Europe becomes Asia, and where the waters part to make Pacific and Atlantic."[75] Du Bois's Siberian trek came to an end when the train reached the Soviet-Mongolian border between three and four o'clock on the morning of November 17. Noticing the concentrations of Soviet troops, Du Bois described the tense line of demarcation as "a border big with signs of war, watched eagerly by the rest of the world."[76]

By sunrise, following a baggage inspection check in the bitter morning cold, he was in Manchukuo. The Asian segment of his overseas sojourn had been meticulously organized by his friend Yasuichi Hikida, an agent for the Japanese imperial government whose deep interests in Afro-Asian cultural and political solidarity endeared him among much of the New York Black intelligentsia.[77] Upon arriving at the capital of Hsinking, a travel-weary Du Bois settled into the Hotel Yamato, taking a long bath and relaxing in the blue kimono and slippers in his room. His hosts gave him a tour of the city, a mix of Chinese influences and modern Japanese developments. He visited Port Arthur, site of the opening battle of the Russo-Japanese War in 1904 that ultimately allowed Japan to claim Manchuria—renamed Manchukuo—in its sphere of influence. He also traveled to the city of Mukden, where in September 1931 Japan staged the explosion that offered the pretense to finally invade and lay claim to its new imperial territory.[78] Du Bois rationalized that while Japan may have taken Manchuria for expansion and economic development, it ultimately kept it out of the hands of the Western powers, who would have inevitably seized it for their own exploitative aspirations. "The people appear happy," Du Bois blithely deduced.[79]

From Dalian on the morning of November 17, Du Bois crossed the Yellow Sea for China. He arrived at Tientsin around sunset and from there went to Peiping (Beijing). On his first day, by his count, he walked ten miles of the city's streets, "a continuous succession of little shops, stores, artisans' work places, restaurants, amusement centers, sidewalk markets, personal services." Over the next three days he marveled at Peiping, the history and culture packed within its walls, the "monuments, buildings, towers, arches, tile, porcelain, jewels, inscriptions, manuscripts and customs, habits, songs and a strange language." Experiencing a sensory overload, he could only remark, "China is inconceivable . . . Never before has a land so affected me. For Africa I had more emotion—a greater wave of understanding and recognition. But China is to the wayfarer of a little week, and I suspect of a little year, incomprehensible." He found Shanghai distasteful. The city, he observed, reeked of empire and was inundated with European capital and racist foreigners.[80] A frank conversation with a group of Chinese business, cultural, and educational representatives about the future of their nation, Du Bois discourteously peppering them with questions about their dependence on Europe and hostile relations with Japan, did not inspire confidence.[81] Nevertheless, he realized that "any attempt to explain the world, without giving a place of extraordinary prominence to China, is futile."[82]

He sailed for China's adversary on December 1, reaching Nagasaki the next day. The visit of America's most prominent Black scholar and race spokesman became a national event in Japan, with newspapers broadcasting his arrival. Hikida's network had carefully planned Du Bois's schedule almost to the minute. He spent time in Kobe, in Osaka—where he received an official welcome from the vice-governor of the province and the mayor—and in Tokyo, where he met with prominent government and educational representatives. In each city, he lectured at local universities. And, as always, he attempted to soak up as much local history and culture as possible. A highlight was

sightseeing at Kyoto and Nara, with its elaborate shrines, temples, and
a bronze statue of Buddha, "fifty feet and more high, dark with ancient metal and with its crown of close-curled African hair," a symbol
of Afro-Asian unity that he found mesmerizing.[83]

The hospitality showered upon Du Bois during his two-week visit
left him overwhelmed and smitten with Japan. He did not see this as a
personal tribute, writing, with false modesty, that he was, after all,
a "person entirely without influence." Instead, he contrived that Japan,
"entirely unofficially, yet with full official knowledge and sanction, un-
dertook to say through me to 12,000,000 people that she recognized a
common brotherhood, a common suffering and a common destiny."[84]
The country, in Du Bois's eyes, represented the future of the colored
world. He left from Yokohama on December 17, his new friends waving him farewell.[85]

Du Bois returned to the United States via Hawaii. He spent
Christmas Day in Honolulu, a paradise on earth, but, as he also noted,
the center of what could very well be the "most idiotic and senseless of
wars—a war with Japan."[86] After almost seven months in Europe and
Asia, he had seen the all too real legacies of war along every stop of his
journey. He had also seen the possibility, perhaps even inevitability, of
future war. As he sailed home across the Pacific Ocean, he realized the
need to try to understand all that he had experienced and observed.

BY INSTINCT, DU BOIS began thinking about what book to write
next. On February 11, 1937, just a month after docking in San Francisco and slowly making his way across the country and back to Atlanta,
he contacted his go-to publisher, Alfred Harcourt. He had an idea for
a slim monograph—"about two hundred pages"—based on his recent
travels, with the working title "A Search for Democracy." He wanted
to illustrate the connections between democracy, fascism, and communism, and "draw into the picture the colored peoples of the world: the
people of China, Japan, and India, and the peoples of Africa." Du Bois
envisioned demonstrating the influence of these global developments
on "incipient war in Europe."[87] He quickly drafted a full manuscript

and continued to tinker with it well into 1937. Neither Harcourt nor any other publishers, however, seemed interested in the book.[88]

Du Bois's travels also gave renewed urgency to his work on *The Black Man and the Wounded World*. He still believed he needed financial support to finish the project to his satisfaction. However, by this point, few organizations, foundations, or philanthropies remained unsolicited. Stretching his imagination, he turned to the possibility of the American Philosophical Society (APS), the oldest learned society in the nation, founded in 1743 by Benjamin Franklin. The APS had recently expanded its grant program, and, in Du Bois's view, questions of race, war, and peace absolutely constituted urgent philosophical matters.

He had initially reached out to the APS on May 25, 1936, just before departing for his overseas trip. At the time, he wrote that he did not want to make his book "a conventional war history, but rather a frank argument on the disastrous effects of war upon backward races." He intended to "take up and finish this work" upon his return,[89] and when he came back to the United States, he had not forgotten about his contact with the APS from almost ten months earlier.

Over the long life span of the book, Du Bois had used his multiple applications and letters of inquiry for funding as ways to think through the project itself. Taken as a whole, they formed a critical part of his evolving historical and political understanding of the war and how he conceptualized writing about it. While speaking to his frustrations with what he believed was a lack of time and resources to complete the book, the grant applications also revealed his ongoing struggle to comprehend the meaning of the war and the place of peoples of African descent in it. As seen in his application to the Imperialism Committee of the American Fund for Public Service in the late 1920s, what he initially imagined as a book about the contributions of Black people to the remaking of democracy in America and throughout the world had also evolved into a potential study—and warning—about the horrors of modern warfare, using the experiences of Black people as a case in point. Du Bois's appeal to the Carnegie Endowment in early 1936 reflected his view of the book as an argument for the futility of war and the imminent threat to peace. The trip around the world further solidified these convictions.

On March 9, 1937, he submitted his formal grant application to the APS, offering a new level of insight, vision, and analytical precision that distinguished this proposal from all the others before it. "Most studies of the war are technical or historical in the narrower sense, that is, detailed events and movements of armies, proximate causes, and political and social results," he wrote. This was, in fact, what much of his manuscript in its current condition looked like. However, he believed, "the World War was an occurrence which calls for broader study than this." The war "brought into the arena all the peoples of the world and especially peoples like the Negroes of the United States, the West Indies and Africa, who were not directly concerned." Supported by two decades of historical developments and a foundational book on the Reconstruction era, the kernel of his argument remained as strong as ever: "The peoples of Africa represented a part of the causes of the War: the demands for colonies, labor, and raw material. They were pawns in industrial imperialism."

But the real pressing need for his book, Du Bois made clear, lay in the growing likelihood of a new global catastrophe looming on the horizon: "The whole prospect of war in the future is thus largely bound up with the results of the World War upon these darker races." He envisioned producing "a study of war which shall be a tract for peace." The 1920s and 1930s had revealed the volatility of the global economy and the recklessness of the imperial system. He'd seen the evidence during his time abroad in Europe and Asia, and with the nations and people of the world interconnected as never before, he believed that "future war will spell suicide." His project would be singular. "We have had some studies of this sort so far as Europe is concerned"—he was likely thinking of the *Economic and Social History of the World War* edited by James Shotwell, the Carnegie rejection still burning— "but nothing that starts with the other end of the scale, with Africa and African labor, and shows the possible future from that point of view." He concluded his application with a revealing explanation for why the book remained unfinished, as well as a plea for why, now, it needed to reach the public:

I began my work in this field as a conventional study of the Negro as a soldier in the World War, and the arrangement of these
facts would have made a book ready for publication many years
ago; but the whole theme has been expanding and developing
in my mind, more especially since my trip around the world in
1936; until I conceive it now on a much broader and more important scale and if I can have leisure and opportunity to finish
this work, I think I can do something which will have influence
on future knowledge with regard to war and colored people.[90]

Du Bois's recent travels had infused *The Black Man and the
Wounded World* with a sense of urgency and focus that it previously
lacked. It was also, in many respects, a quite different book from the
one he'd spent a decade writing and another half decade attempting
to secure funding to support its completion. But in his mind, it was
a better book and, as the world lunged ever so closer to future world
war, the one he desperately needed to write.

It did not take long for the APS to make a decision. The following
month, the APS executive officer Edwin Conklin wrote to Du Bois,
offering regrets that the committee on research could not support his
application. "This decision does not indicate lack of interest in your
proposal," Conklin explained in pro forma language, "but is dependent upon the fact that the sum of the many grants requested is far
more than the appropriation at the disposal of the Committee."[91] Yet
another rejection and, Du Bois surely thought, evasion of the lessons
of history at the cost of the world and its impending doom.

THE LOVELY GEORGIA SPRING weather kept Du Bois in positive
spirits despite the APS rejection.[92] With a full plate, there was no time
to wallow in self-pity. After returning to the United States, he jumped
right into the semester at Atlanta University, teaching a course on
"Race Problems" and another on "Sociology of the American Negro."[93]
He continued to fire off weekly columns for *The Pittsburgh Courier*,
and as always, he stayed on the road, delivering lectures as well as periodically traveling to New York to check in on Nina and tend to other

personal matters. In the midst of it all, he still found time for his multiple research and writing projects, except for *The Black Man and the Wounded World*. In a letter to a Boston family friend, he admitted to being tired but, with good cheer, added, "Life is quite worth living."[94]

However, as summer rolled around, Du Bois longed for a break as well as a change of scenery. To make up for his absence due to the trip abroad and to earn extra money, he taught in the AU summer school.[95] For three days a week through June and most of July, he showed up for his course on "Cooperation," although his mind was more focused on planning his end-of-term vacation. The blazing hot weather only added to his exhaustion and inability to get much work done.[96] He could not wait to head north and rest.

Before eagerly leaving Atlanta on July 24, he tended to various matters, among them temporarily discontinuing his *New York Times* delivery service.[97] But his subscription lasted long enough for him to read the Sunday, July 11, issue. With his recent travels fresh in mind, he would have gravitated to the front-page headline: JAPANESE TAKE TWO TOWNS IN FIGHTING NEAR PEIPING; CHINESE PREPARE FOR WAR.[98]

Since the 1931 Japanese occupation of Manchuria, troop skirmishes between the two countries had become frequent. As Japan continued to exert its imperial ambitions, Chinese resistance increased as well. On the night of July 7, 1937, Japanese and Chinese troops exchanged gunfire near the Marco Polo Bridge just outside Peiping. Tensions quickly escalated, and Japan, taking advantage of the opportunity, prepared for a full-scale invasion. The Chinese were not about to back down. As one government official declared, "This time they will find we will stand and fight."[99]

After returning from a much-needed vacation in Maine, a mentally recharged Du Bois caught up on the Sino-Japanese conflict. "There were premonitions of the present war between China and Japan when I was in Asia last winter," he reflected in his September 25 "Forum of Fact and Opinion" entry for *The Pittsburgh Courier*. He placed the blame on everyone but Japan, accusing Europe of a long campaign of economic aggression and faulting China for not accepting an alliance with "her own cousin" and preferring "to be a coolie

for England." Instead of working toward the inevitable "world dominance of the yellow race," the two countries were engaged in "one
of the great deciding wars of the world. And the future of colored
people is bound up with it."[100] Du Bois made clear that, in the end,
the colored world needed to side with Japan as the best hope for challenging Western imperial aggression, even if it meant tolerating war
in its most ghastly incarnation. His pacifism, as it did in the World
War, once again strained under the pressure of contemporary realities
and political idealism, this time the vision of Japan and Afro-Asian
solidarity as harbinger of Europe's demise. Financial challenges within
The Pittsburgh Courier brought Du Bois's weekly column to an end
at the conclusion of the year. However, he undoubtedly would have
searched for excuses as the Imperial Japanese Army committed geno-
cide in Nanjing, killing upward of three hundred thousand Chinese
soldiers and civilians, burning villages, and raping tens of thousands
of women.[101]

Even as the world again veered toward cataclysm, 1938 started
off on a high note for Du Bois. After wrapping up an invigorating
Midwest speaking tour, he celebrated his seventieth birthday in grand
fashion.[102] His Atlanta University colleagues Rayford Logan and Ira
de Augustine Reid took charge of organizing a "suitable testimonial"
for the distinguished "editor, teacher, scholar, man of letters and crusader for human rights," as they described him in the solicitation letter
sent to potential sponsors of the event. Joel Spingarn was especially
eager to participate. "I should like to pay a tribute to my friend on that
occasion, as I did in February, 1918, on the occasion of his fiftieth
birthday," he informed Reid.[103]

On February 23, prominent men and women, Black and white,
from every corner of the country, all linked to Du Bois by personal
association and fierce admiration, descended on the Atlanta University Center. An extravagant evening banquet followed a late-morning
university-wide convocation honoring him in the Sisters Chapel on
the Spelman campus. At the convocation, the man of the hour delivered remarks reviewing his life and work.

Clad in his Harvard doctoral robe, Du Bois took to the podium, gazing out at the audience filling the pews. Evenly split to his left and right sat presidents Charles Johnson of Fisk, Florence Read of Spelman, Rufus Clement of Atlanta University; his fellow AU professors Ira Reid, Rayford Logan, and William Stanley Braithwaite; and, above the rest, his two most dear living friends, Joel Spingarn and James Weldon Johnson. Du Bois began his address, "A Pageant in Seven Decades, 1868–1938," an autobiographical summation of the intertwined drama of his life and the times that shaped it. His telling of the first four decades hewed closely to his previous reflections in *The Souls of Black Folk* and especially "The Shadow Years," his birthday speech from 1918 that had become the first chapter of *Darkwater.*

As he continued, his professorial voice resonating throughout the chapel, attentive listeners would have recognized the profound importance of the World War in shaping the subsequent twenty years of Du Bois's life and thought. Concluding the survey of his fifth decade, he attempted to summarize the ways in which "the World War touched America," mentioning such key events as the fight for Black officers, the East St. Louis massacre, and the forced retirement of Charles Young. Against this tumultuous backdrop, Du Bois led his audience into his sixth decade, 1918 to 1928, one he admittedly approached "with some misgivings and difficulties of judgment." He recalled going to France after the armistice—"to investigate the treatment of Negro soldiers and keep the record straight"—and organizing the 1919 Pan-African Congress.

Then, abruptly, as if jarred by the weight of history and the wounds of memory, he offered his birthday well-wishers a moment of remarkable self-reflection: "I felt for a moment during the war that I could be without reservation a patriotic American." The government, so it seemed at the time, was making sincere efforts to meet the demands of Black people. "I tried to stand by the country and wrote the widely discussed editorial 'Close Ranks' in which I said to the Negroes: Forget your special grievances for the moment and stand by your country." "I am not sure that I was right but certainly my intentions were," he continued. "I did not believe in war, but I thought that in a fight with America against militarism and for democracy we would be fighting for the emancipation of the Negro race. With the Armistice came disillusion." Referring to his time in France and what would be the genesis of *The Black Man and the Wounded World*, he said, "I saw the mud and dirt of the trenches; I heard from the mouths of soldiers the kind of treatment that black men got in the American army; I was convinced and said that American white officers fought more valiantly against Negroes within our ranks than they did against the Germans. I still believe this was largely true." Only a few individuals in the audience and on the stage, most notably Joel Spingarn and James Weldon Johnson, would have been able to fully appreciate the significance of those words.

After bringing his audience up to the present and his ongoing effort "to spy out in the Universal Gloom a path for the American Negro," Du Bois concluded his speech. At the ripe age of seventy, armed with good health, knowledge, perspective, and the strength of his convictions, he continued to fight. He ended on a philosophical note, telling his well-wishers, "I have never shared what seems to me the essentially childish desire to live forever. Life has its pain and evil—its bitter disappointments; but in healthful length of days there is triumphal fullness of experience and infinite joy in seeing the most interesting of continued stories unfold. Not eternity but time is for the living."[104]

The precarity of life and the sorrow that came with it hit home just a few months after the high of Du Bois's birthday celebration. James Weldon Johnson and his wife, Grace Nail, were enjoying the start of their New England vacation. On the Sunday morning of June 26, following a visit with friends in Maine, James and Grace got into their black 1935 Ford coupe for the drive to their summer home in Great Barrington.

The weather was awful. Grace was behind the wheel. Driving along Main Street in the small town of Wiscasset through rain and heavy mist, their car approached an intersection of the New York, New Haven and Hartford Railroad. Grace did not see the slow-moving eastbound passenger train until too late, and she slammed into the locomotive, crushing the front of the car. Passengers and townspeople quickly rushed to the site of the wreckage. They found Grace, badly injured but still conscious, attempting to get out of the car, but they prevented her from doing so. James, unconscious, bleeding from the head, sat slumped next to her. The local medical examiner arrived at the scene and made the decision to remove James, barely alive, from the mangled automobile. He survived for only a few more minutes.[105]

Du Bois initially did not believe it was true.[106] Like Johnson, he'd also planned to vacation in Massachusetts and Maine and was just about to depart Atlanta for New York. The telegrams informing him about the funeral and asking him to serve as an honorary pallbearer arrived shortly after he got on the road.[107] He did not make it to New York in time to attend the Thursday, June 30, ceremony at Salem Methodist Episcopal Church in Harlem, where more than two thousand mourners, among them many of the most distinguished cultural and political figures in Black America, paid their respects. Walter White, arriving by plane from Columbus, Ohio, where the NAACP national convention was taking place, read some of the hundreds of messages received from around the country. He wept as he returned to his seat. A quarter-mile-long procession of cars traveled to Green-Wood Cemetery in Brooklyn, where Johnson was temporarily entombed until his widow recovered enough to oversee his cremation and final burial.[108]

For Du Bois, Johnson's loss was almost too much to comprehend. They'd shared a tent at the Amenia conference in 1916 and steered the NAACP into maturity. They'd marched, shoulder to shoulder, down Fifth Avenue at the front of the Silent Protest Parade in the wake of the East St. Louis massacre. They'd continued to tirelessly wage battle, with the power of their minds and the force of their pens, against the evils of white supremacy. And Johnson had been one of Du Bois's biggest supporters when it came to *The Black Man and the Wounded World*. Now Du Bois had lost one of his most loyal advocates, faithful admirers, and kindred spirits. It took him almost three months to muster the strength to write to Johnson's widow, who had recovered and was living with family members in New York City. In his September 21, 1938, note, Du Bois fumbled for the right words, offering excuses for his absence at the funeral and lack of communication before admitting, "Above all I was so stunned by the terrible news that I did not know what to write or say once I realized the sad truth."[109]

～

DU BOIS WAS UNDERSTANDABLY not in an optimistic mood as the twentieth anniversary of the armistice approached. The dreams of peace, democracy, and human brotherhood that fired his imagination two decades earlier had faded away, replaced by the reality of a world teetering on the brink of even greater catastrophe.

On Friday, October 28, 1938, he delivered a lecture at Virginia State College on "Germany and the Race Problem,"[110] emphatically stating that Germany currently practiced the worst type of racial prejudice anywhere in the world. If minority groups, African Americans included, failed to take matters seriously, he warned, the crisis facing the Jews would be their fate as well. He took his audience through his personal connections to and his time spent in Germany, first as a graduate student from 1892 to 1894, when Germany was "the cultural center of the world"; next in 1926, where "the toll of the World War was in evidence everywhere" and the nation stood on the edge of ruin; and, lastly, his visit in 1936, where he observed the Third Reich up close and saw the immense power wielded by Hitler and the intense hatred for Jews he'd fomented. Hitler had mastered the art of propaganda, Du Bois noted, stirring up race prejudice to a fever pitch. He pointed specifically to Hitler's use of radio and how it provided him "a chance to dominate thought and opinion in a manner never known before." As a result, Jewish people, especially those of culture, wealth, and status, had been "subjected to the worst insults imaginable. Their possessions have been confiscated, their citizenship nullified, and their future obliterated."[111]

In describing the state of affairs in Germany, Du Bois did not exaggerate. Since Hitler's rise to power, and especially after the 1935 Nuremberg Laws, Jews were fleeing Germany by the tens of thousands. The anti-Semitic rhetoric intensified toward the end of 1937 and into 1938, following the annexation of Austria. The Third Reich passed a wave of new discriminatory laws targeting Jewish citizenship rights, freedom of movement, and economic livelihood. On the very same day that Du Bois spoke at Virginia State College, the German government arrested and deported approximately seventeen thousand Polish Jews, continuing a purge begun earlier in the month. Poland refused to open its borders, leaving the refugees with nowhere to go, stranded in squalid camps, enduring wretched conditions.[112]

The Friday, November 11, Armistice Day issue of *The New York Times* carried a shocking front-page headline: NAZIS SMASH, LOOT AND BURN JEWISH SHOPS AND TEMPLES UNTIL GOEBBELS CALLS HALT. Even for the calm, emotionally detached Du Bois, reading these appalling words had to be stomach churning.[113]

On November 7, seventeen-year-old Herschel Grynszpan, a Polish Jew living in France, walked into the German embassy in Paris and shot Ernst vom Rath, one of the secretaries. News of the assassination raised anti-Semitic passions in Germany to a boiling point, providing Hitler with the pretense for retaliation against the entire Jewish population. Throughout the night of November 9 and into the early-morning hours of the next day, in large cities and small towns, mobs ransacked, destroyed, and torched Jewish homes and businesses with abandon.[114] Jewish men and women were pulled into the streets, paraded to curses and taunts, and beaten without mercy. "The noise of breaking glass and cracking furniture accompanied loud anti-Jewish jeers," *The New York Times* reported.[115] By the end of the pogrom, some 7,500 Jewish businesses lay destroyed and 267 synagogues burned to the ground. Nazi police arrested more than 20,000 Jewish men and swept them off to concentration camps. The 91 Jewish deaths were followed by hundreds of suicides. *Kristallnacht* would be an omen, marking the beginning of the Reich's systematic persecution of the Jewish people.[116] Du Bois, putting down his paper, knew that the worst was yet to come.

In reading about the horrors taking place in Germany, he no doubt thought of Joel Spingarn. Du Bois's deep respect for Jews and their struggle was closely tied to his cherished friend. Their bond served as the personal cornerstone for Du Bois's belief in the necessity of Black-Jewish comradeship.

But as the calendar year turned to 1939, Spingarn was not well. In January, doctors diagnosed him with a brain tumor. An emergency surgery at the Neurological Institute of New York saved his life. But as his brother, Arthur, informed Du Bois in a January 10 update, "His condition is still serious."[117] Arthur, along with other New York friends, kept Du Bois abreast of Spingarn's condition as it gradually deteriorated over the ensuing months.[118] Finally, on the morning of July 26, at his home at 110 East Seventy-Eighth Street, Joel lost the battle. He was sixty-four years of age. In accordance with Jewish custom, the family held a private funeral service in Dutchess County the following day and laid him to rest at Poughkeepsie Rural Cemetery.[119]

Black America paid respects to Spingarn's life and commitment to the cause of racial justice. *The New York Age* lauded him as "a believer in democracy and the rights of the individual and minority groups at a time when such a belief required real courage and sacrifice."[120] An *Amsterdam News* tribute placed him in the same company as Wendell Phillips, William Lloyd Garrison, Elijah Lovejoy, John Brown, and Abraham Lincoln, reminding readers that as men like Spingarn passed from the scene, "they leave a heritage, a heritage that must be carried on if the cause of the Negro is to continue forward and the Democracy of America is to endure."[121] The NAACP offered a moving obituary in the September issue of *The Crisis*. Walter White praised the association's former president as a man who deep in his heart "believed passionately in equal rights for all citizens irrespective of race, color, or creed."[122] Despite Du Bois's frosty relationship with Roy Wilkins, now in charge of his former magazine, he had to be pleased with the editorial devoted to Spingarn who, Wilkins wrote, "deserves to have his name honored and revered as long as there are Americans of color and their friends who believe truly in the democratic way of life."[123]

Unlike the recent sudden deaths of John Hope and James Weldon Johnson, Du Bois had known that Spingarn's time was short.

Nevertheless, Spingarn left a void that could not be filled. To the end, he had remained Du Bois's closest white friend. Their bond had been tested in fire, most notably during the World War and the furor surrounding "Close Ranks" and the military intelligence captaincy. The NAACP had named its highest annual award in Spingarn's honor, and he represented, in Du Bois's eyes, the possibility of democracy and interracial brotherhood. Du Bois's belief in the war as a seminal moment in the future of democracy had been intimately connected with the passionate idealist and full-throated American. Now, gone too soon, Spingarn represented another reminder of the war's tragedy.

~

WHEN DU BOIS PICKED up his September 1, 1939, copy of *The New York Times,* he saw the headline GERMAN ARMY ATTACKS POLAND; CITIES BOMBED, PORT BLOCKADED. He read one alarming story after another—the annexing of Danzig; Britain mobilizing its fleet and evacuating women, children, the elderly, and the infirm from cities like London to the countryside; the prime minister of France, Édouard Daladier, convening an emergency meeting of his cabinet; President Roosevelt putting all army and naval commands on notice; the Soviet parliament ratifying its nonaggression pact with the Reich; Hitler promising in a fiery speech to the Reichstag that "November 1918 shall never be repeated in the history of Germany."[124] The war Du Bois predicted and saw as a virtual certainty was now unleashed upon the world.

As in 1914, the dominoes of a wider conflict quickly began to fall. On September 3, Britain and France declared war on Germany. However, unprepared to fight, they offered no immediate military support to besieged Poland. Overwhelmed by the size and might of the German army, Polish forces steadily retreated toward Warsaw. By September 13, the capital city was under attack and Hitler's goal of a swift victory appeared inevitable.[125]

On September 15, the *Amsterdam News* managing editor Earl Brown sent a telegram to Du Bois inviting him to write a weekly column that might touch upon "war and the Negro people."[126] Du Bois informed Brown that he was busy, but with the world again at war, the possibility of a new weekly column in the most widely read Black newspaper in New York was too tempting an opportunity to pass up.

The inaugural column of "As the Crow Flies" appeared on October 21, as the world trembled over the capitulation of Poland and the reality of war. "Does it make any difference to the American Negroes what the people of Europe do?" Du Bois asked his new readers, emphatically answering, "It does." What he'd observed and lived through in the years preceding, during, and following the first World War offered all the proof. "Unless we look back twenty-five years it is almost impossible to conceive today the depths of race hatred, mob violence and murder which the American Negro went through during and directly after the World War," he wrote, revisiting what he labeled "The Hell of Race Hate" spanning 1915 to 1921. "Never since the red days of Reconstruction did Negroes suffer in the United States as they suffered in these days." He asserted that it was all because of "a World War starting primarily over the partitioning of Africa, spreading to the United States to protect our European credits for arms and food furnished, and resulting in fierce reaction here and elsewhere after the armistice."

He continued with a summary of "The Armistice and After." Looking back at America in the wake of Versailles, he saw "a nation refusing to pay the cost of war and trying to capitalize on the misery of the world." The reckoning came in 1929 with the Depression and economic calamity. "What more is needed than a glance at this history to show how little the world is and how close together; how hard it is for America to escape the disaster of Europe and Asia and how bound up with the prosperity of the world is the future of the Negro race?" he pondered.[127]

Du Bois clearly had his uncompleted book in mind while crafting his first *Amsterdam News* column. He essentially offered a summary of his manuscript and the key historical moments that made up its twenty-one chapters. It had taken a new world war to bring him to this point of clarity.

But what did it mean to write about the roots of the current war, with the wounds of the last still fresh? "Nothing is so difficult to grasp and realize than the near past," Du Bois mused, capturing the core challenge he faced in 1919—and continued to wrestle with in 1939—in writing about the World War and its aftermath. "We are apt to know what happened one hundred years ago and what it meant; but ten years ago—that is a different question." He returned to his trip to Europe and Asia some five years earlier, when he "went up in a high place and looked down upon the world." He saw Germany. Hitler, "a master whose power was forged by the radio," who "hated Jews and Bolsheviks and feared everybody else," made his people, suffering from "hunger, insult and hopelessness," believe to their core "that they were oppressed and in danger from the world." He saw the Soviet Union and its army of amassing troops, alongside them "the feverish activity in industry." He saw China, "exploited and stricken," and Japan, facing her adversaries with "armed suspicion," on the precipice of war, "both of them singularly under the spell of Western civilization."[128] When it came to understanding this second world war, the past was the present.

Throughout the fall of 1939, back in his comfort zone as a columnist, Du Bois used his inaugural *Amsterdam News* pieces to exhibit a mastery of the history of the First World War and how it connected with the current crisis. The newspaper served as a welcome and timely outlet for reaching the public and sharing his prescient knowledge. In many ways, it provided the space, audience, and intellectual freedom that a book, with all its expectations and complications, could not.

But Du Bois still wanted the book. Maybe, just maybe, before the world fully descended into the abyss, he could find a way to complete *The Black Man and the Wounded World*.

On November 30, he wrote once again to the Social Science Research Council, mentioning the possibility of assistance for the "collection and classification" of his personal materials for the autobiographical book he had begun working on. However, his first and most urgent request concerned the long-gestating project on the World War. "I have been collecting this material since my trip to Europe after the Armistice in 1918. Much of it is unique and invaluable." He singled out one area of the manuscript—the draft, camp life, and the labor of Black troops in the South—that could use additional research and that, given his location at Atlanta University, he would be well positioned to conduct. He acknowledged his receipt of the $600 grant in 1936, but said that "this was not enough to complete it," and added, with uncharacteristic modesty, "I should be glad if I could have five hundred dollars of your fund in order to increase the material concerning the South and in general to consolidate my matter and put it in publishable form."[129]

As he gingerly courted the SSRC and waited for a response, the war expanded and hopes for peace evaporated. In the East, China and Japan continued to battle with increased ferocity and no end in sight.[130] The situation in Europe further deteriorated, with the Soviet Union continuing to flex its muscles in the Baltics, seizing Latvia, Estonia, and Lithuania. The November 30 invasion of Finland led to Russia's expulsion from the League of Nations. Designed to prevent world war and atrocity, the international body could do nothing to stop Hitler's aggression. Germany, after occupying Poland, commenced with a campaign of religious and ethnic cleansing, characterized by forcing civilians from their homes, relocating them to slave labor camps, and executing anyone who resisted. Military operations against Great Britain increased, with U-boats inflicting almost daily damage and German bombers testing the boundaries of British airspace. The westward expansion of the war was only a matter of time. On March 18, 1940, as a heavy snow fell, Hitler met with Mussolini at the Brenner Pass in the Alps between Italy and Germany. Hitler dominated the two-and-a-half-hour conversation, touting his nation's military might and informing the prime minister that Germany was poised to launch its western offensive with or without Italian support. Mussolini promised to enter the war on the side of Germany in due time.[131]

While France and Great Britain prepared for battle, the possibility of war became a reality in the United States. In his January 3 State of the Union address, President Franklin Roosevelt attempted to shake the country out of its isolationist mindset, warning, "There is a vast difference between keeping out of war and pretending that this war

is none of our business." He asked Congress for the expansion of foreign trade agreements and increases in defense spending "based not
on panic but on common sense." Above all else he called for national
unity, viewing it as, "in a very real and a very deep sense, the fundamental safeguard of all democracy." "May the year 1940," he concluded,
"be pointed to by our children as another period when democracy
justified its existence as the best instrument of government yet devised
by mankind."[132]

The response from the Social Science Research Council came on
March 23, 1940. "It is with sincere regret that I am writing to inform
you that the Committee at its meeting last week was not able to act
favorably on your application for a grant-in-aid for 1940–41," the
secretary Laura Barrett informed Du Bois, offering no explanation.
He did not need one.[133]

Du Bois was no stranger to disappointment when it came to foundation support for *The Black Man and the Wounded World*. But this
latest rejection, considering the circumstances, hit him differently. He
viewed the book as an urgent, almost last-gasp attempt to warn the
world about the costs of war and an opportunity to salvage the hope of
democracy that Woodrow Wilson championed with such inspiration
and that Franklin Roosevelt invoked once again. After two decades of
confusion, guilt, and frustration, Du Bois had reached the end of the
road. He looked at his manuscript. More than eight hundred pages
and two decades of intellectual labor. The letters, diaries, and photographs from Black veterans he'd stubbornly held on to over the years
and not returned to their rightful owners—all part of a rare, unrivaled
archive. A history lay stacked before him, one he knew needed to be
told. It was too much. And now it was too late.

The next month, April, the war reached the point of no return.
Germany invaded Denmark and Norway. Shortly thereafter, on May
10, the long-anticipated offensive against France began. As in 1914,
Germany attacked through Belgium. But this time France and Britain could not stop the advance. In just two weeks of combat, the
Wehrmacht, with devastating speed, stood poised to trap and crush
both the French and British armies. Only a controversial pause in the

advance at Dunkirk allowed the Allies to evacuate some 330,000 troops and avoid complete destruction. The German army now swung south to complete the task of avenging 1918. French forces rallied and put up a stout defense, but it was not enough. They soon confronted another foe. At 6:00 p.m. on June 10, Mussolini stood on the balcony of Palazzo Venezia and declared war against France and Great Britain. Hours later, Italian troops crossed the Southern Alps and began their own advance. By this time, however, France's fate had already been sealed. On June 14, German troops triumphantly marched into a nearly abandoned Paris. Three days later, the French prime minister Philippe Pétain announced his intention to negotiate a peace settlement with Germany.[134]

At Compiègne on June 21, 1940, where the armistice ending the First World War had been signed, France and Germany met again, this time with their roles reversed. Hitler now sat in the chair once occupied by Marshal Ferdinand Foch. The armistice, allowing Germany to occupy most of northern and western France and all of the coastline, was agreed to on June 22. FRENCH SIGN REICH TRUCE, ROME PACT NEXT, *The New York Times* announced on the front page of its Sunday edition the following day, a headline Du Bois no doubt read with sadness and resignation.[135]

"How great a failure and a failure in what does the World War betoken?" Du Bois had asked this question, remarkable at the time, in *Darkwater*. Now, tragically, twenty years later, with the world again at war, as he accepted the reality that he would not finish *The Black Man and the Wounded World*, he had the answer.

CHAPTER 12

"I hate war."[1]

DU BOIS DEDICATED *Dusk of Dawn: An Essay Toward an Autobiography of a Race Concept*, as he'd promised Amy Spingarn, to her husband, Joel.[2] He was to Du Bois a "scholar and knight," his colleague, comrade, and confidant across the color line. Amy and Joel's brother, Arthur, both thanked Du Bois for the dedication and the personal copy of the book he sent them after its publication in early September 1940. Amy was particularly moved, writing from Amenia that she and her children would forever cherish it: "We know how much Joel valued your friendship and admired your work."[3]

Du Bois shaped *Dusk of Dawn* around the remarks he'd delivered for his seventieth birthday celebration. However, as he explained in the opening "Apology," he wanted the book to be more than mere autobiography and different from his other two self-reflective books, *The Souls of Black Folk* and *Darkwater*, which he characterized as, respectively, "written in tears and blood." With false modesty, he offered that his time on earth held significance only in that "it was part of a Problem," one that he considered "the central problem of the greatest of the world's democracies and so the Problem of the future world."

In the first four chapters of *Dusk of Dawn*, he chronicled his journey from his birth in Great Barrington to the birth of the NAACP and *The Crisis* in 1910. He used chapters 5 through 7 "to consider the conception which is after all my main subject"—the problem of race. He explored the social and scientific construction of race and its meaning for white and Black people alike, proving that the problem of the twentieth century was, in fact, and remained, the problem of the color line.

Returning to his autobiographical pageant, Du Bois titled the penultimate chapter "Propaganda and World War,"[4] describing the era of the World War in the language of someone who had experienced severe trauma. It was a "phantasmagoria of war, race hate and mob-law." The years from 1912, with the election of Woodrow Wilson, to 1919 represented for Black Americans "an extraordinary test for their courage and a time of cruelty, discrimination and wholesale murder." For Du Bois personally, it was a "whirl of circumstances and stress of soul." In 1914, when war burst upon the world, he found himself "thrown into consternation." When the United States finally, "and in a sense inevitably," entered the war, the question of Black participation caused "an extraordinary exacerbation of race hate and turmoil." "There have been few periods in the history of the American Negro," he wrote, "when he has been more discouraged and exasperated."

The war and its aftermath had left Du Bois shell-shocked. "In my effort to reconstruct in memory my thought and the fight of the National Association for the Advancement of Colored People during the World War, I have difficulty in thinking clearly," he confessed. He had compromised his anti-war principles, but, as he tried to rationalize, "in the midst of arms, not only laws but ideas are silent." He believed that America, in defeating German militarism, "would in reality fight for democracy including colored folk and not merely for war investments." He was wrong. He tried to make sense of his actions and decisions. Buoyed by hope, repeating the words from his birthday speech, he "felt for a moment during the war that I could be without reservation a patriotic American." "At other times," he reflected, "I was bowed down and sickened by the public burnings, the treatment of colored troops and the widespread mob law."

The most tormenting episode of confusion came with "Close Ranks," written during, as he recalled, "one of my periods of exaltation." "Who was I to talk of forgetting grievances, when my life had been given to protest against them?" he asked, quoting at length from his August 1918 reply in *The Crisis*, where he doubled down on "Close Ranks" and asserted, "If this is OUR country, then this is OUR war." He then wrote, with uncharacteristic disorientation and shame:

> I am less sure now than then of the soundness of this war attitude. I did not realize the full horror of war and its wide impotence as a method of social reform. Perhaps, despite words, I was thinking narrowly of the interest of my group and was willing to let the world go to hell, if the black man went free. Today I do not know; and I doubt if the triumph of Germany in 1918 could have had worse results than the triumph of the Allies. Possibly passive resistance of my twelve millions to any war activity might have saved the world for black and white. Almost certainly such a proposal on my part would have fallen flat and perhaps slaughtered the American Negro body and soul. I do not know. I am puzzled.

He pointed to the man he had dedicated *Dusk of Dawn* to and "the influence which he had at that time upon my thought and action." "I do not think that any other white man ever touched me emotionally so closely as Joel Spingarn," he confided. Spingarn was "fired with consuming patriotism," which consumed Du Bois as well. "He wanted me and my people not merely as a matter of policy, but in recognition of a fact, to join wholeheartedly in the war." He recounted Spingarn's "bold and far-sighted plan" for the Military Intelligence Branch and his own dalliance with a captaincy. It crumbled, "probably by far the best result," Du Bois viewed in hindsight. Nevertheless, because of Spingarn's "advice and influence," Du Bois, in his words, "became during the World War nearer to feeling myself a real and full American than ever before or since."

As he continued to reminisce about the years spanning the World War, he took readers to the moment immediately after the armistice and the "unexpected change in my life program." "Out of a clear sky," he wrote, "the board of directors of the NAACP asked me to go to France for the purpose of investigating the treatment of Negro soldiers and for collecting and perfecting the historic record of their participation in the war." He again recalled his experiences speaking with Black soldiers and officers and hearing from them in shocked disbelief about the lengths the American army went to enforce white supremacy.

This excavation of memory led him to reflect upon the history he hoped to produce. "The whole history of the American Negro and other black folk in the World War, has never been written." Without offering its name, he referred to *The Black Man and the Wounded World*. "I collected while I was in France and since a mass of documents covering this episode in our history. They deserve publication, not simply as a part of the Negro's history, but as an unforgettable lesson in the spiritual lesions of race conflict during a critical period of American history. I hope sometime that a careful history based on these documents may see the light."[5]

Dusk of Dawn, written at the beginnings of a new world war, demonstrated that the "spiritual lesions of race conflict" continued to fester. Du Bois's chapter-long musing on the history and personal memories of the First World War revealed that his own spiritual lesions remained unhealed as well. The tragedy of the war was compounded by the tragedy of its history, a history that continued to haunt him and the world. He never admitted failure or defeat. But in *Dusk of Dawn*, he painfully accepted that for the foreseeable future, and perhaps even in his lifetime, *The Black Man and the Wounded World* would remain incomplete and unpublished.

~

DU BOIS LAMENTED THE fate of *The Black Man and the Wounded World*, but work kept him busy. He had devoted years to another massive endeavor, an *Encyclopedia Africana* that, if completed, would stand as a crowning achievement. Like his book on the World War, funding support from white philanthropists failed to materialize. Nevertheless, despite its gloomy prospects, he continued to putter along with the project.[6] Tapping into his creative side, he began writing a play titled "Darker Wisdom," later changed to "Sorcery of Color."[7] But the bulk of his attention in 1940 went to his new journal venture, *Phylon*. He eventually secured backing from the Carnegie Foundation, and the inaugural issue appeared in January 1940.[8]

The Second World War soon consumed him and much of the race as well. The landscape for Black soldiers in the nation's armed forces was bleak, and the War Department showed no signs of rethinking its racial policies as preparedness debates became more intense. As the possibility of the United States entering the war loomed, Du Bois's longtime friend and former soldier Rayford Logan played a key role in African American efforts to pressure the government.[9] Recalling his battles with American racism in France, Logan asked, "Would it not be simple justice, in a new war to make the world safe for democracy, to consult with some of the colored veterans of the last fiasco?"[10]

On Wednesday, August 14, Logan appeared before the House of Representatives Committee on Military Affairs for a hearing on a proposed Selective Service bill. He was joined by fellow veteran Charles Hamilton Houston, who had recently stepped down as special counsel for the NAACP, passing the leadership baton to his protégé, Thurgood Marshall. "If we Negroes are going to help protect this country," Houston emphasized, "let us be visible in times of peace and in times of war."[11] Two decades earlier, Du Bois might have testified alongside his colleagues in arguing for full inclusion of African Americans into the nation's military. But times had changed. Just three days after Logan's and Houston's testimony, Du Bois quipped in his *Amsterdam News* column, "History repeats itself: again we are fighting for the privilege of fighting someone's else [sic] battles."[12]

The skepticism of Du Bois and other noninterventionists made little difference as Congress overwhelmingly approved the Selective Service Act on September 16, 1940. All men between the ages of twenty-one and thirty-six had to register for the draft for a twelve-month term of active service. Racial segregation in the military, however, remained firmly intact despite the protests of Walter White, A. Philip Randolph, Rayford Logan, and other civil rights leaders. President Roosevelt tried to appease them by promoting Benjamin O. Davis Sr. to brigadier general, giving him the star denied to Charles Young. FDR also appointed William Hastie—the first Black federal judge and successor to his cousin Charles Hamilton Houston as dean of Howard University School of Law—as civilian aide to the secretary of war, a role similar to the one held by Emmett Scott.[13]

A. Philip Randolph was still not satisfied. On January 25, 1941, he announced his idea for a July 1 protest march of ten thousand African Americans at the nation's capital to "wake up and shock official Washington as it has never been shocked before."[14] Plans for the Washington protest gained momentum throughout the spring and into the summer, with the Brotherhood of Sleeping Car Porters spearheading the organizing charge and Randolph serving as lead evangelist. By May, he envisioned a replication of the Silent Protest Parade of 1917, with some fifty thousand people marching behind muffled drums through the streets of the city to the Lincoln Memorial.[15] Convinced that Randolph meant business, Walter White, Rayford Logan, and a host of other African American civic, labor, religious, and fraternal leaders banded together in early June to form a national coordinating committee. Local groups in more than a dozen cities across the country sold ten-cent buttons to help finance the march and chartered buses and trains. With the full backing of the NAACP and the enthusiasm of the Black press, Randolph upped the stakes and predicted a crowd of one hundred thousand people.[16]

Du Bois remained on the sidelines of the March on Washington Movement. However, in a February 3 letter to Andrew Allison, the secretary of the Fisk Alumni Association, Du Bois made his thoughts crystal clear on the role Black people should play in the war. Allison sought his opinion on whether his alma mater should take a stance on the issue of preparedness and Black participation in the armed forces. Du Bois minced no words. He was glad that Fisk had thus far "not yielded to war hysteria" and joined the throngs of those "beating the tom toms of war." With striking introspection, Du Bois wrote, "I have lived though one period of deliberate and prolonged propaganda for war and partially succumbed to it until I really believed that the first World War was a war to end war and that the interests of colored people in particular were bound up in the defeat of Germany. I have lived to know better and my opposition to war under any circumstances has been immeasurably increased." He still believed that "defensive war is justifiable," but he saw absolutely no cause for the United States to enter the present war. "We are not being attacked; there is no reasonable possibility of our having to defend ourselves." He hoped that Fisk would "stay aloof from this war insanity" and remain focused on those who shared its educational mission "and not to those who are advocates of organized murder" and "the present insane rush to overturn civilization in the name of defending it."[17]

The March on Washington, in Du Bois's view, ultimately played right into the insanity. He refused to be fooled again. "The burning question is does democracy and the American way of life give anyone a right to oppose our entrance into the war," he asked in his June 7 column.[18] The slogan of the march—"We Loyal Colored Americans Demand the Right to Work and Fight for Our Country"—no doubt rubbed him the wrong way. On the question of loyalty, in the June 21 issue of the *Amsterdam News*, he was especially curt: "I am an American. So what?"[19]

Just a week before the July 1 scheduled march date, as tens of thousands of African Americans prepared to descend on the capital, Roosevelt blinked. On June 25, 1941, he issued Executive Order 8802, drafted by Randolph behind the scenes, prohibiting racial discrimination in the defense industries.[20] He also established the Fair Employment Practice Committee (FEPC) to implement the order and provide oversight. Randolph, in response, called off the protest but kept up the fight for Black equality in the armed forces as well as the creation of a permanent FEPC.[21]

Even with the achievement of Executive Order 8802, Du Bois remained unmoved and increasingly annoyed about the war and what it meant for the race. "I have been having a month out of the world of war, and I realize how little important news there really is," he sniffed in the June 28 *Amsterdam News* after returning from a trip to Cuba.[22] As awful as Germany was, on the imperial historical scorecard, its record of atrocity still paled in comparison to that of the

Allied so-called democracies, he bitterly reasoned. He saw the revolt of colonized and racially oppressed people as inevitable, with or without a Nazi victory.[23]

Germany's invasion of Russia, however, changed the equation for him. The delicate partnership between the two nations dissolved over rival claims to the Balkans and Hitler's long-standing desire for Lebensraum and crushing communism in the east. The Führer pushed aside skeptics from within the Reich who warned against opening a second front and the economic and military drain of potentially occupying Soviet territory. By June, a line of more than four million Axis troops amassed along an eighteen-hundred-mile front stretching from the Baltic Sea to the Black Sea. Operation Barbarossa, which commenced in the early-morning hours of June 22, was the largest invasion in modern military history, with Germany betting that its 145 divisions, 3,600 tanks, and 27,000 aircraft would bring Russia to its knees by winter. Hitler initially had every reason to be optimistic. Only a week into the invasion, his forces advanced more than two hundred miles, laid waste to an overwhelmed Red Army, and set sights on Moscow.[24]

"The Russo-German war compels nearly all of us to rearrange our thoughts and forecasting," Du Bois wrote, admitting that the stunning developments left him "puzzled and awhirl." He brooded over the implications for Africa and Asia, declaring that for their fate alone, "Hitler cannot win."[25] Russia had become Du Bois's only silver lining in the outcome of the First World War. "The hopes of the modern world rest on the survival of the new conception of politics and industry which Russia represents," he explained in "As the Crow Flies," a dream now very much in jeopardy.[26]

He had zero confidence in Great Britain and the United States to win the war, much less repair the world. On August 14, Prime Minister Winston Churchill and President Franklin Roosevelt announced the Atlantic Charter. The statement, developed during a two-day meeting on August 9–10 aboard the USS *Augusta* in Placentia Bay, Newfoundland, outlined in eight points a postwar vision of national sovereignty, free trade, labor rights, and disarmament as the basis of a new future where "all the men in all the lands may live out their lives in freedom from want and fear."[27]

Du Bois was not impressed. "I do not like the Roosevelt-Churchill manifesto," he fumed. Highlighting the two nations' ugly record of imperial domination, he punched holes in the lofty verbiage, which reeked of hypocrisy. "But when you consider what England and America have done to Yellow, Brown and Black folk—to the dark majority of the world's people in the last three centuries; can you blame us for suspicions, when the newest plea for peace, makes no single mention nor intimation of the future treatment of the colored world?" He had seen and heard it all before. "What new assurance, what new promise have we, that these countries will or can do better in 1942, than they did in 1918?"[28]

By the fall of 1941, Du Bois could only cry out in frustration at the state of the world. "Death, pain, bereavement, blindness, insanity, poverty—these are the children of war. On these we are silent. We scream 'Who is winning?' Imbeciles! Nobody is winning. Nobody will win. We all lose." He also thought about the main subject of *The Black Man and the Wounded World*. In September, as African Americans were volunteering and being drafted in disproportionate numbers to serve yet again in a Jim Crow military, he wrote, "Again the tragedy of the Negro American soldier festers as it did in the Revolution, the Civil War, the Spanish War and the first World War . . . The sore will never heal, so long as we fight for a Freedom and Democracy which we dare not practice."[29]

~

ON SUNDAY MORNING, December 7, 1941, just before 8:00 a.m., the first wave of 353 planes of the Imperial Japanese Navy Air Service appeared in the skies above Pearl Harbor on the Hawaiian island of Oahu. After Japan signed the Tripartite Pact with Germany and Italy on September 27, 1940, relations with the United States had steadily deteriorated. As Japanese diplomats in Washington, DC, made peace overtures to American officials, military leaders in Tokyo planned for war. Feeling the strain of economic sanctions and a fuel embargo, Japan boldly gambled that a surprise attack would fatally cripple America's naval forces and compel Roosevelt to opt for a quick negotiated settlement over a conflict he lacked the capability to win. For the next hour and fifteen minutes that morning, armor-piercing bombs and aerial torpedoes rained down on vulnerable American fighter bases and battleships. The Pearl Harbor attack killed 2,403 American servicemen and civilians.[30]

At 12:30 p.m. the following day, addressing Congress, FDR called for a declaration of war against Japan. Unlike Woodrow Wilson in his rhetorically extravagant war address, Roosevelt was direct and to the point. "The people of the United States have already formed their opinions and well understand the implications to the very life and safety of our Nation," he stated. Representative Jeannette Rankin, the first woman elected to Congress and a committed pacifist, cast the lone vote against going to war. Four days later, in a speech before the Reichstag, Hitler declared war on the United States, with Congress following suit against Germany hours later.[31]

African Americans would be part of the war whether they liked it or not. However, the question of the meaning of their loyalty and what they would fight for remained unanswered. Twenty-six-year-old James Thompson from Wichita, Kansas, offered his thoughts in a letter published in the January 31, 1942, issue of *The Pittsburgh Courier*, asking, "Should I sacrifice my life to live half American?" Encouraging the race to not "lose sight of our fight for true democracy at home," he suggested the adoption of "the double VV for a double victory. The first V for victory over our enemies from without, the second V for victory over our enemies from within. For surely those who perpetrate these ugly prejudices here are seeking to destroy our democratic form of government just as surely as the Axis forces."[32] In its next issue, the *Courier* invited readers to weigh in on the "Double V" slogan. The resoundingly positive response birthed a powerful rallying cry that captured the sentiments and aspirations of African Americans throughout the country.

The Double V mantra and the debate about African American patriotism pulled the scab off of World War I for Du Bois. Black papers like the *Courier* and *The Philadelphia Tribune* resuscitated the debate around "Close Ranks" and dismissed Du Bois's advice at the time. "Each generation faced by the horror of war is disposed to think that its attitude is wiser and braver than that of generations gone," he wrote with no small hint of elderly condescension and annoyance in his February 14, 1942, "As the Crow Flies" column, "so that there is already rising today controversy about the attitude of Negroes toward the second World War as compared toward that in the First World War." Du Bois went back and reread his infamous *Crisis* editorial from July 1918 and, digging in his heels, expressed "no desire to change a word." He stressed the need to place his statement in the context of the times, pointing to his activities and those of the NAACP to "hammer at discrimination" and fight for Black rights in and outside the military. He mentioned the June 1918 editors' conference, asserting that he "spoke for a united Negro press," its resolutions essentially mirroring his argument in "Close Ranks." Yet again defending himself, he surely hoped that his readers would not notice his selective memory and careful parsing of events from more than two decades earlier. Du Bois conceded, sadly, that "the First World War did not bring us democracy." However, he added, "Nor will the second." So with a mix of resignation and clarity, he wrote, "We close ranks again but only, now as then, to fight for democracy and democracy not only for white folk but for yellow, brown and black."[33]

As discussions about Black loyalty continued, and with additional time to reflect and stew, Du Bois was even more direct a month later. "Listen, fellow white Americans," he shouted through his column. "Yes, yes, yes! We are going to do our bit. In this war as in others we will be neither slackers nor traitors." Black people would again fight for America "not because we think that it is always right, or always just; or even always decent." They would do so for the sole reason that "whatever this country is, it is because of our blood and our toil and our sacrifice." He and the race would "play the game." Nevertheless, he scolded white America, "For Christ's sake stop squawking about democracy and freedom. After all, we are black men and we live in America."[34]

～

THE THOUSANDS OF BLACK MEN pouring into the nation's armed forces could relate to Du Bois's bitter words. The start of World War II for African Americans looked depressingly like a repetition of World

War I. The military funneled the majority of Black volunteers and draftees into service units and labor battalions. The War Department reactivated the Ninety-Second and Ninety-Third divisions but, adhering to the notorious 1925 "Use of Negro Manpower" report, kept them commanded by white officers, many of them vehemently racist. The Black press and civil rights activists placed their hopes in the expanding air corps, which established an all-Black training school at Tuskegee. But by the end of 1942, even at full strength, the men of the Ninety-Ninth Pursuit Squadron had not been deployed overseas, and morale plummeted by the day.[35] There was at least no repetition of Fort Des Moines, as the military accepted African Americans into officers' training schools alongside white candidates. However, most of the men who managed to earn commissions received assignments to noncombat units and, as in World War I, had limited opportunities for promotion. At training camps and bases across the country, especially in the South, the color line ruled as Black troops encountered humiliation in all aspects of their daily experience, from travel to church services to recreation to sleeping quarters. Desperate letters of complaint flooded the White House, the Black newspapers, NAACP headquarters, and the office of William Hastie, who, quickly running out of patience, resigned from the War Department on January 5, 1943.[36]

As the condition of African Americans in the armed forces reached crisis levels, *The Journal of Negro Education* devoted its 1943 summer issue to the "American Negro in World War I and World War II." The Howard professor and journal editor Charles H. Thompson, who had served in the First World War himself, believed that historical perspective was needed "for any real improvement of the Negro's status in our current war effort" and was especially crucial for "the peace that is to follow."[37] The thirty contributors to the issue represented many of the most important past, present, and future voices in the political and intellectual struggle for Black equality.[38] Emmett Scott, touting his special appointment in the War Department—as well as his book—provided the introductory statement on the participation of African Americans in World War I.[39]

Du Bois's article, "The Negro Soldier in Service Abroad During the First World War," drew from his book, albeit one that never reached the public.[40] He pared down the thirty-eight-page draft of chapter 17, "Armistice," from *The Black Man and the Wounded World* to document the discrimination and "drastic regime" of work and confinement Black soldiers and officers suffered through in the months before their demobilization. Using some of the dozens of letters and testimonies in his archive, Du Bois included the words of Black troops themselves to demonstrate the horrific racial prejudice they experienced and contrasted this with the praise heaped on Black troops by the mayors of French towns, whom he also quoted.[41] The article, however brief, showed the tantalizing potential of *The Black Man and the Wounded World* and what it could have been.

If it had been published just a few months later, the special issue of *The Journal of Negro Education* may very well have featured an article comparing racial violence during World War I with that of World War II. The new war triggered social and economic changes on an unprecedented scale, most notably the movement of an estimated 1.5 million African Americans out of the South during the 1940s, dramatically altering the demographics of the nation and of urban America in particular.[42]

White, Black, and brown people competing over jobs, housing, public space, and citizenship rights increasingly led to violent confrontation. The year 1943 threatened to be even worse than 1917. A May 25 rampage of white workers resisting the hiring of African Americans at a Mobile, Alabama, shipyard occurred just before the "Zoot Suit" riot in Los Angeles on June 3, where white sailors and soldiers went on the attack against young Mexican Americans.[43] On June 15, a mini pogrom erupted in Beaumont, Texas, leaving three African Americans dead and hundreds injured.[44] Three days of mayhem from June 20 to 22 in Detroit, the epicenter of the country's war industry, resulted in the deaths of thirty-four people, twenty-five of them African American. Thurgood Marshall likened the actions of the Detroit police, who were responsible for seventeen deaths, to the Gestapo.[45] On the night of August 1, after rumors spread that a New York City police officer killed a Black soldier, Harlem exploded. Despite the pleas of Walter White, Roy Wilkins, and other Black leaders for peace, the spasm of rage could not be contained. It lasted until sunrise on August 2, resulting in six dead, seven hundred injured, and property damage of about five million dollars.[46]

The violence brought back dark memories for Du Bois. "There are riots and riots," he wrote in the *Amsterdam News* following the Harlem eruption, vividly remembering "the wave of rioting that accompanied the First World War, in East St. Louis, Chicago, Washington and elsewhere. They were harsh and bloody." But the "recent wars," in his view, were more ominous for America: "The number of Negroes who are determined to be men has grown since 1917. The opposition has been driven more and more into the open, and stands increasingly revealed as one and the same as the opponents of democracy and the ignorant followers of outworn patterns of prejudice and reaction."[47] Although Du Bois did not fully absolve African Americans of responsibility for the violence and destruction, he ultimately believed that "until the American Negro becomes a free and equal American citizen, democracy in this land is impossible."[48]

The bloodshed of 1943 and the increased militancy of African Americans paved the way for Rayford Logan's volume *What the Negro Wants*. Logan solicited fourteen contributors to write for the book, representing a range of conservative, liberal, and radical viewpoints.[49] He saw the collection as an opportunity to provide an intellectual and political road map for Black people, with an eye toward the postwar world. Du Bois's inclusion was a given.[50]

For his essay, Du Bois offered yet another autobiographical musing, detailing in broad strokes his life and the evolution of his "program" for Black freedom and equality. The World War was the ultimate crucible in the first stage of his program to make Black people full American citizens. "The struggle was bitter," he recalled. He still found it hard to comprehend:

> I was fighting to let the Negroes fight; I, who for a generation had been a professional pacifist; I was fighting for a separate

training camp for Negro officers; I, who was devoting a career to opposing race segregation; I was seeing the Germany which taught me the human brotherhood of white and black, pitted against America which was for me the essence of Jim Crow; and yet I was "rooting" for America; and I had to, even before my own conscience, so utterly crazy had the whole world become and I with it.[51]

In attempting to explain his actions during the war, Du Bois invoked the excuse of temporary insanity that he'd pleaded guilty to in *The Black Man and the Wounded World*. But now, unlike what he wrote more than two decades earlier, the madness was not "divine."

Du Bois claimed that traveling to France after the armistice provided him with "a sort of mental balance." Having seen the devastating costs of war with his own eyes, he came to a firm conclusion: "Western European civilization had nearly caused the death of modern culture in jealous effort to control the wealth and work of colored people."[52] This occasioned the second shift in his program for Black freedom and the push for Pan-Africanism. He credited his visit to Germany and Russia in 1926 with inspiring the "third modification" of his program and its focus on the nexus of race and wealth inequality. The final turn in Du Bois's program came with his return to Atlanta University and the rejuvenation of the Black college as the center for sociological study and systematic planning. "It is the duty of the black race to maintain its cultural advance," he affirmed, "not for itself alone, but for the emancipation of mankind, the realization of democracy and the progress of civilization."[53]

Much to Du Bois's surprise, he needed to find another base of operations to continue his efforts. Following the unexpected death of John Hope in 1936, things had not gone smoothly for him at Atlanta University. His relationship with Florence Read, who wielded unchecked authority over the schools of the Atlanta University Center, became toxic. The new president of AU, Rufus Clement, soon became a target of Du Bois's ire as well. Viewing Clement as insecure and intellectually second-rate, he peppered him with a steady stream of complaints, the most significant regarding an adequate salary for his secretary and research assistant, Irene Diggs. Du Bois's successful organization of a two-day conference of Black land-grant-college presidents in April 1943 to develop a coordinated plan for the social scientific study of racial conditions in the South further grated at Clement's ego. Clement, with Read in his ear, decided that the famous professor and his outsized presence was no longer worth the trouble. On November 23, Du Bois received a letter from Clement stating that the AU board of trustees had voted to retire him from the active faculty effective June 30, 1944.[54]

He was stunned. The decision, he reflected in his *Autobiography*, was "disastrous" and "savored of a deliberate plot." He had envisioned spending the rest of his active years at the university, carrying out his meticulously planned sociological program of studying the race problem and devising its solution. The rug was pulled out from under his feet. More critically, he was in dire financial straits. The Depression had wiped out his life insurance, and less than five thousand dollars sat in his savings account. Mortgage payments remained on the Baltimore family home he had built in 1940, educational expenses for his granddaughter loomed, and he still felt obligated to provide for Nina and Yolande.[55] After receiving bad press and a flood of letters from alumni and other Du Bois allies, the trustees backtracked and, at their April 25 meeting, granted Du Bois a year's salary and a modest annual pension.[56] He grudgingly accepted his fate, but refused to believe that even at the advanced age of seventy-six, he was ready to be put out to pasture.

Old friends Arthur Spingarn and Louis Wright envisioned the NAACP as a gentle landing spot for Du Bois in the twilight of his career. Rejoining the organization he'd helped establish would carry strong symbolic meaning, something the public relations–savvy Walter White recognized.[57] Spingarn and Wright tilled the ground, leading to a May 17 letter from White asking Du Bois to accept a position, with the purpose of preparing "material to be presented on behalf of the American Negro and of the colored peoples of the world to the Peace Conference."[58] Du Bois received job offers from Howard, Fisk, and other schools, but was willing to turn them down for the opportunity to rekindle his relationship with the NAACP, which had grown to more than five hundred thousand members since his 1934 resignation and still held a piece of his heart. On June 28, he met with the board in New York to discuss terms.[59] The next month, White formally signed off on Du Bois's return as "Director of Special Research," with a $5,000 annual salary, beginning September 1, 1944.[60]

∼

IN HIS NEW ROLE with the NAACP, Du Bois approached 1945 as the year that would determine the fate and future of the twentieth-century world. The Allies, after turning the tide of the war in the spring and summer of 1944, had victory in their sights. The failed German offensive in the Ardennes—launched on December 16, 1944, and coming to a bloody, futile end by January 25, 1945—marked Hitler's last gasp. In early February, Roosevelt, Churchill, and Stalin met at Yalta in Crimea to discuss the anticipated defeat and occupation of Germany, Soviet participation in the war against Japan, and the carving up of postwar Europe. The following month, American forces advanced eastward into Germany while the Soviet Red Army hammered its way to Berlin. The two-prong ground assault was accompanied by a devastating Allied bombing campaign that rained fire upon German cities and ultimately killed nearly half a million people, the majority civilians.[61]

The sudden death of Franklin Roosevelt on April 12 from a massive cerebral hemorrhage and the ascension of Harry Truman—the former senator from Missouri and vice president for all of eighty-two days—to commander in chief did not change the inevitable. On April 16, Soviet troops swarmed Berlin, gradually overwhelming the final vestiges of German military resistance. Hitler knew that time had run out, for him and the Third Reich. He planned to avoid a demise similar to that of his ill-fated Axis partner Benito Mussolini, who, after being captured while on the run, was executed on April 28 in a small village in northern Italy. On April 30, alongside his new wife, Eva Braun, the Führer committed suicide in his bunker underneath the Reichstag as the Red Army, less than a mile away, closed in. Other high-ranking German officials, including Goebbels, followed suit. On May 8, the Allies accepted Germany's unconditional surrender.[62]

Even with the jubilation of V-E Day, the war against Japan remained far from over. Fighting in the Pacific had become increasingly savage, assuming all the characteristics of a full-out race war, with both sides engaging in atrocities and taking no prisoners.[63] The U.S. firebombing raid on Tokyo on March 9–10 incinerated sixteen square miles of the city and killed more than one hundred thousand civilians. Combat on the ground was just as ruthless, as American forces clawed their way to vital yet costly victories in Burma and Iwo Jima. Fighting at Okinawa from April to July was especially awful, resulting in more than twenty thousand U.S. combat deaths and roughly one hundred and ten thousand dead Japanese soldiers. In the follow-up conference to the Yalta meeting, taking place at Potsdam from July 17 to August 2, the United States, Great Britain, and the Soviet Union issued a declaration insisting that Japan unconditionally surrender or face "prompt and utter destruction." The United States had outpaced the Soviets in developing a new weapon of devastating capability, and Truman made the fateful decision to use it. On the morning of August 6, 1945, the B-29 bomber *Enola Gay* dropped a ten-thousand-pound uranium-powered fission weapon over the city of Hiroshima. Three days later, an even more destructive plutonium-core atomic bomb obliterated the city of Nagasaki. Combined, the first atomic attacks in world history killed more than 225,000 people, the majority civilians, and ushered in a new, terrifying future. On August 15, 1945, Japan surrendered.[64]

The second World War that Du Bois had lived through, leaving behind approximately seventy-five million dead, as well as ruin on an unimaginable scale, finally came to a close. "Now that the Second World War has ended what have we Americans of Negro descent lost and gained?" he asked in a new weekly column for *The Chicago Defender*. "War itself is always a loss which bears hardest among the segregated and the oppressed, leaving a legacy of death and destruction which is almost incalculable." Compared with his initial optimism after the armistice of 1918, Du Bois was much more sober, clear-eyed, and woeful in judging the end of World War II. Nevertheless, he managed to pull from the smoldering ashes some embers of hope. He welcomed the rise of Asia, and specifically China, "as a great power" and celebrated that the world would now have no choice but to recognize the Soviet Union as a global equal. The growth of independence movements in India and French Indo-China, in Du Bois's view, marked the beginning of the inevitable end of European imperial domination in Asia. He was equally encouraged by the "upheaval in Pan Africa," on the African continent as well as throughout the diaspora. Most important, the war reaffirmed the urgent necessity of democracy, a core aspect of Du Bois's life credo and identity that he refused to abandon. Offering final thoughts, he wrote, "It cannot be said that, balancing these loses and gains, the war has been either a vast success or a terrible failure. It can be said that civilization after this war has a chance to go forward and no group of civilized people have better opportunity to forward the advance of human culture than American Negroes."[65]

ALTHOUGH DU BOIS DID not plan to write the history of Black soldiers again, his postwar agenda in other respects mirrored his activities from a generation earlier, as he devoted his energies to the future of peace and democracy—specifically as it related to the colonial world—and the resumption of his Pan-African movement.

Walter White and others in the NAACP may have expected that the aging Du Bois would return to the association content to live out his remaining years in ceremonial fashion, providing advice to the director when needed and offering a sage word here and there.[66] Du Bois, with seemingly boundless energy, had other thoughts. In his first official report on October 4, 1944, the new director of special research outlined an ambitious agenda containing more than a dozen potential projects, all connected to the future of colonies, color, democracy, and peace.[67] As he wrote in August in one of his last *Amsterdam News* columns, "The greatest question before the world today is this: can we have Democracy in America and Europe so long as the majority of the peoples of the world are in colonial status; kept poor and ignorant and diseased for the profit of the civilized nations of the world? This is the problem to which I propose to devote the remaining years of my active life."[68]

In typical Du Bois fashion, he channeled his thoughts into writing a new book. He began drafting *Color and Democracy: Colonies and Peace* in the fall of 1944 and had the book done and in the hands of readers by April 1945, just weeks before the Allied victory in Europe.[69]

Making clear the incompatibility of colonialism and future peace, *Color and Democracy*'s crisply succinct 143 pages served as Du Bois's manifesto for the postwar world. He began with Dumbarton Oaks, the international conference held from August 21 to October 7, 1944, that created the framework for a new body to replace the moribund League of Nations. "Fears, jealousies, and hopes" came together at the sprawling Washington, DC, estate, he wrote, to craft "a tentative plan for world government designed especially to curb aggression, but also to preserve imperial power and even extend and fortify it." "If this situation is not frankly faced and steps toward remedy are not attempted," he warned, "we shall seek in vain to find peace and security; we shall leave the door wide-open for renewed international strife to secure colonies, and eventually and inevitably for colonial revolt." He advocated for a new Mandates Commission, based on the one established at Versailles for the League of Nations but built on a stronger foundation. He also insisted that the General Assembly allow for colonial delegates "alongside the master peoples in the Assembly." Lastly, he sought a clear statement from each colonial power on their long-term commitments to political and economic equality for their subjects.[70]

While offering specific recommendations, the book represented the latest contribution to Du Bois's lifelong conversation about the meaning of democracy and its relationship to the problem of the color line. "Democracy has failed because so many fear it," he believed,[71] tracing this failure directly back to the First World War, using the bloody evidence of not just one, but two global catastrophes to indict the colonial system and its racist ideological underpinnings. He again wrote with urgency—"We are seeking desperately to save modern civilization from the repetition of two disastrous and world-wide wars"—seeing nothing less at stake than the future of humanity. "If colonial imperialism has caused wars for a century and a half, it can be depended upon to remain as a continual cause of other wars in the century to come."[72]

The arrival of *Color and Democracy* serendipitously coincided with the founding meeting of the United Nations. Du Bois, like most of the rest of the world, had been excluded from the glittering halls of Versailles and treated by the Wilson administration as a nuisance to be tolerated as they crafted the doomed League of Nations. San Francisco, Du Bois believed, would be different.[73] This time he was one of the select group of three thousand representatives officially invited to the conference. He joined Mary McLeod Bethune and Walter White as part of the three-person NAACP team formally accredited as one of the forty-two organizations welcomed as consultants to the American delegation. He saw his role as impressing upon anyone who would listen that "human rights among the great nations and especially among colonies must be respected," lest their disregard spark a future war.[74]

The meeting opened on April 26, 1945, Du Bois watching the proceedings with a sharp eye. But even with his proximity and status, he waged an uphill battle to gain recognition of the rights of peoples of African descent and the colonized populations of the world. Of the fifty nations present, the United States, the Soviet Union, and Great Britain not surprisingly hovered above the rest. Along with placing his hopes on the Soviet Union, Du Bois encouraged China and India to use their influence to push for an explicit statement of racial equality, but the Western superpowers made sure this did not happen, instead adopting a vague, carefully worded commitment to human rights. The meeting also evaded the question of colonial independence. The old Mandates Commission, which Du Bois wanted to see revived and improved, was instead transformed into a Trusteeship Council that in effect reinforced Great Britain's and the United States' imperial spheres of influence in Africa and the Pacific. Du Bois also took note of the aggressive stance toward the Soviet Union that signaled a shift in Truman's foreign policy from that of his recently deceased predecessor. Despite a flurry of press releases, public speeches in San Francisco, and behind-the-scenes lobbying—including by Ralph Bunche, the only Black member of the United States delegation—Du Bois's efforts largely fell on deaf ears. He left San Francisco on May 26, dispirited.[75] "Here, then," he wrote in *The Chicago Defender*, "I seem to see outlined a third World War based on the suppression of Asia and the strangling of Russia. Perhaps I am wrong. God knows I hope I am."[76]

Following the letdown of San Francisco, Du Bois began to focus on the organization of a new Pan-African Congress. The idea became a distinct possibility in early 1944, when Amy Jacques Garvey, who valiantly carried on the work of the UNIA following her husband's death, in 1940, wrote to Du Bois about supporting her efforts and those of fellow Jamaican Harold Moody of the League of Coloured Peoples in developing an "African Freedom Charter" to put before the United Nations.[77] Planning picked up steam at the beginning of 1945 and gained momentum after Du Bois and his longtime Pan-African Congress partner Rayford Logan organized a modestly attended Colonial Conference on April 6 at the Schomburg Library in Harlem.[78]

George Padmore complicated Du Bois's plans. The London-based Trinidadian labor activist and intellectual issued his own call for a Pan-African Congress in the March 17 issue of *The Chicago Defender*, making clear that he and other Black people of the British Empire were ready to take the lead. "Whatever can be said about colored folks in other lands, those living in Great Britain are on the march," he proclaimed. "They are determined to make their voices heard in the council of nations."[79] Du Bois, caught off guard by the announcement and feeling the need to assert his proprietary rights to the movement, wrote to Padmore. "You know, of course, that I am interested in such a meeting and have been connected with attempts along this line since 1918," he gently reminded.[80] Padmore reassured Du Bois of his desire to work with him, but the center of Pan-African gravity had clearly shifted from the offices of the NAACP to the radical trade union circles of London.[81] Correspondence between the two self-appointed spokesmen continued through the summer of 1945 regarding when and where a meeting might take place. Padmore eventually settled on Manchester in October. As the date of the congress neared, Du Bois was subdued about its potential impact, but nevertheless still pleased by the revival of his Pan-African vision.[82] With less than a week to spare, he received approval from the British government and the State Department to travel to London, departing on the morning of October 13.[83]

The Manchester Pan-African Congress opened on the afternoon of October 15. Unlike in 1919, Du Bois was not the driving force, but now an elder statesman. Padmore graciously welcomed him as the father of Pan-Africanism, possessing "a youthful, vigorous mind, younger and more alive than many a youth's," and named him permanent chairman of the congress "as a token of esteem and respect."[84] Du Bois presided over several of the sessions and offered a historical Pan-African retrospective, including his efforts, "without credential or influence," after the First World War to sow the seeds of the movement.[85]

But the six-day congress was indeed about the future. The two hundred attendees and eighty-seven delegates represented a broad cross-section of diasporic organizations and included many of the future leaders of the African anti-colonial struggle, most notably Kwame Nkrumah and Jomo Kenyatta. The final resolution was unequivocal: "We are determined to be free; we want education, the right to earn a decent living; the right to express our thoughts and emotions, and to adopt and create forms of beauty. Without all this, we die even if we live." They believed in peace. However, "if the world is still determined to rule mankind by force, then Africans as a last resort may have to appeal to force, in order to achieve freedom, even if force destroys them and the world."[86]

Du Bois's Pan-African reinvestment factored into the writing of a second postwar book, *The World and Africa*, published in January 1947.[87] In the "Foreword," Du Bois explained his decision for crafting an updated version of his previous two surveys of African history, *The Negro* (1915) and *Black Folk: Then and Now* (1939), pointing specifically to the ruptures of the two world wars.[88] He did not budge from his initial 1915 thesis that the First World War was ultimately a conflict over "spheres of influence in Asia and colonies in Africa."

Thus came the rise of Hitler, along with every attempt on the part of the Western powers to appease him, except with colonial territories. "So war began. Hell broke loose."[89] His sweeping survey of African history in the following chapters challenged the intellectual foundations of white supremacy by decentering Europe and asserting African peoples as historical actors. If Western civilization and world democracy had a future, he asserted in the final chapter, "Andromeda," it hinged on the elevation of Africa and the destruction of colonialism as the key to peace. "No culture whose greatest effort must go to suppress some of the strongest contributions of mankind can have left in itself strength for survival. Peace and tolerance is the only path to eternal progress."[90]

The triumph of another book was offset by the implosion of his role in the NAACP. The main source of Du Bois's problems was again Walter White, the executive secretary's dictatorial methods gnawing at every fiber of Du Bois's democratic sensibilities. He believed that White's petty insults toward him, from the denial of adequate office space to insisting on the right to open his mail, were designed to keep him in his place.[91] The two headstrong leaders elbowed each other for who would be the face and voice of the NAACP before the United Nations.[92] The bad blood escalated when White, who hitched the association to Truman's reelection, demanded that Du Bois refrain from openly expressing his support for the Progressive Party candidate Henry Wallace, pointing to the NAACP's policy of nonpartisanship.[93] Du Bois could take no more. On September 7, 1948, he sent a blistering letter to the board, venting his frustrations at the lack of clear direction regarding his position, the NAACP's tacit endorsement of the Truman administration's foreign policy, and White's hypocrisy when it came to the rule against salaried officials engaging in "political activity."[94] White's anger turned to rage when Du Bois's memo was leaked and published in *The New York Times*.[95] In an icy September 13 memo, White refuted, point by point, all of Du Bois's charges.[96] The same day, the NAACP board voted to terminate Du Bois's employment, effective at the end of the year.[97]

For the second time, Du Bois departed on bad terms from the

organization he had cofounded. His inability to work with Walter White and his belief that the association had ceased to function "in a democratic manner" played a major role.[98] But also underlying his departure from the NAACP was the increasingly repressive Cold War climate and the growing national hysteria around communism.

The sudden American pivot from wartime partners with the Soviet Union to postwar adversaries caused seismic shifts in both geopolitical relations and domestic affairs. Du Bois had witnessed the seeds of conflict being planted at the UN meeting in San Francisco. They came into full bloom on March 5, 1946, at Westminster College in Fulton, Missouri, when the former British prime minister Winston Churchill, with President Harry Truman sitting on the platform listening intently, delivered the "Iron Curtain" speech, menacingly painting communism and the Soviet Union's aspirations in Eastern and Central Europe as a threat to Western democracy. "The speech of Winston Churchill was one of the most discouraging occurrences of modern times," Du Bois wrote in disgust. He hoped against hope that the United States would not be swayed by Churchill's "siren song."[99] The first true test came the following year as civil war in Greece raised the possibility of the country falling into communist hands. On March 12, 1947, in a speech to a joint session of Congress, Truman called for $400 million in military aid to Greece, as well as Turkey, and outlined his doctrine of providing American support for any nation facing the threat of communist intrusion. Du Bois saw Truman's decision as "the most stupid and dangerous proposal ever made by the leader of a great modern nation."[100] The United States increased its anti-communism investment to the tune of $13 billion with the Marshall Plan, passed in early April 1948 with the goal of bolstering the war-shattered economies of Western Europe.

In Du Bois's eyes, the peril of Truman's foreign policy eclipsed the president's commitment to civil rights. Following a wave of postwar violence against Black veterans marked by the blinding of Isaac Woodard by police in South Carolina and the lynching of George Dorsey in Georgia, Truman took action.[101] On December 5, 1946, he established the President's Committee on Civil Rights. One year later, the fifteen-person committee issued its 178-page report, *To Secure These Rights*, which contained thirty-four recommendations, among them a federal anti-lynching bill, the expansion and protection of voting rights, local and state police reform, a permanent Fair Employment Practice Committee, and the elimination of segregation in all areas of American life.[102] Even prior to its release, Truman signaled his commitment when, on June 29, 1947, at the Lincoln Memorial before a crowd of ten thousand, he became the first president to speak at the NAACP national meeting.[103] Truman followed this with a special February 2, 1948, address before Congress, where he endorsed several of the recommendations in *To Secure These Rights*, much to the disgust of Southern Democrats.[104] With his reelection in mind, and facing the threat of African Americans led by A. Philip Randolph protesting a new Selective Service Act, Truman issued Executive Order 9981 on July 26, 1948, officially desegregating the armed forces. Implementation would be slow, but the Jim Crow military that so disillusioned Du Bois in World War I and again in World War II was no more, at least on paper.[105]

Ironically, while Truman pushed forward an agenda for full African American citizenship that surpassed any other president in modern history, he simultaneously ushered in the most severe attack on civil liberties since the World War I era. Policy pronouncements went hand in hand with a wave of domestic repression against anyone and anything with even the thinnest connection to the Soviet Union. The House Committee on Un-American Activities stepped up its investigation of suspected communists, from Hollywood actors and directors to government officials. On March 21, 1947, Truman codified the chilling environment with Executive Order 9835, requiring federal employees to take a loyalty oath and empowering all government agencies to enforce it. Attorney General Tom Clark subsequently began to compile a list of suspected subversive organizations that included a number of African American civil rights groups loosely connected to the Communist Party and the radical left more generally.[106]

The Council of African Affairs (CAA), one of the groups on the attorney general's list, became Du Bois's next institutional home. The legendary entertainer-activist Paul Robeson and former YMCA missionary Max Yergan founded the CAA in 1937. Headquartered in New York City at 23 West Twenty-Sixth Street, the CAA emerged as one of the most important organizations promoting the connections between African Americans and the struggles of colonized and oppressed peoples in Africa, Asia, and other parts of the Black diaspora.[107] Du Bois, who had briefly served on the executive council, admired the work of the CAA and was especially fond of Robeson. Robeson's deep respect for the doctor was mutual.[108] Therefore, when the opportunity to join the CAA as vice chairman presented itself, Du Bois accepted. The non-salaried position did not help alleviate his financial distress, which had been made worse by Nina's deteriorating health, requiring $2,600 in yearly medical costs.[109] But he would have a spacious penthouse office, secretarial assistance, and more than enough room for his massive library, file cabinets, maps, and art.[110]

Even with the CAA firmly in the crosshairs of the government, Du Bois relished the political and intellectual liberation his new position afforded. He monitored such global events as the hard-fought victory of Indian independence, civil war in China between the Western-backed nationalist government of Chiang Kai-shek and the communist forces of Mao Zedong, and upheavals on the African continent, especially the rise of the Afrikaner National Party and the institutionalization of apartheid. He maintained his prolific writing regimen despite *The Chicago Defender* cutting ties with him owing to his leftist affiliations. He also became more tightly connected to a community of white and Black radical activists who were pushing back against the country's reactionary drift. The person most responsible for bringing Du Bois into this circle was the multitalented and politically fearless Shirley Graham, whose affection for the man she considered her soul mate knew no bounds.[111]

❧

DU BOIS'S NEW ASSOCIATIONS brought him into more direct contact with the global peace movement. In 1949, a momentous year for him, he daringly starred in a number of international gatherings. The

Scientific and Cultural Conference for World Peace meeting in New York in late March served as a grand stage for making his peace convictions unambiguously clear. His closing-night speech before twenty thousand people at Madison Square Garden was one of the most rousing oratory performances in his half century of public speaking. "We know and the saner nation knows that we are not traitors nor conspirators; and far from plotting force and violence it is precisely force and violence that we bitterly oppose," the professor roared. "This conference was not called to defend communism nor socialism nor the American way of life. It was called to promote peace!"[112] Riding the wave of the New York conference, he participated in an even larger international peace gathering the following month in Paris, attended by more than two thousand delegates representing seventy-two countries. As one of the featured speakers, he described it as "the greatest demonstration for peace in modern times."[113] Finally, in August, he attended the all-Soviet Conference in Moscow, the only American bold enough to flaunt the inevitable red-baiting that would follow. "The claim of the United States that it represents democracy in contrast to fascism or communism is patently false," he bluntly stated, assuring the approximately one thousand attendees that not all Americans had succumbed to the propaganda of the government and big business.[114]

Du Bois's center-stage presence at the peace congresses in 1949 culminated with the creation of the Peace Information Center (PIC) in February of the following year. He served as chairman of the small group of four white idealists committed to educating the American public about the peace movements of other nations.[115] Their main activities entailed the production of a "Peace-gram" newsletter and circulating the Stockholm Appeal, a global petition launched by the World Peace Council following its March 1950 Stockholm meeting. The work of the PIC became especially urgent when, on June 25, Soviet-backed troops of the North Korean People's Army crossed the 38th parallel and quickly overwhelmed South Korean forces.

Du Bois bemoaned the outbreak of the Korean War, but it could not compare with the heartache of the following day. On June 26, Nina died peacefully in bed following her morning bath.[116] She had suffered through six years of physical pain, severe illness, and eventual incapacitation. But she had also suffered in silence through their fifty-five years of marriage, a union, Du Bois rationalized, that was "not absolutely ideal" but yet "happier than most, so far as I could perceive." His was the perception of a man who viewed Nina—always serious, sexually frigid, uninterested in travel—more as an obligation than a true partner. Yet they remained tethered by the old marriage concept of "until death do us part." Du Bois laid her to rest in Great Barrington next to Burghardt, the boy whose death caused her to view life and the world, her widower reflected, as a "great ocean of dark bitterness." Even with the birth of Yolande, she never recovered from that "unhealable wound." Now, at least, Nina would finally be at peace. And for this, Du Bois, burying his guilt, was glad.[117]

With no time to mourn, and with Shirley Graham's support, he continued his anti-war activism. In July, he publicly clashed with Secretary of State Dean Acheson, who, in *The New York Times*, dismissed the peace movement as a Soviet "propaganda trick," further putting Du Bois and the PIC in the government's crosshairs.[118] He also stepped into the political ring when the American Labor Party unexpectedly approached him to run for the United States Senate on their ticket. "I went into the campaign for Senator knowing well from the first that I did not have a ghost of a chance for election, and that my efforts would bring me ridicule at best and jail at worst," he admitted. Nevertheless, he saw this as an opportunity to engage with the democratic process in a new way and to broadcast his message of peace and civil rights to a wider audience. The eighty-two-year-old candidate delivered ten speeches during the campaign, the highlight an October 24 address at Madison Square Garden before seventeen thousand people. As predicted, he lost in a rout but received a surprising 205,729 votes, four percent of all those cast.[119]

As the senatorial campaign neared its end, Du Bois suddenly confronted a matter of potentially life-shattering concern. On August 11, 1950, the Justice Department ordered the PIC to register under the obscure Foreign Agents Registration Act of 1938. Du Bois was out of the country when the letter arrived, and he subsequently dismissed it as ridiculous. The PIC was an American organization and only acting on behalf of people committed to the cause of world peace. Despite the PIC's request for a meeting to clarify its history and objectives, the Justice Department curtly replied that "no useful purpose would be served in any further discussion" and ordered the organization to register without delay.[120] At an impasse, and hoping to undercut federal authorities, the PIC voted to disband on October 12. The Justice Department, however, refused to budge. On February 9, 1951, federal prosecutors in Washington, DC, unsealed indictments against the five officers of the PIC, including Du Bois, accusing the organization of being an "agent of a foreign principal."[121]

Earlier that day, Du Bois had gone with Shirley Graham to the Queens County courthouse to get a marriage license. After years of friendship, intellectual bonding, and shared political struggle, they decided to make their union permanent, eyeing a February 27 wedding date. From the license bureau, the giddy couple went to Cartier in Manhattan to pick out a ring. They capped off their day with a celebratory lunch at Henri's, one of their favorite French restaurants, enjoying a dessert of crêpes suzette for "the final glow of satisfaction," Graham reminisced. They learned of the indictment later that evening, with Du Bois informing his stunned fiancée by phone. "Dear," she told him, "this changes our plans. We must be married right away." As his wife, Graham would be allowed to visit him in jail if necessary and act as his spokeswoman. Du Bois ultimately agreed. On February 14, they married in a small private ceremony, with the officiating reverend and Graham's son, David, as the only witnesses.[122]

Two days later, on the morning of February 16, Du Bois and his four white PIC codefendants walked up the steps of the federal district court in Washington, DC. Their case sat on the docket with those of other men charged with manslaughter, robbery, and larceny. After the arraignment and setting of a trial date, a marshal led Du Bois down into the court basement where he was fingerprinted, searched for concealed weapons, and then handcuffed. The sight of this created enough commotion among observers that the marshal removed the restraints. The presiding judge set bail at $1,000, and Du Bois was soon free. His only previous experiences with the court system had been a speeding violation and a $25 fine in 1918 after purchasing his first car; now he was an indicted criminal, facing five years in prison.[123]

The months leading up to the trial were, as he recalled, a "gruesome experience."[124] The Talented Tenth largely distanced themselves from the man who had validated their existence and worth. He was most disappointed, although not surprised, by the response from the NAACP national office. Justice Department attorneys convinced Walter White of Du Bois's guilt, and even after the board passed a tepid resolution acknowledging *The Crisis* founder's many years of service, the calculating executive secretary encouraged local branches to stay away from the case. In spite of this, support for Du Bois poured in from every corner of the country, as well as internationally, strengthening his belief in the power of the masses and not the bourgeoisie.[125] With Shirley Graham by his side, he traveled the country, raising critical funds for his defense, discussing the outrageous circumstances of his case while also seizing the opportunity to exhort for peace and true democracy in the United States. He spoke before rapturous audiences, one of the highlights an event at the Chicago Coliseum attended by fifteen thousand people.[126] Du Bois, with age-defying energy and determination, steeled by history and his life experiences, held firm to his principles. In a speech in New York just before the start of his trial, he affirmed, "Peace is not an object in itself; it is a method, a path to an ideal."[127]

Jury selection for the case of *United States v. Peace Information Center* began on November 8, 1951. A panel of eight African Americans and four white people listened to Justice Department attorneys attempt to convince them that, by inference and innuendo, the PIC had ties to European communists. The vigorous defense, spearheaded by the former congressman Vito Marcantonio, quickly exposed the weakness of the government's arguments. On the morning of Tuesday, November 13, the prosecution rested its case. Du Bois stood ready to testify, as did Albert Einstein as a character witness. Marcantonio launched into a withering takedown of the prosecution and argued for an immediate acquittal. The government, he maintained, had proved nothing. Judge Matthew McGuire agreed, ruling in the afternoon that "the Government has failed to support, on the evidence adduced, the allegations laid down in the indictment."[128]

And with that, the case was dismissed. The crowded courtroom teetered on the edge of spontaneous applause before the judge warned against any demonstrations. Shirley Graham nearly fainted. Du Bois was himself numb. Wanting out of the courthouse as quickly as possible, they hopped into a taxi and headed for their hotel, Du Bois slumping into the seat, his eyes closed. They celebrated long into the night with friends and supporters before returning home to New York.[129]

～

THE TRIAL AND ACQUITTAL put a tragic exclamation point on Du Bois's journey to reckon with the meanings of race, war, and democracy that had begun in the chaotic days of World War I more than thirty years earlier. At that time, Du Bois had professed to feeling closer to becoming a full American than at any other moment in his life. Believing in the potential of his country and the possibilities of democracy, he supported the war, doing all he could to encourage all other Black people to do the same. He did so knowing the risks, fully cognizant that America and the world could very well disappoint him. But the reward was tantalizing. Even in the midst of death, destruction, and soul-crushing racism, he saw hope and the inevitability of a brighter future. He would write this history and demonstrate how it was in fact Black folk who fought harder than anyone else to rescue civilization and save white folk from killing themselves. They, and he, embodied the struggle to forge a new world rooted in democracy, freedom, racial justice, and peace.

But the World War, as Du Bois slowly accepted during the 1920s and 1930s, held no redemptive value. For the greatest and most prolific Black scholar of his day, writing its history and trying to make sense of its legacy was maddeningly difficult. And when it became clear that the root causes of the war had not been removed and threatened to sprout into an even more catastrophic conflict, no one would listen. The Second World War left no doubt for Du Bois about his misjudgment that war could ever advance humanity. He would now fight for peace, the only possible foundation for the full realization of democracy and freedom for oppressed peoples. For this, the government of his own country had attempted to end his life by throwing him in jail.

Du Bois recounted his nine-month ordeal in a book he published in 1952, *In Battle for Peace: The Story of My 83rd Birthday.* His life constituted an enduring quest to reconcile the warring ideals of his Black identity and American identity. The trial was an attack on both. In the context of the Cold War, any critiques of war, capitalism, empire, and white supremacy were deemed un-American. This stung him to his core. He felt compelled to explain at length what, for him, it meant to be an American:

> I am a native-born citizen of the United States as my forefathers on both sides have been for two hundred years . . . I have tried to make this nation a better country for my having lived in it. It would not be true for me to say that I "love my country," for it has enslaved, impoverished, murdered and insulted my people. Despite this I know what America has done for the poor, oppressed and hopeless of many other peoples, and what indeed it has done to contradict and atone for its sins against Negroes. I still believe that some day this nation will become a democracy without a color-line. I work and shall work for an America whose aim is not solely to make a few people rich, but rather to stop War, and abolish Poverty, Disease and Ignorance for all men.[130]

Du Bois refused to be coerced into a false patriotism and the trap of unconditional loyalty. "I do not believe that loyalty to the United States involves hatred for other peoples, nor will I promise to support my country 'Right or Wrong.' I will defend this country when it is right. I will condemn it when it is wrong."[131]

If World War I marked the high point of Du Bois's belief in American democracy, his fight to escape conviction and imprisonment for merely advocating peace marked its nadir. "We claim that America leads in democracy," he wrote. "This claim is old and has at times approached truth. It is not true today. For democracy, while logical in theory, is difficult to achieve and maintain in practice."[132] Du Bois's radical conception of democracy that evolved in the years between the world wars and matured in the reactionary political climate of the Cold War made him a threat. "As, then, a citizen of the world as well as of the United States of America, I claim the right to know and think and tell the truth as I see it," he declared. "I believe in Socialism as well as Democracy." Above all else, he wrote, "I hate war."[133]

Du Bois's words in 1952 were a long way from those in 1918, when he counseled Black people in the pages of *The Crisis* to put aside their "special grievances," reminded them, "If this is OUR country, then this is OUR war," and scolded them, "*first* your Country, *then* your Rights!"[134] Since that time, he had been through much. He tried to make sense of it all, using every tool at his disposal, the most powerful being his sharp historical mind and stirring literary pen. The books he produced, from *Darkwater* to *In Battle for Peace*, cataloged his brilliance, his unswerving commitment to Black freedom, as well as his capacity for change. The one book he did not produce, still tucked away in his voluminous files, its pages becoming more faded and brittle by the day, spoke to his struggle to reconcile the contradictions of race, war, Americanness, and democracy, and his complicated place in this nexus. Attempting to write and ultimately failing to complete this book steeled his conviction to fight for peace. He would bear the scars of this battle.

And so, from the First World War to the Cold War, after more than three decades of dogged hope and heartbreaking disappointment, one truth remained: the Black man and the wounded world was, and continued to be, Du Bois himself.

EPILOGUE

"... that what I have done ill or never finished can now be handed on to others for endless days to be finished while I rest."[1]

THE YEARS FOLLOWING Du Bois's acquittal were challenging for him. With Shirley Graham's support, he weathered the anti-communist storm that eliminated his right to travel and made him a political pariah among many of his own race. He enjoyed the comforts of 31 Grace Court—working in his office, entertaining guests such as Paul Robeson in the spacious parlor, sitting in Graham's well-tended garden, watching *Perry Mason* on Sunday evenings.[2] Perhaps a life well suited for any normal octogenarian, but not for the man once recognized as the spokesman of Black America. "The colored children ceased to hear my name," Du Bois lamented.[3]

Nevertheless, he soldiered on, defying his opponents and, seemingly, father time as well. On the occasion of his ninetieth birthday, he declared, "I do not apologize for living long ... High on the ramparts of this blistering hell of life, I sit and see the Truth. I look it full in the face, and I will not lie about it, neither to myself or to the world."[4] In his defiance, Du Bois outlasted most of his generation, friends and adversaries alike.

This included the men involved in the decades-long saga of *The Black Man and the Wounded World*. Major Adam Patterson, his manuscript and documents still in Du Bois's possession, died on July 21, 1949, in Chicago at the age of seventy-two. On April 3, 1950, Carter

G. Woodson, the tireless promoter of Black history who, despite their clashes, held Du Bois's deep respect, succumbed to a heart attack in his Washington, DC, home.[5] When Du Bois learned of Matthew Boutté's passing on October 12, 1957, he no doubt reminisced about their time together in France immediately after the war, walking through the troop encampments at Le Mans and visiting battlefield sites along the Western Front. He also surely would have wanted to attend the funeral at Arlington National Cemetery, where Boutté joined Charles Young for his final resting place.[6] Two months later, on December 12, Du Bois's longtime rival Emmett Scott departed at age eighty-four.[7] His book, with *The Black Man and the Wounded World* never completed, remained the authoritative account of the Black experience in World War I.

The last leg of Du Bois's journey took place in Ghana. His passport restored, he accepted Kwame Nkrumah's invitation to come to Accra to complete the *Encyclopedia Africana*. "I am too old to think about this as anything but a final move," he told Graham,[8] and they bid farewell to the United States on October 5, 1961. Four days earlier, in an act of defiance, Du Bois had officially joined the Communist Party. Arriving in Accra as dignitaries, the couple moved into a luxurious seven-room house and received every possible courtesy from Nkrumah and his government.[9]

Time eventually took its toll. Du Bois valiantly attempted to work on the *Encyclopedia Africana*, but could only do so much.[10] Prostate surgery in 1962 left him physically weakened, but he carried on, quietly and with trademark dignity. Those around him knew the end was near. Du Bois did as well. Late in the evening of August 27, 1963, with Graham by his side, he passed away in his sleep.[11] WE MOURN DU BOIS, A GREAT SON OF AFRICA, blared the front page of the Accra *Evening News*.[12] At the conclusion of an elaborate state funeral two days later, he was laid to rest, buried just outside the western wall of Osu Castle in the land of his ancestors, facing the Atlantic, across from the land of his birth.[13]

When it came to Du Bois's final message, Graham abided by her late husband's wishes from that summer day in Brooklyn on June 26,

1957, when he sat down in his office to write his final message to the world. Graham unsealed the envelope, inscribed with the instruction "To be opened after my death," protecting Du Bois's six-year-old note. His last words, read by the Ghanaian ambassador Michael Dei-Anang just before army officers lowered the bronze casket into the ground, were brief and poignant:

> It is much more difficult in theory, than actually, to say the last goodbye to one's friends and loved ones; and to all the familiar things of this life. I am going to take a long deep and endless sleep. This is not a punishment but a privilege to which I have looked forward for long years. I have loved my work; I have loved people and my play, but always I have been uplifted by the thought that what I have done well will live long and justify my life; that what I have done ill or never finished can now be handed on to others for endless days to be finished while I rest; and that Peace will be my applause.
>
> One thing alone I charge you: Live and believe in Life. Always human beings will live and progress to greater, broader and fuller Life. The only possible death is to lose belief in this truth simply because this greater end comes slowly—just because Time is long.
>
> Good-bye.[14]

～

DU BOIS'S FINAL MESSAGE remains as relevant today as it did in 1963. From the grave, he speaks, his prophetic voice a gift as well as a charge. In telling the story of *The Black Man and the Wounded World*, I have thought about Du Bois's legacy, the work he has handed down for us to complete, and what lessons we can take from his decades-long battles with the history and memory of the First World War.[15]

As breathtakingly prolific as he was, Du Bois left behind an incredible body of unpublished work, comprised of a multitude of partial manuscripts and never-released essays, books, and larger projects, most prominent among them *The Black Man and the Wounded World*.

Considering that he wrote his "final message" in 1957, four years before he accepted Kwame Nkrumah's invitation to come to Ghana, it is entirely plausible that as he pondered death and his legacy, *The Black Man and the Wounded World* lingered on his mind.

Herbert Aptheker assumed the weighty responsibility of completing and bringing to light as many of Du Bois's unfinished works as possible. The young Columbia University–trained historian and member of the Communist Party forged a strong bond with Du Bois after completing his military service in World War II. Before departing the NAACP for the second time, Du Bois allowed Aptheker—who was at the time working on a documentary history of African Americans supported by a Guggenheim fellowship—to share his office. By 1947, Du Bois had entrusted Aptheker to edit his correspondence and arrange for its publication. When Du Bois quickly departed for Ghana in 1961, he gave Aptheker the steel filing cabinets containing the more than a hundred thousand letters and other papers, along with the custodial authority to control their organization. "There's no reason why you and Herbert shouldn't some day publish those things which are worthwhile," he told Shirley Graham with a wry smile shortly before his death. "Some of what I wrote years ago will be better understood when I am dead."[16]

He undoubtedly was thinking about *The Black Man and the Wounded World*. In 1971, Shirley Graham, Aptheker, and Vincent Harding, the pioneering historian, civil rights activist, and founder of the Institute of the Black World in Atlanta, discussed the idea of publishing Du Bois's World War I study, with Harding providing an introduction.[17] Although Aptheker possessed some materials related to *The Black Man and the Wounded World*, the full manuscript and archive resided in a separate collection of Du Bois's papers that had been donated to Fisk University in 1961 before he left for Ghana.[18] After acquiring a microfilm copy of the manuscript from Fisk in early 1972, Aptheker began assessing the content for possible publication by the University of Massachusetts Press.[19]

Aptheker went through at least two of the microfilm reels, taking detailed notes on the scope and content. However, his efforts ended there.[20] Upon examining the state of the manuscript, he encountered the same problem that Du Bois had so many years ago and realized the enormous task of preparing it for publication. "The job is a much bigger one than I had thought at first," he informed the University of Massachusetts Press director, Leone Stein.[21] In the subsequent years, facing strong headwinds, Aptheker valiantly forged ahead with the release of several of Du Bois's other unpublished essays, papers, and speeches, but *The Black Man and the Wounded World* was not among them.[22] It remains Du Bois's most significant work to never reach the public.[23]

Failure is a troubling lens through which to view Du Bois. The term suggests a weakness and flaw at the core of one's identity. Failure for Du Bois, considering his upbringing and the times that shaped him, was never an option.[24] Moreover, he holds an exalted status in the study of Black people and the broader struggle for Black freedom. He remains, as Cornel West once wrote, "the brook of fire through which we all must pass in order to gain access to the intellectual and political weaponry needed to sustain the radical democratic tradition in our time."[25] The association of Du Bois with failure, of any sort, unsettles this. While the voluminous amount of scholarship on his life and work demonstrates that he is not above critique, the lure of hagiography is seductive, as is the reflex, given his long-standing marginalization in the academy, to come to his defense.[26]

Several issues beyond Du Bois's control no doubt factored into his not completing *The Black Man and the Wounded World*. White foundations and philanthropies by and large refused to invest their money in him and his bold interpretation of the war. Potential publishers also saw little market value in the book as he conceived it. And then there was Du Bois himself. Writing constituted his method of thinking, of grappling with the issues and problems of the world, none more daunting than the color line.[27] His intellectual temperament was one of political imagination and artistic experimentation.[28] By nature, he was inclined to indulge in multiple projects and endeavors at the same time, diluting his focus, resulting in a cornucopia of writings that crossed every disciplinary boundary. Many of these works, in various ways, did examine the history and meaning of the First World War. So, even without *The Black Man and the Wounded World*, his contributions to our understanding of the conflict are profound.

But just as we rightfully celebrate his brilliance, vision, and intellectual determination, we cannot simply strip him of agency and responsibility where he did not succeed. Doing so robs him of his full humanity. Du Bois's road to ultimately abandoning *The Black Man and the Wounded World* was littered with choices. He chose to write *Darkwater, The Gift of Black Folk*, and *Dark Princess*. He chose to focus his efforts on the writing of *Black Reconstruction* when time and funding from his Rosenwald fellowship in 1931–1933 afforded him the opportunity to possibly complete *The Black Man and the Wounded World*. He chose to be less than honest with potential publishers, would-be supporters, and, most disheartening, many of the Black veterans who entrusted him with their personal artifacts and historical memories. He chose to be uncompromising in his vision of the book and its focus. And, in the end, as another World War again brought civilization to the brink of destruction, he ultimately made the choice that *The Black Man and the Wounded World* was a project too big, too disillusioning, and too tragic to devote the needed time, energy, and emotional fortitude to complete. Acknowledging these choices is not to cast shame on him, but to instead appreciate his complexity, his vulnerability, and the nature of the challenge he faced in writing his book.

That challenge was the World War, and we should not blame Du Bois for an inability to reckon with its historical magnitude. The war was a truly cataclysmic event in the history of the modern world. For those who lived through it, the conflict marked a moment of profound rupture. Scholars, with the benefit of time and personal distance Du Bois did not have, are continuing to grapple with the significance of World War I and its global implications. And we still have not fully explored its impact on African Americans and other peoples of African descent. Du Bois's twenty-one chapters and nearly one thousand pages of manuscript reflected his attempts to do just this. With a prescience that historians are only now appreciating, he asserted the place of

Black people, and Black soldiers specifically, as central actors in the drama of the World War, an act of radical historical imagination considering the times he lived in. He came to the bold conclusion that the war, far from inaugurating a new epoch of democracy and freedom from future war, reinforced white supremacy, imperialism, capitalist greed, and reckless militarism. The war, as he prophetically wrote in 1919, was indeed a failure.

That failure ultimately proved to be Du Bois's failure as well. His efforts to make sense of the war were not simply historical but deeply personal and moral as well. His support for the war came at great cost, most painfully the accusations that he not only betrayed his principles, but betrayed the race. The World War haunted him. "I felt for a moment as the war progressed that I could be without reservation a patriotic American," he repeated in his final autobiography, which was completed in 1960 and published posthumously in 1968. He carried the weight of this disillusionment for the rest of his life.[29] Du Bois, we might say, suffered from intellectual shell shock when it came to rationalizing a war defined by its irrationality.[30] In writing *The Black Man and the Wounded World*, he sought not only historical clarity, but atonement.

Du Bois finally accepted that true atonement would come not through the publication of his book, but through his actions and political commitments. In this sense, failure was necessary. It was generative. Through his disillusionment, frustration, and guilt, he evolved. World War I and its lessons, personal and historical, fueled his dogged critique of white supremacy, empire, and, most of all, war itself. His maturation into an uncompromising peace activist would not have been possible without his struggle to write *The Black Man and the Wounded World* and the failure that came with it. As Martin Luther King Jr.—another towering African American freedom fighter who paid a high price for his anti-war beliefs—poignantly said in a 1968 speech, "Dr. Du Bois' greatest virtue was his committed empathy with all the oppressed and his divine dissatisfaction with all forms of injustice."[31] This is the Du Bois we must remember.

Du Bois's failure, in addition to allowing us to better understand him, is also instructive in ways that return us to his unfinished work and the challenges we still confront today.

The Black Man and the Wounded World speaks directly to the enduring tension of being Black and being American. The quest to relieve the pain of this tension has defined much of the Black experience in American history. Du Bois believed that the double-consciousness he prophetically articulated in *The Souls of Black Folk* and elsewhere could be reconciled in the crucible of war and patriotism. Unfortunately, he was wrong, and as the years passed, he recognized his error. But we should not see him as selfishly naïve in believing that he and all Black people could be full Americans. Up to his final years, even while facing persecution by the government and branded as un-American, he refused to completely abandon his country. He wrote in his *Autobiography*:

> I know the United States. It is my country and the land of my fathers. It is still a land of magnificent possibilities. It is still the home of noble souls and generous people. But it is selling its birthright. It is betraying its mighty destiny. I was born on its soil and educated in its schools. I have served my country to the best of my ability. I have never knowingly broken its laws or unjustly attacked its reputation. At the same time I have pointed out its injustices and crimes and blamed it, rightly as I believe, for its mistakes. It has given me education and some of its honors, for which I am thankful.[32]

He viewed his unflinching criticism of America as the highest form of duty, citizenship, and patriotic sacrifice. The struggle of African Americans to hold the nation accountable for its sins, while also fighting for its potential, endures to this day.

Du Bois reminds us of the challenges facing American democracy and its fragility. Black people, he asserted, have been among the most faithful believers in the capacity of America to fulfill its democratic promise, only to be met time and time again with dashed expectations and cruel reminders of its limitations. *The Black Man and the*

Wounded World formed part of Du Bois's lifelong project of re-imaging the history of democracy through the lens of Black folk and reclaiming it as a radical ideal. He hoped the World War would be a seminal moment in the history of democracy, the dawn of a new era of social, political, and economic freedom for African Americans and other people of African descent. It did not happen. More than a century after the First World War, many of the same struggles Du Bois confronted—white supremacist violence, creeping fascism, wealth inequality, modern forms of voter disfranchisement, the restriction of women's bodily autonomy, the corrupting influence of money in the electoral process, right-wing assaults on the truth, exorbitant government spending on the military, preparation for endless war—remain urgent matters today.

But Du Bois did not lose faith. He embraced life, believed in the possibility of democracy, and trusted in the certainty of human progress.

And it is this legacy, even more so than the book he did not publish, that Du Bois leaves us with. It is the unfinished work of democracy, of racial equality, of economic justice, and of peace that we are tasked with taking up. Through the whiplash of success and failure, joy and rage, hope and despair, Du Bois continues to inspire, reminding us to fight, live, and love in order to make our wounded world a better place.

NOTES

Prologue

1. Interview with David Graham Du Bois, box 21, folder 18, David Levering Lewis Papers, Special Collections and University Archives, University of Massachusetts Amherst Libraries.

2. Shirley Graham Du Bois, *His Day Is Marching On: A Memoir of W. E. B. Du Bois* (Philadelphia: Lippincott, 1971), 218. This description is also based on photographs of Du Bois in his office taken in 1956 and 1958.

3. W. E. B. Du Bois, "We Remember Him for His Character," W. E. B. Du Bois Papers, Special Collections and University Archives, University of Massachusetts Amherst Libraries (hereafter cited as Du Bois Papers, UM-A); Gerald Horne, *Black and Red: W. E. B. Du Bois and the Afro-American Response to the Cold War, 1944–1963* (Albany: State University of New York Press, 1986); on James Ford and African American participation in the Communist Party more broadly, see Minkah Makalani, *In the Cause of Freedom: Radical Black Internationalism from Harlem to London, 1917–1939* (Chapel Hill: University of North Carolina Press, 2011); Mark Naison, *Communists in Harlem During the Depression* (Urbana: University of Illinois Press, 1983); Mark Solomon, *The Cry Was Unity: Communists and African Americans, 1917–1936* (Jackson: University Press of Mississippi, 1998).

4. Du Bois also wrote a letter to Shirley Graham with instructions for his funeral ceremony, telling her that, moved by Ford's death, "I must do at least this little to ease your task when the end comes." W. E. B. Du Bois to Shirley Graham Du Bois, June 26, 1957, Du Bois Papers, UM-A.

5. My last message, June 1957, Du Bois Papers, UM-A.

Chapter 1

1. "World War and the Color Line," *The Crisis* (November 1914), 28.

2. W. E. B. Du Bois to Charlotte Hirsch, June 3, 1914, Du Bois Papers, UM-A.

3. W. E. B. Du Bois to J. H. Badley, September 25, 1914, Du Bois Papers, UM-A.

4. John Morrow Jr., *The Great War: An Imperial History* (London: Routledge, 2004), 33–36.

5. "Kaiser William's War Speech," *New York Times*, August 5, 1914; on German enthusiasm for the war, see Jeffrey Verhey, *The Spirit of 1914: Militarism, Myth, and Mobilization in Germany* (Cambridge: Cambridge University Press, 2000).

6. "Over 17,000,000 Fighting Men of Eight Nations Now Engaged in the Colossal European War," *New York Times*, August 5, 1914.

7. On lead-up to the outbreak of war, see Barbara W. Tuchman, *The Guns of August* (New York: Ballantine Books, 1994), chaps. 1–9; John Keegan, *The First World War* (New York: Vintage Books, 1998), chaps. 1–3; Michael S. Neiberg, *Dance of the Furies: Europe and the Outbreak of World War I* (Cambridge, MA: Belknap Press of Harvard University Press, 2011); Viscount Grey of Fallodon, *Twenty-Five Years: 1892–1916, Volume II* (New York: Frederick A. Stokes, 1925), 20.

8. On the Schlieffen Plan, see Hans Ehlert, Michael Epkenhans, and Gerhard P. Gross, eds., *The Schlieffen Plan: International Perspectives on the German Strategy for World War I* (Lexington: University Press of Kentucky, 2014).

9. Isabel Hull argues that the atrocities inflicted on the Belgian civilian population by the German army at the start of the war were rooted in a military culture of violent extremism first practiced and perfected in Germany's African colonies. Isabel V. Hull, *Absolute Destruction: Military Culture and the Practices of War in Imperial Germany* (Ithaca, NY: Cornell University Press, 2013).

10. On the opening battles of the war, see Tuchman, *The Guns of August*, chaps. 10–22; Keegan, *The First World War*, chaps. 4–5. The historiographical debate on Germany's war aims dates back to the 1920s and continued through the 1960s. For two key contributions, see Imanuel Geiss, "The Outbreak of the First World War and German War Aims," *Journal of Contemporary History* 1, no. 3 (1966): 75–91; and Friedrich Fischer, *Germany's Aims in the First World War* (New York: W. W. Norton, 1967).

11. See Jay M. Winter and Robert Jean-Louis, *Capital Cities at War: Paris, London, Berlin, 1914–1919* (Cambridge: Cambridge University Press, 1997); Neiberg, *Dance of the Furies*, 154–66.

12. Frances Hoggan to W. E. B. Du Bois, August 15, 1914, Du Bois Papers, UM-A.

13. W. E. B. Du Bois to Frances Hoggan, August 19, 1914, Du Bois Papers, UM-A.

14. W. E. B. Du Bois, *The Autobiography of W. E. B. Du Bois: A Soliloquy on Viewing My Life from the Last Decade of Its First Century* (New York: International Publishers, 1968), 61 (hereafter cited as Du Bois, *Autobiography*).

15. David Levering Lewis, *W. E. B. Du Bois: Biography of a Race, 1868–1919* (New York: Henry Holt, 1993), 31–38 (hereafter cited as Lewis, *W. E. B. Du Bois, Vol. 1*).

16. Ibid.

17. W. E. B. Du Bois, "My Evolving Program for Negro Freedom," in Rayford Logan, ed., *What the Negro Wants* (Chapel Hill: University of North Carolina Press, 1944), 36.

18. Du Bois, *Autobiography*, 136; Lewis, *W. E. B. Du Bois, Vol. 1*, 51, 79–116; "W. E. B. Du Bois at Harvard," *Journal of Blacks in Higher Education*, no. 15 (1997): 126; on Du Bois and humanism, see Lewis R. Gordon, "Du Bois's Humanistic Philosophy of Human Sciences," *Annals of the American Academy of Political and Social Science* 568 (2000): 265–80.

19. On Du Bois's time as a student in Germany and its influence on his life, see Lewis, *W. E. B. Du Bois, Vol. 1*, 117–49; Kwame Anthony Appiah, *Lines of Descent: W. E. B. Du Bois and the Emergence of Identity* (Cambridge, MA: Harvard University Press, 2014); Kenneth D. Barkin, " 'Berlin Days,' 1892–1894: W. E. B. Du Bois and German Political Economy," *boundary 2* 27, no. 3 (Fall 2000): 79–101; Kenneth D. Barkin, "W. E. B. Du Bois' Love Affair with Imperial Germany," *German Studies Review* 28, no. 2 (May 2005): 285–302; Axel R. Schäfer, "W. E. B. Du Bois, German Social Thought, and the Racial Divide in American Progressivism: 1892–1909," *Journal of American History* 88, no. 3 (2001): 925–49.

20. Quarter centennial celebration of my life [fragment], ca. February 23, 1893, Du Bois Papers, U-MA; Herbert Aptheker, ed., *Against Racism: Unpublished Essays, Papers, Addresses, 1887–1961* (Amherst: University of Massachusetts Press, 1985), 26–29.

21. On the history of racial uplift and its ideological dimensions, see Kevin K. Gaines, *Uplifting the Race: Black Leadership, Politics and Culture in the Twentieth Century* (Chapel Hill: University of North Carolina Press, 1996).

22. For a concise summation of Du Bois's early academic career and scholarly work, see Shawn Leigh Alexander, *W. E. B. Du Bois: An American Intellectual and Activist* (Lanham, MD: Rowman & Littlefield, 2015), chap. 2. On Du Bois's Atlanta University studies and contributions to the discipline of sociology more broadly, see Aldon Morris, *The Scholar Denied: W. E. B. Du Bois and the Birth of Modern Sociology* (Berkeley: University of California Press, 2015); Elliott M. Rudwick, "W. E. B. Du Bois and the Atlanta University Studies on the Negro," *Journal of Negro Education* 26, no. 4 (1957): 466–76.

23. On the end of Reconstruction and Democratic redemption, see Nicholas Lemann, *Redemption: The Last Battle of the Civil War* (New York: Farrar, Straus and Giroux, 2006).

24. On post-Reconstruction African American disfranchisement and the role of the Supreme Court more specifically, see Alan Friedlander and Richard A. Gerber, *Welcoming Ruin: The Civil Rights Act of 1875* (Leiden: Brill, 2019); Michael Perman, *Struggle for Mastery: Disfranchisement in the South, 1888–1908* (Chapel Hill: University of North Carolina Press, 2001); R. Volney Riser, *Defying Disfranchisement: Black Voting Rights Activism in the Jim Crow South, 1890–1908* (Baton Rouge: Louisiana State University Press, 2010).

25. On the development of Jim Crow segregation as a legal and cultural system, see Grace Elizabeth Hale, *Making Whiteness: The Culture of Segregation in the South, 1890–1940* (New York: Pantheon, 1998); Howard N. Rabinowitz, *Race Relations in the Urban South, 1865–1890* (Urbana: University of Illinois Press, 1980); C. Vann Woodward, *The Strange Career of Jim Crow: A Commemorative Edition* (New York: Oxford University Press, 2002).

26. On the Southern post–Civil War sharecropping system, see Gerald D. Jaynes, *Branches Without Roots: Genesis of the Black Working Class in the American South, 1862–1882* (New York: Oxford University Press, 1986); Pete Daniel, *The Shadow of Slavery: Peonage in the South, 1901–1969* (Urbana: University of Illinois Press, 1972).

27. On the convict lease system and the criminalization of Blackness in the Jim Crow era more broadly, see Douglas A. Blackmon, *Slavery by Another Name: The Re-Enslavement of Black Americans from the Civil War to World War II* (New York: Doubleday, 2008); Sarah Haley, *No Mercy Here: Gender, Punishment, and the Making of Jim Crow Modernity* (Chapel Hill: University of North Carolina Press, 2016); Talitha L. LeFlouria, *Chained in Silence: Black Women and Convict Labor in the New South* (Chapel Hill: University of North Carolina Press, 2015); Alex Lichtenstein, *Twice the Work of Free Labor: The Political Economy of Convict Labor in the New South* (London: Verso, 1996); Khalil Gibran Muhammad, *The Condemnation of Blackness: Race, Crime, and the Making of Modern Urban America* (Cambridge, MA: Harvard University Press, 2010); David M. Oshinsky, *Worse Than Slavery: Parchman Farm and the Ordeal of Jim Crow Justice* (New York: Free Press, 1996).

28. On the history of post-Reconstruction lynching, see W. Fitzhugh Brundage, *Under Sentence of Death: Lynching in the South* (Chapel Hill: University of North Carolina Press, 1997); Philip Dray, *At the Hands of Persons Unknown: The Lynching of Black America* (New York: Random House, 2002); Stewart E. Tolnay and E. M. Beck, *A Festival of Violence: An Analysis of Southern Lynchings, 1882–1930* (Urbana: University of Illinois Press, 1995); Crystal N. Feimster, *Southern Horrors: Women and the Politics of Rape and Lynching* (Cambridge, MA: Harvard University Press, 2009).

29. W. E. B. Du Bois, *The Souls of Black Folk* (New York: Oxford University Press, 2007), chap. 11, "Of the Passing of the First Born."

30. Du Bois, "My Evolving Program for Negro Freedom," 53.

31. W. E. B. Du Bois, *Dusk of Dawn: An Essay Toward an Autobiography of a Race Concept*, in W. E. B. Du Bois, *Writings* (New York: Library of America, 1986), 602–603.

32. Du Bois, *The Souls of Black Folk*, 3. Du Bois first stated "the problem of the twentieth-century is the problem of the color line" in his role as secretary of the 1900 Pan-African Congress in Paris organized by Henry Sylvester Williams. Lucas Dietrich, "'At the Dawning of the Twentieth Century': W.E.B. Du Bois, A.C. McClurg & Co., and the Early Circulation of *The Souls of Black Folk*," *Book History* 20, no. 1 (2017): 307–29. For a full exploration of *The Souls of Black Folk*, with emphasis on its philosophical and Hegelian influences, see Stephanie J. Shaw, *W. E. B. Du Bois and* The Souls of Black Folk (Chapel Hill: University of North Carolina Press, 2013).

33. Du Bois, *The Souls of Black Folk*, 8.

34. Ibid., 4.

35. Du Bois expounded on his idea of the Talented Tenth in a subsequent 1903 essay. See W. E. B. Du Bois, "The Talented Tenth," in *The Negro Problem: A Series of Articles by Representative American Negroes of To-day* (New York: James Pott, 1903).

36. On the Talented Tenth and Du Bois's gender politics, see Susan Gillman and Alys Eve Weinbaum, eds., *Next to the Color Line: Gender, Sexuality, and W. E. B. Du Bois* (Minneapolis: University of Minnesota Press, 2007); Joy James, *Transcending the Talented Tenth: Black Leaders and American Intellectuals* (New York: Routledge, 1997); Hazel V. Carby, *Race Men* (Cambridge, MA: Harvard University Press, 2009).

37. On Booker T. Washington, see Kenneth Marvin Hamilton, *Booker T. Washington in American Memory* (Urbana: University of Illinois Press, 2017); Louis R. Harlan and Raymond Smock, *Booker T. Washington in Perspective: Essays of Louis R. Harlan* (Jackson: University Press of Mississippi, 1988); Robert J. Norrell, *Up from History: The Life of Booker T. Washington* (Cambridge, MA: Belknap Press of Harvard University Press, 2009); Kevern Verney, *The Art of the Possible: Booker T. Washington and Black Leadership in the United States, 1881–1925* (New York: Routledge, 2001).

38. Du Bois, *The Souls of Black Folk*, 42.

39. On Du Bois's conflict with Booker T. Washington, see Jacqueline M. Moore, *Booker T. Washington, W.E.B. Du Bois, and the Struggle for Racial Uplift* (Wilmington, DE: Scholarly Resources, 2003); Raymond Wolters, *Du Bois and His Rivals* (Columbia: University of Missouri Press, 2002), chap. 2.

40. Lewis, *W. E. B. Du Bois, Vol. 1*, 297–342.

41. On Du Bois and *The Crisis*, see Phillip Luke Sinitiere and Amy Helene Kirschke, *Protest and Propaganda: W. E. B. Du Bois, The CRISIS, and American History* (Columbia: University of Missouri Press, 2014).

42. Dorothy Cowser Yancy, "William Edward Burghardt Du Bois' Atlanta Years: The Human Side—A Study Based Upon Oral Sources," *Journal of Negro History* 63, no. 1 (1978): 59–67.

43. I am grateful to Tiffany Ruby Patterson for encouraging me to use the term "strategic dishonesty" in characterizing Du Bois's behavior. Also see Bonnyeclaire Smith-Stewart, "Hypocrisy in the Life of W.E.B. Du Bois: Reconstructing Selective Memory," *Phylon* 51, no. 1 (2014): 57–75.

44. W. E. B. Du Bois, *In Battle for Peace: The Story of My 83rd Birthday* (New York: Masses and Mainstream, 1952), 12.

45. Du Bois, *Dusk of Dawn*, 741; Manning Marable, *W. E. B. Du Bois: Black Radical Democrat* (London: Routledge, 2004), 77.

46. Du Bois, *Dusk of Dawn*, 741.

47. On Spingarn, as well as his relationship with Du Bois, see Marshall van Deusen, *J. E. Spingarn* (New York: Twayne, 1971); Barbara Joyce Ross, *J. E. Spingarn and the Rise of the NAACP, 1911–1939* (New York: Atheneum, 1972); Lori Harrison-Kahan, "Scholars and Knights: W. E. B. Du Bois, J. E. Spingarn, and the NAACP," *Jewish Social Studies* 18, no. 1 (2011): 63–87.

48. J. E. Spingarn to W. E. B. Du Bois, October 24, 1914, Du Bois Papers, UM-A.

49. W. E. B. Du Bois to J. E. Spingarn, October 28, 1914, Du Bois Papers, UM-A.

50. American Steamship Company, American Line list of passengers, ca. September 1914, Du Bois Papers, UM-A.

51. W. E. B. Du Bois to U.S. consul, Liverpool, England, September 24, 1914; Department of State to W. E. B. Du Bois, September 26, 1914; U.S. consul, Liverpool, England, to W. E. B. Du Bois, October 6, 1914, Du Bois Papers, UM-A.

52. On the Battle of the Marne, see Holger H. Herwig, *The Marne, 1914: The Opening of World War I and the Battle That Changed the World* (New York: Random House, 2009).

53. On the early months of the war, see Robert A. Doughty, *Pyrrhic Victory: French Strategy and Operations in the Great War* (Cambridge, MA: Harvard University Press, 2008), chap. 2.

54. On the war in Africa, see Morrow, *The Great War: An Imperial History*; Byron Farwell, *The Great War in Africa, 1914–1918* (New York: W. W. Norton, 1986); Michelle R. Moyd, *Violent Intermediaries: African Soldiers, Conquest, and Everyday Colonialism in German East Africa* (Athens: Ohio University Press, 2014); Hew Strachan, *The First World War in Africa* (Oxford: Oxford University Press, 2004).

55. Impressions of Germany, ca. 1892, Du Bois Papers, UM-A.

56. "Art and Germany's Savants," *Literary Digest* (October 24, 1914), 791; "Germany Defended by Her Savants," *New York Times*, October 8, 1914.

57. W. E. B. Du Bois to Moritz Schanz, October 9, 1914, Du Bois Papers, UM-A.

58. "World War and the Color Line," *The Crisis* (November 1914), 28–30.

59. Ibid., 28.

60. W. E. B. Du Bois, "The African Roots of War," *Atlantic Monthly* (May 1915).

61. Nina Du Bois to W. E. B. Du Bois, January 3, 1915; Nina Du Bois to W. E. B. Du Bois, ca. February 1915, Du Bois Papers, UM-A.

62. On the Second Battle of Ypres and the use of poison gas, see George H. Cassar, *Trial by Gas: The British Army at the Second Battle of Ypres* (Sterling, VA: Potomac Books, 2014); Nina Du Bois to W. E. B. Du Bois, ca. May 15, 1915, Du Bois Papers, UM-A.

63. Susan R. Grayzel, *At Home and Under Fire: Air Raids and Culture in Britain from the Great War to the Blitz* (Cambridge: Cambridge University Press, 2012).

64. Nina Du Bois to W. E. B. Du Bois, ca. June 20, 1915, Du Bois Papers, UM-A.

65. On the sinking of the *Lusitania*, see Willi Jasper, *Lusitania: The Cultural History of a Catastrophe* (New Haven, CT: Yale University Press, 2016); Erik Larson, *Dead Wake: The Last*

Crossing of the Lusitania (New York: Crown, 2015); "No Need to Fight, If Right," *New York Times*, May 11, 1915.

66. Nina Du Bois to W. E. B. Du Bois, ca. May 15, 1915; Nina Du Bois to W. E. B. Du Bois, ca. May 16, 1915, Du Bois Papers, UM-A.

67. "Lusitania," *The Crisis* (June 1915), 81.

68. Yolande Du Bois to W. E. B. Du Bois, ca. June 1915, Du Bois Papers, UM-A.

69. W. E. B. Du Bois to Yolande Du Bois, June 19, 1915, Du Bois Papers, UM-A.

70. On the lead-up to American entry into the war and the Preparedness Movement, see Michael S. Neiberg, *The Path to War: How the First World War Created Modern America* (New York: Oxford University Press, 2016).

71. On the participation of French African colonial troops in the war, see Richard S. Fogarty, *Race and War in France: Colonial Subjects in the French Army, 1914–1918* (Baltimore: Johns Hopkins University Press, 2008); Joe Lunn, *Memoirs of the Maelstrom: A Senegalese Oral History of the First World War* (Portsmouth, NH: Heinemann, 1999); Myron J. Echenberg, *Colonial Conscripts: Tirailleurs Senegalais in French West Africa, 1857–1960* (Portsmouth, NH: Heinemann, 1991).

72. *The Crisis* (November 1914). On the role of the Black press in framing African participation in the war, see Chad L. Williams, *Torchbearers of Democracy: African American Soldiers in the World War I Era* (Chapel Hill: University of North Carolina Press, 2010), 150–59.

73. On the contradictory identity of African American soldiers as participants in the violence of American imperialism, see Le'Trice D. Donaldson, *Duty Beyond the Battlefield: African American Soldiers Fight for Racial Uplift, Citizenship, and Manhood, 1870–1920* (Carbondale: Southern Illinois University Press, 2020); Willard B. Gatewood, *"Smoked Yankees" and the Struggle for Empire: Letters from Negro Soldiers, 1898–1902* (Urbana: University of Illinois Press, 1971); Paul A. Kramer, *The Blood of Government: Race, Empire, the United States, & the Philippines* (Chapel Hill: University of North Carolina Press, 2006); Adriane Lentz-Smith, *Freedom Struggles: African Americans and World War I* (Cambridge, MA: Harvard University Press, 2010), 56–59; Mary Talusan, *Instruments of Empire: Filipino Musicians, Black Soldiers, and Military Band Music During US Colonization of the Philippines* (Jackson: University Press of Mississippi, 2021).

74. William H. Leckie and Shirley A. Leckie, *The Buffalo Soldiers: A Narrative of the Black Cavalry in the West* (Norman: University of Oklahoma Press, 2012); Frank N. Schubert, *Black Valor: Buffalo Soldiers and the Medal of Honor, 1870–1898* (Wilmington, DE: Scholarly Resources, 1997).

75. James W. Hurst, *Pancho Villa and Black Jack Pershing: The Punitive Expedition in Mexico* (Westport, CT: Praeger, 2007); Joseph A. Stout Jr., *Border Conflict: Villistas, Carrancistas, and the Punitive Expedition, 1915–1920* (Fort Worth: Texas Christian University Press, 1999).

76. On Charles Young's early life and military career, see Donaldson, *Duty Beyond the Battlefield*, 89–100; David P. Kilroy, *For Race and Country: The Life and Career of Colonel Charles Young* (Westport, CT: Praeger, 2003); Brian Shellum, *Black Officer in a Buffalo Soldier Regiment: The Military Career of Charles Young* (Lincoln: University of Nebraska Press, 2010).

77. Wilberforce University to W. E. B. Du Bois, August 17, 1894, Du Bois Papers, UM-A.

78. Du Bois, *Autobiography*, 187.

79. Ibid., 267.

80. Du Bois, for example, chose the former German chancellor Otto von Bismarck as the subject of his Fisk commencement address.

81. Lewis, *W. E. B. Du Bois, Vol. 1*, 176.

82. W. E. B. Du Bois to Charles Young, January 21, 1916, Charles Young Collection, Ohio Historical Society, www.ohiohistory.org (hereafter cited as Young Collection, OHS).

83. Charles Young to Nina Du Bois, July 6, 1915, Du Bois Papers, UM-A.

84. Lewis, *W. E. B. Du Bois, Vol. 1*, 517.

85. *The Crisis* (January 1916), 130.

86. W. E. B. Du Bois, "Conservation of Races," in W. E. B. Du Bois, *Writings* (New York: Library of America, 1986), 821.

87. W. E. B. Du Bois to Yolande Du Bois, February 25, 1916, Du Bois Papers, UM-A; Du Bois to Charles Young, January 14, 1916, Du Bois to Charles Young, January 21, 1916, Young Collection, OHS.

88. Kilroy, *For Race and Country;* "Medal Given to Maj Young," *Boston Globe*, February 23, 1916; "The Boston Meeting," *The Crisis* (April 1916), 309; Presentation of the Spingarn Medal, ca. February 1916, Du Bois Papers, UM-A.

89. W. E. B. Du Bois to Yolande Du Bois, February 25, 1916, Du Bois Papers, UM-A.

90. "Young," *The Crisis* (March 1916), 240–42.

91. "Booker T. Washington," *The Crisis* (December 1915), 82.

92. The Amenia conference, 1925, Du Bois Papers, UM-A.

93. Notes on Amenia conference, ca. 1916, Du Bois Papers, UM-A.

94. For full list of attendees, see The Amenia conference, 1925, Du Bois Papers, UM-A.

95. Maceo Crenshaw Dailey Jr., "The Business Life of Emmett Jay Scott," *Business History Review* 77, no. 4 (2003): 667–86.

96. The Amenia conference, 1925, Du Bois Papers, UM-A.

97. Ibid.

98. Lewis, *W. E. B. Du Bois, Vol. 1*, 517–22; Patricia Sullivan, *Lift Every Voice: The NAACP and the Making of the Civil Rights Movement* (New York: The New Press, 2009), 59–60.

99. J. E. Spingarn to W. E. B. Du Bois, December 12, 1916, Du Bois Papers, UM-A.

100. W. E. B. Du Bois to Frances Hoggan, January 29, 1917; Augustus Dill to James E. Shepard, January 8, 1917, Du Bois Papers, UM-A.

101. W. E. B. Du Bois to Frances Hoggan, January 29, 1917, Du Bois Papers, UM-A.

102. "The Editor, January 5th," *The Crisis* (February 1917), 163.

103. Francis J. Grimké to W. E. B. Du Bois, January 26, 1917; Carrie Clifford to W. E. B. Du Bois, January 20, 1917; George Wm. Cook to Joel E. Spingarn, January 11, 1917; George A. Towns to W. E. B. Du Bois, January 26, 1917. Additional correspondence related to Du Bois's surgery in Du Bois Papers, UM-A.

104. W. E. B. Du Bois, *Darkwater: Voices from Within the Veil* (New York: Oxford University Press, 2007), 11.

105. Du Bois, *Dusk of Dawn*, 734.

106. On Wilson's upbringing, early life, and academic career, see John Milton Cooper Jr., *Woodrow Wilson: A Biography* (New York: Knopf, 2009); A. Scott Berg, *Wilson* (New York: G. P. Putnam's Sons, 2013).

107. W. E. B. Du Bois, "My Impressions of Woodrow Wilson," *Journal of Negro History* 58, no. 4 (1973): 453.

108. Woodrow Wilson, "Democracy and Efficiency," *Atlantic Monthly* (March 1901), 290–91.

109. Du Bois and Wilson first crossed paths in the pages of *The Atlantic Monthly* in 1901, offering contrasting articles on the topic of Reconstruction. Wilson's views reflected the racism of the emerging "Dunning School" of Reconstruction historiography, which painted the era as a failure, whereas Du Bois viewed Reconstruction as a noble attempt at creating a multiracial democracy. See Woodrow Wilson, "Reconstruction and the Southern States," *Atlantic Monthly* (January 1901); John David Smith and J. Vincent Lowery, eds., *The Dunning School: Historians, Race and the Meaning of Reconstruction* (Lexington: University Press of Kentucky, 2013); W. E. B. Du Bois, "The Freedmen's Bureau," *Atlantic Monthly* (March 1901).

110. Du Bois, "My Impressions of Woodrow Wilson," 453–54; on Du Bois's socialist ideological beliefs, see Marable, *W. E. B. Du Bois*, 88–91.

111. "Politics," *The Crisis* (August 1912), 180–81.

112. "An Open Letter to Woodrow Wilson," *The Crisis* (March 1913), 236–37.

113. On Southern progressivism and race, see John Dittmer, *Black Georgia in the Progressive Era, 1900–1920* (Urbana: University of Illinois Press, 1977); Dewey W. Grantham, *Southern Progressivism: The Reconciliation of Progress and Tradition* (Knoxville: University of Tennessee Press, 1983); William A. Link, *The Paradox of Southern Progressivism, 1880–1930* (Chapel Hill: University of North Carolina Press, 1992).

114. On Wilson's racial policies, see Nicholas Patler, *Jim Crow and the Wilson Administration: Protesting Federal Segregation in the Early Twentieth Century* (Boulder: University of Colorado Press, 2004); Eric S. Yellin, *Racism in the Nation's Service: Government Workers and the Color Line in Woodrow Wilson's America* (Chapel Hill: University of North Carolina Press, 2013), chap. 4.

115. He is listed on the 1910 U.S. Census as "Edward Patterson." Thirteenth Census of the United States, 1910, Ancestry.com; Fred L. Borch, "Adam E. Patterson: First African American Judge Advocate in History," *Army Lawyer* (February 1, 2015), 1–2; Adam E. Patterson and M. W. Guy, *The Homeseeker's Guide* (Muskogee, Indian Territory: Commercial Industrial Association, 1907). On the "Exoduster" movement, see Nell Irvin Painter, *Exodusters: The Black Migration to Kansas After Reconstruction* (New York: Knopf, 1977); "Revolt on Patterson," *Washington Post*, July 27, 1913; Yellin, *Racism in the Nation's Service*, 68–70.

116. "Revolt on Patterson," *Washington Post*, July 27, 1913; "Plot to Assassinate New Register of Treas'y," *Chicago Defender*, August 2, 1913; "Senate May Not Confirm Patterson," *Afro-American*, August 2, 1913.

117. "Patterson Shows White Feather," *Afro-American*, August 9, 1913.

118. "Adam E. Patterson," *Washington Bee*, August 9, 1913; "Patterson Declines," *Topeka Plaindealer*, August 15, 1913.

119. "Another Open Letter to Woodrow Wilson," *The Crisis* (September 1913), 232–36.

120. Mark E. Benbow, "Birth of a Quotation: Woodrow Wilson and 'Like Writing History with Lightning,'" *Journal of the Gilded Age and Progressive Era* 9, no. 4 (2010): 509–33.

121. On the rebirth of the Ku Klux Klan, see Nancy MacLean, *Behind the Mask of Chivalry: The Making of the Second Ku Klux Klan* (New York: Oxford University Press, 1994); Linda Gordon, *The Second Coming of the KKK: The Ku Klux Klan of the 1920s and the American Political Tradition* (New York: Liveright, 2017).

122. On Haiti and African American reactions to the U.S. occupation, see Brandon R. Byrd, *The Black Republic: African Americans and the Fate of Haiti* (Philadelphia: University of Pennsylvania Press, 2019).

123. Letter from United States President to W. E. B. Du Bois, October 17, 1916, Du Bois Papers, UM-A.

124. "Mr. Hughes," *The Crisis* (November 1916), 12.

125. On the Zimmermann Telegram, see Thomas Boghardt, *The Zimmermann Telegram: Intelligence, Diplomacy, and America's Entry into World War I* (Annapolis, MD: Naval Institute Press, 2012); Barbara W. Tuchman, *The Zimmermann Telegram* (New York: Viking Press, 1958); Neiberg, *The Path to War*, 219–21.

126. Cooper, *Woodrow Wilson*, 362–80.

127. Ibid., 385–87.

128. "A Joint Resolution of April 6, 1917, Public Resolution 65–1, 40 STAT 1, Declaring That a State of War Exists Between the Imperial German Government and the Government and the People of the United States and Making Provision to Prosecute the Same," https://catalog.archives.gov/id/5916620.

129. Credo, Du Bois Papers, UM-A.

130. Arnold Rampersad, *The Art and Imagination of W. E. B. Du Bois* (Cambridge, MA: Harvard University Press, 1976), 160–61.

131. Marable, *W. E. B. Du Bois*, 94–95.

132. "Speech of Frederick Douglass," *Liberator* 33, no. 30 (July 1863); Du Bois deeply admired Frederick Douglass. He publicly and in unpublished poetry eulogized Douglass after his death in 1895. In November 1903, Du Bois agreed to write a biography of Douglass, but the offer was later rescinded and given to Booker T. Washington. A life-size portrait of Douglass, acquired in 1915, hung for years in Du Bois's office and home until he donated it to Fisk University in 1959. See To keep the memory of Frederick Douglass, March 1895; The passing of Douglass, February 20, 1895; George W. Jacobs & Co. to W. E. B. Du Bois, November 11, 1903; George W. Jacobs & Co. to W. E. B. Du Bois, January 25, 1904; W. E. B. Du Bois to S. J. Wright, December 4, 1959, Du Bois Papers, UM-A. On the connections between Douglass's and Du Bois's thought, see David W. Blight, "Up from 'Twoness': Frederick Douglass and the Meaning of W.E.B. Du Bois's Concept of Double Consciousness," *Canadian Review of American Studies* 21, no. 3 (Winter 1990): 301–19.

133. "The World Last Month," *The Crisis* (May 1917), 8. On the English suffrage movement and World War I, see Laura E. Nym Mayhall, *Militant Suffrage Movement: Citizenship and Resistance in Britain, 1860–1930* (New York: Oxford University Press, 2003), chap. 7.

Chapter 2

1. "The World Last Month," *The Crisis* (September 1917), 215.

2. Darius Young, "'The Saving of Black America's Body and White America's Soul': The Lynching of Ell Persons and the Rise of Black Activism in Memphis," in *An Unseen Light: Black Struggles for Freedom in Memphis, Tennessee*, Aram Goudsouzian and Charles W. McKinney Jr., eds. (Lexington: University Press of Kentucky, 2018), 39–40.

3. Supplement to the Crisis, Volume 14, Number 3, July 1917, Du Bois Papers, UM-A.

4. Ibid.
5. Ibid.
6. Ibid.
7. Ibid.
8. "The Huns," *The Independent*, June 2, 1917.
9. Theodore Kornweibel Jr., "Apathy and Dissent: Black America's Negative Responses to World War I," *South Atlantic Quarterly* 80 (Summer 1981): 322–38; Williams, *Torchbearers of Democracy*, 24; Lentz-Smith, *Freedom Struggles*, 38–41.
10. "Loyalty," *The Crisis* (May 1917), 8.
11. Minutes of the Board of Directors, April 9, 1917, NAACP Papers; "N. A. A. C. P. to Meet in Washington," *Baltimore Afro-American*, April 21, 1917.
12. "A Call to Counsel," *The Crisis* (May 1917), 7.
13. "Attitude of the American Negro," *Chicago Defender*, May 26, 1917.
14. "National Conference of N. A. A. C. P. in Washington," *Chicago Defender*, May 12, 1917; "Great Conference," *Washington Bee*, May 26, 1917; Annual Convention, 1917, proposed resolutions, Papers of the NAACP, Part 1: Meetings of the Board of Directors, Records of Annual Conferences, Major Speeches, and Special Reports, Annual Conference Proceedings, 1910–1950.
15. Proposed Resolutions, ca. May 1917, Du Bois Papers, UM-A; "Resolutions of the Washington Conference," *The Crisis* (June 1917), 59–60.
16. "Messages from the Messenger," *The Messenger* (November 1917), 31.
17. "Social Progress," *The Crisis* (November 1916), 30.
18. "Military Training Camp for Colored Men: An Open Letter from Dr. J. E. Spingarn," February 15, 1917, box 95–8, Joel E. Spingarn Papers, Moorland-Spingarn Research Center, Howard University (hereafter cited as MSRC).
19. "No, Thank You, Dr. Spingarn," *Baltimore Afro-American*, February 24, 1917.
20. "'Jim Crow' Training Camps—No!" *Chicago Defender*, April 28, 1917.
21. W. E. B. Du Bois to Joel E. Spingarn, February 26, 1917, Du Bois Papers, UM-A.
22. "Training Camp Deferred," *Savannah Tribune*, April 28, 1917.
23. *Cleveland Gazette*, March 31, 1917.
24. "Officers," *The Crisis* (June 1917), 60–61.
25. Ibid., 61.
26. "Colored Training Camp," *Iowa Bystander*, June 1, 1917.
27. For more on the Des Moines camp and the background of the cadets, see Hal S. Chase, "Struggle for Equality: Fort Des Moines Training Camp for Colored Soldiers, 1917," *Phylon* 39, no. 4 (1978): 297–310; Bernard F. Harris, "Chipping Away at the Bedrock of Racial Intolerance: Fort Des Moines and Black Officer Training, 1917–1918," *Annals of Iowa* 77, no. 3 (2018): 231–62; Adam P. Wilson, *African American Army Officers of World War I: A Vanguard of Equality in War and Beyond* (Jefferson, NC: McFarland, 2015).
28. Located in Nashville and founded in 1876, Meharry was the first medical school for African Americans in the South. See Herbert Aptheker, ed., *The Correspondence of W. E. B. Du Bois* (Amherst: University of Massachusetts Press, 1973), 298.
29. Addie W. Hunton and Kathryn M. Johnson, *Two Colored Women with the American Expeditionary Forces* (Brooklyn, NY: Brooklyn Eagle Press, 1920), 57.

30. Virgil M. Boutté to Emmett J. Scott, January 26, 1918, Thomas M. Gregory Papers, MSRC.

31. Yellin, *Racism in the Nation's Service*, 110, 143.

32. "South Opposes Negro Soldiers," *Baltimore Afro-American*, April 14, 1917.

33. Tasker H. Bliss to Newton Baker, August 24, 1917, 8142–17, RG 165, United States National Archives and Record Administration, College Park, MD (hereafter cited as NARA).

34. Shellum, *Black Soldier in a Buffalo Soldier Regiment*, 248.

35. Charles Young to W. E. B. Du Bois, June 20, 1917, Du Bois Papers, UM-A.

36. W. E. B. Du Bois to Charles Young, June 28, 1917, Young Collection, OHS.

37. W. E. B. Du Bois to Walter Lippmann, June 29, 1917; W. E. B. Du Bois to Oswald Villard, ca, June 29, 1917, Du Bois Papers, UM-A.

38. Shellum, *Black Officer in a Buffalo Soldier Regiment*, 252–54.

39. Ibid., 251–54.

40. Charles Young to W. P. Bayless, August 12, 1917, Young Collection, OHS.

41. For key works on the Great Migration, see Eric Arnesen, *Black Protest and the Great Migration: A Brief History with Documents* (Boston: Bedford/St. Martin's, 2003); Davarian L. Baldwin, *Chicago's New Negroes: Modernity, the Great Migration, and Black Urban Life* (Chapel Hill: University of North Carolina Press, 2007); James R. Grossman, *Land of Hope: Chicago, Black Southerners, and the Great Migration* (Chicago: Chicago University Press, 1989); Carole Marks, *Farewell—We're Good and Gone: The Great Black Migration* (Bloomington: Indiana University Press, 1989); Joe William Trotter, *The Great Migration in Historical Perspective: New Dimensions of Race, Class, and Gender* (Bloomington: Indiana University Press, 1991); Isabel Wilkerson, *The Warmth of Other Suns: The Epic Story of America's Great Migration* (New York: Random House, 2010).

42. "The Migration of Negroes," *The Crisis* (June 1917), 63–66.

43. On the East St. Louis massacre, see Charles Lumpkins, *American Pogrom: The East St. Louis Race Riot and Black Politics* (Athens: Ohio University Press, 2008); Elliott M. Rudwick, *Race Riot at East St. Louis, July 2, 1917* (Carbondale: Southern Illinois University Press, 1964).

44. Lumpkins, *American Pogrom*, chap. 4; Rudwick, *Race Riot at East St. Louis, July 2, 1917*, chap. 5.

45. Memorandum to the Anti-Lynching Committee of W. E. B. Du Bois on East St. Louis, ca. 1917, Du Bois Papers, UM-A.

46. Ida. B. Wells-Barnett, *The East St. Louis Massacre: The Greatest Outrage of the Century* (Chicago: Negro Fellowship Herald Press, 1917). On the life and activism of Ida B. Wells-Barnett, see Mia Bay, *To Tell the Truth Freely: The Life of Ida B. Wells* (New York: Hill and Wang, 2010); James West Davidson, *"They Say": Ida B. Wells and the Reconstruction of Race* (New York: Oxford University Press, 2007); Paula Giddings, *Ida, a Sword Among Lions: Ida B. Wells and the Campaign Against Lynching* (New York: Amistad, 2008); Linda O. McMurry, *To Keep the Waters Troubled: The Life of Ida B. Wells* (New York: Oxford University Press, 1998); Jacqueline Jones Royster, ed., *Southern Horrors and Other Writings: The Anti-Lynching Campaign of Ida B. Wells, 1892–1900* (Boston: Bedford Books, 1997); Sarah L. Silkey, *Black Woman Reformer: Ida B. Wells, Lynching, and Transatlantic Activism* (Athens: University of Georgia Press, 2015).

47. "The Massacre of East St. Louis," *The Crisis* (September 1917), 220.

48. "Awake America," *The Crisis* (September 1917), 216.

49. James Weldon Johnson, *Along This Way: The Autobiography of James Weldon Johnson* (New York: Viking Press, 1933), 321.

50. "Negroes in Protest March in Fifth Av.," *New York Times*, July 29, 1917; "5,000 March in Silent Parade," *Baltimore Afro-American*, August 4, 1917; "Thousands March in Silent Protest," *Chicago Defender*, August 4, 1917.

51. On tensions between Black soldiers and white Texans, see Garna L. Christian, *Black Soldiers in Jim Crow Texas, 1899–1917* (College Station: Texas A&M University Press, 1995).

52. For full accounts of the Houston Riot, see Robert V. Haynes, *A Night of Violence: The Houston Riot of 1917* (Baton Rouge: Louisiana State University Press, 1976); Lentz-Smith, *Freedom Struggles*, chap. 2.

53. "Houston," *The Crisis* (October 1917), 284–85.

54. The execution and subsequent outrage prompted the War Department to institute a new policy that required the Judge Advocate General's Office to review all death sentences and have them approved by the president of the United States. Two subsequent court-martial proceedings resulted in the execution of six additional soldiers, bringing the total to nineteen. Woodrow Wilson granted clemency to ten soldiers sentenced to death. They were instead sentenced to life in prison, along with thirty-one other soldiers. See Haynes, *A Night of Violence*, 278–79.

55. "Thirteen," *The Crisis* (January 1918), 114.

56. Byron Farwell, *Over There: The United States in the Great War, 1917–1918* (New York: W. W. Norton, 1999).

57. "Jubilee," *The Crisis* (February 1918), 163.

58. Du Bois, *In Battle for Peace*, 1.

59. W. E. B. Du Bois to Mary White Ovington, February 26, 1918, Du Bois Papers, UM-A; Lewis, *W. E. B. Du Bois, Vol. 1*, 545–46.

60. W. E. B. Du Bois to Joel E. Spingarn, September 25, 1917, box 1, folder 10, Joel E. Spingarn Collection, James Weldon Johnson Collection in the Yale Collection of American Literature, Beinecke Rare Book and Manuscript Library (hereafter cited as Spingarn Collection, Yale); W. E. B. Du Bois to secretary of war, October 17, 1917, Du Bois Papers, UM-A.

61. "Baker," *The Crisis* (December 1917), 61–62.

62. Emmett J. Scott, *Scott's Official History of the American Negro in the World War* (New York: Underwood & Underwood, 1919), chap. 3.

63. Emmett Jay Scott, "The Negro in the War Department," *The Crisis* (December 1917), 76.

64. U.S. War Department to Mary White Ovington, February 23, 1918, Du Bois Papers, UM-A. Elliott Rudwick writes that even after the Amenia conference, Emmett Scott remained bitter with Du Bois because of his organization of the Niagara Movement in opposition to Booker T. Washington. See Elliott M. Rudwick, *W. E. B. Du Bois: Propagandist of the Negro Protest*, 2nd ed. (Philadelphia: University of Pennsylvania Press, 1968), 186–87.

65. Morale at the camp plummeted when the white commanding officer, Charles Ballou, ordered the men to swallow their pride and not respond to any racial slights, real or

perceived, from the white residents of Des Moines. Further testing the resolve of the officer candidates, the War Department extended the camp for an additional six weeks, causing many highly qualified cadets to take the option of leaving. See Williams, *Torchbearers of Democracy*, 49–52.

66. Joel E. Spingarn to W. E. B. Du Bois, October 17, 1917, Du Bois Papers, UM-A.

67. Williams, *Torchbearers of Democracy*, 52–55, 79–80, 108–10; Jennifer D. Keene, *Doughboys, the Great War, and the Remaking of America* (Baltimore: Johns Hopkins University Press, 2001), 40; Jeanette Keith, *Rich Man's War, Poor Man's Fight: Race, Class, and Power in the Rural South During the First World War* (Chapel Hill: University of North Carolina Press, 2004), 71–73, 119–23.

68. Carol Byerly, *Fever of War: The Influenza Epidemic in the U.S. Army During World War I* (New York: New York University Press, 2005), chap. 3.

69. Scott, *Scott's Official History*, 472; Virgil M. Boutté to Emmett J. Scott, January 26, 1918, Thomas M. Gregory Papers, MSRC.

70. Robert J. Blakely and Marcus Shepard, *Earl B. Dickerson: A Voice for Freedom and Equality* (Evanston, IL: Northwestern University Press, 2006), 29.

71. On the history of the Ninety-Third Division, see Frank E. Roberts, *The American Foreign Legion: Black Soldiers in the 93rd in World War I* (Annapolis, MD: Naval Institute Press, 2004).

72. Emilie Hapgood to W. E. B. Du Bois, October 11, 1917; W. E. B. Du Bois to Emilie Hapgood, October 17, 1917, Fisk University, John Hope and Aurelia E. Franklin Library, Special Collections, W. E. B. Du Bois Collection (hereafter cited as Du Bois Collection, Fisk), box 6, folder 2; Nikki Brown, *Private Politics and Public Voices: Black Women's Activism from World War I to the New Deal* (Bloomington: Indiana University Press, 2006), 37–40; Nina Mjagkij, *Organizing Black America: An Encyclopedia of African American Associations* (New York: Garland, 2001), 129.

73. "To General H. P. McCain," *The Crisis* (February 1918), 165.

74. "Colonel Young," *The Crisis* (March 1918), 218.

75. "The Negro and the War Department," *The Crisis* (May 1918), 7–8.

76. Shellum, *Black Officer in a Buffalo Soldier Regiment*, 259–60.

77. "The Negro and the War Department," *The Crisis* (May 1918), 7–8.

78. "School of Pharmacy (U. of Ill.) Notes," *NARD Journal* 28, no. 6 (1919): 286; Hunton and Johnson, *Two Colored Women*, 57.

79. Boutté diary, *The Black Man and the Wounded World*, Misc., Unidentified, 1918–1919, Du Bois Collection, Fisk, box 34, folder 38.

80. Blakely and Shepard, *Earl B. Dickerson*, 30; Boutté diary, *The Black Man and the Wounded World*, Misc., Unidentified, 1918–1919, Du Bois Collection, Fisk, box 34, folder 38; Hunton and Johnson, *Two Colored Women*, 57–59.

81. Keegan, *The First World War*, 392–414; Edward G. Lengel, *Thunder and Flames: Americans in the Crucible of Combat, 1917–1918* (Lawrence: University Press of Kansas, 2015); Michael S. Nieberg, *The Second Battle of the Marne* (Bloomington: Indiana University Press, 2008).

82. Roberts, *The American Foreign Legion*. On the history of the 369th Infantry Regiment, as well as the proper spelling of Neadom Roberts's name, see Jeffrey T. Sammons and

John H. Morrow Jr., *Harlem's Rattlers and the Great War: The Undaunted 369th Regiment & the African American Quest for Equality* (Lawrence: University Press of Kansas, 2014).

83. "The Black Soldier," *The Crisis* (June 1918), 60.

84. *The Black Man and the Wounded World*, chaps. 13–14, "The 92nd Division," Notes, Du Bois Collection, Fisk, box 29, folder 2.

85. "Captain Boutte," *The Black Man and the Wounded World*, 350th Machine Gun Battalion, Notes, Du Bois Collection, Fisk, box 30, folder 12.

86. Ibid.; Hunton and Johnson, *Two Colored Women*, 59–61; W. E. B. Du Bois, "An Essay Toward a History of the Black Man in the Great War," *The Crisis* (June 1919), 71.

87. J. Clay Smith Jr., *Emancipation: The Making of the Black Lawyer, 1844–1944* (Philadelphia: University of Pennsylvania Press, 1993), 413–14.

88. Leroy H. Godman to Commanding General, Camp Pontanezen, February 11, 1919, Du Bois Papers, UM-A; Hunton and Johnson, *Two Colored Women*, 61.

89. "Captain Boutte," *The Black Man and the Wounded World*, 350th Machine Gun Battalion, Notes, Du Bois Collection, Fisk, box 30, folder 12. Boutté's diary is silent from July 22 to August 11, 1918, the same time period of his arrest and court-martial. It is likely that, while detained, he did not have access to his diary. Boutté diary, *The Black Man and the Wounded World*, Misc., Unidentified, 1918–1919, Du Bois Collection, Fisk, box 34, folder 38; Du Bois, "An Essay Toward . . . ," 71.

90. Memorandum to Officers from Major General Ballou, July 23, 1918, in John Brother Cade, *Twenty-Two Months with "Uncle Sam": Being the Experiences and Observations of a Negro Student who Volunteered for Military Service Against the Central Powers from June, 1917 to April, 1919* (N.p.: Robinson-Cofer, 1929), 51; Williams, *Torchbearers of Democracy*, 135; Arthur E. Barbeau and Florette Henri, *The Unknown Soldiers: African-American Troops in World War I* (New York: Da Capo Press, 1996), 146–48.

91. Letter from W. E. B. Du Bois to U.S. War Department, March 4, 1918, Du Bois Papers, UM-A.

92. Mark Ellis, *Race, War and Surveillance: African Americans and the United States Government During World War I* (Bloomington: Indiana University Press, 2001), 104–106; Ross, *J. E. Spingarn and the Rise of the NAACP, 1911–1939*, 97–98.

93. See Mark Ellis, "Joel Spingarn's 'Constructive Programme' and the Wartime Antilynching Bill of 1918," *Journal of Policy History* 4, no. 2 (Spring 1992): 134–61.

94. Joel E. Spingarn to Amy Spingarn, June 9, 1918, folder 580, box 95–15, Joel E. Spingarn Papers, MSRC; Ellis, *Race, War and Surveillance*, 161; Spingarn Papers.

95. Lewis, *W. E. B. Du Bois, Vol. 1*, 19–22, 374–75, 530.

96. Board of Directors minutes, May 13, 1918, Papers of the NAACP.

97. Memorandum for Dr. Du Bois, May 22, 1918, Du Bois Papers, UM-A.

98. The memo to Studin was in fact crafted by Joel Spingarn. Churchill to Charles H. Studin, June 3, 1918; Charles H. Studin to Churchill, June 12, 1918, 10218–139, MID, RG 165, NARA.

99. At their June 4 meeting, Spingarn also likely informed Du Bois that federal agents in New York were being tasked with investigating the finances of *The Crisis* and where its support was coming from. See A. B. Bielaski to Charles De Woody, June 4, 1918, 10218–139, MID, RG 165, NARA.

100. Du Bois, *Dusk of Dawn*, in *Writings*, 741.

101. Mark Ellis, "'Closing Ranks' and 'Seeking Honors': W. E. B. Du Bois in World War I," *Journal of American History* 79, no. 1 (1992): 108.

102. Ellis, *Race, War and Surveillance*, 162. On wartime coercion, see Christopher Capozzola, *Uncle Sam Wants You: World War I and the Making of the Modern American Citizen* (New York: Oxford University Press, 2008). For discussion of federal surveillance of *The Crisis*, see Ellis, *Race, War and Surveillance*; William G. Jordan, *Black Newspapers & America's War for Democracy, 1914–1920* (Chapel Hill: University of North Carolina Press, 2001); Theodore Kornweibel, *"Investigate Everything": Federal Efforts to Compel Black Loyalty During World War I* (Bloomington: Indiana University Press, 2002), chap. 5.

103. Emmett J. Scott to George Creel, June 5, 1918, 10214–154; Joel E. Spingarn to M. Churchill, June 22, 1918, 10218–154, MID, RG 165, NARA; Ellis, *Race, War and Surveillance*, 147.

104. For full list of attendees, see Conference of Colored Editors, Washington, DC, June 19 to 21, 1918, List of Conferees, 10218–154, MID, RG 165, NARA.

105. Jordan, *Black Newspapers & America's War for Democracy, 1914–1920*, 122–29.

106. Address to the Government, ca. June 19, 1918, Du Bois Papers, UM-A.

107. Address to the Committee on Public Information, June 21, 1918, 10218–154, MID, RG 165, NARA; "Help Us to Help," *The Crisis* (August 1918). The conferees also wrote an additional "Bill of Particulars," fourteen in number to mirror Wilson's January "Fourteen Points" speech, which was submitted privately to Churchill. The list of demands included many that Du Bois had previously called for in *The Crisis*, such as anti-lynching legislation, additional Black officers, restoring Charles Young to active duty, and clemency for the Houston soldiers. Du Bois, as he later informed Spingarn, drafted the resolutions, which were "adopted unanimously with only verbal corrections." Conference of Colored Editors, Washington, DC, June 19 to 21, 1918, Bill of Particulars to Be Submitted Privately to Bureau Heads in Washington, 10218–154, MID, RG 165, NARA; W. E. B. Du Bois to Joel E. Spingarn, June 24, 1918, box 1, folder 11, Spingarn Collection, Yale; Jordan, *Black Newspapers & America's War for Democracy, 1914–1920*, 122–27.

108. W. E. B. Du Bois to Marlborough Churchill, June 24, 1918, *The Black Man and the Wounded World*, General, Du Bois Collection, Fisk, box 14, folder 35.

109. "Close Ranks," *The Crisis* (July 1918), 111.

110. Letter from W. E. B. Du Bois to Francis E. Young, August 8, 1918, Du Bois Papers, UM-A; Lewis, *W. E. B. Du Bois, Vol. 1*, 555–56; "A Momentous Proposal," *The Crisis* (September 1918), 215–16.

111. The timing and intent of "Close Ranks" has been a matter of historical debate. Arnold Rampersad characterizes "Close Ranks" as one of the many "pragmatic compromises" Du Bois made in his career, reflecting "the delicate balance he maintained between 'visions of beauty, order, and perfection' and the cold reality of American power." In a similar vein, William Jordan argues that the editorial was consistent with Du Bois's wartime accommodationist approach, and that of the Black press more broadly, to questions of race and loyalty. Elliott Rudwick, although in much harsher terms than Jordan, likewise views "Close Ranks" and Du Bois's activities during the war more broadly as accommodationist. Mark Ellis asserts that "Close Ranks" was written with

the captaincy commission in mind and intended to assuage the concerns of military intelligence officials. David Levering Lewis, like Ellis, argues that Du Bois wrote "Close Ranks" to "consummate the bargain" of his deal with Spingarn and the War Department. See Rampersad, *The Art and Imagination of W. E. B. Du Bois*, 201; William Jordan, "'The Damnable Dilemma': African-American Accommodation and Protest During World War I," *Journal of American History* 81, no. 4 (1995): 1562–83; Rudwick, *W. E. B. Du Bois*, 193–207; Ellis, "'Closing Ranks' and 'Seeking Honors'"; Mark Ellis, "W. E. B. Du Bois and the Formation of Black Opinion in World War I: A Comment on 'The Damnable Dilemma,'" *Journal of American History* 81, no. 4 (1995): 1584–90; Lewis, *W. E. B. Du Bois, Vol. 1*, 555.

112. Newton Baker to Colonel Marlborough Churchill, June 26, 1918, box 115, folder 115, Emmett J. Scott Papers, Beulah M. Davis Special Collections Department, Morgan State University (hereafter cited as Scott Papers, MSU).

113. Joel Spingarn to Churchill, July 6, 1918, 10218–154, MID, RG 165, NARA.

114. In private correspondence with Mary White Ovington regarding the commission prior to the July 8, 1918, board meeting, Du Bois apparently expressed his concerns about how he might, as Ovington recounted back to him, "go into the work expecting it to be one thing and find that it had to be quite another." Du Bois was, in fact, not entirely clear what his position would entail, writing to Spingarn that his plans remained "still a little hazy in my mind." Mary White Ovington to W. E. B. Du Bois, July 10, 1918, Du Bois Papers, UM-A; W. E. B. Du Bois to Joel E. Spingarn, June 28, 1918, box 1, folder 11, Spingarn Collection, Yale.

115. NAACP Minutes of the Meeting of the Board of Directors, July 8, 1918, Du Bois Papers, UM-A.

116. W. E. B. Du Bois to J. E. Spingarn, July 9, 1918, Du Bois Papers, UM-A.

117. J. E. Spingarn to Charles H. Studin, July 10, 1918, Du Bois Papers, UM-A.

118. Du Bois, *Dusk of Dawn*, in *Writings*, 740.

119. Ellis, "'Closing Ranks' and 'Seeking Honors,'" 110.

120. "The Outer Pocket," *The Crisis* (August 1918), 218.

121. "Du Bois Editorial Causes Big Stir," *Chicago Defender*, July 20, 1918.

122. Supportive notes arrived from George W. J. Brown, Mary White Ovington, Ida Gibbs Hunt, Georgia Johnson, George G. Bradford, and H. E. Baker. See Du Bois Papers, UM-A.

123. Archibald S. Pinkett to W. E. B. Du Bois, July 11, 1918, Du Bois Papers, UM-A.

124. W. E. B. Du Bois to John Hope, July 12, 1918, Du Bois Papers, UM-A.

125. John Hope to W. E. B. Du Bois, July 22, 1918, Du Bois Papers, UM-A.

126. W. E. B. Du Bois to J. E. Spingarn, July 12, 1918, Du Bois Papers, UM-A.

127. Du Bois provided Spingarn with a detailed accounting of his personal finances, insinuating that his acceptance of the commission and move to Washington, DC, would be cost prohibitive. W. E. B. Du Bois to Joel E. Spingarn, July 19, 1918, box 1, folder 11, Spingarn Collection, Yale.

128. J. E. Spingarn to W. E. B. Du Bois, July 16, 1918, Du Bois Papers, UM-A.

129. W. E. B. Du Bois to Joel E. Spingarn, July 19, 1918, box 1, folder 11, Spingarn Collection, Yale; Du Bois Papers, UM-A; Lewis, *W. E. B. Du Bois, Vol. 1*, 559.

130. Byron Gunner to W. E. B. Du Bois, July 16, 1918, Du Bois Papers, UM-A.

131. Byron Gunner to W. E. B. Du Bois, July 25, 1918, Du Bois Papers, UM-A.

132. *Boston Guardian*, July 20, 1918.

133. *Cleveland Gazette*, July 27, 1918.

134. Hubert Harrison, "The Descent of Dr. Du Bois," in Jeffrey B. Perry, ed., *A Hubert Harrison Reader* (Middletown, CT: Wesleyan University Press, 2001), 170–72.

135. In his July 16 note to Du Bois, Spingarn wrote, "The editorials in the August Crisis will make your policy clearer and pave the way for a wider realization of your programme and your new opportunity." J. E. Spingarn to W. E. B. Du Bois, July 16, 1918, Du Bois Papers, UM-A.

136. "A Philosophy in Time of War," *The Crisis* (August 1918), 164–65.

137. Joel E. Spingarn to Amy Spingarn, July 20, 1918, family letters, Joel E. Spingarn Papers, New York Public Libray (hereafter Joel E. Spingarn Papers, NYPL).

138. Ellis, "'Closing Ranks' and 'Seeking Honors,'" 115–18.

139. Robert Russa Moton to Woodrow Wilson, June 15, 1918; Woodrow Wilson to Robert Russa Moton, June 18, 1918; Secretary of War to Woodrow Wilson, July 19, 1918; From the Committee on Public Information, July 26, 1919, 10218–154, MID, RG 165, NARA.

140. Marlborough Churchill to Hunt, July 30, 1918, box 7, folder 4, Joel E. Spingarn Papers, NYPL; Marlborough Churchill to Joel E. Spingarn, July 30, 1918, box 7, folder 4, Joel E. Spingarn Papers, NYPL.

141. Colonel Marlborough Churchill to W. E. B. Du Bois, July 30, 1918, *The Black Man and the Wounded World*, General, Du Bois Collection, Fisk, box 14, folder 35.

142. J. E. Spingarn to W. E. B. Du Bois, July 30, 1918, Du Bois Papers, UM-A.

143. W. E. B. Du Bois to J. E. Spingarn, August 7, 1918, box 1, folder 11, Spingarn Collection, Yale.

144. Du Bois, *Dusk of Dawn*, in *Writings*, 743.

145. "A Momentous Proposal," *The Crisis* (September 1918), 215–16.

146. "Our Special Grievances," *The Crisis* (September 1918), 216–17.

147. "The Reward," *The Crisis* (September 1918), 217.

Chapter 3

1. W. E. B. Du Bois, "The Black Man in the Revolution of 1914–1918," *The Crisis* (March 1919), 218.

2. Boutté Diary, *The Black Man and the Wounded World*, Misc., Unidentified, 1918–1919, Du Bois Collection, Fisk, box 34, folder 38.

3. William Colson, "The Failure of the 92nd Division," *The Messenger* (September 1919).

4. On the Meuse-Argonne campaign, see Paul F. Braim, *The Test of Battle: The American Expeditionary Forces in the Meuse-Argonne Campaign* (Newark: University of Delaware Press, 1987); Robert H. Ferrell, *America's Deadliest Battle: Meuse-Argonne, 1918* (Lawrence: University Press of Kansas, 2007); Edward G. Lengel, ed., *A Companion to the Meuse-Argonne Campaign* (Chichester, UK: John Wiley & Sons, 2014); Douglas V. Mastriano, *Thunder in the Argonne: A New History of America's Greatest Battle* (Lexington: University Press of Kentucky, 2018). On the impact of the influenza pandemic on the AEF and in the Meuse-Argonne specifically, see Byerly, *Fever of War*, chap. 4.

5. On the 368th in the Meuse-Argonne, see Robert Ferrell, *Unjustly Dishonored: An African American Division in World War I* (Columbia: University of Missouri Press, 2011), chap. 2;

Chad Williams, "African Americans in the Meuse-Argonne Offensive," in Lengel, ed., *A Companion to the Meuse-Argonne Campaign*.

6. Major J. N. Merrill to Commanding Officer, 368th Infantry, October 3, 1918, in *History of Negro Troops in the World War*, Army War College, Historical Section (1942), appendix 33, United States Army Military History Institute.

7. Williams, "African Americans in the Meuse-Argonne Offensive," 170–71.

8. Scott, *Scott's Official History*, in chap. 10; on the Ninety-Second Division's official combat record, see American Battle Monuments Commission, *92d Division: Summary of Operations in the World War* (Washington, DC: United States Government Printing Office, 1944).

9. Boutté diary, *The Black Man and the Wounded World*, Misc., Unidentified, 1918–1919, Du Bois Collection, Fisk, box 34, folder 38.

10. Lewis, *W. E. B. Du Bois, Vol. 1*, 476–77.

11. J. E. Spingarn to W. E. B. Du Bois, October 9, 1918, Du Bois Papers, UM-A.

12. Minutes of the Meeting of the Board of Directors, October 14, 1918, Du Bois Papers, UM-A.

13. Ibid.

14. On the volatile relationship with Villard and tensions surrounding Du Bois's control of *The Crisis*, see Lewis, *W. E. B. Du Bois, Vol. 1*, 395–97, 466–500.

15. Du Bois, *Dusk of Dawn*, 744.

16. The literary scholar Keith Byerman identifies a consistent pattern of "the personal, the intellectual, and the political" intersecting in Du Bois's work. Keith E. Byerman, *Seizing the Word: History, Art, and Self in the Work of W. E. B. Du Bois* (Athens: University of Georgia Press, 1994), xi.

17. On Du Bois's approach to history, see Herbert Aptheker, "Du Bois as Historian," *Negro History Bulletin* 32, no. 4 (1969): 6–16; David W. Blight, "W. E. B. Du Bois and the Struggle for American Historical Memory," in Geneviève Fabre and Robert O'Meally, eds., *History and Memory in African-American Culture* (New York: Oxford University Press, 1994); Robert Gregg, "Giant Steps: W. E. B. Du Bois and the Historical Enterprise," in Michael B. Katz and Thomas J. Sugrue, *W.E.B. Du Bois, Race, and the City: The Philadelphia Negro and Its Legacy* (Philadelphia: University of Pennsylvania Press, 1998).

18. On Du Bois's clashes with Villard and tensions related to *The Crisis*, see Lewis, *W. E. B. Du Bois, Vol. 1*, chap. 17.

19. Minutes of the Meeting of the Board of Directors, October 14, 1918, Du Bois Papers, UM-A.

20. Ibid.

21. Woodson was profiled along with George Edmund Haynes, who the same year received a doctorate in sociology from Columbia University. "Two Doctors of Philosophy," *The Crisis* (July 1912), 119–20.

22. "The Journal of Negro History," *The Crisis* (December 1916), 61. On Woodson's biographical background and approach to the study and teaching of African American history, see Jarvis R. Givens, *Fugitive Pedagogy: Carter G. Woodson and the Art of Black Teaching* (Cambridge, MA: Harvard University Press, 2021); Jacqueline Googin, *Carter G. Woodson: A Life in Black History* (Baton Rouge: Louisiana State University Press, 1993).

23. Givens, *Fugitive Pedagogy*, chaps. 1–2. Woodson's less than friendly feelings toward Du Bois may also have stemmed from their differing experiences at Harvard. Whereas

Du Bois maintained a long-standing friendship with his Harvard mentor Albert Bushnell Hart, Woodson had a much less positive relationship with Hart during his doctoral studies. Additionally, Woodson encountered difficulty completing his dissertation and ultimately never published it, unlike Du Bois, whose thesis "The Suppression of the African Slave Trade" inaugurated the Harvard Historical Studies series. See Googin, *Carter G. Woodson*, 22–29.

24. W. E. B. Du Bois to John Hope, March 26, 1925, Du Bois Papers, UM-A; August Meier and Elliott Rudwick, *Black History and the Historical Profession, 1915–1980* (Urbana: University of Illinois Press, 1986), 12–13.

25. "Memoranda," *The Black Man and the Wounded World*, Proposed Editorial Board, Du Bois Collection, Fisk, box 14, folder 32.

26. Carter G. Woodson to W. E. B. Du Bois, October 27, 1918, *The Black Man and the Wounded World*, Proposed Editorial Board, Du Bois Collection, Fisk, box 14, folder 32.

27. Goggin, *Carter G. Woodson*, 43; Carter G. Woodson to L. Hollingsworth Wood, October 14, 1918, box 10, L. Hollingsworth Wood Papers, Quaker and Special Collections, Haverford College (hereafter cited as Wood Papers, Haverford); Carter G. Woodson to Dr. R. E. Jones, October 14, 1918, box 114, folder 4, Scott Papers, MSU. Robert Elijah Jones was an Episcopal bishop in New Orleans and editor of the *Southwestern Christian Advocate*.

28. Carter G. Woodson to W. E. B. Du Bois, October 27, 1918, *The Black Man and the Wounded World*, Proposed Editorial Board, Du Bois Collection, Fisk, box 14, folder 32.

29. W. E. B. Du Bois to Carter G. Woodson, October 30, 1918, *The Black Man and the Wounded World*, Proposed Editorial Board, Du Bois Collection, Fisk, box 14, folder 32.

30. "Two Doctors of Philosophy," *The Crisis* (July 1912), 119–20; Haynes's doctoral dissertation, "The Negro at Work in New York City," was published by Columbia University Press in 1912 as part of the Studies in History, Economics and Public Law series.

31. "Dr. George E. Haynes Appointed Adviser to Department of Labor," *Chicago Defender*, May 4, 1918; George Edmund Haynes, "Effect of War Conditions on Negro Labor," *Proceedings of the Academy of Political Science in the City of New York* 8, no. 2 (1919): 165–78.

32. W. E. B. Du Bois to Carter G. Woodson, October 30, 1918, *The Black Man and the Wounded World*, Proposed Editorial Board, Du Bois Collection, Fisk, box 14, folder 32.

33. Emmett Scott to W. E. B. Du Bois, August 13, 1918, Du Bois Papers, UM-A.

34. Correspondence with Mr. Scott, Memoranda, *The Black Man and the Wounded World*, Proposed Editorial Board, Du Bois Collection, Fisk, box 14, folder 30.

35. W. E. B. Du Bois to Emmett J. Scott, November 8, 1918, *The Black Man and the Wounded World*, Proposed Editorial Board, Du Bois Collection, Fisk, box 14, folder 30.

36. Carter G. Woodson to W. E. B. Du Bois, November 9, 1918, *The Black Man and the Wounded World*, Proposed Editorial Board, Du Bois Collection, Fisk, box 14, folder 32. Jacqueline Goggin offers detail on Woodson's financial difficulties with the upstart ASNLH and various efforts to both secure funding and promote the organization. See Goggin, *Carter G. Woodson*, 36–44.

37. Emmett J. Scott to W. E. B. Du Bois, November 10, 1918, *The Black Man and the Wounded World*, Proposed Editorial Board, Du Bois Collection, Fisk, box 14, folder 30. Scott made a similar revelation in a conversation with George Foster Peabody about the competing war history projects and Du Bois's invitation. See Lewis, *W. E. B. Du Bois, Vol. 1*, 697n61.

38. On the performance of the Ninety-Third Division, see Roberts, *The American Foreign Legion*; Barbeau and Henri, *The Unknown Soldiers*, chap. 7.

39. Barbeau and Henri, *The Unknown Soldiers*, chap. 6; Scott, *Scott's Official History*, chap. 12; Williams, *Torchbearers of Democracy*, 202.

40. Williams, *Torchbearers of Democracy*, 135.

41. Diary entry, October 25, 1918, box 2, Diary Book #9, Robert Lee Bullard Papers, Manuscript Division, Library of Congress, Washington, DC.

42. Barbeau and Henri, *The Unknown Soldiers*, 137; Memorandum, August 21, 1918, box 44, 92nd Division Headquarters decimal file, RG 120, NARA; Memorandum, R. H. Leavitt to Commanding Generals, 183rd and 184th Brigades, August 22, 1918, box 44, 92nd Division Headquarters decimal file, RG 120, NARA.

43. Fred L. Borch, "Adam E. Patterson: The First African-American Judge Advocate," *Army Lawyer* (February 2015), 1–2; Felix James, "Robert Russa Moton and the Whispering Gallery," *Journal of Negro History* 62, no. 3 (July 1977): 236–37; Letter from Adam E. Patterson to National Association for the Advancement of Colored People, March 14, 1919, Du Bois Papers, UM-A.

44. Williams, *Torchbearers of Democracy*, 189–90.

45. Lewis, *W. E. B. Du Bois, Vol. 1*, 563–64.

46. Ibid., chaps. 15 and 17.

47. Minutes of the Meeting of the Board of Directors, November 11, 1918, NAACP Papers.

48. W. E. B. Du Bois to George Peabody, August 28, 1918, Du Bois Papers, UM-A.

49. NAACP Minutes of the Meeting of the Board of Directors, September 9, 1918, Du Bois Papers, UM-A.

50. Du Bois used the influence of Peabody and Philip Whitwell Wilson of the London *Daily News* to forward the memorandum to the American Commission to Negotiate Peace. Philip Whitwell Wilson to W. E. B. Du Bois, September 26, 1918, Du Bois Papers, UM-A.

51. "The Future of Africa," *The Crisis* (January 1919), 119–21.

52. "The Future of Africa," *The Crisis* (January 1918), 114.

53. Memorandum on the future of Africa, November 19, 1918, Du Bois Papers, UM-A.

54. Minutes of the Board of Directors of the NAACP, November 11, 1918, Du Bois Papers, UM-A.

55. Clarence G. Contee, "Du Bois, the NAACP, and the Pan-African Congress of 1919," *Journal of Negro History* 57, no. 1 (1972): 15–16.

56. Report of the Pan-African Congress, ca. August 1900; To the nations of the world, ca. 1900, Du Bois Papers, UM-A; Lewis, *W. E. B. Du Bois, Vol. 1*, 248–51. On Henry Sylvester Williams, see Marika Sherwood, *Origins of Pan-Africanism: Henry Sylvester Williams, Africa, and the African Diaspora* (New York: Taylor and Francis, 2012).

57. Courtney Young, "Hart, Albert Bushnell," in Gerald Horne and Mary Young, *W.E.B. Du Bois: An Encyclopedia* (Westport, CT: Greenwood Press, 2001), 97–98; Gregg, "Giant Steps."

58. Albert Bushnell Hart to W. E. B. Du Bois, November 15, 1918, Du Bois Papers, UM-A.

59. Charles Young to W. E. B. Du Bois, November 30, 1918, Du Bois Papers, UM-A.

60. W. T. B. Williams to W. E. B. Du Bois, December 9, 1918, Du Bois Papers, UM-A.

61. Evarts Greene to W. E. B. Du Bois, November 19, 1918, Du Bois Papers, UM-A.

62. NYU Dean of the Faculties to W. E. B. Du Bois, November 18, 1918, *The Black Man and the Wounded World*, General, Du Bois Collection, Fisk, box 14, folder 34.

63. Stanford University to W. E. B. Du Bois, November 21, 1918, Du Bois Papers, UM-A.

64. Meier and Rudwick, *Black History and the Historical Profession, 1915–1980*, 77–78.

65. Herbert D. Foster to W. E. B. Du Bois, December 17, 1918, Du Bois Papers, UM-A; Kenneth R. Manning, *Black Apollo of Science: The Life of Ernest Everett Just* (New York: Oxford University Press, 1983).

66. H. Morse Stephens to W. E. B. Du Bois, December 1, 1918, Du Bois Papers, UM-A.

67. Charles Homer Haskins to W. E. B. Du Bois, November 20, 1918, Du Bois Papers, UM-A.

68. W. E. B. Du Bois to Carter G. Woodson, November 12, 1918, *The Black Man and the Wounded World*, Proposed Editorial Board, Du Bois Collection, Fisk, box 14, folder 32.

69. Carter G. Woodson to W. E. B. Du Bois, November 16, 1918, *The Black Man and the Wounded World*, Proposed Editorial Board, Du Bois Collection, Fisk, box 14, folder 32.

70. "Immediate Release. Negro's Part in the Great War to Be Told," November 1918, Du Bois Papers, UM-A.

71. Du Bois had written to Peabody on November 12, informing him of his conversations with Scott and Woodson. W. E. B. Du Bois to George Foster Peabody, November 12, 1918, Du Bois Papers, UM-A.

72. W. E. B. Du Bois to Villard, Peabody, and Wood, November 16, 1918, *The Black Man and the Wounded World*, Proposed Editorial Board, Du Bois Collection, Fisk, box 14, folder 31.

73. Ibid.

74. Carter G. Woodson to L. Hollingsworth Wood, November 23, 1918, box 10, Wood Papers, Haverford.

75. Moorland helped Woodson found the Association for the Study of Negro Life and History in 1915.

76. Jesse Moorland to Du Bois, November 25, 1918, *The Black Man and the Wounded World*, Proposed Editorial Board, Du Bois Collection, Fisk, box 14, folder 29.

77. Du Bois to Moorland, November 29, 1918, *The Black Man and the Wounded World*, Proposed Editorial Board, Du Bois Collection, Fisk, box 14, folder 29.

78. W. E. B. Du Bois to Villard, Peabody, and Wood, November 16, 1918, *The Black Man and the Wounded World*, Proposed Editorial Board, Du Bois Collection, Fisk, box 14, folder 31.

79. "The Denial of Passports," *The Crisis* (February 1919), 237–38.

80. On April 14, 1919, Du Bois recounted his activities surrounding his trip to France and the Pan-African Congress, beginning with the war history book. Notes on the Paris Peace Conference and Pan African Congress, April 14, 1919, Du Bois Papers, UM-A.

81. Ibid.

82. The Military Intelligence Branch (MIB) was redesignated as the Military Intelligence Division (MID) in August 1918. Kornweibel, *"Investigate Everything,"* 236.

83. Walter Loving to Colonel Masteller, April 28, 1919, 10218–279, MID, RG 165, NARA; Ellis, *Race, War and Surveillance*, 187–88.

84. Emmett Scott to Frank Parker Stockbridge, November 29, 1918, *The Black Man and the Wounded World*, General, Du Bois Collection, Fisk, box 15, folder 3.

85. Ibid. Scott also sent Du Bois a letter from Stockbridge, likely outlining their proposed arrangement regarding the book. Emmett Scott to W. E. B. Du Bois, November 29, 1918, *The Black Man and the Wounded World*, Proposed Editorial Board, Du Bois Collection, Fisk, box 14, folder 30.

86. Emmett Scott to W. E. B. Du Bois, November 29, 1918, Du Bois Papers, UM-A.

87. Memo, November 29, 1918, *The Black Man and the Wounded World*, Proposed Editorial Board, Du Bois Collection, Fisk, box 14, folder 30.

88. Invoice from Du Bois to NAACP is dated November 29. However, the timing of Scott's messages to Du Bois indicates that he had to be in Washington, DC, on November 30. Invoice from W. E. B. Du Bois to the NAACP, November 29, 1918, Du Bois Papers, UM-A; Notes on the Paris Peace Conference and Pan African Congress, April 14, 1919, Du Bois Papers, UM-A; Loving to Masteller, April 28, 1919, 10218–279, MID, RG 165, NARA.

89. Loving to Masteller, April 28, 1919, 10218–279, MID, RG 165, NARA.

90. W. E. B. Du Bois to F. P. Stockbridge, November 30, 1918, Du Bois Papers, UM-A.

91. Notes on the Paris Peace Conference and Pan African Congress, April 14, 1919, Du Bois Papers, UM-A.

92. Memo, November 29, 1918, *The Black Man and the Wounded World*, Proposed Editorial Board, Du Bois Collection, Fisk, box 14, folder 30.

93. W. E. B. Du Bois passport application, Roll #: 645; Volume #: Roll 0645-Certificates: 49500–49749, 30 Nov 1918–02 Dec 1918, NARA, Ancestry.com, *U.S., Passport Applications, 1795–1925*; Notes on the Paris Peace Conference and Pan African Congress, April 14, 1919, Du Bois Papers, UM-A.

94. Emmett J. Scott to George Creel, November 30, 1918, box 115, folder 3, Scott Papers, MSU.

95. Ellis, *Race, War and Surveillance*, 188–89.

96. W. E. B. Du Bois to Woodrow Wilson, November 27, 1918, Du Bois Papers; Ellis, *Race, War and Surveillance*, 189; Lewis, *W. E. B. Du Bois, Vol. 1*, 561–62.

97. "Robert Moton," *The Crisis* (May 1919), 9–10.

98. Robert R. Moton to Woodrow Wilson, June 15, 1918; Woodrow Wilson to Robert R. Moton, June 18, 1918; Robert R. Moton to Woodrow Wilson, June 25, 1918; Newton Baker to Woodrow Wilson, July 19, 1918, 10218–154, Woodrow Wilson Statement on "Mob Action," July 25, 1918, MID, RG 165, NARA.

99. Moton to Scott, July 27, 1918, box 1, RG 107. For Moton's influence, see correspondence, box 1, RG 107, NARA.

100. Gerald W. Patton, *War and Race: The Black Officer in the American Military, 1915–1941* (Westport, CT: Greenwood Press, 1981), 103.

101. Notes on the Paris Peace Conference and Pan African Congress, April 14, 1919, Du Bois Papers, UM-A.

102. "A Proposed History and Survey of the American Negro During the Great War," Du Bois Papers, UM-A; Handwritten timeline on the back of "A War History," *The Black Man and the Wounded World*, Misc. Entries Notes, Du Bois Collection, Fisk, box 31, folder 2; Ellis, *Race, War and Surveillance*, 188.

103. W. E. B. Du Bois to F. P. Stockbridge, December 2, 1918, Du Bois Papers, UM-A.

104. Oswald Garrison Villard to W. E. B. Du Bois, November 26, 1918, Du Bois Papers, UM-A.

105. Minutes of the Meeting of the Board of Directors, December 9, 1918; W. E. B. Du Bois to Jessie Redmon Fauset, September 7, 1918, Du Bois Papers, UM-A.

106. Minutes NAACP Board of Directors, December 9, 1918, Du Bois Papers, UM-A.

107. "War History," *The Crisis* (December 1918), 61–62.

108. "My Mission," *The Crisis* (May 1919), 7.

Chapter 4

1. "The Fields of Battle," *The Crisis* (March 1919), 268.

2. Memo, Procedure—To Secure passport by accredited newspaper man to France, November 29, 1918, *The Black Man and the Wounded World*, chap. 16, "The 368th Regiment," Notes, Du Bois Collection, Fisk, box 29, folder 13.

3. Notes on the Paris Peace Conference and Pan African Congress, April 14, 1919, Du Bois Papers, UM-A.

4. "Official Press Representatives to Peace Conference at Paris," *Orizaba Abaziro*, December 8, 1918, Du Bois Papers, UM-A.

5. "Letters from Dr. Du Bois," *The Crisis* (February 1919), 163. Creel may have contacted Emmett Scott to confirm that Du Bois had indeed received approval to travel. Notes on the Paris Peace Conference and Pan African Congress, April 14, 1919, Du Bois Papers, UM-A.

6. George Creel, American Committee on Public Information to Representatives of the Allied Governments and others whom it may concern, November 27, 1918, Du Bois Papers, UM-A.

7. "Newspaper Writers Sail," *New York Times*, December 2, 1918.

8. "Official Press Representatives to Peace Conference at Paris," *Orizaba Abaziro*, December 8, 1918, Du Bois Papers; Robert Russa Moton, *Finding a Way Out* (New York: Doubleday, 1920), 253; James, "Robert Russa Moton and the Whispering Gallery," 235.

9. Robert Russa Moton, "Negro Troops in France," *Southern Workman* 48 (May 1919): 220.

10. "Letters from Dr. Du Bois," *The Crisis* (February 1919), 163–64.

11. Ann Hagedorn, *Savage Peace: Hope and Fear in America, 1919* (New York: Simon & Schuster, 2007), 19–21.

12. "Delegation Is Complete," *New York Times*, November 28, 1918; Cooper, *Woodrow Wilson*, 456–58.

13. On the appropriation of Wilson's ideas of "self-determination," see Erez Manela, *The Wilsonian Moment: Self-Determination and the International Origins of Anticolonial Nationalism* (Oxford: Oxford University Press, 2007); Woodrow Wilson, "Sixth Annual Message," December 2, 1918, American Presidency Project, www.presidency.ucsb.edu/documents/sixth-annual-message-6.

14. David Levering Lewis describes Du Bois and Wilson, regarding their approach to the peace conference and postwar aspirations, as "kindred intellects, both bearers of ecumenical schemes that were visionary for the times." Lewis, *W. E. B. Du Bois, Vol. 1*, 564.

15. "Letters from Dr. Du Bois," *The Crisis* (February 1919), 163–64.

16. Train ticket, December 10, 1918, *The Black Man and the Wounded World*, chap. 15, "The 365th, 366th, and 367th Regiments," Notes, Du Bois Collection, Fisk, box 29, folder 5.

17. "Letters from Dr. Du Bois," *The Crisis* (February 1919), 163–64; Moton, "Negro Troops in France," 219–20.

18. "Letters from Dr. Du Bois," *The Crisis* (February 1919), 163–64; Moton, "Negro Troops in France," 220.

19. James, "Robert Russa Moton and the Whispering Gallery"; "The Black Man in the Revolution of 1914–1918," *The Crisis* (March 1919), 218.

20. Leroy Davis, *A Clashing of the Soul: John Hope and the Dilemma of African American Leadership and Black Higher Education in the Early Twentieth Century* (Athens: University of Georgia Press, 1998), 239–46; Headquarters, Ninety-Second Division, December 16, 1918, box 62, Du Bois Collection, Fisk.

21. John Hope to Lugenia Hope, December 15, 1918, reel 14, John and Lugenia Hope Papers, Yale University.

22. Ridgely Torrence, *The Story of John Hope* (New York: Arno Press, 1969), 214; John Hope to Lugenia Hope, December 16, 1918, reel 14, John and Lugenia Hope Papers, Yale University.

23. William M. Slowe to W. E. B. Du Bois, December 18, 1918, *The Black Man and the Wounded World*, General, Du Bois Collection, Fisk, box 15, folder 3.

24. Du Bois to NAACP, "Bulletin #3," part 1, box 1: C385, folder 2, Papers of the National Association for the Advancement of Colored People, Library of Congress (hereafter cited as NAACP Papers, LOC).

25. Unlike Robert Moton, Du Bois lacked the necessary government connections to secure an official pass to visit Black troops. See Headquarters, Ninety-Second Division, December 16, 1918, Du Bois Collection, Fisk. Du Bois first contacted the AEF general John Pershing on December 9, 1918, for a visitors pass as well as an interview. General John J. Pershing to W. E. B. Du Bois, January 16, 1919, *The Black Man and the Wounded World*, General, Du Bois Collection, Fisk, box 15, folder 1; Loving to Masteller, May 2, 1919, MID, 10218–134, RG 165, NARA; American Battlefield Monuments Commission, *92nd Division*, Summary of Operations in the World War (Washington, DC: United States Government Printing Office, 1944), 28; Notes on the Paris Peace Conference and Pan African Congress, April 14, 1919, Du Bois Papers, UM-A.

26. Du Bois to NAACP, "Bulletin #3," part 1, box 1: C385, folder 2, NAACP Papers, LOC; "In France, 1918," *The Crisis* (March 1919), 215–16.

27. Du Bois to NAACP, "Bulletin #3," part 1, box 1: C385, folder 2, NAACP Papers, LOC.

28. Ibid.

29. "In France, 1918," *The Crisis* (March 1919), 215–16; "Easter 1919," *The Crisis* (April 1919), 267.

30. "Documents of War," *The Crisis* (May 1919), 18–20; Allen J. Greer to Senator Kenneth D. McKellar, December 6, 1918, Du Bois Papers, UM-A.

31. Adam E. Patterson to W. E. B. Du Bois, November 23, 1918, Du Bois Papers, UM-A.

32. In his April 14, 1919, outline of his France travels and activities, Du Bois wrote "Letters from home," which took place just before he left for General Headquarters. It is possible that Patterson's letter was included in this correspondence. Notes on the Paris Peace Conference and Pan African Congress, April 14, 1919, Du Bois Papers, UM-A.

33. Describing his encounter with James "Tim" Brymn in the March 1919 *Crisis* editorial "In France, 1918," Du Bois writes, "Up in the window stood a black Major, a Captain, a Teacher and I—with tears behind our smiling eyes." Adam Patterson was one of a small number of African American officers to achieve the rank of major in the Ninety-Second Division, therefore making it likely that he was with Du Bois, John Hope, and the other unidentified Black captain. "In France, 1918," *The Crisis* (March 1919), 215–16.

34. On the impact of African American military bands and key musicians and the spread of jazz in France more generally, see Reid Badger, *A Life in Ragtime: A Biography of James Reese Europe* (New York: Oxford University Press, 1995); Rachel Anne Gillett, *At Home in Our Sounds: Music, Race, and Cultural Politics in Interwar Paris* (New York: Oxford University Press, 2021), 35–38; Jeffrey H. Jackson, *Making Jazz French: Music and Modern Life in Interwar Paris* (Durham, NC: Duke University Press, 2003), chaps. 1–2; James Nathan Jones, Franklin F. Johnson, and Robert B. Cochrane, "Alfred Jack Thomas: Performer, Composer, Educator," *Black Perspective in Music* 11, no. 1 (1983): 63–75; Arthur W. Little, *From Harlem to the Rhine: The Story of New York's Colored Volunteers* (New York: Covici, Friede, 1936); Celeste Day Moore, *Soundscapes of Liberation: African American Music in Postwar France* (Durham, NC: Duke University Press, 2021), 19–20; William A. Shack, *Harlem in Montmartre: A Paris Jazz Story Between the Great Wars* (Berkeley: University of California Press, 2001), 11–25; Tyler Stovall, *Paris Noir: African Americans in the City of Light* (Boston: Houghton Mifflin Harcourt, 1996); Williams, *Torchbearers of Democracy*, 165.

35. "To the Editorial Board of a Proposed History of the Black Man in the Great War," *The Black Man and the Wounded World*, Themes & Topics, Misc., Unidentified, 1917–1920, Du Bois Collection, Fisk, box 15, folder 16.

36. Loving to Masteller, April 28, 1919, 10218–279, MID, RG 165, NARA.

37. Du Bois was among the estimated two million people who crowded along the Champs-Élysées when Wilson arrived in Paris. He briefly caught a glimpse of the president. "Letters from Dr. Du Bois," *The Crisis* (February 1919), 164; Margaret MacMillan, *Paris 1919: Six Months That Changed the World* (New York: Random House, 2003), 15–16.

38. Walter Lippmann was Wilson's adviser and helped draft the Fourteen Points. Baker was Wilson's press secretary for the Versailles conference. Marable, *W. E. B. Du Bois*, 100; Contee, "Du Bois, the NAACP, and the Pan-African Congress of 1919," 21; W. E. B. Du Bois to NAACP Board of Directors, January 4, 1919, part 1, box 1: C385, folder 2, NAACP Papers, LOC.

39. "My Mission," *The Crisis* (May 1919), 7–9; Lewis, *W. E. B. Du Bois, Vol. 1*, 567.

40. Michael L. Krenn, *Black Diplomacy: African Americans and the State Department, 1945–1969* (Armonk, NY: M. E. Sharpe, 1999), 180n3; Werner Sollors, Caldwell Titcomb, and Thomas A. Underwood, *Blacks at Harvard: A Documentary History of African-American Experience at Harvard and Radcliffe* (New York: New York University Press, 1993), 150.

41. "The Ghetto," *The Crisis* (February 1914), 170.

42. W. E. B. Du Bois to NAACP Board of Directors, January 4, 1919, part 1, box 1: C385, folder 2, NAACP Papers, LOC. On the African American expatriate community in France, see Stovall, *Paris Noir*.

43. George H. Jackson to W. E. B. Du Bois, December 27, 1918, Du Bois Papers, UM-A.

44. Charles Mangin, *La Force Noire* (France: Hachette, 1910); Joe Lunn, "'Les Races Guerrières': Racial Preconceptions in the French Military About West African Soldiers During the First World War," *Journal of Contemporary History* 34, no. 4 (1999): 519–25; Lunn, *Memoirs of the Maelstrom*; Fogarty, *Race and War in France*.

45. On Blaise Diagne and his activities during the war, see Gregory Mann, *Native Sons: West African Veterans and France in the Twentieth Century* (Durham, NC: Duke University Press, 2006), 68–70; Fogarty, *Race and War in France*, 239–41; Lunn, *Memoirs of the Maelstrom*; Séance du 8 Juillet 1915, Annales de la Chambre des Députés, Débats Parlementaires, 11 Legislature, Session Ordinaire de 1915, Du 11 Mai au 30 Juillet, vol. 102, 986–92; Annales de la Chambre des Députés, Débats Parlementaires, 11 Legislature, Session Ordinaire de 1915, Du 11 Mai au 30 Juillet, vol. 102, 1459, Service des Archives de l'Assemblée Nationale, Palais Bourbon, Paris, France.

46. On the history of the *tirailleurs sénégalais* in the war, see Charles John Balesi, *From Adversaries to Comrades-in-Arms: West Africans and the French Military, 1885–1918* (Waltham, MA: Crossroads Press, 1979); Echenberg, *Colonial Conscripts*; Fogarty, *Race and War in France*; Lunn, *Memoirs of the Maelstrom*; Marc Michel, *Les Africains et la Grande Guerre: L'appel à l'Afrique (1914–1918)* (Paris: Karthala, 2003).

47. Lewis, *W. E. B. Du Bois, Vol. 1*, 567.

48. On diaspora and translation in the context of France, see Brent Hayes Edwards, *The Practice of Diaspora: Literature, Translation, and the Rise of Black Internationalism* (Cambridge, MA: Harvard University Press, 2003).

49. L. Linard, "Au sujet des troupes noires américaines," Août 7, 1918, 17N 76, Service Historique de l'Armée de Terre, Château de Vincennes, Paris, France.

50. W. E. B. Du Bois, "Editing 'The Crisis,'" *The Crisis* (March 1951), 149. For a discussion of Diagne's reaction to the memo, see Williams, *Torchbearers of Democracy*, 180–82.

51. Ligue Coloniale Française, Festival invitation, December 1918, Du Bois Papers, UM-A.

52. A photo of Diop appeared in the June issue of *The Crisis*. "Essay Toward a History of the Black Man in the Great War," *The Crisis* (June 1919), 64; Lewis, *W. E. B. Du Bois, Vol. 1*, 566.

53. "Les Revue des Coloniaux," *The Black Man and the Wounded World*, Brochures, Journals, Pamphlets, Programs, Du Bois Collection, Fisk, box 31, folder 6; "Vive la France," *The Crisis* (March 1919), 215; "Grateful France," *The Crisis* (March 1919), 235–36; W. E. B. Du Bois to NAACP Board of Directors, January 4, 1919, part 1, box 1: C385, folder 2, NAACP Papers, LOC. For more on the French civilizing mission, see Alice L. Conklin, *A Mission to Civilize: The Republican Idea of Empire in France and West Africa, 1895–1930* (Stanford, CA: Stanford University Press, 1997); Fogarty, *Race and War in France*.

54. On the place of France in the African American imagination prior to and during World War I, see Trica Danielle Keaton, Tracy Denean Sharpley-Whiting, and Tyler Stovall, *Black France/France Noire: The History and Politics of Blackness* (Durham, NC: Duke University Press, 2012). On French racism in the specific context of the war, see Tyler Stovall, "The Color Line Behind the Lines: Racial Violence in France During the Great War," *American Historical Review* 103 (June 1998): 737–69; William B. Cohen, "French

Racism and Its African Impact," in G. Wesley Johnson, ed., *Double Impact: France and Africa in the Age of Imperialism* (Westport, CT: Greenwood Press, 1985); Jennifer D. Keene, "French and American Racial Stereotypes During the First World War," in William L. Chew III, ed., *National Stereotypes in Perspective: Americans in France, Frenchmen in America* (Atlanta: Rodopi, 2001); Fogarty, *Race and War in France*.

55. Cover, *The Crisis* (March 1919), 215.

56. "Vive la France," *The Crisis* (March 1919), 215.

57. "Memorandum from W. E. B. Du Bois to M. Diagne and others on a pan-african congress to be held in Paris in February 1919," January 1, 1919, Du Bois Papers, UM-A.

58. To the Board of Directors, January 4, 1919, Series 1, box I: C385, folder 2, NAACP Papers, LOC.

59. W. E. B. Du Bois to Joel E. Spingarn, January 15, 1919, box 1, folder 11, Spingarn Collection, Yale; Panthéon de la Guerre pamphlets and brochures, *The Black Man and the Wounded World*, Brochures, Journals, Pamphlets, Programs, Du Bois Collection, Fisk, box 31, folder 6; Lewis, *W. E. B. Du Bois, Vol. 1*, 565–66.

60. Du Bois immediately wrote to Spingarn when he arrived in Brest on December 9. Spingarn did not receive Du Bois's note until December 17. W. E. B. Du Bois to Joel E. Spingarn, December 9, 1918, box 1, folder 11, Spingarn Collection, Yale.

61. W. E. B. Du Bois to NAACP Board of Directors, January 4, 1919, part 1, box 1: C385, folder 2, NAACP Papers, LOC.

62. Memorandum to the Chairman and the Acting Chairman of the N.A.A.C.P., December 24, 1918, Series 1, box I: C385, folder 2, NAACP Papers, LOC.

63. To the Board of Directors, January 4, 1919, Series 1, box I: C385, folder 2, NAACP Papers, LOC; Charles Flint Kellogg, *NAACP: A History of the National Association for the Advancement of Colored People, Volume I, 1909–1920* (Baltimore: Johns Hopkins University Press, 1967), 281.

64. F. P. Schoonmaker to Intelligence Officers, 92nd Division, January 1, 1919, Du Bois Papers, UM-A; James Erwin assumed command of the Ninety-Second Division from Charles Ballou on December 15, 1918.

65. In his January 16, 1919, letter to Du Bois, Pershing wrote, "I note that proper facilities were afforded to you for visiting the troops as you desired, and I hope that you will find your visit in France a pleasant and profitable one." John J. Pershing to W. E. B. Du Bois, January 16, 1919, *The Black Man and the Wounded World*, General, Du Bois Collection, Fisk, box 15, folder 1.

66. Allied Expeditionary Forces—Intelligence Files of Du Bois, 1917–1919, group #: 312, series no.: 21, box no.: 366, folder no.: 5, Du Bois Papers, UM-A; Visitor's Bureau agreement, *The Black Man and the Wounded World*, American Expeditionary Forces, Notes, Du Bois Collection, Fisk, box 30, folder 22.

67. Boutté Diary, *The Black Man and the Wounded World*, Misc., Unidentified, 1918–1919, Du Bois Collection, Fisk, box 34, folder 38.

68. Scott, *Scott's Official History*, 163.

69. Pershing to Foch, November 26, 1918, in Morris J. MacGregor and Bernard C. Nalty, eds., *Blacks in the United States Armed Forces: Basic Documents, Vol. 4* (Wilmington, DE: Scholarly Resources, 1977), 257.

70. Scott, *Scott's Official History*, 163; T. T. Thompson to W. E. B. Du Bois, January 8, 1919, Du Bois Papers, UM-A.

71. Benedict Crowell and Robert Forrest Wilson, *Demobilization: Our Industrial and Military Demobilization After the Armistice, 1918–1920* (New Haven, CT: Yale University Press, 1921).

72. Adam E. Patterson to W. E. B. Du Bois, January 4, 1919, Du Bois Papers, UM-A.

73. Moton, "Negro Troops in France," 224; Moton, *Finding a Way Out*, 253–65; James, "Robert Russa Moton and the Whispering Gallery"; "Head of Tuskegee Sees Colored Units," *Stars and Stripes*, January 3, 1919; "Robert R. Moton," *The Crisis* (May 1919), 9–10; Robert R. Moton to W. E. B. Du Bois, January 19, 1919, Du Bois Papers, UM-A.

74. Du Bois, "An Essay Toward . . . ," 77.

75. W. E. B. Du Bois, "My Impressions of Woodrow Wilson," *Journal of Negro History* 58, no. 4 (1973): 458–59.

76. "Our Success and Failure," *The Crisis* (July 1919), 128.

77. Clinton H. Wooding to W. E. B. Du Bois, May 16, 1919, Du Bois Papers, UM-A.

78. W. E. B. Du Bois, "The Negro Soldier in Service Abroad During the First World War," *Journal of Negro Education* 12, no. 3 (1943): 326; Barbeau and Henri, *The Unknown Soldiers*, 165.

79. Du Bois, "The Negro Soldier in Service Abroad," 326–32.

80. Hunton and Johnson, *Two Colored Women*, 55–57.

81. Louis Pontlock to W. E. B. Du Bois, April 26, 1919, Du Bois Papers, UM-A; Du Bois, "The Negro Soldier in Service Abroad," 326.

82. "An Essay Toward . . . ," 80–83; Ferrell, *Unjustly Dishonored*, 17–41.

83. Louis Pontlock to W. E. B. Du Bois, April 26, 1919, Du Bois Papers, UM-A.

84. Dennison's portrait appeared on the cover of the September 1915 "Chicago" issue of *The Crisis*.

85. Colonel Herschel Tupes, 372nd Infantry, to Commanding General, AEF, August 24, 1918, in *History of Negro Troops in the World War*, Army War College, Historical Section (1942), United States Army Heritage and Education Center, Carlisle, PA (hereafter cited as USAHEC).

86. Concernant les cadres du 372° R.I.U.S., Général Goybet, Août 21, 1918, 16N 204, Service Historique de l'Armée de Terre.

87. Du Bois, "An Essay Toward . . . ," 63.

88. Allan O. Newman to W. E. B. Du Bois, June 12, 1919, Du Bois Papers, UM-A. Photo of Godman in *Scott's Official History*, chap. 19.

89. W. E. B. Du Bois to Otis B. Duncan, April 24, 1919, *The Black Man and the Wounded World*, General, Du Bois Collection, Fisk, box 14, folder 36.

90. Scott, *Scott's Official History*, 434–38.

91. T. T. Thompson to W. E. B. Du Bois, January 8, 1919, Du Bois Papers, UM-A.

92. Captain Virgil M. Boutté to American Expeditionary Forces, General Headquarters, January 26, 1919, Du Bois Papers, UM-A.

93. "Our Success and Failure," *The Crisis* (July 1919), 128.

94. W. E. B. Du Bois to NAACP Board of Directors, January 12, 1919, part 1, box I: C385, folder 2, NAACP Papers, LOC.

95. Boutté also served as Mary Church Terrell's personal guide when she visited the French battlefields in May 1919. Mary Church Terrell, *A Colored Woman in a White World* (Washington, DC: Ransdell, 1940), 346–47.

96. Du Bois, "An Essay Toward . . . ," 84; American Battlefield Monuments Commission, *92nd Division*, 34.

97. "The Fields of Battle," *The Crisis* (April 1919), 268–69.

98. Du Bois, *Autobiography*, 274.

99. "The Fields of Battle," *The Crisis* (April 1919), 268.

100. Letter from the Office of the Mayor, Domfront, France, January 31, 1919; Statement of Mayor of Ville de Domfront, January 22, 1919, Du Bois Papers, UM-A.

101. W. E. B. Du Bois to Blaise Diagne, January 2, 1919, Du Bois Papers, UM-A.

102. "Memorandum to M. Diagne and Others on a Pan-African Congress to Be Held in Paris in February 1919," January 1, 1919; Blaise Diagne to W. E. B. Du Bois, January 5, 1919, Du Bois Papers, UM-A.

103. Rayford W. Logan, "The Historical Aspects of Pan-Africanism: A Personal Chronicle," *African Forum* 1 (Summer 1965): 94; Lewis, *W. E. B. Du Bois, Vol. 1*, 567–68.

104. He also requested $500. Cablegram, W. E. B. Du Bois to John Shillady, January 30, 1919, Series 1, box I: C385, folder 2, NAACP Papers, LOC.

105. Mary White Ovington to Du Bois, February 11, 1919, Du Bois Papers, UM-A; Cablegram, Mary White Ovington to W. E. B. Du Bois, February 14, 1919, Series 1, box I: C385, folder 2, NAACP Papers, LOC.

106. Lewis, *W. E. B. Du Bois, Vol. 1*, 568–69, 575; "The Pan-African Congress," *The Crisis* (April 1919), 271.

107. For an excellent full treatment of the Pan-African Congress, see Sarah Claire Dunstan, "Conflicts of Interest: The 1919 Pan-African Congress and the Wilsonian Moment," *Callaloo* 39, no. 1 (2016): 133–50.

108. Pan-African Conference, Resolutions votées par le Congrès Pan-Africain, ca. February 21, 1919, Du Bois Papers, UM-A.

109. Cooper, *Woodrow Wilson*, 468–71.

110. See Adom Getachew, *Worldmaking After Empire: The Rise and Fall of Self-Determination* (Princeton, NJ: Princeton University Press, 2019), chap. 2.

111. Woodrow Wilson, "Address at the Third Plenary Session of the Peace Conference in Paris, France," February 14, 1919, American Presidency Project, www.presidency.ucsb.edu/documents/address-the-third-plenary-session-the-peace-conference-paris-france.

112. Thomas Knock, *To End All Wars: Woodrow Wilson and the Quest for a New World Order* (New York: Oxford University Press, 1992), chap. 12; Cooper, *Woodrow Wilson*, 475.

113. Pneumatic card from J. E. Spingarn to W. E. B. Du Bois, February 26, 1919, Du Bois Papers, UM-A.

114. Letter from American Commission to Negotiate Peace to W. E. B. Du Bois, February 28, 1919, Du Bois Papers, UM-A.

115. Letter from American Commission to Negotiate Peace to W. E. B. Du Bois, March 8, 1919, Du Bois Papers, UM-A.

116. Du Bois, "My Impressions of Woodrow Wilson," 459; Lewis, *W. E. B. Du Bois, Vol. 1*, 577–78.

117. Du Bois, *Autobiography*, 271.

118. Office of the Mayor of Raon-l'Étape, France, to W. E. B. Du Bois, March 2, 1919; Mayor of Liverdun, France, to W. E. B. Du Bois, March 3, 1919; Mayor of Saint-Dié, France, to W. E. B. Du Bois, March 6, 1919; Mayor of Le Mans, France, to W. E. B. Du Bois, March 12, 1919; Mayor of Serqueux, France, to W. E. B. Du Bois, March 17, 1919; Mayor of Fresne, Marne, to W. E. B. Du Bois, March 18, 1919; Mayor of Loisy, France, to W. E. B. Du Bois, March 20, 1919; Mayor of Marseille, France, to W. E. B. Du Bois, March 21, 1919; Challes-les-Eaux Office of the Mayor to William Stevenson, April 17, 1919, Du Bois Papers, UM-A.

119. Du Bois, "The Black Man in the Revolution of 1914–1918," 218–23.

120. Mary White Ovington to W. E. B. Du Bois, March 7, 1919, Du Bois Papers, UM-A.

121. Minutes of the Meeting of the Board of Directors, March 10, 1919, Part I, Board of Directors File, 1909–1959, Minutes, 1909–1959, reel 1, NAACP Papers, LOC.

122. Mary White Ovington to W. E. B. Du Bois, March 7, 1919, Du Bois Papers, UM-A.

123. Du Bois was originally scheduled to depart from France on March 15. The shipping company, however, had to cancel the trip, and he was rescheduled for March 22. Circular letter from Compagnie generale transatlantique, March 6, 1919, Du Bois Papers, UM-A.

124. Ellis, *Race, War and Surveillance*, 216–17; Du Bois, *Dusk of Dawn*, 746; F. C. Howe to W. E. B. Du Bois, February 26, 1918, Du Bois Papers, UM-A.

125. "Easter, 1919," *The Crisis* (April 1919), 267–68.

126. "For What?," *The Crisis* (April 1919), 268.

127. "Tribute," *The Crisis* (April 1919), 270.

Chapter 5

1. "History," *The Crisis* (May 1919), 11.

2. "Gotham Boys Take Harlem by Storm," *Baltimore Afro-American*, February 21, 1919; "Fifth Av. Cheers Negro Veterans," *New York Times*, February 18, 1919. For other accounts of the 369th Infantry Regiment homecoming parade, see David Levering Lewis, *When Harlem Was in Vogue* (New York: Knopf, 1981); Richard Slotkin, *Lost Battalions: The Great War and the Crisis of American Nationality* (New York: Henry Holt, 2005); Sammons and Morrow, *Harlem's Rattlers*. On African American soldiers' homecoming parades in general, see Williams, *Torchbearers of Democracy*, 213–22.

3. Mary White Ovington to W. E. B. Du Bois, March 7, 1919, Du Bois Papers, UM-A.

4. Williams, *Torchbearers of Democracy*, chap. 5.

5. Mary White Ovington to W. E. B. Du Bois, March 7, 1919, Du Bois Papers, UM-A.

6. Letter from W. E. B. Du Bois to National Association for the Advancement of Colored People, April 14, 1919, Du Bois Papers, UM-A.

7. Report of the director of publications and research, April 8, 1919, Du Bois Papers, UM-A.

8. See Lewis, *W. E. B. Du Bois, Vol. 1*, especially chap. 17, for background on Du Bois's battles over control of *The Crisis*.

9. See Capozzola, *Uncle Sam Wants You*.

10. Cooper, *Woodrow Wilson*, 476.

11. On wartime and postwar labor protest and unrest, see Nell Irvin Painter, *Standing at Armageddon: United States, 1877–1919* (New York: W. W. Norton, 1987); Joseph A. McCartin, *Labor's Great War: The Struggle for Industrial Democracy and the Origins of Modern American Labor Relations, 1912–1921* (Chapel Hill: University of North Carolina Press, 1997).

12. See Robert K. Murray, *Red Scare: A Study in National Hysteria, 1919–1920* (Minneapolis: University of Minnesota Press, 1955); Melvyn P. Leffler, *The Specter of Communism: The United States and the Origins of the Cold War, 1917–1953* (New York: Hill and Wang, 1994).

13. On the domestic upheaval of 1919, see Hagedorn, *Savage Peace*.

14. "Soldier in Uniform Is Beaten in Georgia Town," *Chicago Defender*, May 10, 1919; "Negro Soldier Beat Up in Worth County," *Macon (Ga.) News*, April 20, 1919; Williams, *Torchbearers of Democracy*, 239–40.

15. "Sylvester, Georgia," August 1, 1919, Part 9: Discrimination in U.S. Armed Forces, Series A: General Office Files on Armed Forces' Affairs, 1918–1955, folder General, August–November 1919, NAACP Papers, LOC.

16. On postwar Southern violence against Black veterans, see Lentz-Smith, *Freedom Struggles*, 178–79; Vincent Mikkelson, "Coming from Battle to Face a War: The Lynching of Black Soldiers in the World War I Era," Ph.D. dissertation, Florida State University, 2007; Williams, *Torchbearers of Democracy*, chap. 6.

17. "Soldiers, Attention!," *Chicago Defender*, April 5, 1919.

18. In France, following the armistice, Patterson prepared and circulated the questionnaire "To the Officers of the Ninety-Second Division" with the war history in mind. He also requested that they send a photograph to his Chicago address upon their return to the United States. At least two dozen officers provided responses. The completed questionnaires are interspersed within the various *Black Man and the Wounded World* chapter drafts on the Ninety-Second Division. See *The Black Man and the Wounded World*, Du Bois Collection, Fisk, box 27, folders 8–10; box 28, folders 14–20; box 29, folders 1–14.

19. Patterson to Du Bois, March 20, 1919, Du Bois Papers, UM-A.

20. Rand McNally & Company to Adam E. Patterson, April 3, 1919; Patterson to Du Bois, April 11, 1919, Du Bois Papers, UM-A.

21. "Tentative Subjects for History," *The Black Man and the Wounded World*, Classification Schemes, Du Bois Collection, Fisk, box 26, folder 17.

22. Adam E. Patterson to W. E. B. Du Bois, April 11, 1919, Du Bois Papers, UM-A.

23. Adam E. Patterson to W. E. B. Du Bois, April 12, 1919, Du Bois Papers, UM-A.

24. W. E. B. Du Bois to Adam E. Patterson, April 16, 1919, Du Bois Papers, UM-A.

25. On the "race man" in Chicago, see St. Clair Drake and Horace R. Cayton, *Black Metropolis: A Study of Negro Life in a Northern City* (New York: Harcourt, Brace, 1945).

26. Adam E. Patterson to W. E. B. Du Bois, April 7, 1919, Du Bois Papers, UM-A.

27. David Levering Lewis writes that "Du Bois's letters were remarkable for consistent economy of expression." Lewis, *W. E. B. Du Bois, Vol. 1*, 493.

28. Du Bois to Patterson, April 16, 1919, Du Bois Papers, UM-A.

29. W. E. B. Du Bois to Louis C. Washington, April 4, 1919, *The Black Man and the Wounded World*, General, Du Bois Collection, Fisk, box 15, folder 4.

30. W. E. B. Du Bois to Otis B. Duncan, April 24, 1919; Charles E. Bentley to W. E. B. Du Bois, April 23, 1919, *The Black Man and the Wounded World*, General, Du Bois Collection, Fisk, box 14, folder 34.

31. W. E. B. Du Bois to Napoleon B. Marshall, April 5, 1919, *The Black Man and the Wounded World*, General, Du Bois Collection, Fisk, box 14, folder 41.

32. P. Preston Reynolds, "Dr. Louis T. Wright and the NAACP: Pioneers in Hospital Racial Integration," *American Journal of Public Health* 90, no. 6 (June 2000): 883–92.

33. W. E. B. Du Bois to Louis T. Wright, April 24, 1919, *The Black Man and the Wounded World*, General, Du Bois Collection, Fisk, box 15, folder 4.

34. Leroy H. Godman to W. E. B. Du Bois, n.d., *The Black Man and the Wounded World*, General, Du Bois Collection, Fisk, box 14, folder 38.

35. W. E. B. Du Bois to Frederick P. Keppel, April 15, 1919, *The Black Man and the Wounded World*, General, Du Bois Collection, Fisk, box 14, folder 40; Frederick P. Keppel to W. E. B. Du Bois, April 18, 1919, Du Bois Papers, UM-A.

36. Walter White to Joel E. Spingarn, April 16, 1919; Joel E. Spingarn to Walter White, April 21, 1919, C-75, NAACP Papers, LOC; Minutes of the Meeting of the War History Committee, April 23, 1919, Du Bois Collection, Fisk, box 61; Report of the Secretary for the May 1919 Meeting of the Board, May 6, 1919, Du Bois Papers, UM-A.

37. See Kerri K. Greenidge, *Black Radical: The Life and Times of William Monroe Trotter* (New York: Liveright, 2020), 265–67.

38. "No Passports," *Richmond Planet*, February 15, 1919. Questions about Du Bois's activities and how he secured a passport were especially pronounced in New York's Black radical circles. See "Negro Passports Refused," *The Messenger* (March 1919), 4.

39. "Dr. W. E. B. Du Bois Is Coming," *Richmond Planet*, April 19, 1919; "The Dubois Disclosures," *Richmond Planet*, May 3, 1919.

40. Founded by Bishop Daniel Payne in 1881, the Bethel Literary and Historical Society was one of the most important political institutions for Washington, DC's, African American community. See Willard B. Gatewood, *Aristocrats of Color: The Black Elite, 1880–1920* (Bloomington: Indiana University Press, 1990); Jacqueline M. Moore, *Leading the Race: The Transformation of the Black Elite in the Nation's Capital, 1880–1920* (Charlottesville: University Press of Virginia, 1999).

41. Contee, "Du Bois, the NAACP, and the Pan-African Congress of 1919," 19.

42. "Bethel Literary," *Washington Bee*, May 3, 1919.

43. Walter Loving to Colonel Masteller, May 5, 1919, 10218–138, RG 165, NARA.

44. On the cover imagery of *The Crisis*, see Amy Helene Kirschke, *Art in Crisis: W. E. B. Du Bois and the Struggle for African American Identity and Memory* (Bloomington: Indiana University Press, 2007).

45. "My Mission," *The Crisis* (May 1919), 7–9.

46. "Returning Soldiers," *The Crisis* (May 1919), 13–14.

47. "The Outer Pocket," *The Crisis* (June 1919), 99.

48. On Du Bois's attacks on Moton and Scott, see Wolters, *Du Bois and His Rivals*, 131–40.

49. "Robert R. Moton," *The Crisis* (May 1919), 9–10.

50. Robert Moton, "Negro Troops in France," *Southern Workman* 48 (May 1919): 219–24.

51. Robert R. Moton to W. E. B. Du Bois, April 18, 1919, *The Black Man and the Wounded World*, General, Du Bois Collection, Fisk, box 14, folder 41.

52. "To Mr. Emmett Scott," *The Crisis* (May 1919), 10.
53. "Dr. Du Bois Attacks Emmett J. Scott," *Richmond Planet*, May 10, 1919.
54. Du Bois to Patterson, April 16, 1919, Du Bois Papers, UM-A.
55. W. E. B. Du Bois to Charles E. Bentley, April 19, 1919, *The Black Man and the Wounded World*, General, Du Bois Collection, Fisk, box 14, folder 34.
56. "History," *The Crisis* (May 1919), 11.
57. "Rape," *The Crisis* (May 1919), 12.
58. Du Bois, "Editing 'The Crisis,'" 149.
59. To the Board of Directors, January 4, 1919, box IC 385, folder 2, NAACP Papers, LOC.
60. Robert A. Bowen to M. Churchill, April 25, 1919, 10218–139, MID, RG 165, NARA.
61. NAACP Annual Report, 1919, 65, NAACP Papers, LOC.
62. "The Outer Pocket," *The Crisis* (June 1919), 98–99.
63. Theodore Kornweibel Jr., *"Seeing Red": Federal Campaigns Against Black Militancy, 1919–1925* (Bloomington: Indiana University Press, 1998), 56–59.
64. "The Outer Pocket," *The Crisis* (June 1919), 98–99.
65. Mary White Ovington to W. E. B. Du Bois, April 11, 1919, Du Bois Papers, UM-A.
66. "The Negro at Bay," *The Nation* 128 (June 14, 1919), 931.
67. "The Outer Pocket," *The Crisis* (June 1919), 98–99.
68. Elmer Carter to W. E. B. Du Bois, May 7, 1919, Du Bois Papers, UM-A.
69. Louis Pontlock to W. E. B. Du Bois, April 26, 1919, Du Bois Papers, UM-A.
70. Charles R. Isum to W. E. B. Du Bois, May 17, 1919, Du Bois Papers. UM-A.
71. Resolution on behalf of the colored people of Baltimore, May 14, 1919, Du Bois Papers, UM-A.
72. Report of the Director of Research and Publications of the NAACP and Editor of *The Crisis* for the Year 1919, Du Bois Papers, UM-A.
73. Report of the Director of Research and Publications for the month of May, May 31, 1919, Du Bois Papers, UM-A.
74. He may very well have met with Adam Patterson and possibly other Black officers to discuss the book project. In his April 16 letter to Patterson, Du Bois wrote that he would be in Chicago from May 17 to May 19 and that the two "will then have a consultation and finally put things in shape." W. E. B. Du Bois to Adam Patterson, April 16, 1919, Du Bois Papers, UM-A.
75. "Y.M.C.A. News," *Chicago Defender*, May 17, 1919.
76. "Prof. W. E. B. Du Bois Addressed a Vast Crowd of People at the Wendell Phillips High School," *Chicago Broad Ax*, May 24, 1919.
77. Du Bois, "An Essay Toward . . . ," 79, 85, 86.
78. Ibid., 63.
79. On this point and, in particular, Du Bois's relationship to Georg Wilhelm Friedrich Hegel, see Reiland Rabaka, *Du Bois's Dialectics: Black Radical Politics and the Reconstruction of Critical Social Theory* (Lanham, MD: Lexington Books, 2008); Shaw, *W. E. B. Du Bois and* The Souls of Black Folk; Winfried Siemerling, "W.E.B. Du Bois, Hegel, and the Staging of Alterity," *Callaloo* 24, no. 1 (2001): 325–33; Shamoon Zamir, *Dark Voices: W. E. B. Du Bois and American Thought, 1888–1903* (Chicago: University of Chicago Press, 1995), chap. 4.
80. Du Bois, "An Essay Toward . . . ," 72.

81. Ibid., 87; Mark Whalan, "'The Only Real White Democracy' and the Language of Liberation: The Great War, France, and African American Culture in the 1920s," *Modern Fiction Studies* 51, no. 4 (2005): 775–800.

Chapter 6

1. Du Bois, *Darkwater*.
2. "The Heart of the South," *The Crisis* (May 1917), 18–19. According to the 1910 census, the Black population of Charleston was 31,056. This number likely dropped to at or slightly below 30,000 by 1917 due to the Great Migration. Department of Commerce, Bureau of the Census, *Negro Population in the United States, 1790–1915* (New York: Arno Press, 1968), 773; the NAACP formally received Charleston's branch application on April 1917 and approved it at the May board of directors meeting. Minutes of the Meeting of the Board of Directors, May 14, 1917, Du Bois Papers, UM-A. On Charleston's Black community during the war, see Theodore Hemmingway, "Prelude to Change: Black Carolinians in the War Years, 1914–1920," *Journal of Negro History* 65, no. 3 (1980): 212–27; Peter F. Lau, *Democracy Rising: South Carolina and the Fight for Black Equality Since 1865* (Lexington: University of Kentucky Press, 2015).
3. Henry Romeike, Inc., Newspaper clippings, 1917, Du Bois Papers, U-MA; paper fan with image of "Dr. W. E. B. DuBois and Sightseeing Party, March 1917," Eugene C. Hunt Papers, 1834–1994, Avery Research Center at College of Charleston; "Charleston," *The Crisis* (April 1917); Lewis, *W. E. B. Du Bois, Vol. 1*, 526–28; For more on Du Bois's visit to Charleston, see Ethan J. Kytle and Blain Roberts, *Denmark Vesey's Garden: Slavery and Memory in the Cradle of the Confederacy* (New York: The New Press, 2018), 178–79; Mamie Garvin Fields and Karen Fields, *Lemon Swamp and Other Places: A Carolina Memoir* (New York: Free Press, 1983), 36–37.
4. "Awake," *The Crisis* (April 1917), 270.
5. Lau, *Democracy Rising*, 41–44; Hemmingway, "Prelude to Change"; Katherine Mellen Charron, *Freedom's Teacher: The Life of Septima Clark* (Chapel Hill: University of North Carolina Press, 2009), 85–96.
6. Cameron McWhirter, *Red Summer: The Summer of 1919 and the Awakening of Black America* (New York: Henry Holt, 2011), 41–49; Lau, *Democracy Rising*, 50–52; Charron, *Freedom's Teacher*, 97–100; David F. Krugler, *1919, The Year of Racial Violence: How African Americans Fought Back* (New York: Cambridge University Press, 2015), 43–50.
7. The influence of Du Bois's graduate school adviser Albert Bushnell Hart is evident in this regard. See Albert Bushnell Hart, "Imagination in History," *American Historical Review* 15, no. 2 (January 1910): 246.
8. E. L. Josey and E. J. Josey, "Edward Christopher Williams: Librarian's Librarian," *Negro History Bulletin* 33, no. 3 (1970): 70–77; Adam McKible, "Introduction," in Edward Christopher Williams, *When Washington Was in Vogue: A Love Story (A Lost Novel of the Harlem Renaissance)* (New York: Amistad, 2003), xiii–xxxiv; Adam McKible, "Edward Christopher Williams," in Paul Finkelman and Cary Wintz, eds., *Encyclopedia of the Harlem Renaissance* (London: Routledge, 2004), 1260–61.
9. E. C. Williams to W. E. B. Du Bois, November 15, 1918, *The Black Man and the Wounded World*, General, Du Bois Collection, Fisk, box 15, folder 4.

10. W. E. B. Du Bois to E. C. Williams, April 4, 1919, *The Black Man and the Wounded World*, General, Du Bois Collection, Fisk, box 15, folder 4.

11. W. E. B. Du Bois to E. C. Williams, April 19, 1919; Du Bois to E. C. Williams, May 15, 1919, *The Black Man and the Wounded World*, General, Du Bois Collection, Fisk, box 15, folder 4.

12. W. E. B. Du Bois to E. C. Williams, June 18, 1919, *The Black Man and the Wounded World*, General, Du Bois Collection, Fisk, box 15, folder 4.

13. E. C. Williams to W. E. B. Du Bois, June 17, 1919, *The Black Man and the Wounded World*, General, Du Bois Collection, Fisk, box 15, folder 4; E. C. Williams to W. E. B. Du Bois, June 18, 1919, Du Bois Papers, UM-A.

14. Joseph L. Stevens to W. E. B. Du Bois, June 25, 1919, Du Bois Papers, UM-A.

15. Herman V. Davis to W. E. B. Du Bois, July 5, 1919, Du Bois Papers, UM-A.

16. Frank L. Drye to W. E. B. Du Bois, May 30, 1919, *The Black Man and the Wounded World*, General, Du Bois Collection, Fisk, box 14, folder 36.

17. Walker W. Thomas to The Crisis, July 10, 1919, Du Bois Papers, UM-A.

18. Lt. Robert W. Cheers to Oswald Garrison Villard, June 3, 1919, *The Black Man and the Wounded World*, chap. 16, "The 368th Regiment," Notes, Du Bois Collection, Fisk, box 29, folder 1.

19. The initial guilty verdicts hinged on the testimony of Norris, who declared that Cheers and other officers retreated against orders. Du Bois wrote to Baker and offered to thank him publicly for his defense of the officers. Newton D. Baker to Robert R. Moton, November 1, 1919; W. E. B. Du Bois to Newton D. Baker, November 12, 1919, *The Black Man and the Wounded World*, General, Du Bois Collection, Fisk, box 14, folder 34; also see Williams, "African Americans in the Meuse-Argonne Offensive."

20. Wolters, *Du Bois and His Rivals*, 140–41.

21. James Shepard, who remained on good terms with both Du Bois and the Tuskegee camp, informed Du Bois, "Confidentially the editorial against you last week was written by Tyler . . ." James E. Shepard to W. E. B. Du Bois, ca. June 1919, Du Bois Papers, UM-A. Tyler prepared a much longer vitriolic rebuttal that Scott ultimately condensed and scaled back. "SCOTT FLAYS DUBOIS," box 115, folder #4, Scott Papers, MSU.

22. "Scott Asks DuBois for Bill of Particulars," *New York Age*, May 24, 1919.

23. NAACP officials, most notably Mary White Ovington, recognized the delicacy of Scott serving as keynote speaker and intentionally organized the conference program to keep Scott and Du Bois from appearing together. Harry E. Davis to Mary White Ovington, May 19, 1919, B1, folder 19, NAACP Papers, LOC; Mary White Ovington to Harry E. Davis, May 10, 1919, B1, folder 18, NAACP Papers, LOC; John R. Shillady to Emmett J. Scott, May 20, 1919, B1, folder 19; Emmett J. Scott to John R. Shillady, May 24, 1919, B1, folder 20, NAACP Papers, LOC; Harry E. Davis to Mary White Ovington, May 23, 1919, B1, folder 20, NAACP Papers, LOC; Mary White Ovington to Harry E. Davis, May 26, 1919, NAACP Papers, LOC. For Emmett Scott's speech, see Annual Meeting, 1919, NAACP Papers, LOC.

24. "Our Success and Failure," *The Crisis* (July 1919), 127–30.

25. "Scott Again Scores DuBois," *New York Age*, July 26, 1919. Ralph Tyer, named by Du Bois in his July editorial "Our Success and Failure," also publicly responded to

Du Bois. "Ralph Tyler Answers Du Bois Open Attack," *Cleveland Advocate*, July 12, 1919; "Charges That Dr. Du Bois Published Belated Letters," *Richmond Planet*, July 19, 1919.

26. On American memory of the war, see Stephen Trout, *On the Battlefield of Memory: The First World War and American Remembrance, 1919–1941* (Tuscaloosa: University of Alabama Press, 2010).

27. "Review of The American Negro in the World War," *Journal of Negro History* 4, no. 4 (1919): 466–67.

28. Circular, *The Black Man and the Wounded World*, General, Du Bois Collection, Fisk, box 15, folder 2.

29. Scott, *Scott's Official History*, 10. Scott formally enlisted Woodson's assistance to complete the book. In a March 27, 1919, letter to Frank Parker Stockbridge, Scott wrote, "Mr. Woodson and my whole office force are enthusiastically lined up behind me to put this job over." Considering Woodson's financial needs, he most likely struck a deal with Scott to share profits of the book. Emmett J. Scott to Frank P. Stockbridge, March 27, 1919, box 113, folder #1, Scott Papers, MSU.

30. Scott, *Scott's Official History*, 12.

31. Ibid., 14.

32. Roosevelt died on January 6, 1919.

33. Scott, *Scott's Official History*, 426, 453, 457.

34. Despite offering no public comment, Du Bois closely monitored the release of Scott's book. He kept copies of the publicity and received a copy of the book for review in *The Crisis. The Crisis*, tellingly, did not publish a review. Circular; W. H Rider, L. W. Walter Company to The Crisis, September 20, 1919; Du Bois to W. H. Rider, September 25, 1919, *The Black Man and the Wounded World*, General, Du Bois Collection, Fisk, box 15, folder 2.

35. *The Crisis* (September 1919), 266.

36. Krugler, *1919, The Year of Racial Violence*, 50–58.

37. "The Riot at Longview, Texas," *The Crisis* (October 1919); Krugler, *1919, The Year of Racial Violence*, 58–64.

38. Krugler, *1919, The Year of Racial Violence*, chap. 3; McWhirter, *Red Summer*, chap. 11; Patrick Sauer, "One Hundred Years Ago, a Four-Day Race Riot Engulfed Washington, D.C.," *Smithsonian Magazine*, July 2019, www.smithsonianmag.com/history/one-hundred-years-ago-four-day-race-riot-engulfed-washington-dc-180972666/.

39. "The Riots," *The Crisis* (September 1919), 243.

40. "Protest Sent to Wilson," *New York Times*, July 22, 1919.

41. W. E. B. Du Bois to Louis C. Washington, April 4, 1919, *The Black Man and the Wounded World*, General, Du Bois Collection, Fisk, box 15, folder 4.

42. Chicago Commission of Race Relations, *The Negro in Chicago: A Study of Race Relations and a Race Riot* (Chicago: University of Chicago Press, 1922), 25; William M. Tuttle Jr., *Race Riot: Chicago in the Red Summer of 1919* (New York: Atheneum, 1970), 42.

43. Williams, *Torchbearers of Democracy*, 250–57; Harry Haywood, *Black Bolshevik: Autobiography of an Afro-American Communist* (Chicago: Liberator Press, 1978), 84.

44. Krugler, *1919, The Year of Racial Violence*, chap. 4; McWhirter, *Red Summer*, chaps. 12–13.

45. On postwar NAACP activism in Texas, see Steven A. Reich, "Soldiers of Democracy: Black Texans and the Fight for Citizenship, 1917–1921," *Journal of American History* 82, no. 4 (1996): 1478–504.

46. "Texas Judge Whips John R. Shillady," *New York Times*, August 23, 1919.

47. Herbert J. Seligmann, "The Press Abets the Mob," *The Nation* 109 (1919), 460–61; McWhirter, *Red Summer*, chap. 15.

48. "Shillady and Texas," *The Crisis* (October 1919), 283–84.

49. "Mob Kills Negro, Bogalusa Woman Brands Assailant," *New Orleans Times-Picayune*, September 1, 1919.

50. Ida B. Wells, *Arkansas Race Riot* (Chicago: Hume Job Print, 1920); "The Real Cause of Race Riots," *The Crisis* (December 1919), 56–62.

51. Du Bois, *Autobiography*, 286; Dominic J. Capeci and Jack C. Knight, "Reckoning with Violence: W. E. B. Du Bois and the 1906 Atlanta Race Riot," *Journal of Southern History* 62, no. 4 (1996): 727–66.

52. "Let Us Reason Together," *The Crisis* (September 1919), 231.

53. "The League of Nations," *The Crisis* (May 1919), 10–11.

54. Cooper, *Woodrow Wilson*, 505–34; also see John Milton Cooper Jr., *Breaking the Heart of the World: Woodrow Wilson and the Fight for the League of Nations* (Cambridge: Cambridge University Press, 2001).

55. Du Bois, *Dusk of Dawn*, 747.

56. 1919 board meeting dates: June 9, July 11, August 26, September 8, October 13, November 10, November 24, December 8, NAACP Papers, LOC.

57. "The Riots: An NAACP Investigation," *The Crisis* (September 1919), 243.

58. Du Bois, "An Essay Toward . . . ," 72.

59. William A. Hewlett to W. E. B. Du Bois, August 26, 1919, in Aptheker, ed., *Correspondence*, 234–35.

60. A. Philip Randolph, "A New Crowd—A New Negro," *The Messenger* (May–June 1919), 26–27. On the radicalism of *The Messenger*, see Theodore Kornweibel Jr., *No Crystal Stair: Black Life and the Messenger, 1917–1928* (Westport, CT: Greenwood Press, 1975).

61. On the African Blood Brotherhood, see Robert A. Hill, ed., *The Crusader* (New York: Garland, 1987); Cathy Bergin, "'Unrest Among the Negroes': The African Blood Brotherhood and the Politics of Resistance," *Race & Class* 57, no. 3 (2016): 45–58; Makalani, *In the Cause of Freedom*, chap. 2.

62. "The Horizon," *The Crisis* (June 1919), 100.

63. Ibid., 151; Williams, *Torchbearers of Democracy*, 271–80.

64. U.S. Congress, *Congressional Record*, 66th Congress, 1st Session, August 25, 1919, 4302–306. On the surveillance of African Americans, see Kornweibel, *"Seeing Red."*

65. For example, Du Bois corresponded with Victor Daly, business manager for *The Messenger*, about his war history and Daly provided information. Daly replied that A. Philip Randolph and Chandler Owen, along with other former officers of the Ninety-Second Division, were contemplating their own history of the war that would be "a matter of opinion as well as a mere historical chronicle, of where there are too many on the market." W. E. B. Du Bois to Victor Daly, September 15, 1919; Victor Daly to W. E. B.

Du Bois, September 26, 1919, *The Black Man and the Wounded World*, General, Du Bois Collection, Fisk, box 14, folder 36.

66. "New Leadership for the Negro," *The Messenger* (May–June 1919), 9.
67. On the history of the American Legion, see William Pencak, *For God & Country: The American Legion, 1919–1941* (Boston: Northeastern University Press, 1989); Thomas A. Rumer, *The American Legion: An Official History, 1919–1989* (New York: M. Evans, 1990).
68. "The American Legion," *The Crisis* (September 1919), 233.
69. Letter from Universal Negro Improvement and Conservation Association to W. E. B. Du Bois, ca. April 30, 1915, Du Bois Papers, UM-A.
70. Letter from Marcus Garvey to W. E. B. Du Bois, April 25, 1916, Du Bois Papers, UM-A.
71. Letter from Unidentified correspondent to Marcus Garvey, April 29, 1916, Du Bois Papers, UM-A.
72. David Levering Lewis, *W. E. B. Du Bois: The Fight for Equality in the American Century, 1919–1963* (New York: Henry Holt, 2000), 50–51 (hereafter cited as Lewis, *W. E. B. Du Bois, Vol. 2*).
73. On Garvey's ascendancy on the national stage, see Colin Grant, *Negro with a Hat: The Rise and Fall of Marcus Garvey* (New York: Oxford University Press, 2008).
74. Attachment, Robert A. Hill, ed., *The Marcus Garvey and Universal Negro Improvement Association Papers, Volume 1* (Berkeley: University of California Press, 1983), 333.
75. UNIA Meeting at Carnegie Hall, *Garvey Papers, Vol. 1*, 502.
76. Editorial Letter by Marcus Garvey, *Garvey Papers, Vol. 2*, 42.
77. Garvey inflated membership numbers for the UNIA. By the end of 1919, international membership was likely well over the three hundred thousand estimated by Du Bois, but far less than the two million Garvey boasted. Grant, *Negro with a Hat*, 165. On the presence of the UNIA in the South, see Mary G. Rolinson, *Grassroots Garveyism: The Universal Negro Improvement Association in the Rural South, 1920–1927* (Chapel Hill: University of North Carolina Press, 2007).
78. "Synopsis of UNIA Meeting," "Address Denouncing W. E. B. Du Bois," *Garvey Papers, Vol. 1*, 392–99.
79. James Burghardt to W. E. B. Du Bois, August 21, 1919; W. E. B. Du Bois to James Burghardt, August 27, 1919, Du Bois Papers, UM-A.
80. Lewis, *W. E. B. Du Bois, Vol. 2*, 11.
81. W. E. B. Du Bois to Alfred Harcourt, July 15, 1919; Alfred Harcourt to W. E. B. Du Bois, July 17, 1919, *The Black Man and the Wounded World*, General, Du Bois Collection, Fisk, box 14, folder 39.
82. Memoranda—1917–1918, September 1918, Du Bois Papers, UM-A.
83. Memoranda—1918–1920, December 1920, Du Bois Papers, UM-A.
84. *Darkwater* draft, box 1, folder 18, Du Bois Collection, Beinecke Library, Yale University.
85. Lewis, *W. E. B. Du Bois, Vol. 2*, 11–13.
86. Du Bois, *Darkwater*, 1.
87. Ibid., chap. 2.
88. Ibid., 20.
89. Ibid., chap. 2.

90. The first four paragraphs and the final paragraph of the chapter were the same as "The African Roots of War." A published version of the "Memorandum on the Future of Africa" appeared in the January 1919 issue of *The Crisis* as "The Future of Africa."
91. Du Bois, *Darkwater*, chap. 3.
92. Ibid., chaps. 4, 6, 7, 8.
93. Ibid., chap. 9.

Chapter 7

1. *The Black Man and the Wounded World*, chap. 8, "The Challenge," Du Bois Collection, Fisk, box 25, folder 5.
2. Lewis, *W. E. B. Du Bois, Vol. 2*, 32–33; *The Brownies' Book* (January 1920). For more background on the creation of *The Brownies' Book*, see Christina Schaffer, *The Brownies' Book: Inspiring Racial Pride in African-American Children* (Frankfurt: Internationaler Verlag der Wissenschaften, 2012); Katherine Capshaw Smith, "*The Crisis* Children's Page, *The Brownies' Book*, and the Fantastic," in Sinitiere and Kirschke, *Protest and Propaganda*.
3. On Du Bois's relationship with Johnson, see Lewis, *W. E. B. Du Bois, Vol. 2*, 183.
4. Georgia Douglass Johnson, "Recruit," *The Brownies' Book* (January 1920), 32, www.loc.gov/item/22001351/.
5. Ibid.
6. Ibid., 25.
7. Minutes, July 11, 1919, Du Bois Papers, UM-A.
8. "The War History," *The Crisis* (October 1919), 286–87.
9. E. Holsey Waller to the editor of *The Crisis*, November 19, 1919; J. E. Washington to W. E. B. Du Bois, September 29, 1919; James A. Lowe to W. E. B. Du Bois, November 12, 1919; De Haven Hinkson to W. E. B. Du Bois, February 21, 1920; R. E. Ray to W. E. B. Du Bois, March 6, 1920, Du Bois Papers, UM-A.
10. W. E. B. Du Bois to C. S. Jennifer, March 18, 1920; W. E. B. Du Bois to Edward Banks, March 31, 1920, Du Bois Papers, UM-A.
11. W. E. B. Du Bois to Gilbert H. Moody, January 7, 1920, Du Bois Papers, UM-A.
12. Obadiah Foster, *The Modern Warfare and My Experience in France* (Washington, DC: Goins Printing Company, 1919).
13. W. E. B. Du Bois to Obadiah M. Foster, December 27, 1919; Obadiah M. Foster to W. E. B. Du Bois, December 30, 1919, Du Bois Papers, UM-A.
14. United States Adjutant General's Office, Letter from United States War Department to Hettie Lewis, March 27, 1919; Hettie B. Lewis to W. E. B. Du Bois, October 1, 1919, Du Bois Papers, UM-A.
15. Charlotte Brickhouse to W. E. B. Du Bois, November 18, 1919; A. C. Whitney to W. E. B. Du Bois, November 28, 1919; W. E. B. Du Bois to R. M. Johnson, November 22, 1919, Du Bois Papers, UM-A.
16. Adam E. Patterson to W. E. B. Du Bois, ca. March 1920, Du Bois Papers, UM-A.
17. W. E. B. Du Bois to Adam Patterson, March 2, 1920, Du Bois Papers, UM-A.
18. E. C. Williams to W. E. B. Du Bois, August 20, 1919, *The Black Man and the Wounded World*, *Crisis* Material, Notes, Du Bois Collection, Fisk, box 30, folder 31. In the poten-

tial publishing plan they sketched out, Du Bois would pen volume one, a regular edition costing $2.00, along with a subscription edition at $3.00. Volumes two and three, composed of documents, maps, and pictures, at a cost of $3.00 each, would list Williams as co-contributor.

19. W. E. B. Du Bois to E. C. Williams, January 7, 1920, Du Bois Papers, UM-A.

20. James Watson Gerard served as the American ambassador to Germany prior to U.S. entry in the World War. See James Watson Gerard, *My Four Years in Germany* (New York: George H. Doran, 1917); James Watson Gerard, *Face to Face with Kaiserism* (New York: George H. Doran, 1918). Du Bois misspelled Ludendorff's name as "von Ludenberg."

21. In a short "to-do list," Du Bois notes the "Willy-Nicky letters," a set of messages relayed between third cousins Wilhelm II, the German emperor, and Nicholas II, the emperor of Russia, on the eve of the war. To-do list, ca. 1919, Du Bois Papers, UM-A.

22. Karl Kautsky, "Imperialism and the War," *International Socialist Review* (November 1914). On Kautsky, see Gary P. Steenson, *Karl Kautsky, 1854–1938: Marxism in the Classical Years* (Pittsburgh: University of Pittsburgh Press, 1978).

23. Peter Novick, *That Noble Dream: The "Objectivity Question" and the American Historical Profession* (Cambridge: Cambridge University Press, 1988).

24. E. C. Williams to W. E. B. Du Bois, A Few General Works on the Great War, ca. 1920, Du Bois Papers, UM-A.

25. *Harper's Pictorial Library of the World War* (New York: Harper & Brothers, 1920); Arthur Conan Doyle, *A History of the Great War* (New York: George H. Doran, 1915–1920). Other titles suggested by Williams included John Buchan's massive history of the war, which ran in twenty-four installments beginning in 1915; Francis A. March, *History of the World War*, published in 1918; and the widely publicized five-volume *History of the World War*, by Frank H. Simonds, a writer for the *New-York Tribune*. On Buchan, see Keith Grieves, "*Nelson's History of the War*: John Buchan as a Contemporary Military Historian, 1915–22," *Journal of Contemporary History* 28, no. 3 (July 1993): 533–51.

26. *Harper's Pictorial Library of the World War, Volume 10* (1920), 137.

27. Jacques Chambrun and Charles Marenches, *American Army in the European Conflict* (New York: Macmillan, 1919), 29.

28. Hampton Institute, *Brief Sketch of the Record of the American Negro and Indian in the Great War* (Boston: The Committee, 1919); Miles V. Lynk, *Negro Pictorial Review of the Great World War* (Memphis: Twentieth Century Art, 1919).

29. John A. Jamieson et al., *Complete History of the Colored Soldiers in the War* (New York: Bennett and Churchill, 1919), foreword.

30. For further discussion of this book and other publications by Black veterans, see Williams, *Torchbearers of Democracy*, 310–12.

31. Lewis, *W. E.B Du Bois, Vol. 1*, 205.

32. Index of world war I research material, ca. 1920, W. E. B. Du Bois Papers, UM-A.

33. W. E. B. Du Bois to E. C. Williams, January 7, 1920 [April 6, 1920], Du Bois Papers, UM-A.

34. *The Black Man and the Wounded World*, Classification Schemes, Du Bois Collection, Fisk, box 26, folders 18–19; *The Black Man and the Wounded World*, Crisis Material, Notes, Du Bois Collection, Fisk, box 30, folders 29–30.

35. Index of world war I research material, ca. 1920, W. E. B. Du Bois Papers, UM-A.

36. Du Bois, "An Essay Toward . . ."

37. *The Black Man and the Wounded World*, chap. 14, "92nd Division," Du Bois Collection, Fisk, box 27, folder 9.

38. *The Black Man and the Wounded World*, chap. 15, "The 365th, 366th and 367th Regiments," Notes, Du Bois Collection, Fisk, box 29, folder 4.

39. James W. Johnson, Terrell Palmer, and Samuel K. Murray, *Modern Artillerymen* (Camp Dix, New Jersey, March 1919).

40. James William Johnson to the editor of *The Crisis*, April 28, 1919, Du Bois Papers, UM-A.

41. W. E. B. Du Bois to James W. Johnson, July 24, 1920; James W. Johnson to W. E. B. Du Bois, August 4, 1920, Du Bois Papers, UM-A.

42. W. E. B. Du Bois to L. H. Godman, January 7, 1920; Leroy H. Godman to W. E. B. Du Bois, February 10, 1920, Du Bois Papers, UM-A.

43. W. E. B. Du Bois to Edward Banks, March 31, 1920, Du Bois Papers, UM-A.

44. Wellington Willard to W. E. B. Du Bois, May 6, 1919; J. Wellington Willard to W. E. B. Du Bois, July 21, 1920, Du Bois Papers, UM-A.

45. Lewis, *W. E. B. Du Bois, Vol. 1*, 553.

46. On April 24, 1920, Du Bois wrote to Joel Spingarn, "Would it be possible or advisable in my history to publish in full the memorandum which you sent to General Churchill on the special bureau for Negroes in the Intelligence Bureau?" He added, "It seems to me that the time has come for that to be published either wholly or in part or possibly in general outline." The timing of Du Bois's letter to Spingarn corresponds with when he drafted chapter 8 of the war history. W. E. B. Du Bois to Joel E. Spingarn, April 24, 1920, box 1, folder 11, Spingarn Collection, Yale.

47. *The Black Man and the Wounded World*, chap. 8, "The Challenge," Du Bois Collection, Fisk, box 27, folder 5.

48. Sullivan, *Lift Every Voice*, 89–92.

49. "Dr. Du Bois Is Awarded the Spingarn Medal," *Chicago Defender*, June 5, 1920.

50. "The Atlanta Conference," *The Crisis* (July 1920), 133; W. E. B. Du Bois receiving Spingarn Medal, Atlanta University, June 1, 1920, Du Bois Papers, UM-A; Lewis, *W. E. B. Du Bois, Vol. 2*, 24–25.

51. Nahum Dimitri Chandler, *Toward an African Future—Of the Limit of World* (Albany: State University of New York Press, 2021), 14.

52. W. E. B. Du Bois, *The Negro* (Philadelphia: University of Pennsylvania Press, 2001), 232. Robert Gregg notes that Du Bois completed *The Negro* at the same time as he was writing "The African Roots of War." Robert Gregg, "Afterword," in Du Bois, *The Negro*, 255n16.

53. Lentz-Smith, *Freedom Struggles*, chap. 5.

54. On the making of the modern African diaspora, see Kim D. Butler, "Defining Diaspora, Refining a Discourse," *Diaspora* 10, no. 2 (2001): 189–219; Colin Palmer, "Defining and Studying the Modern African Diaspora, *Perspectives: The Newsmagazine of the American Historical Association* (September 1998); Tiffany Ruby Patterson and Robin D. G. Kelley, "Unfinished Migrations: Reflections on the African Diaspora and the Making of the Modern World," *African Studies Review* 43, no. 1 (2000): 11–45.

55. See Wilson J. Moses, "Culture, Civilization, and Decline of the West: The Afrocentrism

of W. E. B. Du Bois," in Bernard W. Bell, Emily R. Grosholz, and James B. Stewart, eds., *W. E. B. Du Bois on Race and Culture: Philosophy, Politics, and Poetics* (New York: Routledge, 1996).

56. *The Black Man and the Wounded World*, chap. 3, "World of Black Folk," Du Bois Collection, Fisk, box 26, folder 24.

57. *The Black Man and the Wounded World*, chap. 4, "Black France," Du Bois Collection, Fisk, box 27, folder 1.

58. Alphonse Séché, *Les Noirs: D'après des Documents Officiels* (Paris, 1919); Fogarty, *Race and War in France*, 15.

59. Séché, *Les Noirs*, 38; *The Black Man and the Wounded World*, chap. 4, "Black France," Notes, Du Bois Collection, Fisk, box 27, folder 13.

60. For example, the smiling West African *tirailleur* was used to advertise the popular chocolate drink Banania. Black anti-colonial activists, such as Leopold Senghor and Frantz Fanon, specifically targeted this imagery in their critiques of French racism and imperialism. See Brett A. Berliner, *Ambivalent Desire: The Exotic Black Other in Jazz-Age France* (Amherst: University of Massachusetts Press, 2002); Anne Donadey, " 'Y'a Bon Banania': Ethics and Cultural Criticism in the Colonial Context," *French Cultural Studies* 11, no. 31 (2000): 9–29; Frantz Fanon, *Black Skin, White Masks* (New York: Grove Press, 1967); Alison S. Fell, "Beyond the Bonhomme Banania: Lucie Cousturier's Encounters with West African Soldiers During the First World War," in Alisa Miller, Laura Rowe, and James Kitchen, *Other Combatants, Other Fronts: Competing Histories of the First World War* (Newcastle-upon-Tyne, UK: Cambridge Scholars, 2011); Dana S. Hale, *Races on Display: French Representations of Colonized Peoples, 1886–1940* (Bloomington: Indiana University Press, 2008), chap. 5.

61. Jennifer D. Keene, "W.E.B. Du Bois and the Wounded World: Seeking Meaning in the First World War for African-Americans," *Peace and Change* 26, no. 2 (2001): 145–46.

62. *The Black Man and the Wounded World*, chap. 4, "Black France," Du Bois Collection, Fisk, box 27, folder 1.

63. Memorandum to the Board of Directors from the Director of Publications and Research, October 27, 1920, Du Bois Papers, UM-A.

64. Waller served as the first president of the NAACP's Baltimore branch. He notably supported Du Bois during his controversy surrounding the military intelligence captaincy during the war. Garnett R. Waller to W. E. B. Du Bois, November 6, 1920, Du Bois Papers, UM-A.

65. Pace graduated from Atlanta University in 1903. *The Moon Illustrated Weekly* was Du Bois's first attempt at magazine publishing and editorship. Pace is most well known for founding Black Swan Records, the first African American–owned record company with national distribution. Du Bois gave Pace the idea for the company's name, was an early investor, and served on the board of directors. Lewis, *W. E. B. Du Bois, Vol. 1*, 217, 324–25; Harry H. Pace to W. E. B. Du Bois, December 27, 1920; certificate for one share of the capital stock of the Black Swan Phonograph Co. Inc., December 18, 1921, Du Bois Papers, UM-A.

66. Harry H. Pace to W. E. B. Du Bois, November 5, 1920, Du Bois Papers, UM-A.

67. E. Burton Ceruti to W. E. B. Du Bois, November 13, 1920, Du Bois Papers, UM-A.

68. The Second Pan-African Congress, Bulletin I, March 1921, Application, Bulletins, 1921, Du Bois Collection, Fisk, box 12, folder 27; "Pan-Africa," *The Crisis* (May 1921), 5; "The Second Pan-African Congress," *The Crisis* (July 1921), 119–20.

69. Office of the Provost Marshal General, Second Report of the Provost Marshal General to the Secretary of War on the Operations of the Selective Service System to December 20, 1918 (Washington, DC: Government Printing Office, 1919); Office of the Provost Marshal General, Second Report of the Provost Marshal General to the Secretary of War on the Operations of the Selective Service System to July 15, 1919 (Washington, DC: Government Printing Office, 1920); *The Black Man and the Wounded World*, n.d. (unpublished), Brochures, Journals, Pamphlets, Programs, Du Bois Collection, Fisk, box 31, folder 8.

70. *The Black Man and the Wounded World*, chap. 15, "The 365th, 366th, and 367th Regiments," Notes, Du Bois Collection, Fisk, box 29, folder 4.

71. B. C. Franklin, "The Tulsa Race Riot and Three of Its Victims," National Museum of African American History and Culture, www.si.edu/object/nmaahc_2015.176.1.

72. On the Tulsa riot, see Scott Ellsworth, *Death in a Promised Land: The Tulsa Race Riot of 1921* (Baton Rouge: Louisiana State University Press, 1981); Randall Kennedy and Alfred L. Brophy, *Reconstructing the Dreamland: The Tulsa Race Riot of 1921: Race, Reparations and Reconciliation* (New York: Oxford University Press, 2003); Tim Madigan, *The Burning: Massacre, Destruction, and the Tulsa Race Riot of 1921* (New York: Thomas Dunne Books/ St. Martin's Press, 2001); Mary E. Jones Parrish, Scott Ellsworth, Anneliese M. Bruner, and John Hope Franklin, *The Nation Must Awake: My Witness to the Tulsa Race Massacre of 1921* (San Antonio, TX: Trinity University Press, 2021).

73. "Forty-Four Blocks of Negro Property Destroyed by the Mob at Tulsa, Oklahoma," *The Crisis* (July 1921), 115.

74. "Pan-Africa," *The Crisis* (August 1921), 149.

75. On Logan's background, see Kenneth Robert Janken, *Rayford W. Logan and the Dilemma of the African-American Intellectual* (Amherst: University of Massachusetts Press, 1993), chaps. 1–2; Lewis, *W. E. B. Du Bois, Vol. 2*, 37.

76. Lewis, *W. E. B. Du Bois, Vol. 1*, 435–37. David Levering Lewis discusses Du Bois's friendships with women, as well as his multiple extramarital affairs, in his two-volume biography.

77. "110 Delegates to the Pan-African Congress by Countries," *The Crisis* (December 1921), 68–69.

78. Jessie Fauset, "Impressions of the Second Pan African Congress," *The Crisis* (November 1921), 12–18; W. E. B. Du Bois, "A Second Journey to Pan-Africa," *The New Republic* 29 (December 7, 1921), 39–41; Lewis, *W. E. B. Du Bois, Vol. 2*, 37–50.

79. "To the World," *The Crisis* (November 1921), 5–10.

80. Du Bois, "A Second Journey to Pan-Africa," 41.

81. *The Brownies' Book*, vol. 2, no. 12, December 1921, Du Bois Papers, UM-A.

Chapter 8

1. "Dr. Du Bois Heard in Los Angeles," *California Eagle*, March 4, 1923.

2. W. E. B. Du Bois to Charles Young, May 18, 1921, Du Bois Papers, UM-A.

3. David Levering Lewis notes that Young was among "the pantheon" of Du Bois's male "soul mates" that also included John Hope, Joel Spingarn, James Weldon Johnson, George Crawford, Thomas Bell, and Wendell Dabney. Lewis, *W. E. B. Du Bois, Vol. 2*, 385.

4. Letter from Charles Young to W. E. B. Du Bois, April 21, 1921, Du Bois Papers, UM-A.

5. W. E. B. Du Bois to Charles Young, May 18, 1921, Du Bois Papers, UM-A.

6. On the UNIA's activities in Liberia, see Grant, *Negro with a Hat*, chap. 12.

7. On the National Congress of British West Africa and the 1920 Conference of Africans of British West Africa, see G. I. C. Eluwa, "The National Congress of British West Africa: A Study in African Nationalism," *Présence Africaine* 77, no. 1 (1971): 131–49; J. Ayodele Langley, *Pan-Africanism and Nationalism in West Africa, 1900–1945: A Study in Ideology and Social Classes* (Oxford: Clarendon Press, 1973); *Correspondence Relating to the National Congress of British West Africa, Ordered by His Excellency the Governor to Be Printed* (Accra, Ghana: Government Press, 1920).

8. W. E. B. Du Bois to Colonel Charles Young, May 18, 1921; Colonel Charles Young to W. E. B. Du Bois, April 21, 1921, Du Bois Papers, UM-A.

9. See Sammons and Morrow, *Harlem's Rattlers*, 144.

10. Charles Young to W. E. B. Du Bois, April 30, 1919, Du Bois Papers, UM-A.

11. Lewis, *W. E. B. Du Bois, Vol. 2*, 100–102; Charles Young to W. E. B. Du Bois, April 30, 1919, Du Bois Papers, UM-A.

12. W. E. B. Du Bois to Robert Lansing, November 12, 1919, *The Black Man and the Wounded World*, General, Du Bois Collection, Fisk, box 14, folder 40.

13. Du Bois to Charles Young, May 18, 1921, Du Bois Papers, UM-A.

14. Charles Young to W. E. B. Du Bois, July 20, 1920, Du Bois Papers, UM-A.

15. Charles Young to W. E. B. Du Bois, January 14, 1921, Du Bois Papers, UM-A.

16. Shellum, *Black Officer in a Buffalo Soldier Regiment*, 274–78.

17. Armintie Young to W. E. B. Du Bois, January 13, 1922, Du Bois Papers, UM-A.

18. Nina Du Bois to W. E. B. Du Bois, January 23, 1922; Letter from Nina Du Bois to W. E. B. Du Bois, January 31, 1922, Du Bois Papers, UM-A.

19. "Charles Young," *The Crisis* (February 1922), 155.

20. Shellum, *Black Officer in a Buffalo Soldier Regiment*, 99, 128, 213.

21. W. E. B. Du Bois to S. B. Pearson, February 23, 1922, Du Bois Papers, UM-A.

22. Lectures: Spring 1922, ca. March 1922, Du Bois Papers, UM-A.

23. Memorandum on lectures by W. E. B. Du Bois, 1922, ca. January 1922, Du Bois Papers, UM-A.

24. Grant, *Negro with a Hat*, chap. 11.

25. Speech by Marcus Garvey, August 1, 1921, *Negro World*, August 6, 1921, in Hill, ed., *Garvey Papers, Vol. 3*, 577.

26. W. E. B. Du Bois, "Marcus Garvey," *The Crisis* (December 1920), 60.

27. "The Demagog," *The Crisis* (April 1922), 252. On Du Bois's feud with Garvey, see Wolters, *Du Bois and His Rivals*, chap. 5; Lewis, *W. E. B. Du Bois, Vol. 2*, chap. 2.

28. Between April 7 and April 27, Du Bois did not have any scheduled lectures. Memorandum on lectures by W. E. B. Du Bois, 1922, ca. January 1922, Du Bois Papers, UM-A.

29. On the history of the British West Indies Regiment, see W. F. Elkins, "A Source of Black Nationalism in the Caribbean: The Revolt of the British West Indies Regiment

at Taranto, Italy," *Science & Society* 34, no. 1 (1970): 99–103; Glenford D. Howe, "In the Crucible of Race: Race, Power, and Military Socialization of West Indian Recruits During the First World War," *Journal of Caribbean Studies* 10, no. 3 (Summer–Fall 1995): 163–81; C. L. Joseph, "The British West Indies Regiment 1914–1918," *Journal of Caribbean History* 2 (1971): 94–124; Anna Maguire, "'I Felt Like a Man': West Indian Troops Under Fire During the First World War," *Slavery & Abolition* 39, no. 3 (2018): 602–21; Richard Smith, *Jamaican Volunteers in the First World War: Race, Masculinity and the Development of a National Consciousness* (Manchester: Manchester University Press, 2004).

30. England's use of African "natives" as laborers and the role of Black South African troops in the East African campaign received less attention in the chapter draft. *The Black Man and the Wounded World*, chap. 5, "Black England," Du Bois Collection, Fisk, box 27, folder 2.

31. E. C. Williams to Du Bois, May 3, 1922, *The Black Man and the Wounded World*, General, Du Bois Collection, Fisk, box 15, folder 4.

32. In her June 1921 review of *Two Colored Women* in *The Crisis*, Jessie Fauset described it as "the first intimate and authentic account of the life of the colored soldier who fought for his country in France" and "a guide-book to memory." "On the Bookshelf," *The Crisis* (June 1921), 60–61. A first edition of the book digitized for the Internet Archive contains Du Bois's signature. This was likely his personal copy.

33. Kathryn M. Johnson to NAACP Board of Directors, ca. July 1916; NAACP Board of Directors to Kathryn M. Johnson, August 15, 1916; Kathryn M. Johnson to W. E. B. Du Bois, September 6, 1916, Du Bois Papers, UM-A.

34. On Black women's wartime activism, see Brown, *Private Politics and Public Voices*; Darlene Clark Hine, "The Call That Never Came: Black Women Nurses and World War I," *Indiana Military History Journal* 15 (January 1983): 23–26; Andrea Patterson, "Black Nurses in the Great War: Fighting for and with the American Military in the Struggle for Civil Rights," *Canadian Journal of History* 47, no. 3 (2012): 545–66.

35. For more on Johnson and Hunton, see Brown, *Private Politics and Public Voices*, chap. 4; Lentz-Smith, *Freedom Struggles*, chap. 1; Nina Mjagkij, *Light in the Darkness: African Americans and the YMCA, 1852–1946* (Lexington: University Press of Kentucky, 1993), chap. 5; Scott, *Scott's Official History*, chap. 17 (written by Alice Dunbar-Nelson).

36. Hunton and Johnson, *Two Colored Women*, preface.

37. Letter from Clinton J. Peterson to W. E. B. Du Bois, August 2, 1920, Du Bois Papers, UM-A.

38. Letter from Clinton J. Peterson to W. E. B. Du Bois, January 22, 1922, Du Bois Papers, UM-A.

39. Madeline G. Allison to Clinton J. Peterson, January 25, 1922, Du Bois Papers, UM-A.

40. W. E. B. Du Bois to Clinton J. Peterson, February 20, 1922, Du Bois Papers, UM-A.

41. *The Black Man and the Wounded World*, chap. 12, "The 15th New York," Notes, Du Bois Collection, Fisk, box 28, folders 11–13; William Haywood to W. E. B. Du Bois, April 6, 1922; *The Black Man and the Wounded World*, chap. 12, "The 15th New York," Notes, Du Bois Collection, Fisk, box 28, folder 13.

42. On the spread of the Ku Klux Klan in the 1920s and its anti-Catholicism, see Gordon, *The Second Coming of the KKK*; Felix Harcourt, *Ku Klux Kulture: America and the Klan in the 1920s* (Chicago: University of Chicago Press, 2017); William D. Jenkins, *Steel Valley Klan:*

The Ku Klux Klan in Ohio's Mahoning Valley (Kent, OH: Kent State University Press, 1990); Shawn Lay, *Hooded Knights on the Niagara: The Ku Klux Klan in Buffalo, New York* (New York: New York University Press, 1995); MacLean, *Behind the Mask of Chivalry*; Leonard Joseph Moore, *Citizen Klansmen: The Ku Klux Klan in Indiana, 1921–1928* (Chapel Hill: University of North Carolina Press, 1997); Mark Paul Richard, *Not a Catholic Nation: The Ku Klux Klan Confronts New England in the 1920s* (Amherst: University of Massachusetts Press, 2015).

43. Letter from Knights of Columbus Historical Commission to W. E. B. Du Bois, May 10, 1922, Du Bois Papers, UM-A.

44. Ibid.

45. W. E. B. Du Bois to Knights of Columbus Historical Commission, May 11, 1922, Du Bois Papers, UM-A.

46. W. E. B. Du Bois to Knights of Columbus Historical Commission, May 20, 1922; Knights of Columbus Historical Commission to W. E. B. Du Bois, May 24, 1922, Du Bois Papers, UM-A.

47. W. E. B. Du Bois to Knights of Columbus Historical Commission, June 6, 1922, Du Bois Papers, UM-A.

48. W. E. B. Du Bois to Edward F. McSweeney, October 15, 1923, Du Bois Papers, UM-A.

49. Memorandum on criticisms of 'The gift of Black folk,' October 15, 1923, Du Bois Papers, UM-A.

50. Du Bois, *The Gift of Black Folk*, 29–30.

51. Ibid., 54–56.

52. James Weldon Johnson, *Along This Way*, 363–64.

53. On the NAACP anti-lynching campaign and significance of *Moore v. Dempsey*, see Megan Ming Francis, *Civil Rights and the Making of the Modern American State* (New York: Cambridge University Press, 2014), chaps. 4–5; Mark Schneider, *"We Return Fighting": The Civil Rights Movement in the Jazz Age* (Boston: Northeastern University Press, 2002), chaps. 5, 12, and 14; Sullivan, *Lift Every Voice*, 105–11.

54. Along with the manuscript and documents, Du Bois included for reference "a few copies of histories already published covering various parts of the work of Negro troops," likely among them works by Emmett Scott, Kelly Miller, William Allison Sweeny, and Kathryn Johnson and Addie Hunton. Report of the director of publication, November 1922, Du Bois Papers, UM-A; Minutes of the Meeting of the Board of Directors, December 11, 1922, NAACP Papers, LOC.

55. W. E. B. Du Bois to Open Forum Speakers Bureau, January 11, 1923, Du Bois Papers, UM-A; Open Forum Speakers Bureau was established in Boston in 1914. Arthur Mountain, "The Open Forum Movement," *American Review* 1 (1923): 464–67. On the history of the Open Forum lecture movement, see Arthur S. Meyers, *Democracy in the Making: The Open Forum Lecture Movement* (Lanham, MD: University Press of America, 2012), and specifically chapter 6 on Du Bois.

56. Lectures by W. E. Burghardt Du Bois, 1923, Du Bois Papers, UM-A.

57. "Wayfaring," *The Crisis* (May 1923), 7.

58. "The Message," *The Crisis* (May 1923), 7–8.

59. "The Outer Pocket," *The Crisis* (May 1923), 84.

60. "Negroes Boldest and Most Fearless Champion of Civil Rights Reaches L.A.," *California Eagle*, February 24, 1923.

61. "Dr. DuBois Heard in Los Angeles," *California Eagle*, March 4, 1923.

62. Ibid.

63. Throughout the spring and summer of 1923, the titles of Du Bois's lectures, as well as his book, alternated between "The Black Man *in* the Wounded World" and "The Black Man *and* the Wounded World" (emphasis mine). By the end of 1923, the title was definitively "The Black Man and the Wounded World."

64. "Audiences," *The Crisis* (May 1923), 8.

65. Letter from United States Army Quartermaster General to Ada M. Young, March 3, 1922, Du Bois Papers, UM-A; Shellum, *Black Officer in a Buffalo Soldier Regiment*, 283.

66. Letter from W. E. B. Du Bois to Ada Young, April 12, 1923, Du Bois Papers, UM-A.

67. Letter from W. E. B. Du Bois written on behalf of Ada Young to W. A. Hamilton, May 9, 1923, Du Bois Papers. UM-A.

68. Letter from American Legion Colonel Charles Young Post 398 to W. E. B. Du Bois, June 19, 1922; Letter from W. E. B. Du Bois to Ada M. Young, June 26, 1922, Du Bois Papers, UM-A.

69. Letter from W. E. B. Du Bois to Shelby Davidson, May 21, 1923; Letter from Shelby Davidson to W. E. B. Du Bois, May 23, 1923, Du Bois Papers, UM-A.

70. "Major Patterson Resumes Practice," *Chicago Defender*, January 24, 1920; "Maj. Patterson Loses Position," *Chicago Defender*, January 26, 1924; "Mayor Wm. E. Dever Orders Maj. Patterson Reinstated," *Chicago Defender*, March 1, 1924.

71. Adam E. Patterson to W. E. B. Du Bois, May 15, 1923, Du Bois Papers, UM-A.

72. W. E. B. Du Bois to Adam E. Patterson, May 22, 1923, Du Bois Papers, UM-A.

73. "Col. Charles Young's Body Arrives Here," *New York Amsterdam News*, May 23, 1923; "New Yorkers Pay Last Tribute to Col. Young," *Chicago Defender*, June 2, 1923.

74. Badger, *A Life in Ragtime*, 218–19.

75. "The Great Hall of the College of the City of New York, Messrs. George B. Post & Sons, Architects," *American Architect* (March 31, 1909), 110–11.

76. "Col. Charles Young's Body Arrives Here," *New York Amsterdam News*, May 23, 1923; "New Yorkers Pay Last Tribute to Col. Young," *Chicago Defender*, June 2, 1923.

77. "Whole United States Will Honor Col. Young at Services in Arlington Cemetery on Friday," *Baltimore Afro-American*, June 1, 1923.

78. Walter F. White to W. E. B. Du Bois, May 16, 1923, Du Bois Papers, UM-A.

79. "New Yorkers Pay Last Tribute to Col. Young," *Chicago Defender*, June 2, 1923; Lewis, *W. E. B. Du Bois, Vol. 2*, 100–102.

80. "Color Did Not Bar Col. Young," *New York Amsterdam News*, May 30, 1923.

81. Ibid.

82. "New Yorkers Pay Last Tribute to Col. Young," *Chicago Defender*, June 2, 1923; "Whole United States Will Honor Col. Young at Services in Arlington Cemetery on Friday," *Baltimore Afro-American*, June 1, 1923; "New York's Final Tribute Is Laid at Bier of Late Col. Charles Young, U.S.A.," *New York Age*, June 2, 1923.

83. "Crowds in Phila. Honor Col. Young," *Baltimore Afro-American*, June 8, 1923.

84. "Young Funeral on Next Friday," *Baltimore Afro-American*, May 25, 1923; "Colored Schools Close for Col. Young Funeral," *Washington Post*, June 1, 1923; "60,000 in Washington Pay Final Tribute to Col. Charles Young on Friday," *Baltimore Afro-American*, June 8, 1923; Shellum, *Black Officer in a Buffalo Solider Regiment*, 283–84.

85. Henry Ossian Flipper was the first African American to graduate from West Point in 1877. Johnson Chesnut Whittaker enrolled in 1876 and briefly roomed with Flipper. On April 5, 1880, he was found unconscious, having been beaten and tied to his bed. West Point officials accused him of faking his attack to avoid taking a final exam required for graduation. He was subsequently court-martialed and expelled. In 1883 President Chester Arthur overturned the conviction, and in 1995 President Bill Clinton awarded Whittaker a posthumous commission. On the first African Americans at West Point, see Tom Carhart, *Barricades: The First African-American West Point Cadets and Their Constant Fight for Survival* (Xlibris, 2020).

86. "Charles Young," *The Crisis* (July 1923), 104–106.

87. "The Horizon," *The Crisis* (April 1922), 270; Vanessa Northington Gamble, *Making a Place for Ourselves: The Black Hospital Movement, 1920–1945* (New York: Oxford University Press, 1995), 75.

88. Gamble, *Making a Place for Ourselves*, 75–80.

89. Jennifer D. Keene, "The Long Journey Home: African American World War I Veterans and Veterans' Policies," in Stephen R. Ortiz, ed., *Veterans' Policies, Veterans' Politics* (Gainesville: University Press of Florida, 2012), 159–60.

90. Isaac Webb to W. E. B. Du Bois, June 29, 1923, Du Bois Papers, UM-A.

91. Mary Kaplan, *The Tuskegee Veterans Hospital and Its Black Physicians: The Early Years* (Jefferson, NC: McFarland, 2016), 24. Ralph Ellison, in his 1952 novel *Invisible Man*, evokes the experiences of shell-shocked Southern Black veterans confined to an insane asylum.

92. Paul R. D. Lawrie, *Forging a Laboring Race: The African American Worker in the Progressive Imagination* (New York: New York University Press, 2016), chap. 4.

93. "The Horizon," *The Crisis* (April 1923), 270.

94. Letter from Albon L. Hosley to B. J. Davis, May 30, 1923, Du Bois Papers, UM-A; Keene, "The Long Journey Home," 161.

95. "The Fear of Efficiency," *The Crisis* (June 1923), 55–56.

96. "The Tuskegee Hospital," *The Crisis* (July 1923). Albon Hosley, Robert Moton's personal secretary at Tuskegee, provided Du Bois with detailed information about developments surrounding the hospital, which Du Bois used for this editorial. Albon L. Hosley to W. E. B. Du Bois, June 1, 1923, Du Bois Papers, UM-A.

97. Letter from Albon L. Hosley to W. E. B. Du Bois, July 14, 1923, Du Bois Papers, UM-A.

98. Albon L. Hosley to W. E. B. Du Bois, July 14, 1923, Du Bois Papers, UM-A; Secretary Report, September 1923, NAACP Papers, LOC; Pete Daniel, "Black Power in the 1920s: The Case of Tuskegee Veterans Hospital," *Journal of Southern History* 36, no. 3 (1970): 378–79; "The Tuskegee Hospital Muddle," *The Crisis* (September 1923), 216–18; Gamble, *Making a Place for Ourselves*, 91–93.

99. "Tuskegee Situation Tests President," July 20, 1923, *Baltimore Afro-American*.

100. "Hines Probes Klan Use of U.S. Sheets at Tuskegee," *Baltimore Afro-American*, July 27, 1923.

101. "Fear Race Clash at Tuskegee," *Chicago Defender*, July 14, 1923.

102. Walter White, *A Man Called White: The Autobiography of Walter White* (New York: Viking Press, 1948), 70.

103. "Why Negro Veterans Lack Negro Doctors," *The Outlook* (July 18, 1923), 396–98.

104. Letter from Annie Howe to W. E. B. Du Bois, July 27, 1923, Du Bois Papers, UM-A.

105. W. E. B. Du Bois to Annie Howe, August 1, 1923, Du Bois Papers, UM-A.

106. Gamble, *Making a Place for Ourselves*, 100.

107. W. E. B. Du Bois to Otis B. Duncan, June 19, 1923, Du Bois Papers, UM-A.

108. Lewis, *W. E. B. Du Bois, Vol. 1*, 459–61; David Krasner, "'The Pageant Is the Thing': Black Nationalism and The Star of Ethiopia," in Jeffrey D. Mason and J. Ellen Gainor, eds., *Performing America: Cultural Nationalism in American Theater* (Ann Arbor: University of Michigan Press, 1998), 106–22.

109. On Chicago's place in the New Negro renaissance, see Davarian Baldwin, *Chicago's New Negroes: Modernity, the Great Migration, and Black Urban Life* (Chapel Hill: University of North Carolina Press, 2007).

110. W. E. B. Du Bois to Otis B. Duncan, June 19, 1923, Du Bois Papers, UM-A.

111. Otis B. Duncan to W. E. B. Du Bois, June 22, 1923, Du Bois Papers, UM-A.

112. W. E. B. Du Bois to Otis B. Duncan, July 9, 1923; Memorandum on a proposed pageant and history entitled "the Black man and the wounded world" and designed to illustrate the part which the Negro race took in the Great War, ca. 1923, Du Bois Papers, UM-A.

113. Du Bois to Camille Cohen Jones, August 8, 1923, Du Bois Papers, UM-A.

114. Lewis, *W. E. B. Du Bois, Vol. 2*, 109–11.

115. "The Houston Martyrs," *The Crisis* (December 1923), 73.

116. "The Houston Martyrs," *The Crisis* (November 1923), 7.

117. "Sick and in Prison," *The Crisis* (December 1923), 59. The December issue also included an accompanying article, "The Houston Martyrs," *The Crisis* (December 1923), 72–74.

118. "The January Crisis," *The Crisis* (December 1923).

Chapter 9

1. *The Black Man and the Wounded World*, chap. 1, "Interpretations," Du Bois Collection, Fisk, box 26, folder 22.

2. Letter from Denison House to John Alcindor, October 8, 1922, Du Bois Papers, UM-A.

3. "Sketches from Abroad: Le Grand Voyage," *The Crisis* (March 1924), 203–205.

4. "Pan-Africa in Portugal," *The Crisis* (February 1924), 170; Lewis, *W. E. B. Du Bois, Vol. 2*, 109–17.

5. "Sketches from Abroad: Le Grand Voyage," *The Crisis* (March 1924), 203–205; The journey of W. E. B. Du Bois: and invitation to victuals, 1924, Du Bois Papers, UM-A; Lewis, *W. E. B. Du Bois, Vol. 2*, 118.

6. "Sketches from Abroad: Le Grand Voyage," *The Crisis* (March 1924), 203; Lewis, *W. E. B. Du Bois, Vol. 2*, 118; W. E. B. Du Bois, "The Primitive Black Man," *The Nation* 119 (December 17, 1924), 675–76.

7. W. E. B. Du Bois to William H. Lewis, September 20, 1923; William H. Lewis to W. E. B. Du Bois, October 4, 1923; William H. Lewis to Calvin Coolidge, October 4, 1923; William H. Lewis to W. E. B. Du Bois, October 11, 1923; W. E. B. Du Bois to William H. Lewis, October 13, 1923; Calvin Coolidge to Charles D. B. King, December 28, 1923, Du Bois Papers, UM-A; "An Appointment," *The Crisis* (March 1924); Lewis, *W. E. B. Du Bois, Vol. 2*, 112.

8. W. E. B. Du Bois to C. D. B. King, 1924, Du Bois Papers, UM-A; Lewis, *W. E. B. Du Bois, Vol. 2*, 120–21.

9. G. I. C. Eluwa, "Background to the Emergence of the National Congress of British West Africa," *African Studies Review* 14, no. 2 (1971): 205–18. Also see David A. Kimble, *A Political History of Ghana: The Rise of Gold Coast Nationalism, 1850–1928* (Oxford: Clarendon Press, 1963).

10. W. E. B. Du Bois, "The Black Man and the Wounded World: A History of the Negro Race in the World War and After," *The Crisis* (January 1924), 110–14; *The Black Man and the Wounded World*, chap. 1, "Interpretations," Du Bois Collection, Fisk, box 26, folder 22; Lewis, *W. E. B. Du Bois, Vol. 2*, 254; Keene, "W. E. B. Du Bois and the Wounded World," 138.

11. See *The Black Man and the Wounded World*, Subscriptions, Du Bois Collection, Fisk, box 15, folders 6–11; Bradford G. Williams to Du Bois, January 14, 1924, *The Black Man and the Wounded World*, Subscriptions, T-Y, Du Bois Collection, Fisk, box 15, folder 11.

12. W. E. B. Du Bois to Mildred C. Smith, March 21, 1924; Du Bois's talks during his lecture tour focused mostly on the Pan-African Congress and the future of Liberia. Lectures by W. E. B. Du Bois: Spring 1924, ca. April 1924, Du Bois Papers, UM-A.

13. Pero Gaglo Dagbovie, "'Most Honorable Mention . . . Belongs to Washington, DC': The Carter G. Woodson Home and the Early Black History Movement in the Nation's Capital," *Journal of African American History* 96, no. 3 (2011): 295–324.

14. W. E. B. Du Bois to Carter G. Woodson, April 24, 1924, Du Bois Papers, UM-A.

15. Associated Publishers to W. E. B. Du Bois, April 28, 1924, Du Bois Papers, UM-A.

16. See Mark Whalan, *The Great War and the Culture of the New Negro* (Gainesville: University Press of Florida, 2008); Williams, *Torchbearers of Democracy*, 324–44.

17. W. E. B. Du Bois, "The Black Man and the Wounded World," *The Crisis* (May 1924), 36–38.

18. "The World in Council," *The Crisis* (September 1911), 196.

19. On Gustav Spiller and the Ethical movement, see Ian MacKillop, *The British Ethical Societies* (Cambridge: Cambridge University Press, 1986).

20. At the congress, Du Bois delivered a paper in the sixth session on "The Negro Race in the United States," surveying their history and their progress since emancipation and, in a clear rebuke to the program of Booker T. Washington, arguing before the international audience that "intellectual emancipation should proceed hand-in-hand with economic independence." Universal Races Congress, First Universal Races Congress pamphlet, 1911, Du Bois Papers, UM-A; Record of the Proceedings of the First Universal Races Congress, 1911, Du Bois Collection, Fisk, box 6, folder 23; Lewis, *W. E. B. Du Bois, Vol. 1*, 439–43.

21. John David Smith, "W.E.B. Du Bois, Felix von Luschan, and Racial Reform at the Fin de Siècle," *Amerikastudien / American Studies* 47, no. 1 (2002): 23–38.

22. On Lloyd George's Mansion House speech and significance, see Timothy Boyle, "New Light on Lloyd George's Mansion House Speech," *Historical Journal* 23, no. 2 (1980): 431–33; Keith Wilson, "The Agadir Crisis, the Mansion House Speech, and the Double-Edgedness of Agreements," *Historical Journal* 15, no. 3 (1972): 513–32.

23. On the Agadir Crisis, see Gregory D. Miller, *The Shadow of the Past* (Ithaca, NY: Cornell University Press, 2011), chap. 6.

24. On the crucial period between July 28 and August 28, 1914, see Neiberg, *Dance of the Furies*.

25. Du Bois, "The Black Man and the Wounded World," *The Crisis* (May 1924), 36–38; For the full chapter draft, see *The Black Man and the Wounded World*, chap. 2, "The Story of the War," Du Bois Collection, Fisk, box 26, folder 23.

26. The combined total of potential subscribers from the January and May calls numbered at least 114. *The Black Man and the Wounded World*, Subscriptions, Du Bois Collection, Fisk, box 15, folders 6–11.

27. Blair T. Hunt to Du Bois, May 13, 1924, *The Black Man and the Wounded World*, Subscriptions, H–J, Du Bois Collection, Fisk, box 15, folder 8.

28. Du Bois, *Dusk of Dawn*, 759.

29. Following his return from Liberia, Du Bois attacked Garvey in *The Crisis*, beginning with "A Lunatic or a Traitor" in the May 1924 issue. "A Lunatic or a Traitor," *The Crisis* (May 1924), 8–9. On the feud between Du Bois and Garvey, see Lewis, *W. E. B. Du Bois, Vol. 2*, 148–52; Wolters, *Du Bois and His Rivals*, chap. 5.

30. The revolt at Fisk, ostensibly about the choking influence of white leadership and money, and the power of Black students and alumni to shape their institutions, expanded to other colleges as well. McKenzie resigned as Fisk president on April 16, 1925. See Lewis, *W. E. B. Du Bois, Vol. 2*, 132–48.

31. See Douglas Flamming, "*The Star of Ethiopia* and the NAACP: Pageantry, Politics, and the Los Angeles African American Community," in Tom Sitton and William Deverell, eds., *Metropolis in the Making: Los Angeles in the 1920s* (Berkeley: University of California Press, 2001).

32. On Bullard's background and career during the World War, see Sebastian H. Lukasik, "Lieutenant General Robert L. Bullard," in David T. Zabecki and Douglas V. Mastriano, *Pershing's Lieutenants: American Military Leadership in World War I* (London: Bloomsbury, 2020).

33. Henry E. Armstrong, "General Bullard 'Hopes' Not to Arouse Controversy," *New York Times*, December 27, 1925.

34. Robert Lee Bullard, *Personalities and Reminiscences of the War* (New York: Doubleday, Page, 1925), 291–98.

35. "Bullard a 'Damnable Liar,'" *New York Amsterdam News*, June 10, 1925.

36. "Bullard Was Named for Bob Lee," *Chicago Defender*, June 13, 1925.

37. In refuting Bullard's claims against the 368th, the *Courier* also quoted from Du Bois's 1919 "Essay Toward a History of the Black Man in the Great War," an indication that six years later, Du Bois's views and research on the Black war experience remained authoritative and highly relevant. "'Take Back Lies,' Bullard Is Told," *Pittsburgh Courier*, June 20, 1925.

38. "Voice of the People," *Chicago Daily Tribune*, June 12, 1925.

39. "Bullard's Charges Against Colored Soldiers Resented by A.E.F. Military Leaders," *Houston Informer*, June 20, 1925, in NAACP Papers, LOC.

40. G. H. Hammond Jr. to W. E. B. Du Bois, June 10, 1925, Du Bois Papers, UM-A.

41. Walter Chenault to W. E. B. Du Bois, June 16, 1925, Du Bois Papers, UM-A.

42. Haywood and Fish had no connection to the Ninety-Second Division. They recognized, however, that Bullard's accusations tarnished the legacy of all Black soldiers as well as the white officers who led them. Their reputation was at stake as well. In February of the following year, Fish introduced a bill in Congress for the erection of a monument in Séchault, France, in honor of the Ninety-Third Division. Fish encouraged the NAACP to take up his bill with the same fervor as the Dyer anti-lynching bill, arguing to James Weldon Johnson that if the bill passed, the monument "would be a conclusive answer for all time to the arraignment of colored soldiers by General Bullard." Hamilton Fish to James Weldon Johnson, March 20, 1926; Report from Secretary, July 1925 meeting, NAACP Papers, LOC.

43. "Resolutions Score Bullard and Coolidge," *Baltimore Afro-American*, July 18, 1925.

44. "Major Adam Patterson Gives Some Inside Facts to Refute Bullard's Attack on Soldiers," *Chicago Defender*, June 13, 1925.

45. Many of the photographs belonged to other veterans, who pressured Patterson to request their return. Adam E. Patterson to W. E. B. Du Bois, May 7, 1925; W. E. B. Du Bois to Adam E. Patterson, May 13, 1925, *The Black Man and the Wounded World*, General, Du Bois Collection, Fisk, box 15, folder 1.

46. Letter from A. E. Patterson to W. E. B. Du Bois, June 16, 1925, Du Bois Papers, UM-A.

47. W. E. B. Du Bois to Adam E. Patterson, July 8, 1925, Du Bois Papers, UM-A.

48. W. E. B. Du Bois to A. E. Patterson, July 16, 1925, Du Bois Papers, UM-A.

49. W. E. B. Du Bois to A. E. Patterson, July 22, 1925, Du Bois Papers, UM-A.

50. A. E. Patterson to W. E. B. Du Bois, August 4, 1925, Du Bois Papers, UM-A.

51. "Bullard," *The Crisis* (September 1925).

52. "Negro Manpower in War," October 30, 1925, USAHEC.

53. Major General Hanson Ely to Chief of Staff, November 10, 1925, USAHEC.

54. W. E. B. Du Bois to Charles E. Bentley, September 11, 1925, Du Bois Papers, UM-A.

55. Benjamin F. Seldon to W. E. B. Du Bois, September 6, 1925; W. E. B. Du Bois to Abram R. Reeves, September 24, 1925; National Council of the Young Men's Christian Associations of the United States of America to W. E. B. Du Bois, September 19, 1925; W. E. B. Du Bois to Leroy H. Godman, September 17, 1924; W. E. B. Du Bois to L. H. Godman, October 28, 1925; L. H. Godman to W. E. B. Du Bois [fragment], October 31, 1925; L. H. Godman to W. E. B. Du Bois, December 2, 1925, Du Bois Papers, UM-A.

56. *The Black Man and the Wounded World*, chap. 16, "The 368th Regiment," Du Bois Collection, Fisk, box 27, folder 10.

57. Ibid.

58. The Macmillan Company to W. E. B. Du Bois, July 29, 1925, Du Bois Papers, UM-A.

59. W. E. B. Du Bois to the Macmillan Company, September 10, 1925, Du Bois Papers, UM-A.

60. The Macmillan Company to W. E. B. Du Bois, September 17, 1925, Du Bois Papers, UM-A.

61. See Keith L. Nelson, "The 'Black Horror on the Rhine': Race as a Factor in Post–World War I Diplomacy," *Journal of Modern History* 42, no. 4 (1970): 606–27; Julia Roos, "Nationalism, Racism and Propaganda in Early Weimar Germany: Contradictions in the Campaign Against the 'Black Horror on the Rhine,'" *German History* 30, no. 1 (2012): 45–74.

62. On the Dawes Plan, see Conan Fischer, *The Ruhr Crisis, 1923–1924* (Oxford: Oxford University Press, 2003); Stephen A. Schuker, *The End of French Predominance in Europe: The Financial Crisis of 1924 and the Adoption of the Dawes Plan* (Chapel Hill: University of North Carolina Press, 1978).

63. See Zara Steiner, *The Lights That Failed: European International History, 1919–1933* (Oxford: Oxford University Press, 2007), 387–410; Patrick O. Cohrs, *The Unfinished Peace After World War I: America, Britain and the Stabilisation of Europe, 1919–1932* (New York: Cambridge University Press, 2006); William Mulligan, *The Great War for Peace* (New Haven, CT: Yale University Press, 2014).

64. "Peace on Earth," *The Crisis* (March 1926), 215–16.

65. W. E. B. Du Bois to Carter G. Woodson, March 19, 1926, Du Bois Papers, UM-A.

66. Carter G. Woodson to W. E. B. Du Bois, March 20, 1926, Du Bois Papers, UM-A.

67. The Macmillan Company to W. E. B. Du Bois, March 25, 1926; W. E. B. Du Bois to the Macmillan Company, March 26, 1926; the Macmillan Company to W. E. B. Du Bois, March 30, 1926, Du Bois Papers, UM-A.

68. Du Bois, *Dusk of Dawn*, 760.

69. For Du Bois's immediate postwar thoughts on the Russian Revolution, see "Forward," *The Crisis* (September 1919), 234–35.

70. Russia and America: An Interpretation, 1950, Du Bois Papers, UM-A.

71. For an example of Du Bois's correspondence in 1926 related to the proposed "Battalions of Labor" chapter, see Leon C. James to W. E. B. Du Bois, May 14, 1926; Leon C. James to J. E. Moorland [fragment], July 9, 1919, Du Bois Papers, UM-A; *The Black Man and the Wounded World*, chap. 10, "Battalions of Labor," Du Bois Collection, Fisk, box 27, folder 6. *Sidelights on Negro Soldiers* offered an especially useful view of domestic camp conditions for Black labor troops, which Williams investigated while working with the Federal Council of Churches and the Phelps-Stokes Fund. See Charles H. Williams, *Sidelights on Negro Soldiers* (Boston: B. J. Brimmer, 1923).

72. On June 21, he contacted a representative of the Italy America Society for any information they may have had on Black troops in the Italian army during the war. W. E. B. Du Bois to Irene Di Robilant, June 21, 1926; Augusto Villa to Irene Di Robilant, June 26, 1926, Du Bois Papers, UM-A.

73. Du Bois, *Dusk of Dawn*, 763.

74. Russia and America: An Interpretation, 1950, Du Bois Papers, UM-A.

75. Du Bois, *Dusk of Dawn*, 762.

76. "Russia, 1926," *The Crisis* (November 1926), 8.

77. Russia and America: An Interpretation, 1950, Du Bois Papers, UM-A.

78. Du Bois, *Dusk of Dawn*, 762–64; "Russia, 1926," *The Crisis* (November 1926), 8.

79. W. E. B. Du Bois to R. R. Taylor, January 3, 1927, Du Bois Papers, UM-A.

80. R. R. Taylor to W. E. B. Du Bois, March 9, 1927; W. E. B. Du Bois to R. R. Taylor, March 14, 1927, Du Bois Papers, UM-A.

81. *The Black Man and the Wounded World*, Misc. Entries, Du Bois Collection, Fisk, box 31, folder 1.

82. James William Johnson to W. E. B. Du Bois, May 28, 1927, Du Bois Papers, UM-A.

83. W. E. B. Du Bois to James William Johnson, June 2, 1927, Du Bois Papers, UM-A.

84. James William Johnson to W. E. B. Du Bois, June 7, 1927, Du Bois Papers, UM-A.

85. W. E. B. Du Bois to James Dillard, June 15, 1927, Du Bois Papers, UM-A.

86. See Eric Anderson and Alfred A. Moss, *Dangerous Donations: Northern Philanthropy and Southern Black Education, 1902–1930* (Columbia: University of Missouri Press, 1999). Du Bois's relationship with various philanthropies and his constant struggle for funding is a consistent theme through David Levering Lewis's two-volume biography. With a focus on the 1930s and Du Bois's efforts at international reform, see Maribel Morey, "W. E. B. Du Bois's International Lens on Modern US Philanthropy and His Fleeting Hopes for Reform," in Aldon Morris et al., *The Oxford Handbook of W. E. B. Du Bois* (Oxford: Oxford Academic Press, 2022).

87. J. H. Dillard to W. E. B. Du Bois, June 25, 1927; W. E. B. Du Bois to James Dillard, July 8, 1927; J. H. Dillard to W. E. B. Du Bois, July 12, 1927; J. H. Dillard to W. E. B. Du Bois, August 3, 1927, Du Bois Papers, UM-A.

88. J. H. Dillard to W. E. B. Du Bois, September 17, 1927, Du Bois Papers, UM-A.

89. W. E. B. Du Bois to James Dillard, September 27, 1927, Du Bois Papers, UM-A.

90. W. E. B. Du Bois to the Rockefeller Foundation, November 18, 1927, Du Bois Papers, UM-A.

91. The Rockefeller Foundation to W. E. B. Du Bois, November 26, 1927, Du Bois Papers, UM-A.

92. Lewis, *W. E. B. Du Bois, Vol. 2*, 230–31; W. E. B. Du Bois to Mrs. Matthew V. Boutté, December 27, 1927, Du Bois Papers, UM-A.

93. The committee consisted of Clarence Darrow (chair), John Hurst, Mary McLeod Bethune, James Cobb, Lillian Alexander (secretary), and Arthur Spingarn. Du Bois Testimonial Committee. Circular letter from Du Bois Testimonial Committee, 1928; Du Bois Testimonial Committee. Circular letter from Du Bois Testimonial Committee, February 1928, Du Bois Papers, UM-A.

94. The property still required $5,000 worth of renovations. W. E. B. Du Bois to Alice Davis Crawford, February 28, 1928, Du Bois Papers, UM-A.

95. Lewis, *W. E. B. Du Bois, Vol. 2*, 220–26; Mason Stokes, "Father of the Bride: Du Bois and the Making of Black Heterosexuality," in Gillman and Weinbaum, *Next to the Color Line*.

96. On Alain Locke and the New Negro, see Alain Locke, ed., *The New Negro: An Interpretation* (New York: Albert and Charles Boni, 1925); Jeffrey C. Stewart, *The New Negro: The Life of Alain Locke* (New York: Oxford University Press, 2018). On the Harlem Renaissance and the New Negro movement more generally, see Lewis, *When Harlem Was in Vogue*; Cary D. Wintz and Paul Finkelman, eds., *Encyclopedia of the Harlem Renaissance* (New York: Routledge, 2004); Davarian L. Baldwin and Minkah Makalani, *Escape from New York: The New Negro Renaissance Beyond Harlem* (Minneapolis: University of Minnesota Press, 2013).

97. W. E. B. Du Bois, "The Criteria of Negro Art," *The Crisis* (October 1926), 290–97.

98. Since 1919, Du Bois had closely followed India's struggle against British colonial rule and kept readers abreast in *The Crisis*. His friendship with the militant nationalist Lala Lajpat Rai, whom he befriended during the war, played an important role in his knowledge of India and its politics. See Lewis, *W. E. B. Du Bois, Vol. 2*, 218–19.

99. For more in-depth treatments of *Dark Princess*, see Homi K. Bhabha, "The Black Savant and the Dark Princess," *ESQ: A Journal of the American Renaissance* 50, no. 1 (2004): 137–55; Laila Soraya Haidarali, "Browning the Dark Princess: Asian Indian Embodiment of 'New Negro Womanhood,'" *Journal of American Ethnic History* 32, no. 1 (2012): 24–69; Bill V. Mullen, "Du Bois, Dark Princess, and the Afro-Asian International," *Positions: East Asia Cultures Critique* 11, no. 1 (2003): 217–39; Payal K. Patel, "On the Path of the Maharajah of Bwodpur: The Global Problem of the Color Line in W. E. B. Du Bois's *Dark Princess*," *CR: The New Centennial Review* 15, no. 2 (2015): 119–56.

100. Unidentified correspondent to James William Johnson, September 28, 1927, Du Bois Papers, UM-A.

101. James W. Johnson to W. E. B. Du Bois, May 23, 1928, Du Bois Papers, UM-A.

102. W. E. B. Du Bois to James W. Johnson, May 26, 1928, Du Bois Papers, UM-A.

103. James W. Johnson to W. E. B. Du Bois, June 4, 1928, Du Bois Papers, UM-A.

104. Correspondence between W. E. B. Du Bois and James W. Johnson, May 23, 1928–August 17, 1928, Du Bois Papers, UM-A.

105. Around this same time Du Bois spoke with his former *Crisis* coeditor Jessie Fauset about the book. Their conversation led Du Bois to approach Mary Childs Nerney, the executive secretary of the NAACP during its formative years of 1912 to 1916. Nerney had connections to Henry Ford, and Du Bois hoped that she might be able to induce the automobile giant, who initially opposed the war but profited handsomely from it once the United States entered, to finance *The Black Man and the Wounded World*. Nothing came of their correspondence. W. E. B. Du Bois to Mary Childs Nerney, August 11, 1928; Mary Childs Nerney to W. E. B. Du Bois, October 12, 1928, Du Bois Papers, UM-A.

106. W. E. B. Du Bois to John Simon Guggenheim Memorial Foundation, August 11, 1928, Du Bois Papers, UM-A.

107. John Simon Guggenheim Memorial Foundation to W. E. B. Du Bois, August 13, 1928, Du Bois Papers, UM-A.

Chapter 10

1. W. E. B. Du Bois to the World Tomorrow, June 24, 1930, Du Bois Papers, UM-A.

2. Du Bois, *Autobiography*, 91–92.

3. W. E. B. Du Bois, "The Possibility of Democracy in America," *The Crisis* (September 1928), 295.

4. W. E. B. Du Bois, "The Possibility of Democracy in America," *The Crisis* (October 1928), 336.

5. Ibid., 336–38.

6. Du Bois, "Possibility of Democracy in America," Du Bois Papers, UM-A.

7. "On the Fence," *The Crisis* (November 1928), 381; Lewis, *W. E. B. Du Bois, Vol. 2*, 247.

8. On Herbert Hoover, with particular attention to his views on race and African Americans, see John M. Barry, *Rising Tide: The Great Mississippi Flood of 1927 and How It Changed America* (New York: Simon & Schuster, 1997); George F. Garcia, "Herbert Hoover and the Issue of Race," *Annals of Iowa* 44, no. 7 (1979): 507–15. William E. Leuchtenburg, *Herbert Hoover* (New York: Henry Holt, 2009), chaps. 1–5; Donald J. Lisio, *Hoover, Blacks, and Lily-Whites: A Study of Southern Strategies* (Chapel Hill: University of North Carolina Press, 1985).

9. Blueprints for the Johnsons' home, "Five Acres," in Great Barrington, Massachusetts, by J. Mc.A. Vance, circa 1926, box 124, folder 1107, Series V; Johnsons, W.E.B. Du Bois, Nina Du Bois, John B. Nail, John E. Nail, and Grayce Fairfax Nail, Great Barrington, Massachusetts, circa 1928, box 109, folder 960, Series IX, James Weldon Johnson and Grace Nail Johnson Papers, Beinecke Rare Book and Manuscript Library, Yale University.

10. On the relationship between the NAACP and the AFPS, see Sullivan, *Lift Every Voice.*

11. Ibid., 113–14; Gloria Garrett Samson, *The American Fund for Public Service: Charles Garland and Radical Philanthropy, 1922–1941* (Westport, CT: Greenwood Press, 1996), 1–3, 33.

12. The fund largely financed the NAACP's valiant yet unsuccessful campaign to pass the Dyer anti-lynching bill and underwrote the Legal Defense Fund that was established during the Ossian Sweet case. Samson, *The American Fund for Public Service,* 151–52.

13. W. E. B. Du Bois to the American Fund for Public Service Imperialism Committee, January 10, 1929, Du Bois Papers, UM-A.

14. W. E. B. Du Bois to the American Fund for Public Service Imperialism Committee, January 17, 1929, Du Bois Papers, UM-A.

15. W. E. B. Du Bois to the American Fund for Public Service Imperialism Committee, January 25, 1929; Memorandum from W. E. B. Du Bois to the American Fund for Public Service Imperialism Committee, February 9, 1929, Du Bois Papers, UM-A.

16. W. E. B. Du Bois to the American Fund for Public Service Imperialism Committee, January 25, 1929; Memorandum from W. E. B. Du Bois to the American Fund for Public Service Imperialism Committee, April 5, 1929, Du Bois Papers, UM-A.

17. Memorandum from W. E. B. Du Bois to the American Fund for Public Service Imperialism Committee, Du Bois Collection, Fisk, box 14, folder 33.

18. American Fund for Public Service Imperialism Committee to W. E. B. Du Bois, April 3, 1929, Du Bois Papers, UM-A.

19. Memorandum from W. E. B. Du Bois to the American Fund for Public Service Imperialism Committee, March 27, 1929, Du Bois Papers, UM-A.

20. Memorandum from W. E. B. Du Bois to the American Fund for Public Service Imperialism Committee, April 5, 1929, Du Bois Papers, UM-A.

21. American Fund for Public Service Imperialism Committee, Letter from American Fund for Public Service Imperialism Committee to W. E. B. Du Bois, May 1, 1929, Du Bois Papers, UM-A.

22. W. E. B. Du Bois to the American Fund for Public Service Imperialism Committee, March 27, 1929, Du Bois Papers, UM-A.

23. W. E. B. Du Bois to Albert Bushnell Hart, November 20, 1924, Du Bois Papers, UM-A.

24. Albert Bushnell Hart to W. E. B. Du Bois, October 10, 1929, Du Bois Papers, UM-A.

25. W. E. B. Du Bois to Albert Bushnell Hart, October 11, 1929, Du Bois Papers, UM-A.

26. Ibid.

27. Albert Bushnell Hart to W. E. B. Du Bois, October 17, 1929, Du Bois Papers, UM-A.

28. Devere Allen to W. E. B. Du Bois, July 25, 1929, Du Bois Papers, UM-A.

29. Kirby Page to W. E. B. Du Bois, October 1, 1929, Du Bois Papers, UM-A.

30. On the "war guilt" debate in the historical profession, see Novick, *That Noble Dream*, 207–24; Roy Turnbaugh, "Harry Elmer Barnes and World War I Revisionism: An Absence of Dialogue," *Peace & Change* 5 (Fall 1978): 63–69.

31. "War-Guilt Soundings: A Summary of 429 Opinions," *The World Tomorrow* (October 1930), 395.

32. David M. Kennedy, *Freedom from Fear: The American People in Depression and War, 1929–1945* (New York: Oxford University Press, 1999), chap. 2.

33. W. E. B. Du Bois to the World Tomorrow, June 24, 1930, Du Bois Papers, UM-A.

34. Lisa M. Budreau, "The Politics of Remembrance: The Gold Star Mothers' Pilgrimage and America's Fading Memory of the Great War," *Journal of Military History* 72, no. 2 (April 2008): 371–411.

35. "Stay Out of France," *Chicago Defender*, April 19, 1930.

36. Report of the Acting Secretary (for the April Meeting of the Board), no date, Part 01: Meetings of the Board of Directors, Records of Annual Conferences, Major Speeches, and Special Reports, NAACP Papers, LOC.

37. William E. King to W. E. B. Du Bois, May 9, 1930; Letter from W. E. B. Du Bois to William E. King, May 13, 1930, Du Bois Papers, UM-A.

38. "Stay Out of France," *Chicago Defender*, April 19, 1930.

39. Ibid.

40. Colonel Benjamin O. Davis served with the Ninth Cavalry in the Philippines during the World War. As with the other Black regiments of the Regular Army, he was not given the opportunity to serve in France. Slowly rising through the ranks to become a colonel in early 1930, Davis's postwar years included a stint with the Ohio National Guard and teaching military tactics at Wilberforce University and Tuskegee Institute. See Marvin Fletcher, *America's First Black General: Benjamin O. Davis, Sr., 1880–1970* (Lawrence: University of Kansas Press, 1989), 56–75.

41. Rebecca Jo Plant and Frances M. Clarke, "'The Crowning Insult': Federal Segregation and the Gold Star Mother and Widow Pilgrimages of the Early 1930s," *Journal of American History* 102, no. 2 (2015): 406–32.

42. Even Du Bois's rival, Emmett J. Scott, included a chapter in his 1919 book on the contributions of Black women in the war, which was penned by Alice Dunbar-Nelson, who had served as a field representative with the Women's Committee of the Council of National Defense. Alice Dunbar-Nelson, "Negro Women in War Work," chap. 27 in Scott, *Scott's Official History*. On the activism of Black women in World War I, see Brown, *Private Politics and Public Voices*. On the broader history of Black women's activism, see Martha S. Jones, *Vanguard: How Black Women Broke Barriers, Won the Vote, and Insisted on Equality for All* (New York: Basic Books, 2020); Deborah G. White, *Too Heavy a Load: Black Women in Defense of Themselves, 1894–1994* (New York: W. W. Norton, 1999).

43. Jane Olcott, *The Work of Colored Women* (New York: Colored Work Committee, War Work Council, National Board, Young Women's Christian Associations, 1919).

44. *The Black Man and the Wounded World*, chap. 18, "The War Within the War," Du Bois Collection, Fisk, box 27, folder 12.

45. Edwin Rogers Embree and Julia Waxman, *Investment in People: The Story of the Julius Rosenwald Fund* (New York: Harper, 1949), chap. 6.

46. In October 1929, Du Bois had asked Embree if the Rosenwald Fund would be in a position to help offset the financial woes of *The Crisis* to the tune of $10,000. In the end, Embree agreed to grant the NAACP $2,500 over a three-year period, with half of the money going to the cash-strapped magazine. W. E. B. Du Bois to Julius Rosenwald Fund, October 4, 1929; W. E. B. Du Bois to the Crisis Finance Committee, March 26, 1930; W. E. B. Du Bois to Julius Rosenwald Fund, June 3, 1930, Du Bois Papers, UM-A.

47. Du Bois to Julius Rosenwald Fund, December 19, 1930, Du Bois Papers, UM-A.

48. Ibid.

49. Ibid.

50. Anna J. Cooper to W. E. B. Du Bois, December 31, 1929, Du Bois Papers, UM-A; Lewis, *W. E. B. Du Bois, Vol. 2*, 359–60.

51. Edwin R. Embree to W. E. B. Du Bois, January 3, 1931, Du Bois Papers, UM-A.

52. Memorandum from W. E. B. Du Bois to Rosenwald Fund, January 9, 1931, Du Bois Papers, UM-A.

53. In prior correspondence, Embree had given Du Bois every indication that he would receive some type of support. Du Bois proposed four possible subvention plans: $10,000 for two years; $5,000 for one year; $5,000 for two years; $2,500 for one year. Embree countered with the possibility of a two-year award of $5,000 for the first year and $2,500 for the second year. W. E. B. Du Bois to James Weldon Johnson, December 23, 1930; Edwin Embree to Du Bois, January 17, 1931; W. E. B. Du Bois to Rosenwald Fund, January 23, 1931, Du Bois Papers, UM-A.

54. Edwin Embree to Du Bois, February 16, 1931, Du Bois Papers, UM-A.

55. W. E. B. Du Bois to Rosenwald Fund, February 24, 1931, Du Bois Papers, UM-A.

56. Memo from Du Bois to NAACP Board, May 9, 1931; Memorandum from W. E. B. Du Bois to the NAACP Board of Directors, May 12, 1931, Du Bois Papers, UM-A.

57. "56,312 Cars Cross Bridge on First Day," *New York Times*, October 26, 1931; Commercial Credit Corporation. Conditional sales contract, May 24, 1928, Du Bois Papers, UM-A.

58. The economics of war, October 26, 1931, Du Bois Papers, UM-A.

59. Harcourt, Brace and Company to W. E. B. Du Bois, September 11, 1931, Du Bois Papers, UM-A.

60. W. E. B. Du Bois to Harcourt, Brace and Company, September 23, 1931, Du Bois Papers, UM-A.

61. Harcourt, Brace and Company to W. E. B. Du Bois, October 6, 1931, Du Bois Papers, UM-A.

62. Outline of Du Bois's book on Reconstruction, ca. October 21, 1931, Du Bois Papers, UM-A.

63. Harcourt, Brace and Company to W. E. B. Du Bois, October 22, 1931, Du Bois Papers, UM-A.

64. W. E. B. Du Bois to Harcourt, Brace and Company, October 28, 1931, Du Bois Papers, UM-A.

65. Kennedy, *Freedom from Fear*, chap. 3.

66. See Cheryl Lynn Greenberg, *To Ask for an Equal Chance: African Americans in the Great Depression* (Lanham, MD: Rowman & Littlefield, 2009).

67. Lewis, *W. E. B. Du Bois, Vol. 2*, 211–12.

68. Cheryl Lynn Greenberg, *"Or Does It Explode?": Black Harlem in the Great Depression* (New York: Oxford University Press, 1991).

69. "Boutte Seeking Work for Harlem's 'Vets'," *New York Amsterdam News*, March 9, 1932.

70. "Jim-Crow Absent in Veterans Camp," *New York Amsterdam News*, June 15, 1932.

71. "Senate Committee Warned of Needs of American Negro in Plea for Direct Relief Legislation," *New Journal and Guide*, July 2, 1932.

72. "369th Vet Blames G.O.P. for Defeat of Bonus Bill," *Baltimore Afro-American*, June 25, 1932.

73. "Herbert Hoover," *The Crisis* (November 1932), 363.

74. Nancy J. Weiss, *Farewell to the Party of Lincoln: Black Politics in the Age of F.D.R.* (Princeton, NJ: Princeton University Press, 1983), chap. 1.

75. On the rise of Hitler and the 1932 election, see Thomas Childers, *The Third Reich: A History of Nazi Germany* (New York: Simon & Schuster, 2017), chaps. 1–6; Richard J. Evans, *The Coming of the Third Reich* (New York: Penguin Press, 2004), 1–283; William L. Shirer, *The Rise and Fall of the Third Reich: A History of Nazi Germany* (New York: Simon & Schuster, 1960).

76. Lewis, *W. E. B. Du Bois, Vol. 2*, 288–89.

77. "Again Howard," *The Crisis* (April 1932), 131.

78. W. E. B. Du Bois to Arthur Spingarn, October 18, 1932, Du Bois Papers, UM-A.

79. "Howard Again," *The Crisis* (January 1933), 20.

80. Lewis, *W. E. B. Du Bois, Vol. 2*, 283–95, 300–301.

81. Ibid., 302–304; W. E. B. Du Bois to Joel Spingarn, February 22, 1933, Du Bois Papers, UM-A.

82. W. E. B. Du Bois to Joel Spingarn, February 22, 1933, Du Bois Papers, UM-A.

83. On the Scottsboro case, see James E. Goodman, *Stories of Scottsboro* (New York: Vintage Books, 1995); Dan T. Carter, *Scottsboro: A Tragedy of the American South* (Baton Rouge: Louisiana State University Press, 1969); Gerald Horne, *Black Revolutionary: William Patterson and the Globalization of the African American Freedom Struggle* (Urbana: University of Illinois Press, 2013).

84. "Colored Editors on Communism," *The Crisis* (June 1932), 190–91.

85. "Karl Marx and the Negro," *The Crisis* (March 1933), 55–56.

86. "Marxism and the Negro Problem," *The Crisis* (May 1933), 103–104, 118.

87. On Du Bois's engagement with Marxism, see Charisse Burden-Stelly and Gerald Horne, *W. E. B. Du Bois: A Life in American History* (Santa Barbara, CA: ABC-CLIO, 2019); Bill V. Mullen, *Un-American: W.E.B. Du Bois and the Century of World Revolution* (Philadelphia: Temple University Press, 2015), chap. 2; Cedric J. Robinson, *Black Marxism: The Making of the Black Radical Tradition*, 3rd ed. (Chapel Hill: University of North Carolina Press, 2021), chap. 9; Michael J. Saman, "Du Bois and Marx, Du Bois and Marxism," *Du Bois Review* 17, no. 1 (2020): 33–54.

88. W. E. B. Du Bois to Nina Du Bois, March 17, 1933, Du Bois Papers, UM-A.

89. See Eben Miller, *Born Along the Color Line: The 1933 Amenia Conference and the Rise of a National Civil Rights Movement* (New York: Oxford University Press, 2012); Jonathan Scott Holloway, *Confronting the Veil: Abram Harris, Jr., E. Franklin Frazier, and Ralph Bunche, 1919–1941* (Chapel Hill: University of North Carolina Press, 2002); Risa L. Goluboff, *The Lost Promise of Civil Rights* (Cambridge, MA: Harvard University Press, 2007), 179.

90. "Youth and Age at Amenia," *The Crisis* (October 1933), 226–27; Miller, *Born Along the Color Line.*

91. Lewis, *W. E. B. Du Bois, Vol. 2*, 335–48; "Segregation," *The Crisis* (January 1934), 20.

92. Kenneth R. Janken, *Walter White: Mr. NAACP* (New York: The New Press, 2003), 188.

93. "The N. A. A. C. P. and Race Segregation," *The Crisis* (February 1934), 52–53.

94. Ibid.; "A Free Forum," *The Crisis* (February 1934), 52.

95. Greenidge, *Black Radical*, 350–51. Greenidge, in her definitive biography, presents Trotter's death as a suicide, although debate exists as to whether it was an accident. Also see Stephen R. Fox, *The Guardian of Boston: William Monroe Trotter* (New York: Atheneum, 1970).

96. W. E. B. Du Bois, "William Monroe Trotter," *The Crisis* (May 1934), 134.

97. "The Board of Directors on Segregation," *The Crisis* (May 1934), 149.

98. At the same meeting, Mary White Ovington offered a motion giving Du Bois ownership of *The Crisis* and the NAACP severing its ties with the magazine. It failed to garner support. Letter from Mary White Ovington to W. E. B. Du Bois, May 18, 1934, Du Bois Papers, UM-A.

99. Telegram from W. E. B. Du Bois to J. E. Spingarn, May 21, 1934, Du Bois Papers, UM-A.

100. W. E. B. Du Bois to NAACP Board of Directors, June 1, 1934, Du Bois Papers, UM-A.

101. Louis T. Wright to W. E. B. Du Bois, June 16, 1934, Du Bois Papers, UM-A.

102. W. E. B. Du Bois to NAACP Board of Directors, June 26, 1934, Du Bois Papers, UM-A. The NAACP Board formally accepted his resignation on July 9, 1934. Clerk of the Board to W. E. B. Du Bois, July 16, 1934, Du Bois Resignation/Rejoining, Du Bois Collection, Fisk, box 6, folder 28.

103. W. E. B. Du Bois to Edwin Embree, June 3, 1933, Du Bois Papers, UM-A.

104. W. E. B. Du Bois to John Hope, September 14, 1933, Du Bois Papers, UM-A.

105. W. E. B. Du Bois to John Hope, December 13, 1933, Du Bois Papers, UM-A.

106. Alfred Harcourt to the Carnegie Corporation, December 18, 1933; Carnegie Corporation of New York to W. E. B. Du Bois, January 2, 1934; Carnegie Corporation of New York to W. E. B. Du Bois, March 16, 1934; Carnegie Corporation of New York to W. E. B. Du Bois, March 26, 1934, Du Bois Papers, UM-A.

107. Lewis, *W. E. B. Du Bois, Vol. 2*, 362–63.

108. W. E. B. Du Bois to Ruth Anna Fisher, March 26, 1934, Du Bois Papers, UM-A.

109. W. E. B. Du Bois to Harcourt, Brace & Company, May 12, 1934, Du Bois Papers, UM-A.

110. Harcourt, Brace & Company to W. E. B. Du Bois, June 14, 1934, Du Bois Papers, UM-A.

111. W. E. B. Du Bois to Harcourt, Brace & Company, July 17, 1934; Harcourt, Brace & Company to W. E. B. Du Bois, July 23, 1934, Du Bois Papers, UM-A.

112. W. E. B. Du Bois to Harcourt, Brace & Company, November 17, 1934, Du Bois Papers, UM-A.

113. W. E. B. Du Bois, *Black Reconstruction in America* (New York: Simon & Schuster, 1995), 708.

114. Ibid., 725.

115. Shirley Graham to W. E. B. Du Bois, September 9, 1935, Du Bois Papers, UM-A.

116. James Weldon Johnson to W. E. B. Du Bois, June 25, 1935, Du Bois Papers, UM-A.

117. Review of Black Reconstruction, by Benjamin Brawley, ca. June 8, 1935, Du Bois Papers, UM-A.

118. Emmett J. Scott to W. E. B. Du Bois, June 27, 1935, Du Bois Papers, UM-A.

119. W. E. B. Du Bois to J. Emmett Scott, July 9, 1935, Du Bois Papers, UM-A. For more on the development, publication, promotion, and reception of *Black Reconstruction*, see Claire Parfait, "Rewriting History: The Publication of W. E. B. Du Bois's *Black Reconstruction in America* (1935)," *Book History* 12 (2009): 266–94.

120. Du Bois, *Black Reconstruction*, 706.

121. Ibid., 708.

122. Ibid., 713.

Chapter 11

1. Du Bois grant submission to the American Philosophical Society, March 9, 1937, *The Black Man and the Wounded World*, General, Du Bois Collection, Fisk, box 14, folder 33.

2. Shirley Graham Du Bois, *His Day Is Marching On*, 44.

3. W. E. B. Du Bois to Carita V. Owens, February 8, 1928, Du Bois Papers, UM-A.

4. Receipt from the *Atlanta Constitution*, January 30, 1933, Du Bois Papers, UM-A.

5. Evans, *The Coming of the Third Reich*, 301–12.

6. "Comment Varied as Hitler Rises," *Atlanta Constitution*, January 31, 1933.

7. "Hitler Pledges Fight in Cabinet," *New York Times*, January 31, 1933.

8. "The Jews," *The Crisis* (May 1933), 117.

9. "As the Crow Flies," *The Crisis* (October 1933), 221. Also see Harold Brackman, "'A Calamity Almost Beyond Comprehension': Nazi Anti-Semitism and the Holocaust in the Thought of W. E. B. Du Bois," *American Jewish History* 88, no. 1 (March 2000): 53–93; Benjamin Sevitch, "W. E. B. Du Bois and the Jews: A Lifetime of Opposing Anti-Semitism," *Journal of African American History* 87 (Summer 2002): 323–37.

10. Childers, *The Third Reich*, 254–55; Evans, *The Coming of the Third Reich*, chaps. 5 and 6.

11. Childers, *The Third Reich*, 370–72; Richard J. Evans, *The Third Reich in Power, 1933–1939* (New York: Penguin Press, 2005), 618–19.

12. "Peace," *The Crisis* (December 1933), 293.

13. "As the Crow Flies," *The Crisis* (February 1934), 31.

14. On Du Bois's multiple connections to the social sciences, see Britt Rusert and Whitney Battle-Baptiste, eds., *W.E.B. Du Bois's Data Portraits: Visualizing Black America* (New York: Princeton Architectural Press, 2018); Aldon Morris, *The Scholar Denied: W. E. B. Du Bois and the Birth of Modern Sociology* (Berkeley: University of California Press, 2017); Robert E. Prasch, "W. E. B. Du Bois's Contributions to U.S. Economics (1893–1910)," *Du Bois Review* 5, no. 2 (2008): 309–24; Faye V. Harrison and Donald Nonini, "Introduction to W.E.B. Du Bois and Anthropology," *Critique of Anthropology* 12, no. 3 (1992): 229–37.

15. Social Science Research Council (U.S.). Grants in aid of research in the social sciences, 1934, Du Bois Papers, UM-A.

16. W. E. B. Du Bois to Social Science Research Council, July 19, 1934, Du Bois Papers, UM-A.

17. Social Science Research Council to W. E. B. Du Bois, August 2, 1934; Social Science Research Council to W. E. B. Du Bois, September 12, 1934; W. E. B. Du Bois to Social Science Research Council, October 17, 1934; Social Science Research Council to W. E. B. Du Bois, October 19, 1934, Du Bois Papers, UM-A.

18. Proposal for book on Negro troops, ca. 1935, Du Bois Papers, UM-A.

19. Social Science Research Council to W. E. B. Du Bois, March 20, 1935; Unidentified correspondent to Social Science Research Council, March 21, 1935, Du Bois Papers, UM-A.

20. W. E. B. Du Bois to Social Science Research Council, March 27, 1935, Du Bois Papers, UM-A.

21. John Hope to W. E. B. Du Bois, April 12, 1935, Du Bois Papers, UM-A.

22. Social Science Research Council to W. E. B. Du Bois, April 1, 1935; Social Science Research Council to W. E. B. Du Bois, July 1, 1935, Du Bois Papers, UM-A.

23. "Gustav Oberlaender," *Immigrant Entrepreneurship*, www.immigrantentrepreneurship.org /entries/gustav-oberlaender/; Oberlaender Trust brochure, 1932, Du Bois Papers, UM-A.

24. Proposal to Increase the Friendship and Sympathy Between Germany and the United States and Germany and the World, ca. April 24, 1931, Du Bois Papers, UM-A.

25. W. E. B. Du Bois to John Hope, January 30, 1935, Du Bois Papers, UM-A.

26. Oberlaender Trust to W. E. B. Du Bois, April 17, 1935, Du Bois Papers, UM-A.

27. W. E. B. Du Bois to Oberlaender Trust, May 3, 1935, Du Bois Papers, UM-A.

28. Oberlaender Trust to W. E. B. Du Bois, June 12, 1935, Du Bois Papers, UM-A.

29. Lewis, *W. E. B. Du Bois, Vol. 2*, 388.

30. Italian defense ministers discussed the possibility of invading Ethiopia as early as 1932. On the history of the Italian-Ethiopian War, see George W. Baer, *The Coming of the Italian-Ethiopian War* (Cambridge, MA: Harvard University Press, 1967).

31. "Italy and Abyssinia," *The Crisis* (June 1926), 62–63.

32. See Joseph Fronczak, "Local People's Global Politics: A Transnational History of the Hands Off Ethiopia Movement of 1935," *Diplomatic History* 39, no. 2 (2015): 245–74.

33. W. E. B. Du Bois to John Hope, April 22, 1935; The American Committee on the Ethiopian Crisis to W. E. B. Du Bois, August 9, 1935, Du Bois Papers, UM-A.

34. The American League Against War and Fascism to W. E. B. Du Bois, September 17, 1935; W. E. B. Du Bois to John Hope, October 1, 1935, Du Bois Papers, UM-A; "7,000 Here Protest Ethiopian Invasion," *New York Times*, September 26, 1935; "10,000 Protest Mussolini's War in East Africa," *New York Amsterdam News*, September 28, 1935. On African American responses to the Italian-Ethiopian War, see Robin D. G. Kelley, "'This Ain't Ethiopia, But It'll Do': African Americans and the Spanish Civil War," in *Race Rebels: Culture, Politics, and the Black Working Class* (New York: Free Press, 1996); William R. Scott, *The Sons of Sheba's Race: African-Americans and the Italo-Ethiopian War, 1935–1941* (Bloomington: Indiana University Press, 1993).

35. W. E. B. Du Bois, "Inter-Racial Implications of the Ethiopian Crisis: A Negro View," *Foreign Affairs* 14, no. 1 (October 1935): 82–92.

36. Ibid.; Lisa Anderson, "James T. Shotwell: A Life Devoted to Organizing Peace," *Columbia Magazine*, December 8, 2005, https://magazine.columbia.edu/article/james-t-shotwell-life-devoted-organizing-peace.

37. James T. Shotwell, ed., *Economic and Social History of the World War: Outline of Plan, European Series* (Washington, DC: Carnegie Endowment for International Peace, 1924), 1–2.

38. "World War Story Fills 152 Volumes," *New York Times*, March 15, 1937, 25; Harold Josephson, *James T. Shotwell and the Rise of Internationalism in America* (Rutherford, NJ: Fairleigh Dickinson University Press, 1974).

39. W. E. B. Du Bois to the Carnegie Endowment for International Peace, January 16, 1936, Du Bois Papers, UM-A.

40. Carnegie Endowment for International Peace to W. E. B. Du Bois, January 27, 1936, Du Bois Papers, UM-A.

41. W. E. B. Du Bois to the Carnegie Endowment for International Peace, February 4, 1936, Du Bois Papers, UM-A.

42. W. E. B. Du Bois to Southern Railroad System, February 3, 1936, Du Bois Papers, UM-A.

43. W. E. B. Du Bois to Nina Du Bois, February 21, 1936; W. E. B. Du Bois to Virginia Alexander, February 21, 1936, Du Bois Papers, UM-A.

44. Lincoln Congregational Temple program for February 9, 1936, January 14, 1936; Adult Education Council of Chicago instructions for engagement, ca. February 1936; Lectures, February 1936, Du Bois Papers, UM-A.

45. W. E. B. Du Bois to Mildred Bryant Jones, February 21, 1936, Du Bois Papers, UM-A.

46. W. E. B. Du Bois to Virginia Alexander, February 21, 1936, Du Bois Papers, UM-A. On the relationship between Du Bois and Alexander, see Lewis, *W. E. B. Du Bois, Vol. 2*, 272–74.

47. "Bury Dr. John Hope Here Today," *Atlanta Daily World*, February 23, 1936; "Dr. John Hope Laid to Rest on Campus Before Hundreds," *Atlanta Daily World*, February 24, 1936; W. E. B. Du Bois to Nina Du Bois, February 26, 1936, Du Bois Papers, UM-A.

48. "Forum of Fact and Opinion," *Pittsburgh Courier*, March 28, 1936.

49. *The Black Man and the Wounded World*, 1936 (unpublished), Introduction, Table of Contents, Du Bois Collection, Fisk, box 26, folder 20.

50. W. E. B. Du Bois to the Carnegie Endowment for International Peace, February 26, 1936, Du Bois Papers, UM-A.

51. Carnegie Endowment for International Peace to W. E. B. Du Bois, March 12, 1936, Du Bois Papers, UM-A; Josephson, *James T. Shotwell and the Rise of Internationalism in America*, 231.

52. William Safire, ed., *Lend Me Your Ears: Great Speeches in History* (Newburyport, MA: Rosetta Books, 2014), 242–44.

53. Nina Du Bois to W. E. B. Du Bois, June 26, 1936, Du Bois Papers, UM-A.

54. *Pittsburgh Courier* to W. E. B. Du Bois, April 11, 1936, Du Bois Papers, UM-A.

55. W. E. B. Du Bois to Oberlaender Trust, December 19, 1935; Oberlaender Trust to W. E. B. Du Bois, April 9, 1936, Du Bois Papers, UM-A.

56. Harold Moody to W. E. B. Du Bois, June 12, 1936; travel memo, 1936; note from W. E. B. Du Bois to Diedrich Westermann, June 24, 1936, Du Bois Papers, UM-A.

57. Childers, *The Third Reich*, 378–79; Evans, *The Third Reich in Power*, 632–37; "Roosevelt to

Mix Fishing and Work," *New York Times*, March 29, 1936. On the Roosevelt administration's views of Hitler and his ascendancy, see David McKean, *Watching Darkness Fall: FDR, His Ambsassadors, and the Rise of Adolf Hitler* (New York: St. Martin's Press, 2021).

58. Childers, *The Third Reich*, 356–57, 380; Lewis, *W. E. B. Du Bois, Vol. 2*, 395–97.

59. Victor D. Lindeman to W. E. B. Du Bois, March 26, 1936; W. E. B. Du Bois to Victor D. Lindeman, March 31, 1936; Victor D. Lindeman to W. E. B. Du Bois, March 31, 1936; American Committee for Anti-Nazi Literature to W. E. B. Du Bois, April 22, 1936; W. E. B. Du Bois to American Committee for Anti-Nazi Literature, May 5, 1936; American Committee for Anti-Nazi Literature to W. E. B. Du Bois, May 11, 1936, Du Bois Papers, UM-A.

60. Travel memo, 1936, Du Bois Papers, UM-A.

61. Although Du Bois was not present for the Olympic Games in Berlin, he still provided secondhand observations for *The Pittsburgh Courier*, especially noting that the American sprinter Jesse Owens, who won four gold medals, was "without doubt the most popular single athlete in the Olympic Games of 1936." "Forum of Fact and Opinion," *Pittsburgh Courier*, October 24, 1936. On the role of the Olympic Games in further legitimizing the Third Reich, see Childers, *The Third Reich*, 380.

62. "Forum of Fact and Opinion," *Pittsburgh Courier*, October 24, 1936; Lewis, *W. E. B. Du Bois, Vol. 2*, 403–404.

63. "Forum of Fact and Opinion," *Pittsburgh Courier*, November 14, 1936.

64. "Forum of Fact and Opinion," *Pittsburgh Courier*, October 3, 1936; "Forum of Fact and Opinion," *Pittsburgh Courier*, October 10, 1936.

65. October 17, 1936; Einteilung de Sitzplätze im Richard Wagner Bühnenfestspielhaus zu Bayreuth, ca. 1936; Ticket to *Der Ring des Nibelungen*, August 1936; Bayreuther Bühnenfestspiele. Ticket to *Lohengrin*, August 19, 1936; Bayreuther Bühnenfestspiele. *Der Ring des Nibelungen* program: *Das Rheingold*, August 21, 1936, Du Bois Papers, UM-A.

66. "Forum of Fact and Opinion," *Pittsburgh Courier*, October 31, 1936; Lewis, *W. E. B. Du Bois, Vol. 2*, 404–405.

67. "Forum of Fact and Opinion," *Pittsburgh Courier*, January 9, 1937.

68. "Forum of Fact and Opinion," *Pittsburgh Courier*, November 7, 1936.

69. "Forum of Fact and Opinion," *Pittsburgh Courier*, December 12, 1936.

70. "Forum of Fact and Opinion," *Pittsburgh Courier*, January 7, 1937.

71. Trans-Siberian Express: Shortest, most economical and comfortable route between Europe and the Far East, ca. 1936, Du Bois Papers, UM-A.

72. "Forum of Fact and Opinion," *Pittsburgh Courier*, January 23, 1937.

73. Nina Du Bois to W. E. B. Du Bois, November 21, 1936, Du Bois Papers, UM-A.

74. "Forum of Fact and Opinion," *Pittsburgh Courier*, January 16, 1937.

75. "Forum of Fact and Opinion," *Pittsburgh Courier*, January 23, 1937.

76. "Forum of Fact and Opinion," *Pittsburgh Courier*, February 6, 1937.

77. Lewis, *W. E. B. Du Bois, Vol. 2*, 390–93. For more on Yasuichi Hikida, see Gerald Horne, *Facing the Rising Sun: African Americans, Japan, and the Rise of Afro-Asian Solidarity* (New York: New York University Press, 2018).

78. W. E. B. Du Bois to Ellen Irene Diggs, November 16, 1936, Du Bois Papers, UM-A.

79. "Forum of Fact and Opinion," *Pittsburgh Courier*, February 13, 1937.

80. "Forum of Fact and Opinion," *Pittsburgh Courier*, February 27, 1937.

81. "Forum of Fact and Opinion," *Pittsburgh Courier*, March 6, 1937.

82. Lewis, *W. E. B. Du Bois, Vol. 2*, 413–14; "Forum of Fact and Opinion," *Pittsburgh Courier*, February 20, 1937.

83. Lewis, *W. E. B. Du Bois, Vol. 2*, 414–17; "Forum of Fact and Opinion," *Pittsburgh Courier*, March 13, 1937.

84. "Forum of Fact and Opinion," *Pittsburgh Courier*, March 13, 1937.

85. C. J. Tagashira to W. E. B. Du Bois, November 7, 1936, Du Bois Papers, UM-A; "Forum of Fact and Opinion," *Pittsburgh Courier*, March 20, 1937.

86. W. E. B. Du Bois to Louie Shivery, December 24, 1936, Du Bois Papers, UM-A; "Forum of Fact and Opinion," *Pittsburgh Courier*, April 3, 1937.

87. W. E. B. Du Bois to Harcourt, Brace and Company, February 11, 1937, Du Bois Papers, UM-A.

88. A world search for democracy, ca. 1937, Du Bois Papers, UM-A; Lewis, *W. E. B. Du Bois, Vol. 2*, 389. Lisa McLeod offers the best analysis of "A World Search for Democracy." See Lisa McLeod, "Du Bois's 'A World Search for Democracy': The Democratic Roots of Socialism," *Socialism and Democracy* 32, no. 3 (November 2018): 105–24.

89. W. E. B. Du Bois to American Philosophical Society, May 25, 1936; C. F. Skinner to Du Bois, May 28, 1936, *The Black Man and the Wounded World*, General, Du Bois Collection, Fisk, box 14, folder 33.

90. Du Bois grant submission to the American Philosophical Society, March 9, 1937, *The Black Man and the Wounded World*, General, Du Bois Collection, Fisk, box 14, folder 33.

91. Executive Officer Conklin to Du Bois, April 12, 1937, *The Black Man and the Wounded World*, General, Du Bois Collection, Fisk, box 14, folder 33.

92. W. E. B. Du Bois to Nina Du Bois, April 15, 1937, Du Bois Papers, UM-A.

93. Semester II sociology course calendar, 1937, Du Bois Papers, UM-A.

94. W. E. B. Du Bois to Emma Groves, April 13, 1937, Du Bois Papers, UM-A.

95. W. E. B. Du Bois to Emma Groves, July 1, 1937, Du Bois Papers, UM-A.

96. W. E. B. Du Bois to Nina Du Bois, June 28, 1937, Du Bois Papers, UM-A.

97. W. E. B. Du Bois to *New York Times*, July 19, 1937, Du Bois Papers, UM-A.

98. "Japanese Take Two Towns in Fighting Near Peiping; Chinese Prepare for War," *New York Times*, July 11, 1937.

99. "Chinese for War to Curb Japanese," *New York Times*, July 11, 1937. On the lead-up to and outbreak of the Second Sino-Japanese War, see Rana Mitter, *Forgotten Ally: China's World War II, 1937–1945* (Boston: Houghton Mifflin Harcourt, 2013), chaps. 1–4.

100. "Forum of Fact and Opinion," *Pittsburgh Courier*, September 25, 1937; "Forum of Fact and Opinion," *Pittsburgh Courier*, October 23, 1937.

101. Mitter, *Forgotten Ally*, chap. 7; on Du Bois's problematic views of Japan and the Second Sino-Japanese War specifically, see Nahum Dimitri Chandler, "A Persistent Parallax: On the Writings of W. E. Burghardt Du Bois on Japan and China, 1936–1937," *CR: The New Centennial Review* 12, no. 1 (Spring 2012): 291–316; Horne, *Facing the Rising Sun*; Seok-Won Lee, "The Paradox of Racial Liberation: W. E. B. Du Bois and Pan-Asianism in Wartime Japan, 1931–1945," *Inter-Asia Cultural Studies* 16, no. 4 (2015): 513–30; Lewis, *Du Bois, Vol. 2*, 418–19; Bill V. Mullen and Cathryn Watson, eds., *W. E. B.*

Du Bois on Asia: Crossing the World Color Line (Jackson: University Press of Mississippi, 2005); Yuichiro Onishi, *Afro-Asian Solidarity in 20th-Century Black America, Japan and Okinawa* (New York: New York University Press, 2013), chap. 2.

102. Monthly calendar, February 1938–April 1938; Speaking tour travel itinerary, February 1938, Du Bois Papers, UM-A.

103. J. E. Spingarn to Ira De Augustine Reid, January 18, 1938; J. E. Spingarn to Rayford Logan, February 15, 1938, Du Bois Papers, UM-A.

104. A Pageant in seven decades, 1868–1938, Du Bois Papers, UM-A.

105. "Fatal Accident at Wiscasset," *Lincoln County News*, June 30, 1938; "Negro Leader Dies in Crossing Crash," *New York Times*, June 27, 1938; "James Weldon Johnson Killed by Train," *Chicago Defender*, July 2, 1938; "J. Weldon Johnson Dies in Auto Crash," *Baltimore Afro-American*, July 2, 1938; "Funeral of James W. Johnson Thursday," *New York Amsterdam News*, July 2, 1939; "Noted Negro Killed in Auto-Train Crash," *Boston Globe*, June 27, 1938; "'I Didn't See the Train': Mrs. James Weldon Johnson Describes Accident Which Killed Her Husband," *Baltimore Afro-American*, July 16, 1938; "Railroad Crossing Where James Weldon Johnson Met His Death," *Baltimore Afro-American*, July 16, 1938; "Poet Never Knew What Hit Him," *Baltimore Afro-American*, July 16, 1938; "Johnson's Death Car Total Wreck," *Baltimore Afro-American*, July 16, 1938.

106. "James Weldon Johnson Killed in Auto-Train Accident, Report," *Atlanta Daily World*, June 27, 1938.

107. Telegram from American Society of Composers, Authors and Publishers to W. E. B. Du Bois, June 28, 1938, Du Bois Papers, UM-A.

108. Report of the funeral of James Weldon Johnson [fragment], ca. 1938, Du Bois Papers, UM-A.

109. W. E. B. Du Bois to Grace N. Johnson, September 21, 1938, Du Bois Papers, UM-A.

110. W. E. B. Du Bois to Virginia State College, October 19, 1938, Du Bois Papers, UM-A.

111. "Du Bois Fears German-Type Prejudice . . . ," *Atlanta Daily World*, November 1, 1938.

112. Childers, *The Third Reich*, 355–62; Evans, *The Third Reich in Power*, 506–79.

113. Earlier in the year he transferred his *New York Times* subscription to Atlanta. *New York Times* to W. E. B. Du Bois, March 16, 1938, Du Bois Papers, UM-A.

114. On *Kristallnacht*, see Alan E. Steinweis, *Kristallnacht 1938* (Cambridge, MA: Belknap Press of Harvard University Press, 2009).

115. Historians have demonstrated that while Hitler and Goebbels helped set *Kristallnacht* in motion, the broader German population, fueled by anti-Semitism, was equally if not more responsible for the pogrom. See ibid.; "Nazis Smash, Loot and Burn Jewish Shops and Temples Until Goebbels Calls Halt," *New York Times*, November 11, 1938.

116. Childers, *The Third Reich*, 367.

117. "Spingarn Goes Under Knife to Save Life," *New York Amsterdam News*, January 7, 1939; W. E. B. Du Bois to Arthur Spingarn, January 9, 1939; Arthur Spingarn to W. E. B. Du Bois, January 10, 1939, Du Bois Papers, UM-A.

118. Arthur Spingarn to W. E. B. Du Bois, March 25, 1939; Lillian Alexander to W. E. B. Du Bois, April 8, 1939, Du Bois Papers, UM-A.

119. "President Spingarn Dies," *The Crisis* (September 1939), 270.

120. Ibid.

121. "The Passing of Col. Spingarn," *New York Amsterdam News*, August 5, 1939.

122. "President Spingarn Dies," *The Crisis* (September 1939), 269–70.

123. "J. E. Spingarn—Man of Courage," *The Crisis* (September 1939), 273.

124. "Hitler Tells the Reichstag 'Bomb Will Be Met by Bomb,'" *New York Times*, September 1, 1939.

125. Richard J. Evans, *The Third Reich at War* (New York: Penguin Press, 2009), 3–9.

126. *New York Amsterdam News* to W. E. B. Du Bois, September 15, 1939, Du Bois Papers, UM-A.

127. "As the Crow Flies," *New York Amsterdam News*, October 21, 1939.

128. "As the Crow Flies," *New York Amsterdam News*, November 4, 1939.

129. W. E. B. Du Bois to Social Science Research Council, November 30, 1939, Du Bois Papers, UM-A.

130. See Mitter, *Forgotten Ally*.

131. Martin Gilbert, *The Second World War: A Complete History* (New York: Henry Holt, 1989), 1–60; Ian Kershaw, *Hitler: 1936–1945 Nemesis* (New York: W. W. Norton, 2000), 291–92.

132. Franklin D. Roosevelt, Annual Message to the Congress, January 3, 1940, American Presidency Project, www.presidency.ucsb.edu/documents/annual-message-the-congress.

133. Social Science Research Council to W. E. B. Du Bois, March 23, 1940, Du Bois Papers, UM-A.

134. Gilbert, *The Second World War*, 61–94.

135. "French Sign Reich Truce, Rome Pact Next," *New York Times*, June 23, 1940; Gilbert, *The Second World War*, 100–102; Kershaw, *Hitler*, 298–99.

Chapter 12

1. Du Bois, *In Battle for Peace*, 164.

2. Arthur Spingarn to W. E. B. Du Bois, September 7, 1939, Du Bois Papers, UM-A.

3. Arthur B. Spingarn to W. E. B. Du Bois, September 24, 1940; Amy Spingarn to W. E. B. Du Bois, September 26, 1940, Du Bois Papers, UM-A.

4. Scholars of Du Bois and *Dusk of Dawn* have focused much more on what the book reveals about Du Bois's conceptualization of race to the exclusion of his historical and personal reckoning with the First World War. For example, see Appiah, *Lines of Descent*, 141–42; Eric Porter, *The Problem of the Future World* (Durham, NC: Duke University Press, 2010), chap. 1.

5. Du Bois, *Dusk of Dawn*, 746.

6. On the history of the "Encyclopedia Africana," see Henry Louis Gates Jr., "W. E. B. Du Bois and the Encyclopedia Africana, 1909–63," *Annals of the American Academy of Political and Social Science* 568 (March 2000): 203–19; Clarence G. Contee, "The Encyclopedia Africana Project of W. E. B. Du Bois," *African Historical Studies* 4, no. 1 (1971): 77–91. Du Bois's best hopes for funding the "Encyclopedia Africana" vanished in April 1938, when the General Education Board decided not to fund the project. He continued to work on the project with Rayford Logan's assistance, but by early 1939 he realized that funding support was unlikely. W. E. B. Du Bois to Rayford W. Logan, January 4, 1939; W. E. B. Du Bois to Anson Phelps Stokes, Guy B. Johnson, and Rayford W. Logan, March 1, 1940, Du Bois Papers, UM-A.

7.   The darker wisdom: prophecies in tale and play, seeking to pierce the gloom of 1940, 1941, Du Bois Papers, UM-A.

8.   Lewis, *W. E. B. Du Bois, Vol. 2*, 477–86; for an excellent discussion of *Phylon* and its significance in Du Bois's intellectual and political thought, see Porter, *The Problem of the Future World*, chap. 1.

9.   Rayford Logan served as chairman of the Committee on Participation of Negroes in the National Defense Program (CPNNDP). Organized by the *Pittsburgh Courier*, the CPNNDP was a lobbying group composed of representatives from various civil rights organizations, fraternities and sororities, Black American Legion posts, and professional societies. The CPNNDP developed a broad agenda to press for military and civil reforms, which included, among other demands, expanded opportunities for Black officers, the elevation of Benjamin O. Davis Sr. to brigadier general, and the recruitment of air force cadets. "Here's What We Want in Defense Program," *Norfolk Journal and Guide*, July 6, 1940; Kenneth Janken, *Rayford Logan*, 114–17.

10. "Segregation in Army Is a Basic Weakness," *New York Amsterdam News*, September 23, 1939.

11. United States Congress. House Committee on Military Affairs, *Selective Compulsory Military Training and Service Hearings Before the United States House Committee on Military Affairs, Seventy-Sixth Congress, Third Session, on July 10, 11, 24–26, 30, 31, Aug. 2, 12–14, 1940* (Washington, DC: U.S. Government Printing Office, 1940), 585–90.

12. "As the Crow Flies," *New York Amsterdam News*, August 17, 1940.

13. "B. O. Davis Becomes First Negro General," *Chicago Defender*, November 2, 1940.

14. "10,000 Should March on D.C., Says Randolph," *Baltimore Afro-American*, January 25, 1941.

15. "'March of Mourning' Set for Nation's Capitol," *Chicago Defender*, May 17, 1941.

16. "Plans for March on Washington Near Completion," *New Journal and Guide*, June 21, 1941; Beth Tompkins Bates, *Pullman Porters and the Rise of Protest Politics in Black America, 1925–1945* (Chapel Hill: University of North Carolina Press, 2001), 152–57.

17. W. E. B. Du Bois to Andrew J. Allison, February 3, 1941, Du Bois Papers, UM-A.

18. "As the Crow Flies," *New York Amsterdam News*, June 7, 1941.

19. "As the Crow Flies," *New York Amsterdam News*, June 21, 1941.

20. Bates, *Pullman Porters and the Rise of Protest Politics in Black America, 1925–1945*, 157–61.

21. David Lucander, *Winning the War for Democracy: The March on Washington Movement, 1941–1946* (Urbana: University of Illinois Press, 2014).

22. "As the Crow Flies," *New York Amsterdam News*, May 31, 1941.

23. Lewis, *W. E. B. Du Bois, Vol. 2*; W. E. B. Du Bois, "Neuropa: Hitler's New World Order," *Journal of Negro Education* 10, no. 3 (July 1941): 380–86.

24. Childers, *The Third Reich*, 469–82; Evans, *The Third Reich at War*, 162–66, 178–82; David Stahel, *Operation Barbarossa and Germany's Defeat in the East* (Cambridge: Cambridge University Press, 2009).

25. "As the Crow Flies," *New York Amsterdam News*, July 12, 1941.

26. "As the Crow Flies," *New York Amsterdam News*, July 26, 1941.

27. On the Atlantic Charter, see Douglas Brinkley and David R. Facey-Crowther, *The Atlantic Charter* (New York: St. Martin's Press, 1994); Elizabeth Borgwardt, *A New Deal for the World* (Cambridge, MA: Harvard University Press, 2007), chaps. 1–2.

28. "As the Crow Flies," *New York Amsterdam News*, September 6, 1941.

29. "As the Crow Flies," *New York Amsterdam News*, September 13, 1941; Bernard C. Nalty, *Strength for the Fight: A History of Black Americans in the Military* (New York: Free Press, 1986), 141.

30. On the Pearl Harbor attack, see Robert William Love, *Pearl Harbor Revisited* (New York: St. Martin's Press, 1995); Michael Slackman, *Target—Pearl Harbor* (Honolulu: University of Hawaii Press, 1990); Carl Smith, *Pearl Harbor 1941: The Day of Infamy* (Westport, CT: Praeger, 2004); Steve Twomey, *Countdown to Pearl Harbor: The Twelve Days to the Attack* (New York: Simon & Schuster, 2016).

31. Franklin D. Roosevelt, "Address to Congress Requesting a Declaration of War with Japan," December 8, 1941, American Presidency Project, www.presidency.ucsb.edu /documents/address-congress-requesting-declaration-war-with-japan; Mary Barmeyer O'Brien, *Jeannette Rankin: Bright Star in the Big Sky* (Guilford, CT: TwoDot, 2015), 45–47; Kennedy, *Freedom from Fear*, 523.

32. "Should I Sacrifice to Live 'Half-American?'," *Pittsburgh Courier*, January 31, 1942.

33. "As the Crow Flies," *New York Amsterdam News*, February 14, 1942.

34. "As the Crow Flies," *New York Amsterdam News*, March 14, 1942.

35. J. Todd Moye, *Freedom Flyers: The Tuskegee Airmen of World War II* (New York: Oxford University Press, 2012), chap. 3.

36. Phillip McGuire, ed., *Taps for a Jim Crow Army: Letters from Black Soldiers in World War II* (Lexington: University Press of Kentucky, 2015), 154–55; William H. Hastie to secretary of war, January 5, 1943, in Morris J. MacGregor and Bernard C. Nalty, *Blacks in the United States Armed Forces: Basic Documents, Volume 5* (Wilmington, DE: Scholarly Resources, 1977), 178–82.

37. Charles H. Thompson, "Editorial Note: The American Negro in World War I and World War II," *Journal of Negro Education* 12, no. 3 (1943): 263.

38. The issue included, in order of their articles, the following contributors: Horace Mann Bond, Emmett J. Scott, Campbell C. Johnson, Howard H. Long, William H. Hastie, W. E. B. Du Bois, Charles H. Garvin, John W. Davis, Walter White, Percival L. Prattis, Charles H. Houston, Thomas N. Roberts, Herman Branson, Robert C. Weaver, Giles A. Hubert, Leon A. Ransom, Kenneth B. Clark, Lewis K. McMillan, Carroll L. Miller, Mary A. Morton, Roscoe E. Lewis, Claude A. Barnett, Walter G. Daniel, Marion T. Wright, Edgar Love, Ira De A. Reid, Merze Tate, Rufus E. Clement, Caroline F. Ware, Margaret C. McCulloch, Lawrence D. Reddick, and Dorothy B. Porter. An asterisk indicated individuals who "Participated in World War I." "Front Matter," *Journal of Negro Education* 12, no. 3, The American Negro in World War I and World War II (Summer 1943).

39. Emmett J. Scott, "The Participation of Negroes in World War I: An Introductory Statement," *Journal of Negro Education* 12, no. 3, The American Negro in World War I and World War II (Summer 1943): 288–97.

40. Chas. H. Thompson to W. E. B. Du Bois, December 28, 1942, *Journal of Negro Education*, 1941–1943, 1945–1946, Du Bois Collection, Fisk, box 13, folder 40.

41. W. E. B. Du Bois, "The Negro Soldier in Service Abroad During the First World War," *Journal of Negro Education* 12, no. 3 (1943): 324–34. For the full chapter 17 draft, see *The Black Man and the Wounded World*, chap. 17, "Propaganda and Armistice," Du Bois Collection, Fisk, box 27, folder 11.

42. James N. Gregory, *The Southern Diaspora: How the Great Migrations of Black and White Southerners Transformed America* (Chapel Hill: University of North Carolina Press, 2005), 15–18, 32–38. Also see Wilkerson, *The Warmth of Other Suns.*

43. Luis Alvarez, *The Power of the Zoot: Youth Culture and Resistance During World War II* (Berkeley: University of California Press, 2008); Eduardo Obregón Pagán, *Murder at the Sleepy Lagoon* (Chapel Hill: University of North Carolina Press, 2003).

44. James A. Burran, "Violence in an 'Arsenal of Democracy': The Beaumont Race Riot, 1943," in Bruce A. Glasrud, ed., *Anti-Black Violence in Twentieth-Century Texas* (College Station: Texas A&M University Press, 2015), 116–30.

45. Thomas J. Sugrue, *Origins of the Urban Crisis: Race and Inequality in Postwar Detroit* (Princeton, NJ: Princeton University Press, 1996), chap. 1; Walter White and Thurgood Marshall, *What Caused the Detroit Riot?* (New York: NAACP, 1943); Thurgood Marshall, "The Gestapo in Detroit," *The Crisis* 50, no. 8 (1943): 232; Rachel Marie-Crane Williams, *Run Home If You Don't Want to Be Killed: The Detroit Uprising of 1943* (Chapel Hill: University of North Carolina Press, 2021).

46. Nat Brandt, *Harlem at War: The Black Experience in WWII* (Syracuse, NY: Syracuse University Press, 1996); Dominic J. Capeci, *The Harlem Riot of 1943* (Philadelphia: Temple University Press, 1977).

47. "As the Crow Flies," *New York Amsterdam News,* October 9, 1943.

48. "As the Crow Flies," *New York Amsterdam News,* July 24, 1943.

49. Logan, *What the Negro Wants,* preface.

50. The other contributors included: Leslie Pinckney Hill, Charles Wesley, Roy Wilkins, A. Philip Randolph, Willard S. Townsend, Doxey A. Wilkerson, Gordon B. Hancock, Mary McLeod Bethune, Frederick D. Patterson, George S. Schuyler, Langston Hughes, and Sterling A. Brown. Their collective unanimity on the need for full Black equality so rankled W. T. Couch, director of the University of North Carolina Press, that he initially rejected the manuscript. Couch, after being threatened by a lawsuit from Logan, ultimately agreed to publish the book but insisted upon writing his own introduction to the volume, making clear his objection to the views of the contributors and expressing his personal belief in white superiority. For an in-depth examination of the book and the controversy surrounding it, see Kenneth Janken, *Rayford Logan,* chap. 6.

51. Du Bois, "My Evolving Program for Negro Freedom," 58–59.

52. Ibid., 59.

53. Ibid., 70.

54. Rufus E. Clement to W. E. B. Du Bois, November 23, 1943, Du Bois Papers, UM-A.

55. Du Bois, *Autobiography,* 322–24; W. E. B. Du Bois to Yolande Du Bois Williams, June 13, 1944, Du Bois Papers, UM-A.

56. "Probe Ouster of Dr. DuBois at Atlanta U.," *Chicago Defender,* May 6, 1944; Melville J. Herskovits to Kendall Weisiger, April 17, 1944; Louis T. Wright to Kendall Weisiger, April 20, 1944; Actions of the board of trustees of Atlanta University in connection with the retirement of Dr. W. E. B. Du Bois, May 1, 1944, Du Bois Papers, UM-A; Lewis, *W. E. B. Du Bois, Vol. 2,* 493–95.

57. NAACP to W. E. B. Du Bois, May 23, 1944; NAACP to W. E. B. Du Bois, July 18, 1944, Du Bois Papers, UM-A.

58. NAACP to W. E. B. Du Bois, May 17, 1944, Du Bois Papers, UM-A.

59. W. E. B. Du Bois to NAACP, June 1, 1944; W. E. B. Du Bois to NAACP, June 19, 1944; NAACP to W. E. B. Du Bois, June 23, 1944, Du Bois Papers, UM-A.

60. W. E. B. Du Bois to NAACP, July 5, 1944; NAACP to W. E. B. Du Bois, July 21, 1944, Du Bois Papers, UM-A.

61. Gilbert, *The Second World War*, chaps. 39–41, 43–45.

62. Childers, *The Third Reich*, 556–67; Evans, *The Third Reich at War*, chaps. 5–7; Gilbert, *The Second World War*, chaps. 39–41, 43–45.

63. See John W. Dower, *War Without Mercy: Race and Power in the Pacific War* (New York: Pantheon, 1986).

64. Kennedy, *Freedom from Fear*, 809–51.

65. "The Winds of Time," *Chicago Defender*, September 15, 1945, in Herbert Aptheker, ed., *Newspaper Columns by W. E. B. Du Bois, Vol. 2* (White Plains, NY: Kraus-Thomson Organization, 1986), 654–55.

66. Du Bois, *Autobiography*, 327.

67. A Report on the Department of Special Research, October 4, 1944, Du Bois Papers, UM-A.

68. "As the Crow Flies," *New York Amsterdam News*, August 19, 1944.

69. Hugh H. Smythe to W. E. B. Du Bois, December 1, 1944; W. E. B. Du Bois to Howard University, January 5, 1945, Du Bois Papers, UM-A.

70. Du Bois, *Color and Democracy*, 245–50, 328.

71. Ibid., 287–302.

72. Ibid., 303, 308, 311; Porter, *The Problem of the Future World*, 78.

73. "The Winds of Time," *Chicago Defender*, April 28, 1945, in Aptheker, *Newspaper Columns, Vol. 2*, 633.

74. Aptheker, *Newspaper Columns*, May 19, 1945, 639–41.

75. Lewis, *W. E. B. Du Bois, Vol. 2*, 507–10; Brenda Gayle Plummer, *Rising Wind: Black Americans and U.S. Foreign Affairs, 1935–1960* (Chapel Hill: University of North Carolina Press, 1996), chap. 4; Report of the NAACP Department of Special Research, June 11, 1945, Du Bois Papers, UM-A.

76. "The Winds of Time," *Chicago Defender*, June 23, 1945, in Aptheker, *Newspaper Columns, Vol. 2*, 644–45.

77. Amy Jacques Garvey to W. E. B. Du Bois, April 4, 1944, Du Bois Papers, UM-A; Ula Yvette Taylor, *The Veiled Garvey: The Life & Times of Amy Jacques Garvey* (Chapel Hill: University of North Carolina Press, 2002). Du Bois saw this as an opportunity for a larger Pan-African meeting that would be convened by himself, Garvey, and Moody, as well as Paul Robeson and Max Yergen of the Council on African Affairs. Postwar Pan-African Conference proposal, ca. April 8, 1944, Du Bois Papers, UM-A.

78. Rayford W. Logan to W. E. B. Du Bois, November 23, 1944; W. E. B. Du Bois to Rayford W. Logan, November 24, 1944; Harold Moody and Amy Jacques Garvey endorsed the Colonial Conference and offered Du Bois support. Report of the NAACP Department of Special Research, February 13, 1945; Letter from W. E. B. Du Bois to League of Coloured Peoples, February 15, 1945; Letter from League of Coloured Peoples to W. E. B. Du Bois, February 23, 1945; Letter from Amy Ashwood Garvey to W. E. B. Du Bois, February 1, 1945; Speakers at the Colonial Conference, April 1945, Du Bois Papers, UM-A.

79. George Padmore, "Call for Pan-African Parley in Paris Drafted by British Colonial Leaders," *Chicago Defender*, March 17, 1945.

80. W. E. B. Du Bois to George Padmore, March 22, 1945, Du Bois Papers, UM-A.

81. George Padmore to W. E. B. Du Bois, April 12, 1945, Du Bois Papers, UM-A; Penny Von Eschen, *Race Against Empire: Black Americans and Anticolonialism, 1937–1957* (Ithaca, NY: Cornell University Press, 1997), 45–52.

82. "Winds of Time," *Chicago Defender*, September 29, 1945, in Aptheker, *Newspaper Columns, Vol. 2*, 656–57.

83. W. E. B. Du Bois to George Padmore, October 5, 1945; Great Britain Passport Department to W. E. B. Du Bois, October 6, 1945; United States House of Representatives to W. E. B. Du Bois, October 8, 1945; W. E. B. Du Bois to Emma Groves, October 12, 1945, Du Bois Papers, UM-A.

84. George Padmore, *History of the Pan-African Congress: Colonial and Coloured Unity, a Programme of Action* (London: Hammersmith Bookshop, 1963), 32, 40.

85. Ibid., 13.

86. Fifth Pan-African Congress final resolution, ca. October 1945, Du Bois Papers, UM-A.

87. Du Bois initially proposed the book, at the time titled "Africa and Two World Wars," to Henry Holt and Company, who ultimately passed due to high wartime publication costs. W. E. B. Du Bois to Henry Holt and Company, December 14, 1944; Henry Holt and Company to W. E. B. Du Bois, December 18, 1944, Du Bois Papers, UM-A.

88. Du Bois, *The World and Africa*, 1.

89. Ibid., 4–9.

90. Ibid., 164.

91. White began to voice his concerns about Du Bois at the end of 1945, writing in a December memo, "Certain actions by yourself seriously interfered with the smooth operation of the NAACP as a whole." Du Bois responded in a sharply written three-page letter. Walter White to W. E. B. Du Bois, December 21, 1945; W. E. B. Du Bois to Walter White, January 3, 1946; Du Bois Resignation/Rejoining, Du Bois Collection, Fisk, box 6, folder 28.

92. Alexander, *W. E. B. Du Bois: An American Intellectual and Activist*, 104; Lewis, *W. E. B. Du Bois, Vol. 2*, 531; W. E. B. Du Bois to Walter White, July 1, 1948, Du Bois Papers, UM-A.

93. See "The Winds of Time," *Chicago Defender*, February 21, 1948, in Aptheker, *Newspaper Columns, Vol. 2*, 763–64; Memo from Walter White to W. E. B. Du Bois, July 9, 1948, Du Bois Papers, UM-A.

94. W. E. B. Du Bois to National Association for the Advancement of Colored People, September 7, 1948, Du Bois Papers, UM-A.

95. "Racial Unit Scored as Aiding Truman," *New York Times*, September 9, 1948.

96. Walter White to W. E. B. Du Bois, September 13, 1948, Du Bois Papers, UM-A.

97. Motion passed by the NAACP to terminate W. E. B. Du Bois's employment, September 13, 1948, Du Bois Papers, UM-A.

98. Du Bois, *Autobiography*, 337.

99. "The Winds of Time," *Chicago Defender*, March 23, 1946, in Aptheker, *Newspaper Columns, Vol. 2*, 680.

100. "The Winds of Time," *Chicago Defender*, April 19, 1947, in Aptheker, *Newspaper Columns, Vol. 2*, 711.

101. See Richard Gergel, *Unexampled Courage: The Blinding of Sgt. Isaac Woodard and the Awakening of President Harry S. Truman and Judge J. Waties Waring* (New York: Sarah Crichton Books/Farrar, Straus and Giroux, 2019).

102. The report played a key role in undermining support for Du Bois's United Nations *Appeal.*

103. "Truman Demands We Fight Harder to Spur Equality," *New York Times,* June 30, 1947; "President Truman's Speech to NAACP on Human Rights," *New York Times,* June 30, 1947.

104. "Anti-Lynching Law, Civil Liberties Unit Sought by Truman," *New York Times,* February 3, 1948; "The Text of President Truman's Message on Civil Rights," *New York Times,* February 3, 1948; Kari Frederickson, *Dixiecrat Revolt and the End of the Solid South, 1932–1968* (Chapel Hill: University of North Carolina Press, 2001).

105. Jon E. Taylor, *Freedom to Serve: Truman, Civil Rights, and Executive Order 9981* (New York: Routledge, 2013); Mary Dudziak, *Cold War Civil Rights: Race and the Image of American Democracy* (Princeton, NJ: Princeton University Press, 2011), 85–86.

106. On the Cold War and the Red Scare, see Melvyn P. Leffler, *The Specter of Communism: The United States and the Origins of the Cold War, 1917–1953* (New York: Hill and Wang, 1994); Ted Morgan, *Reds: McCarthyism in Twentieth-Century America* (New York: Random House, 2003); Peter L. Steinberg, *The Great "Red Menace": United States Prosecution of American Communists, 1947–1952* (Westport, CT: Greenwood Press, 1984). On government persecution of African Americans during this period, see Gerald Horne, *Black Liberation/Red Scare: Ben Davis and the Communist Party* (Newark: University of Delaware Press, 1994); James Zeigler, *Red Scare Racism and Cold War Black Radicalism* (Jackson: University Press of Mississippi, 2015).

107. Alphaeus Hunton Jr. joined in 1943 as educational director and became executive director in the summer of 1948 after Yergen was ousted from the position following an ugly fight over the nonpartisan status of the organization and alleged communist ties. For more on the Council of African Affairs, see Von Eschen, *Race Against Empire.*

108. On the relationship between Du Bois and Robeson, see Murali Balaji, *Professor and the Pupil: The Politics and Friendship of W. E. B. Du Bois and Paul Robeson* (New York: Nation Books, 2007).

109. Alexander, *W. E. B. Du Bois,* 107–108.

110. Du Bois, *Autobiography,* 345; Letter from Council on African Affairs to W. E. B. Du Bois, December 25, 1948, Du Bois Papers, UM-A; Du Bois's position with the CAA was facilitated by Herbert Aptheker and Doxey Wilkerson. Lewis, *W. E. B. Du Bois, Vol. 2;* Graham Du Bois, *His Day Is Marching On,* 98.

111. Gerald Horne, *Race Woman: The Lives of Shirley Graham Du Bois* (New York: New York University Press, 2000), chap. 5; Erik S. McDuffie, *Sojourning for Freedom: Black Women, American Communism, and the Making of Black Left Feminism* (Durham, NC: Duke University Press, 2011).

112. Du Bois, *In Battle for Peace,* 27–28.

113. Ibid., 28.

114. Du Bois, *Autobiography,* 355; Du Bois, *In Battle for Peace,* 182–86; Alexander, *W. E. B. Du Bois,* 114; for an in-depth contextual examination of Du Bois's peace activities, see Charisse Burden-Stelly, "In Battle for Peace During 'Scoundrel Time': W. E. B. Du Bois

and United States Repression of Radical Black Peace Activism," *Du Bois Review* 16, no. 2 (2019): 555–74.

115. Du Bois, *In Battle for Peace*, 35.

116. Announcement of the death of Nina Gomer Du Bois, July 26, 1950; W. E. B. Du Bois to Ernest R. Alexander, July 6, 1950, Du Bois Papers, UM-A.

117. Du Bois, *Autobiography*, 280–81; As the crow flies, July 8, 1950, Du Bois Papers, UM-A; Graham Du Bois, *His Day Is Marching On*, 124–27.

118. "Text of the Acheson Statement," *New York Times*, July 13, 1950; W. E. B. Du Bois to United States Department of State, July 14, 1950, Du Bois Papers, UM-A.

119. Du Bois, *In Battle for Peace*, 43–50.

120. Ibid., 51–59.

121. "5 of 'Peace' Group Here Indicted," *New York Times*, February 10, 1951; Lewis, *W. E. B. Du Bois, Vol. 2*; Alexander, *W. E. B. Du Bois*; Du Bois, *In Battle for Peace*.

122. Horne, *Race Woman*, 134; Du Bois, *In Battle for Peace*, 57–59.

123. Du Bois, *In Battle for Peace*, 70–71.

124. Ibid., 71.

125. Burden-Stelly, "In Battle for Peace During 'Scoundrel Time,'" 567–68.

126. Du Bois, *Autobiography*, 377.

127. Du Bois, *In Battle for Peace*, 86, 90–91.

128. Ibid., chaps. 12–13.

129. Ibid., 146–47; Moos, Elizabeth. Report on W. E. B. Du Bois's indictment and trial, ca. December 1951, Du Bois Papers, UM-A; Graham Du Bois, *His Day Is Marching On*, 170–73.

130. Du Bois, *In Battle for Peace*, 162–63.

131. Ibid., 163.

132. Ibid., 165.

133. Ibid., 164.

134. "Close Ranks," *The Crisis* (July 1918), 111; "A Philosophy in Time of War," *The Crisis* (August 1918), 164–65; "Our Special Grievances," *The Crisis* (September 1918), 216–17.

Epilogue

1. My last message, June 1957, Du Bois Papers, UM-A.

2. Graham Du Bois, *His Day Is Marching On*, 219.

3. Du Bois, *Autobiography*, 395.

4. Graham Du Bois, *His Day Is Marching On*, 231.

5. "Dr. Carter G. Woodson, Historian, Found Dead," *Chicago Defender*, April 8, 1950.

6. "Military Burial for Dr. Boutte," *New York Amsterdam News*, October 19, 1957.

7. "Emmett J. Scott, Educator, Was 84," *New York Times*, December 14, 1957.

8. Graham Du Bois, *His Day Is Marching On*, 319–20.

9. Ibid., 191.

10. Contee, "The Encyclopedia Africana Project of W. E. B. Du Bois," 77–91.

11. Graham Du Bois, *His Day Is Marching On*, 367.

12. Evening News, volume VI, number 1,703, August 30, 1963, Du Bois Papers, UM-A.

13. Lewis, *W. E. B Du Bois, Vol. 1*, 1–10.

14. Ibid., 9; My last message, June 1957, Du Bois Papers, UM-A.

15. I take my cue here from the work of Lawrie Balfour, Robert Gooding-Williams, and other scholars who connect Du Bois and his work to contemporary struggles for racial justice and democracy. See Lawrie Balfour, "Inheriting Du Bois," *Du Bois Review* 8, no. 2 (2011): 409–16; Robert Gooding-Williams, *In the Shadow of Du Bois: Afro-Modern Political Thought in America* (Cambridge, MA: Harvard University Press, 2009).

16. Graham Du Bois, *His Day Is Marching On*, 363; Gary Murrell, "Herbert Aptheker's Struggle to Publish W. E. B. Du Bois," in Phillip Luke Sinitiere, ed., *Citizen of the World: The Late Career and Legacy of W. E. B. Du Bois* (Evanston, IL: Northwestern University Press, 2019), 202–205.

17. Shirley Graham Du Bois to Vincent Harding, December 9, 1971, box 2, folder 2, Bernard Jaffe Papers, University of Massachusetts Amherst Libraries; February 3, 1972, box 20, folder 15, Papers of Shirley Graham Du Bois, Schlesinger Library, Radcliffe Institute, Harvard University; Vincent Harding to Herbert Aptheker, July 26, 1971; Herbert Aptheker to Vincent Harding, July 28, 1971, box 38, folder 2, Stanford University Library Special Collections. I am grateful to Phillip Luke Sinitiere for bringing this to my attention and sharing with me some of the correspondence between Shirley Graham Du Bois, Vincent Harding, and Herbert Aptheker.

18. Fisk University Library to W. E. B. Du Bois, May 17, 1961; Fisk University Library to Shirley Du Bois, September 19, 1961; the private library and personal papers of W. E. B. Du Bois, September 20, 1961, Du Bois Papers, UM-A.

19. Herbert Aptheker to Shirley Graham Du Bois, February 9, 1972, box 20, folder 15, Papers of Shirley Graham Du Bois, Schlesinger Library, Radcliffe Institute, Harvard University; Herbert Aptheker to Katherine Emerson, May 9, 1975, University of Massachusetts Press administrative records, University of Massachusetts Amherst Libraries. Again, I thank Phillip Sinitiere for sharing these documents with me.

20. Box: Acquisitions-Authors, C to D, Folder: "Du Bois, Seven Critiques of Negro Education," University of Massachusetts Press administrative records, University of Massachusetts Amherst Libraries.

21. Herbert Aptheker to Leone Stein, May 21, 1972, Box: Acquisitions-Authors, C to D, Folder: "Du Bois, Seven Critiques of Negro Education," University of Massachusetts Press administrative records, University of Massachusetts Amherst Libraries.

22. See Murrell, "Herbert Aptheker's Struggle to Publish W. E. B. Du Bois"; Herbert Aptheker, *Against Racism*.

23. The only other unfinished and unpublished project of comparable scale to *The Black Man and the Wounded World* was the *Encyclopedia Africana*. *Africana: The Encyclopedia of the African and African-American Experience* was published in 1999 as a one-volume edition. Coedited by Henry Louis Gates Jr. and Kwame Anthony Appiah, it was inspired by Du Bois's *Encyclopedia Africana* and approached as a completion of his unfinished work. An expanded five-volume edition, more in line with Du Bois's vision of the encyclopedia, was published in 2005. In 1950, Du Bois completed a 350-page manuscript for a book titled "Russia and America: An Interpretation" that was rejected by Harcourt, Brace and Company and has remained unpublished. See Russia and America: an interpreta-

tion, 1950; Harcourt, Brace, and Company to W. E. B. Du Bois, July 13, 1950, Du Bois Papers, UM-A; Mullen, *Un-American*, 85–95; Lewis, *W. E. B. Du Bois, Vol. 2*, 557.

24. On this evolution, Scott Sandage writes, "Failure had become what it remains in the new millennium: the most damning incarnation of the connection between achievement and personal identity." See Scott A. Sandage, *Born Losers: A History of Failure in America* (Cambridge, MA: Harvard University Press, 2005), 5.

25. Cornel West, "Black Strivings in a Twilight Civilization," in Henry Louis Gates Jr. and Cornel West, *The Future of the Race* (New York: Knopf, 1996), 55.

26. Chad Williams, "W. E. B. Du Bois, World War I and the Question of Failure," *Black Perspectives*, February 19, 2018, www.aaihs.org/w-e-b-du-bois-world-war-i-and-the-question -of-failure/.

27. This point is eloquently made by Nahum Chandler. See Nahum D. Chandler, "The Figure of W. E. B. Du Bois as a Problem for Thought," *CR: The New Centennial Review* 6, no. 3 (Winter 2006): 31.

28. See Rampersad, *The Art and Imagination of W. E. B. Du Bois.*

29. Du Bois, *Autobiography*, 274.

30. On the irrationality of the war, see Paul Fussell, *The Great War and Modern Memory* (New York: Oxford University Press, 1975).

31. "Honoring Dr. Du Bois," Du Bois Papers, UM-A.

32. Du Bois, *Autobiography*, 419.

ACKNOWLEDGMENTS

ON A PICTURESQUE FALL New England day in October 2000, I visited the University of Massachusetts–Amherst. I was at the time a young, eager graduate student, embarking on my first research trip for a dissertation on African American soldiers and World War I. I did not know what to expect when I arrived at the towering and appropriately named W. E. B. Du Bois Library to examine the mysteriously labeled "Du Bois World War I materials." Maybe it was some of his writings from *The Crisis*. Or possibly a folder of newspaper clippings. My hopes were tempered, but perhaps I would get lucky.

I approached the special collections department and anxiously placed my request with the reference librarian. I sat down at an empty table and waited. The librarian returned several minutes later with, to my surprise, six microfilm reels. With my curiosity now fully piqued, I spooled the film of the first reel through the reader and, slowly, turned the handle. Frame by frame, the chapters of *The Black Man and the Wounded World*, along with Du Bois's research and correspondence related to the book, began to unfold before my eyes. I was stunned and captivated. From that moment, I knew that I wanted to learn more about Du Bois's unfinished book and ultimately tell the story of why it never saw the light of day.

The journey from that serendipitous research visit when I first encountered *The Black Man and the Wounded World* to the completion of this project has been a long one, full of its own twists and turns, highs and lows, frustrations and thrills. There were times when I wondered, as if by some cruel twist of fate, whether my own book would meet the same outcome as Du Bois's. The support and encouragement of so many people over the years ensured that this would not be the case.

I have been fortunate to have in my corner an extraordinary literary agent, Tanya McKinnon. From our first phone conversation in September 2016 (shout-out to Robin D. G. Kelley for dropping my name), she saw the potential of this book and encouraged me to think big. Her commitment to supporting Black authors and ensuring that we have the publishing opportunities to tell our stories is truly inspiring.

Eric Chinski has been a generous, patient, and wise editor. He afforded me the time and space to write my book as I saw fit, while also gently pushing me to make hard choices about what needed and did not need to be in the manuscript. His reassurance made what could have easily been a tortuous revision process an enjoyable one. I am grateful to the entire production and marketing team at Far-rar, Straus and Giroux, especially Tara Sharma, Carrie Hsieh, and the cover designer Thomas Colligan. I am especially thankful for the sharp copyediting eyes of Maxine Bartow.

This project was supported by grants and fellowships from the American Council of Learned Societies, the Mandel Center for the Humanities at Brandeis University, and the Radcliffe Institute for Advanced Study at Harvard University. My time as a Radcliffe fellow was especially valuable, as I benefited from the genius and collegiality of a remarkable cohort of interdisciplinary scholars and artists. I would like to thank Lizabeth Cohen, Sharon Bromberg-Lin, Alison Ney, and the late Judith Vichniac for their leadership; Jane Kamensky for making the time to read my book proposal; and my luminous colleagues in the Africana Studies working group—Erica R. Edwards, Ifeoma Fafunwa, Françoise Hamlin, Shireen Hassim, Steffani Jemison, Leah Wright Rigueur, Quito Swan, and Patricia J. Williams.

Any historian will tell you that we are nothing without the commitment, imagination, and skill of librarians and archivists. I am indebted to the staff of Quaker and Special Collections at Haverford College, the Beinecke Rare Book and Manuscript Library at Yale University, New York Public Library Special Collections, the Rare Book and Special Collections of the Library of Congress, and the Brandeis University Library. Many thanks to Edith Murungi at the Morgan State University Special Collections Department for providing me with materials from the Emmett J. Scott Collection. I have profound admiration for the dedicated team at University of Massachusetts–

Amherst who have spearheaded the Credo project and the digitization of the Du Bois Papers, which made my research incalculably easier. Each of my visits to Fisk University, where Du Bois's original *The Black Man and the Wounded World* materials are located, was a revelation. The Special Collections and Archives of the John Hope and Aurelia E. Franklin Library at Fisk is a treasure trove and powerful reminder of the rich and all too often unexplored history contained within Historically Black Colleges and Universities. I am grateful to the entire library staff, most notably Robert Spinelli, who assisted me with final research and permissions.

I have presented aspects of this work at various conferences and invited talks over the years. I am thankful to the attentive audiences at Boston University, Duke University, Hamilton College, the Hutchins Center for African and African American Research at Harvard University, State University of New York at Binghamton, and Vanderbilt University. The insightful comments, probing questions, and useful suggestions I received during these presentations made this project stronger.

The list of people who have supported me and this book over the years is long, and even with the luxury of several pages, I would still run the risk of omitting someone. Please know that your friendship, camaraderie, and inspiration, from near and far, has upheld me and given me the strength to keep pressing forward.

A few individuals merit special acknowledgment. Nell Irvin Painter remains my most trusted adviser. She recognized my excitement—and naivete—when I first encountered Du Bois's World War I materials. Counseling patience, she kept me focused on completing my dissertation and first book, without which I would not have had the expertise and confidence to tackle Du Bois years later. Few historians of World War I rise to the stature of Jennifer D. Keene. Her work on the Black experience in World War I, including Du Bois and *The Black Man and the Wounded World*, has set a high bar that I constantly aspire to reach. Shawn Leigh Alexander, Michael Neiberg, and Phillip Luke Sinitiere kindly read all or parts of early drafts of the manuscript. I especially want to thank Phil for his feedback, as well as for sharing some of his research on Du Bois. David Levering Lewis, who also read a full draft of the manuscript, knows better than any historian how daunting a book on the life and mind of W. E. B. Du Bois can be. With his customary grace, he encouraged me to take on this project and solve the mystery of Du Bois's unfinished tome. I remain awestruck by his brilliance and thankful beyond words for his support.

I have been lucky to be surrounded by wonderful students and colleagues at Brandeis University while completing this book. Veronica Saltzman provided stellar research assistance. Many thanks to my fellow faculty members, past and present, in the Department of History and, most treasured, in the African and African American Studies Department—Greg Childs, Abby Cooper, Aliyyah Abdur-Rahman, Anita Hill, Jasmine Johnson, Wangui Muigai, Wellington Nyangoni, Betsy Plumb, Carina Ray, Shoniqua Roach, Faith Smith, Amber Spry, Ibrahim Sundiata, and Derron Wallace. Serving as chair of this esteemed department will always stand as one of the highlights of my career.

Family has been my bedrock. My passion for history is rooted in our familial past and the generations of loved ones that have made whatever modest success I have achieved in the present possible. To all my aunts, uncles, and cousins; my brother, Lenny; and my dear sister, Kelli: you have stayed by my side and in my heart throughout the journey of completing this book. I have been blessed with three incredible children. Gabriel, Michael, and Layla, my pride and joy: nothing will ever surpass the delight I feel every day of being your father and watching you grow. Madeleine, I could not dream of a better wife, partner, confidant, and friend. Thank you for putting up with me—and Du Bois's ghost!

I have dedicated this book to my mother and father, Jayne and Carl. In the summer of 2020, as the death toll from the COVID-19 pandemic continued to skyrocket and took a particularly devastating toll on Black families, I, like so many people with advanced aged parents, feared the worst. The thought of them not being here to read this book, after having poured so much support and encouragement into me over the years, drove me to write the final chapters and revise the full manuscript. The only explanation I can offer for how I managed to finish *The Wounded World*, considering the circumstances, is love. I owe them everything and more.

INDEX

Du Bois's ambitions for, 283; Du
Bois's correspondence with soldiers
for, 159–60; Du Bois's French
expedition and meeting of soldiers
for, 121–22, 128–36, 139–40,
164–65, 167, 168; Du Bois's outline
for, 111; Du Bois's professionalism
and, 183, 223; Du Bois's travels and,
369–71; Duncan and, 136, 160,
276–77; Embree's advice on, 330;
"An Essay Toward a History of the
Black Man in the Great War,"
177–78, 180, 184, 186, 202,
223–25, 257; funding for, 89, 102,
129, 161, 285–86, 295–96,
306–309, 327–31, 353–59, 362,
369–71, 382–84, 425, 426; Gannett
and, 319–20; *The Gift of Black
Folk* and, 254–56; Guggenheim
Foundation and, 313–14; Hart
and, 100, 170, 322; Haynes and,
92, 93, 97, 111; interest among
African Americans for, 286–88;
"Interpretations" introduction in,
283–87, 360; James Weldon Johnson
and, 318–20, 327, 331, 376; James
William Johnson's loan of materials
for, 224–25, 306, 312–13; Littell
and, 299–300, 302; NAACP and,
88–94, 97, 102, 104, 111, 112,
128–29, 137, 143, 145, 154, 161,
168, 201, 236, 237, 256–58,
285–86, 331; narrative and
argument in, 258; Ninety-Second
Division in, 221–24, 251, 305,
319, 361; Oberlaender Trust and,
355–56; organization of research
in, 222–23; and other histories of
the Black war experience, 189–90,
222; pageant idea and, 276–77;
Pan-African Congress and, 236–38,
277; Patterson and, 120–21, 129,
132, 157–59, 183–84, 190, 219–20,
264–65, 294–98, 305, 306, 313;
production challenges and, 183,
425; publishers and, 157–58, 208;
research assistants for, 101–102,
169; Rockefeller Foundation and,

307–309; Rosenwald Fund and,
327–31, 426; scholarly foundation
for, 221; Scott and, 90, 92–94, 97,
100, 103–108, 111, 123, 144, 145,
167, 168, 187; Scott's book and, 93,
94, 103–105, 145, 173, 190–92,
219, 222; Shotwell and, 358–62;
Social Science Research Council and,
353–55, 382–84; Stockbridge and,
106–108, 110–11, 123, 167, 168;
"The Story of the War" chapter in,
288–91, 360; subscription pledges
for, 237, 286, 290, 291; Taylor and,
305; 368th Infantry Regiment in,
225, 299, 361; unfinished status of,
384, 385, 390, 420, 422, 425–28;
veterans' contributions to, 173–75,
185–86, 218–19, 236, 253, 264–65,
305–306, 313, 426; veterans'
support for, 175, 176, 219; Villard's
idea for, 88–89; war documents
exposé and, 170; "The War Within
the War" chapter in, 327; Williams
and, 184–85, 218, 220–23, 234,
236, 251–52; Woodson and, 90–94,
97, 100, 102–105, 108, 111, 123,
144, 145, 168, 287–88, 301–302,
305; "The World of Black Folk"
chapter in, 231–32, 360; Young and,
100, 246, 248
Black Manhattan (Johnson),
327
Black press, 162, 187, 188, 202, 398;
editors' conferences, 69–70, 227,
337
Black Reconstruction (Du Bois),
328–29, 331–34, 339, 346–50, 353,
354, 358, 426
Black people, 13–14; migration of,
52–53, 193, 197, 226, 229, 335;
radical, 202, 204, 274
Black soldiers: in Civil War, 39; French
colonial troops, 124–27, 233–35,
262, 300; in Houston rebellion,
56–58, 61, 96, 226, 278; "Use
of Negro Manpower" report on,
297–98, 398; in World War II,
396–99

A NOTE ABOUT THE AUTHOR

Chad L. Williams is the Samuel J. and Augusta Spector Professor of History and African and African American Studies at Brandeis University. He is the author of the award-winning book *Torchbearers of Democracy: African American Soldiers in the World War I Era* and the coeditor of *Charleston Syllabus: Readings on Race, Racism, and Racial Violence*. His writings and op-eds have appeared in *The Atlantic, The Washington Post, Time,* and *The Conversation.* He lives in Needham, Massachusetts.